EMMA GOLDMAN IN 1912

# LIVING
# MY LIFE

EMMA GOLDMAN

IN TWO VOLUMES

Vol. II

DOVER PUBLICATIONS, INC.

NEW YORK

This Dover edition, first published in 1970, is
an unabridged republication of the work originally
published in 1931 by Alfred Knopf, Inc., New York.

International Standard Book Number: 0-486-22544-5
Library of Congress Catalog Card Number: 74-105452

Manufactured in the United States of America
Dover Publications, Inc.
180 Varick Street
New York, N.Y. 10014

# ILLUSTRATIONS

## (*Volume Two*)

# CHAPTER XXXIX

O N MY RETURN EAST I LEARNED OF THE DEATH OF VOLTAIRINE DE
Cleyre. Her end affected me very deeply; her whole life had been
a continuous chain of suffering. Death had come after an operation
for an abcess on the brain which had impaired her memory. A second
operation, her friends had been informed, would have deprived her
of the power of speech. Voltairine, always stoical in pain, preferred
death. Her end, on June 19, was a great loss to our movement and to
those who valued her strong personality and unusual talents.

In compliance with her last request Voltairine was buried in Waldheim Cemetery, near the graves of our Chicago comrades. Their
martyrdom had awakened Voltairine's soul as it had so many other
fine spirits. But few had so completely consecrated themselves to their
cause as she, and fewer still had her genius to serve the ideal with
singleness of purpose.

Arrived in Chicago, I went out to Waldheim with Annie Livshis,
a dear common friend. Voltairine had made her home with Annie and
Jake Livshis, and she had been tenderly nursed by our devoted comrades to the very last. I went to the cemetery with red carnations in
my arms, while Annie carried red geraniums to be added to those she
had already planted on the fresh grave. These were the only monument Voltairine had ever wanted.

Voltairine de Cleyre was born of a Quaker mother and a French
father. The latter, in his youth an admirer of Voltaire, had named his
daughter after the great philosopher. Later her father, having turned
conservative, had placed her in a Catholic convent school, from which
Voltairine subsequently escaped, rebelling against the authority of
both. She was exceptionally gifted as poet, writer, and lecturer. She
would have gained high position and renown had she been one to
market her talents, but she would not accept even the simplest com-

forts for her activities in the various social movements. She shared the fate of the lowly whom she sought to teach and inspire. Revolutionary vestal, she lived as the poorest of the poor in dreary and wretched surroundings, taxing her body to the utmost, sustained only by her ideal.

Voltairine began her public career as a pacifist, and for many years she sternly set her face against revolutionary methods. But greater familiarity with European developments, the Russian Revolution of 1905, the rapid growth of capitalism in her own country, with all its resultant violence and injustice, and particularly the Mexican Revolution, subsequently changed her attitude. After an inner struggle, Voltairine's intellectual integrity compelled her to admit her error frankly and to stand up bravely for the new vision. She did so in a number of essays and especially when she took up work for the Mexican Revolution, which she considered of most vital consequence. She devoted herself entirely to it, writing, lecturing, and collecting funds. In her the movement for liberty and humanism, especially the anarchist cause, lost one of its most gifted and tireless workers.

As I stood beside Voltairine's grave, in the shadow of the monument dedicated to the memory of our comrades, I felt that another martyr had been added to them. She was the prototype of the sculptured Waldheim figure, beautiful in her spiritual defiance and filled with the revolt of a flaming ideal.

The year 1912, rich with varied experiences, closed with three important events: the appearance of Sasha's book, the twenty-fifth anniversary of the eleventh of November, and the seventieth birthday of Peter Kropotkin.

Sasha was reading the final proofs of his *Prison Memoirs*. In renewed agony he was living through again every detail of the fourteen years, and experiencing harrowing doubt as to whether he had succeeded in making them real in his work. He kept revising until our bill for author's corrections mounted to four hundred and fifty dollars. He was worried and exhausted, yet he hung on, going over his proofs again and again. The final chapters had to be taken from him almost by force to save him from the curse of his tormenting anxiety.

And now the book was ready at last. Verily, not a book, but a life suffered in the solitude of interminable prison days and nights, with all their pain and grief, their disillusionments, despair, and hope. Tears of joy sprang to my eyes as I held the precious volume in my

hands. I felt it my triumph as well as Sasha's — *our* fulfilment of
twenty years, giving the promise of Sasha's real resurrection from his
prison nightmare, and my own release from the gnawing regret of not
having shared his fate.

*Prison Memoirs of an Anarchist* was widely reviewed and acclaimed
a work of art and a deeply moving human document. " A story of
prison life by an author who spent fourteen years behind the bars
gathering his material ought to have value as a human document,"
commented the New York *Tribune*. "When the writer, furthermore,
wields his pen in the manner of the Slavic realists and is compared
by critics with such men as Dostoyevsky and Andreieff, his work must
possess a tremendous fascination as well as a social value."

The literary critic of the New York *Globe* stated that "nothing
could exceed the uncanny spell exercised by this story. Berkman has
succeeded in making you live his prison experiences with him, and his
book is probably as complete a self-revelation as is humanly possible."

Such praise from the capitalist press helped to accentuate my disappointment over Jack London's attitude towards Sasha's book. Having been requested to write a preface for it, Jack had asked to see
the manuscript. After he had read it, he wrote us in his impetuous
way how tremendously he was impressed by it. But his preface turned
out to be a lame apology for the fact that he, a socialist, was writing
an introduction to the work of an anarchist. At the same time it was
a condemnation of Sasha's ideas. Jack London had not failed to see
the human and the literary qualities of the book. What he wrote was
even more laudatory than most of the reviews. But London insisted on
using his preface for a long discussion of his own social theories versus
anarchism. Inasmuch as Sasha's book did not deal with theories, but
with life, Jack's attitude was absurd. His argument was summarized in
his dictum: "The man who can't shoot straight can't think straight."
Evidently Jack assumed that the world's best thinkers were also the
best shots.

Sasha, who had gone to see Jack, pointed out that the great Danish
critic Georg Brandes, though not an anarchist, had written a sympathetic preface to Peter Kropotkin's *Memoirs of a Revolutionist* without attempting to air his own theories. As artist and humanist Brandes
had appreciated the big personality of Kropotkin.

" Brandes was not writing in America," London replied. " If he
had been, he would most likely have displayed a different attitude."

Sasha understood; Jack London feared offending his publishers and incurring the censure of his party. The artist in Jack longed to soar, but the man in him kept his feet on the ground. His own best literary efforts, as he himself said, were buried in his trunk because his publishers wanted only works sure to bring financial results. And there were Glen Ellen and also other responsibilities to meet. Jack left no doubt on the matter, by remarking: "I have a family to support." Perhaps he did not realize how self-condemnatory his justification was.

Sasha refused Jack's preface. Instead we asked our friend Hutchins Hapgood to write an introduction to *Prison Memoirs*. He had never proclaimed himself an adherent of any ism, nor did he sign his letters: "Yours for the revolution," as Jack London used to do. He was, however, enough of a literary rebel and social iconoclast to appreciate the spirit of Sasha's book.

Jack London was not the only one who condemned while praising. There were others, even in our own ranks, among them S. Yanofsky, the editor of the *Freie Arbeiter Stimme*. He was one of the speakers at the banquet given to celebrate the appearance of Sasha's book. He was the only one of the five hundred guests who interjected a discordant note into the otherwise beautifully harmonious evening. Yanofsky paid high tribute to Sasha's *Memoirs* as the "mature product of a mature mind," but he "regretted the useless and futile act of a silly boy." I felt outraged by the man's denouncing the *Attentat* on the occasion of the birth of Sasha's book, a work conceived in that heroic moment of July 1892 and nourished by tears and blood throughout the dark and terrible years that followed. When I was called upon to speak, I turned upon the man who presumed to represent a great ideal and yet who was lacking in the least understanding of one so truly the idealist.

"To you the impressionable youth of Alexander Berkman appears silly," I said, "and his *Attentat* futile. You are by no means the first to take such a stand towards the idealist whose humanity can tolerate no injustice and endure no wrong. From time immemorial the wise and practical have denounced every heroic spirit. Yet it has not been they who have influenced our lives. The idealists and visionaries, foolish enough to throw caution to the winds and express their ardour and faith in some supreme deed, have advanced mankind and have enriched the world. The one whose work we are here to celebrate happens to be such a futile visionary. His act was the protest of a sensitive spirit that would rather perish for his ideal than continue for a lifetime as a smug inhabitant of a complaisant and callous world. If our comrade did not perish, it was certainly not due to the mercy of those who had openly declared he should not survive his living grave. It was due entirely to the same traits that inspired Alexander Berkman's act: his unwavering purpose, his indomitable will, and his faith in the ultimate triumph of his ideal. These elements have gone into the making of the 'silly' youth, into his act and into his martyrdom of fourteen years. It is these same elements that have inspired the creation of *Prison Memoirs*. Whatever greatness and humanity the book possesses, they are woven of these elements. There is no gap between the silly youth and the mature man. There is a continuous flow, a red thread that winds like a leitmotif throughout the entire life of Alexander Berkman."

November 11, 1887—November 11, 1912! Twenty-five years, an infinitesimal fraction of time in the upward march of the race, but an eternity for him who dies many deaths in the course of his life. The twenty-fifth anniversary of the Chicago martyrdom intensified my feeling for the men I had never personally known, but who by their death had become the most decisive influence in my existence. The spirit of Parsons, Spies, Lingg, and their co-workers seemed to hover over me and give deeper meaning to the events that had inspired my spiritual birth and growth.

November 11, 1912 came at last. Numerous labour organizations and anarchist groups worked feverishly to make the anniversary an impressive memorial. They arrived in large numbers in the hall, their flaming red banners covering the balconies and walls. The platform was decorated in red and black. The life-size portraits of our comrades were hung with wreaths. The presence of the hateful Anarchist Squad only helped to increase the bitter resentment of the crowd against the forces that had crushed the Haymarket victims.

I was one of the many speakers eager to pay tribute to our precious dead and to recall once more the valour and heroism of their lives. I awaited my turn, stirred to the roots by the historic occasion, its great social significance and personal meaning to me. Memories of the distant past flitted through my mind—Rochester and a woman's voice ringing like music in my ears: "You will love our men when you learn to know them, and you will make their cause your own!" In times of ascent to heights, in days of faint-heartedness and doubt, in hours of prison isolation, of antagonism and censure from one's own kind, in failure of love, in friendships broken and betrayed — always their cause was mine, their sacrifice my support.

I stood erect before the dense mass of people. Its tense feeling mingled with mine, and all our hate and all our love were concentrated in my voice. "They are not dead," I cried; "they are not dead, the men we have come to honour tonight! Out of their quivering bodies dangling from the noose, new lives have emerged to take up the strains throttled on the scaffold. With a thousand voices they proclaim that our martyrs are not dead!"

Preparatory work was beginning for the celebration of the seventieth birthday of Peter Kropotkin. He was a prominent figure in the realm of learning, recognized as such by the foremost men of the world. But to us he meant much more than that. We saw in him the father of modern anarchism, its revolutionary spokesman and brilliant exponent of its relation to science, philosophy, and progressive thought. As a personality he towered high above most of his contemporaries by virtue of his humanity and faith in the masses. Anarchism to him was not an ideal for the select few. It was a constructive social theory, destined to usher in a new world for all of mankind. For this he had lived and laboured all his life. The seventieth anniversary of such a person was therefore of great moment to all who knew and loved him.

Months before, we had written to his admirers in European countries, and to our own leading comrades, for contributions to the Kropotkin-birthday edition of *Mother Earth*. Everybody responded generously. Now the December issue was ready, containing tributes to Peter Kropotkin by Georg Brandes, Edward Carpenter, Professor George D. Herron, Tom Mann, J. Morrison-Davidson, Bayard Boyesen, Anna Strunsky Walling and her husband, Rose Strunsky, Leonard D. Abbott, and leading anarchists throughout the world. In conjunction with the special Kropotkin issue of our magazine a big meeting took place in Carnegie Hall, arranged by us in co-operation with the *Freie Arbeiter Stimme* Association. As on the pages of *Mother Earth*, every speaker paid tribute to Kropotkin, our common teacher and inspiration.

Peter was deeply moved by these expressions of love and affection. In token of appreciation he sent us the following letter:

DEAR COMRADES AND FRIENDS:

First of all, let me express to you my warmest, heartiest thanks for all the kind words and thoughts you have addressed to me, and then to voice through your pages the same heartiest thanks to all the comrades and friends who have sent me such warm and friendly letters and telegrams on the occasion of my seventieth birthday.

I need not tell you, nor could I word it on paper, how deeply I was touched by all these expressions of sympathy, and how I felt that "something brotherly" which keeps us anarchists united by a feeling far deeper than the mere sense of solidarity in a party; and I am sure that that feeling of brotherhood will have some day its effect, when history will call upon us to show what we are worth, and how far we can act in harmony for the reconstruction of society upon a new basis of equality and freedom.

And then let me add that if all of us have contributed to some extent to the work of liberation of exploited mankind, it is because our ideas have been more or less the expression of the ideas that are germinating in the very depths of the masses of the people. The more I live, the more am I convinced that no truthful and useful social science, and no useful and truthful social action is possible but the science which bases its conclusions, and the action which bases its acts, upon the thoughts and the inspirations of the masses. All sociological science and all social actions which do not do that must remain sterile.

With full heart with you,

PETER KROPOTKIN

The effect on Ben of his San Diego experience proved to be stronger and more lasting than any of us had expected. He remained in the throes of those harrowing days and he became a victim of the *idée fixe* that he must return there. He followed his activities with even more than his wonted energy, working as if driven by furies and driving everybody else in turn. I became to him a means rather than an end, the end being meetings, meetings, meetings, and plans for more meetings. But I saw that he did not really live in his work, or in our love. His whole being was centred on San Diego, and it became almost a hallucination with him. He taxed my powers of endurance, and often my affection, by his constant insistence on starting for the Coast. His restlessness kept increasing and he was not content until we were finally on our way.

Our Los Angeles friends were strongly opposed to our returning to San Diego. They said that Ben's obsession was nothing but bravado, and that I was weak in giving in to his irrational scheme. They even brought the matter to the attention of the audience at our last meeting, urging a unanimous vote against our going.

I knew that our friends were concerned only for our safety, but I could not agree with them. I did not feel about San Diego as Ben did; to me it was but one of the many towns in the United States where free speech had been gagged and its defenders maltreated. To such places I always kept returning until the right of free speech was again established there. That was one of the motives for my wanting to go back to San Diego, but it was by no means the strongest motive. I was certain that Ben would not be freed from the hold of that city unless he returned to the scene of the May outrage. My love for him had grown more intense with the years. I could not permit him to go to San Diego alone. I therefore informed my comrades that I would go with Ben, no matter what might be awaiting us there. It seemed incredible that any group of people, however savage in time of excite-ment, would repeat such brutalities after the lapse of a year, particu-larly since the Vigilantes and San Diego had been placed in the pillory by country-wide condemnation.

An active worker in our ranks volunteered to precede us to San Diego, secure a hall, and advertise my lecture, which was again to be on " An Enemy of the People." Before long he notified us that all was well and promising.

After our last meeting in Los Angeles we were taken by our friends Dr. and Mrs. Percival T. Gerson to the railroad station. On the way Ben's excitement reached such a pitch that the doctor suggested a sanatorium instead of San Diego. But Ben insisted that nothing would cure him except to go back. In the train he became deathly pale, and large drops of perspiration poured over his face. His body shook with nervousness and fear. All night he tossed about sleeplessly in his berth.

Except for my concern about him I was singularly calm. I was wide awake and sat up reading *Comrade Yetta* by "Albert Edwards." An interesting book always made me forget a difficult situation. This volume was by Arthur Bullard, one of our friends who had

co-operated with us during Babushka's visit to New York. His powerful story and its Russian theme brought back to me the days gone by.
The last two hours of our trip Ben was fast asleep, and I was so lost
in the past that I was unaware we were nearing San Diego. The bustle
of our fellow-passengers recalled me to reality. I dressed hurriedly
and then woke Ben.

It was early dawn, and only a few passengers got off the train. The
platform was deserted as we made our way towards the exit. But
before we had proceeded far, five men suddenly confronted us. Four
of them exposed detective badges and informed us that we were under
arrest. I demanded the reason for our detention, but they gruffly
ordered us to come with them.

San Diego was asleep as we walked to the police station. Something
in the appearance of the man accompanying the officers seemed familiar to me. I strove to remember where I had seen him before. Then
it dawned on me that it was he who had come to my room in the U. S.
Grant Hotel to tell me that I was wanted by the authorities. I recognized him as the reporter who had caused our former difficulties there.
He was a leader of the Vigilantes!

Ben and I were locked up. There was nothing to be done but await
developments. I again took up my book. Weary, I put my head on the
little cell table and dozed off.

"You must have been very tired to sleep like that," the matron
said as she woke me. "Didn't you hear the racket?" She looked
fixedly at me. "Better have some coffee," she added, not unkindly.
"You may need your strength before the day is over."

Noises and yelling came from the street. "The Vigilantes," the
matron said in a low voice. There were loud cries outside and I could
hear voices calling: "Reitman! We want Reitman!" Then came the
tooting of automobile horns and the shriek of the riot signal. And
again cries of "Reitman!" My heart sank.

The riot call boomed and howled. The noises beat like tomtoms on
my brain. Why had I ever let Ben come, I thought; it was madness,
madness! They could not forgive him for returning. They wanted his
life!

In a frenzy I rapped on my cell door. The matron arrived and with
her the Chief of Police and several detectives.

"I want to see Dr. Reitman!" I demanded.

"That's what we've come for," the Chief replied. "He wants you
to consent to being taken out of town, and your other comrade too."

"What other comrade?"

"The chap who arranged your meeting. He's in the jail, and lucky for him he is."

"You're playing the benefactor again," I retorted; "but you won't dupe me this time. Take those two out of town. *I* will not go under your protection."

"All right," he growled. "Come and talk to Reitman yourself."

The pale horror staring at me out of Ben's eyes made me realize the meaning of fear as I had never seen it before. "Let's get out of town," he whispered, trembling. "We can't hold the meeting anyway. Chief Wilson promises to get us away safe. Please say yes."

I had completely forgotten our meeting. It was my objection to leaving under police protection that made me urge Ben to go himself.

"It is your life that is in danger," I said; "they don't want me. No harm will come to me. But in any case I can't run away."

"All right, I'll stay too," he replied determinedly.

I struggled with myself for a moment. I knew that if I let him stay, I should jeopardize his life and possibly also the safety of the other comrade. There was no other way out; I should have to consent.

No play was ever staged with greater melodrama than our rescue from the San Diego jail and our ride to the railroad station. At the head of the procession marched a dozen policemen, each carrying a shot-gun, with revolvers sticking in their belts. Then came the Chief of Police and the Chief of Detectives, heavily armed, Ben between them. I followed with two officers on each side. Behind me was our young comrade. And behind him more police.

Our appearance was greeted with savage howls. As far as the eye could reach, there was a swaying, jostling human pack. The shrill cries of women mingled with the voices of the men, drunk with the lust of blood. The more venturesome of them tried to make a rush for Ben.

"Back, back!" shouted the Chief. "The prisoners are under the protection of the law. I demand respect for the law. Get back!"

Some applauded him, others jeered. He proudly led the procession through the phalanxes of police, accompanied by the yelling of the frenzied crowd.

Automobiles were waiting us, gaily bedecked with American flags. One of them had rifles posted at every corner. Police and plain-clothes men stood on the running-board. I recognized the reporter among them. We were piled into this armed citadel, Chief Wilson standing over us like a stage hero, with a shot-gun pointed at the mob. Cameras from houses and tree-tops began to click, the sirens screamed, the riot call boomed again, and off we dashed, followed by the other cars and the angry bellowing of the mob.

At the railroad station we were pushed into a Pullman, six policemen crowding around Ben. Just as the train was about to start, a man ran in, shoved the officers aside, and spat full in Ben's face. Then he rushed out again.

"That's Porter," Ben cried, "the leader of last year's attack on me!"

I thought of the savagery of the mob, terrifying yet fascinating at the same time. I realized why Ben's previous experience had so obsessed him until it had driven him back to San Diego. I felt the overwhelming power of the crowd's concentrated passion. I knew I should find no peace until I had returned to it, to subdue it or to be destroyed.

I would go back, I promised myself, but not with Ben. There was no relying on him in a critical moment. I knew he had imaginative flights, but strength of will he had not. He was impulsive, but he lacked stamina and a sense of responsibility. These traits of his character had repeatedly clouded our lives and made me tremble for our love. I grieved to realize that Ben was not of heroic stuff. He was not of the texture of Sasha, who had courage enough for a dozen men and extraordinary coolness and presence of mind in moments of danger.

Perhaps courage, I thought, is nothing remarkable in those who know no fear. I was sure Sasha had never known fear. And I, during the McKinley panic, had I feared for my life? No, I had had no fear for myself, though I had often felt it for others. It was always this, and my exaggerated sense of responsibility, that compelled me to do things I hated to do. Are we really courageous, we who do not know fear, if we remain firm in the face of danger? Ben was consumed with terror, yet he went back to San Diego. Was that not real courage? Inwardly I strove to exonerate Ben, to find some justification for his readiness to run away.

The train sped on. Ben's face was close to mine, his voice whispering endearments, his eyes gazing pleadingly into mine. As so often before, all my doubts and all my pain dissolved in my love for my impossible boy.

In Los Angeles and San Francisco we were fêted as heroes, though we had both shamefully run away. I did not feel very comfortable about it, but I was gratified by the exceptional interest in my lectures. The two that drew the largest audiences were those on "Victims of Morality" and on *Prison Memoirs of an Anarchist.*

Upon our return to New York Ben urged a larger house to give us better living-quarters and also enough room for a combination office and book-shop. He was sure he could build up a good trade to help make *Mother Earth* independent of tours. Ben was anxious to have his mother under the same roof with him, especially now that she was not well.

We found a place at 74 East One Hundred and Nineteenth Street, a ten-room house in good condition. The parlour, conveniently seating a hundred people, was the very thing we needed for small sessions and social gatherings; the basement was light and spacious enough for an office and book-shop; the upper floors would afford privacy for each of us. I had never dreamed of such comfort, yet the cost of the rent and heating was lower than our previous expenditures for these items. The large house would need someone to look after it, because I should be busy revising my drama lectures for publication.

I decided to invite my friend Rhoda Smith as housekeeper. She was a few years younger than I and full of the light-heartedness of the French race. But beneath her lightness were the sterling qualities of kindness and dependability. She was a splendid housekeeper and cook, and, like most French women, very skilful with her hands. No less deft was she with her tongue, especially when she had looked a little too deeply into her glass. Her language, always very spicy, would then become hot. Not everyone could stand its flavour or its sting.

We needed a secretary for our office work, and Ben suggested a friend of his, Miss M. Eleanor Fitzgerald. I had first met her in Chicago, during our free-speech campaign. She was a striking girl with red hair, delicate skin, and blue-green eyes. Very fond of Ben, she had no inkling of his ways with women. She did not know of my relationship with Ben and she was considerably shocked when I told her that we were very much more to each other than merely manager and lecturer. Miss Fitzgerald (or "Lioness," as Ben called her, because of her red mane of hair) was a most likable person, with something very fine and large about her. In fact, she was the only real personality among all the obsessions Ben had imposed on me through the years. Ben kept stressing the need of a secretary. "Lioness" was very competent, he assured me; she had held several responsible positions, and had recently become manager of a sanatorium in South Dakota. She was interested in our work and she would be glad to give up her job and join us in New York.

Our new quarters were ready and we began breaking up our old home. When I had first moved into 210 East Thirteenth Street, in 1903, to share the flat with the Horrs, we were the first tenants in the recently built house. Since then the police had repeatedly tried to have me put out, but my landlord remained steadfast, arguing that I had never given cause for complaint, and that I was the oldest tenant. The others, indeed, had changed so often in nationality, character, and station that I had lost count. From business men to day-labourers, from preachers to gamblers, from Jewish women with wigs on their heads to street girls flaunting their charms on the stoop, they were a constant human tide coming in, staying awhile, and ebbing again.

There were no facilities for heating at 210, except the kitchen stove, and my room was farthest from it. It faced the yard and looked right into the windows of a large printing house. The nerve-racking buzz of its linotypes and presses never let up. My room was the living-room, dining-room, and *Mother Earth* office, all in one. I slept in a little alcove behind my bookcase. There was always someone sleeping in front, someone who had stayed too late and lived too far away or who was too shaky on his feet and needing cold compresses or who had no home to go to.

All the other tenants of the house were in the habit of applying to us when ill or in trouble. Our most frequent callers, usually in the wee hours of the morning, were the gamblers. Expecting a raid, they would run up the fire-escape to ask us to hide their paraphernalia. "In your place," they once told me, "the police may look for bombs, but never for chips." Everyone in distress came to us in 210 as to an oasis in the desert of their lives. It was flattering, but at the same time wearying, never to have any privacy by day or at night.

Our little flat had grown very dear to me; a good deal of my life had been spent in it. It had witnessed a decade of the most varied activities, and men and women famous in the annals of life had laughed and cried there. The Russian campaigns of Catherine Breshkovskaya and of Tchaikovsky, the Orleneff work, free-speech fights and revolutionary propaganda, not to speak of the many personal dramas, with all their griefs and joys, had flowed through the historic place. The entire kaleidoscope of human tragedy and comedy had been reflected in colourful variegation within the walls of 210. No wonder my good friend Hutch Hapgood often urged that together we write the story of that "home of lost dogs." He was especially insistent on emphasizing its romance and pathos whenever we both felt young and gay and desperately flirted our way into each other's hearts. Alas, I was fond of his wife, and he of Ben, and so we remained shamelessly faithful, and the story unwritten.

Ten years had streamed by in a rushing current, with little leisure to reflect on how dear the place had grown to me. Only when the time came to leave it did I realize how rooted I had become at 210. Taking a last look at the empty rooms, I walked out with a feeling of deep loss. Ten most interesting years of my life left behind!

ALEXANDER BERKMAN
AT THE AGE OF TWENTY-ONE, IN 1892

# CHAPTER XL

AT LAST WE WERE INSTALLED IN OUR NEW QUARTERS. BEN AND Miss Fitzgerald were in charge of the office, Rhoda of the house, while Sasha and I took care of the magazine. With each one busy in his own sphere, the differences in character and attitude had more scope for expression without mutual invasiveness. We all found "Fitzi," as we called our new co-worker, a most charming woman, and Rhoda also liked her, though she often took delight in shocking our romantic friend by her peppery jokes and stories.

Ben was happy to have his mother with him. She had two sons, but her entire world was centred in Ben. Her mental horizon was very narrow; she was unable even to read or write and felt no interest in anything except the little home Ben had made for her. In Chicago she had lived among her pots and kettles, untouched by the stream outside. She loved her son and she was always most patient with his moods, no matter how irrational they were. He was her idol who could do no wrong. As to his numerous affairs with women, she was sure it was they who led her child astray. She had hoped her son would become a successful doctor, honoured, respected, and rich. Instead he had dropped his practice when he had barely begun it, "took up" with a woman nine years his senior, and got himself involved with a dangerous lot of anarchists. Ben's mother was always respectful when she met me, but I could sense her keen dislike.

I understood her very well : she was one of the millions whose minds have been stunted by the limitations of their lives. Her approval or disapproval would have mattered little to me if it had not been that Ben was as madly obsessed by his mother as she by him. He realized how little there was in common between them. Her attitude and manner jarred on him and would drive him away whenever he came to Chicago to visit her. Yet her hold was beyond his control. She was constantly on his mind, his passion for her a menace to his love for any other woman. His mother-complex had caused me much suffering and even despair. Yet I loved Ben in spite of all our differences. I longed for peace and harmony with him. I wanted to see him happy and contented, and I consented to his plan to bring his mother to New York.

She was given the best room in the house, supplied with her own furniture, so as to make her feel more at home. Ben always took his breakfast alone with her, with no one near to disturb their idyll. At our common meals she was given the seat of honour and treated by everybody with utmost consideration. But she felt ill at ease, out of her environment. She longed for her old Chicago place and she became dissatisfied and unhappy. Then, one unfortunate day, Ben began to read *Sons and Lovers* by D. H. Lawrence. From the very first page he lived in the book with his mother. He saw in it the story of himself and of her. The office, our work, and our life were blotted out. He could think of nothing but the story and his mother, and he began to imagine that I — and everyone else — was treating her badly. He would have to take her away, he decided; he must give up everything and live only for his mother.

I was in the midst of my drama manuscript. There were lectures on hand, a large undertaking for *Mother Earth,* and the campaign in behalf of J. M. Rangel, Charles Cline, and their I.W.W. comrades arrested in Texas while on their way to Mexico to participate in the revolution in that country. All of the men were Mexicans except Cline, who was an American. They had been attacked by an armed posse, and in the skirmish three of the Mexicans and a deputy sheriff had lost their lives. Now fourteen men, including Rangel and Cline, were awaiting trial on charges of murder. Publicity was needed to arouse the workers of the East to the peril of the situation. I reasoned, I argued, I pleaded with Ben not to permit Lawrence's book to rob him of his senses. But to no avail. Scenes with Ben became more frequent and violent. Our life was daily growing more impossible. A way out had to be found. I could not share my misery with anyone, least of all with Sasha, who had from the beginning been opposed to the scheme of the house and a life with Ben and his mother under the same roof.

The break came. Ben had started again the old plaint about his mother. I listened in silence for a while, and then something snapped in me. The desire seized me to make an end of Ben as far as I was concerned, to do something that would shut out for ever every thought and every memory of this creature who had possessed me all these years. In blind fury I picked up a chair and hurled it at him. It whirled through space and came crashing down at his feet.

He made a step towards me, then stopped and stared at me in wonder and fright.

"Enough!" I cried, beside myself with pain and anger. "I've had enough of you and your mother. Go, take her away — today, this very hour!"

He walked out without a word.

Ben rented a small flat for his mother and went to live with her. He began again attending to the office. We still had that much in common, but the rest seemed dead. I found forgetfulness in more intensive work. I lectured several times a week, participated in the campaign for the I. W. W. boys arrested in connexion with the miners' strike in Canada, and at the same time continued working on my drama book, dictating the manuscript to Fitzi.

I had come to know her better since she had joined the *Mother Earth* group. She was a rare personality, cast in a generous spiritual mould. Her father was Irish, but on her mother's side she came from American pioneer stock, the earliest settlers in Wisconsin. From them Fitzi had inherited her independence and self-reliance. At the age of fifteen she had joined the Seventh Day Adventists, defying the ire of her father. But her search for truth did not terminate there. Her idea of God, as she often said, was much more beautiful and more tolerant than the Adventist conception. So one day she stood up in the midst of the religious service, announced to the assembly that she had not found the truth among them, and walked out of the little country church and out of the ranks of the believers. She became interested in free-thought and radical activities. Socialism disappointed her as being essentially another Church with new dogmas. Her large nature found greater attraction in the freedom and scope of anarchist ideas. I grew to love Fitzi for her inherent idealism and understanding spirit, and we gradually came very close to each other.

The close of the year was at hand, and we had not yet held a house-warming in our new place. New Year's was decided upon as the right moment for our party of friends and active supporters of *Mother Earth* to help kick out the Old with all its trouble and pain and gaily meet the New no matter what it might bring. Rhoda was all excitement and she worked hard and late to make ready for the festive occasion. New Year's Eve brought the procession of friends, among them poets, writers, rebels, and Bohemians of various attitude, behaviour, and habit. They argued about philosophy, social theories, art, and sex. They ate the delicious things Rhoda had prepared and drank the wines our generous Italian comrades had supplied. Everybody danced and grew gay. But my thoughts were with Ben, whose birthday it was. He was thirty-five and I nearing forty-four. That was a tragic difference in age. I felt lonely and unutterably sad.

Still young was the new year when the country began to echo with new outrages against labour. The horrors in West Virginia were followed by cruelties in the hop-fields of Wheatfield, California, in the mines of Trinidad, Colorado, and in Calumet, Michigan. The police, the militia, and gangs of armed citizens were carrying on a reign of despotism.

In Wheatfield twenty-three thousand hop-pickers, who had come in answer to a newspaper advertisement, found themselves confronted by conditions not decent even for cattle. They were kept at work all day without rest or proper food, even without drinking-water. To quench their thirst in the scorching heat they were compelled to buy lemonade at five cents a glass from members of the Durst family, the owners of the hop-field. Unable to endure such a state of affairs, the pickers sent a delegate to Durst. The delegate was assaulted and beaten up, whereupon the men struck. The local authorities, aided by the Burns Detective Agency, the Citizens' Alliance, and subsequently the National Guard, terrorized the strikers. They broke up a gathering of the workers and opened fire without provocation. Two men were killed and a number wounded; the District Attorney and a deputy sheriff also lost their lives. Many of the strikers were put through the " third degree," one of them, grilled without sleep for fourteen days to extract a confession, attempted suicide. Another, who had lost his arm in the police attack, hanged himself.

The latest victim of these American Black Hundreds was Mother Jones, a famous native agitator. In truly tsarist manner she was deported from Trinidad at the order of General Chase, who threatened to imprison her *incommunicado* if she dared to return. In Calumet, Moyer, the president of the Western Federation of Miners, was shot

in the back and driven out of town. Similar happenings in various
parts of the country decided me to give a lecture dealing with the
right of labour to self-defence. The Radical Library of Philadelphia
invited me to speak on that subject in the Labor Temple. Before I
reached the hall, the police drove everybody out and locked the place.
I delivered my talk none the less, in the quarters of the Radical Library, as well as in New York and in a number of other cities.

My relation with Ben, which had grown more strained, finally
became unbearable. Ben was no less unhappy than I. He decided to
return with his mother to Chicago and take up the practice of medicine again. I did not try to detain him.

For the first time I was to give a full course of lectures on " The
Social Significance of the Modern Drama " in New York, both in
English and in Yiddish. The Berkeley Theatre on Forty-fourth Street
was rented for the purpose. It was disheartening to start out on an
important venture without Ben, for the first time in six years. His
departure, which had given me a feeling of release, now resistlessly
drew me to him. He was ever present in my thoughts, and my hunger
for him kept growing. Nights I would determine to cut myself loose
once and for all and not even accept his letters. The morning would
find me eagerly scanning my mail for the handwriting so electrifying
in its effect on me. No man I had loved had ever so paralysed my
will before. I fought against it with all my strength, but my heart
wildly called for Ben.

I could see from his letters that he was going through the same
purgatory as I, and that he also could not free himself. He yearned to
return to me. His attempt to take up the practice of medicine had
failed; I had made him see his profession in a new light, he wrote, and
he felt how inadequate it was to give relief. He knew that the poor
needed better working- and living-conditions; they needed sunshine,
fresh air, and rest. What could powders and pills do for them? A
great many physicians realize that the health of their patients does
not depend on their prescriptions. They know the true remedy, but
they prefer to grow rich on the credulity of the poor. He could never
again become one of those, Ben wrote. I had spoiled him for that. I
and my work had become too vital a part of his life. He loved me.
He knew it now better than at any time since we had first met. He
knew he had been impossible in his behaviour in New York. He had
never felt free or at ease with my friends. They had not shown faith

in him, and that had made him more antagonistic towards them. And I, too, had seemed changed when in New York; I made him feel inferior to Sasha, and I was more critical of him than when we were alone on tour. We must try again, he pleaded; we must go away, just by ourselves, on tour. He wanted nothing else.

His letters were like a narcotic. They put my brain to sleep, but they made my heart beat faster. I clung to the assurance of his love.

Again, in the winter, the country was in the throes of unemployment. Over a quarter of a million persons were out of work in New York, and other cities were stricken in no lesser degree. The suffering was augmented by the extraordinarily severe weather. The papers minimized the appalling state of affairs; the politicians and reformers remained lukewarm. A few palliatives and the threadbare suggestion of an investigation were all they could offer to meet the widespread misery.

The militant elements resolved upon action. The anarchists and the I.W.W.'s organized the unemployed and secured considerable relief for them. At my Berkeley Theatre lectures and other meetings appeals for the jobless met with generous response. But it was a mere drop in the ocean of need.

Then an unexpected thing happened, which gave the situation compelling publicity. Out of the ranks of starved and frozen humanity the slogan came to visit religious institutions. The unemployed, led by a vivid youth named Frank Tannenbaum, began a march on the churches of New York.

We all had loved Frank for his wide-awakeness and his unassuming ways. He had spent much of his free time in our office, reading and helping in the work connected with *Mother Earth*. His fine qualities held out the hope that Frank would some day play an important part in the labour struggle. None of us had expected however that our studious, quiet friend would so quickly respond to the call of the hour.

Whether out of fear or because of the realization of the significance of the march on the churches, several of them gave shelter, food, and money to the bands of unemployed. Emboldened by their success, one hundred and eighty-nine jobless men, with Frank at their head, went to one of the Catholic churches in the city. Instead of receiving them with loving-kindness a priest at St. Alphonsus Church, turned traitor to his God, who had commanded that one give all to the poor. In connivance with two detectives the priest trapped Frank Tannenbaum and had him and several of the unemployed arrested.

Frank was condemned to serve a year in the penitentiary and to pay a five-hundred-dollar fine, which meant an additional five hundred days' imprisonment. He made a splendid stand, his speech in his own defence being intelligent and defiant.

The most outrageous aspect of the Tannenbaum arrest and conviction was the silence maintained by the so-called sponsors of the oppressed. Not a finger did the socialists raise to awaken the public to the obvious conspiracy on the part of the authorities and the St. Alphonsus Church to " make an example " of Frank Tannenbaum. The New York *Call,* a socialist daily, sneered at the convicted boys and even said that Frank Tannenbaum had deserved a spanking.

The Socialist Party and some prominent I.W.W. leaders tried to paralyse the activities of the jobless. This only helped to increase the zeal of the Conference of the Unemployed, which consisted of various labour and radical organizations. A mass meeting at Union Square was decided upon and the date fixed for March 21. Neither the Socialists nor the I.W.W.'s would participate. It was Sasha who was the active spirit of the movement. He had a double share to perform, as I was hard at work finishing my manuscript, lecturing frequently, and supervising our office.

The mass meeting was large and spirited; it reminded me of a similar event in the same place and for the same purpose, the demonstration of August 1893. Apparently nothing had changed since then. Now as then capitalism was relentless, the State crushing every individual and social right, and the Church in league with them. Now as then those daring to give voice to the suffering of the dumb multitude were persecuted and jailed, and the masses too seemed to have remained as ever in their submissive helplessness. The thought was depressing and made me want to run away from the square. But I stayed. I stayed because deep down in me there was the certainty that there is no sameness in nature. Eternal change, I knew, is for ever at work, life always is in flux, new currents flowing from the dried-up springs of the old. I stayed, and I spoke to the huge crowd as I could speak only when really lifted out of myself.

I left the square after my speech, while Sasha remained at the meeting. When he came home, I learned that the demonstration had ended in a parade up Fifth Avenue, the vast assembly marching and carrying a large black flag as a symbol of their revolt. It must have been a menacing sight to the dwellers on Fifth Avenue no less than to the police, for the latter did not interfere. The unemployed marched all the way to the Ferrer Center, from Fourteenth to One Hundred and Seventh Street, where they were treated to a substantial meal, given tobacco and cigarettes, and provided with temporary lodgings.

This demonstration was the beginning of a city-wide campaign for the unemployed. Sasha, whose valour had endeared him to everyone who knew about his life, was its organizing and directing influence. In his tireless efforts he had the support of a large number of our young rebels, who vigorously worked with him.

My Berkeley Theatre series brought some interesting and amusing experiences. One was the help I was able to give a stranded group of Welsh players; the other an offer to go on the vaudeville stage. My drama lectures afforded me free access to the theatres, and thus I happened to attend the initial performance of a play called *Change,* by J. O. Francis, a Welsh dramatist. It proved to be the most powerful social drama I had seen in the English language. The appalling conditions of the Welsh miners and their desperate struggle to wrench a few pitiful pennies from their masters was as moving as Zola's *Germinal.* Besides this theme the play also treated the age-long struggle between the stubborn acquiescence of the old generation in things as they are and the bold aspirations of the young. *Change* was a stirring work of social significance and it was magnificently interpreted by the Welsh group. No wonder that most reviewers damned the play. A friend informed me that the Welsh troupe was stranded, and asked me to interest the radical element in its behalf.

At a special matinée performance, which I had helped to arrange, I met a number of New York dramatists and literati. One very popular playwright expressed surprise that such an arch-destructionist as I should care for creative drama. I tried to explain to him that anarchism represented the urge of expression in every phase of life and art. Seeing his uncomprehending look, I remarked: "Even those who only *think* they are dramatists will have opportunity in a free society. If they lack real talent, they will still have other honourable professions to choose from, like shoemaking, for instance."

After the performance many of those present expressed their willingness to come to the rescue of the stranded players. I arranged to bring the matter also to the attention of my Sunday audiences and made an appeal in *Mother Earth*. The following Sunday I delivered a lecture on *Change*. The entire Welsh company were present as my guests, and I succeeded in arousing enough interest to keep their theatre going for several weeks. Not the least help to them were the advance notices which our friends in every city gave them when they were touring the country.

At the close of my drama course I was approached by a representative of the Victoria Theatre, a vaudeville house owned by Oscar Hammerstein. He offered me an engagement to appear twice a day, naming a thousand dollars as my approximate weekly salary. I laughed it off at first. The suggestion of going on the vaudeville stage did not appeal to me. But the man kept on urging the advantages of reaching large audiences not to mention the money I would earn. I dismissed the proposal as ridiculous, but gradually the idea of the opportunities the venture would give prevailed upon me. The poverty of the unemployed affected the receipts of our meetings; most people could not afford such luxuries as books or lectures now. The hope that our new quarters might diminish our expenses had also failed to materialize. Several weeks on the vaudeville stage would free me from the everlasting economic grind. They might give me a year to myself, to cut loose from everybody and everything, a year to drift, to read books for their inherent value and not merely for the use they might be to my lectures. This hope silenced all my objections, and I went to Hammerstein's.

The manager informed me that he would have to try me out first, to see what was the drawing power of my name. We went back-stage, where he introduced me to some of the performers. It was a motley crowd of dancers, acrobats, and men with trained dogs. "I'll have to sandwich you in," the manager said. He was not sure whether I was to come on before the high kicker or after the trained dogs. At any rate I could not have more than ten minutes. From behind the curtain I watched the pitiful efforts to amuse the public, the horrible contortions of the dancer, whose flabby body was laced into youthful appearance, the cracked voice of the singer, the cheap jokes of the funny man, and the coarse hilarity of the crowd. Then I fled. I knew I could not stand up in such an atmosphere to plead my ideas, not for all the money in the world.

The last Sunday at the Berkeley Theatre was turned into a gala

night. Leonard D. Abbott presided, and among the speakers were the
noted actress Mary Shaw, the first to defy American purists with
her performances of *Ghosts* and of *Mrs. Warren's Profession;* Fola
La Follette, gifted and frankly outspoken; and George Middleton,
who had a volume of one-act plays to his credit. They dwelt on what
the drama meant to them, and what a powerful factor it was in
awakening social consciousness in people who might not be reached
in any other way. They were very appreciative of my work, and I
was grateful to them for making me feel that my efforts had brought
some of the American intelligentsia into closer rapport with the
struggle of the masses. The evening strengthened my conviction that
whatever contribution I had made in that direction had been due in
part to my never having permitted anyone to "sandwich" me in.

My Berkeley lectures brought me a valuable gift in the form of my
drama notes in typewriting. Stenographers had often tried to take
down my speeches, but in vain. My delivery was too rapid, they said,
especially when I was carried away by my theme. A young man named
Paul Munter was the first in his profession to beat my flow of words
with his stenographic speed. He attended my entire series, for six
weeks, and at the end presented me with my course in perfectly typewritten sheets.

Paul's gift proved to be of great value in the preparation of my
manuscript of *The Social Significance of the Modern Drama*. Thanks
to it the work was less difficult than the writing of my essays, though
I had been in a more tranquil state of mind then; I still had hopes of
a harmonious life with Ben. Little was left of that hope now. Perhaps therefore I clung more tenaciously to its remaining shreds.
Ben's pleading letters from Chicago added fuel to the smouldering
fires of my longing. After two months I began to realize the wisdom
of the Russian peasant saying: "If you drink, you'll die, and if you
don't drink, you'll die. Better drink and die."

To be away from Ben meant sleepless nights, restless days, sickening yearning. To be near him involved conflict and strife, daily denial
of my pride. But it also meant ecstasy and renewed vigour for my
work. I would have Ben and go with him on tour again, I decided.
If the price was high, I would pay it; but I would drink, I would
drink!

Sasha had never been more thoughtful and considerate than during the months of my struggle to free myself from Ben. He was

stimulatingly helpful with the revision of my drama book; in fact, I let him do most of it himself. I felt the work safe in his hands: he was scrupulously conscientious about not changing the spirit or tendency of my writing. We also collaborated on *Mother Earth*. There were wonderful nights when we would prepare copy for the printer and drink strong coffee to keep us going till the break of day. They brought us closer to each other than we had been for a long time past — not that anything could ever loosen our common bonds or affect our friendship, which had stood the test of so many fires.

Depending upon Sasha to read the proofs of my book, and with Fitzi in charge of the office, I could now start on tour. Fitzi had proved herself not only very efficient, but a real friend as well, a beautiful soul, whose interest in our labours made me ashamed of my early doubts of her. Sasha had also realized that his former objections to the "stranger" were groundless. They had become friends and worked harmoniously together. Everything was ready for my departure.

My drama book was off the press, looking quite attractive in its simple attire. It was the first English volume of its kind to point out the social meaning of thirty-two plays by eighteen authors of different countries. My only regret was that my own adopted land had to be left out. I had tried diligently to find some American dramatist who could be placed alongside the great Europeans, but I could discover no one. Commendable beginnings there were by Eugene Walter, Rachel Crothers, Charles Klein, George Middleton, and Butler Davenport. The dramatic master, however, was not yet in sight. He would no doubt appear some day, but meanwhile I had to be content with calling the attention of America to the works of the foremost playwrights of Europe and the social significance of modern dramatic art.

At a lecture in Toledo a visiting-card had been left on my table. It was from Robert Henri, who had requested that I let him know what lectures I was planning to deliver in New York. I had heard of Henri, had seen his exhibitions, and had been told that he was a man of advanced social views. Subsequently, at a Sunday lecture in New York, a tall, well-built man came up and introduced himself as Robert Henri. "I enjoy your magazine," he said, "especially the articles on Walt Whitman. I love Walt, and I follow everything that is written about him."

I learned to know Henri as an exceptional personality, a free and generous nature. He was in fact an anarchist in his conception of art and its relation to life. When we started the Ferrer evening classes, he quickly responded to the invitation to instruct our art students. He also interested George Bellows and John Sloan, and together they helped to create a spirit of freedom in the art class which probably did not exist anywhere else in New York at that time.

Later Robert Henri asked me to sit for my portrait. I was very busy at the time; besides, several people had already tried to paint me, with little success. Henri said he wanted to depict the "real Emma Goldman." "But which is the real one?" I asked; "I have never been able to unearth her." His beautiful studio in Gramercy Park, far removed from the dirt and noise of the city, and the sweet hospitality of Mrs. Henri were balm to me. There were talks on art, literature, and libertarian education. Henri was well versed in these subjects; he possessed, moreover, unusual intuition for every sincere striving. During those illuminating hours I learned of the art-school he had started some years before. "The students are left entirely to themselves," he said, "to develop whatever is in them. I merely answer questions or give suggestions on the solution of their more difficult problems." He never sought to impose his ideas on his pupils.

I was naturally anxious to see the portrait, but, knowing Henri's sensitiveness about showing unfinished work, I did not ask for it. I was not in New York when the painting was done, but some time later my sister Helena wrote me that she had seen it at an exhibition in Rochester. "I should not have known it was you if your name had not been under it," she told me. Several other friends agreed with her. I was certain, however, that Henri had tried to portray what he conceived to be the "real Emma Goldman." I never saw the painting, but I prized the memory of the sittings, which had given me so much of value.

# CHAPTER XLI

THE TRAIN WAS SPEEDING TOWARDS CHICAGO. MY HEART WAS outwinging it, all aflutter with the yearning to join Ben at last. I was scheduled to deliver twelve lectures and give a drama course in the city. During my stay I came upon the new literary publication called the *Little Review,* and shortly afterwards I met its editor, Margaret C. Anderson. I felt like a desert wanderer who unexpectedly discovers a stream of fresh water. At last a magazine to sound a note of rebellion in creative endeavour! The *Little Review* lacked clarity on social questions, but it was alive to new art forms and was free from the mawkish sentimentality of most American publications. Its main appeal to me lay in its strong and fearless critique of conventional standards, something I had been looking for in the United States for twenty-five years. "Who is this Margaret Anderson?" I inquired of the friend who had shown me a copy of the magazine. "A charming American girl," he replied, " and she is anxious to interview you." I told him I did not care to be interviewed, but that I did want to meet the editor of the *Little Review.*

When Miss Anderson came to my hotel, I went to the elevator to meet her. I was surprised to see a *chic* society girl, and, thinking that I must have misunderstood the name, I turned back to my room. "Oh, Miss Goldman," the girl called, " I am Margaret Anderson!" Her butterfly appearance was disappointing, so radically different from my mental picture of the *Little Review* editor. My tone was cold as I asked her into my room, but it did not seem to affect my visitor in the least. "I came to invite you to my place," she said impetuously, "just to rest and relax a little; you look so tired and you are always surrounded by so many people." At her home I would need to see no one, she ran on, I should be entirely undisturbed and could do as I pleased. "You can bathe in the lake, take walks, or just lie perfectly

still," she coaxed; "I will wait on you and play for you." She had a
taxi waiting for us to go at once. I was overwhelmed by the wordy
avalanche and I felt remorseful at the frigid reception I had given
the generous girl.

In a large apartment facing Lake Michigan I found, besides Miss
Anderson, the latter's sister with her two children, and a girl named
Harriet Dean. The entire furniture consisted of a piano, piano-stool,
several broken cots, a table, and some kitchen chairs. However this
strange *ménage* managed to pay the undoubtedly large rent, there
was evidently no money for anything else. In some mysterious way,
though, Margaret Anderson and her friend procured flowers, fruit,
and dainties for me.

Harriet Dean was as much a novel type to me as Margaret, yet
the two were entirely unlike. Harriet was athletic, masculine-looking,
reserved, and self-conscious. Margaret, on the contrary, was feminine in the extreme, constantly bubbling over with enthusiasm. A few
hours with her entirely changed my first impression and made me
realize that underneath her apparent lightness was depth and strength
of character to pursue whatever aim in life she might choose. Before
long I saw that the girls were not actuated by any sense of social injustice, like the young Russian intelligentsia, for instance. Strongly indi-
vidualized, they had broken the shackles of their middle-class homes
to find release from family bondage and bourgeois tradition. I regretted their lack of social consciousness, but as rebels for their own
liberation Margaret Anderson and Harriet Dean strengthened my
faith in the possibilities of my adopted country.

My visit with them was entertaining and restful. I was happy to
find two young American women who were seriously interested in
modern ideas. We spent our time talking and discussing. In the evening Margaret would play the piano and I would sing Russian folk-
songs or relate to the girls some episodes of my life.

Margaret's playing was not that of a trained artist. There was
a certain original and vibrant quality in it, particularly when no
strangers were present. At such moments she was able to give full
expression to all her emotion and intensity. Music stirred me profoundly, but Margaret's playing exerted a peculiar effect, like the
sight of the sea, which always made me uneasy and restless. I had
never learned to swim and I feared deep water, yet on the beach I
would be filled with a desire to reach out towards the waves and

become submerged in their embrace. Whenever I heard Margaret play, I was overcome by the same sensation and an uneasy craving. The days spent at her home on Lake Michigan passed all too quickly, but during the rest of my stay in Chicago Margaret and " Deansie " were never away from my side for very long.

Through Margaret I met most of the contributors to the *Little Review,* among them Ben Hecht, Maxwell Bodenheim, Caesar, Alexander Kaun, Allen Tanner, and others. Able writers they were, yet none of them possessed the all-absorbing ardour and daring of Margaret Anderson.

Harriet Monroe, of the *Poetry Magazine,* and Maurice Browne, of the Little Theatre, belonged to the same circle. I was particularly interested in the new dramatic experiment of Mr. Browne. He had talent and sincerity, but he was too dominated by the past to make the Little Theatre an effective influence. The Greek drama and the classics were certainly of great value, I often told him, but thoughtful people were nowadays seeking dramatic expression of the human problems of our own day. As a matter of fact, no one in Chicago outside of Mr. Browne's troupe and their small circle of adherents was aware of the existence of the Little Theatre. Life simply passed it by. The greater the pity, because Maurice Browne was very much in earnest about his efforts.

On this visit in Chicago I was fortunate to hear some very fine music. Percy Grainger, Alma Gluck, Mary Garden, and Casals concerted in the city during my stay. Such an array of artists was a rare treat.

Alma Gluck gripped me with her first tones. Her Hebrew chants especially gave full sway to the range of her rich voice. The sorrows of six thousand years were made poignantly real by her exquisite singing.

Mary Garden I had seen on previous occasions. Once in St. Louis she had been denied a theatre for her performance of *Salome,* which the moral busybodies had declared indecent. Some reporter had called Mary Garden's attention to the similarity of her fight for free expression to that of Emma Goldman, and Mary had spoken in high praise of me. She knew nothing about anarchism, she had said, or anything about my ideas, but she admired my stand for freedom. I wrote her my appreciation. In reply she asked me to let her know next time we happened to be in the same city. Later, in Portland,

Mary had recognized me in the front row just as some admirers had presented her with a huge basket of roses. Stepping to the edge of the stage, she picked out the largest and reddest ones and threw them into my lap with an airy kiss. Years before, in 1900, when in Paris, she had delighted me by her rendering of Charpentier's *Louise* and Massenet's *Thais*. But never had I seen her so lovely and fascinating as in the opera *Pelléas et Mélisande,* which I attended in the Chicago Auditorium with Margaret Anderson. She was youth, naïvité, and the earth-spirit exquisitely blended into one.

The greatest musical event during my stay in Chicago was the playing of the Spanish 'cellist Casals. I had always loved the 'cello best, but until I heard this conjuror, I had guessed little of its possibilities. Casal's touch unlocked its treasures, made it vibrate like the human soul and sing in velvet tones.

Unexpectedly came the shocking news of the massacre of workers in Ludlow, Colorado, of the shooting of strikers and the burning of women and children in their tents. Drama lectures appeared trifling, with the flames of Ludlow rising to the sky.

The coal-miners in southern Colorado had been on strike for months. The Colorado Fuel and Iron Company, a Rockefeller combine, appealed to the State for "protection" while at the same time they were shipping thugs and gunmen to the coal region. The miners were evicted from their huts, which were on company property. With their wives and children they pitched tents and prepared for the long winter. The Rockefeller interests prevailed upon Governor Ammon to call out the militia to "keep order."

Arriving in Denver with Ben, I learned that the labour leaders would be glad to accept funds I might raise at my lectures, but that they did not care to have it known that they were in any way connected with my efforts. No more encouragement did I receive from our own comrades in Ludlow. The authorities would not permit me to come to the city, they wrote, and if I did get there, the papers would proclaim that I was behind the strike. It was painful to know that I was not wanted by the very people for whom I had worked all my life.

Fortunately I had an independent forum, *Mother Earth* and my lectures. On my own platform I should be free to denounce the Ludlow crime and point out its lesson to labour. We started our meetings, and within two weeks I was able to demonstrate that a few militants imbued with idealism could focus greater attention on a pressing social issue than large organizations that lacked the courage to speak out. My lectures helped to turn the full light of publicity on Ludlow. Ludlow, Wheatland, the invasion of Mexico by Federal troops — they were all streams from the same source. I discussed them before audiences reaching into the thousands, and we succeeded in raising large sums for the various struggles.

On our arrival in Denver we had found twenty-seven I.W.W. boys in jail. They had been arrested as a result of a free-speech campaign and had been tortured in the sweat-box for refusing to work on the rock-pile. Our efforts in their behalf were successful. On their release they marched through the streets with banners and songs to our hall, where they were received in the spirit of comradeship and solidarity.

One of the interesting experiences of my Denver stay was meeting Julia Marlowe Sothern and Gustave Frohman. We discussed modern plays. Frohman was sure they did not interest the theatre-going public, and I argued that New York had also another public, more intelligent and appreciative than the one in the habit of flocking to Broadway. That public, I insisted, would support a theatre giving the dramas of Ibsen, Strindberg, Hauptmann, Shaw, and the Russians. I offered to prove that a repertory theatre, with prices running from fifty cents to a dollar and a half, could be made self-sustaining. Mr. Frohman thought I was an impractical optimist. He was interested, however, and he promised to talk the matter over further with me when we were both back in New York.

I had seen Miss Marlowe and Sothern in *The Sunken Bell,* by Gerhart Hauptmann. I did not care for his Heinrich, but Julia Marlowe as Rautendelein was sublime, and she was equally great as Katharina in *The Taming of the Shrew* and also as Juliet. Miss Marlowe must have been nearing forty at the time. She was rather heavy for youthful parts, yet her superb acting at no time broke the illusion of Rautendelein, the lithe, wild mountain-spirit, or the unsophisticated naïveté of Juliet, the child-woman.

Sothern was stiff and uninteresting, but Julia made up for both by her charm, grace, and unaffectedness. She sent flowers to my lectures and a kindly greeting to " ease the task of always having to be before the public." Well she knew how painful it often was.

While Ben and I were busy with our meetings in the West, Sasha was engaged in strenuous activities in New York. With Fitzi, Leonard

D. Abbott, the comrades of anarchist groups, and the young members of the Ferrer School he was conducting the unemployed movement and the anti-militarist campaign. Their persistency in fighting for free speech in New York had resulted in the repeated breaking up of their gatherings by mounted police, involving incredible brutality and violence. But their perseverance and defiance of arbitrary official regulations in the end impressed public opinion and they won the right of assembly in Union Square without police permission. From Sasha's brief notes I could only guess what was happening in New York, but soon the newspapers were filled with accounts of the work of the Anti-Militarist League, which Sasha had founded, and the demonstrations in behalf of the Ludlow miners held in New York and in Tarrytown, Rockefeller's citadel. It was wonderful to me to see Sasha's old spirit rising to the battle, and to observe his extraordinary skill in organizing and handling the work.

The New York activities resulted in a number of arrests, among them that of Becky Edelsohn and several boys from the Ferrer School. Sasha wrote that Becky had been splendid at her trial, where she had conducted her own defence. On being convicted she had declared a forty-eight-hour hunger strike in protest. It was the first time that a political prisoner had done this in America. I had always known Becky to be brave, though her lack of responsibility and perseverance in her personal life had for years been a source of irritation to me. I was therefore very glad to see her show such strength of character. It is often the exceptional moment that discovers unsuspected qualities.

Liberal and radical elements in New York were co-operating in protest against the Ludlow butchery. The " Silent Parade " in front of Rockefeller's office, organized by Upton Sinclair and his wife, and the various other demonstrations were arousing the East to the appalling conditions in Colorado.

I eagerly scanned the papers from New York. I had no anxiety about Sasha, for I knew how dependable and cool he was in times of danger. But I longed to be at his side, in my beloved city, to take part with him in those stirring activities. My engagements, however, kept me in the West. Then came the news of an explosion in a tenement-house on Lexington Avenue which cost the lives of three men — Arthur Carron, Charles Berg, and Karl Hanson — and of an unknown woman. The names were unfamiliar to me. The press was filled with the wildest rumours. The bomb, it was reported, had been intended for Rockefeller, whom the speakers at the New York meetings had charged with direct responsibility for the Ludlow massacres. The premature explosion had probably saved his life, the papers declared. Sasha's name was dragged into the case, and the police were looking for him and the owner of the Lexington apartment, our comrade Louise Berger. Word came from Sasha that the three men who had lost their lives in the explosion were comrades who had worked with him in the Tarrytown campaign. They had been badly beaten up by the police at one of the Union Square demonstrations. The bomb might have been intended for Rockefeller, Sasha wrote, but in any case the men had kept their intentions to themselves, for neither he nor anyone else knew how the explosion had occurred.

Comrades, idealists, manufacturing a bomb in a congested tenement-house! I was aghast at such irresponsibility. But the next moment I remembered a similiar event in my own life. It came back with paralysing horror. In my mind I saw my little room in Peppi's flat, on Fifth Street, its window-blinds drawn, Sasha experimenting with a bomb, and me watching. I had silenced my fear for the tenants, in case of an accident, by repeating to myself that the end justified the means. With accusing clarity I now relived that nerve-racking week in July 1892. In the zeal of fanaticism I had believed that the end justifies the means! It took years of experience and suffering to emancipate myself from the mad idea. Acts of violence committed as a protest against unbearable social wrongs — I still believed them inevitable. I understood the spiritual forces culminating in such *Attentats* as Sasha's, Bresci's, Angiolillo's, Czolgosz's, and those of others whose lives I had studied. They had been urged on by their great love for humanity and their acute sensitiveness to injustice. I had always taken my place with them as against every form of organized oppression. But though my sympathies were with the man who protested against social crimes by a resort to extreme measures, I nevertheless felt now that I could never again participate in or approve of methods that jeopardized innocent lives.

I was worried about Sasha. He was the spirit of the tremendous campaign in the East, and I feared the police would involve him in their dragnet. I wanted to return to New York, but his letters held me back. He was perfectly safe, he wrote, and there were plenty of people to help him in the work. He had succeeded in obtaining the bodies of the dead comrades for cremation, and he was planning a monster demonstration at Union Square. The authorities definitely declared in the press that no public funeral would be permitted. All the radical groups, including the I.W.W., repudiated Sasha's intention. Even Bill Haywood warned him to desist from his plan because he was " sure to cause another eleventh of November." But Sasha's group refused to be terrorized. He publicly announced that he would stand responsible for anything that might happen at the meeting, on condition that no police officers be permitted within the lines of the demonstration.

The public funeral took place in spite of official prohibition. Union Square seethed with a crowd of twenty thousand people. At the last moment the police had decided not to permit Sasha, who was to preside at the demonstration, to reach the square. Detectives and reporters besieged our house. Sasha appeared on the front stoop to talk to them and they asked to see the urn containing the cremated remains of the Lexington Avenue victims. He stepped back into the house and then slipped out through the back and some neighbouring yards. He had taken the precaution to order a red automobile to wait for him in a nearby street. At a furious pace it was driven to Union Square. For blocks all approaches to the square were crowded. It seemed impossible to reach the platform. But before Sasha could open the door of the machine, police officers — in their excitement undoubtedly taking the automobile to be that of the Fire Chief — obsequiously cleared a lane for the auto right through the crowd to the very front of the platform. When Sasha stepped out, the officers were amazed to see who it was. He quickly ascended the platform. It was too late for the police to do anything without causing a blood bath.

Now the remains of the dead comrades, Sasha wrote me, were deposited in a specially designed urn in the form of a clenched fist rising from the depths. The urn was exposed in the office of *Mother Earth,* which had been decorated with wreaths and red and black banners. Thousands passed through our quarters to pay the last tribute to Carron, Berg, and Hanson.

I was happy to learn that the perilous situation in New York had ended so favourably. But when I received copies of the July issue of *Mother Earth,* I was dismayed at its contents. The Union Square speeches were published there in full; with the exception of Sasha's own address and those of Leonard D. Abbott and Elizabeth Gurley

Flynn, the harangues were of a most violent character. I had tried always to keep our magazine free from such language, and now the whole number was filled with prattle about force and dynamite. I was so furious that I wanted the entire issue thrown into the fire. But it was too late; the magazine had gone out to the subscribers.

The persistent efforts of one man in Portland, Oregon, exerted an influence in that town that for its potency could hardly be equalled in any other American city. I refer to my friend Charles Erskine Scott Wood. By position he belonged to the ultra-conservative set, yet he was among the most unflinching opponents of the social layer from which he sprang. It was owing to his efforts that the Public Library was granted to so dangerous a person as I was considered to be. Mr. Wood presided at my first lecture, which was on " Intellectual Proletarians," and his presence brought an enormous audience.

Portland was in the throes of a prohibition campaign. My talk on " Victims of Morality," which touched on this subject, resulted in an uproar. It was one of the most exciting evenings in my public career. The prohibitionists and the pro-liquorists almost came to blows on the occasion.

The following day a man called on Mr. Wood and offered to buy my lecture notes, not the part dealing with the suppression of sex, but the one where I had enlarged on the right of grown-ups to choose their drinks. The caller represented the Saloon-Keepers' League, and his organization wanted my notes as propaganda in their anti-prohibition campaign. Mr. Wood informed him that he would submit the offer to me, but that I was a " queer creature " and would probably not consent to having only half of my lecture published. " But she will be paid," the man cried, " and any price she wants! " Needless to say, I declined to appear as an agent of the Saloon-Keepers' League.

The power of the Montana copper-kings, faithfully supported by the Catholic Church, made Butte and other smelting-towns in the State barren ground except for the sweet hospitality of my friends Annie and Abe Edelstadt, the latter a brother of our dead poet. The system of espionage had been perfected by the bosses. Their employees were surrounded by spies not only when at work, but also in their free hours. The " spotters " dogged every step of the men and made detailed reports on their behaviour. In consequence those modern slaves lived in fear of displeasing their masters and losing their jobs. The situation was aggravated by reaction in the union ranks. The Western Federation of Miners, long in the control of corrupt and unscrupulous officials, helped to silence the voice of labour protest. But pressure from above begets rebellion. The break had to come. The aroused workers dynamited the Union Hall, drove their leaders out of town, and organized a new union along revolutionary lines.

It was a changed atmosphere that greeted us on our arrival in Butte. No particular efforts were necessary to arouse interest in my lectures. The people came in a body and openly demonstrated their independence. They fearlessly asked questions and participated in the discussion. If any " spotters " were in the audience, they were unknown to the men, who would have certainly given them short shrift.

Very significant also was the presence of many women, especially at my lecture on " Birth-control." Formerly they would not have dared to inquire about such matters even privately; now they stood up in a public assembly and frankly avowed their hatred of their position as domestic drudges and child-bearers. It was an extraordinary manifestation, most encouraging to me.

All through the years no decent hall had been accessible to us in Chicago. I had often been compelled to speak in dreadful places, generally in the rear of a saloon. That did not, however, prevent the so-called better class from attending my lectures. Not rarely the street in front of the hall would be lined with automobiles, thus providing a chance for the Wobblies, and even for some of my own comrades, to protest against my " educating the bourgeoisie." My last lecture in Chicago in April had been nearly broken up by a drunken man who had drifted in from the saloon and who insisted on taking charge of the proceedings. At the close of the meeting two strangers left their visiting-cards with Ben. They asked him to let them know when I would return to Chicago and promised to secure an appropriate place for my future lectures.

Having received many promises, few of which had ever been fulfilled, I had little faith in this one. Nevertheless I wrote the strangers that I would meet them on my way back from the Coast. After leaving Butte I proceeded to Chicago, where I also intended to visit Margaret Anderson and Deansie. The men proved to be a rich advertising-agent and a stock-broker! We discussed the best means of organizing a series of drama lectures and it was decided to secure the Fine Arts recital hall. The men offered to finance the venture and I wondered why they should do it, unless it be that wealthy Jews love to engage in " uplift " work. I made it clear to them that I must remain as free to speak in the fashionable place as in the back room of a saloon. It was agreed that I should wire my lecture dates later on.

When I arrived in New York I was confronted with a serious financial situation. Sasha's activities among the unemployed, together with the anti-militarist and Ludlow campaigns, had swallowed up most of the funds I had sent to our office from my tour. We could not meet the obligations of *Mother Earth,* much less the expense of the house, which in my absence had been turned into a free-for-all lodging- and feeding-place. We were in debt to our printer and to the mailing-house, and money was owed to every store-keeper in the neighbour-hood. The strain of the agitation he had carried on, the danger and the responsibility he had faced, had left Sasha in a high-strung and irritable state. He was sensitive to my criticism, and hurt that I should even mention money matters. I had hoped for rest, harmony, and peace after six months of constant lecturing and the struggle involved in my tour. Instead I was swamped with new cares.

I was dazed by the situation and I felt very indignant with Sasha. Entirely absorbed in his own propaganda, he had given me no thought. He was the revolutionist of old, with the same fanatical belief in the Cause. His sole concern was the movement, and I was to him but a means for it. He was nothing more to himself than that; how could I expect to be any more to him?

Sasha did not understand my resentment. He grew impatient at my mentioning money matters. He had spent our funds for the move-ment; the latter was more important than my drama lectures, he said. I spoke bitterly to him, telling him that without my drama lec-tures he would have had no means to finance his activities. The clash made us both unhappy. Sasha withdrew into himself.

The only ones I could turn to in my misery were my dear nephew Saxe and my old friend Max. Both were very understanding, but neither of them was worldly enough to be of much assistance to me. I should have to face the situation alone.

I decided to give up our house and to declare myself bankrupt. My friend Gilbert E. Roe, to whom I confided my troubles, laughed at my strange notion. " Bankruptcy is resorted to by those who want to get out of paying debts," he said; " it will involve you in year-long litigation, and your creditors will attach every penny you make to the end of your days." He offered to lend me money, but I could not accept his generosity.

Then a new idea struck me. I would tell the printer exactly how I stood. The frank and open way is always the best, I decided. My creditors proved to be very accommodating. They lost no sleep over the money I owed them, they said; I could be depended on to make good. It was finally arranged that I pay my indebtedness in monthly instalments. Our mailing-house even declined my promissory notes. " Pay what you can and when you can," the manager said; " your word is good enough for us."

I resolved to start from the bottom up again; to rent a small place — one room for an office, the other for my living-quarters — and to accept every lecture engagement I could secure, and practise the strictest economy in order to keep up *Mother Earth* and my work. I wired Ben dates for my dramatic course in Chicago, and then I went out to look for a new home. It was a discouraging task; the Lexington Avenue explosion and the publicity given to Sasha's activities were fresh in the public mind, and the landlords were timid. But at last I found a two-room loft on One Hundred and Twenty-fifth Street, and I set to work to make it fit for my use.

Sasha and Fitzi came to help me get my new place in order, but our relations were strained. Yet Sasha was too deeply rooted in my being to permit me to remain angry with him very long. There was also something else to change my resentful attitude. The realization had come to me that it was not Sasha, but I who was at fault. Not only since my return from the last tour, but all through the eight years since his release from prison, it was I who had been responsible for the breaks that came between us. I had committed a great wrong against him. Instead of giving him a chance to find his way back to life, after his resurrection, I had brought him into my atmosphere, into an environment that could only be galling to him. I had done this in the mistaken belief, usual with mothers, that they know best what is good for their children; fearing the latter will be crushed in the world outside, they desperately try to shield them from the experiences so essential to their growth. I had committed the same mistake in regard to Sasha. Not only had I not urged him to launch out for

542 Sasha finds sympathy and love

himself, but I had trembled at every step he made, because I could not see him exposed to new suffering and hardships. Yet I had saved him from nothing; I had only awakened his resentment. Perhaps he was not even aware of it, yet it was always there, breaking out in one form or another. Sasha had always wanted his own work and his own place. I had offered him everything one human being can give to another, but I had not helped him to what he wanted and needed most. There was no blinking the hard fact. But now that Sasha had found a woman who could give him both love and understanding, it was my opportunity to repair the wrong I had done him.

I would enable them to go on a cross-country tour, I decided. Once Sasha reached California, he could carry out his dream of a paper of his own.

Fitzi and Sasha eagerly responded to my suggestion for a tour. I arranged with my young friend Anna Baron, who used to do part-time typing for us, to take care of the business side of the *Mother Earth* office. Max and Saxe were to look after the editorial work of the magazine. There were also Hippolyte and other friends to help. Sasha felt rejuvenated, and there was no further friction between us.

One day my friend Bolton Hall called on me. I had worked hard and he no doubt noticed my exhausted condition. "Why not go out to the little farm in Ossining?" he suggested. "Not for worlds," I replied, "as long as my pest is there." "What pest?" he queried in wonder. "Why, Micky, whom for years I have tried vainly to escape." "You mean Herman Mikhailovitch, the timid-looking fellow who used to help in the *Mother Earth* office and the Ferrer Center?" "The very one," I told him; "his apparent timidity has been my curse for a long time." Dear Bolton looked his blank surprise. "Tell me about it," he urged.

I related the story to Bolton. Herman had been a reader of *Mother Earth* for a long time, had faithfully paid his subscription, and often ordered literature. He lived in Brooklyn, but none of us had ever met him. Then one day I received a letter from Omaha asking permission to arrange my meetings there. It was from Herman. Glad that someone in that city had offered to assist, I wired him to go ahead. On my arrival there I found our unknown comrade in rags and looking starved. Ben helped him and we also procured his release when he was locked up for distributing our handbills announcing my meetings. Before I left the city I enabled him to join the painters' union and secure a job. In Minneapolis three days later we were un-expectedly faced by Herman. He wanted to organize my meetings along the route, he declared. I assured him that I appreciated his offer, but that I already had one manager; two would be too much to endure. Herman said nothing more, but when we reached the next town, he was there, and again in the next and in the next. There was no shaking him off; he was either ahead of us or at our rear. The pro-ceeds from my lectures were not sufficient to pay his railroad fare, and I feared lest Herman meet some accident while stealing rides. He be-came an additional worry and burden. In Seattle I could not stand it any more. He would find a job, he said, if I would secure him for a few weeks. I did, and he solemnly promised to remain in Seattle. When we came to Spokane, who should meet us but Herman Mikhailovitch? He did not like the West, he declared, and had decided to return to New York. For the rest of our tour Herman stuck like glue. He was a good worker, ready to do anything to help my meetings; and he was shrewd enough to make himself indispensable to Ben. I gave a sigh of relief when we finally arrived in New York.

Nothing was heard from Herman for some time. Then he showed up again, all in rags. He was working in a laundry, he told me, eighteen hours a day for five dollars a week. In the midst of his story he fell to the floor in a faint. A hurried agreement with Sasha and Hippolyte, to the effect that Herman could earn his keep by assisting in the office, saved him from returning to the laundry, and incidentally also from further fainting spells. He was an intelligent chap, but fame affects some people worse than liquor. Touring with us, getting arrested, and seeing his name in the papers had turned Herman's head. His condition became worse after Ben put him up as one of his stars at a hobo meeting. Herman shared honours with Chuck Connor, the Chinatown celebrity, Sadakichi Hartmann, of weird dance fame, Hutchins Hapgood, widely known for his books on the underworld, Arthur Bullard, intellectual Bohemian and globe-trotter, Ben Reit-man, pseudo-king of Hoboland, and others of the over- and under-world *milieu*.

Herman, now christened Micky, delivered himself of an oration on that occasion, speaking with unchallenged authority on tramping as a superior art. " Everywhere you are forced to sell your labour," he declared, " but on the open road you are free from work. I have pledged myself to be the master of my soul. Rather than work for a boss, I will let others work for me unless I can choose my occupation." He was hailed as a hero and accepted by the fraternity as one of their own.

The next day the papers had write-ups about Micky, " the Irish Jew who had taken a pledge never to work." Micky walked on air, his head held high, his chest expanded, and looking the world contemptuously in the face. In our office he wisely refrained from flaunting his fame — until Ben and I went on tour. Then he declared that he had his own life to live and great things to perform. The boys promptly told him they could not survive such importance in the same house.

In Omaha I was faced by Micky again. He would not be an expense, he assured me; he only wanted to be connected with my work. I could not deny him that. Micky continued as my shadow, ever on my heels, from town to town. I admired his perseverance, though he got on my nerves fearfully. His presence became all-pervading. Then he began to gossip about my New York friends and particularly about Ben, who had been especially patient with him. That broke the camel's back, and Micky fled from my sight.

When we were back in New York, Ben brought the cheerful news that Micky had landed in the city that very day, half-starved and frozen from a long tramp. " Rig him out, give him money, shelter, and food," I said, " only don't bring him here; his attentions are entirely too much for me." Ben did as I asked, but he never stopped talking of poor Micky's plight, and on Christmas Eve he brought him to me as a gift. A snow-storm was raging, and we had a spare room. How could I send the poor creature away?

No sooner did Micky feel secure than he again began to demonstrate his superiority, criticizing, reprimanding, and straining everybody's patience to the breaking-point. In rage one day he raised a cane against Saxe, who had grown tired of listening to his bragging. My presence saved Micky from the sound thrashing he deserved. I told him categorically that he would have to find another place. When we returned from a meeting that night, we found our furnace sabotaged and Micky locked in his room. He was on a hunger strike, his note on my desk informed me, and he would keep it up until I would consent to his remaining in the house. The boys offered to throw him bodily into the street, but I refused to let them do so, hoping Micky would change his mind.

Four days passed, and he was still locked in. I took a pail of water and resolutely climbed up to his room. He opened as soon as he heard my voice. I told him that if he would not get up within five minutes, I would give him a cold shower-bath. He began to weep and to charge me with being cruel. He loved me more than anyone else, he declared; he was my true friend, but now he must die, since I would not requite his affection. He would die right there, and I must help him do so. The boys had suggested that Micky's pranks were due to jealousy, and I had laughed at the silly notion. At last poor Micky's secret was out! But I remained stern. " A nice kind of love is yours, to want to burden me with your death," I said; " don't you think there are worthier causes to go to the electric chair for? " I told him to get up, take a bath, put on clean clothes, and have some food; later on we would decide on the best way for him to commit suicide. He asked permission to go out on the farm and I gladly consented. But, once there, he began pestering me with letters, two and three of them every day, complaining of cold and hunger and threatening suicide again.

" No doubt Micky knows you have a sick conscience," Bolton teased me; " and, besides, consider his unrequited love," he added with a merry twinkle in his eye. " But I'll get him off the farm all right, and I promise not to leave him destitute." Bolton wrote Micky that he had been informed of his illness and poverty, and that there-upon he had notified the authorities of the poorhouse: an officer would call for him in a few days. By return mail Bolton received a reply from Micky to the effect that he was no pauper, and that he had saved enough money to take him to the Coast. Micky left. " Clever man, this Micky," Bolton commented, " but I didn't know you could be so easily imposed on."

The little place at Ossining was at last free from the pest, and I longed for a much-needed rest. But in the confusion I had quite forgotten that young Donald, the son of my dear friend Gertie Vose, was living in the house that I was giving up. Sasha had written me when I was in the West that the boy had come to him with a letter from his mother, and that he had taken him in. Gertie Vose was an old rebel whom I had met in 1897, but I had not seen her son in eighteen years. When I met him again in our house he produced on me a very disagreeable effect, which was probably due to his high-pitched voice or to his shifting look, which seemed to avoid my eyes. But he was Gertie's son, alone and out of work. He seemed undernourished and he was wretchedly dressed. I proposed that he go out for a rest to our little place in Ossining. He told me that he had intended to return home after the Tarrytown campaign, but he was waiting for his mother to send him the fare. He seemed appreciative of my offer, and the next day he left for the farm.

In my new quarters I took up my activities again. Readjustment to the altered conditions involved many hardships, but they were made more bearable by the presence of my good friend Stewart Kerr, who had a room above my little office. He had formerly shared with us our apartment at 210 East Thirteenth Street; of a considerate and non-invasive nature, Stewart was touchingly thoughtful of my welfare and very helpful in numerous ways. It was comforting to have him as my neighbour, the two of us being the only tenants living in the little house.

I was busy preparing the new drama course I had promised to deliver in Chicago and a series of lectures on the war. Three months had passed since its outbreak in Europe. Outside of *Mother Earth* and our anti-militarist campaign in New York I had not been able to raise my voice in the West against the slaughter, except on one occasion, in Butte, when I had spoken from an automobile to a large crowd and denounced the criminal stupidity of war. I felt that but for the socialist betrayal of their ideals, the great catastrophe would have been impossible. In Germany the party counted twelve million adherents. What a power to prevent the declaration of hostilities! But for a quarter of a century the Marxists had trained the workers in obedience and patriotism, trained them to rely on parliamentary activity and, particularly, to trust their socialist leaders blindly. And now most of those leaders had joined hands with the Kaiser! Instead of making common cause with the international proletariat, they had called upon the German workers to rise to the defence of " their " fatherland, the fatherland of the disinherited and degraded. Instead of declaring the general strike and thus paralysing war preparations, they had voted the Government money for slaughter. The socialists of the other countries, with certain notable exceptions, had followed their example. No wonder, for the German social democracy had for decades been the pride and inspiration of the socialists throughout the world.

My drama course under the auspices of my two wealthy patrons proved to be a most disagreeable experience. Mr. L., the advertising genius, had taken it upon himself to " edit " the announcements I had sent. Indeed, he had changed their entire character, handling the subjects of my lectures as if they had been chewing-gum ads.

Then happened something to shock the tender sensibilities of my patrons. My first drama talk fell on November 10, a day of momentous importance to me. It had been the last day on earth of my comrades martyred in Chicago twenty-seven years before. I introduced my lecture by contrasting the changes in the public attitude towards anarchism between 1887 and 1914. The vision of our precious dead was before me, bearing witness to the last prophecy of August Spies : " Our silence will be more powerful than the voices you strangle today." In 1887 Chicago's sole answer to anarchism was the gallows; in 1914 it was eagerly listening to the ideas for which Parsons and his comrades had died. During my brief introduction I saw one of my backers and his family, in the first row, uncomfortably fidgeting in their seats; some people in the rear ostentatiously left the hall. Unconcernedly I went on with the subject of the evening, " The American Drama."

Subsequently my backers informed Ben that I had " missed the opportunity of a lifetime." They had induced the " wealth and influence of Chicago " to attend my lectures, " the rich Rosenwalds among them." They would have helped to secure my drama work for the rest of my life, and then " Emma Goldman had to spoil in ten minutes all that we had worked weeks to achieve."

I felt as if I had been put up on the block for sale. The incident had a most depressing effect on me. Try as I would, I could not get my usual intensity into my further drama talks. It was different when I discussed the war. In my own hall, under no obligations to anyone, I could freely express my abhorrence of slaughter and frankly discuss whatever phase of the social question I took up. At the close of my drama course we reimbursed my " patrons " for their outlay. I did not regret the experience; it taught me that patronage is paralysing to one's integrity and independence.

My stay in Chicago was lent charm by my two young friends Margaret and Deansie. Both consecrated themselves to me and turned the office of the *Little Review* over to my needs. The girls were as poor as church mice, never sure of their next meal, much less able to pay the printer or the landlord. Yet there were always fresh flowers on the desk to cheer me. Since the unforgettable days I had spent with Margaret in the spring when we had both enjoyed the hospitality of Mr. and Mrs. Roe at their home in Pelham Manor, something very new and precious had grown up between us. Three weeks of almost daily association with her, her fine understanding and intuition, had increased our mutual affection.

Chicago had charm, but I could not linger. Other voices were calling, calling me to take up the struggle again. I still had a number of cities to cover. Sasha and Fitzi had left on their lecture tour, and I was urgently needed at home.

# CHAPTER XLII

HELENA AND OUR YOUNG FOLKS IN ROCHESTER ALWAYS BROUGHT me back to that city even when I did not have to lecture there. This year there were additional reasons for visiting my home town: an opportunity to speak on the war, and the great family event of David Hochstein's first concert with the local symphony orchestra.

The Victoria Theatre had been secured for my lecture by an anarchist workman known as Dashuta. An idealist of the best type, he had paid out of his meagre savings the entire expense of the meeting and he had used all his leisure to make the lecture widely known. His help meant infinitely more to me than the "security for life" offered by the Chicago rich.

On my arrival in Rochester I found my people in anxious suspense over David's forthcoming concert. Well I knew how my sister Helena yearned for the dreams and aspirations of her own frustrated life to be realized in her youngest son. At the first signs of his talent my timid sister had developed determination and strength to defy every difficulty that beset the beloved child's artistic career. She drudged and saved to enable her children, particularly David, to have the opportunities she herself had been deprived of in life, and she was consumed by a great longing to give herself to the uttermost. On my visits she would sometimes pour out her heart to me, never complaining, but only regretting that she was able to do "so little" for her dear ones.

Now the crowning moment of her struggle had arrived. David had returned from Europe the finished artist she had slaved to help him become. Her heart trembled for his triumph. The cold critics, the unappreciative audience — what would her darling's playing mean to them? Would they understand his genius? She refused seats in a box.

"It might disturb him to see me," she said. She would feel more comfortable with Jacob in the gallery.

I had heard David in New York and I knew how his playing had impressed everyone. He was truly an artist. Handsome and of good appearance, he made a striking figure on the platform. I felt no anxiety about his Rochester engagement. My sister's excitement, however, had communicated itself to me, and all during the concert my thoughts were with her whose fierce love and hope were now being fulfilled. David's violin charmed the audience and he was acclaimed with an enthusiasm seldom accorded a young artist in his native town.

Arriving in New York, I was approached by the Newspaper Enterprise Association, controlled by the Scripps-Howard newspapers, for an essay on how the American people could help establish peace on earth and good will towards men. The subject, if treated adequately, would have required a volume, but I was asked to "keep it down" to a thousand words. The opportunity to reach a large audience, however, was too valuable to miss. In my article I pointed out that the first step to good will demands a reversal of Christ's command to "render unto Cæsar the things which are Cæsar's and unto God the things that are God's." Ceasing to pay tribute to despots in heaven and on earth, I wrote, would tend towards peace among men.

On my return from a short tour I was surprised to find Donald Vose still in New York. He looked more shabby than I had seen him last, and though it was cold December, he was without an overcoat. Every day he came to our office and remained for hours "to warm up," as he said. "What about the money you expected?" I asked him; "did it ever come?" He had received it, he told me, but he had been promised a good job in New York and he had decided to stay on. Nothing had come of it, however, and now his fare was used up and he had to write home for more. It sounded plausible, yet somehow I was not impressed. His constant presence was getting on my nerves.

Soon reports began to drift in that Donald was spending money on drink and that he was nightly treating his companions. I thought at first that it was mere gossip; the boy apparently could not afford an overcoat; where would he get money for drink? But the reports became more frequent, and I got suspicious. I knew his mother Gertie to be too poor to support her son, as were also most of her friends. Writing her would only make her uneasy, and I therefore communicated with some of our friends in the West. They investigated the matter in Seattle, Tacoma, and the Home Colony, where Gertie lived. No money was being supplied to Donald from any of those places. My apprehensions increased. Shortly afterwards Donald came to tell me that his fare had arrived at last and that he was returning West. I was relieved and I felt also a little ashamed of my distrust.

A week after Donald's departure we read about the arrest of Matthew A. Schmidt in New York and of David Caplan on Puget Sound. We knew that the two men were " wanted " in connexion with the Los Angeles *Times* explosion. The "gentlemen's agreement" made by the State of California to refrain from further prosecution of labour men after the McNamara confession was broken again. Donald Vose came to my mind, and my old suspicions were revived. Various circumstances pointed to his connexion with the arrest of the men. It seemed preposterous to think a child of Gertie Vose capable of treachery, yet I could not free myself from the thought that Donald was somehow responsible for the arrests.

Soon no room was left for doubt. Proofs sent to us by dependable friends on the Coast disclosed that Donald Vose was in the pay of Detective William J. Burns and that he had betrayed Matthew A. Schmidt and David Caplan. The son of our old comrade Gertie, raised in anarchist circles and a guest in our house, turned Judas! It was a staggering blow, one of the worst I had received in my twenty-five years of public life.

The first step I decided upon was a frank avowal in *Mother Earth* of the facts in the case and an explanation of how Donald Vose had happened to live in our house. But it would crush my dear friend Gertie to learn that her own child was a spy! Gertie had been so happy that her son was now " in the right atmosphere," and that he would take up the work for which she had spent her life. I wondered how the clear-thinking and observant woman could have remained so blind to the true nature of her son. She never would have sent him to our house if she had had the slightest inkling of his true nature. I hesitated to disclose the truth about Donald. Yet sooner or later Gertie would have to face the fact; moreover, there was so much involved in Donald's relation to us and to our work that I could not keep the matter under cover. Our people must be warned against him, I finally decided.

I wrote an article for our magazine giving the whole history of the case. But before it was set up, I received the request from those connected with the defence of Schmidt and Caplan to delay publishing anything about Donald because he was expected to testify at the trial. I had always hated subterfuge, but I could not ignore the wishes of the people in charge of the defence of Caplan and Schmidt.

The tenth anniversary of *Mother Earth* was approaching. It seemed nothing short of a miracle for our magazine to have survived a whole decade. It had faced the condemnation of enemies and the unfriendly criticism of well-wishers and had had a hard struggle to keep alive. Even most of those who had helped at its birth had expressed misgivings about its continued existence. Their fears were not groundless, in view of the reckless founding of the magazine. Blissful ignorance of the publishing business, combined with the ridiculous nest-egg of two hundred and fifty dollars — how could anyone hope to succeed with such a start? But my friends had overlooked the most important factors in the heritage of *Mother Earth,* a Yiddish perseverance and a boundless enthusiasm. These had proved to be stronger than gilt-edged securities, large income, or even popular support. From the very beginning I had outlined for it a twofold purpose: to voice without fear every unpopular progressive cause, and to aim for unity between revolutionary effort and artistic expression. To achieve these ends I had to keep *Mother Earth* untrammelled by party policies, even by anarchist policies, free from sectarian favouritism and from every outside influence, however well-intentioned. For this I was charged even by some of my comrades with using the magazine for my personal ends, and by socialists with being in the employ of capitalism and of the Catholic Church.

Its survival was due in no little measure to the devotion of a small band of comrades and friends who helped to realize my dream of an independent radical spokesman in the United States. The tributes paid at the tenth anniversary by readers in America and abroad testified to the niche in people's hearts my child had made for itself. Some of the praise was especially touching because it came from persons with whom I had been compelled to clash swords over the war.

After my return from the Neo-Malthusian Conference, held in Paris in 1900, I had added to my lecture series the subject of birth-control. I did not discuss methods, because the question of limiting offspring represented in my estimation only one aspect of the social struggle and I did not care to risk arrest for it. Moreover, I was so continually on the brink of prison because of my general activities that it seemed unjustifiable to court extra trouble. Information on methods I gave only when privately requested for it. Margaret Sanger's difficulties with the postal authorities over her publication of *The Woman Rebel,* and the arrest of William Sanger for giving his wife's pamphlet on methods of birth-control to a Comstock agent, made me aware that the time had come when I must either stop lecturing on the subject or do it practical justice. I felt that I must share with them the consequences of the birth-control issue.

Neither my birth-control discussion nor Margaret Sanger's efforts were pioneer work. The trail was blazed in the United States by the grand old fighter Moses Harman, his daughter Lillian, Ezra Heywood, Dr. Foote and his son, E. C. Walker, and their collaborators of a previous generation. Ida Craddock, one of the bravest champions of women's emancipation, had paid the supreme price. Hounded by Comstock and faced with a five-year sentence, she had taken her own life. She and the Moses Harman group were the pioneers and heroes of the battle for free motherhood, for the right of the child to be born well. The matter of priority, however, in no way lessened the value of Margaret Sanger's work. She was the only woman in America in recent years to give information to women on birth-control and she had revived the subject in her publication after many years of silence.

E. C. Walker, president of the Sunrise Club, had invited me to speak at one of its fortnightly dinners. His organization was among the few libertarian forums in New York open to free expression. I had often lectured there on various social topics. On this occasion I chose birth-control as my theme, intending openly to discuss methods of contraception. I faced one of the largest audiences in the history of the club, numbering about six hundred persons, among them physicians, lawyers, artists, and men and women of liberal views. Most of them were earnest people who had come together to lend moral support to the test case that this first public discussion represented. Everyone felt certain that my arrest would follow, and some friends had come prepared to go bail for me. I carried a book with me in case I should have to spend the night in the station-house. That possibility did not disturb me, but I did feel uneasy because I knew that some of the diners had come out of curiosity, for the sex thrills they expected to experience on this evening.

I introduced my subject by reviewing the historical and social aspects of birth-control and then continued with a discussion of a number of contraceptives, their application and effects. I spoke in the direct and frank manner that I should use in dealing with ordinary disinfection and prophylaxis. The questions and the discussion that followed showed that I had taken the right approach. Several physicians complimented me on having presented so difficult and delicate a subject in a " clean and natural manner."

No arrest followed. Some friends feared I might be picked up on my way home, and insisted on seeing me to my door. Days passed and the authorities had taken no steps in the matter. It was the more surprising in view of the arrest of William Sanger for something he had not said nor written himself. People wondered why I, who had been so frequently arrested when I had not broken the law, should be allowed to go unpunished when I had done so deliberately. Perhaps Comstock's failure to act was due to the fact that he knew that those who were in the habit of attending the Sunrise Club gatherings were probably already in possession of contraceptives. I must therefore deliver the lecture at my own Sunday meetings, I decided.

Our hall was packed, mostly with young people, among them students from Columbia University. The interest evinced by my audience was even greater than at the Sunrise dinner, the questions put by the young folks of a more direct and personal nature. I did not mince matters, yet there was no arrest. Evidently I should have to make another test — on the East Side.

I had to postpone the matter for a while because of previous engagements. Students from the Union Theological Seminary, frequent attendants at my Sunday lectures, had invited me to address them. I had consented after having warned the boys that they were likely to meet with opposition from the faculty. As soon as it became known that the heathen was to invade the theological sanctum, a tempest broke out which lasted beyond the day set for my lecture. The students insisted on their right of hearing whom they pleased until the faculty gave in, and another date was agreed upon.

In the mean time I had to deliver another lecture, on the " Failure of Christianity," with particular reference to Billy Sunday, whom I considered the modern clown of religion and whose circus was in Paterson at the time. In view of the tsarist methods employed by the authorities in dealing with strike meetings and radical gatherings, the police protection given Billy and his performances was doubly out-rageous. Our comrades in Paterson were planning some protest, and they invited me to speak. I felt that it would not be fair to discuss Billy Sunday without first learning the calibre of the man and seeing what he was passing out as religion. I went with Ben to Paterson to hear the self-appointed voice of Christ.

Never did Christianity appear to me so divested of meaning and decency. Billy Sunday's vulgar manner, his coarse suggestiveness, erotic flagellation, and disgusting lasciviousness, clad in theological phraseology, stripped religion of the least spiritual significance. I was too nauseated to hear him to the end. Fresh air brought relief from the atmosphere of the lewd mouthings and sexual contortions with which he goaded his audience to salacious hysteria.

Some days later I lectured in Paterson on the " Failure of Chris-tianity " and cited Billy Sunday as the symbol of its inner collapse. The next morning's newspapers stated that I had provoked the wrath of God by my blasphemy. I learned that the hall in which I had spoken had caught fire after I had left and burned to the ground.

My tour this year met with no police interference until we reached Portland, Oregon, although the subjects I treated were anything but tame : anti-war topics, the fight for Caplan and Schmidt, freedom in love, birth-control, and the problem most tabooed in polite society, homosexuality. Nor did Comstock and his purists try to suppress me, although I openly discussed methods of contraception before various audiences.

Censorship came from some of my own comrades because I was treating such " unnatural " themes as homosexuality. Anarchism was already enough misunderstood, and anarchists considered depraved; it was inadvisable to add to the misconceptions by taking up per-verted sex-forms, they argued. Believing in freedom of opinion, even if it went against me, I minded the censors in my own ranks as little as I did those in the enemy's camp. In fact, censorship from com-rades had the same effect on me as police persecution; it made me surer of myself, more determined to plead for every victim, be it one of social wrong or of moral prejudice.

The men and women who used to come to see me after my lectures on homosexuality, and who confided to me their anguish and their isolation, were often of finer grain than those who had cast them out. Most of them had reached an adequate understanding of their differentiation only after years of struggle to stifle what they had considered a disease and a shameful affliction. One young woman confessed to me that in the twenty-five years of her life she had never known a day when the nearness of a man, her own father and brothers even, did not make her ill. The more she had tried to respond to sexual approach, the more repugnant men became to her. She had hated herself, she said, because she could not love her father and her brothers as she loved her mother. She suffered excruciating remorse, but her revulsion only increased. At the age of eighteen she had accepted an offer of marriage in the hope that a long engagement might help her grow accustomed to a man and cure her of her " disease." It turned out a ghastly failure and nearly drove her insane. She could not face marriage and she dared not confide in her fiancé or friends. She had never met anyone, she told me, who suffered from a similar affliction, nor had she ever read books dealing with the subject. My lecture had set her free; I had given her back her self-respect.

This woman was only one of the many who sought me out. Their pitiful stories made the social ostracism of the invert seem more dreadful than I had ever realized before. To me anarchism was not a mere theory for a distant future; it was a living influence to free us from inhibitions, internal no less than external, and from the destructive barriers that separate man from man.

Los Angeles, San Diego, and San Francisco were record-breaking in the size of our meetings and the interest shown. In Los Angeles I was invited by the Women's City Club. Five hundred members of my sex, from the deepest red to the dullest grey, came to hear me speak on " Feminism." They could not excuse my critical attitude towards the bombastic and impossible claims of the suffragists as to the wonderful things they would do when they got political power. They branded me as an enemy of woman's freedom, and club-members stood up and denounced me.

The incident reminded me of a similar occasion when I had lectured on woman's inhumanity to man. Always on the side of the under dog, I resented my sex's placing every evil at the door of the male. I pointed out that if he were really as great a sinner as he was being painted by the ladies, woman shared the responsibility with him. The mother is the first influence in his life, the first to cultivate his conceit and self-importance. Sisters and wives follow in the mother's footsteps, not to mention mistresses, who complete the work begun by the mother. Woman is naturally perverse, I argued; from the very birth of her male child until he reaches a ripe age, the mother leaves nothing undone to keep him tied to her. Yet she hates to see him weak and she craves the manly man. She idolizes in him the very traits that help to enslave her — his strength, his egotism, and his exaggerated vanity. The inconsistencies of my sex keep the poor male dangling between the idol and the brute, the darling and the beast, the helpless child and the conqueror of worlds. It is really woman's inhumanity to man that makes him what he is. When she has learned to be as self-centred and as determined as he, when she gains the courage to delve into life as he does and pay the price for it, she will achieve her liberation, and incidentally also help him become free. Whereupon my women hearers would rise up against me and cry: " You're a man's woman and not one of us."

Our experience in San Diego two years previously, in 1913, had exerted the same effect on me as the night ride in 1912 had on Ben. I was set on returning to deliver my suppressed lecture. In 1914 one of our friends had gone to San Diego to try to secure a hall. The socialists, who had their own place, refused to have anything to do with me. Other radical groups were equally brave, so that my plan had to be abandoned. Only temporarily, I had promised myself, however.

This year, 1915, I was fortunate in having to deal with real men instead of with mere apologies in male attire. One of them was George Edwards, the musician who had offered us the Conservatory of Music on the occasion of our first trouble with the Vigilantes. The other was Dr. A. Lyle de Jarnette, a Baptist minister who had resigned from the Church and had founded the Open Forum. Edwards had become a thorough anarchist who devoted his time and abilities to the movement. He had set to music Voltairine de Cleyre's *The Hurricane,* Olive Schreiner's *Dream of Wild Bees,* and " The Grand Inquisitor " from Dostoyevsky's *Brothers Karamazov.* Now he was determined to help me come back to San Diego and establish the right of free speech there. Dr. Jarnette had organized the Open Forum as a protest against Vigilante suppression. The association had since grown into a large and vital body. Arrangements were made for me to deliver three lectures there, in an attempt to break the San Diego conspiracy.

The recently electer mayor of the city, reputed to be a liberal, had

assured the Open Forum that I would be allowed to speak, and that
no Vigilante interference would be permitted. It was a new tone for
San Diego, probably due to the circumstance that its exposition had
greatly suffered as a result of the three-year boycott. But our former
experiences in the city did not justify too much trust in official declara-
tions. We preferred to prepare ourselves for possible emergencies.

I had long before decided that I would return to San Diego without
Ben. I had planned to go alone, but fortunately Sasha was in Los
Angeles at the time. I knew I could count on his poise in a difficult
situation and on his utter fearlessness in the face of the gravest danger.
Sasha and my romantic admirer Leon Bass left for San Diego two
days ahead of me to look over the field. Accompanied by Fitzi and
Ben Capes, I departed quietly from Los Angeles in an auto. Nearing
the Vigilante city, the picture of Ben surrounded by fourteen thugs
rose before me. They had covered the same route, with Ben at the
mercy of savages who were beating and humiliating him. I thought
of him writhing in pain, with no one to succour him or alleviate his
terror. Barely three years had passed. I was free, with dear friends
at my side, securely riding through the balmy night. I could enjoy the
beauty around me, the golden Pacific on one side, majestic mountains
on the other, their fantastic formations towering above us. The very
glory of this magnificent country-side must have been mockery to
Ben, a mockery in league with his torturers. May 14, 1912 — June 20,
1915 — what an incredible change! Yet what might be awaiting us
in San Diego?

We arrived at four-thirty in the morning and drove straight to the
small hotel where Sasha had engaged rooms for us. He reported that
the hall-keeper had declared that I could not speak in his place, but
that Dr. Jarnette and the other members of the Open Forum were
determined to see our plans through. The hall was theirs by yearly
lease, the key was in their hands, and it had been decided to take
possession of the hall and guard every entrance.

When our meeting opened, at eleven in the morning, we became
aware that a number of Vigilantes were present. The situation was
tense, the atmosphere charged with suppressed excitement. It furnished a fitting background for my subject, which was Ibsen's *Enemy
of the People*. Our men were on the alert, and no untoward incident
took place, the Vigilantes evidently not daring to start any hostile
demonstration.

The afternoon lecture was on Nietzsche, and again the hall was crowded, but this time the Vigilantes remained away. In the evening I spoke on the struggle of Margaret and William Sanger, dealing with the importance of birth-control. The day ended without any disturbance. I felt that our triumph was due mostly to the comrades martyred for free speech three years previously — to Joseph Mikolasek, who had been murdered in the fight, and the hundreds of I.W.W.'s and other victims, including Ben, who had been beaten, thrown into prison and driven out of town. The thought of them steeled me and urged me on.

Ben insisted on visiting San Diego again, and he returned there later on, not in any public capacity, but just to convince himself that he was not afraid. He went to the exposition in the company of his mother and several friends. No one paid any attention to them. The Vigilante conspiracy had been broken.

Among my numerous friends in Los Angeles none was more helpful in my work and welfare than Dr. Percival T. Gerson, together with his wife. They interested scores of people in my lectures, gave me the opportunity to address gatherings in their home, and entertained me lavishly. It was also Dr. Gerson who procured for me an invitation to speak before the Severance Club, named in honour of Caroline M. Severance, co-worker of Susan B. Anthony, Julia Howe, and the group of militants of the preceding generation.

Before I began my lecture, I was introduced to a man who, in the absence of the president, had been asked to preside. There was nothing striking about him as he sat buried in my volume of *Anarchism and Other Essays*. In his opening remarks this chairman, whose name was Tracy Becker, astonished the audience by the announcement that he had been connected with the District Attorney's office in Buffalo when President McKinley was killed. Until very recently he had considered Emma Goldman a criminal, he said — not one who had courage to do murder herself, but one who unscrupulously played on weak minds and induced them to commit crimes. During the trial of Leon Czolgosz he felt certain, he continued, that it was I who had instigated the assassination of the President and he had thought that I ought to be made to pay the extreme penalty. Since he had read my books and had talked to some of my friends, he realized his mistake and he now hoped that I would forgive him the injustice he had done me.

Dead silence followed his remarks, and everybody's eyes were turned on me. I felt frozen by the sudden resurrection of the Buffalo tragedy, and in an unsteady voice, at first, I declared that since we are all links in the social chain, no one can avoid responsibility for such deeds as that of Leon Czolgosz; not even the chairman. He who remains indifferent to the conditions that result in violent acts of protest cannot escape his share of blame for them. Even those of us who see clearly and work for fundamental changes are not entirely exempt from guilt. Too absorbed in efforts for the future, we often turn a deaf ear to those who reach out for sympathetic understanding and who hunger for the fellowship of kindred spirits. Leon Czolgosz had been one of such.

I talked with growing feeling as I proceeded to describe the bleak background of the boy, his early environment and life. I related the impressions of the Buffalo newspaper woman who had sought me out to tell me what she had experienced during Czolgosz's trial, and I pointed out the motives of Leon's act and martyrdom. I felt no resentment against the man who had confessed his eagerness to send me to the electric chair. Indeed, I rather admired him for frankly admitting his error. But he had revived in my memory the fury of that period, and I was in no mood to meet him or to listen to his idle pleasantries.

The San Francisco Exposition was at its height, and the population of the city had almost doubled. Our meetings, totalling forty within one month, successfully competed with the gate receipts of the big show. The great event was my appearance at the Congress of Religious Philosophies. The astonishing thing was made possible by Mr. Power, who was in charge of the sessions of the congress. He had known me in the East, and when he learned of my presence in San Francisco, he invited me to speak.

The public conclave of the religious philosophers took place in the Civic Auditorium, one of the largest halls in the West. The place of the chairman, a reverend gentleman who suddenly fell ill when he heard that I was to speak, was taken by a member of the newspaper fraternity. I was thus between the devil and the deep sea, and I began my talk on atheism by saying so. My introduction put the audience in a light mood. Surrounded on the platform by gentlemen of the cloth of every known denomination, I needed all my humour to rise to the solemnity of the occasion.

Atheism is rather a delicate subject to handle under such circum-

stances, but somehow I managed to pull through. I saw consternation
on the faces of the theologians, who protested that my treatment of
religion was scandalous. But the vast audience evidently enjoyed it,
for its hilarious approval came perilously near breaking up the congress when I got through. I was followed by a rabbi, who began by
saying that " in spite of all Miss Goldman has said against religion,
she is the most religious person I know."

BEN L. REITMAN

ON MY ARRIVAL IN NEW YORK AFTER MY PROTRACTED WESTERN lecture tour I hoped to get a long-needed rest. But the fates and Sasha willed it otherwise. He had just returned from Los Angeles to work in the East in behalf of Matthew A. Schmidt and David Caplan, and he immediately drew me into his intensive campaign.

Sasha's presence on the Coast during my last San Diego experience was due to a rather unexpectedly happy turn of affairs. When he had started out on his Western lecture tour, in the fall of 1914, he had not intended to go farther than Colorado. That was owing to his arrest on the very eve of his leaving New York. Fitzi had preceded him to Pittsburgh to make the preliminary arrangements for the meetings. Sasha's New York friends had meanwhile arranged a farewell party in his honour. At midnight the company, returning home, sang revolutionary songs. A policeman ordered them to cease singing, and in the altercation that followed he lifted his night-stick to strike Bill Shatoff, our old friend and co-worker. Sasha's presence of mind undoubtedly saved Bill from serious injury. He gripped the policeman's upraised arm so that the latter let the club fall out of his hand. More officers arrived and the whole company were arrested. In the morning they were condemned to short terms in the workhouse for " disturbing the peace," except Sasha, who was charged with assaulting an officer and inciting to riot. The magistrate insisted on his standing trial there and then, saying that his sentence would not exceed two years. The policeman had come to court with his entire arm painted with iodine and bandaged, and his statement to the judge was to the effect that Sasha had attacked him without the least provocation and that only the arrival of more police had saved his life. It was clearly the intention to " railroad " Sasha. The police, having failed to stop his unemployment activities and Ludlow strike protests, were evidently determined to wreak vengeance on him this time.

Sasha refused to have the case proceed before the police magistrate. The charges against him, classed as felonies, gave him the legal right of trial by jury. Moreover, he was scheduled to speak the same evening in Pittsburgh, and he decided to take his chances in criminal court.

Our friend Gilbert E. Roe bailed him out and promised to look after the case during his absence. Sasha departed for Pittsburgh, but when he reached Denver, he was warned by Roe to go no farther west, so as to be able to return to New York within forty-eight hours if he was called for trial. The situation looked serious, Sasha being in danger of a five-year prison term.

For weeks he remained lecturing in Colorado, anxious to go to California to aid in the defence of Matthew A. Schmidt and David Caplan, who were awaiting trial in Los Angeles in connexion with the *Times* building explosion. Then one day he received a telegram from New York, reading: "Case against you dismissed. You are free to go where you please. Congratulations."

It was Gilbert E. Roe who had managed to have the indictments against Sasha quashed by convincing the new District Attorney of New York that the charges were the result of police enmity.

Now Sasha was in New York, working strenuously in behalf of the Caplan-Schmidt defence. On the Coast he had organized a wide publicity campaign in their behalf, and as a result of his efforts the International Workers' Defence League had requested him to tour the country and form defence branches along the route. It was just the kind of activity Sasha was particularly fitted for, and he devoted himself passionately to saving the two indicted men from the fate that had been his in Pennsylvania.

Equipped with credentials from various labour organizations, he had left Los Angeles, stopping at all the larger industrial cities on his way east, so that by the time he reached New York he had already rallied a goodly part of organized labour to the support of the prisoners in the Los Angeles jail.

Sasha immediately enlisted me for the Caplan-Schmidt campaign, as he did everyone else he could get into the work. It was good to have him near again and to co-operate with him. The Caplan-Schmidt mass meeting he organized, at which we were both to speak, and the numerous other efforts for the defence he was making were too important to let me consider my need of rest. The reactionary forces on the Coast arrayed against labour were feverishly active. They were poisoning the public mind against the men about to be tried; to prejudice the case they were spreading the rumour that David Caplan had turned State's evidence. The preposterous story had just made its appearance in the New York newspapers. Aware of the effect of such statements even upon the radicals, it became necessary to take a stand against the outrageous slander. I had known David fifteen years and had been closely connected with him in the movement during that time; I was absolutely convinced of his integrity.

When the date of the Caplan-Schmidt trial became known, Sasha returned to the Coast to start a bulletin, as part of the publicity he was making for the case.

The conflagration in Europe was spreading; already six countries had been swept by it. America was also beginning to catch fire. The jingo and military cliques were growing restive. " Sixteen months of war," they cried, " and our country is still keeping aloof! " The clamour for " preparedness " began, people joining in who but yesterday waxed hot against the atrocities of organized slaughter. The situation called for more energetic anti-war agitation. It became doubly necessary when we learned of the attitude of Peter Kropotkin.

Rumours had been filtering through from England that Peter had declared himself in favour of the war. We ridiculed the idea, certain that it was a newspaper fabrication to charge our Grand Old Man with pro-war sentiments. Kropotkin, the anarchist, humanitarian, and gentlest of beings — it was preposterous to believe that he could favour the European holocaust. But presently we were informed that Kropotkin had taken sides with the Allies, defending them with the same vehemence that the Haeckels and the Hauptmanns were championing " their " fatherland. He was justifying all measures to crush the " Prussian menace," as those in the opposite camp were urging the destruction of the Allies. It was a staggering blow to our movement, and especially to those of us who knew and loved Peter. But our devotion to our teacher and our affection for him could not alter our convictions nor change our attitude to the war as a struggle of financial and economic interests foreign to the worker and as the most destructive factor of what is vital and worth while in the world.

We determined to repudiate Peter's stand, and fortunately we were not alone in this. Many others felt as we did, distressing as it was to turn against the man who had so long been our inspiration. Enrico Malatesta showed far greater understanding and consistency than Peter, and with him were Rudolph Rocker, Alexander Schapiro, Thomas H. Keell, and other native and Jewish-speaking anarchists in Great Britain. In France Sébastien Faure, A. Armand, and members of the anarchist and syndicalist movements, in Holland Domela Nieuwenhuis and his co-workers maintained a firm attitude against the wholesale murder. In Germany Gustav Landauer, Erich Mühsam, Fritz Oerter, Fritz Kater, and scores of other comrades retained their senses. To be sure, we were but a handful in comparison with the war-drunk millions, but we succeeded in circulating throughout the world the manifesto issued by our International Bureau, and we increased our energies at home to expose the true nature of militarism.

Our first step was the publication in *Mother Earth* of Peter Kropotkin's pamphlet on "Capitalism and War," embodying a logical and convincing refutation of his new position. In numerous meetings and protests we pointed out the character, significance, and effects of war, my lecture on "Preparedness" showing that "readiness," far far from assuring peace, has at all times and in all countries been instrumental in precipitating armed conflicts. The lecture was repeatedly delivered before large and representative audiences, and it was among the first warnings in America against the military conspiracy behind the protestations of peace.

Our people in the States were awakening to the growing danger, and demands for speakers and for literature began pouring into our office from every part of the country. We were not rich in good English agitators, but the situation was urgent, and I was continually busy filling the gap.

I went about the country, speaking almost every evening, my days occupied with numerous calls on my time and energy. At last even my unusual powers of endurance gave way. Returning to New York after a lecture in Cleveland, I was taken ill with the grippe. I was too ill to be transferred to a hospital. After I had spent two weeks in bed, the physician in charge ordered me taken to a decent hotel room, my own quarters lacking all comforts. On my arrival at the hotel I was too weak to register, and Stella, my niece, wrote my name in the guest book. The clerk looked at it and then retired to an inner office. He returned to say that a mistake had been made; there was no vacant room for me in the place. It was a cold and grey day, the rain coming down in torrents, but I was compelled to return to my old quarters.

The incident resulted in strong protests in the press. One communication in particular attracted my attention; it was a long and caustic letter upbraiding the hotel people for their inhumanity to a patient. The statement, signed " Harry Weinberger, Attorney-at-Law, New York," was by a man I did not know personally, but whose name I had heard mentioned as that of an active single-taxer and member of the Brooklyn Philosophical Society.

In the mean time Matthew Schmidt had been sacrificed to the vengeance of the Merchants' and Manufacturers' Association, the Los Angeles *Times,* and the State of California. One of the main witnesses against him was Donald Vose. In open court, face to face with his victim, he admitted being in the employ of Detective William J. Burns. As his agent Vose had ferreted out the whereabouts of David Caplan. He enjoyed the hospitality of the latter for two weeks, gained his confidence, and learned that Schmidt was somewhere in New York. Then he was ordered east by Burns, instructed to frequent anarchist circles and be on the alert for the first chance to reach Matthew Schmidt. On the witness-stand Vose boasted that the prisoner at the bar had confessed his guilt to him. Schmidt was convicted, the jury recommending imprisonment for life.

There was no more reason for withholding the publication of what I considered Donald Vose's perfidy. The January 1916 issue of *Mother Earth* contained the too-long-delayed article about him.

Gertie Vose stood by her son. I understood her maternal feeling, but in my estimation it did not excuse a rebel of thirty years' standing. I never wanted to see her again.

Conviction did not break the strong spirit of Matthew A. Schmidt or influence his faith in the ideals for which he was to be buried for the rest of his life. His statement in court, setting forth the causes behind the social war, was illuminating in its clarity, simplicity, and courage. Though facing a life sentence, he did not lose his rich humour. In the midst of his recital of the real facts in the case he turned to the jury with the remark : " Let me ask you, gentlemen, do you believe a man like Donald Vose? You wouldn't whip your dog on the testimony of such a creature; no honest man would. Any man who would believe Vose would not deserve to have a dog."

Interest in our ideas was growing throughout the country. New anarchist publications began to appear: *Revolt* in New York, with Hippolyte Havel as its editor; the *Alarm* in Chicago, issued by a local group of comrades, and the *Blast* in San Francisco, with Sasha and Fitzi at its head. Directly or indirectly I was connected with all of them. It was, however, the *Blast* that was closest to my heart. Sasha had always wanted a forum from which to speak to the masses, an anarchist weekly labour paper to arouse the workers to conscious revolutionary activity. His fighting spirit and able pen were enough to assure the *Blast* vitality and courage. The co-operation of Robert Minor, the powerful cartoonist, added much to the value of the publication.

Robert Minor had wandered far since the days when I first met him in St. Louis. He had definitely broken with the milk-and-water brand of socialism and had given up a lucrative position on the New York *World* for a twenty-five-dollar-a-week job on the socialist daily *Call.* "This will free me," he once told me, "from making cartoons that show the blessings of the capitalistic régime and injure the cause of labour." In the course of time Bob had developed into a revolutionist and subsequently into an anarchist. He devoted his energy and abilities to our movement. *Mother Earth, Revolt,* and the *Blast* were considerably strengthened by his trenchant brush and pen.

From Philadelphia, Washington, and Pittsburgh came calls for a series of lectures to extend over several months. The initiative of our comrades was a satisfying and stimulating sign; such a venture had never before been tried with one speaker, but our friends were eager to attempt it. I realized the strain it would involve to travel continually from town to town, lecture every evening, then rush back to speak at my Friday and Sunday meetings in New York. But I welcomed the opportunity to awaken interest in the Los Angeles case, agitate against the war, and help circulate our various publications.

My English lectures in Philadelphia were hardly worth the weekly effort. They were poorly attended; the few who did come were sluggish and inert, like the social atmosphere in the City of Brotherly Love. There were only two persons whose friendship recompensed me for the otherwise dreary experience, Harry Boland and Horace Traubel.

Harry was an old devotee and always generously helpful in every struggle I made. Horace Traubel I had first met at a Walt Whitman dinner in 1903. He had impressed me as the outstanding personality among the Whitmanites. I enjoyed the hours spent in his sanctum, filled with Whitman material and books, as well as with the files of his own unique paper, the *Conservator*. Most interesting were his reminiscences of the Good Gray Poet, whose latter years of life Horace had shared. I got more from him of Walt than from any biographer I had read, and I also got much of Horace Traubel, who revealed himself and his own humanity in his talks about his beloved poet.

Another man brought close to me by Horace was Eugene V. Debs. I had met him previously on several occasions and had clashed swords with him in a friendly way over our political differences, but I knew little of his real personality. Horace, an intimate friend of Debs's, made him vibrant to me in the heights and depths of his character. The comradeship I felt for Horace ripened into a beautiful friendship during my visits to Philadelphia. The city's empty boast of brotherly love was redeemed by none so much as by Horace Traubel, whose love embraced mankind.

Results in Washington, D. C., surprised everybody and, most of all, our active workers Lillian Kisliuk and her father. Lillian had for years lived in the capital, but had always been sceptical about the success of lectures in her city, and particularly about having two a week. It was her enthusiasm for our ideas, however, that had induced her to undertake the task.

The Pittsburgh arrangements were in charge of our very able friend Jacob Margolis, who was assisted by a group of young American comrades, among them Grace Loan, very vivid and intense, her husband, Tom, and his brother, Walter. The Loans were most refreshing by their genuineness and zeal, and they gave promise of great usefulness to our cause. They had all worked like beavers to make my meetings a success, but unfortunately the result was not commensurate with their efforts. On the whole, however, my series of meetings in the stronghold of the steel-trust were well worth while, especially because Jacob Margolis had succeeded in inducing a club of lawyers to invite me to address them.

I had heretofore faced the representatives of the law only as a prisoner. On this occasion it was my turn — not to pay back in kind, but to tell the judges and prosecutors among my hearers what I thought of their profession. I confess I did it with glee, without re-morse or pity for the predicament of the gentlemen who had to listen without being able to punish me even for contempt of court.

My lectures in New York that winter included the subject of birth-control. I had definitely decided some time previously to make public the knowledge of contraceptives, particularly at my Yiddish meetings, because the women on the East Side needed that information most. Even if I were not vitally interested in the matter, the conviction of William Sanger and his condemnation to prison would have impelled me to take up the question. Sanger had not been actively engaged in the birth-control movement. He was an artist, and he had been tricked by a Comstock agent into giving him a pamphlet which his wife, Mar-garet Sanger, was circulating. He could have pleaded ignorance and thus avoided punishment. His bold defence in court earned him the deserved appreciation of all right-thinking people.

My lectures and attempts at lecturing on birth-control finally re-sulted in my arrest, whereupon a public protest was arranged in Car-negie Hall. It was an impressive gathering, with our friend and ardent co-worker Leonard D. Abbott presiding. He presented the historical aspects of the subject, while Doctors William J. Robinson and J. S. Goldwater spoke from the medical point of view. Dr. Robinson was an old champion of the cause; together with the venerable Abraham Jacobi, he was the pioneer of birth-control in the New York Academy of Medicine. Theodore Schroeder and Bolton Hall illuminated the legal side of family limitation, and Anna Strunsky Walling, John Reed, and a number of other speakers dwelt on its social and human value as a liberating factor, particularly in the lives of proletarians.

My trial, after several preliminary hearings, was set for April 20. On the eve of that day a banquet took place at the Brevoort Hotel, arranged by Anna Sloan and other friends. Members of the profes-sions and of various social tendencies were present. Our good old comrade H. M. Kelly spoke for anarchism, Rose Pastor Stokes for socialism, and Whidden Graham for the single-taxers. The world of art was represented by Robert Henri, George Bellows, Robert Minor, John Sloan, Randall Davey, and Boardman Robinson. Dr. Goldwater and other physicians participated. John Francis Tucker, of the Twi-light Club, was toast-master and he lived up to his reputation as one of the wittiest men in New York. An entertaining discussion was pro-vided by John Cowper Powys, the British writer, and Alexander

Harvey, an editor of *Current Literature*. Powys expressed himself as appalled by his ignorance of birth-control methods, but he insisted that though he personally was not interested in the matter, yet he belonged to the occasion because of his constitutional objection to any suppression of free expression.

When at the close I was given the floor to reply to the various points raised, I called the attention of the guests to the fact that the presence of Mr. Powys at a banquet given to an anarchist was by no means his first libertarian gesture. He had given striking proof of his intellectual integrity some years previously in Chicago when he had refused to speak at the Hebrew Institute because that institution had denied its premises to Alexander Berkman. The latter had been announced to speak on the Caplan-Schmidt case. At the last moment the directors of the Institute closed its doors. Thereupon the Chicago workers had boycotted the reactionary organization and founded their own Workmen's Institute. Shortly afterwards Mr. Powys had arrived to deliver a series of lectures at the Hebrew Institute. When informed of the attitude of its directors to Berkman, Mr. Powys had cancelled his engagements. His action was especially commendable because all he knew of Berkman was the misrepresentations he had read in the press.

Rose Pastor Stokes demonstrated direct action at the banquet. She announced that she had with her typewritten sheets containing information on contraceptives and that she was ready to hand them out to anyone who wanted them. The majority did.

In court the next day, April 20, I pleaded my own case. The District Attorney interrupted me continually by taking exceptions, in which he was sustained by two of my three judges. Presiding Judge O'Keefe proved to be unexpectedly fair. After some tilts with the young prosecutor I took the stand in my own behalf. It gave me the opportunity to expose the ignorance of the detectives who testified against me and to deliver in open court a defence of birth-control.

I spoke for an hour, closing with the declaration that if it was a crime to work for healthy motherhood and happy child-life, I was proud to be considered a criminal. Judge O'Keefe, reluctantly I thought, pronounced me guilty and sentenced me to pay a fine of one hundred dollars or serve fifteen days in the workhouse. On principle I refused to pay the fine, stating that I preferred to go to jail. It called forth an approving demonstration, and the court attendants cleared the room. I was hurried off to the Tombs, whence I was taken to the Queens County Jail.

Our following Sunday meeting, which I could not attend, since my forum was now a cell, was turned into a protest against my conviction. Among the speakers was Ben, who announced that pamphlets containing information about contraceptives were on the literature table and could be taken free of charge. Before he had got off the platform, the last of the pamphlets had been snatched up. Ben was arrested on the spot and held for trial.

In Queens County Jail, as on Blackwell's Island years previously, I saw it demonstrated that the average social offender is made, not born. One must have the consolation of an ideal to survive the forces designed to crush the prisoner. Having such an ideal, the fifteen days were a lark to me. I read more than I had for months outside, prepared material for six lectures on American literature, and still had time for my fellow prisoners.

Little did the New York authorities foresee the results of the arrests of Ben and me. The Carnegie Hall meeting had awakened interest throughout the country in the idea of birth-control. Protests and public demands for the right to contraceptive information were reported from numerous cities. In San Francisco forty leading women signed a declaration to the effect that they would get out pamphlets and be ready to go to prison. Some proceeded to carry out the plan and they were arrested, but their cases were discharged by the judge, who stated that there was no ordinance in the city to prohibit the propagation of birth-control information.

The next Carnegie Hall meeting was held as a greeting upon my release. The occasion was under the auspices of prominent persons in New York, but the actual organization work was done by Ben and his " staff," as he called our active boys and girls. Birth-control had ceased to be a mere theoretic issue; it became an important phase of the social struggle, which could be advanced more by deeds than by words. Every speaker stressed this point. It was again Rose Pastor Stokes who carried wishes into action. She distributed leaflets on contraceptives from the platform of the famous hall.

The sole disturbing element was Max Eastman, who declared a few minutes before the opening of the meeting that he would not preside if Ben Reitman should be allowed to speak. In view of Eastman's socialistic ideas and his past insistence on the right of free speech this ultimatum shocked everyone on the committee. The fact that Ben was under indictment for the very thing for which the meeting had been called made Mr. Eastman's attitude all the more incomprehensible.

I suggested to him to withdraw, but his friends persuaded him to preside. The incident once more proved how poorly some alleged radicals in America have grasped the true meaning of freedom and how little they care about its actual application in life. The " cultural " leader of socialism in the United States and editor of the *Liberator* permitted personal dislikes to stand in the way of what he claimed to be his " high ideal."

Ben's trial took place on May 8 in Special Sessions, before Judges Russell, Moss, and McInerney. The last-named was the man who had sent William Sanger to prison for a month. Ben pleaded his own case, making a splendid defence for birth-control. He was found guilty, of course, and sentenced to the workhouse for sixty days, because, as Judge Moss put it, he had " acted with deliberation, premeditation, and forethought, in defiance of the law." Ben cheerfully admitted the imputation.

His conviction was followed by a large protest meeting in Union Square. A touring-car was our platform, and we spoke to the working masses that were streaming out from the factories and shops. Bolton Hall presided; Ida Rauh and Jessie Ashley handed out the forbidden pamphlets. At the close of the meeting they were all arrested, including the chairman.

In the excitement of the birth-control campaign I did not forget other important issues. The European slaughter was continuing, and the American militarists were growing bloodthirsty at the smell of the red stream. Our numbers were few, our means limited, but we concentrated our best energies to stem the tide of war.

The Easter uprising in Ireland was culminating tragically. I had entertained no illusions about the rebellion, heroic as it was; it lacked the conscious aim of complete emancipation from economic and political rule. My sympathies were naturally on the side of the revolting masses and against British imperialism, which had oppressed Ireland for so many centuries.

Extensive reading of Irish literature had endeared the Gaelic people to me. I loved them as painted by Yeats and Lady Gregory, Murray and Robinson, and above all by Synge. They had shown me the remarkable similarity between the Irish peasant and the Russian moujik I knew so well. In their naïve simplicity and lack of sophistication, in the motif of their folk-melodies, and in their primitive attitude towards law-breaking, which sees in the offender an unfortunate rather than a criminal, they were brothers. The Irish poets seemed to me more expressive even than the Russian writers, their language being their people's own tongue. The debt I owed to Celtic literature and to my Irish friends in America, and my feeling for the oppressed everywhere, combined in my attitude to the uprising. In *Mother Earth* and on the platform I voiced my solidarity with the people risen in rebellion.

The quality of some of the victims of British imperialism was made vivid to me by Padraic Colum. He had been in close touch with the martyred leaders and spoke with knowledge and understanding of the events of Easter week. Lovingly he remembered Padraic H. Pearse, the poet and teacher, James Connolly, the proletarian rebel, and Francis Sheehy-Skeffington, a most gentle and genuine soul. Colum's description made the men live again and moved me profoundly. At my request he wrote an account of the events for *Mother Earth,* which was published in our magazine together with Padraic H. Pearse's stirring poem " The Pæan of Freedom."

No less than Great Britain our own country writhed in the throes of reaction. After Matthew A. Schmidt had been condemned to life imprisonment there came the conviction of David Caplan, who was sentenced to ten years in the California State prison at San Quentin. The quarters of the Magón brothers, champions of Mexican liberty, were raided in Los Angeles, and Ricardo and Enrico Magón arrested. In northern Minnesota thirty thousand iron-ore miners were waging a desperate struggle for more bearable conditions of existence. The mine-owners, aided by the Government, sought to break the strike by arresting its leaders, including Carlo Tresca, Frank H. Little, George Andreychin, and others active in behalf of the toilers. Arrests followed arrests throughout the country, accompanied by the utmost police brutality and encouraged by the subservience of the courts to the demands of capital.

Ben was meanwhile serving his sentence in the Queens County Jail. His letters breathed a serenity I had never known him to feel before. I was due to leave on my tour. There were many friends to look after Ben in my absence, and we planned to have him join me in California upon his release. There was no reason for anxiety about him, and he himself urged me to go, yet I was loath to leave him in prison. For eight years he had shared the pain and joy of my struggle. How would it be, I wondered, to tour again without Ben, without his elemental activity, which had helped so much to make my meetings a success? And how should I bear the strain of the struggle without Ben's affection and the comfort of his presence? The thought chilled me, yet the larger purpose, which was my life, was too vital to be affected by personal needs. I left alone.

# CHAPTER XLIV

I N DENVER I HAD THE RATHER UNUSUAL EXPERIENCE OF SEEING A judge preside at my lecture on birth-control. It was Ben B. Lindsey. He spoke with conviction on the importance of family limitation and he paid high tribute to my efforts. I had first met the Judge and his very attractive wife several years previously and I had spent time with them whenever I visited Denver. Through friends I had learned of the shameful treatment he had received at the hands of his political enemies. They had not only circulated the most scurrilous reports about his public and private integrity, but they had even directed their attacks against Mrs. Lindsey, anonymously threatening and terrorizing her. Yet I found Judge Lindsey free from bitterness, generous towards his enemies, and determined to pursue his own course.

While in the city, I had the opportunity of attending a lecture by Dr. Stanley Hall on " Moral Prophylaxis." I was familiar with his work and I believed him to be a pioneer in the field of sex psychology. In his writings I had found the subject illumined sympathetically and with understanding. Dr. Hall was introduced by a minister, which circumstance may have handicapped his freedom of expression. He talked badly and endlessly on the need of the churches' taking up sex instruction as " a safeguard for chastity, morality, and religion," and he voiced antiquated notions that had no bearing either on sex or on psychology. It made me sad to see him grown so feeble, particularly mentally, since we had met at the celebration of the twentieth anniversary of Clark University and at my own lectures. I felt sorry for the American people who were accepting such infantile stuff as authoritative information.

My lectures in Los Angeles were organized by Sasha, who had specially come for the purpose from San Francisco, where he was publishing the *Blast*. He had worked energetically, and my meetings proved to be successful in every way. Yet I missed Ben, Ben with all his weaknesses, his irresponsibility and ways that were so often harsh. But my longings were stilled by the urgent needs of the Los Angeles situation.

My lecture on "Preparedness" happened to fall on the day of the Preparedness Parade. We could have chosen no more opportune date had we known in advance of the planned militarist demonstration. In the afternoon the people of Los Angeles were treated to a patriotic spectacle, at which they were assured that "the lover of peace must go armed to the teeth," while in the evening they heard it emphasized that "he who goes armed is the greatest menace to peace." Some patriots had come to our meeting with the intention of breaking it up. They changed their minds, however, when they saw that our audience was not in a mood to listen to jingo appeals.

The brothers Ricardo and Enrico Flores Magón were being held in the Los Angeles jail, and the local comrades had so far not succeeded in bailing them out. Twice before had these men been railroaded to prison for their bold advocacy of liberty for the Mexican people. During their ten years' residence in the United States they had been imprisoned five years. Now Mexican influence in America sought to send them up for the third time. The people who knew and loved the Magóns were too poor to bail them out, while those who had means believed them to be the dangerous criminals they were pictured by the press. Even some of my American friends, I found, had been influenced by the newspaper ravings. Sasha and I set to work to secure the needed ten-thousand-dollar bond. Because of the official denunciation of everything Mexican our task proved to be extremely difficult. We even had to compile material to show that the only offence of the Magóns consisted in their selfless devotion to the cause of Mexican liberty. After much effort we succeeded in procuring their release on bond. The happy surprise on the faces of Ricardo and Enrico, who doubted the possibility of bailing them out, was the highest appreciation of our work in their behalf.

An impressive scene took place in court when the Magón brothers appeared for their hearing. The court-room was filled with Mexicans. When the judge entered, not one of them stood up, but when the Magóns were led in, they rose to a man and bowed low before them. It was a magnificent gesture that demonstrated the place these two brothers held in the hearts of those simple people.

In San Francisco Sasha and Fitzi had prepared everything to make my month's stay in the city pleasant and useful. My first lectures were most satisfactory, and they held out much promise for the rest of my series. I had my own apartment, as I was expecting Ben to join me in July. But I spent a great deal of my free time with Sasha and Fitzi in their place.

On Saturday, July 22, 1916, I was lunching with them. It was a golden California day, and the three of us were in a bright mood. We were a long time over our luncheon, Sasha regaling us with a humorous account of Fitzi's culinary exploits. The telephone rang, and he stepped into his office to answer it. When he returned, I noticed the extremely serious expression on his face, and I intuitively felt that something had happened.

" A bomb exploded in the Preparedness Parade this afternoon," he said; " there are killed and wounded." " I hope they aren't going to hold the anarchists responsible for it," I cried out. " How could they? " Fitzi retorted. " How could they not? " Sasha answered; " they always have."

My lecture on " Preparedness " had originally been scheduled for the 20th. But we learned that the liberal and progressive labour elements had arranged an anti-preparedness mass meeting for the same evening, and, not wishing to conflict with the occasion, postponed my talk for the 22nd. It struck me now that we had barely escaped being involved in the explosion; had my meeting taken place as scheduled, prior to the tragedy, everyone connected with my work would have undoubtedly been held responsible for the bomb. The telephone call had come from a newspaper man who wanted to know what we had to say about the explosion — the usual question of reporters and detectives on such occasions.

On the way to my apartment I heard newsboys calling out extra editions. I bought the papers and found what I had expected — glaring headlines about an " Anarchist Bomb " all over the front pages. The papers demanded the immediate arrest of the speakers at the anti-preparedness meeting of July 20. Hearst's *Examiner* was especially bloodthirsty. The panic that followed on the heels of the explosion exposed strikingly the lack of courage, not only of the average person, but of the radicals and liberals as well. Before the 22nd of July they had filled our hall every evening for two weeks, waxing enthusiastic over my lectures. Now at the first sign of danger they ran to cover like a pack of sheep at the approach of a storm.

On the evening following the explosion there were just fifty people at my meeting, the rest of the audience consisting of detectives. The atmosphere was very tense, everybody fidgeting about, apparently in terror of another bomb. In my lecture I dealt with the tragedy of the afternoon as proving more convincingly than theoretic dissertations that violence begets violence. Labour on the Coast had been opposed to the preparedness parade, and union members had been asked not to participate. It was an open secret in San Francisco that the police and the newspapers had been warned that something violent might happen if the Chamber of Commerce kept insisting on the public demonstration of its mailed fist. Yet the " patriots " had permitted the parade to take place, deliberately exposing the participants to danger. The indifference to human life on the part of those who had staged the spectacle gave a foretaste of how cheaply life would be considered should America enter the war.

A reign of official terror followed the explosion. Revolutionary workers and anarchists were, as always, the first victims. Four labour men and one woman were immediately arrested. They were Thomas J. Mooney and his wife, Rena, Warren K. Billings, Edward D. Nolan, and Israel Weinberg.

Thomas Mooney, long a member of Moulders' Union, Local 164, was known throughout California as an energetic fighter in the cause of the workers. For many years he had been an effective factor in various strikes. Because of his incorruptibility he was cordially hated by every employer and labour politician on the Coast. The United Railways had tried, a few years previously, to put Mooney behind the bars, but even the farmer jury had refused to credit the frame-up against him. Recently he had sought to organize again the motormen and conductors of the street-car combine. He had attempted, unsuccessfully, to call a strike of the platform-men a few weeks before the parade, and the United Railways marked him for their victim. They posted bulletins on the car barns, warning their men to have nothing to do with the " dynamiter Mooney," on pain of immediate discharge.

On the night following the posting of the bulletins, some power-towers of the company were blown up, and those who knew smiled at the obvious attempt of the railway bosses to " get " Mooney by the peculiarly " timely " branding of him as a dynamiter.

Warren K. Billings, formerly president of the Boot and Shoe Workers' Union, had for years been active in labour struggles, and the employers had once before succeeded in railroading him to prison on a trumped-up charge in connexion with strike troubles in San Francisco.

Edward D. Nolan was a man greatly admired and respected by labour elements on the Coast for his clear social vision, intelligence, and energy. He had, a few days previous to the preparedness parade, returned from Baltimore, where he had been sent as a delegate to the Machinists' convention. Nolan was also chief of the pickets in the local machinists' strike, and he had long since been put on the employers' black-list.

Israel Weinberg was a member of the executive board of the Jitney Bus Operators' Union, which had incurred the enmity of the United Railways by seriously embarrassing its receipts. The street-car company was trying to drive the jitneys off the principal streets, and the opportunity to discredit the Jitney Bus Union by charging a prominent member with murder was not to be lost by District Attorney Fickert of San Francisco, whom the railways had helped to office that he might quash the indictments against their corrupt officials — which he promptly did as soon as elected.

Mrs. Rena Mooney, the wife of Tom Mooney, was a well-known music-teacher. An energetic and devoted woman, her arrest was a police *coup* to prevent her efforts in behalf of Tom.

To charge these men with responsibility for the preparedness-parade explosion was a deliberate attempt to strike Labour a deadly blow through its most energetic and uncompromising representatives. We expected a concerted response in behalf of the accused from the liberal and radical elements, regardless of political differences. Instead we were confronted by complete silence on the part of the very people who had for years known and collaborated with Mooney, Nolan, and their fellow-prisoners.

The McNamara confession was still haunting, ghostlike, the waking and sleeping hours of their erstwhile friends among the labour politicians. There was not a single prominent man in the unions on the Coast who now dared speak up for his arrested brothers. There was no one to offer a penny for their defence. Not one word appeared even in *Organized Labor,* the organ of the powerful building trades, of which Olaf Tweetmore was editor. Not a word in the *Labor Clarion,* the official weekly of the San Francisco Labor Council and of the State Federation of Labor. Even Fremont Older, who had so staunchly defended the McNamaras and who had always bravely championed every unpopular cause, was silent now, in the face of the evident Chamber of Commerce conspiracy to hang innocent men.

It was a desperate situation. Only Sasha and I dared speak up for the prisoners. But we were known as anarchists and it was a question whether the accused, of whom only Israel was an anarchist, would wish to have us affiliated with their defence; they might feel that our names would hurt their case rather than do them good. I myself knew them but slightly, and Warren K. Billings I had never met. But we could not sit by idly and be a party to the conspiracy of silence. We should have come to their assistance even if we had thought them guilty of the charges, but Sasha knew all of the accused well and he was absolutely certain of their innocence. He considered none of them capable of throwing a bomb into a crowd of people. His assurance was sufficient guarantee for me that they had had no connexion whatever with the preparedness-parade explosion.

During the two weeks following the tragedy of July 22 the *Blast* and my meetings were the only expression of protest against the terrorist campaign carried on by the local authorities, at the behest of the Chamber of Commerce. Robert Minor, summoned by Sasha from Los Angeles, came to help in our preparations for the defence of the accused innocent men.

Ben, who had arrived from New York upon the completion of his prison term, was violently opposed to my remaining in San Francisco to finish my lecture series. My meetings were under police surveillance, the hall filled with hordes of detectives, whose presence kept my audiences away. He could not stand defeat; the mere handful of faithful friends in our hall, holding a thousand, was too much for him. Something else also seemed to be on his mind. He was more than usually restless and he besought me to discontinue my lectures and leave the city. But I could not go back on my engagements and I stayed on. I succeeded in raising at my meetings a hundred dollars and in borrowing a considerable sum for the defence of the arrested labour men. But so terrified was San Francisco that no attorney of standing would accept the case of the prisoners, who had already been condemned by every paper in the city.

It required several weeks of the most strenuous effort on our part to awaken some semblance of interest even among the radicals. With Sasha, Bob Minor, and Fitzi in charge of the activities, I now felt free to continue my tour, though I was very uneasy about their own fate.

The *Blast's* unconditional support of Mooney and his comrades had already subjected Sasha and his associates, Fitzi and our good " Swede " Carl, to the scrutiny of the police authorities. Some days after the explosion, detectives had forcibly entered the *Blast* office and had for hours ransacked it, taking away everything they could lay their hands on, including the California subscription list of *Mother Earth*. They had taken Sasha and Fitzi to headquarters, severely grilled them on their activities, and threatened to arrest them.

The sublime and the ridiculous often overlap each other. At the height of all the worry and anxiety about the San Francisco situation, while on my way to Portland with Ben, he was seized with one of his periodic fits to " nurse his soul, tabulate his ideas, and get acquainted with himself." His plaint was again that he could not continue for ever a " mere office boy," carrying bundles and selling literature; he had other ambitions; he wanted to write. He had wanted to write all along, he said, but I had never given him the chance. Sasha, he declared, was my god, Sasha's life and work my religion. In every difficulty that had arisen between him and Sasha I had always sided with the latter, he said. Ben had never been permitted his way in anything; I had even denied him his longing for a child. He insisted he had not forgotten that I had told him I had made my choice and that I could not allow a child to handicap my work in the movement. My attitude had hung over him like a pall, he declared, and it had made him afraid to confess that he had been living with another girl. His yearning for a child, always very strong, had become more compelling since he had met that girl. During his imprisonment in the Queens County Jail he had determined to allow nothing to stand in the way of the fulfilment of his great wish.

" But you have a child," I said, " your little Helen! Have you ever shown paternal love for her, or even the least interest, except on Valentine's Day, when I would pick out your cards for her? "

He was only a mere youth when the child was born, he replied; and the whole thing had been an accident. Now he was thirty-eight, with a " conscious feeling for fatherhood."

I knew there was no use in arguing. Unlike his confession in the first year of our love, which had struck me like a bolt of lightning out of a clear sky, this new disclosure hardly shocked or wounded me. The other had left scars too deep to heal or ever to allow me freedom from doubt. I had always guessed his deceptions; so accurately, indeed, that he called me a Sherlock Holmes " from whose eyes nothing is hidden."

Peculiar irony of circumstances! In New York Ben had started a "Sunday-school class," which exposed me to the ridicule of my comrades. " A Sunday-school in an anarchist office!" they laughed; " Jesus in the sanctum of the atheist." I sided with Ben. Free speech included his right to Jesus, I said. I knew that Ben was no more a Christian than the millions of others who proclaim themselves followers of the Nazarene. It was rather the personality of the "Son of Man" that appealed to Ben, as it had ever since his early youth. His religious sentimentalism would do no thinking person any harm, I thought. Most of his Sunday-school pupils were girls who were much more attracted to their teacher than to his Lord. I felt that Ben's religious emotionalism was stronger than his anarchistic convictions, and I could not deny him his right of expression.

To maintain consistency in a world of crass contradictions is not easy, and I had frequently been anything but consistent in regard to Ben. His love-affairs with all sorts of women had caused me too many emotional upheavals to allow me to act always in consonance with my ideas. Time, however, is a great leveller of feeling. I no longer cared about Ben's erotic adventures, and his newest confession did not affect me deeply. But it was indeed the height of tragicomedy that my stand in favour of Ben's Sunday-school in the *Mother Earth* office should result in an affair with one of his girl pupils. And then my anxiety about leaving Ben in the jail and going on tour without him at the very time he was absorbed in his new obsession! It was all so absurd and grotesque — I felt unutterably weary and possessed only of a desire to get away somewhere and forget the failure of my personal life, to forget even the cruel urge to struggle for an ideal.

I decided to go to Provincetown for a month, to visit with Stella and her baby. With them I would rest and perhaps find peace, peace.

Stella a mother! It seemed such a short while since she herself had been a little baby, the one ray of sunshine in my bleak Rochester days. When she was about to give birth to her child, I longed to be with her in that supreme moment. Instead I had been obliged to lecture in Philadelphia, while my heart palpitated with anxiety for my dear Stella in the throes of bringing forth new life. Time had passed with giant strides, and now I beheld Stella radiant in her young motherhood, and her little one, six months old, a striking replica of what my niece had looked at that age.

The charm of Provincetown, Stella's care, and the baby's loveliness filled my visit with a delight I had not known in years. There was also Teddy Ballantine, Stella's husband, a man of fine texture, vital and interesting, and the frequent calls of persons of outstanding individuality, such as Susan Glaspell, George Cram Cook, and my old friends Hutch Hapgood and Neith Boyce, the latter a most intriguing personality. There were also John Reed and adventurous Louise Bryant, more sophisticated than she had been in Portland two years before. There was beautiful Mary Pine, already doomed by consumption, her transparent skin and the lustre of her eyes heightened by a mass of copper hair. There was crude Harry Kemp, comically clumsy and awkward alongside of ethereal Mary. Variegated in mind and heart was that Provincetown group, and its company stimulating, but no one exerted such a restful effect on me as did Max, who had come at my invitation to spend a few weeks with me. He had remained unchanged, his fine spirit and intuitive understanding even more mellowed with the years. Kind and wise, he always found the right word to soothe distress. An hour with him was like a spring day, and I found solace and peace at his side. A month spent with him, in the circle of Stella's little family, would make me strong to conquer the world.

Alas, there was no month and no conquest! The eternal struggle for liberty was calling. Letters and telegrams from Sasha cried for help to save the five lives endangered in San Francisco. Could I think of rest, he indignantly demanded, while Tom Mooney and his comrades were facing death? Had I forgotten San Francisco, the terrorized prejudice against the victims in jail there, the cowardice of the labour leaders, the lack of funds for the defence of the prisoners, and the impossibility of securing a good lawyer for them? A note of desperation, unusual with Sasha, sounded in his letters, and he besought me to return to New York to secure for the defence a man prominent in the legal profession. That failing, I should go to Kansas City and try to prevail upon Frank P. Walsh to take the case.

My peace was gone; the forces of reaction had broken in on my golden freedom and had robbed me of the rest I needed so much. I even resented Sasha's strange impatience, but somehow I felt guilty. I was tormented by the feeling that I had broken faith with the victims of a social system which I had fought for twenty-seven years. Days

of inner conflict and of galling indecision followed. Then came Sasha's
telegram informing me that Billings had been convicted and sentenced
to prison for life. There was no more hesitancy on my part. I prepared to leave for New York.

On the last day of my Provincetown stay I went for a walk with
Max across the dunes. The tide was out. The sun hung like a golden
disk, no ripple on the transparent blue of the ocean in the distance.
The sand seemed a sheet of white stretched far out and disappearing
into the coloured crystal of the waters. Nature breathed repose and
wondrous peace. My mind, too, was at rest; peace had come with my
resolve. Max was frolicsome, and I felt in tune with his mood. We
slowly made our way across the vast expanse towards the sea. Obliv-
ous of the world of strife outside, we were held rapt by the spell of
the enchantment around us. Fishermen returning laden with their
spoils recalled us to the lateness of the day. With light step we
started on our way back, our gay song ringing in the air.

We were barely half-way across to the beach when we caught the
sound of gurgling water rising from somewhere. Sudden apprehension silenced our song. We turned to look back, and then Max gripped
my hand and we ran for the shore. The tide was welling in with a
fast sweep. It rose from a cove that emptied into the sea at that point.
It was already close behind us, the waves rushing over the sand with
increasing speed and volume. The terror of being caught drove us on.
Now and then our feet would sink in the soft sand, but the foaming
peril at our back kept steeling the instinctive will to live.

Terrified, we reached the bottom of a hill. With a last effort we
scrambled up and fell exhausted on the green soil. We were safe
at last!

On our way to New York we stopped off in Concord. I had always
wanted to visit the home of America's past cultural epoch. The museum,
the historic houses, and the cemetery were the only remaining witnesses of its days of glory. The inhabitants gave little indication that
the quaint old town had once been a centre of poetry, letters, and philosophy. There was no sign that men and women had existed in
Concord to whom liberty was a living ideal. The present reality was
more ghostlike than the dead.

We visited Frank B. Sanborn, the biographer of Henry David
Thoreau, the last of the great Concord circle. It was Sanborn who,

half a century before, had introduced John Brown to Thoreau, Emerson, and Alcott. He looked the typical aristocrat of intellect, his manner simple and gracious. With evident pride he spoke of the days when together with his sister he had, at the point of a gun, driven the tax-collectors from his homestead. He talked with reverence of Thoreau, the great lover of man and of beast, the rebel against the encroachments of the State on the rights of the individual, the supporter of John Brown when even his own friends had denied him. In detail Sanborn described to us the meeting Thoreau had carried through in memory of the black man's champion, in spite of almost unanimous opposition from the Concord coterie.

Sanborn's estimate of Thoreau bore out my conception of the latter as the precursor of anarchism in the United States. To my surprise, Thoreau's biographer was scandalized at my remark. " No, indeed! " he cried; " anarchism means violence and revolution. It means Czolgosz. Thoreau was an extreme non-resistant." We spent several hours trying to enlighten this contemporary of the most anarchistic period of American thought about the meaning of anarchism.

From Provincetown I had written Frank P. Walsh about the San Francisco situation, telling him that I would go to Kansas City to talk the matter over further if there was any chance of his taking charge of the Mooney defence. His reply awaited me in New York. He could not accept my suggestion, Walsh wrote; he was involved in an important criminal case in his own city, and he had also undertaken to line up the liberal elements in the East for the Woodrow Wilson campaign. He was of course interested in the San Francisco labour cases, his letter continued; he would soon be in New York and take the question up with me; perhaps he would be able to make some useful suggestions.

Frank P. Walsh was the most vital person I had met in Kansas City. He did not flaunt his radicalism in public, but he could always be depended upon 'to aid an unpopular cause. By nature he was a fighter; his sympathies were with the persecuted. I was aware of his interest in the labour struggle, and his letter therefore greatly disappointed me. Moreover, it was puzzling. If he could come to New York to take charge of the Wilson campaign, he could not be so tied up at home. Or did he consider electioneering more important than the five lives in peril on the Coast, I wondered. I was sure he was not familiar with the real state of affairs in San Francisco, and I decided to put the situation clearly before him. Perhaps it would induce him to change his mind.

At the Wilson campaign headquarters in New York, presided over by Frank P. Walsh, George West, and other intellectuals, I had a long talk with Walsh about the Mooney case. He seemed much impressed and he assured me that he would like to step in and do something for the prisoners. It was a serious situation, he said, but a far graver issue was facing the country — the war. The militarist elements were anxious for Wilson to get out of office so they could have their own man as President. It was up to all liberal-minded and peace-loving persons to re-elect Woodrow Wilson, Walsh emphasized. Even the anarchists, he thought, ought to set aside at this crucial moment their objections to participation in politics and help keep Wilson in the White House because " he has kept us out of war so far." It was my duty in particular, Walsh insisted, not to neglect the chance to demonstrate that my efforts against war were not mere talk. I could effectively silence the charge that I preached violence and destruction by proving that I was indeed the true champion of peace.

I was not a little surprised to find Frank P. Walsh such a defender of politics, after the very decided stand he had taken in behalf of the Mexican Revolution. I had once gone to Kansas City to solicit his contribution to that struggle, and he had eagerly responded, at the same time expressing his belief that action speaks louder than words. It was a far cry indeed from that attitude to his present notion that investing Woodrow Wilson with more political power would " save the world."

I left Walsh with a feeling of impatience at the credulity of this radically minded man and his co-workers in the Wilson campaign. It was an additional proof to me of the political blindness and social muddle-headedness of American liberals.

I knew no one in the New York legal profession whom I could approach in connexion with the Mooney case. I therefore had to inform Sasha of my failure. He replied that he himself was coming to New York to see what could be done. The International Workers' Defence League of San Francisco had requested him to go east to secure an able attorney and to rouse the labour elements to the peril of the arrested men.

In the latter part of October Bolton Hall's trial in connexion with our birth-control meeting at Union Square the previous May took place. A number of witnesses, including myself, testified that the defendant had given no contraceptive information on that occasion, and Bolton Hall was found not guilty. On leaving the court-room I was arrested on the same charge of which Hall had just been acquitted.

Persecution of birth-control advocates went merrily on. Margaret Sanger, her sister Ethel Byrne, a trained nurse, and their assistant, Fanya Mandell, were rounded up in a raid on Mrs. Sanger's clinic in Brooklyn. They had been tricked by a woman detective, who posed as the mother of four children, to give her contraceptives. Among the other cases were those of Jessie Ashley and of several I.W.W. boys. The guardians of law and morality throughout the country were determined to suppress the spread of information on birth-control.

The various hearings and trials in connexion with this matter proved that at least the judges were being educated. One of them declared that he distinguished between persons who gave out birth-control information free because of personal conviction and those who sold it. Certainly no such differentiation had been made previously, in William Sanger's case, in Ben's, or in mine. Even more striking proof that the agitation for family limitation was beginning to have an effect was given by Judge Wadhams during the trial of a woman charged with theft. Her husband, tubercular and out of work for a long time, was unable to support his large family. In summing up the causes that had led the prisoner to crime Judge Wadhams remarked that many nations in Europe had adopted birth-regulation with seemingly excellent results. " I believe we are living in an age of ignorance," he continued, " which at some future time will be looked upon aghast as we now look back on the dark ages. We have before us the case of a family increasing in numbers, with a tubercular husband, the woman with a child at her breast and with other small children at her skirts, in poverty and want."

We had reason to feel that it was worth going to jail if the urgency of limiting offspring was getting to be admitted even by the bench. Direct action, and not parlour discussion, was responsible for these results.

Early in November Sasha arrived in New York, and in less than two weeks he was able to rally to the support of the San Francisco fight nearly all of the organized Jewish labour, as well as a number of American trade unions. He was equally successful in his efforts to secure an attorney. By aid of some friends he prevailed upon W. Bourke Cockran, the famous lawyer and orator, to examine the transcript of the Billings case. Cockran was so impressed by Sasha's presentation of it and so aroused by the obvious frame-up that he offered to go to the Coast without a fee and take charge of the defence of Mooney, Nolan, and the other San Francisco prisoners. Sasha also prevailed upon the United Hebrew Trades, the largest and most influential central Jewish labour organization in the country, to call a mass meeting in Carnegie Hall to protest against the conspiracy of big business in California. The delegates of that body being fully occupied with their own duties, the entire brunt of organizing the mass meeting and securing speakers fell to Sasha and the active and efficient young comrades who were helping him in the campaign. Unfortunately, I could give him no assistance, owing to my lecture engagements in various points between New York and the Middle West. I promised, however, to speak at Carnegie Hall, even if it necessitated my return from Chicago to do so.

After seventeen lectures in that city and four in Milwaukee I hastened back to New York, arriving on the morning of December 2, the day of the big gathering. In the afternoon a demonstration took place on Union Square, a protest in favour of Mooney and his comrades and also in behalf of Carlo Tresca and his fellow victims of the Minnesota steel interests at the Messaba Range strike. The evening meeting in Carnegie Hall was attended by a very large audience, which was addressed by Frank P. Walsh, Max Eastman, Max Pine, secretary of the Hebrew Trades, Arturo Giovannitti, poet and labour leader, Sasha, and myself. It fell to me to make the appeal for funds, and the assembly generously responded with aid for the Californians' defence. The same night I left for the West to continue my interrupted tour.

At my lecture in Cleveland on "Family Limitation" Ben conceived the idea of calling for volunteers to distribute birth-control pamphlets. A number of people responded. At the end of the meeting Ben was arrested. A hundred persons, each carrying the forbidden pamphlet, followed him to the jail, but only Ben was held for trial. We immediately organized a Free Speech League, which combined with the local birth-control organization to fight the case.

Cleveland had for years been a free-speech stronghold, owing to the libertarian conditions established there by the single-tax mayor, the late Tom Johnson. Brave citizens of different political views had since zealously guarded those liberties. Among them I had many friends, but none more helpful than Mr. and Mrs. Carr, Fred Shoulder, Adeleine Champney, and our old philosopher Jacobs. They had always exerted themselves to make my public work successful and to enhance my leisure hours by charming fellowship. It was therefore a severe shock to see this exceptional city go back on its traditions. But the ready response to our call to organize a fight against the suppression held out the hope that the right of free expression would again prevail in Tom Johnson's home town.

Similar experiences attended my lectures in various cities, as well as those of other advocates of family limitation. Sometimes it was Ben who was arrested, at other times I and the friends who were actively co-operating with us, or other lecturers who were trying to enlighten the people on the proscribed issue. In San Francisco the *Blast* was held up by the post-office on account of an article on birth-control and because of *lèse-majesté* against Woodrow Wilson. Birth-control had become a burning issue, and the authorities exerted every effort to silence its advocates. Nor did they shrink from foul means to accomplish their ends. In Rochester Ben was arrested for having sold at one of our meetings a copy of Dr. William J. Robinson's *Family Limitation* and Margaret Sanger's pamphlet *What Every Woman Should Know*. The arresting officers were seemingly ignorant that those publications were being openly sold in book-shops. But it soon appeared that there was method in their madness. At the police station a pamphlet on contraceptives was " found " between the pages of Dr. Robinson's book. We knew some detective had placed it there to " get " Ben. And, indeed, he was held for trial.

While still on tour, I received a telegram from Harry Weinberger, my New York attorney, informing me that I had been denied a jury trial. On January 8 my case came up before three judges. Presiding Judge Cullen warned me severely that he would not permit any theories of the defendant to be aired in court. But he might have saved himself the trouble, because my case collapsed before either my lawyer or I had a chance to say anything. The evidence given by the detectives to the effect that I had distributed birth-control pamphlets on Union Square in May was so obviously contradictory that even the Court refused to take it seriously. I was acquitted.

Ben was not so fortunate, however, in regard to the Cleveland

charge against him. He had been subpœnaed for my trial, and as his own
was to take place the following day, he had wired his Cleveland
attorney and bondsman to secure a postponement. They replied that
he need have no anxiety, and that they would get him an extension
of time. To make doubly sure, Ben telegraphed and also sent a copy
of the subpœna to the Cleveland court. But on the afternoon of
January 9 he received word from his lawyer, informing him that, far
from consenting to a postponement, Judge Dan Cull had issued a
warrant for Ben's arrest for contempt of court. Ben took the first
train to Cleveland. The next morning his case was called. Judge Cull
" graciously " consented to dismiss the charge of contempt of court
and to try Ben only on the birth-control case. The Judge was a Roman
Catholic and rigidly opposed to any form of sex hygiene. He talked at
length about the carnal sins of the flesh and denounced birth-control
and anarchism. Of the twelve jurymen five were Catholics. The others
were apparently loath to convict, for they held out for thirteen hours
without coming to an agreement. The Court sent them back, however,
with instructions to remain out until they could bring in a verdict. Long
hours in a stuffy room will cause most juries to grow unanimous. Ben
was found guilty and sentenced to six months in the workhouse and to
pay a thousand dollars' fine. It was the heaviest penalty imposed for
a birth-control offence. Ben made a frank avowal of his belief in
family limitation, and on the advice of counsel he appealed the case.

The result of the trial was due mainly to the absence of proper
publicity. Margaret Sanger had lectured in the city a short time previously, and it had been expected that she would take note of the
situation and urge her hearers to rally to Ben's support. Her refusal
to do so had incensed our friends at the inexcusable breach of solidarity, but unfortunately no time had been left to arouse public sentiment in regard to Ben's case.

It was not the first occasion on which Mrs. Sanger had failed to
aid birth-control advocates caught in the meshes of the law. While
my trial in New York was pending, she was touring the country and
lecturing at meetings arranged by our comrades, largely at my suggestion. Strange to say, Mrs. Sanger, who had begun her birth-control
work in our quarters on One Hundred and Nineteenth Street, would
not even mention my approaching trial. Once, at a meeting in the
Bandbox Theatre, she was called to account for her silence by Robert
Minor. She upbraided him for daring to interfere with her affairs.

In Chicago Ben Capes had to resort to questions from the floor during a meeting to compel Mrs. Sanger to refer to my work for birth-control. Similar occurrences happened in Detroit, Denver, and San Francisco. From numerous places friends wrote me that Mrs Sanger had given the impression that she considered the issue as her own private concern. Subsequently Mr. and Mrs. Sanger publicly repudiated birth-control leagues organized by us, as well as our entire campaign for family limitation.

The lack of backing for Ben in Cleveland taught us the need of an organized protest in connexion with his coming trial in Rochester. On the eve of it a large meeting took place, the local speaker, Dr. Mary E. Dickinson, sharing the platform with Dolly Sloan, Ida Rauh, and Harry Weinberger, all of whom had come from New York for the occasion. The next day an effective demonstration was staged in court. Willis K. Gillette proved to be a very exceptional judge. I almost envied Ben the opportunity of being tried before a man who believed that the court is a place where the defendant should feel unafraid to speak out. With such a judge and with the fighting persistency of an attorney like Harry Weinberger, Ben was sure of fair treatment. He declared that he did not believe in the law that forbids giving birth-control information. He had broken it before and he would do it again, he said. But in the case on trial he was innocent, he maintained, because he did not know how the contraceptive pamphlet had happened to be in Dr. Robinson's book. He was acquitted.

We felt that we had reason for some satisfaction with our share in the campaign. We had presented the ideas of family limitation throughout the length and breadth of the country, bringing the knowledge of methods into the lives of the people who needed them most. We were ready now to leave the field to those who were proclaiming birth-control as the only panacea for all social ills. I myself had never considered it in that light; it was unquestionably an important issue, but by no means the most vital one.

In San Francisco the *Blast* had been suppressed and its office raided twice because of the paper's anti-war work and its efforts in behalf of Mooney. During the last raid Fitzi was brutally handled and her arm almost broken by an official ruffian. It became impossible to continue the publication on the Coast, and Fitzi brought it to New York, where she joined Sasha in his activities for the California defence.

Tom Mooney had been convicted and sentenced to death. Neither the eloquence of W. Bourke Cockran, nor the absolute demonstration that the leading witnesses of the prosecution had perjured themselves availed nothing. The grip of the Chamber of Commerce upon official justice in California proved to be stronger than the most unshakable evidence in favour of the labour defendant. There was hardly a citizen in San Francisco who did not know that the State's witnesses, the McDonalds and the Oxmans, were of the very dregs of debased humanity, their testimony bought and paid for by District Attorney Charles Fickert, the willing tool of the employers. But innocence did not count. The bosses who had declared themselves for the " open shop " had determined to hang Tom Mooney, as a warning to other labour organizers, and Mooney's doom was sealed.

Nor was the State of California the only section of the country where law and order had centred all their might to crush the workers and effectively stifle further protest on the part of the disinherited and humiliated. In Everett, Washington, seventy-four I.W.W. boys were fighting for their lives, and in every other State of the Union the jails and prisons were filled with men convicted for their ideals.

The political sky in the United States was darkening with heavy clouds, and the portents were daily growing more disquieting, yet the masses at large remained inert. Then, unexpectedly, the light of hope broke in the east. It came from Russia, the land tsar-ridden for centuries. The day so long yearned for had arrived at last — the Revolution had come!

# CHAPTER XLV

THE HATED ROMANOVS WERE AT LAST HURLED FROM THEIR throne, the Tsar and his cohorts shorn of power. It was not the result of a political *coup d'état;* the great achievement was accomplished by the rebellion of the entire people. Only yesterday inarticulate, crushed, as they had been for centuries, under the heel of a ruthless absolutism, insulted and degraded, the Russian masses had risen to demand their heritage and to proclaim to the whole world that autocracy and tyranny were for ever at an end in their country. The glorious tidings were the first sign of life in the vast European cemetery of war and destruction. They inspired all liberty-loving people with new hope and enthusiasm, yet no one felt the spirit of the Revolution as did the natives of Russia scattered all over the globe. They saw their beloved *Matushka Rossiya* now extend to them the promise of manhood and aspiration.

Russia was free; yet not truly so. Political independence was but the first step on the road to the new life. Of what use are " rights," I thought, if the economic conditions remain unchanged. I had known the blessings of democracy too long to have faith in political scene-shifting. Far more abiding was my faith in the people themselves, in the Russian masses now awakened to the consciousness of their power and to the realization of their opportunities. The imprisoned and exiled martyrs who had struggled to free Russia were now being resurrected, and some of their dreams realized. They were returning from the icy wastes of Siberia, from dungeons and banishment. They were coming back to unite with the people and to help them build a new Russia, economically and socially.

America also was contributing its quota. At the first news of the Tsar's overthrow thousands of exiles hastened back to their native country, now the Land of Promise. Many had lived in the United

States for decades and acquired families and homes. But their hearts dwelt more in Russia than in the country they were enriching by their labour, which nevertheless scorned them as " foreigners." Russia was welcoming them, her doors wide open to receive her sons and daughters. Like swallows at the first sign of spring they began to fly back, orthodox and revolutionists for once on common ground — their love and longing for their native soil.

Our own old yearning, Sasha's and mine, began to stir again in our hearts. All through the years we had been close to the pulse of Russia, close to her spirit and her superhuman struggle for liberation. But our lives were rooted in our adopted land. We had learned to love her physical grandeur and her beauty and to admire the men and women who were fighting for freedom, the Americans of the best calibre. I felt myself one of them, an American in the truest sense, spiritually rather than by the grace of a mere scrap of paper. For twenty-eight years I had lived, dreamed, and worked for that America. Sasha, too, was torn between the urge to return to Russia and the necessity of continuing his campaign to save the life of Mooney, whose fatal hour was fast approaching. Could he forsake the doomed man and the others whose fate hung in the balance?

Then came Wilson's decision that the United States must join the European slaughter to make the world safe for democracy. Russia had great need of her revolutionary exiles, but Sasha and I now felt that America needed us more. We decided to remain.

The declaration of war by the United States dismayed and over-awed most of the middle-class pacifists. Some even suggested that we terminate our anti-militarist activities. A certain woman, a member of the Colony Club of New York, who had repeatedly offered to supply money for anti-war work in the European countries now demanded that we discontinue our agitation. Having declined her previous offers, I felt free to tell her that true charity begins at home. I could see no reason for giving up the stand on war that I had maintained for a quarter of a century, just because Woodrow Wilson had tired of his watchful waiting. I could not alter my convictions merely because he had ceased to be " too proud " to let American boys do the fighting, while he and other statesmen remained at home.

With the collapse of the pseudo-radicals the entire burden of anti-war activity fell upon the more courageous militant elements. Our group in particular redoubled its efforts, and I was kept feverishly busy travelling between New York and nearby cities, speaking and organizing the campaign.

A contingent of Russian exiles and refugees was preparing to leave for their native land, and we helped to equip its members with provisions, clothing, and money. Most of them were anarchists, and all of them were eager to participate in the upbuilding of their country on a foundation of human brotherhood and equality. The work of organizing the return to Russia was in charge of our comrade William Shatoff, familiarly known as Bill.

This revolutionary anarchist, compelled to take refuge in America from the tyranny of the Russian autocracy, had during his ten years' sojourn in the United States shared the life of the true proletarian and was always in the thick of the struggle for the betterment of the workers' condition. Having worked as a labourer, longshoreman, machinist, and printer, Bill was familiar with the hardships, insecurity, and humiliation that characterize the existence of the immigrant toiler. Many a weaker man would have perished spiritually, but Bill had the vision of an ideal, an inexhaustible energy, and a keen intellect. He devoted his life to the enlightenment of the Russian refugees. He was a splendid organizer, an eloquent speaker, and a man of courage. These qualities enabled him to gather into one great body the various small groups of Russians in America. He was eminently successful in helping to weld them into a powerful and solidaric organization, known as the Union of Russian Workers, which embraced the United States and Canada. Its aim was the education and revolutionary development of the vast numbers of Russian workers whom the Greek Catholic Church in America sought to ensnare, as it had done at home. Bill Shatoff and the comrades active with him had for years worked to awaken their dark Russian brothers to their economic situation and to enlighten them on the importance of organized cooperation. Most of them were unskilled men, labouring long hours and ruthlessly exploited at most arduous toil in mines and mills and on the railroads. Thanks to Bill's energy and devotion, these masses were gradually united into a strong body of rebels.

Shatoff was also for a time manager of the Ferrer Center, and in that capacity his intelligence and enthusiasm proved as efficient as in everything else he undertook.

No less fine was our Bill in the personal relationships of life. Charming and jovial, he was a splendid companion, dependable in every emergency and especially in difficult situations. A staunch and brave friend, Bill insisted on accompanying Sasha when the latter was in danger of attack by San Francisco detectives because of his work in behalf of Mooney. On Sasha's journey to various cities Bill acted as his self-constituted body-guard, and it afforded me great relief to know that any person attempting to do violence to Sasha would meet with the additional resistance of our stout-hearted Bill.

With the first news of the miracle that had taken place in Russia, Shatoff began organizing the thousands of his radical compatriots eager to return home. Like a true captain of a ship he had determined to see everyone safely on his way, without thought of himself. He would go last, he told us, when we urged that his experience and abilities would be more valuable in Russia than in America. He remained until his own departure had grown almost perilous.

I had known for some time of the presence in New York of Mme Alexandra Kolontay and Leon Trotsky. From the former I had received several letters and a copy of her book on woman's share in the world's work. She had asked me to meet her, but I had been unable to spare the time. Later on I had invited her to dinner, but she was prevented by illness from coming. Leon Trotsky I had also never met before, but I happened to be in the city when an announcement was made of a farewell meeting which he was to address before leaving for Russia. I attended the gathering. After several rather dull speakers Trotsky was introduced. A man of medium height, with haggard cheeks, reddish hair, and straggling red beard stepped briskly forward. His speech, first in Russian and then in German, was powerful and electrifying. I did not agree with his political attitude; he was a Menshevik (Social Democrat), and as such far removed from us. But his analysis of the causes of the war was brilliant, his denunciation of the ineffective Provisional Government in Russia scathing, and his presentation of the conditions that led up to the Revolution illuminating. He closed his two hours' talk with an eloquent tribute to the working masses of his native land. The audience was roused to a high pitch of enthusiasm, and Sasha and I heartily joined in the ovation given the speaker. We fully shared his profound faith in the future of Russia.

After the meeting we met Trotsky to bid him good-bye. He knew about us and he inquired when we meant to come to Russia to help in the work of reconstruction. " We will surely meet there," he remarked.

I discussed with Sasha the unexpected turn of events that made us feel closer to Trotsky, the Menshevik, than to Peter Kropotkin, our comrade, teacher, and friend. The war was producing strange bedfellows, and we wondered whether we should still feel near to Trotsky when in the course of time we should reach Russia, for we had only postponed, not given up, our return there.

Shortly after Trotsky's departure the first group of our comrades sailed. We gave them a joyous send-off at a large party attended by many of our American friends, who also generously contributed to the needs of the men. Sasha had conceived the idea of a manifesto to the Russian workers, peasants, and soldiers, and we wrote it just in time to send it with the group. Among them were a number of men and women who had worked with us in our various campaigns in the *Blast* and *Mother Earth*. The manifesto was entrusted to Louise Berger and S.F., our closest and most dependable friends. It was an appeal to the masses of Russia to voice their protest to Washington against the condemnation of Tom Mooney and Warren K. Billings. We thought it the only method left to save the innocently convicted men.

In the spirit of her military preparations America was rivalling the most despotic countries of the Old World. Conscription, resorted to by Great Britain only after eighteen months of war, was decided upon by Wilson within one month after the United States had decided to enter the European conflict. Washington was not so squeamish about the rights of its citizens as the British Parliament had been. The academic author of *The New Freedom* did not hesitate to destroy every democratic principle at one blow. He had assured the world that America was moved by the highest humanitarian motives, her aim being to democratize Germany. What if he had to Prussianize the United States in order to achieve it? Free-born Americans had to be forcibly pressed into the military mould, herded like cattle, and shipped across the waters to fertilize the fields of France. Their sacrifice would earn them the glory of having demonstrated the superiority of *My Country, 'Tis of Thee* over *Die Wacht am Rhein*. No American president had ever before succeeded in so humbugging the people as Woodrow Wilson, who wrote and talked democracy, acted despotically, privately and officially, and yet managed to keep up the myth that he was championing humanity and freedom.

We had no illusions about the outcome of the conscription bill pending before Congress. We regarded the measure as a complete denial of every human right, the death-knell to liberty of conscience, and we determined to fight it unconditionally. We did not expect to be able to stem the tidal wave of hatred and violence which compulsory service was bound to bring, but we felt that we had at least to make known at large that there were some in the United States who owned their souls and who meant to preserve their integrity, no matter what the cost.

We decided to call a conference in the *Mother Earth* office to broach the organization of a No-Conscription League and draw up a manifesto to clarify to the people of America the menace of conscription. We also planned a large mass meeting as a protest against compelling American men to sign their own death-warrants in the form of forced military registration.

Because of previously arranged lecture dates in Springfield, Massachusetts, I was unfortunately not able to be present at the conference, set for May 9. But as Sasha, Fitzi, Leonard D. Abbott, and other clear-headed friends would attend, I felt no anxiety about the outcome. It was suggested that the conference should take up the question of whether the No-Conscription League should urge men not to register. *En route* to Springfield I wrote a short statement giving my attitude on the matter. I sent it with a note to Fitzi asking her to read it at the gathering. I took the position that, as a woman and therefore myself not subject to military service, I could not advise people on the matter. Whether or not one is to lend oneself as a tool for the business of killing should properly be left to the individual conscience. As an anarchist I could not presume to decide the fate of others, I wrote. But I could say to those who refused to be coerced into military service that I would plead their cause and stand by their act against all odds.

By the time I returned from Springfield the No-Conscription League had been organized and the Harlem River Casino rented for a mass meeting to take place on May 18. Those who had participated at the conference had agreed with my attitude regarding registration.

In the midst of our activities Sasha met with a serious accident. I was living again in the little room behind the *Mother Earth* office in One Hundred and Twenty-fifth Street, while Sasha and Fitzi had moved the *Blast* to the room on the upper floor, formerly occupied by our friend Stewart Kerr. There was no telephone connexion in the house except in my office, and one day Sasha, hurrying to answer a call, slipped and fell down the whole length of the steep stairway. Upon examination the ligaments of his left foot were found torn, and a physician ordered him to bed. Sasha would not listen to it; with the amount of work on hand and with only a few comrades to look after it, he could not rest, he said. Though in great pain and able only to hop about on crutches, he was bent on attending the meeting at the Harlem River Casino.

On May 18 Fitzi and I resorted to every feminine trick we could think of to persuade our cripple to remain at home, but he insisted on coming with us. He was helped by two husky comrades down the stairs and lifted into a taxi, and the same performance was repeated later at the hall.

Almost ten thousand people filled the place, among them many newly rigged-out soldiers and their woman friends, a very boisterous lot indeed. Several hundred policemen and detectives were scattered through the hall. When the session opened, a few young " patriots " tried to rush the stage entrance. Their attempt was foiled, because we had prepared for such a contingency.

Leonard D. Abbott presided, and on the platform were Harry Weinberger, Louis Fraina, Sasha, myself, and a number of other opponents of forced military service. Men and women of varying political views supported our stand on this occasion. Every speaker vigorously denounced the conscription bill which was awaiting the President's signature. Sasha was particularly splendid. Resting his injured leg on a chair and supporting himself with one hand on the table, he breathed strength and defiance. Always a man of great self-control, his poise on this occasion was remarkable. No one in the vast audience could have guessed that he was in pain, or that he gave a single thought to his helpless condition if we should fail to carry the meeting to a peaceful end. With great clarity and sustained power Sasha spoke as I had never heard him before.

The future heroes were noisy all through the speeches, but when I stepped on the platform, pandemonium broke loose. They jeered and hooted, intoned *The Star-Spangled Banner,* and frantically waved small American flags. Above the din the voice of a recruit shouted: " I want the floor! " The patience of the audience had been sorely tried all evening by the interrupters. Now men rose from every part of the house and called to the disturber to shut up or be kicked out. I knew what such a thing would lead to, with the police waiting for a chance to aid the patriotic ruffians. Moreover, I did not want to deny free speech even to the soldier. Raising my voice, I appealed to the assembly to permit the man to speak. " We who have come here to protest against coercion and to demand the right to think and act in accordance with our consciences," I urged, " should recognize the right of an opponent to speak and we should listen quietly and grant him the respect we demand for ourselves. The young man no doubt believes in the justice of his cause as we do in ours, and he has pledged his life for it. I suggest therefore that we all rise in appreciation of his evident sincerity and that we hear him out in silence." The audience rose to a man.

The soldier had probably never before faced such a large assembly. He looked frightened and he began in a quavering voice that barely carried to the platform, although he was sitting near it. He stammered something about " German money " and " traitors," got confused, and came to a sudden stop. Then, turning to his comrades, he cried: " Oh, hell! Let's get out of here! " Out the whole gang slunk, waving their little flags and followed by laughter and applause.

Returning from the meeting home we heard newsboys shouting extra night editions — the conscription bill had become a law! Registration day was set for June 4. The thought struck me that on that day American democracy would be carried to its grave.

We felt that May 18 was the beginning of a period of historic importance. To Sasha and myself the day had also a profound personal meaning. It was the twelfth anniversary of his resurrection from the Western Penitentiary of Pennsylvania, the first time in years that he and I were together in the same city and on the same platform.

Streams of callers besieged our office from morning till late at night; young men, mostly, seeking advice on whether they should register. We knew, of course, that among them were also decoys sent to trick us into saying that they should not. The majority, however, were frightened youths, fearfully wrought up and at sea as to what to do.

They were helpless creatures about to be sacrificed to Moloch. Our sympathies were with them, but we felt that we had no right to decide the vital issue for them. There were also distracted mothers, imploring us to save their boys. By the hundreds they came, wrote, or telephoned. All day long our telephone rang; our offices were filled with people, and stacks of mail arrived from every part of the country asking for information about the No-Conscription League, pledging support and urging us to go on with the work. In this bedlam we had to prepare copy for the current issues of *Mother Earth* and the *Blast,* write our manifesto, and send out circulars announcing our forthcoming meeting. At night, when trying to get some sleep, we would be rung out of bed by reporters wanting to know our next step.

Anti-conscription meetings were also taking place outside of New York and I was busy organizing branches of the No-Conscription League. At such a gathering in Philadelphia the police came down with drawn clubs and threatened to beat up the audience if I dared mention conscription. I proceeded to talk about the freedom the masses in Russia had gained. At the close of the meeting fifty persons retired to a private place, where we organized a No-Conscription League. Similar experiences were repeated in many cities.

A week after the Harlem River Casino meeting I received a telegram from Tom Mooney indicating the hoplessness of further legal proceedings in his case and urging an appeal to the people of the country. His telegram read:

San Francisco
May 25, 1917

Superior Court today held Oxman for trial. Chief Justice Angellotti said evidence of Oxman's guilt overwhelming. Special committee appointed by San Francisco Labor Council and Building Trades Council appeared in person before Attorney General Webb requesting answer on his disposition of Judge Griffin's request confessing error in my case. Attorney General said that records did not show error and it would be impossible confess same.

Powerful publicity, monster demonstrations, absolutely necessary for successful outcome. California lynch-law crowd fighting desperately to save themselves.

This precludes new trial unless the unforeseen happens. Give these facts wide publicity.

Tom Mooney

The conviction of Warren K. Billings, in spite of absolute proof of his innocence, had caused the defence to investigate the witnesses for the prosecution. Virtually every one of them was proved to be a tool of District Attorney Charles Fickert, and several confessed that their testimony for the State was purchased by threats and bribery. The jury also was found to have been tampered with by agents of the Chamber of Commerce. It was too late to save Billings, but it warned the defence of what it had to expect in the trial of Tom Mooney.

Fickert realized that some of his old witnesses, exposed as per- jurers and professional prostitutes, could not be used against Mooney. He therefore prepared others of a similar calibre, the star among them being a certain Frank C. Oxman, an alleged Western cattleman. It was mainly on the evidence of Oxman that Mooney was convicted. He testified that he was in San Francisco on Preparedness Day, and he identified Mooney as the man whom he saw placing a suit-case (supposedly of explosives) on a street-corner along the route of the march. An investigation proved that Oxman had not been in San Francisco on the date of the parade. Moreover, a letter by Oxman to his friend F. E. Rigall was produced, in which Oxman urged him to earn "a piece of money" by coming to testify against Mooney. Rigall was at the time in Niagara Falls and had never been in San Francisco. The proof of Oxman's perjury was so overwhelming that District Attorney Fickert was compelled to bring him to trial.

Notwithstanding all these developments, in spite even of the ad- mission of the trial judge, Franklin A. Griffin, that Mooney had been convicted on false testimony, the Supreme Court of California refused to intervene. Mooney was doomed to die!

The country-wide campaign that Sasha had started for Mooney almost a year previously had meanwhile borne fruit. The case had been taken up by radical and progressive labour organizations through- out the land, and many liberal organizations as well as influential individuals had become interested. Work to save the convicted man from the gallows continued without abatement.

At the peace meeting in Madison Square Garden, arranged jointly by the more radical anti-war organizations on June 1, several of our young comrades were arrested for distributing announcements for our Hunt's Point Palace meeting on June 4. Learning of it, we dis- patched a letter to the District Attorney, taking entire responsibility for what the arrested boys had done. We pointed out that if it was a crime to give out the handbill, we, its authors, were the guilty persons. The letter was signed by Sasha and me, and we enclosed a special-delivery stamp for an immediate reply. But no answer came and no action was taken against us.

The arrested boys included Morris Becker, Louis Kramer, Joseph Walker, and Louis Sternberg. They were charged with conspiracy to advise people not to submit to the Conscription Law. Their trial took place before Federal Judge Julius M. Mayer. Kramer and Becker were convicted, the jury recommending clemency for the latter. The Judge's idea of clemency was a scurrilous denunciation of the defendants. He called Kramer a coward and gave him the limit of the law, two years in the Federal penitentiary at Atlanta and ten thousand dollars' fine. Becker received one year and eight months and was also condemned to pay a similar fine. The other two boys, Sternberg and Walker, were acquitted. Harry Weinberger had conducted their defence in his usual able way and he appealed their case. Louis Kramer, while in the Tombs awaiting transfer to Atlanta, refused to register for the draft and was sentenced to serve an additional year.

The June issue of *Mother Earth* appeared draped in black, its cover representing a tomb bearing the inscription: " IN MEMORIAM — AMERICAN DEMOCRACY." The sombre attire of the magazine was striking and effective. No words could express more eloquently the tragedy that turned America, the erstwhile torch-bearer of freedom, into a grave-digger of her former ideals.

We strained our capital to the last penny to issue an extra large edition. We wanted to mail copies to every Federal officer, to every editor, in the country and to distribute the magazine among young workers and college students. Our twenty thousand copies barely sufficed to supply our own needs. It made us feel our poverty more than ever before. Fortunately an unexpected ally came to our assistance: the New York newspapers! They had reprinted whole passages from our anti-conscription manifesto, some even reproducing the entire text and thus bringing it to the attention of millions of readers. Now they copiously quoted from our June issue and editorially commented at length on its contents.

The press throughout the country raved at our defiance of law and presidential orders. We duly appreciated their help in making our voices resound through the land, our voices that but yesterday had called in vain. Incidentally the papers also gave wide publicity to our meeting scheduled for June 4.

Our busy and exciting life was not conducive to Sasha's speedy recovery. He continued to suffer much pain and discomfort. Most of his writing had to be done in bed or with his leg perched up on a chair. He could barely hop about on crutches, but he was again adamant in his decision to attend the mass meeting. We knew he was suffering, but he cracked jokes and scolded Fitzi and me because we were making "too much fuss."

When we got within half a dozen blocks of Hunt's Point Palace, our taxi had to come to a stop. Before us was a human dam, as far as the eye could see, a densely packed, swaying mass, counting tens of thousands. On the outskirts were police on horse and on foot, and great numbers of soldiers in khaki. They were shouting orders, swearing, and pushing the crowd from the sidewalks to the street and back again. The taxi could not proceed, and it was hopeless to try to get Sasha to the hall on his crutches. We had to make a detour around vacant lots until we reached the back entrance of the Palace. There we came upon a score of patrol wagons armed with search-lights and machine-guns. The officers stationed at the stage door, failing to recognize us, refused to let us pass. A reporter who knew us whispered to the police sergeant in charge. "Oh, all right," he shouted, "but nobody else will be admitted. The place is overcrowded."

The sergeant had lied; the house was only half filled. The police were keeping the people from getting in, and at seven o'clock they had ordered the doors locked. While they were denying the right of entry to workers, they permitted scores of half-drunken sailors and soldiers to enter the hall. The balcony and the front seats were filled with them. They talked loudly, made vulgar remarks, jeered, hooted, and otherwise behaved as befits men who are preparing to make the world safe for democracy.

In the room behind the stage were officials from the Department of Justice, members of the Federal attorney's office, United States marshals, detectives from the "Anarchist Squad," and reporters. The scene looked as if set for bloodshed. The representatives of law and order were obviously keyed up for trouble.

Among the "alien enemies" in the hall and on the platform were men and women prominent in the field of education, art, and letters. One of them was the distinguished Irish rebel Mrs. Sheehy-Skeffington, the widow of the pacifist author murdered in the Dublin uprising the previous year. A lover of peace and an eloquent pleader for freedom and justice, she was a sweet and gentle soul. In her was personified the spirit of our gathering, the respect for human life and liberty that was seeking public expression that evening.

When the meeting was opened and Leonard D. Abbott took the chair, he was greeted by the soldiers and sailors with catcalls, whistles, and stamping of feet. This failing of the desired effect, the uniformed men in the gallery began throwing on the platform electric lamps which they had unscrewed from the fixtures. Several bulbs struck a vase holding a bunch of red carnations, sending vase and flowers crashing to the floor. Confusion followed, the audience rising in indignant protest and demanding that the police put the ruffians out. John Reed, who was with us, called on the police captain to order the disturbers removed, but that official declined to intervene.

After repeated appeals from the chairman, supported by some women in the audience, comparative quiet was restored. But not for long. Every speaker had to go through the same ordeal. Even the mothers of prospective soldiers, who poured out their anguish and wrath, were jeered by the savages in Uncle Sam's uniform.

Stella was one of the mothers to address the audience. It was the first time she had to face such an assembly and endure insults. Her own son was still too young to be subject to conscription, but she shared the woe and grief of other, less fortunate, parents, and she could articulate the protest of those who had no opportunity to speak. She held her own against the interruptions and carried the audience with her by the earnestness and fervour of her talk.

Sasha was the next speaker; others were to follow him, and I was to speak last. Sasha refused to be helped to the platform. Slowly and with great effort he managed to climb up the several steps and then walked across the stage to the chair placed for him near the footlights. Again, as on May 18, he had to stand on one leg, resting the other on the chair and supporting himself with one hand on the table. He stood erect, his head held high, his jaw set, his eyes clear and unflinchingly turned on the disturbers. The audience rose and greeted Sasha with prolonged applause, a token of their appreciation of his appearance in spite of his injury. The enthusiastic demonstration seemed to enrage the patriots, most of whom were obviously under the influence of drink. Renewed shouts, whistles, stamping, and hysterical cries of the women accompanying the soldiers greeted Sasha. Above the clamour a hoarse voice cried: "No more! We've had enough!" But Sasha would not be daunted. He began to speak, louder and louder, berating the hoodlums, now reasoning with them, now holding them up to scorn. His words seemed to impress them. They became quiet. Then, suddenly, a husky brute in front shouted: "Let's charge the platform! Let's get the slacker!" In an instant the audience were on their feet. Some ran up to grab the soldier. I rushed to Sasha's side. In my highest pitch I cried: " Friends, friends — wait, wait!" The suddenness of my appearance attracted everyone's attention. " The soldiers and sailors have been sent here to cause trouble," I admonished the people, "and the police are in league with them. If we lose our heads there will be bloodshed, and it will be our blood they will shed!" There were cries of "She's right!" "It's true!" I took advantage of the momentous pause. "Your presence here," I continued, "and the presence of the multitude outside shouting their approval of every word they can catch, are convincing proof that you do not believe in violence, and it equally proves that you understand that war is the most fiendish violence. War kills deliberately, ruthlessly, and destroys innocent lives. No, it is not we who have come to create a riot here. We must refuse to be provoked to it. Intelligence and a passionate faith are more convincing than armed police, machine-guns, and rowdies in soldiers' coats. We have demonstrated it tonight. We still have many speakers, some of them with illustrious American names. But nothing they or I could say will add to the splendid example you have given. Therefore I declare the meeting closed. File out orderly, intone our inspiring revolutionary songs, and leave the soldiers to their tragic fate, which at present they are too ignorant to realize."

The strains of the *Internationale* rose above the approval shouted by the audience, and the song was taken up by the many-throated mass outside. Patiently they had waited for five hours and every word that had reached them through the open windows had found a strong echo in their hearts. All through the meeting their applause had thundered back to us, and now their jubilant song.

In the committee room a reporter of the New York *World* rushed up to me. "Your presence of mind saved the situation," he congratulated me. "But what will you report in your paper?" I asked. " Will you tell of the rough-house the soldiers tried to make, and the refusal of the police to stop them?" He would, he said, but I was certain that no truthful report would be published, even if he should have the courage to write it.

The next morning the *World* proclaimed that " Rioting accompanied the meeting of the No-Conscription League at Hunt's Point Palace. Many were injured and twelve arrests made. Soldiers in uniform sneered at the speakers. After adjournment the real riot began in the adjacent streets."

The alleged riot was of editorial making and seemed a deliberate attempt to stop further protests against conscription. The police took the hint. They issued orders to the hall-keepers not to rent their premises for any meeting to be addressed by Alexander Berkman or Emma Goldman. Not even the owners of places we had been using for years dared disobey. They were sorry, they said; they did not fear arrest, but the soldiers had threatened their lives and property. We secured Forward Hall, on East Broadway, which belonged to the Jewish Socialist Party. It was small for our purpose, barely big enough to seat a thousand people, but no other place was to be had in entire New York. The awed silence of the pacifist and anti-military organizations which followed the passing of the registration bill made it doubly imperative for us to continue the work. We scheduled a mass meeting for June 14.

It was not necessary for us to print announcements. We merely called up the newspapers, and they did the rest. They denounced our impudence in continuing anti-war activities, and they sharply criticized the authorities for failing to stop us. As a matter of fact, the police were working overtime waylaying draft-evaders. They arrested thousands, but many more had refused to register. The press did not report the actual state of affairs; it did not care to make it known that large numbers of Americans had the manhood to defy the government. We knew through our own channels that thousands had determined not to shoulder a gun against people who were as innocent as themselves in causing the world-slaughter.

One day, while I was dictating letters to my secretary, an old man came into the *Mother Earth* office and asked for Berkman. Sasha was engaged in the rear room. Engrossed in work, I did not take the time even to invite the caller to sit down. I pointed to the back, indicating that he might enter. In a few minutes Sasha called me in. He introduced the visitor as James Hallbeck, for years a subscriber of *Mother Earth* and the *Blast,* whom he had met in San Francisco. The name was familiar to me and I remembered the man's ready response to our appeals. Sasha told me that the comrade wanted to make a contribution to our work. We needed money for our campaign desperately and I was glad that someone had come forward with an offer. The indifferent reception I had given Hallbeck made me somewhat embarrassed when he handed me his cheque. I apologized by explaining how busy we were, but he assured me that he understood and that it was perfectly all right. He had very little time, he said, and, hastily bidding us good-bye, he edged his way out. When I looked at the cheque, I discovered to my amazement that it was for three thousand dollars. I was sure the old comrade had made a mistake and I quickly went to call him back. But he shook his head and assured me that there was no error about it. I begged him to return to the office and tell us something about himself. I could not take the money without knowing whether he had enough left to secure his old age.

He told us that he had emigrated from Sweden to America sixty years previously. A rebel since his youth, the judicial murder of our Chicago comrades had made him an anarchist. For a quarter of a century he had lived in California as a wine-grower and he had saved a little money. His own needs were small, and he had no kin in the United States, never having married. His three sisters in the old country were in comfortable circumstances, and they would also get a modest legacy after his death. He was very much interested in the No-Conscription campaign, and, being too old to participate actively, he had decided to put a little money at our disposal for the work. We need have no scruples about accepting the cheque, he assured us. " I am eighty," he added, " and I have not much longer to live. I want to feel that whatever I can spare will benefit the cause I have believed in during the largest part of my life. I don't want the State or the Church to profit by my death." Our venerable comrade's simple manner, his devotion to our work and generous gesture, affected us too profoundly for banal expressions of thanks. Our hand-clasp showed our appreciation, and he left us as unostentatiously as he had come. His cheque was deposited in the bank as a fund for anti-war activities.

June 14, the day of our Forward Hall meeting, arrived. In the late afternoon I was called on the telephone, and a strange voice warned me against attending the gathering. The man had overheard a plot to kill me, he informed me. I asked for his name, but he declined to give it; nor would he consent to see me. I thanked him for his interest in my welfare and hung up the receiver.

Jocularly I told Sasha and Fitzi that I must prepare my will. " But

I shall probably reach a disgusting old age," I remarked. To be prepared for any eventuality, however, I decided to leave a note directing that "the $3000 contributed by James Hallbeck should remain in charge of Alexander Berkman, my lifelong friend and comrade in battle, to be applied to anti-war work and the support of imprisoned conscientious objectors." The *Mother Earth* fund, consisting of $329, was to pay our office debts; our stock of books was to be sold and the proceeds used for the needs of the movement. My personal library I bequeathed to my youngest brother and Stella. My only property, the little farm in Ossining, which my friend Bolton Hall had recently deeded to me, I left to Ian Keith Ballantine, Stella's little boy. Sasha and Fitzi witnessed the document with their signatures.

Reaching East Broadway, where Forward Hall is located, we were met, not by ordinary plotters, but by the entire police department. At least it seemed so to us, judging by the number of New York's "finest" that lined the street and the whole of Rutgers Square adjacent to our meeting-place. The crowd had been pushed back to the farthest end of the square. Those who had succeeded in getting into the building found themselves locked in and held as prisoners, as it were. No conspirators having designs upon my life had the ghost of a chance to get near me or Sasha, so closely were we encircled by husky officers, who hurried us into the building.

The hall was filled to suffocation. There were police galore and an array of Federal officials, but no soldiers. Forward Hall had probably never before held such a large American attendance. People seemed to realize that free expression on the war and conscription had become a rarity, and they were eager to lend their support.

The meeting was very spirited and our program was carried out without a hitch. But at the close every man in the hall who appeared subject to the draft was detained by the officers, and those who could not show a registration card were placed under arrest. It was apparently the intention of the Federal authorities to use our meeting as a trap. We therefore resolved to hold no more public gatherings unless we could make sure that those who had not complied with the registration law would keep away. We decided to concentrate more on the printed word.

On the following afternoon we were all busy in our offices. Sasha and Fitzi were on the upper floor, preparing the next issue of the *Blast*. I worked with my new secretary, Pauline, while our friend

Carl, the "Swede," was mailing our circulars. He was a staunch and dependable comrade who had been with us for a long time, first in Chicago, where he had helped with my lectures, then in San Francisco, where he was associated with the *Blast,* and now in New York. Carl was among the most trustworthy and level-headed men in our ranks. Nothing could ruffle his even temper or make him give up a task once undertaken. He was being assisted in the office by two other active comrades, Walter Merchant and W. P. Bales, who were true American rebels.

Above the hum of conversation and the clicking of the typewriter we suddenly heard the heavy stamping of feet on the stairway, and before any one of us had a chance to see what was the matter, a dozen men burst into my office. The leader of the party excitedly cried: "Emma Goldman, you're under arrest! And so is Berkman; where is he?" It was United States Marshal Thomas D. McCarthy. I knew him by sight; of late he had always stationed himself near the platform at our No-Conscription meetings, his whole attitude one of impatient readiness to spring upon the speakers. The newspapers had reported him as saying that he had repeatedly wired Washington for orders to arrest us.

"I hope you will get the medal you crave," I said to him. "Just the same, you might let me see your warrant." Instead he held out a copy of the June *Mother Earth* and demanded whether I was the author of the No-Conscription article it contained. "Obviously," I answered. "since my name is signed to it. Furthermore, I take the responsibility for everything else in the magazine. But where is your warrant?"

McCarthy declared that no warrant was necessary for us; *Mother Earth* contained enough treasonable matter to land us in jail for years. He had come to get us and we had better hurry up.

Leisurely I walked towards the stairs and called: "Sasha, Fitzi— some visitors are here to arrest us." McCarthy and several of his men roughly pushed me aside and dashed up to the *Blast* office. The deputy marshals took possession of my desk and began examining the books and pamphlets on our shelves, throwing them in a pile on the floor. A detective grabbed W. P. Bales, the youngest of our group, and announced that he was also under arrest. Walter Merchant and Carl were commanded to stand back until the search was over.

I started for my room to change my dress, aware that a night's free lodging was in store for me. One of the men rushed up to detain

me, taking hold of my arm. I wrenched myself loose. "If your chief
didn't have the guts to come up here without a body-guard of thugs,"
I said to him, "he should at least have instructed you not to act like
one. I'm not going to run away. I only want to dress for the reception
awaiting us, and I don't propose to let you act as my maid." The men
ransacking my desk laughed coarsely. "She's a caution," one remarked,
"but it's all right, officer, let her go to her room." When I emerged
with my book and small toilet outfit, I found that Fitzi and Sasha,
who was still on crutches, were already down. McCarthy was with
them.

"I want the membership list of the No-Conscription League," he
demanded.

"We ourselves are always ready to receive our friends the police,"
I retorted; "but we are careful not to take chances with the names
and addresses of those who cannot afford the honour of an arrest.
We don't keep the No-Conscription list in our office, and you can't
find out where it is."

The procession started down the stairs to the waiting automobiles,
McCarthy and his assistants in front, Sasha and I behind them. In
the rear two deputy marshals leading Bales, followed by officers of the
"bomb squad." With Sasha I was given the place of honour in the
Chief Marshal's car. We fairly flew through the congested streets,
frightening people by the screeching of the horn and sending them
scampering in all directions. It was after six o'clock and masses of
workers were streaming from the factories, but McCarthy would not
permit the chauffeur to slacken up, nor did he heed the frantic signals
of the traffic policemen along the route. When I called his attention
to the fact that he was breaking the speed regulations and endangering
the lives of the pedestrians, he replied importantly: "I represent the
United States Government."

In the Federal Building we were joined by Harry Weinberger, our
pugnacious lawyer and unfailing friend. He asked for immediate arraignment and release on bail, but our arrest had purposely been staged
for the late afternoon after the official closing hour. We were ordered
to the Tombs prison.

The following morning we were taken before United States Commissioner Hitchcock. The prosecutor, Federal Attorney for the District of New York, Harold A. Content, charged us with "conspiracy
against the draft" and demanded that our bail be set high. The

commissioner fixed the bonds at twenty-five thousand dollars each. Mr. Weinberger protested, but in vain.

In the Tombs we were held *incommunicado* for several days. Subsequently we learned that the raiders had seized everything they could lay their hands on in the offices of *Mother Earth* and the *Blast,* including subscription lists, cheque-books, and copies of our publications. They had also confiscated our correspondence files, manuscripts intended for publication in book form, as well as my typewritten lectures on American literature and other valuable material that we had spent years in accumulating. The treasonable matter consisted of works by Peter Kropotkin, Enrico Malatesta, Max Stirner, William Morris, Frank Harris, C. E. S. Wood, George Bernard Shaw, Ibsen, Strindberg, Edward Carpenter, the great Russian writers, and other such dangerous explosives.

Our friends hastened to our aid in a spirit of most splendid solidarity. Our dear comrades Michael and Annie Cohn were in the lead with large sums of money. Agnes Inglis of Detroit sent financial help, as did scores of others from various parts of the country. Equally inspiring was the attitude of many poor working-men. They not only contributed their meagre savings, but even offered their trinkets to help raise the fifty-thousand-dollar bond demanded by the United States Government.

I wanted Sasha bailed out first because of his injured leg, which still needed treatment; I did not mind remaining in the Tombs, for I was resting and enjoying an absorbing book Margaret Anderson had sent me. It was *A Portrait of the Artist As a Young Man,* by James Joyce. I had not read that author before and I was fascinated by his power and originality.

The Federal authorities were not anxious to let us out of prison. The three hundred thousand dollars' worth of real estate offered as our bond was refused on a flimsy technicality by Assistant Federal Attorney Content, who declared that nothing but cash would be accepted. There was enough on hand to bail out one of us. Sasha, always gallant, refused to come out first, and therefore the bond was given for me and I was released.

Although the newspapers could easily verify who had contributed towards my bail, the New York *World* had the temerity to print a story in its issue of June 22 to the effect that " a report is current that the Kaiser furnished the $25,000 for Emma's release." It was an indication of the extent to which the press would go to help dispose of undesirable elements.

The Federal grand jury brought in an indictment charging us with conspiracy to defeat the "selective" draft. The maximum penalty for this offence was two years' imprisonment and ten thousand dollars' fine. Our trial was set for June 27. I had only five days to prepare for my defence, while Sasha was still in the Tombs. It was imperative to concentrate all our energies on raising his bail.

But there was Ben, once more unable to face a vital issue and emotionally torn betwixt and between. No court decision had yet been handed down on his appeal from the Cleveland conviction. He had returned to New York when we began our No-Conscription campaign, and with his usual energy he had thrown himself into the work. All went well for some weeks, and then Ben again became, as he had so often before, a prey to his emotional upheavals. This time it was the young woman of his Sunday class. She was neither in danger nor in want, and her child was not expected for months to come. But Ben succumbed. At the very height of our anti-war campaign he left for Chicago to join the prospective mother. His failure to remain at his post at such a critical moment both exasperated and pained me. In vain I sought to explain away his apparent lack of stamina and courage by remembering that he could not have foreseen our arrest. Yet he had not returned when he knew that we were already in custody. Did it not prove breach of faith? The thought that Ben would deny me in my hour of need was tormenting. I felt deeply grieved and humiliated at the same time.

At last we succeeded in procuring the twenty-five-thousand-dollar cash bond demanded for Sasha, and on June 25 he was released from the Tombs. We were entirely at one regarding our trial. We did not believe in the law and its machinery, and we knew that we could expect no justice. We would therefore completely ignore what was to us a mere farce; we would refuse to participate in the court proceedings. Should this method prove impractical, we would plead our own case, not in order to defend ourselves, but to give public utterance to our ideas. We decided to go into court without an attorney. Our resolve was not due to any dissatisfaction with our counsel, Harry Weinberger. On the contrary, we could have wished for no abler attorney and more devoted friend. He had already rendered us services far beyond any monetary recompense, and he had done so although fully aware that we could not pay adequately. We fully appreciated Harry and we felt safe in his hands. But our trial would have meaning only if we could turn the court-room into a forum for the presentation of the ideas we had been fighting for throughout all our conscious years. No lawyer could help us in this, and we were not interested in anything else.

Harry Weinberger understood our attitude, but he strongly advised us against meeting the prosecution with folded arms. It would make no impression whatever in an American court, he said; we should be given the maximum penalty, and nothing would be gained for our principles. But if we would plead our own case, he would give us every legal assistance and suggestion possible.

The day before our trial I met by appointment a number of people at the Brevoort Hotel, before whom I placed our intention of ignoring the prosecution. Among those present were Frank Harris, John Reed, Max Eastman, Gilbert E. Roe, and several others. After I had explained why I had called the conference, Frank Harris, with whom I had been friendly for years, became enthusiastic with the idea. " Emma Goldman and Alexander Berkman, the arch-champions of active resistance, meeting their enemies with folded arms — fine! Splendid! " he cried. In any European court such a stand would prove to be a magnificent gesture, he declared; but an American judge would only consider us flagrantly contemptuous, and the newspapermen would as little know what to make of us as the scribes of two thousand years ago had made of the Carpenter of Nazareth. Frank did not think we would be given a chance to carry out our plan, but in any event he was with us and we could fully count on his support.

John Reed did not believe in deliberately stepping into the lion's den. If one must go, one should fight all the way through, he thought. Whatever our decision, however, he would help in every way he could.

Max Eastman was not impressed by our suggestion. His opinion was that we could achieve more by a legal fight, with the aid of a competent lawyer to conduct our defence. It was more important, he held, that we should be free to continue our anti-war work than to go to prison without having tried every legal recourse.

It was Tuesday, June 27, at 10 a.m., when, together with Sasha, still on crutches, I walked through the crowded court-room in the Federal Building to face the prosecution. Judge Julius M. Mayer and

Assistant United States District Attorney Harold A. Content, their Prussianism carefully hidden, like wrinkles on a woman's face, under the thick paint of Americanism, were in their appointed places. Surrounding them were the lesser stars in the play about to be staged. In the background was a mob of soldiers, State and Federal officials, court attendants looking like hold-up men, and a contingent of reporters. American flags and bunting added to the high spots of the scene. Only a few of our friends had been admitted.

I moved for postponement on the grounds that my co-defendant, Alexander Berkman, suffering from an injury to his leg, was unable to stand the strain of a prolonged trial. As we had been released on bail only a few days, we had had no time to familiarize ourselves with the indictment, I also declared. Attorney Content protested, and Judge Mayer denied my motion.

Thereupon I said that, in view of the evident intention of the Government to turn the prosecution into persecution, we preferred to take no part whatever in the proceedings. His Honour had apparently never heard of such a thing before. He looked puzzled. Then he announced that he would appoint counsel to defend us. "In our free United States even the poorest are accorded the benefit of legal defence," he said. Upon our refusal the Court ruled that our trial should proceed after the noon recess. During luncheon we conferred with Harry Weinberger and other friends and returned to court in fighting trim.

June 27 happened to be my forty-eighth birthday. It marked twenty-eight years of my life spent in an active struggle against compulsion and injustice. The United States now symbolizing concentrated coercion, I could not have wished for a more appropriate celebration than to meet its challenge. It gave me much joy to feel that my friends had, in the excitement of the moment, not forgotten the event. On my return to court they presented me with flowers and gifts. The demonstration of their love and esteem on this special occasion moved me profoundly.

Active participation in our trial having been thrust upon us, Sasha and I determined to use it to best advantage. We decided to wring from our enemies every chance to propagate our ideas. Should we succeed, it would be the first time since 1887 that anarchism had raised its voice in an American court. Nothing else was worth considering in comparison with such an achievement.

I had known Sasha twenty-eight years. As far as one human being can foretell how another will act under stress or when confronted with the unexpected, I had always believed that I could in reference to him. But Sasha as a brilliant lawyer was a revelation even to me, his oldest friend. At the end of the first day I almost pitied the unfortunate talesmen whom he had been catechizing for hours. Like bullets Sasha fired his questions at the prospective jurymen, examining them on social, political, and religious matters, making them writhe at the exposure of their ignorance and prejudice, and almost convincing the victims themselves that they were not fit to try intelligent men. His flashes of humour and charming manners captivated the spectators.

When Sasha had finished quizzing the jurymen, they could hardly restrain their expression of relief. I followed to question them on marriage, divorce, sex enlightenment of the young, and birth-control. Would my radical views on these matters prevent their rendering an unbiased verdict? It was with the greatest difficulty that I was able to get my questions across. I was often interrupted by the Federal Attorney, became involved in verbal clashes with him, and was repeatedly admonished by the Judge to confine myself to "relevant" matters.

We knew very well that the twelve men we had finally selected could not and would not render an unbiased verdict. But by our examination of the talesmen we had succeeded in uncovering the social issues involved in the trial, had created a libertarian atmosphere, and had broached problems never before mentioned in a New York court.

Attorney Content opened his case by stating that he would prove that in our writings and speeches we had urged men not to register. As evidence he produced copies of *Mother Earth,* the *Blast,* and our No-Conscription manifesto. Cheerfully we admitted our authorship of every word, insisting, however, that the prosecution quote page and line where advice not to register was given. Unable to do so, Content called Fitzi to the witness-stand and tried to make her say that we had worked for profit. Though utterly irrelevant to the crime charged against us, the Court permitted the procedure. In her quiet, unruffled manner Fitzi very soon punctured this bubble.

The next "proof," played up as a trump card, was the insinuation of German money. "Emma Goldman deposited three thousand dollars in the bank a few days prior to her arrest. Where did that money come from?" the prosecutor demanded triumphantly. Everybody present pricked up his ears, and the reporters got busy with their pencils. We laughed inwardly. We could picture to ourselves their faces, now bursting with vindictiveness, when our venerable comrade James Hallbeck should testify. Our one regret was that we should have to call the poor soul into the stuffy court-room on such a scorching July day.

He came, a simple and unassuming little man, with a large heart and brave spirit. He recited his story on the witness-stand exactly as he had told it to us when he had brought his generous gift. " But why did you give Emma Goldman three thousand dollars? " Content demanded in a rage. " Nobody just throws away so much money."

" No, I did not throw it away," he answered with dignity. Emma Goldman and Alexander Berkman were his comrades, he explained. They were doing the work he believed in, but was too old to do. That was why he gave them the money. The German-money fuse fizzled out.

The next card was not original. It had been played in my first round with the State of New York in 1893. A detective, who in this case claimed also to be a stenographer, produced notes purporting to be a verbatim report of my speech at the Harlem River Casino. He quoted me as having said on that occasion: " We believe in violence, and we will use violence."

On cross-examination we brought out the fact that the detective had made his notes while standing on a shaky table, and that the highest number he could take was one hundred a minute. We confronted him with the champion stenographer, Paul Munter. The latter testified that it was difficult even for him to take Emma Goldman, especially in any intense speech, and yet his record was one hundred and eighty words a minute. Munter was followed by the proprietor of the Harlem River Casino. Though called by the prosecution, he told the Court that he had not heard me use the expression imputed to me, and he had listened very attentively to my talk. The meeting had been perfectly orderly in spite of a group of soldiers who had tried to cause trouble, he stated, " and it was Emma Goldman who saved the situation on that occasion." A sergeant of the Coast Guard corroborated his testimony.

The uninitiated wondered why the prosecution should stress what I had said on the 18th of May, *before* conscription had become a law, while no reference was made to my speeches *after* the bill had been passed. We knew the reason. At our last meetings we had had stenographers who sat on the platform in everybody's view. But we had been unable to secure a competent man for May 18. The State had evidently been apprised of that fact; therefore the stenographic detective was very convenient for the prosecution.

We produced a number of witnesses to show that the phrase " we believe in violence and we will use violence " had never been uttered by me or any other speaker at our gatherings. Our first witness was Leonard D. Abbott, admired by everybody for his charm and respected even by the most conservative for his sincerity. He had presided at the meetings of May 18 and June 4. He denied emphatically that I had used the words attributed to me at the Harlem River Casino or anywhere else. In fact, he told the Court, he had been somewhat disappointed with my speech, because he had expected a more extreme attitude. As to my having advised young men not to register, that could easily be disproved by a letter I had sent to the gathering at the *Mother Earth* office on May 9, Leonard stated.

His testimony was supported by a conscientious objector who related that he had gone to our office for advice about registration and had been told by us that we preferred to leave registration or military service to the conscience of those eligible for the draft. After him came Helen Boardman, Martha Gruening, Rebecca Shelley, Anna Sloan, and Nina Liederman. These women had all worked with us from the very beginning of the No-Conscription campaign, and they reiterated that they had never heard us urge anyone not to register.

The Federal Attorney demanded that we produce the original text of my letter, insinuating that the contents had been changed in the transcription. He knew that the original copy, like most of our other papers and documents, had been confiscated in the raid and was now in his possession. Yet he had the effrontery to make the demand. He did not produce the letter; it would have belied the charge against me.

However, the prosecution was resourceful; other devices were tried out. Now it was an attempt to play on the prejudices of the jury by creating the impression that our witnesses were mostly foreigners. Much to the chagrin of Federal Attorney Content, it soon developed that most of them had a background older than his own. Helen Boardman, for instance, was the sort of foreigner whose ancestors had come over in the Mayflower, and Anna Sloan was of old Irish-American stock. He had the same poor luck with our men witnesses, among whom were John Reed, Lincoln Steffens, Bolton Hall, and other " real " Americans.

Sasha followed the prosecution with a brief outline of our case. He declared that the charge of conspiracy was the height of absurdity, considering that he and his co-defendant had openly propagated anti-militarism for twenty-eight years. It was therefore a conspiracy known to a hundred millions of our population. As Sasha continued talking, presenting our case with keen logic and incisive manner, some of the jurymen seemed impressed and showed lively interest. Content did not fail to take note of it. At the first opportunity he picked up a copy of *Mother Earth* of July 1914. I had quite forgotten that several copies of that issue had been left in our office. Some of the boys and girls who had participated in the unemployment campaign that Sasha had organized and in the demonstration after the Lexington tenement explosion had long drifted out of our ranks. Most of them had proved worthless, carried away by momentary excitement, but their violent effusions had unfortunately remained in cold print and they were now taken advantage of by the prosecution. Content proceeded to read the choicest bits, straining to impress the jury that all of us sponsored physical force and the use of dynamite. "It is true, Miss Goldman was at that time absent on a tour," he remarked, "and she could therefore not be held responsible for the articles in this particular number." It was an attempt to throw the entire burden on Sasha. I was on my feet before he got through. "The prosecutor knows perfectly well," I declared, "that I am the owner and publisher of *Mother Earth,* and that I am responsible for everything that appears in the magazine, whether I happen to be present at its publication or not." I demanded whether we were being tried for ancient history; otherwise it was difficult to understand why an issue that had appeared three years before the United States went into the war, which had neither been held up by the postal authorities nor objected to by the State of New York, should now be used in the case. It was irrelevant, I declared. But my objections were ruled out by His Honour.

Every day increased the tension in court. The atmosphere grew more antagonistic, the official attendants more insulting. Our friends were either kept out or treated roughly when they succeeded in gaining admittance. On the street below, a recruiting station had been erected, and patriotic harangues mingled with the music of a military band. Each time the national anthem was struck up, everybody in court was commanded to rise, the soldiers present standing at attention. One of our girls refused to get up and she was dragged out of the room by force. A boy was literally kicked out. Sasha and I remained seated throughout the display of patriotism by the mailed fist. What could the officials do? They could not very well order us removed from this Punch and Judy show; we at least had that advantage.

After endlessly repetitious "evidence" of our crime, which in reality proved nothing, the prosecution closed its case. The last round in the contest between ideas and organized stupidity was set for July 9. This left us about forty-eight hours to prepare our arraignment of the forces that had plunged the world into a vale of tears and blood. Since the beginning of our trial we had been compelled to keep up a terrific pace, and we felt exhausted. For the past week we had enjoyed the hospitality of Leonard D. Abbott and his wife, Rose Yuster, and now we pilgrimed to Stella's little place at Darien for a short rest.

I woke the next morning with the bright sunshine streaming into my room and wide stretches of blue hanging over the luscious green of trees and lawn. The air was pungent with the aroma of the earth, the lake was vibrant with soft music, and all of nature breathed enchantment. I, too, was under her magic spell.

On our return to court Monday, July 9, we found the stage set for the last act of the tragicomedy that had already lasted a week. Judge Mayer, Federal Attorney Content, and a large company of performers in the badly constructed plot were already on the stage. The house was filled with invited official guests and *claqueurs* to lead the applause. Scores of pressmen were present to review the show. Not many of our friends had been able to gain admittance, but there were more than on previous days.

Prosecutor Content could in no way compare in ability and forcefulness with his colleague who had prosecuted me in 1893; he had been drab and colourless all through the trial and stereotyped in his address to the jury. At one moment he had attempted to climb to oratorical heights. "You think this woman before you is the real Emma Goldman," he declared, "this well-bred lady, courteous, and with a pleasant smile on her face? No! The real Emma Goldman can be seen only on the platform. There she is in her true element, sweeping all caution to the winds! There she inflames the young and drives them to violent deeds. If you could see Emma Goldman at her meetings, you would realize that she is a menace to our well-ordered institutions." It was therefore the jury's duty to save the country from *that* Emma Goldman by bringing in a verdict of guilty.

Sasha followed the prosecutor. He held the close attention of the men in the box, as well as of the entire court-room, for two hours. That was no small feat in an atmosphere oozing with prejudice and hate. His playful and witty handling of the so-called evidence to prove our "crime" caused much merriment and often loud laughter. This was promptly stopped by stern rebukes from the bench. The testimony of the government thoroughly demolished, Sasha proceeded with an *exposé* of anarchism, masterly in its simple directness and clarity.

I spoke after Sasha, for an hour. I discussed the farce of a government undertaking to carry democracy abroad by suppressing the last vestiges of it at home. I took up the contention of Judge Mayer that only such ideas are permissible as are "within the law." Thus he had instructed the jurymen when he had asked them if they were prejudiced against those who propagate unpopular ideas. I pointed out that there had never been an ideal, however humane and peaceful, which in its time had been considered "within the law." I named Jesus, Socrates, Galileo, Giordano Bruno. "Were they ' within the law ' ? " I asked. "And the men who set America free from British rule, the Jeffersons and the Patrick Henrys? The William Lloyd Garrisons, the John Browns, the David Thoreaus and Wendell Phillipses — were they within the law? "

At that moment the strains of the *Marseillaise* floated through the window, and the Russian Mission marched past on its way to the City Hall. I seized upon the occasion. "Gentlemen of the jury," I said, " do you hear the stirring melody? It was born in the greatest of all revolutions, and it was most emphatically not within the law! And that delegation your government is now honouring as the representatives of new Russia. Only five months ago every one of them was considered what you have been told we are: criminals — not within the law! "

During the proceedings His Honour was assiduously reading. His desk was littered with the literature confiscated in our offices, and he seemed absorbed — now in Sasha's *Memoirs,* now in my *Essays,* now in *Mother Earth.* His application had led some friends to believe that the Judge was interested in our ideas and inclined to be fair.

Judge Mayer fully rose to our expectations. In his charge to the jury he declared with much solemnity: " In the conduct of this case, the defendants have shown remarkable ability. An ability which might have been utilized for the great benefit of this country, had they seen fit to employ themselves in behalf of it rather than against it. In this country of ours we regard as enemies those who advocate the abolition of our government and those who counsel disobedience to our laws by those of minds less strong. American liberty was won by the forefathers, it was maintained by the Civil War, and today there are the thousands who have already gone, or are getting ready to go, to foreign lands to represent their country in the battle for liberty." He then instructed the jury that " whether the defendants are right or wrong can have no bearing on the verdict. The duty of the jury is merely to weigh the evidence presented as to the innocence or guilt of the defendants of the crime as charged."

The jury filed out. The sun had set. The electric lights looked yellow in the dusk. Flies buzzed, their swirl mingling with the whisperings in the room. The minutes crept on, clammy with the day's heat. The jury returned; its deliberation had lasted just thirty-nine minutes.

" What is your verdict? " the foreman was asked.

" Guilty," he answered.

I was on my feet. "I move that the verdict be set aside as absolutely contrary to the evidence."

" Motion denied," Judge Mayer said.

" I further move," I went on, "that sentence be deferred for a few days, and that our bail be continued at the sum already fixed in our case."

" Denied," ruled the Judge.

His Honour asked the usual meaningless question as to whether the defendants had anything to say why sentence should not be imposed.

Sasha replied: " I think it only fair to suspend sentence and give us a chance to clear up our affairs. We have been convicted because we are anarchists, and the proceeding has been very unjust." I also added my protest.

" In the United States, law is an imperishable thing," the Court declared in imposing sentence, " and for such people as would nullify our laws we have no place in our country. In a case such as this I can but inflict the maximum sentence which is permitted by our laws."

Two years in prison with a fine of ten thousand dollars each. The Judge also instructed the Federal Attorney to send the records of the trial to the immigration authorities in Washington with his recommendation to deport us at the expiration of our prison terms.

His Honour had done his duty. He had served his country well and merited a rest. He declared court adjourned and turned to leave the bench.

But I was not through. "One moment, please," I called out. Judge Mayer turned to face me. "Are we to be spirited away at such neck-breaking speed? If so, we want to know it now. We want everybody here to know it."

"You have ninety days in which to file an appeal."

"Never mind the ninety days," I retorted. "How about the next hour or two? Can we have that to gather up a few necessary things?"

"The prisoners are in the custody of the United States Marshal," was the curt answer.

The Judge again turned to leave. Again I brought him to a stop. "One more word!" He stared at me, his heavy-set face flushed. I stared back. I bowed and said: "I want to thank you for your leniency and kindness in refusing us a stay of two days, a stay you would have accorded the most heinous criminal. I thank you once more."

His Honour grew white, anger spreading over his face. Nervously he fumbled with the papers on his desk. He moved his lips as if to speak, then abruptly turned and left the bench.

# CHAPTER XLVI

THE AUTOMOBILE SPED ON. IT WAS FILLED WITH DEPUTY MAR-
shals, with me in their midst. Twenty minutes later we reached
the Baltimore and Ohio Station. The hand of time seemed set back
twenty-five years. I visioned myself at the same station a quarter of a
century ago, straining towards the disappearing train which was bearing Sasha away, leaving me desolate and alone. A gruff voice startled
me. " Are you seeing ghosts? " it demanded.

I was in a compartment, a big man and a woman at my side, the
deputy marshal and his wife. Then I was left with the woman.

The day's heat, the excitement, and three hours' wait in the Federal
Building had exhausted me. I felt worn and sticky in my sweaty
clothes. I started for the wash-room, and the woman followed me. I
objected. She regretted she could not let me go unattended; her instructions were not to permit me out of sight. She had a rather kindly
face. I assured her that I would not try to escape, and she consented
to close the door half-way. Having cleaned up, I crawled into my berth
and immediately fell asleep.

I was awakened by the loud voices of my keepers. The man's coat
was already off and he was proceeding to undress. " You don't mean
you're going to sleep here? " I demanded.

" Sure," he answered, " what's wrong? My wife is here. You've got
nothing to fear."

What more could morality wish for than the presence of the
deputy's wife? It wasn't fear, I told him; it was disgust.

The watchful eyes of the law were closed in sleep, but its mouth was
wide open, emitting a rattle of snores. The air was putrid. Anxious
thoughts about Sasha beset me. A quarter of a century had passed,
crammed with events and rich in the interplay of light and shade.
The painful frustration with Ben — friendships shattered — others

that had never lost their bloom. The earth-spirit often in conflict with the impelling aspirations of the ideal, and Sasha ever dependable all through the long span of time and always my comrade in the struggle. The thought was soothing, and the strain of weeks found relief in blessed sleep.

My male escort stayed away from the compartment most of the day, his presence gracing only our meals, which were brought to us from the diner. At the luncheon I asked the deputy marshal why I was being taken to the Missouri State Prison, at Jefferson City. There was no Federal prison for women, he explained; there used to be one, but it was discontinued because it " did not pay."

" And male federals, do they pay? " I inquired.

" Sure," he said; " there are so many of them that the U. S. Government is planning another prison. One of them is in Atlanta, Georgia," he added, " and that is where your friend Berkman has been taken."

I led him to talk about Atlanta. He assured me that it was a very strict place, and that " Berk " would have a bad time of it if he did not behave himself. Then he remarked with a sneer: " He's an old hand at prisons, ain't he? "

" Yes, but he has survived, and he will prove a match for Atlanta, too, with all its strictness," I retorted hotly.

The lady deputy kept to herself. It gave me a chance to write, read, and think. We changed trains at St. Louis, which afforded me an opportunity for a little exercise while waiting for the local to Jefferson City. I peered eagerly about to discover a familiar face, but I realized that our comrades in St. Louis could not have known when I would reach their town.

Arriving in Jefferson City, my escorts offered to take me to the penitentiary in a taxi. I requested that we walk. It might be my last chance for a long while, I thought. They readily consented, no doubt because they could pocket the price and charge it to their expense accounts.

When my guardians had delivered me to the head matron of the prison, they assured me that they had enjoyed my company. They had not believed that an anarchist would give so little trouble, they remarked. The wife added that she had grown to like me and was sorry to leave me behind. Rather a doubtful compliment, I felt.

With the exception of my two weeks in Queens County Jail, I had

somehow managed to steer clear of prisons since my " rest-cure " on
Blackwell's Island. There had been numerous arrests and several
trials, but no other convictions. A disgusting record for one who
could boast of the never-failing attention of every police department
in the country.

"Any disease?" the head matron demanded abruptly.

I was somewhat taken aback at the unexpected concern over my
health. I answered her that I had nothing to complain of except that
I needed a bath and a cold drink.

"Don't be impudent and pretend you don't know what I mean," she
sternly reproved me. " I mean the disease immoral women have. Most
of those delivered here have it."

"Venereal disease is not particular whom it strikes," I told her;
"the most respectable people have been known to be victims of it. I
don't happen to have it, which is due perhaps much more to luck than
to virtue."

She looked scandalized. She was so self-righteous and prim, she
needed to be shocked, and I was catty enough to enjoy watching the
effect.

After having been subjected to the routine search for dope and
cigarettes, I was given a bath and informed that I could keep my own
underwear, shoes and stockings.

My cell contained a cot with stiff but clean sheets and blankets, a
table and a chair, a stationary wash-stand with running water, and,
blessing of blessings, a toilet built in a little alcove, hidden from
view by a curtain. So far my new home was a decided improvement
over Blackwell's Island. Two things marred my pleasant discovery.
My cell faced a wall that shut off the air and light, and all through
the night the clock in the prison yard struck every fifteen minutes,
whereupon stentorian voices would call out: " All's well." I tossed
about, wondering how long it would take to get used to this new
torture.

Twenty-four hours in the prison gave me an approximate idea of
its routine. The institution had a number of progressive features:
more frequent visits, the opportunity to order foodstuffs, the privilege of writing letters three times a week, according to the grade one
had reached, recreation in the yard daily and twice on Sunday, a
bucketful of hot water every evening, and permission to receive
packages and printed matter. These were great advantages over

conditions in Blackwell's Island. The recreation was especially gratifying. The yard was small and had but little protection from the sun,
but the prisoners were free to walk about, talk, play, and sing, without
interference from the matron who presided in the yard. On the other
hand, the prevailing labour system required definite tasks. The latter
were so difficult to accomplish that they kept the inmates in constant
trepidation. I was informed that I would be excused from making
the complete task, but that was small comfort. With a woman serving
a life sentence on one side of me, and another doomed to fifteen years,
both forced to do the full amount of work, I did not care to take
advantage of my exemption. At the same time I feared that I might
never be able to accomplish the task. The subject was the main topic
of discussion and the greatest worry of the inmates.

After a week spent in the shop I began suffering excruciating pain
in the back of my neck. My condition was aggravated by the first news
from New York. Fitzi's letter conveyed what I already knew, that
Sasha had been taken to Atlanta. It was far away, she wrote, and it
would prevent our friends from visiting him. She had many worries
and hardships to face. The Federal authorities, in co-operation with
the New York police, had terrorized the proprietor of our office. He
had ordered Fitzi to remove *Mother Earth* and the *Blast,* without
even giving her a week's notice. After much effort she had succeeded
in finding quarters on Lafayette Street, but it was questionable whether
she would be permitted to remain there. The patriotic hysteria was increasing, the press and the police vying with each other to exterminate
every radical activity. Dear, brave Fitzi, and our valiant "Swede"!
They had had to carry the whole burden since our arrest. But faithfully they had kept at their post, concerned only about us, with never
any complaint about their own difficulties. Even now Fitzi wrote
nothing about herself. Dear, sweet soul.

Other letters and several telegrams were more cheering. Harry
Weinberger wrote that Judge Mayer had refused to sign the application for our appeal, nor would any other Federal judge give his
signature. But Harry was sure that he could induce one of the Supreme
Court justices to accept the papers, and that would enable us to be
released on bail.

A letter came from Frank Harris, offering to send me reading-
matter and anything else permitted in the prison. Another was from
my jovial old friend William Marion Reedy. Now that I was living

in his State, he wrote, and was his neighbour, as it were, he was anxious to secure for me the right kind of hospitality. He and Mr. Painter, the warden of the penitentiary, had been college chums, and he had written him that he ought to be proud to have Emma Goldman as his guest. He had cautioned him to treat her right, or he would go after him. I should consider myself lucky, his letter read, to have two years' freedom from my hectic activities. It would mean a good rest and it should also mean the autobiography he had long ago advised me to write. "Now is your chance: you have a home, three meals a day and leisure — all free of charge. Write your life. You have lived it as no other woman. Tell us about it." He had already shipped a box containing paper and pencils, he informed me, and he would persuade Mr. Painter to let me have a typewriter. I must "buckle down and write the book," he concluded.

Like many another, my dear old friend Bill had caught the war fever. Yet he was big enough to continue his interest and friendship, regardless of my stand. But his idea of writing in prison caused me to smile. It showed how little even such a clear-headed man realized the effect of imprisonment; to believe that one could adequately express one's thoughts in captivity, after nine hours' daily drudgery. Just the same, his letter made me very happy.

There were loving messages from Stella, my sisters, and even my dear old mother, who wrote in Yiddish. Very touching were the letters of our St. Louis comrades. They would look after my needs, they wrote; they were so near Jefferson City, they would send me fresh food every day. They would be happy if they could do the same for Sasha, but he was too far away. They hoped friends living in the South would look after his needs.

Two weeks after I had been delivered to the prison, the same deputy marshal and his wife arrived to take me back to New York. Irrepressible Harry Weinberger had succeeded in getting Supreme Court Justice Louis D. Brandeis to sign the application for our appeal, which admitted Sasha and me to bail and temporary freedom. The appeal included also the cases of Morris Becker and Louis Kramer. Harry had scored a victory over Judge Mayer. I was sure that our liberty would be of short duration; still, it was good to return to our friends and resume the work where it had been interrupted by our arrest.

It was with emotions quite different from those I had felt on my way to prison that I boarded the train for New York. My escorts, too, seemed changed. The deputy informed me that there would be no need this time to watch me so closely. Only his wife would share my compartment. He wanted me to feel as free as if I were travelling alone, and he hoped that I would have no complaints to make to the reporters. I understood. At the station in St. Louis I was given an ovation by a group of comrades, and of course there were also representatives of the press. The deputy became demonstratively magnanimous. I could invite my people to the station restaurant, he suggested, while he would remain at a neighbouring table. I enjoyed the dear companionship of my friends.

The return journey had many pleasant features, the main one being the absence of the deputy. His wife also did not intrude, both remaining outside my compartment. The door was left ajar, more to afford me air than to keep me in view. It was an unusually close day, and I had a foretaste of what was to be meted out to such a godless creature when I should have joined the departed.

In the Tombs the keepers received the prodigal daughter with glad acclaim. It was late and the prison had closed for the day, but I was permitted a bath. The head matron was an old friend of mine, of the birth-control fight days. She believed in family limitation, she had confided to me, and she had been kind and solicitous, once even attending our Carnegie Hall meeting as my guest. When the other matrons left, she engaged me in conversation and remarked that she saw no reason to be excited about what the Germans had done to the Belgians. England had treated Ireland no better during hundreds of years and recently again during the Easter uprising. She was Irish, and she had no use for the Allies. I explained that my sympathies were not with any of the warring countries, but with the people of every land, because they alone have to pay the terrible price. She looked rather disappointed, but she gave me clean sheets for my bunk, and I liked her as a good Irish soul.

In the morning friends came to see me, among them Harry Weinberger, Stella, and Fitzi. I inquired about Sasha. Had he been brought back, and how was his leg? Fitzi averted her face.

"What is it?" I asked anxiously.

"Sasha is in the Tombs," she replied in a dead voice; "he will be safer there for a while."

Her tone and manner filled me with apprehension. Urged to tell me the worst, she informed me that Sasha was wanted in San Francisco. He had been indicted for murder in connexion with the Mooney case. The Chamber of Commerce and the District Attorney had carried out their threat to "get" Sasha. They were going to have revenge for the splendid work he had done to expose the frame-up against five lives. Billings had already been put out of the way, immured for life, and Tom Mooney was facing death. Their next prey was Sasha. I knew they meant to murder him. Instinctively I raised my hand as if to ward off a blow.

I fully realized only when I was bailed out what Fitzi had meant by saying that Sasha would be safer in the Tombs. Released on bail, he would be in danger of being kidnapped and spirited away to California. Such things had happened before. After Sasha's arrest in 1892, our comrade Mollock had been secretly taken from New Jersey by Pennsylvania detectives who hoped to connect him with the attack on Frick. In 1906 Haywood, Moyer, and Pettibone had been abducted from Colorado to Idaho, and in 1910 the McNamara brothers had met with a like fate in Indiana. If the Government dared resort to such methods with members of powerful labour organizations, native-born at that, why not with a "foreign" anarchist? It was clear we could not risk bailing Sasha out. No time was to be lost if his extradition was to be prevented. Governor Whitman was a reactionary and would probably oblige the unscrupulous crew on the Coast; nothing but a mighty protest on the part of organized labour could stop him.

We immediately set to work, Fitzi, the "Swede," and I. We called a group of people together to organize a publicity committee. Then we invited the labour leaders at the head of the Jewish trade unions. A large gathering was held, attended by men and women influential in the world of labour and letters, which resulted in the formation of an active committee, with Dolly Sloan as secretary-treasurer.

The response of the United Hebrew Trades was immediate and whole-hearted, and the joint board of the Amalgamated Clothing Workers of America followed suit. The former offered to head the appeal for Sasha and to get us a hearing by every union.

Sasha's life was at stake. Conferences with labour men, canvassing unions, arranging meetings and theatre benefits, circularizing organizations, press interviews, and a vast correspondence crowded every minute of those nerve-racking days.

Sasha himself was in gay spirits. To see his visitors he had to be taken from the Tombs to the Federal Building and back again, which afforded him a walk in the fresh air. He had not yet been able to discard his crutches, and hobbling along was rather uncomfortable. But when one faces the possible loss of one's life, promenading even on crutches is a great boon. Marshal McCarthy supervised our visits and he acted rather decently. He made no objections when we brought many friends to see Sasha and he did not have us watched too obviously. In fact, he tried his best to gain our good will. On one occasion he remarked to me : " I know you hate me, Emma Goldman, but just you wait until the espionage bill is passed; then you'll thank me for having arrested you and Berkman in the early stages of the game. Now you get only two years, but later you would get twenty. Own up, wasn't I your friend ? "

" None better," I admitted; " I'll see that you get a vote of thanks."

Our visits with Sasha were turned into merry family reunion. His genial humour and equanimity in the face of imminent danger gained him the respect even of the members of the Marshal's office. They asked for copies of his *Memoirs* and later they told us how greatly the book had impressed them. After that they became very cordial, and we were delighted for Sasha's sake.

Gradually our work was bringing results. The United Hebrew Trades issued a strong appeal to organized labour to rally to the support of Sasha. The joint board of the cloakmakers' union voted five hundred dollars for our campaign and promised to contribute more. The Joint Board of Furriers, the International Brotherhood of Bookbinders, Typographical Union Local 83, and other organizations co-operated with us in the most solidaric manner. They proposed that a representative delegation of at least a hundred labour men be sent to Governor Whitman to protest against Sasha's extradition to California, and steps were immediately taken to put before Whitman the facts of the judicial crime already perpetrated in San Francisco.

Uncertain how long I should remain at liberty, I had not taken an apartment. I shared with Fitzi her flat and spent an occasional week-end with Stella in Darien. One day Dolly Sloan asked me to stay with her while her husband was absent from the city. Their studio was large, very quaint and charming; and I enjoyed Dolly's hospitality. She was an energetic little lady and most eager to help in our campaign for Sasha, but she was not physically strong enough to endure the continual strain, and she often had to take to bed. Unfortunately, I had so much to do and was feeling so bad myself that I could give her little time. She was not bedridden, however, and was able to get about a great deal.

One morning I left her apparently in improved condition. She had had a good night's sleep and she intended remaining home to rest. I worked all day in the office, and in the evening I canvassed several organizations meeting in different parts of the city. The last was the union of the stage mechanics and electrical workers. They were supposed to meet at midnight, but I had to wait three hours in a narrow, stuffy passage piled up with boxes, one of which served me as a seat. When I was finally given the floor, I could see hostility written on every face. It was like swimming against a heavy tide to speak in the atmosphere thick with prejudice and the smell of bad tobacco and stale beer. When I had concluded my address, quite a number of those present expressed themselves as willing to support the campaign for Sasha, but the politicians in official positions were opposed. Berkman was an enemy of the country, they argued, and they would have nothing to do with him. I left them to fight the matter out among themselves.

Returning to Sloan's studio, I could not unlock the door. I rang in vain for a long time, then knocked loudly. At last I heard someone turn the key on the inside, and a woman was facing me. I recognized Pearl, the former wife of Robert Minor. She demanded whether I could not see the new lock on the door and did not guess that it was to keep me out. She was taking care of Mrs. Sloan and I was not wanted in the house. In astonishment I stared at her, then pushed her aside and walked in. The door to Dolly's room was ajar and I saw her lying on her bed evidently in a stupor. I was alarmed by her condition and turned to the woman for an explanation. She merely reiterated that Mrs. Sloan had ordered her to change the lock. But I knew she was lying.

I went out into the street. The day was breaking; I did not want to go to wake Fitzi, who needed sleep so badly. I walked over to Union Square. Once more I had been shut out, a homeless creature, as in the days I had believed gone for ever.

I rented a furnished room. Fitzi agreed with me that Dolly could have had nothing to do with the changing of the lock. It was known to everybody that Pearl Minor was bitterly opposed to all Bob's friends.

For some unaccountable reason she had a special grudge against me. It was stupid of her, but I was aware that she was the product of an orphanage, her mind and heart warped by her miserable childhood.

In the midst of those trying days there came another and far greater shock. I learned that my nephew David Hochstein had waived exemption and volunteered for the army. His mother, all unconscious of the blow awaiting her, was on her way to New York to meet him. My sister had only recently lost her husband after a short illness. I could not bear to think how the news about David would affect her. David, her beloved son, in whom she had concentrated all her hopes — a soldier! His young life to be given for something Helena had always hated as the crime of crimes!

Life's a fiendish contradiction! To think that David, Helena's child, should of his own free will offer himself for the army. He had never been politically or socially conscious, and I was therefore not surprised when told that he had registered. I was sure he would not be drafted. His break-down from tuberculosis a few years previously, though arrested, had yet left his lungs in such a condition that he was certain to be exempted. The news that he had submitted himself to the examination board in New York instead of in Rochester, and that he had said nothing about the state of his health, came as a shock. I could not believe that the boy had deliberately done so, that he believed in the war or in his country's ethical claims. Helena's children were too much like their parents to think that wars are worth fighting or that they solve anything. What, then, could have been the reason, I wondered, to induce David voluntarily to join the army? Perhaps something personal, or the popular maelstrom had caught him too unawares to resist. Whatever the cause, it was appalling that this richly endowed youth, with a brilliant artistic career just begun, should be among the first to offer himself.

I visited Helena at Darien. Her appearance told me more than words. The frightened expression in her eyes made me fear that she would not survive the blow of the vain sacrifice of her boy. I found David also there, and I longed to talk to him. But I remained dumb. Notwithstanding his family affection for me and my love for him, we had remained distant. How could I now hope to reach his mind? I had proclaimed that the choice of military service must be left to the conscience of every man. How could I attempt to impose my views on David, even if I could hope to persuade him, which I did not? I remained tongue-tied. But I argued hotly with Helena that her son was only one of the many, and her tears but a drop in the ocean already shed by the mothers of the world. Yet abstract theories are not for those whose tragedies are open wounds. I saw the agony in my sister's face and I knew there was nothing I could say or do to bring her relief. I returned to New York to continue our campaign for Sasha.

Every day brought new evidence of the love and esteem he enjoyed on the East Side. The radical Yiddish press outdid itself in championing his cause. Particularly did S. Yanofsky, the editor of the *Freie Arbeiter Stimme,* exert himself. That was especially gratifying because he had never been very comradely with either Sasha or me, and in our stand on the war we had completely drifted apart. Abe Cahan, the editor of the socialist *Forward,* was also very sympathetic and stressed the urgency of coming to Sasha's support. In fact, everyone in the radical Jewish circles heartily co-operated with us. A special group to aid our efforts was composed of the Yiddish writers and poets, among them Abraham Raisin, Nadir, and Sholom Asch.

With these strong drawing cards we organized a series of affairs, a theatre performance to raise funds, on which occasion Asch and Raisin spoke between the acts; a mass meeting in Cooper Union at which Sidney Hillman, president of the Amalgamated Clothing Workers, Alex Cohen, Morris Sigman, and other prominent labor men publicly protested in behalf of Sasha. Large meetings took place in Forward Hall and in the Brooklyn Labor Lyceum. For the same purpose were organized also a number of English meetings. The New York *Call,* the socialist daily, wrote forcibly against Sasha's extradition. It was peculiar to see the paper wax so enthusiastic in the campaign, considering that it had remained silent during our arrest and trial.

Fortunately there was no police interference, and our gatherings were attended by thousands of people. Much encouraged, we arranged a special affair at the Kessler Theatre. But Marshal McCarthy had apparently decided that I had already enjoyed too much freedom of speech and should therefore be stopped " for her own good." He announced that he would prohibit the meeting if I should attempt to address the audience. The purpose of the gathering being too important to risk having it disrupted, I promised to comply.

S. Yanofsky, a very clever man with a vitriolic tongue, was the last speaker. He talked eloquently of the Billings-Mooney case and the attempt of the San Francisco bosses to drag Sasha into their net. Then he proceeded to pay his respects to Marshal McCarthy. "He has gagged Emma," he declared, "too stupid to realize that her voice will now carry far beyond the walls of this theatre." At that moment I stepped upon the stage with a handkerchief stuck in my mouth. The audience shrieked with laughter, stamped their feet, and screamed. "You can't stop *that* speech," they shouted.

McCarthy looked sheepish, but I had kept my promise.

The agitation in behalf of Sasha was spreading. More labour bodies were constantly added to our list, among them the important New Jersey State Federation. This feat was accomplished by our Fitzi, and it had been no easy task to reach that by no means radical organization. She charmed people into sympathy and action — not merely by her Irish name and beautiful auburn hair, but by her fine and suave personality. Little did anyone outside of her immediate friends sense the Celtic temperament behind her tranquil manner.

Our activities in New York multiplied to such an extent that I could not accept the numerous invitations which came from other cities to address meetings arranged in behalf of Sasha. I had to select the most important calls, among them that for three lectures in Chicago.

Max Pine, general secretary, and M. Finestone, assistant secretary, of the United Hebrew Trades, were desirous of having Morris Hillquit, the socialist attorney, go to Albany with our delegation, to address Governor Whitman against Sasha's extradition. I had known Morris Hillquit for many years. When I first came to New York, I used to attend the joint gatherings of anarchists and socialists, among whom there were also the two brothers Hilkowitch. One occasion of those days had been particularly memorable. It was a Yom Kippur celebration held as a protest against Jewish orthodoxy. Speeches on free thought, dances, and plenty of eats took the place of the traditional fast and prayers. The religious Jews resented our desecration of their holiest Day of Atonement, and their sons came down in strong force to meet our boys in pitched battle. Sasha, who always loved a fight, was, of course, the leader and easily the most effective in repulsing the attack. While the affray was going on in the street, anarchist and socialist orators were holding forth inside the hall, young Morris Hilkowitch having the floor at the time. Over two decades had passed since then — Hilkowitch had changed his name to the more euphonious Hillquit and had become a successful lawyer, a leading Marxian theoretician, and an important personage in the Socialist Party. Socialism had never appealed to me, though there were many socialists among my friends. I liked them because they were freer and bigger than their creed. Mr. Hillquit I knew very slightly, but I considered his writings as lacking in vision. We had no common ground; he had risen high in the estimation of respectable society, while I remained a pariah.

The war, and particularly America's entry into the dance of death, had shifted many positions and contacts. People formerly closely allied in ideas and effort were now far apart, while others widely separated in the past found now a strong bond. Morris Hillquit had dared to stand out against the war. No wonder he now discovered himself in the same boat with Alexander Berkman, Emma Goldman, and their associates. The frenzied attacks on him by our common enemies and his erstwhile comrades bridged the chasm of the past as well as our theoretic differences. Indeed, I felt much closer to Hillquit than to many of my own comrades whose social vision had been gassed. Nevertheless, I experienced a sense of strangeness to come face to face with the man for the first time in twenty-seven years.

Hillquit was probably no more than three or four years older than Sasha, but he looked at least fifteen years his senior. His hair was thickly streaked with grey, his face lined, and his eyes weary. He had won success, renown, and wealth. Sasha's life had been a Golgotha, yet how different the two men appeared! However, Hillquit had remained simple in his ways, his manner was gracious, and I soon felt at home with him.

He was not very reassuring about Sasha's chances. At any other time, he said, it would not have been difficult to defeat extradition. In the present war hysteria, with Sasha convicted on a Federal conspiracy charge, the outlook was not very promising.

His candidacy for the mayoralty of New York on the Socialist ticket kept Mr. Hillquit exceedingly busy, but he unhesitatingly responded to the invitation to appear before Governor Whitman with the labour delegation. His campaign meetings were the first gatherings of the kind I had ever attended without being sickened by their inanity. I had no more faith in what Hillquit might achieve if elected mayor than anyone else in his place, though I did not doubt the sincerity of his intentions. His electoral campaign had great anti-war propaganda value. It presented the only chance in the hysteria-crazed country for some freedom of speech, and as an experienced orator and clever lawyer Morris Hillquit knew how to steer safely between dangerous patriotic cliffs.

I was glad that he made such good use of his election opportunities, yet I had to decline the invitation of his brother to participate in the work. I had told him how much I had enjoyed hearing the brilliant Morris and his speeches against war. " Why not join us, then ? " he suggested; " you could be of great help in our campaign." He sought to persuade me to set aside my opposition to political action on that exceptional occasion. " Think of the good you could do by helping stem the tide of the war madness," he urged.

But I had grown to like Morris too much to assist him to a political job. One might wish such a thing on one's enemies, not on one's friends.

Our activities for Sasha and the San Francisco cases received unexpected and far-reaching impetus through news from Russia: demonstrations in their behalf had taken place in Petrograd and Kronstadt. It was the answer to the message we had sent to the councils of workers, soldiers, and sailors by the refugees that had departed in May and June. We had followed it up with cables that our good friend Isaac A. Hourwich and our efficient secretary Pauline had succeeded in getting through to Russia after we had learned of Sasha's indictment in San Francisco. With joyful heart I visited Sasha, knowing what the demonstration of solidarity in Russia would mean to him. I tried to appear calm, but he soon sensed that something must have happened. At hearing the glorious tidings his face lit up and his eyes filled with wonder. But, as usual when profoundly stirred, he was silent. We sat quietly, our hearts beating in unison with gratitude to our *Matushka Rossiya*.

The problem was now how to use the demonstrations in Russia to best advantage. We had wide connexions and channels to bring the matter to the attention of the labour bodies, by meetings and circulars, but other means were needed to interest those who were in a position to intercede for our friends in San Francisco. Sasha suggested that I confer with his friend Ed Morgan, a former socialist, now an Industrial Worker of the World. He had been very active in behalf of Mooney and he might prove of great help in his case, Sasha thought.

I had known Morgan for some time. He was a good-hearted fellow, genuine and tireless when given a task. But I was not sure of his abilities and he was fearfully long-winded. I had no doubts about his willingness to do what we should request, but I was dubious about his chances of accomplishing anything vital in Washington. I was wrong. Ed Morgan proved a wizard. In a short time he succeeded in getting more publicity for our purpose than we had got in months. His first step in the capital had been to find out President Wilson's favourite morning papers, his second to bombard them with news items about the agitation in Russia over the San Francisco frame-up. Then Morgan buttonholed influential officials in Washington, made them familiar with the happenings on the Coast, and enlisted their sympathies. The net results of this one man's efforts were a Federal investigation ordered by President Wilson into the labour situation in San Francisco.

I had seen too many official investigations to expect much from this one; still, it held out the hope that the skeleton in the family closet of Big Business and Fickert and Co. would at last be dragged into the light of day. Morgan and many of our trade-union associates were more optimistic. They looked for the complete exoneration and release of Billings, Mooney, and their co-defendants, as well as of Sasha. I could not share their faith, but it did not lessen my admiration for Ed Morgan's splendid achievement.

Shortly afterwards came further news from Russia of still greater moment. A resolution proposed by the sailors of Kronstadt and adopted at a monster meeting called for the arrest of Mr. Francis, the American Ambassador in Russia, who was to be held as hostage until the San Francisco victims and Sasha should be free. A delegation of armed sailors had marched to the American Embassy in Petrograd to carry out the decision. Our old comrade Louise Berger, who with other Russian refugees had returned to her native land after the outbreak of the Revolution, served as their interpreter. Mr. Francis had solemnly assured the delegation that it was all a mistake, and that the lives of Mooney, Billings, and Berkman were in no danger. But the sailors were insistent, and Mr. Francis in their presence cabled to Washington and promised to exert himself further with the American Government to secure the release of the San Francisco prisoners.

The threat of the sailors evidently had an effect on the Ambassador, with the result that President Wilson was moved to prompt action. Whatever the message of the President to Governor Whitman, our delegation found the latter in a very receptive mood. Moreover, quantity is always appreciated by aspiring politicians, and the labour dele-

gation consisted of a hundred men, representing nearly a million organized workers of New York. With them were Morris Hillquit and
Harry Weinberger, who impressed upon the Governor that Alexander
Berkman did not stand alone, and that his extradition would be resented by labour all through the United States. Mr. Whitman thereupon decided to telegraph District Attorney Fickert for the records
of the case and promised to postpone final action until he had thoroughly acquainted himself with the indictment against Sasha.

It was a victory indeed, though it did only temporarily delay proceedings. But instead of sending the requested documents, the San
Francisco prosecutor wired Albany that " the Berkman extradition
would not be pressed for the present." We had known all along that
Fickert could not afford to produce the records, since they did not
contain a scintilla of evidence to connect Sasha with the explosion.

The demand for extradition not having been granted within the
legally allowed thirty days, Sasha could not be detained in prison
longer. The Warden of the Tombs was anxious to get rid of him;
he had already upset the prison routine too much, the administration
said. His numerous visitors and the stacks of letters and messages he
was receiving added to the burdens of the prison officials, not to speak
of the excitement among the other prisoners who had become interested in the Berkman case. " Take him away, for the love of Mike,"
the Warden urged; " you are out on bail, so why don't you raise
his? " I assured him that the bond was on hand, and I should love
nothing better than to relieve him of the worry Sasha's presence was
causing him. But my friend had decided to sign himself back to the
Tombs for another thirty days to keep the promise made by his
attorney. San Francisco had informed Governor Whitman that they
needed more time to prepare the record requested by him. Though
Sasha could not lawfully be compelled to wait for them, Weinberger
had consented to prove that we had nothing to be afraid of in Fickert's
records. The Warden stared incredulously. An anarchist feeling bound
to live up to a pledge which he had not even given himself! " You
people are a crazy lot! " he said. " Who ever heard of a man's insisting on remaining in prison when he has a chance to get out? " But he
would treat Sasha right, he added, and maybe I would speak a good
word for him to Mr. Hillquit, who was sure to be the next mayor
of New York. I tried to tell him that I had no influence with the future socialist mayor, but it was to no purpose. It was sheer anarchist

cussedness, the Warden reiterated, not to help a fellow who had been such a friend to us.

America, only seven months in the war, had already outstripped in brutality every European land with three years' experience in the business of slaughter. Non-combatants and conscientious objectors from every social stratum were filling the jails and prisons. The new Espionage Law turned the country into a lunatic asylum, with every State and Federal official, as well as a large part of the civilian population, running amuck. They spread terror and destruction. Disruption of public meetings and wholesale arrests, sentences of incredible severity, suppression of radical publications and indictments of their staffs, beating of workers — even murder — became the chief patriotic pastime.

In Bisbee, Arizona, twelve hundred I.W.W.'s were manhandled and driven across the border. In Tulsa, Oklahoma, seventeen of their comrades were tarred and feathered and in a half-dead condition left in the sage-brush. In Kentucky Dr. Bigelow, a single-taxer and pacifist, was kidnapped and whipped for a speech he was *about* to deliver. In Milwaukee a group of anarchists and socialists met an even more terrible fate. Their activities had aroused the ire and envy of an unfrocked Catholic priest. He was especially enraged over the audacity of the young Italians who heckled him at his open-air meetings. He set the police on them and they charged the crowd with drawn clubs and guns. Antonio Fornasier, an anarchist, was instantly killed. Augusta Marinelli, another comrade, was mortally wounded, dying in the hospital five days later. In the general shooting several officers were slightly injured. Arrests followed. The Italian club-rooms were raided, literature and pictures destroyed. Eleven persons, including a woman, were held responsible for the riot caused by the uniformed ruffians. While the Italians were under arrest, an explosion took place in the police station. The perpetrators were unknown, but the prisoners were tried for that bomb. The jury was out just seventeen minutes, returning a verdict of guilty. The ten men and Mary Baldini were given twenty-five years each, and the State appropriated Mary's five-year-old child, although her people were willing and able to take care of it.

Through the length and breadth of the country stalked the madness of jingoism. One hundred and sixty I.W.W.'s were arrested in Chicago and held for trial on charges of treason. Among them were Bill Haywood, Elizabeth Gurley Flynn, Arturo Giovannitti, Carlo Tresca, and our old comrade Cassius V. Cook. Dr. William J. Robinson, editor of the New York *Critic and Guide,* was imprisoned for expressing his opinion on war. Harry D. Wallace, president of the League of Humanity and author of *Shanghaied in the European War,* was sentenced to twenty years' imprisonment for a lecture delivered in Davenport, Iowa. Another victim of this frightfulness was Louise Olivereau, an idealist of the finest type of American womanhood, who was condemned in Colorado to forty-five years' imprisonment for a circular in which she voiced her abhorrence of human slaughter. There was hardly a city or town in the wide United States where the jails did not contain some men and women who would not be terrorized into patriotic slaughter.

The most appalling crime was the murder of Frank Little, a member of the executive board of the I.W.W., and of another poor fellow who happened to bear a German name. Frank Little was a cripple, but that did not deter the masked bandits. In the dead of night they dragged the helpless man from his bed in Butte, Montana, carried him to an isolated spot, and strung him to a railroad trestle. The other " alien enemy " was similarly lynched, whereupon it was found that the man's room was decorated with a large American flag and his money was invested in Liberty Bonds.

The assaults on life and on free speech were supplemented by the suppression of the printed word. Under the Espionage Law and similar statutes passed in the war fever the Postmaster General had been constituted absolute dictator over the press. Even private distribution had become impossible for any paper opposed to the war. *Mother Earth* became the first victim, soon followed by the *Blast,* the *Masses,* and other publications, and by indictments against their editorial staffs.

The reactionaries were not the only element responsible for the patriotic orgy. Sam Gompers handed over the American Federation of Labor to the war baiters. The liberal intelligentsia, with Walter Lippman, Louis F. Post, and George Creel in the lead, socialists like Charles Edward Russell, Arthur Bullard, English Walling, Phelps Stokes, John Spargo, Simons, and Ghent, all shared in the glory. The Socialist war phobia, the resolutions of their Minneapolis Conference, their patriotic special train, draped in red, white, and blue, their urging

of every worker to support the war, all helped to destroy reason and
justice in the United States.

On the other hand, the Industrial Workers of the World and those
socialists who had not gone back on their ideals had by their blind
self-sufficiency in the past also helped to sow the seeds of the crop they
were now reaping. As long as persecution had been directed only
against anarchists, they had refused to take notice or even to comment
on the matter in their press. Not one of the I.W.W. papers had
protested against our arrest and conviction. At the Socialist meetings
not a single speaker would denounce the suppression of the *Blast* and
*Mother Earth*. The New York *Call* thought the issue of free speech,
when it was not itself directly concerned, deserving only of a few
perfunctory lines. When Daniel Kiefer, the staunch fighter for freedom, had sent in a protest, it appeared in the *Call* thoroughly expur-
gated, with every reference to our magazines, to Sasha, and to me
left out. The silly people were unable to foresee that the reactionary
measures, always aimed first at the most unpopular ideas and their
exponents, must in the course of time inevitably also be applied to
them. Now the American Huns no longer discriminated between one
radical group and another: liberals, I.W.W.'s, socialists, preachers,
and college professors were being made to pay for their former short-
sightedness.

In comparison with the patriotic crime wave the suppression of
*Mother Earth* was a matter of insignificance. But to me it proved
a greater blow than the prospect of spending two years in prison.
No offspring of flesh and blood could absorb its mother as this child
of mine had drained me. A struggle of over a decade, exhausting tours
for its support, much worry and grief, had gone into the maintenance
of *Mother Earth,* and now with one blow its life had been snuffed out!
We decided to continue it in another form. The circular letter I had
sent out to our subscribers and friends, informing them of the suppression of the magazine and of the new publication I was contem-
plating, brought many promises of help. Some, however, declined to
have anything to do with the matter. It was reckless to defy the war
sentiment of the country, they wrote. They could not give their support to such a purpose — they could not afford to get into trouble.
Too well I knew that consistency and courage, like genius, are the
rarest of gifts. Ben, of my own intimate circle, was sadly lacking in

both. Having endured him for a decade, how could I condemn others for running to cover in danger?

A new project was sure to make Ben enthusiastic. The idea of a *Mother Earth Bulletin* caught his fancy, and his usual energy was put into motion at once to bring the publication about. But we had drifted apart too far. He wanted the *Bulletin* kept free from the war; there were so many other matters to discuss, he argued, and continued opposition to the Government was sure to ruin what we had built up during so many years. We must be more cautious, more practical, he insisted. Such an attitude seemed incredible in one who had been quite reckless in his anti-war talks. It was strange and ludicrous to see Ben in that rôle. His change, like everything else about him, was without reason or consistency.

Our strained relations could not last. One day the storm burst, and Ben left. For good. Listless and dry-eyed, I sank into a chair. Fitzi was near me, soothingly stroking my head.

TAUBE GOLDMAN
EMMA GOLDMAN'S MOTHER

# CHAPTER XLVII

THE *MOTHER EARTH BULLETIN* LOOKED SMALL COMPARED WITH our previous publication, but it was the best we could do in those harassing days. The political sky was daily growing darker, the atmosphere charged with hate and violence, and no sign of relief anywhere in the wide United States. And again it was Russia to shed the first ray of hope upon an otherwise hopeless world.

The October Revolution suddenly rent the clouds, its flames spreading to the remotest corners of the earth, carrying the message of fulfilment of the supreme promise the February Revolution had held out.

The Lvovs and the Miliukovs had pitted their feeble strength against the great giant, a people risen in rebellion, and had been crushed in their turn, like the Tsar before them. Even Kerensky and his party had also failed to learn the great lesson; they forgot their pledges to the peasants and workers as soon as they had ascended to power. For decades the Social Revolutionists — next to the anarchists, although far more numerous and better organized — had been the most potent leaven in Russia. Their lofty ideal and aims, their heroism and martyrdom, had been the luminous beacon to draw thousands to their banner. For a brief period their party and its leaders, Kerensky, Tchernov, and others, had remained attuned to the spirit of the February days. They had abolished the death-penalty, thrown open the prisons of the living dead, and brought hope to every peasant's hut and worker's hovel, to every man and woman in bondage. They had proclaimed freedom of speech, press, and assembly for the first time in the history of Russia, grand gestures that met with the acclaim of all liberty-loving people in the world.

To the masses, however, the political changes had represented only the outward symbol of the real liberty to come — cessation of war, access to the land, and reorganization of the economic life. These were to them the fundamental and essential values of the Revolution. But Kerensky and his party had failed to rise to the situation. They had ignored the popular need, and the onrushing tide swept them away. The October Revolution was the culmination of passionate dreams and longings, the bursting of the people's wrath against the party that it had trusted and that had failed.

The American press, never able to see beneath the surface, denounced the October upheaval as German propaganda, and its protagonists, Lenin, Trotsky, and their co-workers, as the Kaiser's hirelings. For months the scribes fabricated fantastic inventions about Bolshevik Russia. Their ignorance of the forces that had led up to the October Revolution was as appalling as their puerile attempts to interpret the movement headed by Lenin. Hardly a single newspaper evidenced the least understanding of bolshevism as a social conception entertained by men of brilliant minds, with the zeal and courage of martyrs.

Unfortunately the American press did not stand alone in the misrepresentation of the Bolsheviki. Most of the liberals and socialists were with them. It was the more urgent for the anarchists and other real revolutionists to take up cudgels for the vilified men and their part in hastening events in Russia. In the columns of the *Mother Earth Bulletin,* from the platform, and by every other means we defended the Bolsheviki against calumny and slander. Though they were Marxists and therefore governmentalists, I sided with them because they had repudiated war and had the wisdom to stress the fact that political freedom without corresponding economic equality is an empty boast. I quoted from Lenin's pamphlet *Political Parties and the Problems of the Proletariat* to prove that his demands were essentially what the Social Revolutionists had wanted, but had been too timid to carry out. Lenin strove for a democratic republic managed by soviets of workers, soldiers, and peasant deputies. He demanded the immediate convocation of the Constituent Assembly, speedy general peace, no indemnities and no annexations, and the abolition of secret treaties. His program included the return of the land to the peasant population according to need and actual working ability, control of industries by the proletariat, the formation of an International in every land for the complete abolition of the existing governments and capitalism, and the establishment of human solidarity and brotherhood.

Most of these demands were entirely in keeping with anarchist ideas and were therefore entitled to our support. But while I hailed and honoured the Bolsheviki as comrades in a common fight, I refused to credit them with what had been accomplished by the efforts of the entire Russian people. The October Revolution, like the February overthrow, was the achievement of the masses, their own glorious work.

Again I longed to return to Russia and to participate in the task of re-creating her new life. Yet once more I was detained by my adopted country, firmly held by two years' prison sentence. However, I still had two months at my disposal before the decision of the United States Supreme Court should be handed down, and I could accomplish something in the meantime.

The United States Supreme Court, always slow in its grinding, had often required years to bring forth its Solomonic wisdom. But it was war time, and press and pulpit were howling for the pound of flesh to be cut from the anarchists and other rebels. The august body in Washington responded quickly. December 10 was to be the decisive day — Lawyers' Day, really, for no fewer than seven members of the profession would argue the unconstitutionality of conscription and the question of conspiracy involved in the cases of Kramer and Becker, Berkman and Goldman.

Our attorney, Harry Weinberger, had gone to Washington. His brief contained a thorough analysis of the various phases of the situation, but what appealed most to us was the progressive view taken by him of the human values and the social vision that were the key-note of his argument. To us it was a foregone conclusion that most of the gentlemen of the Supreme Court were too old and feeble to stand out against the patriotic clamour. But the few remaining days till December 10 were mine, and I decided to employ them for a hurried tour; I would carry the message of the Russian Revolution to the people and tell them the truth about the Bolsheviki.

The Mooney prosecution was in trouble; the Federal investigators were looking too searchingly into its crooked game. Added to this was the movement in San Francisco for Fickert's recall. The District Attorney had also cause for chagrin because of the refusal of Governor Whitman to deliver Sasha until the records in his case should be forthcoming. It was a rotten deal to give a man who had already served his masters so well in the Billings-Mooney trials. But Fickert did not despair. He would prove that his loyalty to big business could not be dampened. He still had three other criminals in his clutches — Rena Mooney, Israel Weinberg, and Edward D. Nolan. He would first get rid of them; then, when the Supreme Court should have decided Berkman's fate, he would secure him also. For the sake of one's duty one must learn to practise patience, and the San Francisco District Attorney could afford to bide his time. He notified Albany that he would temporarily withdraw his demand for the extradition of Alexander Berkman.

Sasha had to put up a twenty-five-thousand-dollar bond in the Federal conspiracy case. The esteem and popularity which he enjoyed among the workers immediately brought the Yiddish labour organizations and individual friends to his rescue. But it took much more time and a great deal of effort to overcome the red tape of the law. At last that was also mastered, and Sasha was once more a free man. It was no small satisfaction to everyone connected with our work to have him in our midst again. As to Sasha, he resembled a boy playing hooky from school. He was light-hearted and gay, though he knew, as we all did, that he would soon have to go to another prison for a longer stay. His leg had not yet healed and he needed a rest. I proposed that he take advantage of his short respite and go to the country, but he could not think of it, he said, so long as San Francisco was holding its victims. Our agitation had considerably shaken Fickert's self-assurance. His failure to secure Sasha's extradition had been followed by other misfortunes. Weinberg had been acquitted after the jury had deliberated for three minutes only, and the exposure of the prosecution's evidence as perjury had compelled the District Attorney to drop proceedings against Rena Mooney and Ed Nolan. But, the overwhelming proofs of frame-up notwithstanding, the two labour men had not escaped his clever manipulations. Two innocent men, one immured for life, the other facing death! How, then, could Sasha permit himself a vacation? It was impossible, he decided. A few days after his release he was again immersed in the San Francisco campaign.

A new worker in the Mooney field now appeared, Lucy Robbins. I had met her on my tours, but somehow we had not been close. I knew, however, that Lucy was an efficient organizer, and that she had been active in the labour and radical movements. While I was lecturing in Los Angeles in 1915, Lucy and Bob Robbins had looked me up. I had found them delightful company, and a friendship sprang up between us. Lucy disproved the male contention regarding woman's lack of mechanical ability. She was a born engineer and among the first in the country to devise and build an auto-house, which for comfort and charm excelled many a worker's apartment. It was unique, with its diminutive cupboards and dressers, and contained even a bath. In addition Lucy and Bob carried with them a complete printing outfit. In this ingenious house on wheels they made their way from coast to coast, with Lucy as the chauffeur. At points along the route they solicited printing orders, filled them on the spot, and thus earned their living-expenses. Their travelling companions were a phonograph and two little dogs, one of which was an uncompromising anti-Semite. As soon as any Jewish melody would be played, the four-footed Jew-hater would start up an unearthly howl and he would not desist until the offensive music stopped. That was the only disturbing element in the otherwise happy life of my new friends on their perambulations.

They arrived in New York for a brief stay, but when they learned that they could be of help in our campaign for Mooney, they at once volunteered to remain. They put their wheeled castle in storage and went to live in a little room in the Lafayette Street house where our office was located. Lucy soon proved herself as capable in interesting unions and organizing big affairs as she had been as an architect, constructor, mechanic, and Jack of all trades. She understood *Realpolitik* long before the term had become a vogue. She would grow impatient with our idea that neither love nor war justifies all means. We, on the other hand, were anything but sympathetic with her tendency to get results even if the goal were lost in the process. We scrapped a great deal, but it did not lessen our regard for Lucy as a good worker and friend. She was a vital creature with unlimited energy, whom no one could escape. I was happy that Sasha and Fitzi now had Lucy as their aide-de-camp. I felt sure that the three of them would make things hum.

Harry Weinberger brought the news that the Supreme Court was not likely to reach our cases until the middle of January, and he also informed us that we should be given a month's time after the decision before being called upon to surrender. That was encouraging in view of the difficulty of holding out-of-town meetings near Christmas.

Our stand against conscription and our condemnation to prison had gained us many new friends, among them Helen Keller. I had long wanted to meet this remarkable woman who had overcome the most appalling physical disabilities. I had attended one of her lectures, which was to me an affecting experience. Helen Keller's phenomenal conquest had strengthened my faith in the almost illimitable power of the human will.

When we had begun our campaign, I wrote to her asking her support. Not receiving a reply for a long time, I concluded that her own life was too difficult to permit interest in the tragedies of the world. Weeks later came a message from her that filled me with shame for having doubted her. Far from being self-absorbed, Helen Keller proved herself capable of an all-embracing love for humanity and profound feeling for its woe and despair. She had been absent with her teacher-companion in the country, she wrote, where she had heard of our arrest.

" My heart was troubled," the letter continued, " and I wanted to do something and I was trying to make up my mind what to do when your letter came. Believe me, my very heart-pulse is in the revolution that is to inaugurate a freer, happier society. Can you imagine what it is to sit idling these days of fierce action, of revolution and daring possibilities? I am so full of longing to serve, to love and be loved, to help things along, and to give happiness. It seems as if the very intensity of my desire must bring fulfilment, but, alas, nothing happens. Why have I this passionate desire to be a part of a noble struggle when fate has sentenced me to days of ineffectual waiting? There is no answer. It is tantalizing almost to the point of frenzy. But one thing is sure — you can always count upon my love and support. Those who are blinded in eye because they refuse to see tell us that in times like these wise men hold their tongues. But you are not holding your tongue, nor are the I.W.W. comrades holding their tongues — blessings upon you and them. No, Comrade, you must not hold your tongue, your work must go on, although all the earthly powers combine against it. Never were courage and fortitude so terribly needed as now. . . ."

This letter was soon followed by our meeting, which took place at a ball given by the *Masses*. The affair was to serve as a demonstration of solidarity with the indicted group of the publication — Max Eastman, John Reed, Floyd Dell, and Art Young. I was glad to learn that Helen Keller was present. The marvellous woman, bereft of the most vital human senses, could nevertheless, by her psychic strength, see and hear and articulate. The electric current of her vibrant fingers on my lips and her sensitized hand over mine spoke more than mere tongue. It eliminated physical barriers and held one in the spell of the beauty of her inner world.

1917 had been a year of most intense activity, and it deserved to receive a fitting farewell. Our New Year's party in Stella's and Teddy's quarters appropriately performed the pagan rites. For once we forgot the present and ignored what tomorrow might bring. The bottles popped, the glasses clinked, and hearts grew young in play and dance. The beautiful clog-dancing of our Julia, Ian's coloured mammy, and her friends enhanced the general hilarity. Faithful and loving was our Julia, full of frolic and fun. She was the soul of our circle and my right hand in making the mountains of sandwiches our friends devoured. Gaily we welcomed the new year. Life was alluring and every hour of freedom precious. Atlanta and Jefferson were far away.

My short lecture tour that followed was hectic and exciting, with no halls large enough to hold the crowds, enthusiasm for Russia running high everywhere.

In Chicago I had nine meetings arranged by the Non-Partisan Radical League, with William Nathanson, Bilov, and Slater as its active members. And of course there was Ben, making a success of his medical practice, but, like Raskolnikov, always stealing back to the scene of his old crimes.

Never before had Chicago shown such spontaneous fervour and response as at my lectures on Russia. Additional interest was lent to the occasion by the decision of the United States Supreme Court, handed down January 15, declaring the Draft Law constitutional. Forcible conscription, compelling the youth of the country to die across the seas, received the approving seal of the highest court in the land. Protest against human slaughter was declared outlawed. God and the ancient gentlemen had spoken, and their infinite wisdom and mercy were the supreme law.

So sure had we been that the decision would reflect the general war psychosis and sustain the lower courts that we had two weeks previously bidden our friends farewell in the *Bulletin*. We wrote:

> Be of good cheer, good friends and comrades. We are going to prison with light hearts. To us it is more satisfactory to stay behind bars than to remain MUZZLED in freedom. Our spirit will not be daunted, nor our will broken. We will return to our work in due time.

This is our farewell to you. The light of Liberty burns low just now. But do not despair, friends. Keep the spark alive. The night cannot last forever. Soon there will come a rift in the darkness, and the New Day break even in this country. May each of us feel that we have contributed our mite toward the great Awakening.

EMMA GOLDMAN
ALEXANDER BERKMAN

After Chicago came Detroit, where the success of my four meetings was assured by the organizing skill of my friends Jake Fishman and his handsome and capable wife, Minnie. People came *en masse,* reflecting the new-born hope, whose name was Russia, awakened in the breasts of these American wage-slaves. My announcement of the Political Prisoners' Amnesty League which I was planning to organize in New York before entering the Jefferson prison was received with frenzied acclaim, and a large sum was added to the fund started in Chicago.

In Ann Arbor it was Agnes Inglis, an old friend and a splendid worker, who had made the necessary arrangements for my two lectures. But the noble Daughters of the American Revolution willed it otherwise. Some of those ancient females protested to the mayor, and he, poor soul, happened to be of German parentage. What could he do but carry out the spirit of true American independence? My meetings were suppressed.

The end of January terminated the hopes many of our friends had naïvely entertained. The Supreme Court declined to grant us a rehearing or to delay the course of legal justice further. February 5 was set for our recommitment to prison. Seven more days of freedom, the nearness of loved ones, the association of faithful friends — we poured ourselves into every second. Our last evening in New York was devoted to our final public appearance and to the organization of the Political Prisoners' Amnesty League.

Delegates of the Union of Russian Workers from every part of the United States and Canada were holding a conference in New York. Sasha and I had been invited as the guests of honour. An ovation greeted us on our appearance, the entire assembly rising to welcome us. Sasha was the first speaker. In honour of the October Revolution and as a token of special appreciation of the conference he meant to say a few words in Russian. He indeed began in that language, but he got no further than "*Dorogiye tovaristchi* (Dear comrades)," continuing in English. I thought I could do better, but I was mistaken. So completely had we become identified with the life and speech of America that we had lost the fluent use of our native tongue. Yet we had always kept in touch with Russian affairs and literature and had co-operated with radical Russian efforts in the United States. We promised our audience, however, to address them the next time in their own beautiful language — perchance in the land of liberty.

The frosty day had played havoc with Stella's gas, but greater conspiracies had been concocted by candlelight. Ours was the formation of the Political Prisoners' Amnesty League. Leonard D. Abbott, Dr. C. Andrews, Prince Hopkins, Lillian Brown, Lucy and Bob Robbins, and others of our co-workers were present at the birth of the new organization. Prince Hopkins was chosen permanent chairman, with Leonard as treasurer, and Fitzi as secretary. The funds I had collected for the purpose in Chicago and Detroit were turned over as the starting capital of the new body. It was late, or rather early February 4, when our friends bade us hail and farewell. There were still the proofs to be read of my brochure *The Truth about the Bolsheviki,* but Fitzi considerately undertook to see the pamphlet safely through.

A few hours later we proceeded to the Federal Building to surrender. I offered to make the trip to the prison by myself and pay my own fare, but my suggestion met with the incredulous smiles of the officials. The deputy marshal and his lady again shared my compartment on our way to the Jefferson City penitentiary.

My fellow-prisoners greeted me as a long-lost sister. They were very sorry that the Supreme Court had decided against me, but since I had to serve my sentence, they had hoped that I would be returned to Jefferson City. I might help to bring about some improvements, they thought, if I could manage to get at Mr. Painter, the Warden. He was considered "a good man," but they rarely saw him, and they were sure he did not know what was going on in the female wing.

Already during my first stay of two weeks I had realized that the inmates in the Missouri penitentiary, like those at Blackwell's Island, were recruited from the lowest social strata. With the exception of my cell neighbour, who was a woman above the average, the ninety-odd prisoners were poor wretches of the world of poverty and drabness. Coloured or white, most of them had been driven to crime by conditions that had greeted them at birth. My first impression was strengthened by daily contact with the inmates during a period of twenty-one months. The contentions of criminal psychologists notwithstanding, I found no criminals among them, but only unfortunates, broken, hapless, and hopeless human beings.

The Jefferson City prison was a model in many respects. The cells were double the size of the pest holes of 1893, though they were not light enough, except on very sunny days, unless one was so fortunate as to have a cell directly facing a window. Most of them had neither light nor ventilation. Perhaps Southern people do not care for much fresh air; the precious element certainly seemed tabooed in my new boarding-house. Only in extremely hot weather were the corridor windows opened. Our life was very democratic in the sense that we all received the same treatment, were made to inhale the same vitiated air and bathe in the same tub. The great advantage, however, was that one was not compelled to share one's cell with anyone else. This blessing could be appreciated by those only who had endured the ordeal of the continuous proximity of another human being.

The contract labour system had been officially abolished in the penitentiary, I was told. The State was now the employer, but the obligatory task the new boss imposed was not much lighter than the toil the private contractor had exacted. Two months were allowed to learn the trade, which consisted in sewing jackets, overalls, auto coats, and suspenders. The tasks varied from forty-five to a hundred and twenty-one jackets a day, or from nine to eighteen dozen suspenders. While the actual machine work on the different tasks was the same, some of them required double physical exertion. The full complement of work was demanded without regard to age or physical condition. Even illness, unless of a very serious nature, was not considered sufficient cause for relieving the worker. Unless one had previous experience in sewing, or a special aptitude for it, the achievement of the task was a source of constant trouble and worry. There was no consideration for human variations, no allowance for physical limitations, except for a few favourites of the officials, who were usually the most worthless.

The shop was dreaded by all the inmates, particularly on account of the foreman. He was a boy of twenty-one who had been in charge of the treadmill since he was sixteen. An ambitious young man, he was very clever in pressing the tasks out of the women. If insults failed, the threat of punishment brought results. The women were so terrorized by him that they rarely dared to speak up. If anyone did, she became his special target for persecution. He was not even averse to robbing them of a part of their work and then reporting them for impudence, thus increasing their punishment for being short of the task. Four unfavourable marks a month meant a drop in the grade, which in return brought a loss of "good time."

The Missouri penitentiary was run on the merit system, of which Grade A was the highest. To attain that goal meant to have one's sentence reduced almost by half, at least so far as the State prisoners were concerned. We Federals might work ourselves to death without benefiting by our efforts. The only reduction of time we were allowed was the usual two months off each year. The dread of failing to reach Class A whipped the non-Federals beyond their strength in an attempt to accomplish the task.

The foreman was of course but a cog in the prison machine, the centre of which was the State of Missouri. It was doing business with private firms, drawing its customers from every part of the United States, as I soon discovered by the labels we had to sew on the things we manufactured. Even poor old Abe had been turned into a sweater of convict labour: the Lincoln Jobbing House of Milwaukee had the picture of the Liberator on its label, bearing the legend: "True to his country, true to our trade." The firms bought our labour for a song and they were therefore in a position to undersell those employing union labour. In other words, the State of Missouri was slave-driving and tormenting us, and in addition also acting as scab on the organized workers. In this commendable enterprise the official bully in our shop was very useful. Captain Gilvan, the acting warden, and Lilah Smith, the head matron, made up the triple alliance in control of the prison régime.

Gilvan used to administer flogging when that method of reformation was in vogue in Missouri. Other forms of punishment had since taken its place: deprivation of recreation, being locked up for forty-eight hours, usually from Saturday to Monday, on a diet of bread and water, and the "blind" cell. The latter measured about four feet by eight and was entirely dark; only one blanket was permitted and the daily food-allowance consisted of two slices of bread and two cups of water. In that cell prisoners were kept from three to twenty-two days. There were also bullrings, which, however, were not used on white women during my stay.

Captain Gilvan loved to punish the inmates in the blind cell and to hang them up by the wrists. " You must make the task," he would bellow; " no such thing as ' can't.' I punish cheerfully, mark you that ! " He forbade us to leave our work without permission, even to go to the toilet. Once in the shop, after a more than usually brutal outbreak on his part, I approached him. " I must tell you that the task is sheer torture, especially for the older women," I said; " the insufficient food and constant punishment make things even worse." The Captain turned livid. "Look here, Goldman," he growled; " you're up to mischief. I have suspected it since your arrival. The convicts have never complained before, and they have always made the task. It's you who's putting notions into their heads. You had better look out. We have been kind to you, but if you do not stop your agitation, we will punish you like the rest, do you hear ? "

" That's all right, Captain," I replied, " but I repeat that the task is barbarous and no one can make it regularly without breaking down."

He walked away, followed by Miss Smith, and I returned to my machine.

The shop matron, Miss Anna Gunther, was a very decent sort. She would patiently listen to the complaints of the women, often excuse them from work if they were ill, and even overlook a shortage in the task. She had been exceedingly kind to me, and I felt guilty over having left my place without permission. She did not reproach me, but said that I had been rash to talk to the Captain as I had. Miss Anna was a dear soul, the only moral prop the inmates had. Alas, she was only a subordinate.

The reigning queen was Lilah Smith. A woman in the forties, she had been employed in penal institutions since her teens. Of small stature, but compactly built, in appearance she suggested rigidity and coldness. She had an ingratiating manner, but underneath were the hardness and severity of the Puritan, hating implacably every emotion that had dried up in her own being. Neither pity nor compassion dwelt in Lilah's breast, and she was ruthless when she sensed them in any-one else. The fact that my fellow-prisoners liked and trusted me was enough to damn me in her eyes. Aware that I was in the good graces of the Warden, she never showed her antagonism openly. Hers was the insidious way.

The nerve-racking noises in the shop and the furious drive of the work laid me low the first month. My old stomach complaint became aggravated, and I suffered great pain in my neck and spine. The prison physician had anything but a good reputation among the inmates. He knew nothing, they claimed, and was too afraid of Miss Smith to excuse a prisoner from the shop, however ill she might be. I had seen inmates barely able to keep on their feet sent back to work by the doctor. The female department had no dispensary where patients could be examined. Even the seriously ill were kept in their cells. I hated to go to the doctor, but my agony became so unbearable that I had to see him. His gentle manner surprised me. He had been told that I was feeling bad, he said; why hadn't I come sooner? I must have a rest and not resume work until permitted by him, he ordered. His unexpected interest was certainly a far cry from the treatment other prisoners were receiving from him. I wondered whether his kindness to me was not due to the intercession of Warden Painter.

The doctor came to my cell every day, massaged my neck, entertained me with amusing stories, and even ordered a special broth. My improvement was slow, particularly because of the depressing effect of my cell. Its dirty grey walls, the lack of light and ventilation, and my inability to read or do anything else to while away the time made the day oppressively long. Former occupants of the cell had made pitiful attempts to beautify their prison house by family photos and newspaper pictures of their matinée idols. Black-and-yellow patches had been left on the wall, their fantastic outlines adding to my nervous restlessness. Another factor in my misery was the sudden stoppage of my mail; not a word came from anybody for ten days.

Two weeks in the cell made me realize why prisoners preferred the torture of the task. Some sort of occupation is the only escape from despair. None of the inmates enjoyed being idle. The shop, terrible as it was, was better than being locked up in the cells. I returned to work. It was a bitter struggle between physical pain, which drove me to my cot, and mental torment, which forced me back to the shop.

At last I was handed a large package of mail with a note from Mr. Painter saying that he had had to submit my incoming and outgoing correspondence to a Federal inspector in Kansas City, by orders from Washington. It made me feel very important to be considered dangerous even while in prison. Just the same, I wished that Washington were less attentive now, when every line I sent out or received was being read by the head matron and the Warden.

Subsequently I learned the cause of the renewed concern of the Federal authorities in my thoughts and expressions. Mr. Painter had

given me permission to write a weekly letter to my attorney, Harry
Weinberger. I had commented to the latter on Senator Phelan's
speech in Congress against Tom Mooney. Thousands of appeals had
been pouring in on the Governor of California to save Mooney's life.
For a United States Senator to deliver himself of a vindictive attack
at such a moment was both disgraceful and cruel. Naturally my remarks were not very complimentary to Mr. Phelan. I had forgotten
that America since entering the war had turned every official into a
Gessler, and that homage to his hat had become a national duty.

My mail contained much distressing news along with affection and
cheer. Fitzi's apartment had been raided. At night, while she and our
young secretary, Pauline, were asleep, Federal agents and detectives
had broken into the house and rushed into her room before the girls
had a chance to get dressed. The officers were looking for an I.W.W.
conscript who had deserted, they claimed. Fitzi knew nothing about
the man, but that did not stop the raiders from ransacking her desk,
examining letters, and confiscating everything, including the plates of
Voltairine de Cleyre's *Selected Works,* which we had published after
her death.

Stella's letter evidenced her anxiety about the *Mother Earth* Book-
shop, which she and our faithful " Swede " had started in Greenwich
Village. Suspicious-looking individuals had been constantly at their
heels, and conditions were getting so appalling that people hardly
dared to breathe. The March number of the *Bulletin,* which Stella had
sent, came as a harbinger of spring. It contained an account of Harry
Weinberger's visit in Atlanta with Sasha and our two boys. Sasha had
impressed on him the urgent need of continuing the fight for Tom
Mooney's life. Cessation of our efforts for him might prove disastrous,
he had warned Harry. My brave pal! How deeply he felt for the San
Francisco victims and how ardently he had laboured for them! Even
now he showed more concern for Mooney than for his own fate. It was
bracing to feel his spirit in the *Bulletin,* and that of the other friends
who had contributed. It was a wrench to decide to let the paper die,
but, knowing Stella was in danger, I wrote her to discontinue its publication and close the book-shop.

In shipping us so far from New York, Washington had no doubt
meant to make our lot the harder. There could have been no other
reason for burying Sasha in Atlanta, when he could have been sent
to Leavenworth, which is more accessible than the State of Georgia.

Jefferson City being only three hours' ride from St. Louis and an important railroad centre, I had more applications for visits than I could fill. I should have laughed over the frustration of Uncle Sam were it not that he had succeeded in striking Sasha. Conditions in Atlanta, I was informed, were nothing short of feudal. After fourteen years in the Pennsylvania purgatory Sasha was again being made to suffer more than I.

My first visitor was Prince Hopkins, chairman of the Political Prisoners' Amnesty League. He was on tour for that body, organizing branches, collecting data on the number of victims in prison, and raising funds. Hopkins inquired whether there was any other work in the prison I might do to save my health, and he offered to see the Warden. I told him that one of the women in the linen-mending room was to be released in the near future, and that there would be a vacancy. Soon after my visitor had left, I received a letter from him saying that Mr. Painter had promised to speak to Miss Smith about changing my employment, but a later note from the Warden was to the effect that the head matron had previously selected someone else for the job.

Ben Capes came to see me, a veritable beam of sunshine, his joyous nature shedding balm. My activities outside had been too absorbing for me fully to appreciate the boy, or perhaps one clings more hungrily in prison to one's kindred. Ben's friendship had never seemed more precious than on this visit. He sent in an enormous box of delicacies from the most expensive Jefferson City grocery, and my fellow-prisoners expressed the hope that my other visitors might prove equally extravagant. Our lean Tuesdays and Fridays, when fish was served that was neither fresh nor plentiful, would cease to be our hungry days. The food was never wholesome or sufficient for hard-working people, but Tuesdays and Fridays meant practically starvation.

Prison life tends to make one wondrously resourceful. Some of the women had devised an original dumb-waiter, consisting of a bag attached by strings to a broomstick. The contraption would be passed through the bars of an upper-tier cell, and I, directly underneath, would fish the bag in, fill it with sandwiches and goodies, then push it out far enough to enable my upper neighbour to pull the bag up again. The same procedure would be repeated with my neighbour below. Then the things would be passed from cell to cell along each gallery. The orderlies shared in the bounty, and by their help I was able also to feed the occupants of the rear tiers.

Various friends kept me supplied with eatables, especially St. Louis comrades. They even ordered a spring mattress for my cot and arranged with a Jefferson City grocer to send me anything I ordered. It was this helpful solidarity that enabled me to share with my prison companions.

The visit of Benny Capes increased my disappointment in " Big Ben." The grief he had caused me, especially in the course of the last two years of our life, undermined my faith in him and filled my cup with bitterness. I had determined after his last departure from New York to break the bond that had chained me so long. Two years in prison would, I hoped, help me do it. But Ben kept on writing as if nothing had happened. His letters, breathing the old assurance of his love, were like coals of fire. I could not believe him any more, yet I wanted to believe. I refused his plea to permit him to visit me. I even intended to ask him to stop writing, but he himself was facing a prison sentence, incurred during the period of our association, and that still linked him to me. His approaching fatherhood added fuel to my emotional stress. His minute description of the feelings engendered in him, and his delight in the little garments prepared for the expected child, afforded me a glimpse into an unsuspected aspect of Ben's character. Whether it was the defeat of my own motherhood or the pain that another should have given Ben what I would not, his rhapsodies increased my resentment against him and everyone connected with him. The announcement of the birth of his son also contained the information that the Appellate Court in Cleveland had sustained the verdict against him. He was leaving for that city, Ben wrote, to serve his sentence of six months in the workhouse. He was to be torn away from what he had looked forward to so eagerly and go to prison. Once more an inner voice spoke for him, submerging everything else in my heart.

At last I was assigned to a cell facing a window, which permitted the sun to look in upon me occasionally. The Warden had also instructed the head matron to allow me to take three baths a week. These privileges soon changed my condition for the better. He had furthermore promised to have my cell whitewashed, but he could not keep his word. The whole prison badly needed a new coat of paint, but Mr. Painter had failed to secure an appropriation for it. He could not make an exception of me, and I agreed with him. I devised something else to cover up the hideous patches on the walls — *crêpe* paper of a lovely green which Stella had sent me. With it I panelled the entire cell, and presently it began to look quite attractive, its cosiness enhanced by beautiful Japanese prints I had received from Teddy and a shelf of books I had accumulated.

There was no library in the female department, nor were we allowed to take out books from the men's wing. Once I asked Miss Smith why we could not get reading-matter from the male library. " Because I can't trust the girls to go there alone," she said, " and I have no time to accompany them. They would be sure to start flirtations." " What harm would that do ? " I remarked naïvely, and Lilah was scandalized.

I requested Stella to see some publishers and also to induce our friends to send me books and magazines. Before long, four leading New York houses supplied me with many volumes. Most of them were above the understanding of my fellow inmates, but they soon learned to appreciate good novels.

The beneficial effect of reading was demonstrated to me by a Chinese girl who was serving a long term for killing her husband. She was a lonely creature, always keeping to herself and never communicating with the other prisoners. Up and down she would walk in the yard, muttering to herself. She was showing the first signs of insanity.

One day I received a Chinese magazine from comrades in Peking, with my picture on the front page. More ignorant of Chinese than the girl was of English, I gave her the journal. The sight of the familiar script brought tears to her eyes. The next day she tried to tell me in her broken English how wonderful it was to have something to read and how interesting the publication was. "You gland ladee," she kept repeating; " says muchee you zhis," pointing to the magazine. We became friends and she confided to me how she had come to kill the man she loved. They had become Christians. The minister who had married them told them that Christians in wedlock are bound by God for life, one man to one woman. Then she discovered that her husband had other women, and when she protested, he beat her up. He had often told her that he would always have other women besides her, and she killed him for that. Since then she believed all " Chlistians " false and she would never trust them again. She had thought that I, too, was a " Chlistian," but she read in the magazine that I was a non-believer. She would trust me, she said, but she objected to my friendly relations with the coloured inmates. They were inferior and dishonest, she was convinced. I pointed out that some people made the same objections to her race, and that in California

Chinese had been mobbed. She knew it, but she vehemently insisted that Chinese "no smell, no ignolant, diflent people."

Heathen that I was, I lost the privilege of recreation on Sunday afternoons because I failed to attend chapel services. I had minded the deprivation a great deal when I occupied the dark and damp cell, but now I welcomed it. It was quiet in the block, with the women out in the yard, and I was able to immerse myself in reading and writing. Among the books sent me was one from my friend Alice Stone Blackwell, containing the letters of Catherine Breshkovskaya and a biographic sketch of her. It was symbolic of the eternal recurrence of the struggle for freedom that I should be able to read the account of our Little Grandmother's exile under the tsars while I myself was a prisoner. Great as her persecution had been, she had never been forced to do hard labour, nor had any other women politicals in Russia. How surprised Catherine would be if I were to describe to her our shop, as bad a *katorga* as any in the Romanov autocracy! In one of her letters to Miss Blackwell, Babushka commented: "You, dearest, can write without fearing to be arrested, imprisoned, or exiled." In another she waxed enthusiastic over *The New Freedom,* by the former Princeton professor, now President of the United States. I wondered what the dear old lady would say if she could see with her own eyes what her hero in the White House had done to the country — the abrogation of all liberties, the raids, arrests, and reactionary fury his régime had brought in its wake.

The news of Breshkovskaya's arrival in America filled me with hope that an authentic word would at last be said for Soviet Russia and an effective protest voiced against conditions in America. I knew that Babushka was opposed, no less than I, to the socialism of the Bolsheviki; she would therefore be equally critical of their drift towards dictatorship and centralization. But she would appreciate their services to the October Revolution and she would defend them against the lies and calumnies in the American press. Surely the grand old lady would hold Woodrow Wilson to account for his share in the conspiracy to crush the Revolution. The anticipation of what she would do somewhat eased the poignancy of my own helplessness in prison.

The reports of her first public appearance in Carnegie Hall, under the auspices of Cleveland Dodge and other plutocrats, and her bitter denunciation of the Bolsheviki came as a fearful shock. Catherine Breshkovskaya, one of those whose revolutionary work for the past fifty years had paved the way for the October upheaval, was now surrounded by the worst enemies of Russia, working hand in glove with White generals and Jew-baiters, as well as with the reactionary element in the United States. It seemed incredible. I wrote Stella for accurate information, meanwhile continuing to cling to my faith in her who had been my inspiration and guiding star. Her simple grandeur, the charm and beauty of her personality, which I had learned to love during our common work in 1904 and 1905, had too deeply impressed me for me to give Babushka up so easily. I would write her. I would tell her of my own stand regarding Soviet Russia; I would assure her that I believed in her right of criticism, but I would plead with her not to lend herself as an unwitting tool to those who were trying to crush the Revolution. Stella was coming to visit me and I would have her smuggle out my letter to Babushka, type it, and deliver it to her in person.

I had attained to the highest ambition of my fellow sufferers in the penitentiary: I was placed in Grade A. Not entirely through my own efforts, though, for I was still unable to make the full task. I was indebted for it to the kindness of several coloured girls in the shop. Whether it was due to greater physical strength, or because they had been longer at the tasks, most of the Negro inmates succeeded better than the white women. Some of them had acquired such dexterity that they were often able to finish their tasks by three o'clock in the afternoon. Poor and friendless and desperately in need of a little money, they would help out those who fell behind. For this service they were entitled to five cents per jacket. Unfortunately, most of the whites were too poor to pay. I was considered the millionaire; my exchequer was often called upon to extend " loans," and I gladly complied. But the girls helping me with my work would not accept remuneration. They even felt hurt at the very suggestion of it. I was sharing my food and books with them, they protested; how could they take money from me? They agreed with my little Italian friend, Jennie de Lucia, who had constituted herself my maid. " No take money from you," she had declared, and the other women all echoed her sentiment. Thanks to those kind souls, I reached Grade A, which entitled me to send out three letters a week — really four, including the extra letter I had been writing regularly to my counsellor.

On the eve of June 27 my coloured friends presented me with a full task of jackets for the following day. They had remembered my birthday. " It would be so nice if Miss Emma could keep out of the shop on that day," they had said. The next morning my table was covered with letters, telegrams, and flowers from my own kin and comrades, as well as with innumerable packages from friends in different parts of the country. I was proud to have so much love and attention, but nothing touched me so deeply as the gift of my fellow-sufferers in prison.

The Fourth of July was approaching and the women were all aflutter. They had been promised a cinema, recreation twice on that day, and also a dance. Not with male partners — the good Lord forbid! — but among themselves. They could order soft drinks from the grocery, and it was to be a festive day. Alas, the cinema proved inane and the holiday dinner poor. The women became disgruntled, particularly because of the refusal of Miss Smith to release a coloured girl from the blind cell, put there on the complaint of one of the matron's favourites, also coloured, who was suspected as a stool-pigeon and cordially disliked. It was too much to see her dolled up and running the Fourth of July show, while her victim was on bread and water. Several of the women made for the informer, and the grand day ended in a free-for-all fight. Miss Smith was compelled to punish her favourite as well as her assailants, and they were all locked up in the dungeon.

In my next letter I commented on the events of the patriotic day. My epistle was held up and then returned to me with instructions that no account of anything happening in prison could be sent out. I had often before discussed local matters in letters that Mr. Painter had permitted to pass, and I concluded that my Fourth of July narrative had not gone further than the head matron.

A three days' visit from my dear Stella proved a more real holiday for me than the Fourth of July. I was able to hand her my letter for Babushka, several notes my cell neighbours wanted smuggled out, and samples of the fake shop labels. They were three days of freedom from the shop, spent with my beloved child in our own world, a visit long awaited and quickly passed, to be followed by the reaction of the prison routine.

In my letter to Babushka I had begged her not to think that I denied her the right of criticism of Soviet Russia, or that I wished her to gloss over the faults of the Bolsheviki. I pointed out that I differed with them in ideas and that my stand against every form of dictatorship was irrevocable. But that was not important, I insisted, while every government was at the throat of the Bolsheviki. I pleaded with her to bethink herself, not to go back on her glorious past and the high hopes of Russia's present generation.

Babushka had grown feebler and whiter, Stella told me, but she had remained the old rebel and fighter, her heart aflame for the people as of yore. Still, it was true that she was permitting reactionary elements to make use of her. It was impossible to doubt Babushka's integrity or to think her capable of conscious betrayal, but I could not approve her attitude towards the soviets. Granted that her criticism was justified, I reasoned, why did she not proclaim it from a radical platform to the workers, instead of addressing the wretched gang that was conniving to undo the achievements of the Revolution? I could not forgive her that, and I scorned her suggestion that I would some day be on her side and work with her against the Bolsheviki, who were defying the entire reactionary world. And how could a woman like Breshkovskaya remain unseeing and inarticulate in the face of the dreadful situation in America, I wondered. Not since Peter Kropotkin's attitude on the World War had anything so affected me as her tacit approval of the frightfulness around her.

As for those native liberals and socialists who were serving as war drummers for the Government, I felt only disgust for the Russells, Bensons, Simonses, Ghents, Stokeses, Greels, and Gomperses. They had never been anything but political trimmers; they were merely fulfilling their destiny. It was more difficult to understand the Germanophobia of men like George D. Herron, English Walling, Arthur Bullard, and Louis F. Post. Someone had sent me Herron's book *The Need of Crushing Germany*. Never had I read a more bloodthirsty and vicious misrepresentation of a people. And that from the man who had left the Church because of his revolutionary internationalism!

Similarly Arthur Bullard in his volume *Mobilising America* repeated the falsifications spread by him and his worthy companions John Greel and Company. Bullard, the erstwhile enthusiast of the University Settlement, who had done such valiant work in Russia in 1905, had now thrown his ideals and literary talent on the dung-heap of reaction. I almost felt glad that his friend Kellogg Durland had not lived to join those spokesmen of murder and destruction. His death by his own hand, resulting from a frustrated love-affair, had at least the merit of striking only the two persons concerned, but the betrayal of their ideals by the American intelligentsia was a calamity to the whole country. I could not help feeling that this group was even more responsible for the widespread atrocities in the United States than the out-and-out jingoes.

It was the more joy to see that some few had retained their sanity and courage. Randolph Bourne, whose brilliant analysis of war we had reprinted in *Mother Earth,* continued to expose the lack of character and judgment among the liberal intelligentsia. With him were Professors Cattell and Dana, both dismissed from Columbia University for their heresies, as well as other academicians who had refused to silence their disbelief in war. Most gratifying also was the young radical generation and the mettle most of them had shown. Neither prison nor torture could induce them to take up arms. Max Frucht and Elwood B. Moore, of Detroit, and H. Austin Simons, the Chicago poet, had declared themselves willing to undergo any penalty rather than become soldiers. They went to prison, as did Philip Grosser, Roger Baldwin, and scores of others.

Roger Baldwin had proved a great surprise. In former years he had impressed me as rather confused in his social views, a person who tried to be all things to all men. His stand at his trial for evading the draft, his frank avowal of anarchism, and his unreserved repudiation of the right of the State to coerce the individual had made me conscious of guilt towards him. I wrote him confessing my unkind judgment and assuring him that his example had given me a salutary lesson of the need of greater care in the appraisement of people.

The prisons and military barracks were filled with conscientious objectors who were defying the most harrowing treatment. The most conspicuous case among them was that of Philip Grosser.

He had registered as an objector to war on political grounds, and he had declined to sign an enlistment card. Though it constituted a Federal civil offence, the youth was turned over to the military authorities and sentenced to thirty years' imprisonment for refusal to obey military orders. He was subjected to every form of torture, including chaining to the cell door, underground dungeon, and physical violence. Incarcerated in various prisons, he was finally sent to the Federal military penitentiary on Alcatraz Island, California, where he determinedly continued his refusal to participate in anything connected with militarism. Most of his time there he spent in the dark and damp cell of the hell-hole known as Uncle Sam's Devil's Island.

# CHAPTER XLVIII

THE ESPIONAGE ACT RESULTED IN FILLING THE CIVIL AND MILI-
tary prisons of the country with men sentenced to incredibly long
terms; Bill Haywood received twenty years, his hundred and ten
I.W.W. co-defendants from one to ten years, Eugene V. Debs ten
years, Kate Richards O'Hare five. These were but a few among the
hundreds railroaded to living deaths.

Then came the arrest of a group of our young comrades in New
York, comprising Mollie Steimer, Jacob Abrams, Samuel Lipman, Hy-
man Lachowsky, and Jacob Schwartz. Their offence consisted in circulating a printed protest against American intervention in Russia.
Every one of those youths was subjected to the severest third degree,
and Schwartz fell dangerously ill as a result of savage beating. They
were kept in the Tombs, where large numbers of other radicals were
also awaiting trial or deportation, among them our faithful " Swede."
Their brave, determined stand for an ideal's sake glaringly contrasted
with Ben's inconsistency. His attempt to offer his medical services to
the army had capped the climax. If his prison term were at last served,
I felt, it would give me the strength to emancipate myself from him,
to become free from my emotional bondage. In this hope I had pestered Stella and Fitzi to raise his fine, so that he should not have to
serve more time in payment. But my fear had been groundless; the
fine was remitted before his release. Ben did not even have the grace
to inform me or the girls in New York about it. I received the news
from Agnes Inglis, one of my dearest and most considerate friends,
who came to visit me in prison. Later Ben wrote me; he told all about
his son, his mother, his wife, and his plans and urged me to see him.
I did not consider that his letter required a reply.

Agnes Inglis was the type to whom friendship was a sacrament.
Never once did she fail me after we first came in close contact in 1914.

She had been attracted to my work, she once told me, by my pamphlet *What I Believe.* She belonged to a wealthy family of orthodox Presbyterians, and it involved a great inner conflict to free herself from the middle-class morality and traditions of her environment, but with rare spiritual courage she overcame her heritage and gradually developed into a woman of independent and original attitude. She gave most generously of her time, energy, and means to every progressive cause and always participated in our campaigns for free speech. Agnes combined her active interest in the social struggle with a broad humanity in personal relations. I had come to appreciate her qualities as comrade and friend, and it was a great treat to have her visit me for two days.

Before she left the city, she called once more at the penitentiary, and the head matron brought her to the shop. I had not expected her and was startled when I saw Agnes standing in the door of our treadmill. Her affrighted eyes roved all over the place, finally settling on me. She started to walk towards my machine, but I stopped her with a gesture and then waved her my good-bye. I could not endure a demonstration of our affection in the presence of my shop-mates, who had so little of it in their own lives.

The war for democracy was celebrating its triumphs at home as abroad. One of its characteristic features was the dooming of Mollie Steimer's group to long prison terms. They were all mere youths. Yet United States District Judge Henry D. Clayton, a veritable Jeffreys, sentenced the boys to twenty years' imprisonment and Mollie to fifteen, with deportation at the expiration of their terms. Jacob Schwartz had been saved His Honour's mercy; he had died on the day of the opening of the trial, from injuries inflicted upon him by police blackjacks. In his Tombs cell was found an unfinished note in Yiddish, written in his dying hour. It read:

> Farewell, comrades. When you appear before the Court I will be with you no longer. Struggle without fear, fight bravely. I am sorry to have to leave you. But this is life itself. After your long martyr—

" The intelligence, courage, and fortitude shown by our comrades at their trial, particularly by Mollie Steimer," a friend wrote to me, " was profoundly impressive." Even the newspaper men could not help referring to the dignity and strength of the girl and her co-defendants.

These comrades had come from the working masses and were hardly known even to us. By their simple act and magnificent bearing they had added their names to the galaxy of heroic figures in the struggle for humanity.

The torrent of war news would have submerged the important case on trial before Judge Clayton but for the acumen of counsel for the defence. Harry Weinberger realized the significance of the underlying issues and he called on the witness-stand men of national reputation, thereby compelling the press to take notice. He subpœnaed Raymond Robins, one of the heads of the American Red Cross in Russia, and Mr. George Creel, of the Federal Information Bureau, who had been responsible for the so-called " Sisson documents." Thus the truth was exposed about the deliberate attempt to prejudice the world against Russia by forgeries which were to serve as ground for military intervention against the Revolution. Weinberger showed that President Woodrow Wilson had, without the knowledge of the people of the United States and without the consent of Congress, illegally sent American troops to Vladivostok and Archangel. Under those circumstances, he declared, the defendants had done a just and laudable act in calling public attention by their protest against waging war with Russia, with which America was officially at peace.

The influenza epidemic raging through the country had reached our prison, and thirty-five inmates were stricken down. In the absence of any hospital facilities, the patients were kept in their cells, exposing the other inmates to infection. At the first sign of the disease I had offered my services to the physician. He knew I was a trained nurse and he welcomed my aid. He promised to see Miss Smith about letting me take care of the sick, but days passed without bringing results. Later I learned that the head matron had refused to take me out of the shop. I was already enjoying too many privileges, she had said, and she would not stand for more.

Not being officially permitted to nurse, I sought means to aid the sick unofficially. Since the influenza invasion our cells were being left unlocked at night. The two girls assigned to nursing were so hard-worked that they would sleep all through the night, and the orderlies were my friends. That offered me a chance to make hurried calls from cell to cell and do what little was possible to make the patients more comfortable.

On November 11, at ten in the morning, the electric power in our shop was switched off, the machines stopped, and we were informed that there would be no further work that day. We were sent to our cells, and after lunch we were marched to the yard for recreation. It was an unheard-of event in the prison and everyone wondered what it could mean. My thoughts dwelt in the days of 1887. I had intended to strike against work on the anniversary that marked the birth of my social consciousness. But there were so few women able to go to the shop that I did not want to add to the number of absentees. The unexpected holiday gave me the opportunity to be alone for spiritual communion with my martyred Chicago comrades.

During recreation in the yard I missed Minnie Eddy, one of the inmates. She was the most unfortunate creature in the prison, constantly in trouble about her work. Though she tried very hard to complete the allotted task, she seldom succeeded. If she rushed, her work was bad; if she slowed down, she failed to finish the day's work. She was bullied by the foreman, reprimanded by the head matron, and often punished. In her desperation Minnie spent the few cents she received from her sister to pay for help. She was very appreciative of the least kindness and she became inseparable from me. Of late she had been complaining of dizziness and severe pain in the head. One day she had fainted away at her machine. It was apparent that Minnie was seriously ill. Yet Miss Smith refused to exempt her from work. The woman was shamming, the matron claimed, though we knew better. The doctor, by no means a brave or aggressive man, would not dispute Lilah.

Failing to see Minnie in the yard, I assumed that she had probably received permission to remain in the cell. But when we returned from recreation, I discovered that she was in punishment, locked up on bread and water. We expected her to be released the next day.

Late in the evening the prison silence was torn by deafening noises coming from the male wing. The men were banging on bars, whistling, and shouting. The women grew nervous, and the block matron hastened over to reassure them. The declaration of armistice was being celebrated she said. "What armistice?" I asked. "It's Armistice Day," she replied; "that's why you have been given a holiday." At first I hardly grasped the full significance of the information, and then I, too, became possessed of a desire to scream and shout, to do something to give vent to my agitation. "Miss Anna, Miss Anna!"

I called the matron back. " Come here, please, come here! " She approached again. "You mean that hostilities have been stopped, that the war has come to an end and the prisons will be opened for those who refused to take part in the slaughter? Tell me, tell me!" She put her hand soothingly on mine. " I have never seen you so excited before," she said; " a woman of your age, working yourself up to such a pitch over such a thing!" She was a kindly soul, but she knew nothing outside her prison duties.

Minnie Eddy was not released the next day, as I had hoped she would be. On the contrary, suspecting that someone was secretly feeding her, the head matron ordered her transferred to the blind cell. I pleaded with Miss Smith that Minnie might die if she continued on bread and water and was forced to sleep on the damp floor. Lilah told me gruffly to mind my own business. I waited another few days and then I notified the Warden that I had something urgent to see him about. Miss Smith no doubt suspected the contents of my sealed envelope, but she did not dare hold back letters addressed to Mr. Painter. He came, and I reported Minnie's case to him. The same evening Minnie was sent back to her cell.

On Thanksgiving, she was allowed to come to the dining-room for the special dinner, which consisted of pork of questionable quality. Starved for days, she ate ravenously. A week before, her sister had sent her a basket of fruit, and as a privilege Minnie was permitted to receive it. Most of it had meanwhile become decayed, and I warned her not to touch it, promising to send her eggs and other things from my supply. At midnight the coloured orderly woke me to say that she had heard Minnie cry in pain, and when she had reached her cell, she had found the woman in a faint on the floor. Her door was locked and she did not dare call Miss Smith. I insisted that she must be summoned. After a while we heard groaning in Minnie's cell, followed by sobbing, and then the matron's receding steps. The orderly reported that Miss Smith had poured cold water over Minnie, struck her several times, and ordered her to get up from the floor.

The following day Minnie was placed in an isolated rear cell, with only a mattress on the floor. She became delirious, her cries resounding through the corridor. We learned that she had refused nourishment and that an attempt at forcible feeding had been made. But it was too late. She died on the twenty-second day of her punishment.

The misery and tragedies of prison life were aggravated by sad news from the outside. My brother Herman's wife, our beautiful Ray, had died from heart-trouble. Helena also was in a terrible state of mind. No word from David had reached her for weeks, and she was beside herself with dread that something might have happened to him.

A ray of light came with the commutation of Tom Mooney's death-sentence to life imprisonment. It was a travesty on justice to immure a man for life who had been proved innocent by the State's own witnesses. Nevertheless, the commutation was an achievement, due mostly, I felt, to the effective work our people had done. Without the campaign Sasha, Fitzi, and Bob Minor had inaugurated in San Francisco and New York, there would have been no demonstrations in Russia and other European countries. It was the international scope of the Mooney-Billings case that had impressed President Wilson to the extent of inducing him to cause a Federal investigation. The same moral force had prompted him to intercede with the Governor of California for Mooney's life. The agitation organized by Sasha and his associates had at last snatched Tom Mooney from death. Time was thereby gained for further work to give Mooney and Billings liberty. I was happy at these developments and proud of Sasha and the success of his strenuous efforts. I fervently wished that he might be free to bring to completion the victory which had come near costing his own life.

The prison had been quarantined and all visits stopped, excepting of course the incoming and released prisoners. Several new ones arrived, among them Ella. She was sent up on a Federal charge and she brought to me what I had been missing so much — intellectual companionship with a kindred spirit. My fellow inmates had been kind to me and I had not lacked affection, but we belonged to different worlds. It would have only made them self-conscious of their lack of development had I broached my ideas to them or discussed the books I read. But Ella, though still in her teens, shared my conception of life and values.

She was a proletarian child, familiar with poverty and hardship, strong, and socially conscious. Gentle and sympathetic, she was like a beam of sunshine, bringing cheer to her fellow prisoners and great joy to me. The women reached out for her hungrily, though she was an enigma to them. "What are you here for," one inmate asked Ella — "picking pockets?" "No." "Soliciting men?" "No." "Selling Dope?" "No," laughed Ella, "for none of these things." "Well, what else could you have done to have got eighteen months? " "I am an anarchist," Ella replied. The girls thought it funny to go to prison for " just being something."

Christmas was approaching and my companions were in nervous wonderment as to what the day of days would bring them. Nowhere is Christianity so utterly devoid of meaning as in prison, nowhere its precepts so systematically defied, but myths are more potent than facts. Fearfully strong is their hold on the suffering and despairing. Few of the women could expect anything from the outside; some had not even a single human being to give them a thought. Yet they clung to the hope that the day of their Saviour's birth would bring them some kindness. The majority of the convicts, of infantile mentality, talked of Santa Claus and the stocking with naïve faith. It served to help them over their degradation and misery. Forsaken by God, by man forgot, it was their only refuge.

Long before Christmas, gifts began to arrive for me. Members of my family, comrades, and friends fairly deluged me with presents. Soon my cell began to look like a department store, and every day brought additional packages. As usual, our dear Benny Capes, in response to my request for trinkets for the inmates, sent a huge consignment. Bracelets, ear-rings, necklaces, rings, and brooches, enough to make the Woolworth stock feel ashamed, and lace collars, handkerchiefs, stockings, and other things sufficient to compete with any store on Fourteenth Street. Others were equally generous. My old friends Michael and Annie Cohn were particularly lavish. An invalid for years and in constant torment, Annie was yet most thoughtful of others. She was indeed a rare spirit of brave patience and selfless kindness. Our staunch friends for a quarter of a century, Annie and Michael had always been among the first to come to our assistance whenever aid was needed, co-operating in our efforts in the movement, sharing our burdens, helping and giving without stint. Hardly a week had passed since my imprisonment without a cheering letter and gifts from them. For Christmas Annie sent me a special parcel — everything prepared with her own hands, as Michael affectionately wrote. Wonderful Annie, a martyr to physical ailments, steadily growing worse, her suffering increasing, living only in her devotion to others!

It was a problem to divide the gifts so as to give each what she might like best, without arousing envy or suspicion of preference and favouritism. I called to my aid three of my neighbours, and with their expert advice and help I played Santa Claus. On Christmas Eve, while our fellow-prisoners were attending the movies, a matron accompanied us to unlock the doors, our aprons piled high with gifts. With gleeful secrecy we flitted along the tiers, visiting each cell in turn. When the women returned from the cinema, the cell-block resounded with exclamations of happy astonishment. " Santa Claus 's been here! He's brung me something grand! " " Me, too! Me, too! " re-echoed from cell to cell. My Christmas in the Missouri penitentiary brought me greater joy than many previous ones outside. I was thankful to the friends who had enabled me to bring a gleam of sunshine into the dark lives of my fellow-sufferers.

On New Year's again the prison was filled with noisy hilarity. Fortunate indeed are they whom each year brings nearer to the passionately longed-for hour of release. Not so the poor creatures sent up for life. No hope or cheer for them in the new day or new year. Little Aggie kept to her cell, wailing over her fate. A piteous sight the poor woman was, withered at thirty-three, her years spent in the penitentiary since she was eighteen. She had been condemned to death for killing her husband. The murder was the result of a drunken card-row between Aggie's husband and the boarder. It probably was not the young bride who had wielded the fatal poker, but her " own man " had managed to wriggle out of responsibility. He had turned State's evidence and had helped to send the child to her doom. Her extreme youth had saved her from the noose; her sentence was commuted to life imprisonment. I found Aggie one of the sweetest and kindest of beings, capable of strong attachments. After she had been in prison ten years, she was permitted to keep a dog some visitor had given her. His name was Riggles, and an ugly beast he was. But to Aggie he was beauty personified, the most precious thing she possessed and her only tie in life. No mother could have given greater love and attention to her child than Aggie gave her pet. She would never ask anything for herself, but for Riggles she would beg. The brightening of her otherwise dead eyes when she would take Riggles into her arms was a key to the heart-hunger of the unfortunate the law's stupidity had stamped a hardened criminal.

And there was my other neighbour Mrs. Schweiger, a " bad woman," as the head matron called her. A devout Catholic, tragically mismated, she could find no escape in divorce. Ill health, which unfitted her for child-bearing, added to the misery and loneliness of her life. Her husband sought distraction with other women, and she was left to brood and weep, a prisoner in her own home. In a fit of homicidal melancholia she had emptied a pistol into him. She was of German parentage, which did not add to Lilah Smith's liking for her.

With the New Year came the shock of David's death. For months rumours of the boy's end had hung like a pall over his family. Helena's appeals to Washington for news of her son had brought no results. The United States Government had done its duty; it had shipped David with thousands of others to the fields of France. It could not be bothered by the anguish of those left behind. It was from an officer returned from France that Stella had learned of Dave's tragic fate.

The boy had preferred a responsible position, though dangerous, to the safety of the military orchestra to which he had been assigned, his comrade reported to Stella. He lost his life on October 15, 1918, in the Bois de Rappe, in the Argonne forest, killed one month before Armistice Day, in the prime and glory of his youth. My poor sister was still ignorant of the blow awaiting her. She would be informed as soon as official confirmation was received, Stella's letter said. I foresaw the effect of the terrible news on Helena and I felt sickening apprehension for her sake.

For the first time in months I had a caller again, our dear friend and co-worker M. Eleanor Fitzgerald — " Fitzi." Following our imprisonment she had accepted a position with the Provincetown Players, where she worked as arduously as she had with us. At the same time she continued her activities in the Mooney-Billings campaign, the Political Prisoners' Amnesty League, and as well took care of our boys in prison. I realized only when I saw her again how hard she must have been working. She looked worn and fatigued, and I regretted having scolded her in a letter because she had not written me in a long time.

She came to Jefferson on her way back home from the Mooney Conference in Chicago. She had also gone to see Sasha in Atlanta. Her visit with him, she told me, had proved most unsatisfactory, because it had been very brief and under a rigid watch. But she had managed to smuggle out a note from him to me. I had had no direct word from Sasha since the last day of our trial, a year before, and the familiar handwriting brought a lump to my throat. Fitzi's replies to my questions were evasive, and I suspected that all was not well with Sasha. He was having a frightful time of it, she reluctantly admitted. He had been put in the dungeon for circulating a protest to the Warden against the brutal clubbing of defenceless prisoners. He had earned the bitter enmity of the officers by denouncing the unprovoked murder of a young Negro inmate who was shot in the back for "impudence." All his Christmas parcels, except one, had been denied him. The other gifts sent to him had graced the dinner-table of the officials. He looked haggard and sick, Fitzi said. " But you know Sasha," she hastened to add; " nothing can break his spirit or dampen his sense of humour. He joked and laughed while I was with him and I joined in, choking back my tears." Yes, I knew Sasha, and I was certain he would survive. Only eight months more — had he not shown his powers of endurance during his fourteen years in Pennsylvania?

Fitzi could tell me little that was encouraging about the Mooney Conference in Chicago, which she had helped to organize. Most of the labour politicians were busy side-tracking the Mooney activities, she informed me. There was a disheartening lack of unanimity in favour of a general strike in behalf of Mooney and Billings. Moreover, there was evidently a deliberate attempt to hush up publicity. More " diplomatic " methods were to be used to liberate the men. The participation of anarchists was to be discouraged. They had been the first to sound the alarm in the San Francisco cases, and Sasha had consecrated himself to the work, even at the jeopardy of his own life. Now the anarchists and their efforts were to be eliminated from the fight. It was not the first time, nor would it be the last, that anarchists burned their fingers in pulling the chestnuts out of the fire for others, but if Billings and Mooney should regain their freedom, we should feel our work amply repaid. Fitzi, of course, had no intention of relaxing her efforts to bring about a general strike, and I knew that the brave girl would do her best.

The hardest thing to bear in prison is one's utter powerlessness to do aught for one's loved ones in distress. My sister Helena had given me more affection and care than my parents. Without her my childhood would have been even more barren. She had saved me many blows and had soothed my youth's sorrows and pains. Yet in her own greatest need I could do nothing to help her.

If only I could believe that my sister was still able, as in the past, to feel the suffering of humanity at large, then I would point out to her that there were other stricken mothers, their loss no less poignant than hers, and other tragedies more appalling even than David's untimely death. In former days Helena would have understood, and her own grief might have been mellowed by universal suffering. Would she now? From the letters of my sister Lena and of Stella I could see that Helena's springs of social sympathy had dried up with the tears she had shed for her son.

Time is the greatest healer, and it might also heal my sister's wounds, I thought. I held to that ray of hope and I looked forward to my approaching release, when I might take my darling away somewhere and perhaps bring her a little peace by loving communion.

My sorrow was augmented by still another loss, that of my friend Jessie Ashley, valiant rebel. No other American woman of her position had allied herself so completely with the revolutionary movement as Jessie. She had taken a vital part in the I.W.W. activities, the free-speech and birth-control campaigns, giving personal service and much of her means. She had been with us in the No-Conscription League and in every move we had made against the draft and the war. When Sasha and I were held under fifty-thousand-dollar bail, Jessie Ashley was the first to contribute ten thousand dollars in cash towards our bond. The news of her death after a short illness had come unexpectedly. David and Jessie — one of my own blood, the other much closer in spirit — their passing affected me deeply. Yet it was the horrible fate of two other persons, known to me by name only, that proved even a greater blow — that of Rosa Luxemburg and Karl Liebknecht.

Social democracy had been their goal, and anarchists their special *bête noire*. They had fought us and our ideas, not always even by fair means. At last social democracy triumphed in Germany. Popular wrath had frightened the Kaiser out of the country, and the brief revolution had made an end to the house of Hohenzollern. Germany was proclaimed a republic, with the socialists at the political helm. But, oh, the cruel irony of the shades of Marx! Luxemburg and Liebknecht, who had helped to build up the Socialist Party of Germany, were crushed by the régime of their orthodox comrades risen to power.

With Easter came spring's awakening, flooding my cell with warmth and filling it with the perfume of flowers. Life was gaining new meaning — only six more months to liberty!

April added another political, Mrs. Kate Richards O'Hare, to our company. I had met her once before, when she had called at the prison on her visit to Jefferson City to see Governor Gardner. She had been convicted under the Espionage Law, but she was emphatic that the Supreme Court would reverse the verdict, and that in any event she would not serve time in our place. I had been disagreeably impressed by her dogmatic manner and her belief that exceptions would be made in her behalf, but I wished her luck. When I came upon her dressed in the penitentiary uniform of striped gingham, waiting to fall in line with us as we were marching to the dining-room, I felt sorry indeed that her expectations had miscarried. I wanted to take her by the hand and say something that would ease her first and most trying prison hours, but talking or demonstration of feeling was strictly tabooed. Moreover, Mrs. O'Hare looked rather forbidding. Of tall stature, she carried herself with hauteur, her expression appearing more rigid because of her steel-grey hair. I found it difficult to say something warm even when we reached the yard.

Mrs. O'Hare was a socialist. I had read the little publication she had been issuing together with her husband, and I considered her socialism a colourless brand. Had we met on the outside, we should have probably argued furiously and have remained strangers for the rest of our lives. In prison we soon found common ground and human interest in our daily association, which proved more vital than our theoretical differences. I also discovered a very warm heart beneath Kate's outer coldness and found her a woman of simplicity and tender feeling. We quickly became friends, and my fondness for her increased in proportion as her personality unfolded itself to me.

Soon we politicals — Kate, Ella, and I — were nicknamed " the trinity." We spent much time together and became very neighbourly. Kate had the cell on my right, and Ella was next to her. We did not ignore our fellow-prisoners or deny ourselves to them, but intellectually Kate and Ella created a new world for me, and I basked in its interests, its friendship and affection.

Kate O'Hare had been taken away from her four children, the youngest of whom was about eight — an ordeal that would have taxed the strength of many a woman. Kate, however, was splendid. She

knew that her children were well cared for by their father, Frank
O'Hare. Besides, in point of intelligence and maturity her children
were far above their age. They were their mother's real comrades
and not merely the offspring of her womb. Their spirit was Kate's
greatest moral support.

Frank O'Hare visited Kate every week and occasionally even more
often, keeping her in touch with her friends and their work. He mimeo-
graphed her letters and circulated them through the land. The bitter
edge of incarceration was thus taken away from Kate. An additional
factor to help her over the hardest period was her extraordinary
adaptability. She was able to fit into any situation and to go about
everything in her quiet, methodical manner. Even the dreadful noises
in the shop, and its maddening grind, seemed to have little effect on
her. Nevertheless, she suffered a break-down before she had been with
us two months. She had over-estimated her strength when she attempted to master the task sooner than any one of us had been able
to do it.

But Kate kept her courage and she was greatly sustained by Frank,
who had already begun to work for her pardon. She had been convicted for an anti-war speech, but the O'Hares had big political connexions. It was therefore reasonably certain that Kate would not have
to serve long. I myself had declined the offer of friends to gain clemency for me. But it was different with Kate, who believed in the political machine. I hoped, however, that in her appeal would also be included the other political prisoners.

Meanwhile Kate was bringing about changes in the Missouri penitentiary which I had in vain been trying for fourteen months to
accomplish. She had an advantage in the presence of her husband near-
by, in St. Louis, and access to the press, and we often banteringly discussed which of the two was of more value. Her letters to O'Hare,
criticizing the lack of a library for the women, and her condemnation
of our food, standing for two hours before being served, had appeared in the *Post Dispatch* and brought immediate improvement.
The head matron announced that books could henceforth be had from
the men's department, and the food was served hot, " for the first
time in the ten years I've been here," as Aggie commented.

In the interim an unusual feature was introduced by the Warden
independently of Kate's influence. It was announced that we were to
have picnics every second Saturday in the city park. So extraordinary

was the innovation that we felt inclined to consider it a joke, too good to be true. But when we were assured that the first outing would actually take place the following Saturday, that we could spend the whole afternoon in the park, where the male band would play dance music, the women lost their heads and forgot all about the prison rules. They laughed and wept, shouted, and acted generally as if they had gone mad. The week was tense with excitement, everyone working to exhaustion to make the task, so as not to be left behind when the great day should arrive. During recreation the sole talk was of the picnic, and in the evenings the cell block was filled with whispered conversation about the impending event — how to fix up to look nice, how it would feel to walk about in the park. And would the band boys be near enough to talk to? No débutante was ever more wrought up over her first ball than the poor creatures, most of whom had not stepped out of the prison walls for a decade.

The picnic did take place, but to us — to Kate, Ella, and me — it was a ghastly experience. There were heavily armed guards behind and in front of us, and not a step was permitted outside the prescribed area. Guards surrounded the prison orchestra, while the matrons let no woman out of sight the moment dancing began. The supper was most depressing. The whole thing was a farce and an insult to human dignity. But to our unfortunate fellow-convicts it was like manna to the Jews in the desert.

In my next letter to Stella I quoted Tennyson's *Light Brigade*. In the course of the week the Warden sent for me to ask what I had meant by my reference. I told him that I should prefer to remain in my cell Saturday afternoon rather than picnic by the grace of an armed force. There was no danger of any woman's escaping, with the open country-side offering no place to hide. " Don't you see, Mr. Painter," I appealed to him, " it is not the park which will prove an influence for good? It will be your trust in the women, their feeling that at least once in two weeks they are given a chance to eliminate the prison from their consciousness. That sense of freedom and release will create a new morale among the inmates."

The following Saturday there were fewer guards and they did not flaunt their weapons in our faces. Limit restrictions were abolished, and the entire park was ours. The band boys were permitted to meet the girls at the soda-water stand and to treat them to pop and ginger ale. Our suppers in the park were gradually discarded, having proved too hard a task for the two matrons to supervise. But none of us minded it, since we were given another two hours of recreation in the prison yard after supper. The inmates had now something to look forward to and live for. Their state of mind changed; they worked with more zest, and their former distress and irritableness decreased.

One day an unexpected visitor was announced — S. Yanofsky, the editor of our Yiddish anarchist weekly in New York. He was on a lecture tour to California and he could not pass Jefferson City without seeing me, he said. I was pleased to know that my bitter opponent and censor of yester-year had gone out of his way to pay me a visit. His stand on the war, and particularly his worship of Woodrow Wilson, had completely alienated me from him. It was discouraging that a man of his ability and perspicacity should be carried away by the general psychosis. But, after all, his inconsistency was no worse than that of Peter Kropotkin, who had taken the lead which all the other pro-war anarchists had followed. Yanofsky, however, had gone even further in his enthusiasm for the Allies. He had written a veritable panegyric on Woodrow Wilson and had waxed poetic about " the pride of the Atlantic," that it might carry his hero to European shores for the great feast of peace. Such idolatry of one old gentleman for another outraged not only my principles, but also my conception of good taste.

Our conviction and the shameful manner in which we had been spirited out of New York must have touched something very deep in Yanofsky's heart. He wrote and spoke in our defence, helped to raise funds, and evidenced great concern over our fate. But it was mainly our struggle to rescue Sasha from the San Francisco trap that had established closer rapport between Yanofsky and me. His wholehearted co-operation and his genuine interest in Sasha had shown him capable of devoted comradeship I had never suspected in him before.

My mail had again been held up for ten days. The contents of two letters I had written had been found to be of a treasonable nature. I had ridiculed in them the Congressional committee that was investigating bolshevism in America; I had also attacked the high-handed autocracy of Attorney General A. Mitchell Palmer and his régime, as well as Messrs. Lusk and Overman, the New York State Senators delving into radicalism. Those Rip van Winkles had suddenly awakened to find that some of their countrymen had actually been thinking and reading about social conditions, and that other subversive elements had even dared to write books on the subject. It was a crime to be nipped in the bud if American institutions were to be saved. Of the insidious works those of Goldman and Berkman were the worst, and *Prison Memoirs of an Anarchist,* and *Anarchism and Other Essays* deserved to be put on the Index Expurgatorius.

My delayed mail brought news from Harry Weinberger about the treatment of Sasha in the Atlanta Federal prison and of our counsel's protest to Washington in connexion with it. Sasha had been confined in an underground dungeon, deprived of all his privileges, including mail and reading-matter, and kept on a reduced diet. The solitary was breaking down his health, and Weinberger had threatened a campaign of publicity against the palpable persecution of his client by the prison administration. Our comrades Morris Becker and Louis Kramer, as well as several other politicals in Atlanta, were sharing a similar fate.

Among my letters was also one containing details of the harrowing death of the brilliant German anarchist Gustav Landauer. Another prominent victim had been added to the number that included Rosa Luxemburg, Karl Liebknecht, and Kurt Eisner. Landauer had been arrested in connexion with the revolution in Bavaria. Not satisfied with shooting him, the reactionary fury had resorted to the dagger to finish up its ghastly job.

Gustav Landauer was one of the intellectual spirits of the *" Jungen "* (the " Young "), the group that had seceded from the German Social Democratic Party in the early nineties. Together with the other rebels he had founded the anarchist weekly, *Der Sozialist.* Gifted as a poet and writer, the author of a number of books of sociological and literary value, he soon made his publication one of the most vital in Germany.

In 1900 Landauer had drifted from the Kropotkin communist-anarchist attitude to the individualism of Proudhon, which change also involved a new conception of tactics. Instead of direct revolutionary mass action he favoured passive resistance, advocating cultural and co-operative efforts as the only constructive means of fundamental social change. It was sheer irony of fate that Gustav Landauer, turned Tolstoyan, should lose his life in connexion with a revolutionary uprising.

While the Kaiser's socialists were busy annihilating their own political kin, the fate of their country was decided at Versailles. The labour pains of the peace negotiators were long and distressing, the result a still-born child more hideous in a measure than the war. Its fearful effect on the German people and the rest of the world completely vindicated our stand against the slaughter which was to end all slaughter. And Woodrow Wilson, that innocent at the diplomatic gaming-table, how easily he had been duped by the European sharks! The President of the mighty United States had held the world in the palm of his hand. Yet how pathetic was his failure, how complete his collapse! I kept wondering how our worshipful American intelligentsia felt at seeing their idol no longer protected by his Presbyterian mask. The war to end war terminated in a peace that carried a rich promise of more terrible wars.

Among my literary correspondents I greatly enjoyed Frank Harris and Alexander Harvey. Harris had always been very thoughtful, supplying me with his magazine and also frequently writing to me. Owing to his stand on the war, few of his epistles had reached me the previous year, nor any copies of *Pearsons'*, of which Frank was the editor. But in 1919 I was permitted to receive my mail more regularly. I liked Harris's publication more for its brilliant editorials than its social attitude. We were too far apart in our conception of the changes necessary to bring humanity relief. Frank was opposed to the abuse of power; I to the thing itself. His ideal was a benevolent despot ruling with a wise head and generous hand; I argued that " there ain't no such animal " and could not be. We often clashed, yet never in an unkind way. His charm was not in his ideas, but in his literary quality, in his incisive and witty pen and his caustic comments on men and affairs.

Our first clash, however, was not over theories. I had read his *The Bomb* and had been profoundly moved by its dramatic power. The true historic background was wanting, but as fiction the book was of a high order, and I felt it would help to dispel the ignorant prejudices against my Chicago comrades. I had included the volume among the literature we sold at my lectures, and it had been reviewed by Sasha in *Mother Earth* and advertised in our columns.

We had been roundly condemned for it by Mrs. Lucy Parsons, the widow of Albert Parsons. She denounced *The Bomb* because Harris had not kept to the actual facts, and also because Albert emerged from the pages of the book a rather colourless person. Frank Harris claimed to have written, not a history, but a novel of a dramatic event. I had no quarrel with him on that score. But Mrs. Parsons was entirely right in repudiating Harris's erroneous conception of Albert Parsons.

I had expressed my surprise to Frank at his apparent failure to appreciate the personality of Parsons. Far from being colourless or weak, he should have been, together with Louis Lingg, the hero of the drama. Parsons had deliberately walked into the arena to share the fate of his comrades. He had done more; he scorned a chance to save his own life by accepting a pardon because it did not include the lives of the other men.

In reply Frank explained that he had made Lingg the outstanding personality in his novel because he had been impressed by the determination, fearlessness, and stoicism of the boy. He had admired Lingg's contempt for his enemies, and his proud choice of death by his own hand. Since he could not have two heroes in one story, he had given preference to Lingg. In my next letter I called his attention to the fact that the best Russian writers, such as Tolstoy and Dostoyevsky, often had more than one hero in their works. Moreover, the sharp contrast between Parsons and Lingg would have only enhanced the dramatic interest of *The Bomb* had the true grandeur of Albert Parsons been faithfully portrayed. Harris admitted that the values of the Haymarket tragedy had by no means been exhausted in his book; perhaps some day he would write a story from another angle, with Albert Parsons as the dominant figure.

Alexander Harvey's correspondence greatly amused me. He worshipped at the shrine of Greek and Latin culture; nothing that had come to us since counted for much in his estimation. " Believe me," one of his letters read, " the truest conscientious objector was Sophocles. The decay of the ancients goes hand in hand with the loss of liberty. You yourself remind me of Antigone. There is something splendid and Greek in your life and in your gospel." I wanted him to explain the existence of slavery in his beloved old world, and I asked for enlightenment on how it happened that I, who had never looked at a Latin or Greek grammar, should yet prize liberty above everything else. His only explanation was several volumes of Greek plays in English translation.

My library had been greatly enlarged by many books friends had

sent me, among them works by Edward Carpenter, Sigmund Freud,
Bertrand Russell, Blasco Ibañez, Barbusse, and Latzko, and *Ten
Days that Shook the World*. John Reed's story, engrossingly thrilling,
helped me to forget my surroundings. I ceased to be a captive in the
Missouri penitentiary and I felt myself transferred to Russia, caught
by her fierce storm, swept along by its momentum, and identified with
the forces that had brought about the miraculous change. Reed's
narrative was unlike anything else I had read about the October Revolution — ten glorious days, indeed, a social earthquake whose tremors
were shaking the entire world.

While still in the atmosphere of Russia, I received — significant
coincidence! — a basketful of deep-red roses, ordered by Bill Shatoff,
of Petrograd. Bill, our co-worker in many fights in America, our jovial
comrade and friend, in the very midst of the Revolution, surrounded
by enemies within and without, facing danger and death, thinking of
flowers for me!

HELENA HOCHSTEIN AND HER SON DAVID

## CHAPTER XLIX

L IFE IN PRISON, UNLESS ONE HAS VITAL INTERESTS OUTSIDE, IS
deadly dull. Until Kate arrived, our existence in Jefferson had
been no exception. But the publicity campaign kept up by Frank
O'Hare by means of his wife's letters brought many surprises and
unexpected results. After the library and the hot food came an influx
of convict plumbers, carpenters, and mechanics to install shower-baths.
Then the walls of our wing were whitewashed and preparations were
being made to whitewash the cells. Presently Kate received an offer
to be excused from the shop. " Is it only because of the pull you have
outside? " I asked her. " My friends have tried hard to relieve me
from machine work, but I am still pegging away at it." " You have
never been together with Mr. Painter on a political job," Kate
laughed; " we are friends." " You mean you know each other from
behind the scenes? " I questioned. " Precisely," giggled Kate, " and
now you understand why Mr. Painter is willing to do things for me."
Kate refused to be released from the shop; it would spoil her chance
of keeping up her criticism of evils that needed to be reformed.

Meanwhile it became known that an investigator was to visit the
penitentiary. The usual investigating fraternity inspires prisoners with
anything but confidence. This man, however, was from the *Survey,*
the liberal research magazine. Winthrop Lane had published a report
of the unique strike of the politicals in the Leavenworth disciplinary
barracks, and we had been impressed by his sympathetic understanding
of the protestants in prison; his coming was therefore looked forward
to with interested suspense.

When I was called down to the office, I was surprised to find myself
alone with Mr. Lane. It was a pleasant experience to be able to con-
verse with a human being without the surveillance of the head matron, which we always had to endure at visits. Mr. Lane had already

investigated the blocks and the punishment cells in the men's wing, and we discussed penal institutions in general. I did not suggest that he visit the shop, assuming that he would do so as a matter of course. But to my amazement Mr. Lane failed to come to see the women at work. Whatever his report about our place, it would be wanting, I feared, without his personal observation of the very thing that caused all the hardships and trouble in the prison.

My fiftieth birthday I spent in the Missouri penitentiary. What more fitting place for the rebel to celebrate such an occasion? Fifty years! I felt as if I had five hundred on my back, so replete with events had been my life. While at liberty I had hardly noticed age creeping up, perhaps because I had counted my real birth from 1889, when, as a girl of twenty, I had first come to New York. Like our Sasha, who would jestingly give his age minus his fourteen years in the Western Penitentiary, I used to say that my first twenty years should not be held against me, for I had merely existed then. The prison, however, and still more the misery abroad in every land, the savage persecution of radicals in America, the tortures social protestants were enduring everywhere, had an ageing effect on me. The mirror lies only to those who want to be deceived.

Fifty years — thirty of them in the firing line — had they borne fruit or had I merely been repeating Don Quixote's idle chase? Had my efforts served only to fill my inner void, to find an outlet for the turbulence of my being? Or was it really the ideal that had dictated my conscious course? Such thoughts and queries swirled through my brain as I pedalled my sewing-machine on June 27, 1919.

The week before, I had again fallen ill and had been told by the physician to stay in my cell. Feeling particularly weak on my birthday, I had remained in bed, hoping that Dr. McNearney would understand that I needed a rest. To my astonishment an orderly came to tell me that the doctor had ordered me back to the shop. I was certain that McNearney knew nothing about it, and that it was the head matron's doing. But I was too weary of the continual struggle with her, and I dragged myself to work. At noon I discovered that the lady had imposed an additional punishment on me. She had not delivered the flowers, packages, and stack of mail received for me. In the evening I found half of the flowers and plants wilted from the excessive heat.

It was provoking — they had committed no offence, and I thought it petty revenge to have denied them drink and air. I proceeded to clean and bathe them in salt water. Some raised their drooping heads and seemed to revive. They nodded tender birthday messages from my darling Stella and from many other known and unknown well-wishers. A beautiful pink rose rambler plant had come from my troubadour of many years, Leon Bass. No adversity in domestic and business life could dim his interest in our ideas or his devotion to me. Leon was a true knight of old, serving without thought of reward. His solicitude for my welfare was most touching and a rare trait among radicals, who seem to think that people in public life have no personal needs or desires.

Many familiar names were among those of the fifty signers of the birthday message I received from New York and the thirty-five signatures of another from Los Angeles. A box of oranges from a friend's own grove in California; luscious apples and preserves from Butler Davenport, my friend for years, whose dramas were performed in the quaint little theatres built by himself on his estates in Connecticut and in New York. From East and West the congratulatory messages came, expressing appreciation of my work and what I had meant to the writers.

My own family's affection for me had grown with the years. Sister Lena had blossomed out like a flower in her love for me. Her life, filled with hardships and pain, might have corroded the heart of many another woman. But Lena had become more gentle and understanding, even humble. "I do not presume to compare my love for you with Helena's," she once wrote me, "but I love you just the same." It made me remorseful to think of the poor affection I had given her in the past. My old mother had also come very close to me of late years. She kept sending me gifts, things made by her own trembling hands. Her birthday letter, written in Yiddish, was filled with affection for her most wayward child.

The thought of Helena was the only cloud on my birthday sky. Her daughter Minnie had come all the way from Manila to help her mother over their great loss. But my sister was wrapped in her precious dead, and the living could do nothing to loosen its hold. Helena alone had failed me on the day she had always filled with her love before. But I understood.

I felt myself very rich indeed. An abundance of affection and loyalty was my share, and it bore witness that my life and work had been worth the suffering and travail.

A few months after Kate had arrived she was granted the privilege of her typewriter, and my correspondents had been blessing her ever since. "Such a relief," they wrote, "not to have to spend hours in puzzling out your hieroglyphics." On a previous occasion, when I had acquired a Blickensdoerfer, they had also rejoiced to be free from the ordeal of trying to decipher my letters. Alas, their glee had been premature, because my typing did not prove more legible than my handwriting. I was trying hard to improve, stoically enduring the pains in my neck from constant practice, but the heartless lot did not begin to appreciate it. They had even suggested I should be psycho-analyzed for the peculiar complex that made me strike the wrong keys. They kept on finding fault with my most perfect copy. But when Kate became my "secretary," all complaints ceased.

She was thorough in everything, particularly in mechanical things, and adept at handling machines, however intricate. Her father had been a mechanic, and Kate had grown up in his shop, dabbling in machinery since she had been a tot. Later she had become her parent's assistant, and her greatest pride was her membership in the Machinists' Union. But what is a union card among friends? Out of her bigness of heart, Kate scabbed for me. Besides the day's task and her own mail after work hours, she also did my letters. Shamelessly I took advantage of her good nature and exploited her for my correspondence. The Federal authorities had robbed me of my forum and of *Mother Earth,* and letters became my platform. Censorships had taught me to express proscribed ideas in guileless disguise.

With my good old comrade Jacob Margolis I argued hotly the merits and demerits of Soviet Russia. I agreed with him on the danger to the Revolution from the dictatorship of the proletariat, but I fought his lack of faith in the men who had helped October to birth and who were defending its gains against a hostile world. I stressed the point that the time would undoubtedly come when the anarchists would have to take issue with the Lenin-Trotsky group, but not while Russia was in danger from enemies within and without. My comrade replied that he certainly had no intention of siding with the interventionists. He was concerned, however, in keeping anarchism free from any affiliations with the political school that had always fought us in the past and would crush us in Russia just as soon as they should feel their State machine strong enough for it. Our controversy continued for a considerable time, proving as stimulating as a personal talk with Jake. Other letters to New York friends were in defence of Robert Minor, our co-worker in various campaigns. His cabled articles on Russia, which had appeared in one of the New York dailies, caused much indignation in radical ranks. While some of his criticisms of the Bolsheviki were plausible, they contained passages obviously not from Bob's pen. I felt that his reports were being doctored. I urged that it was infantile to suspect everybody as a traitor who did not fully accept the dicta of Lenin, Trotsky, or Zinoviev. They were human, like the rest of us, and likely to make mistakes. To call attention to the latter could not harm the Revolution. As for the apparently garbled accounts, we should have to wait for Robert Minor's return to America, when he could explain things.

On his return to America, Minor proved that his European articles had been deliberately altered in New York editorial rooms to hurt Russia and to injure his standing in radical ranks. He planned to see Sasha and me as soon as we should be released and to give us a full report of the situation in Russia.

An article in the *Liberator* signed "X" contained a violent attack on the anarchists in Russia. Stella had been assured by Max Eastman that a refutation from me would be published, and I devoted several Sundays to an analysis of the charges made against my Russian comrades. I pointed out that the writer had not adduced a single proof for his assertions, that he had shown gross ignorance of his subject, and that he had even lacked the courage to sign his name. I demanded that he come out in the open so that we could argue the matter fairly. A letter from Max Eastman spoke highly of my article and assured me that it would soon appear. But he did not keep his promise, and my refutation was not published.

I was not surprised. On a previous occasion Max Eastman had demonstrated his peculiar conception of free speech and press. His poetic soul had always craved these rights for himself and his group, but not for anarchists. Max Eastman was living up to the good old Marxist tradition.

Lack of fairness to an opponent is essentially a sign of weakness. And, truth to tell, Max Eastman was neither strong nor brave. His spiritual somersault at his trial, and his sudden glorification of the policies of America's "greatest statesman in the White House," testified to it. Well, what of it? He possessed other gifts worthy a king's ransom: he was a poet and handsome. Better a Napoleon in his own domain than a common soldier in the social battle.

It saddened me to learn that Catherine Breshkovskaya had left America without replying to my appeal. Nor had she expressed any protest against the crimes committed by Uncle Sam in the name of lofty ideals. Miss Alice Stone Blackwell had questioned her silence in the face of so much wrong. In reply the veteran fighter had said that she could not jeopardize her chances of helping the destitute children of Russia, for which purpose she had come to the United States.

Kate's repeated complaints about unfairness to the Federal prisoners finally brought an official investigator to question us. We were compelled to make the same task as the State prisoners and we were equally punished in case of failure. But we did not receive the same benefits. Advancement to Grade A gave the Federals only the right of a third letter a week whereas the State prisoners were rewarded by the reduction of five months on each year and were also made eligible to parole. The investigator interviewed us separately. His efforts were apparently exhausted by a significant remark to Kate. "You and Miss Goldman," he said, "must have stiffened the backs of these girls. I always find it difficult to get prisoners to talk frankly. But this time they expressed themselves freely and they all told the same story." The Federals desperately clung to the hope that the investigation would bring results. I did not try to discourage them, though I knew that even Mr. Lane, of the *Survey,* had failed to have his critical article on conditions in our prison accepted by the magazine.

A new batch of letters from Frank Harris served to strengthen the mutual-admiration society that had sprung up between us. I had been greatly impressed by his *Contemporary Portraits,* naming those of Carlyle, Whistler, Davidson, Middleton, and Sir Richard Burton as the most successful. Among the short stories I had chosen *Montes the Matador, The Stigmata,* and *Magic Glasses.* I wrote Frank that I regarded them as his literary masterpieces. I knew that he was inclined to feel hurt if one did not consider all his works great, and I feared that my preferences might impair our friendship. But Frank

Harris heaped coals of fire on my sinful head by calling me "a great
and unerring critic." "You will be out soon," one of his letters read,
"which delights my soul; but I will still be boiling in the fires of the
Philistines. Why do they not deport me? I would thus save passage
money." He asked permission to arrange a banquet in my honour
when I should be released. He had made no mention of Sasha, and I
informed him that, though I appreciated his offer, I could not accept
any testimonial of a public character that did not also include my
old pal.

A similar reception was being planned by Mrs. Margaret Sanger,
as Stella notified me. I felt much surprised at it. Friendship is best
tested in time of danger. While Sasha's fate was hanging in the balance in connexion with San Francisco, Mrs. Sanger had offered no
help and showed no interest. She had been good enough to permit her
name on the list of his publicity committee, but every leading radical
had done no less. Outside of that she had kept cautiously in the background, though she had always claimed to be a very particular friend
of Sasha. I had no desire to hurt Mrs. Sanger, but I had to decline
her proposal.

On August 28, 1919 Sasha and I had completed twenty months of
our two-year sentence. Wicked anarchists though we were, we had
earned four months each for good behaviour. We had done our bit
much longer than many of the boys in the dug-outs. We should have
been honourably discharged from service and allowed to return from
the prison front. But Judge Julius Mayer had willed it otherwise by
placing a high valuation on our heads. Twenty thousand dollars' fine!
A United States commissioner was sent to the penitentiary to question
me about my financial standing. He looked incredulous when I told
him that anarchist propaganda is a pleasure and not a paying business. He grew still more dubious when I explained that the Kaiser,
having been unseemly hurried in his departure from Germany, had
neglected to make provision for our welfare. The commissioner decided to "look into the matter." Meanwhile Berkman and I would
have to serve an extra month in payment of our fine, he declared. Two
months for twenty thousand dollars! When did Sasha and I ever
expect to earn so much money in so short a time?

Only thirty days. Then release from the hateful shop, the control,
the surveillance, the thousand humiliations prison involves. Back to
life and work again — with Sasha. Back to my family, comrades, and

friends. An alluring fantasy, soon dispelled by the immigration authorities. Ellis Island was waiting for the two distinguished guests. I wondered who would compete for my favours next. Would it be Russia, the long-awaited, or America, my old flame? In our uncertain fortunes only one thing was certain: Sasha and I would meet the future as we had always met it in the past.

The last days were drawing near. I had but one thing to regret: the friends I should have to leave behind. Little Ella, grown into my heart as my own child, still had six months to serve. I was less anxious about Kate, who was sure of a pardon before long. Ella would then have no one with her, and I grieved to part from her. And there were also poor little Aggie, the lifer, the coloured orderly Addie, serving ten years, and the other unfortunates who had become dear to me. I had tried to interest some of my women friends in New York in Addie. Several had responded and offered to give her a job when she was paroled. Did I know what she was "in for," they had inquired, "and would she be all right?" I could never bring myself to ask my fellow-prisoners on what charges they had been sent up. I would wait until they confided to me of their own accord. I told Addie what my correspondents had said. "I don't blame them at all," she commented; "they might think I'm here for stealin' or usin' dope. Tell 'em I'm here for killin' my man, who played me false." Convicts have their own code of ethics, I wrote back, and they can be trusted to live up to them, which is more than could be said of a great many people outside. Alice Stone Blackwell had asked no questions; she had secured employment for Addie and she would even pay her fare. But there the head matron had stepped in. She frightened Addie by telling her that "Emma Goldman's friends are Bolsheviki and bad women." She would only queer her chances for parole if the board should learn that she had such sponsors. Addie implored me to do nothing further in her case.

During my imprisonment death had robbed me of two more friends, Horace Traubel and Edith de Long Jarmuth. I had not known of their illness, and the news was a great shock. The poetic beauty of Horace's life accompanied him even to his grave. The church caught fire just as his friends had gathered to pay their last tribute. Red flames shooting on high greeted his remains. It seemed appropriately symbolic of Horace Traubel, the rebel and man.

Edith de Long Jarmuth, Japanese-looking with her blue-black hair, almond-shaped eyes, and marble-white skin, was like a lotus flower in alien soil. She was a strange and ethereal figure in her wealthy and heavy bourgeois home in Seattle. Later her apartment on Riverside Drive in New York became the rendezvous of radicals and intellectual Bohemians. Edith was their magnet, and she felt alive to their ideas and work. Her own interests, however, had no social roots; they sprang from her yearning for the exotic and the picturesque. In life as in art Edith was a dreamer who lacked creative strength. One loved her more for what she was than for what she did. Her personality and native charm were her greatest gifts.

Saturday, September 28, 1919, I left the Missouri penitentiary, accompanied by my faithful Stella, who had come from New York for the occasion. Only technically free, I was taken to the Federal Building to make an affidavit that I possessed no real estate or cash. The Federal agent looked me up and down. "You're dressed so swell, funny you claim to be poor," he commented. "I am a multimillionaire in friends," I replied.

The fifteen-thousand-dollar bond demanded by the Government pending inquiries by the Immigration Bureau was secured, and I was at last at liberty.

PRISON LABELS

## CHAPTER L

IN ST. LOUIS WE WERE ALMOST MOBBED BY FRIENDS, REPORTERS, and camera-men who had come to meet us at the station. I could not bear to see many people and I was eager to be left alone.

Stella grew uneasy on hearing that on our way east I intended to stop off in Chicago, where Ben was living. She implored me to give up the idea. "You will only lose the peace you have gained through months of struggle to free yourself from Ben," she pleaded. There was no need for anxiety, I assured her. In the isolation and loneliness of the cell one finds the courage to face the nakedness of one's soul. If one survives the ordeal, one is less hurt by the nakedness of other souls. I had worked my way through much anguish and travail to a better understanding of my relation with Ben. I had dreamed of having ecstatic love without the pettiness and jarring conditioned in it. But I learned to see that the great and the small, the beautiful and the mean, that had made up our life were inseparable springs from the same source, flowing to a common outlet. In my clarified perception the fine things in Ben now stood out in bolder relief, and the little no longer mattered. One so primitive as he, who was always moved by his emotions, could not do things half-way. He gave without measure or restraint. His best years, his tremendous zest for work, he had devoted to me. It is not unusual for woman to do as much for the man she loves. Thousands of my sex had sacrificed their own talents and ambitions for the sake of the man. But few men have done so for women. Ben was one of the few; he had dedicated himself completely to my interests. Emotionalism had guided his passion as it had his life. But, like nature unleashed, he would destroy with one hand the lavish gifts of the other. I had revelled in the beauty and strength of his giving, and I had recoiled from and struggled against the self-centred egotism which ignored and annihilated obstacles in the soul of the loved one. Erotically Ben and I were of the same earth, but in a cultural sense we were separated by centuries of time. With him social impulses, sympathy with mankind, ideas, and ideals were moods of the moment, and as fleeting. He had no means of sensing basic verities or inner need to convert them into his own.

My life was linked with that of the race. Its spiritual heritage was mine, and its values were transmuted into my being. The eternal struggle of man was rooted within me. That made the abyss between us.

In the solitude of prison I had lived away from the disturbing presence of Ben. Often my heart had called for him, but I had silenced its cry. I had promised myself after our last break never to see him again until I should have made order out of my emotional chaos. I had fulfilled my pledge; nothing was now left of the conflict that had lasted so many years. Neither love nor hate. Only a new friendliness and a clearer appreciation of what the man had given me. I was no longer afraid to meet Ben.

In Chicago he called, bringing a large bouquet of flowers. It was the same old Ben, instinctively reaching out and his eyes opening wide in wonder at meeting no response. No change in him nor understanding for mine. He wanted to give me a party at his home. Would I come, he asked. " Of course," I said, " I will come to meet your wife and your child." I went. The dead had buried their dead, and I felt serene.

In Rochester my people received me with their usual affection. Helena had been in Maine, whence she had written me: "I don't know how I got here. Minnie brought me. How anybody can think to divert me from my great sorrow, I cannot understand. The more I see of nature and people, the greater my loss. My misfortune goes everywhere with me." On our way to Rochester Stella had described Helena's condition and had cautioned me to be prepared. But my worst mental picture was not so horrible as the sight my dear sister presented. Emaciated to the bone, she was a bent old woman, moving with lifeless steps. Her face was shrunken and ashy, unutterable despair in her hollow eyes. I held her close to me, her poor little body convulsed with sobs. She had done nothing but weep since the news of David's death, my people told me; her life was ebbing out in tears.

"Take me away, let me live with you in New York," she pleaded. It had been her dream in our youth to be always near me. Now the moment had come to realize it, she reiterated. I was filled with pity and fear. My existence was so precarious, new uncertainties and dangers were already facing me. Could Helena stand such a life? But everything else had failed to save her from herself. She needed something to occupy her mind, physical exertion especially. Perhaps looking after her daughter and me would take her away from her dead. It was a last hope, and I held it out to her. I told her I would rent an apartment in New York at once, and soon Minnie could bring her to me. She sighed deeply and seemed somewhat consoled.

With Helena's collapse the care of two families had fallen upon my sister Lena. She worked for everybody without complaint; she drudged far beyond her strength and asked no reward. Lena was of the stuff of the millions who go through life unpraised by poet, unsung by lyre, heroic in their silent strength. The gloom I had found on my home-coming was broken only by the golden glow of Ian, our adorable baby of four, and by the sprightly energy of my mother, who was eighty-one. She was in poor health, but still busy with her charity interests, and she was the moving spirit in the numerous lodges to which she belonged. She was the *grande dame par excellence,* more careful of her toilet than her daughters. Always strong and self-assertive, Mother had, since Father's death, become a veritable autocrat. No statesman or diplomat excelled her in wit, shrewdness, and force of character. Whenever I visited Rochester, Mother had new conquests to report. For years the orthodox Jews of the city had discussed the need of an orphanage and a home for the indigent aged. Mother did not waste words; she located two sites, purchased them on the spot, and for months canvassed the Jewish neighbourhood for contributions to pay off the mortgage and build the institutions the others had only talked about. There was no prouder queen than Mother on the opening day of the new orphanage. She invited me to " come and speak a piece " on the great occasion. I had once told her that my aim was to enable the workers to reap the fruit of their labours, and every child to enjoy our social wealth. A mischievous twinkle had come into her still sparkling eyes as she replied: " Yes, my daughter, that is all very good for the future; but what is to become of our orphans now, and the old and decrepit who are alone in the world? Tell me that." And I had no answer to give.

One of her exploits had been to put the Rochester manufacturer of shrouds out of business because of exorbitant charges. The owner of the business, a woman, had a monopoly of furnishing the burial garments without which no orthodox Jew may be laid to final rest. An old woman of the poorest class needed a shroud, but her family could not pay the high price asked for it. When my mother learned of it, she at once proceeded in her usual energetic manner. She called on the heartless creature who had enriched herself on the dead, and demanded that the garment be supplied at once without pay, threatening to ruin her in case of refusal. The manufacturer remained unmoved, and my mother set to work forthwith. She bought white material and with her own hands made a shroud for the pauper; then she called on the largest dry-goods store in the city and succeeded in convincing the owner of the riches he would store up in heaven if he would sell the material in quantities at cost price. " Anything for you, Mrs. Goldman," the man had said, Mother reported proudly. Then she organized a group of Jewish women to sew the shrouds, and she made it known in the community that the garments would be furnished for ten cents apiece. The clever scheme brought about the bankruptcy of the monopolist.

Many anecdotes circulated about my mother, characteristic of her vitality and broad sympathies, but none amused me so much as the story of how Mrs. Taube Goldman had put the chairlady of a powerful lodge " in her place." At one of the meetings Mother had talked rather too long. Another member asked for the floor, and the chairlady timidly suggested that Mrs. Goldman had already exceeded her time. Drawing herself up to full stature, my mother defiantly announced: " The whole United States Government could not stop my daughter Emma Goldman from speaking, and a fine chance you have to make her mother shut up! "

Mother had not always known how to express her affection to her children, except to our " baby " brother, whom she had always loved best. But I remembered the occasion on which she gave me the greatest proof in her power that she also loved me. Mysteriously she had taken me aside to tell me that she had made her will and that she had deeded me her most cherished treasure. Would I promise to make use of it after her death? From a bureau drawer Mother took out her jewel-case and solemnly held it out to me. " Here, my daughter, is what I am leaving you," she said as she handed me the medals she had received from various charity organizations. Repressing my laughter with difficulty, I assured her that I had already received too many medals of my own, though less shiny than hers; I could not very well wear any more, but I would keep hers in loving esteem.

Harry Weinberger had gone to Atlanta to meet Sasha on his release. The fates had never been kind to him in prison; this time they robbed him of three days. Instead of September 28, Sasha was released on October 1. A number of detectives faced him on his discharge, among them representatives of Prosecutor Fickert of San Francisco. They attempted to claim Sasha as their prisoner, but Federal officers declared that they had prior claim upon him. Friends supplied his fifteen-thousand-dollar bond for appearance before the immigration authorities, and at last Sasha was again in our midst. He looked haggard and pale, but otherwise apparently his usual stoical and humorous self. But soon we realized that it was only the flush of his release and the joy of being free, for Sasha was very ill. Uncle Sam's prison had succeeded in accomplishing in twenty-one months what the Western Penitentiary of Pennsylvania had failed to do in fourteen years. Atlanta had broken his health and had sent him back a physical wreck, with the horrors of his experience burned into his soul.

Sasha had been kept in an underground dungeon for protesting against the brutalities practised on the other inmates. The cell was too small to move about in and fetid with the bucket of excrement that was emptied only once in twenty-four hours. He was allowed only two small slices of bread and one cup of water a day. Later on, for interceding for a coloured prisoner, he was again punished by the "hole," which measured two and a half feet by four and a half, and where he could not even stand up straight. The "hole" was provided with double doors, one iron-barred, the other "blind," thus entirely excluding all light and air. In that cell, known as "the tomb," one is subjected to gradual suffocation. It is the worst punishment known in the Atlanta penitentiary, and it is designed to break the prisoner's spirit and force him to beg for mercy. Sasha refused to do so. To keep from suffocating he had to lie flat on the floor with his mouth close to the groove where the double doors fit into the stone casing. Only thus could he keep alive. Released from "the tomb," he was for three months deprived of his mail privileges, allowed no books or other reading-matter, and not permitted any exercise whatever. After that he remained continuously in solitary and isolation for seven-and-a-half months, from February 21 to the day of his discharge, October 1.

The memory of Atlanta haunted Sasha upon his release. At night he would wake up in a cold sweat, tortured by the nightmare of his recent experience. His prison phantoms were no new misery to me, but Fitzi had not seen him in such a state, and it unnerved her. She had gone through much suffering and worry since 1916, and she was run down and depressed. Together with the responsibilities of her position in the Provincetown Playhouse, she had carried almost the entire brunt of the preparations for the Mooney general strike, the amnesty campaign, and the National Amnesty Day. The raising of funds for bail and trials and the care of imprisoned politicals had fallen mostly to her. With the help of a handful of comrades, among them Pauline, Hilda and Sam Kovner, Minna Lowensohn, and Rose Nathanson, Fitzi had accomplished a tremendous amount of work.

More wearing than the physical exertion involved in these activities had been her deep disappointment in the new element that had come into the Billings-Mooney fight. The labour politicians had well-nigh emasculated the militant spirit of the campaign for the California men. Owing to their faint-heartedness, the general strike, set for the first week of July, had completely failed. The same conservative elements had voted against and ruined the chances of a successful general strike in October. Some of the radical organizations were not much more encouraging; they had refused to include in the proposed protest the other political and labour prisoners. Fitzi had justly stressed the argument that the demand for a general amnesty would strengthen the movement for Mooney and Billings, but even so militant a man as Ed Nolan had at first voted against her proposal, though later he changed his attitude and supported her stand. The lack of vision and backbone on the part of the majority of the labour organizations had caused a split and had greatly injured all the rebels in prison.

Sasha's condition was growing steadily worse. An examination by our friend Dr. Wovschin showed the need of an operation, but with stubborn indifference Sasha ignored the physician's advice. Fitzi and I had to conspire with the doctor to take our patient by surprise. Late one afternoon Wovschin arrived with an assistant for a second examination. Sasha was away, we knew not where. On his return we learned that he had been invited to a veritable Jewish feast, specially prepared for him by the mother of Anna Baron, our former *Mother Earth* secretary. Dr. Wovschin was disgusted; he had never operated on anyone immediately after a grand repast. But it had to be now or never. The physician succeeded in coaxing Sasha on to the table under the pretext of having to look him over once more. Then he quickly proceeded to give him ether. Sasha, resisting the anæsthetic, put up a fierce fight, shouting that the Deputy Warden was trying to kill him and swearing to finish the s.o.b. I had unfortunately been detained by an important engagement, and when I hastened back home, I met Fitzi on the street running to a drug store. White as a ghost, she told me that enough ether had already been given Sasha to put several men to sleep, but more was still needed. I found the room looking like a battle-field. The eye-glasses of the assistant physician were smashed and his face lacerated. Dr. Wovschin had also not escaped damage. Sasha was on the table, already unconscious, but still gritting his teeth and denouncing the Deputy Warden. I took his hand in mine and spoke soothingly to him. Presently I felt my pressure returned, and then he quieted down.

When he came to after the operation, he opened his eyes and stared in terror at the foot of the bed. " The goddam Deputy! " he cried, about to leap at his throat. We held him down, assuring him that he was among friends. " Fitzi and I are near you, dear," I whispered; " no one will harm you." He looked incredulously at me. " I can see him plainly right there," he insisted. It took much effort to persuade him that he was only imagining himself still in Atlanta. He gazed steadily into my eyes. " If you say so, it must be true, and I believe you," he said at last, " but how strange is the human mind! " He went peacefully off to sleep.

On my return from Jefferson City I found destroyed what we had slowly built up through a long period of years. The literature confiscated in the raid had not been returned to us, and *Mother Earth,* the *Blast,* Sasha's *Prison Memoirs,* and my essays were under the ban. The large sums of money raised while we were in prison, including the three thousand dollars contributed by our old Swedish comrade, had gone for appeals in cases of conscientious objectors, in the political-amnesty activities, and in other work. We had nothing left, neither literature, money, nor even a home. The war tornado had swept the field clean, and we had to begin everything anew.

Among my first callers was Mollie Steimer, who came accompanied by another comrade. I had never met either of them before, but Mollie's remarkable stand at her trial, and all I knew about her, made me feel as if she had always been in my life. I was glad to meet the brave girl face to face and to tell her of my admiration and love. She was diminutive and quaint-looking, altogether Japanese in features and stature. But she had shown exceptional strength and she was typical of the Russian revolutionists in her earnestness and the severity of her dress.

Mollie and her escort informed me that they had come as delegates of their group to ask me to write for their *Bulletin,* which they were publishing underground. Unfortunately I could not comply with their request. Even if I were not already overburdened with too much work, I could not ally myself with secret activities. I told them that I had thought of continuing *Mother Earth sub rosa,* but had discarded the plan because of the hazard it involved for others. I was not afraid of danger if I could meet it in the open, but I did not want to be trapped by spies and informers, who are always found in secret revolutionary bodies. Mollie understood my attitude. She had not yet recovered from the shock she had experienced at the treachery of Rosansky, the boy who had delivered her and her comrades to the police. She felt, however, that, with every breath of freedom suppressed in the country, our ideas must be spread even at the risk of possible betrayal. I held that the results of such methods are not commensurate with the risk, and I refused to have anything to do with such inadequate efforts. My visitors were much disappointed, the young man even indignant. I disliked hurting them, but I could not alter my decision.

An additional disagreement between us was due to my attitude to Soviet Russia. My young comrades thought that the Bolsheviki, representing a government, should be treated by anarchists like other governments. I insisted that Soviet Russia, the object of attack by the combined reactionists of the world, was not at all to be considered as an ordinary government. I did not object to criticism of the Bolsheviki, but I could not approve active opposition to them, anyway not until they should be in a less dangerous situation.

I longed to take little Mollie in my arms, but she looked stern in her youthful fervour. I let her depart with just a friendly handshake.

She was a wonderful girl, with an iron will and a tender heart, but she was fearfully set in her ideas. "A sort of Alexander Berkman in skirts," I jokingly remarked to Stella. Mollie was a true factory child of revolutionary spirit. She had gone to work at the age of thirteen and she had continued in the shop until she fell into the hands of the authorities. She was essentially of the idealistic youth of Russia in times of the Tsar, who sacrificed their lives before they had scarcely begun to live. What a fearful fate — from the factory to the Missouri prison for fifteen years, with no joy in between for my lovely young comrade!

I found a cozy apartment, and soon Minnie arrived with her mother, and the three of us moved in. For a while it seemed as if Helena would get herself in hand. She was busy attending to the *ménage,* sewing and mending. To afford her more work, I used to invite many friends to dinner. Dutifully my sister would prepare the food, serve it attractively, and charm everybody with her personality. But soon the novelty wore off and the old woe was again upon her. It was no use — her life was crushed, she kept on saying; it had lost meaning and purpose. Everything in her was dead, dead as David in the Bois de Rappe. She could not continue, she insisted, she must make an end of it, and I must help her out of her purgatory. Day after day she would repeat her piteous appeal, and call me cruel and inconsistent for my refusal. I had always claimed that everyone had a right to do with his life what he willed, and that persons suffering from incurable disease should not be compelled to live. And yet I was refusing her the relief I would give even a sick animal.

It was madness, and yet I felt that Helena was right. I was inconsistent. I saw her dying by inches with a desperate determination to escape from life. It would be an act of humanity to help her do so. I had no doubt as to the justification of making an end to one's misery or aiding another in it when there is no hope of recovery. Moved by Helena's plea, I would decide to comply with her wishes; and yet I could not bring myself to cut short her life — the life of one who had been mother, sister, friend to me, everything I had had in my childhood. I continued to struggle with her in the silent hours of the night. In the day-time, when I had to leave her, I would go through sickening terror lest on my return home I should find her dashed on the sidewalk. I could not absent myself unless I knew that someone was staying with her when Minnie and I were out.

My deportation hearing, twice postponed, was finally set for October 27. Sasha had already made his statement prior to leaving Atlanta. He had refused to answer the questions of the Federal immigration agent, who had called on him in the prison to give him " a hearing " in the matter of deportation. Instead he had issued a declaration of his position, in which he said:

> The purpose of the present hearing is to determine my "attitude of mind." It does not, admittedly, concern itself with my actions, past or present. It is purely an inquiry into my views and opinions.
> I deny the right of anyone—individually or collectively—to set up an inquisition of thought. Thought is, or should be, free. My social views and political opinions are my personal concern. I owe no one responsibility for them. Responsibility begins only with the effect of thought expressed in action. Not before. Free thought, necessarily involving freedom of speech and press, I may tersely define thus: no opinion a law—no opinion a crime. For the government to attempt to control thought, to prescribe certain opinions or proscribe others, is the height of despotism.
> This proposed hearing is an invasion of my conscience. I therefore refuse, most emphatically, to participate in it.
>                                        ALEXANDER BERKMAN

Sasha, not being a citizen and not caring about that side of the issue, nevertheless joined me in my fight against deportation because he considered such governmental methods as the worst form of autocracy. I also had an additional reason for contesting the Washington scheme to drive me out of the country. The United States Government still owed me an explanation for the shady methods it had employed in 1909 to rob me of my citizenship. And I was determined to have them disclosed.

I had always longed to revisit Russia, and after the February-October Revolution I had definitely decided to return to my native land to help in its reconstruction. But I wanted to go of my own free will, at my own expense, and I denied the right of the government to force me. I was aware of its brutal strength, but I did not propose to submit without a fight. I was no more deceived in its outcome than I had been in regard to our trial. Now, as then, I was concerned primarily in publicly disclosing the utter hollowness of American political claims and the pretence that heralded citizenship is a sacred and inalienable right.

At my hearing before the immigration officials I found the inquisitors sitting at a desk piled high with my dossier. The documents, classified, tabulated, and numbered, were passed on to me for inspection. They consisted of anarchist publications in different languages, most of them long out of print, and of reports of speeches I had delivered a decade previously. No objection had been made to them at the time by the police or the Federal authorities. Now they were being offered as proof of my criminal past and as justification for banishing me from the country. It was a farce I could not participate in, and I consequently refused to answer any questions. I remained silent throughout the " hearing," at the end of which I handed to my examiners a statement, reading in part:

> If the present proceedings are for the purpose of proving some alleged offence committed by me, some evil or antisocial act, then I protest against the secrecy and third-degree methods of this so-called "trial." But if I am not charged with any specific offence or act, if—as I have reason to believe—this is purely an inquiry into my social and political opinions, then I protest still more vigorously against these proceedings, as utterly tyrannical and diametrically opposed to the fundamental guarantees of a true democracy. Every human being is entitled to hold any opinion that appeals to her or him without making herself or himself liable to persecution. . . .
>
> The free expression of the hopes and aspirations of a people is the greatest and only safety in a sane society. In truth, it is such free expression and discussion alone that can point the most beneficial path for human progress and development. But the object of deportations and of the Anti-Anarchist Law, as of all similar repressive measures, is the very opposite. It is to stifle the voice of the people, to muzzle every aspiration of labour. That is the real and terrible menace of the star-chamber proceedings and of the tendency of exiling those who do not fit into the scheme of things our industrial lords are so eager to perpetuate.
>
> With all the power and intensity of my being I protest against the conspiracy of imperialist capitalism against the life and the liberty of the American people.            EMMA GOLDMAN

The newspapers reported Mollie Steimer to be on a hunger-strike. We all felt very anxious about her, because the police, State and Federal, had been hounding our comrade ever since she had been released on bail. Within eleven months she had been arrested eight times, kept in station-houses for a night or a week, released and re-arrested without definite charges being preferred against her. In the recent raid of the Russian People's House, where the Workers' Council had their offices, Mollie had been hauled in by the immigration authorities, held for eight days, and then released on a thousand-dollar bond. Later, while walking on the street with a friend, she was accosted by two detectives and told that " the boss wanted " her. She was held in the office of the head of the New York " bomb squad " for three hours without being questioned, then taken to the stationhouse and locked up. The following morning she read in the press that she was charged with " inciting to riot." She was transferred to the Tombs and after a week's detention released on five thousand dollars' bail. She had barely reached her home when she was visited by three detectives with a Federal warrant for her arrest and taken to Ellis Island. There she had been held ever since. The entire machinery of the United States Government was being employed to crush the slip of a girl, weighing less than eighty pounds.

Fifteen years in prison were facing Mollie, and I wanted to prevail upon her not to waste her strength by a hunger-strike. As her counsellor, Harry Weinberger was permitted to visit her, and the commissioner allowed me to accompany him. We found her in a very weakened condition, but her will indomitable. She showed no trace of any ill feeling as a result of our previous disagreement. On the contrary, she was very glad to see me, sweet and friendly.

She was being kept locked up all the time, Mollie informed us, denied the right to mingle with the other politicals and to associate with those to be deported. She had repeatedly protested in vain, and finally she had decided on a hunger-strike. I agreed that her provocation was certainly extreme, but I urged that her life was too important to our movement to jeopardize her health. Would she terminate her strike if we should persuade the commissioner to change his treatment of her? She was reluctant at first, but finally consented. This time I did not hesitate to take my splendid comrade in my arms. She was like a little child to me whom I longed to shield from the cruelty of the world.

We succeeded in prevailing upon the commissioner to permit Mollie the right of association with her comrades. To save his face he promised " to look into the matter first," and make a change provided Miss Steimer would " meet him half-way." We sent Mollie the message and got her consent to supply her with food.

The same evening a reception dinner for Sasha and me was taking place at the Brevoort Hotel, arranged by our indefatigable Dolly Sloan. We had opposed the plan of an exclusive affair; we preferred Carnegie Hall or some large theatre where a popular admission price would permit large numbers to attend. But no place in Greater New York could be secured except the Brevoort, whose management alone lived up to their hospitable traditions. The evening was somewhat marred by the inevitable exclusion of many friends who had travelled from afar to be with us on the occasion. But the fine spirit of the evening made up for that disappointment. Lola Ridge, our gifted rebel poet, inspired the audience by reciting a graphic poem she had dedicated to Sasha and me, and the other speakers were equally generous in paying tribute to us. Even our old co-worker Harry M. Kelly, who had drifted away from us because of the World War, was again in our midst, the same kindly soul.

I spoke of our heroic young rebels on Ellis Island and of Mollie, whose courage and revolutionary integrity put many a man to shame. The Mollies of the rising generation had sprung from the soil we older anarchists had helped to plough, I said. They were our children of the spirit and they would carry further their heritage. In this proud consciousness we might look with assurance towards the future.

A similar affair in behalf of Kate Richards O'Hare was arranged by the group of radical women that were working for Kate's pardon. Crystal Eastman presided, the speakers of the evening including Elizabeth Gurley Flynn and me. I talked about Kate's life in the Jefferson City prison and of the good she had achieved for the unfortunates there. I dwelt on the fine spirit of her comradeship, and I related some personal details of our sojourn in the penitentiary that illustrated Kate's character. Her complex about her hair particularly amused the audience. Not for anything would she appear in the shop without an elaborate coiffure. The ritual required considerable time and effort, and, as there was no opportunity for it in the morning, Kate used to devote the last evening hours to it. Once I was awakened at night by Kate lustily swearing. " What is it, Kate? " I called to her. " Stuck again by a hairpin, darn it," she replied. " You will be vain," I teased her. " Sure," she retorted; " how else am I to show off my beauty? Nothing in this world can be had without a price, as you well know yourself." " Well, I would not pay for such foolishness as curled hair." " Why, E. G., how you talk. Just ask your male friends, and you'll find out that a fine coiffure is more important than the best speech." The diners roared, and I was sure most of them agreed with Kate.

The gods had never been miserly in providing me with care and work. No sooner had Sasha left his sick-bed than another patient was on hand: Stella was laid up and had to be nursed. My only chance for rest was when some friends managed to kidnap me, as my friend Aline Barnsdall presently did.

I had first met her at my lectures in Chicago. She was keenly interested in the drama and she had staged some modern plays in that city. We spent many pleasant hours together, and I had an opportunity of learning that she was also wide awake to social problems, particularly to free motherhood and birth-control. Her interest in the Mooney-Billings case proved that her attitude was not mere theory. She had been among the first to contribute to the defence and she had also extended a large loan for the purpose. It was not until I was sent to prison, however, that Aline made me feel that she really cared for me. Her coming to Chicago from the Coast to welcome me on my release brought her very near and helped to cement our friendship, begun four years before. On her arrival in New York she carried me off and made me forget for a while the troubles of the world.

One day, as we sat discussing my approaching deportation, I happened to quote Ibsen to the effect that it is the struggle for the ideal that counts, rather than the attainment of it. My life had been rich and colourful, and I had nothing to regret. "What about material results?" Aline suddenly asked. "Nothing except my good looks," I replied jestingly. My friend grew thoughtful and then inquired whether I would be able to cash a cheque. I could, I told her, but it were better for her not to have my name in her cheque-book. Aline declared that she had the right to dispose of her money as she pleased; the government had no business to control such things. Then she handed me a cheque for five thousand dollars, to be applied to the fight against my deportation or for my needs if I should be compelled to leave the country.

I did not trust myself to thank Aline for her gracious gesture; I had to get my emotions in hand first. Later in the evening I told her that the most disturbing feeling in regard to my deportation was the dread of dependence. Never once since I had come to America had I known the fear of not being able to stand on my own feet. I should rather keep my independence in poverty than give it up for wealth. It was the only treasure which I guarded as a miser does his possessions. To be driven out of the land I had called my own, where I had toiled and suffered for years, was not a cheerful prospect. But to come to other shores penniless and without the hope of immediate adjustment was for me a calamity indeed. It was not the dread of poverty or want; it was the fear of having to do the bidding of those who have the power to withhold the means of existence. This spectre had worried me most. " Your cheque is not an ordinary gift," I said to Aline; " it will be the means of keeping me free, and it will enable me to retain my independence and self-respect. Do you understand? " She nodded, and my heart expanded in gratitude no words could express.

A year had passed since the Armistice, and political amnesty had been granted in every European country. America alone failed to open her prison doors. Instead, official raids and arrests increased. There was hardly a city where workers known as Russians or suspected of sympathy with radical ideas were not being picked up, taken at their work-benches or on the street. Behind these raids stood Attorney General Mitchell Palmer, panicky at the thought of radicals. Many of the arrests were accompanied by brutal manhandling of the victims. New York, Chicago, Pittsburgh, Detroit, Seattle, and other industrial centres had their detention houses and jails filled with these " criminals." I was besieged by requests for lectures. The Federal deportation mania was terrorizing the foreign workers of the country, and there were many calls upon me to speak on the matter and enlighten the people on the subject.

Our own fate was hanging in the balance, and Sasha was still an invalid. It seemed preposterous to begin a lecture tour, yet I could not refuse. I had a foreboding that it would be my last opportunity to raise my voice against the shame of my adopted land. I consulted Sasha and he agreed that I ought to go. I suggested that he come with me; it would help him to forget Atlanta and enable him to be with our comrades for perhaps the last time, and he consented.

Our friends and counsel unconditionally opposed our undertaking the campaign. The question of our deportation was still under consideration by the Federal Government, and it was therefore inadvisable to prejudice our case, they argued. But Sasha and I felt that it was the psychological moment to speak out in behalf of Russia. We could not allow personal interests to influence our decision.

From New York to Detroit and thence to Chicago we made a whirl-wind tour, our movements watched by local and Federal agents, every utterance noted down and attempts made to silence us. Unperturbed we continued. It was our last supreme effort and we felt our die had been cast.

Notwithstanding sensational press reports of police interference, warnings to keep away from our gatherings, and similar methods cal-culated to deter our audiences from attending, our meetings in Detroit, as well as in Chicago, were crowded by thousands. No ordinary assem-blies, these; monster demonstrations they were, a tempest of vehement indignation against government absolutism and of homage to our-selves. It was the eloquent voice of the awakened collective soul, thrilled by new hope and aspiration. We merely articulated its yearn-ings and dreams.

During the farewell dinner given us by our friends in Chicago, on December 2, reporters dashed in with the news of Henry Clay Frick's death. We had not heard of it before, but the newspaper men suspected that the banquet was to celebrate the event. "Mr. Frick has just died," a blustering young reporter addressed Sasha. "What have you got to say?" "Deported by God," Sasha answered dryly. I added that Mr. Frick had collected his debt in full from Alexander Berkman, but he had died without making good his own obligations. "What do you mean?" the reporters demanded. "Just this: Henry Clay Frick was a man of the passing hour. Neither in life nor in death would he have been remembered long. It was Alexander Berkman who made him known, and Frick will live only in connexion with Berkman's name. His entire fortune could not pay for such glory."

The next morning brought a telegram from Harry Weinberger informing us that the Federal Department of Labor had ordered our deportation, and that we must surrender on December 5. We had two more days of freedom and another lecture on hand. There was much to attend to in New York, and Sasha left to arrange our affairs there. I remained for the last meeting. However the storm might rage and the waves mount high, I was determined to face it to the end.

The next day I took the fastest train for New York, Kitty Beck and Ben Capes accompanying me. It was a royal send-off that was given me on leaving Chicago. Our friends and comrades almost mo-nopolized the station platform, the sea of faces expressive of the most precious token of complete solidarity and affection.

I was on the fastest American train, travelling in state with my two companions. "A sleeper or compartment on what may be your last trip in the U. S.?" my friends had declared; " never!" A drawing-room was none too good, and champagne to go with it. Somehow Benny had managed to unearth a couple of bottles in spite of Prohibition. He was an old hand at getting on the good side of porters, and he captured our darky's heart. Our porter had been busying himself about our room and sniffing the air all the time. " Great stuff," he grinned, closing one eye. " Bet your life, George," Benny admitted; " can you get us a bucket of ice?" "Yah, sah, a whole chest." We had not enough bottles to fill a refrigerator, Ben told him, but he might " come in on the swag " if he would bring an extra glass. The sly Negro proved to be a philosopher and artist. His observations on life were keen and his mimicry of the passengers and their foibles masterly.

Kitty and I, left alone, talked into the wee hours of the morning. Her life had been very tragic, perhaps because nature had made her all too lavish. Giving was to her a ritual, to serve to the uttermost her only impulse. Whether it was the man she loved, a friend, or a beggar, a stray cat or a dog, Kitty always emptied the fullness of her heart. She could exact nothing for herself, yet I have seldom known a being so in need of affection. Those in her life accepted from her as a matter of course; few, if any, of them understood the craving of her own heart. Kitty was born to give, not to receive. That was at once her supreme achievement and her defeat.

At the Grand Central terminal in New York friends awaited us, including Sasha, Fitzi, Stella, Harry, and other intimates. There was no time left even to go to my apartment to bid my dear Helena good-bye. We piled into taxis and drove straight to Ellis Island. There Sasha and I surrendered, while Harry Weinberger prepared to demand the return of the thirty thousand dollars deposited as our bond.

"That is the end, Emma Goldman, isn't it? " a reporter remarked. "It may only be the beginning," I flashed back.

# CHAPTER LI

THE ROOM I WAS ASSIGNED TO ON THE ISLAND ALREADY CONTAINED two occupants, Ethel Bernstein and Dora Lipkin, who had been rounded up at the raid of the Union of Russian Workers. The documents discovered there consisted of English grammars and text-books on arithmetic. The raiders had beaten up and arrested those found on the premises for possessing such inflammatory literature.

To my amazement I learned that the official who had signed the order for our deportation was Louis F. Post, Assistant Secretary of Labor. It seemed incredible. Louis F. Post, ardent single-taxer, champion of free speech and press, former editor of the *Public,* a fearless liberal weekly, the man who had flayed the authorities for their brutal methods during the McKinley panic, who had defended me, and who had insisted that even Leon Czolgosz should be safeguarded in his constitutional rights — he now a champion of deportation? The radical who had offered to preside at a meeting arranged after my release in connexion with the McKinley tragedy, now favouring such methods? I had been a guest at his home and entertained by him and Mrs. Post. We had discussed anarchism and he had admitted its idealist values, though he had doubted the practicability of their application. He had assisted us in various free-speech fights and he had vigorously protested by pen and voice against John Turner's deportation. And he, Louis F. Post, had now signed the first order for deporting radicals!

Some of my friends suggested that Louis F. Post, being an official of the Federal Government, could not go back on his oath to support the mandates of the law. They failed to consider that in accepting office and taking the oath he had gone back on the ideals he had professed and worked for during all his previous years. If he were a man of integrity, Louis F. Post should have remained true to himself and should have resigned when Wilson forced the country into war.

He should have resigned at least when he found himself compelled to order the deportation of people for the opinions they entertained. I felt that Post had covered himself with ignominy.

The lack of stamina and backbone on the part of such American radicals was tragic. But why expect a braver stand from Louis F. Post than from his teacher Henry George, the father of single-tax, who had failed my Chicago comrades at the eleventh hour? His voice carried great weight at the time and he could have helped to save the men in whose innocence he had believed. But political ambition proved stronger than his sense of justice. Louis F. Post was now following in the footsteps of his admired single-tax apostle.

I sought comfort in the thought that there still were some single-taxers of integrity and moral strength. Bolton Hall, Harry Weinberger, Frank Stephens (my comrades in many free-speech fights), Daniel Kiefer, and scores of others had stood their ground — against war and the new despotism. Frank Stephens, arrested as a conscientious objector, had in protest even declined to accept bail. Daniel Kiefer was another libertarian of true metal. Liberty was a living force in his private life as in his public activities. He was one of the first single-taxers to take an active part against America's entry into the war and against the " selective" draft. He heartily abhorred renegades of the type of Mitchell Palmer, Newton D. Baker, and other weak-kneed Quakers and pacifists. Nor did he spare his friend Louis F. Post for his betrayal.

Judge Julius M. Mayer, of the United States District Court, dismissed Harry Weinberger's writ of habeas corpus and refused to admit us to bail. But the hearing elicited valuable information. The attorney for the United States Government stated that Jacob Kershner had been dead for years; in fact, he was dead at the time his citizenship was revoked, in 1909. The official admission definitely stamped the action of the Federal authorities as a deliberate attempt to deprive me of citizenship by disfranchising the *dead* Jacob Kershner.

Our counsel was not one to accept defeat easily. Beaten at one place, he would train his guns upon another. The United States Supreme Court was his next objective. He would apply for a writ of error, he informed us, and he would insist on our being admitted to bail. Then we could proceed with the fight for my citizenship. Harry was irrepressible, and I was glad to take advantage of every hour left me on American soil.

Sasha and I had long before decided to write a pamphlet on deportation. We knew that the Ellis Island authorities would confiscate such a manuscript, and it therefore became necessary to prepare and send it out secretly. We wrote at night, our room-mates keeping watch. In the morning, during our joint walks, we would discuss what we had written and exchange suggestions. Sasha made the final revision and gave it to friends to smuggle out.

Each day brought scores of new candidates for deportation. From various States they came, most of them without clothes or money. They had been kept in jails for months and were then shipped to New York just as they were at the time of their unexpected arrest. In that condition they were facing a long voyage in the winter. We bombarded our people with requests for clothing, blankets, shoes, and other wearing-apparel. Soon supplies began to arrive, and great was the rejoicing among the prospective deportees.

The condition of the emigrants on Ellis Island was nothing short of frightful. Their quarters were congested, the food was abominable, and they were treated like felons. These unfortunates had cut their moorings in the homeland and had pilgrimed to the United States as the land of promise, liberty, and opportunity. Instead they found themselves locked up, ill-treated, and kept in uncertainty for months. I marvelled that things had changed so little since my Castle Garden days of 1886. The emigrants were not permitted to mingle with us, but we managed to get from them notes that strained all our linguistic acquirements, almost every European language being represented. It was little enough we were in a position to do for them. We interested our American friends and did the best we could to show the forsaken strangers that not all of the United States was represented by official barbarians. We were loaded with work, and neither Sasha nor I could complain of ennui.

An attack of neuralgia proved very timely. The island dentist failed to alleviate my pain; the commissioner, however, refused to let my own dentist attend me. My agony becoming unbearable, I made a vigorous protest, and finally the island authorities promised to communicate with Washington for instructions. For forty-eight hours my teeth became a Federal issue. Secret diplomacy at last solved the great problem. Washington consented to let me go to my dentist, accompanied by a male guard and a matron.

The dentist's reception room became my rendezvous. Fitzi, Stella, Helena, Yegor, our little Ian, dear old Max, and other friends

gathered there. Waiting for treatment became a joy, time passing
all too quickly.

Harry Weinberger was meeting with unexpected difficulties in
Washington, due to bureaucratic pettiness and red tape. The Clerk
of the Court refused to accept his papers because they were not in
printed form. Harry successfully appealed to Chief Justice White. On
December 11 he was permitted to argue his motion, but the Court
denied us the writ of error. A stay of deportation for Sasha was also
refused. The documents in my case were ordered printed and returned
within one week.

I decided that if Sasha was to be driven out of the country, I would
go with him. He had come into my life with my spiritual awakening,
he had grown into my very being, and his long Golgotha would for
ever remain our common bond. He had been my comrade, friend, and
co-worker through a period of thirty years; it was unthinkable that he
should join the Revolution and I remain behind.

"You are staying to make the fight, aren't you?" Sasha asked me
at recreation that day. I could do much for the deportees, he added,
as well as for Russia, if I should establish my right to remain in the
United States. The same old Sasha, I thought; always considering
propaganda values first. I could hardly restrain the pang I felt over his
detachment even at such a moment. Yet I knew the real Sasha; I knew
that although he would not admit it even to himself, there was a great
deal of the all-too-human underneath his rigid revolutionary exterior.
"It's no use, old scout," I said; "you can't get rid of me so easily.
I have made my decision, and I am going with you." He gripped hard
my hand, but he said not a word.

Few days remained to us on the hospitable United States shores,
and our girls were busy as beavers with the final preparations. No
effort was too hard for my darling Stella, no task too difficult for
Fitzi. They went about their work with aching hearts, yet they were
always cheery when with us. Separation from them and from Max,
Helena, and other loved ones was poignant indeed. Some day we might
all meet again, however — all except Helena. I entertained no such
hopes concerning my poor sister. I had a feeling she could not last
much longer, and I knew she intuitively echoed my thought. We clung
to each other desperately.

Saturday, December 20, was a hectic day, with vague indications
that it might be our last. We had been assured by the Ellis Island

authorities that we were not likely to be sent away before Christmas, certainly not for several days to come. Meanwhile we were photographed, finger-printed, and tabulated like convicted criminals. The day was filled with visits from numerous friends who came individually and in groups. Self-evidently, reporters also did not fail to honour us. Did we know when we were going, and where? And what were my plans about Russia? " I will organize a Society of Russian Friends of American Freedom," I told them. " The American Friends of Russia have done much to help liberate that country. It is now the turn of free Russia to come to the aid of America."

Harry Weinberger was still very hopeful and full of fight. He would soon get me back to America, he insisted, and I should keep myself ready for it. Bob Minor smiled incredulously. He was greatly moved by our approaching departure; we had fought together in many battles and he was fond of me. Sasha he literally idolized and he felt his deportation as a severe personal loss. The pain of separation from Fitzi was somewhat mitigated by her decision to join us in Soviet Russia at the first opportunity. Our visitors were about to leave when Weinberger was officially notified that we were to remain on the island for several more days. We were glad of it and we arranged with our friends to come again, perhaps for the last time, on Monday, no callers being allowed on the island on the Lord's day.

I returned to the pen I was sharing with my two girl comrades. The State charge of criminal anarchy against Ethel had been withdrawn, but she was to be deported just the same. She had been brought to America as a child; her entire family were in the country, as well as the man she loved, Samuel Lipman, sentenced to twenty years at Leavenworth. She had no affiliations in Russia and was unfamiliar with its language. But she was cheerful, saying that she had good cause to be proud: she was barely eighteen, yet she had already succeeded in making the powerful United States Government afraid of her.

Dora Lipkin's mother and sisters lived in Chicago. They were working people too poor to afford a trip to New York, and the girl knew that she would have to leave without even bidding her loved ones good-bye. Like Ethel, she had been in the country for a long time, slaving in factories and adding to the country's wealth. Now she was being kicked out, but fortunately her lover was also among the men to be deported.

I had not met either of the girls before, but our two weeks on Ellis

Island had established a strong bond between us. This evening my room-mates again kept watch while I was hurriedly answering important mail and penning my last farewell to our people. It was almost midnight when suddenly I caught the sound of approaching footsteps. " Look out, someone's coming! " Ethel whispered. I snatched up my papers and letters and hid them under my pillow. Then we threw ourselves on our beds, covered up, and pretended to be asleep.

The steps halted at our room. There came the rattling of keys; the door was unlocked and noisily thrown open. Two guards and a matron entered. " Get up now," they commanded, " get your things ready! " The girls grew nervous. Ethel was shaking as in fever and helplessly rummaging among her bags. The guards became impatient. " Hurry, there! Hurry! " they ordered roughly. I could not restrain my indignation. " Leave us so we can get dressed! " I demanded. They walked out, the door remaining ajar. I was anxious about my letters. I did not want them to fall into the hands of the authorities, nor did I care to destroy them. Maybe I should find someone to entrust them to, I thought. I stuck them into the bosom of my dress and wrapped myself in a large shawl.

In a long corridor, dimly lit and unheated, we found the men deportees assembled, little Morris Becker among them. He had been delivered to the island only that afternoon with a number of other Russian boys. One of them was on crutches; another, suffering from an ulcerated stomach, had been carried from his bed in the island hospital. Sasha was busy helping the sick men pack their parcels and bundles. They had been hurried out of their cells without being allowed even time to gather up all their things. Routed from sleep at midnight, they were driven bag and baggage into the corridor. Some were still half-asleep, unable to realize what was happening.

I felt tired and cold. No chairs or benches were about, and we stood shivering in the barn-like place. The suddenness of the attack took the men by surprise and they filled the corridor with a hubbub of exclamations and questions and excited expostulations. Some had been promised a review of their cases, others were waiting to be bailed out pending final decision. They had received no notice of the nearness of their deportation and they were overwhelmed by the midnight assault. They stood helplessly about, at a loss what to do. Sasha gathered them in groups and suggested that an attempt be made to reach their relatives in the city. The men grasped desperately at that last hope and appointed him their representative and spokesman. He succeeded in prevailing upon the island commissioner to permit the men to telegraph, at their own expense, to their friends in New York for money and necessaries.

Messenger boys hurried back and forth, collecting special-delivery letters and wires hastily scribbled. The chance of reaching their people cheered the forlorn men. The island officials encouraged them and gathered in their messages, themselves collecting pay for delivery and assuring them that there was plenty of time to receive replies.

Hardly had the last wire been sent when the corridor filled with State and Federal detectives, officers of the Immigration Bureau and Coast Guards. I recognized Caminetti, Commissioner General of Immigration, at their head. The uniformed men stationed themselves along the walls, and then came the command: " Line up! " A sudden hush fell upon the room. " March! " It echoed through the corridor.

Deep snow lay on the ground; the air was cut by a biting wind. A row of armed civilians and soldiers stood along the road to the bank. Dimly the outlines of a barge were visible through the morning mist. One by one the deportees marched, flanked on each side by the uniformed men, curses and threats accompanying the thud of their feet on the frozen ground. When the last man had crossed the gangplank, the girls and I were ordered to follow, officers in front and in back of us.

We were led to a cabin. A large fire roared in the iron stove, filling the air with heat and fumes. We felt suffocating. There was no air nor water. Then came a violent lurch; we were on our way.

I looked at my watch. It was 4:20 A.M. on the day of our Lord, December 21, 1919. On the deck above us I could hear the men tramping up and down in the wintry blast. I felt dizzy, visioning a transport of politicals doomed to Siberia, the *étape* of former Russian days. Russia of the past rose before me and I saw the revolutionary martyrs being driven into exile. But no, it was New York, it was America, the land of liberty! Through the port-hole I could see the great city receding into the distance, its sky-line of buildings traceable by their rearing heads. It was my beloved city, the metropolis of the New World. It was America, indeed, America repeating the terrible scenes of tsarist Russia! I glanced up — the Statue of Liberty!

Dawn was breaking when our barge pulled up alongside of the large ship. We were quickly transferred and assigned to a cabin. It was six o'clock. Exhausted, I crawled into my bunk and immediately fell asleep.

I was awakened by someone pulling at my covers. A white figure stood at my berth, probably the stewardess. Was I ill, she asked, to remain in bed so long. It was already six o'clock in the evening. I had shut out the hideous sights in twelve hours of blessed sleep. Stepping into the corridor, I was startled by someone roughly grabbing me by the shoulder. "Where are you going?" a soldier demanded. "To the toilet, if you must know it. Any objection?" He loosed his hold and followed me; he waited till I emerged again, and accompanied me back to the cabin. My girl companions informed me that guards had been stationed at our door since our arrival, and that they had also been escorted to the place of pressing needs every time they left the cabin.

At noon the next day we were conducted by the sentry to the officers' dining-room. At a large table sat the captain and his retinue, civilian and military. A separate table was assigned to us.

After lunch I requested to see the Federal official in charge of the deportees. He proved to be F. W. Berkshire, an immigration inspector detailed to manage the *Buford* expedition. Did we like our cabin and was the food good, he inquired solicitously. We had no complaints to make, I told him, but how about our men comrades? Could we take our meals with them and meet them on deck? "Impossible," Berkshire said. I then demanded to see Alexander Berkman. Also impossible. Thereupon I informed the inspector that I had no desire to cause trouble, but that I would give him twenty-four hours to change his mind about allowing me to talk to my friend. If my demand should be refused, at the expiration of that time I would go on a hunger-strike.

In the morning Sasha was brought under escort to see me. It seemed weeks since I had beheld his dear face. He told me that the conditions of the men were harrowing. They were cooped up in the hold of the ship, forty-nine in a place barely large enough for half that number. The rest of them were in two other compartments. The bunks, three tiers high, were old and worn out; those in the lower ones bumped their heads against the wire netting of the uppers every time they turned around. The boat, built at the end of the last century, had been used as a transport in the Spanish-American War and later discarded as unsafe. The floor of the steerage was wet all the time, the beds and blankets damp. Only salt water was to be had for washing, and no soap. The food was abominable, especially the bread, half-baked and uneatable. And, worst of all, there were only two toilets for the two hundred and forty-six men.

Sasha advised against pressing our request to eat with the men. It would be better to save what we could from our food for the sick boys who could not stomach the rations given them. Meanwhile he was trying to see what improvements he could secure. He was negotiating with Berkshire a list of demands he had submitted. I was happy to see Sasha full of vital energy again. He had forgotten his own physical troubles the moment he saw that the others were depending on him.

The officers celebrated Christmas in the dining-room in grand style. Ethel and Dora were too ill to leave their berths, and I could not bear to be alone with our jailers. Their Christmas feast was the veriest mockery to me. During the day we were taken out on deck, but not allowed to see the men. Insistence by Sasha and myself finally resulted in permission for him and Dora's friend to visit us.

Friction had developed between the deportees and those in charge of the *Buford*. The men were given no exercise in the fresh air, and Sasha had protested in the name of his comrades. The Federal representative, Immigration Inspector Berkshire, seemed willing to grant the demands, but he evidently stood in awe of those commanding a large force of soldiers. The inspector referred the men to the " chief," but Sasha refused to apply to the latter on the ground that the deportees were political and not military prisoners. Prisoners they were, indeed, continuously locked below deck, with sentries stationed day and night at the doors. Berkshire seemed to realize that our comrades were determined, and no doubt he felt that their resentment of the treatment they were receiving was justified. On Christmas Day he informed Sasha that the " higher authorities " had granted the demanded exercise.

Even then we were not allowed to associate with them. Political prisoners in other countries could freely mingle together during recreation hours regardless of sex, but American puritanism considered such things improper. To save morality we were kept locked in our cabin while the men were out for an airing. They had to remain on the lowest deck, with the waves often sweeping the boat and drenching them.

We were in rough waters, and many of the deportees fell ill. The coarse and badly cooked food was causing general stomach-complaints, and the dampness of the bunks laid many of the men low with rheumatism. The ship's doctor, too busy to attend the increasing number of patients, called upon Sasha to aid him. My offer to serve as nurse had been refused, but my hands were fully occupied with my two girl companions, who had to keep to their beds almost all the time. It was a very strained atmosphere those Christmas days, with forebodings of impending strife.

Our guards were extremely antagonistic, but with the passing of time I seemed to detect a gradual change. At first very forbidding and taciturn, their severity presently began to decrease. They entered into conversation with us, always on the alert, however, for the approach of an officer. Soon they confided to me that they had been tricked. The order for duty had reached them only the day previous to embarkation. They were in ignorance about the purpose and probable length of the voyage, and they had no idea of our destination. They had been told that they were to guard dangerous criminals being shipped somewhere. They were bitter against their officers, and some cursed them openly.

The sentry who had so roughly grabbed me the first day was holding out longest against us. One evening I kept watching him as he paced up and down in front of our cabin. He looked exhausted with the endless walking and I suggested that he sit down for a while. When I placed a camp-chair before him, his reserve broke down. " I daren't," he whispered, " the sergeant may be along." I offered to change rôles with him: I would remain on the look-out. " My God!" he exclaimed, unable to restrain himself any longer, " they told us you were a desperado, that you had killed McKinley and are always plotting against someone." From that moment he became very friendly, ready to do us any service. He had apparently spoken of the incident to his buddies, and they began to hang around our door, eager to show us some kindness. Our cabin had also a special attraction for them: my good-looking young companion Ethel. The soldiers were wild about her, discussed anarchism every free moment at their disposal, and became greatly interested in our fate. They hated their superiors. They would like to drop them into the sea, they said, because they were treated as chattel slaves and punished on every pretext.

One of the lieutenants also was very courteous and humane. He borrowed from me some books, and when he returned them, I found a note containing the news that Kalinin had become President of

Soviet Russia and hinting that we were not to be taken to any parts occupied by the Whites. Uncertainty as to our exact destination had all the time been a source of great anxiety and worry among the deportees. The information of the friendly officer proved a great relief in allaying our worst fears.

Meanwhile our men comrades were busy " agitating " their guards and fraternizing with them. The soldiers offered them their extra shoes and clothing for sale — " Might come handy in Russia," they said. Sasha's tact and his rich stock of humorous stories helped to win the hearts of Uncle Sam's boys. Posting a sentry as their look-out, they would crowd into his compartment and ask for funny yarns. He knew how to arouse their interest, and presently they began to put questions about the Bolsheviki and the soviets. They were eager to know what changes the Revolution had made, and they heard with amazement that in the Red Army the soldiers themselves elected their officers, and that even a commissar or general did not dare insult a private. They thought it wonderful that officers and men were on a footing of equality, and that all shared the same rations.

The steerage quarters were cold and wet. Many of the deportees had been given no opportunity to provide themselves with warm clothing, and there was much suffering as a result. Sasha suggested that those who had supplies should share what they could spare with their less fortunate comrades, and the men responded beautifully. Bags, suit-cases, and trunks were unpacked, everyone donating whatever he did not absolutely require for himself. Coats, underwear, hats, socks, and other apparel were piled up in one of the compartments below deck, and a commission was selected for distribution. The story of the proceedings, as told to me by Sasha, strikingly evidenced the splendid solidarity and fellow-feeling of the deportees. Themselves not too well provided for, they gave of their very last. The distribution had proved so fair and just that there had not been a single complaint.

The strains of Russian melodies, ringing from a hundred throats, were resounding through the *Buford.* The men were on deck, and their lusty voices rose above the rolling of the waves, reaching us in our cabin. The powerful baritone of the leader intoned the first stanzas, and then the entire crowd joined in the chorus. Revolutionary songs they sang, forbidden old Russian folk-tunes surcharged with the grief and yearning of the peasant, or echoing Nekrassov's women who heroically followed their lovers to prison and exile. All aboard grew silent, even the guards ceasing their march and listening with strained ears to the heart-rending melodies.

Sasha had become chummy with the assistant steward, and by means of him we organized a mail service. Copious notes passed every day between us, and we kept each other informed of happenings. Our friend, whom we had christened " Mac," became so devoted that he began to take a personal interest in our fate. He was very clever and ingenious, and he managed to appear at the most unexpected moments, just when he was needed. He seemed suddenly to develop the habit of walking with his hands under his apron, and he never came to us without some little gift hidden about his person. Delicacies from the pantry, sweet morsels from the captain's table, even fried chicken and pastry, we would find stuck away under our beds or in Sasha's bunk. And then one day he brought to Sasha several soldiers who confided to him that they had come as delegates of their comrades in arms. They had a serious mission. It was an offer to supply the deportees with guns and ammunition, to arrest all those in charge, turn the command of the *Buford* over to Sasha, and sail with all aboard to Soviet Russia.

It was January 5, 1920 when we reached the English Channel. The mail-bag carried away by the pilot contained our first letters to the United States. For the sake of safety they were addressed to Frank Harris, Alexander Harvey, and other American friends whose correspondence was subject to less scrutiny than that of our own people. Mr. Berkshire had also consented to let us send a cable to America. The favour was rather costly, amounting to eight dollars, but it was worth the relief our friends would feel at the message that we were alive and still safe.

When we left the English Channel, we were followed by an Allied destroyer. Twofold fear on the part of the *Buford* authorities was responsible for the presence of the warship. Our men had repeatedly complained about the quality of the bread rationed to them. Their protest ignored, they had threatened to strike. Mr. Berkshire brought Sasha " strict orders from the Colonel" for the deportees to submit. The men laughed in his face. " Berkman is the only ' Colonel ' *we* recognize," they shouted. The military chief sent for Sasha. He stormed about the disorganization of the ship's discipline, raved about the deportees fraternizing with the soldiers, and threatened to have the men searched for hidden weapons. Sasha boldly declared that his comrades would resist. The Colonel did not press the matter, and it was evident that he felt he could not rely on the force under his command. Sasha offered to solve the difficulty by putting two of the deportees, who were cooks, in charge of the bakery, without pay. The Colonel was loath to accept what he considered a reflection upon his supreme authority, but Sasha insisted and he won Berkshire to his side. Sasha's plan was finally adopted, and henceforth everyone enjoyed bread of the best quality. What might have proved serious trouble had thus been averted, but the talk of a strike, and the organized stand of our comrades, had had its effect on the commanding officers. Confidence in their exclusive power shaken, an Allied destroyer was a useful thing to have near. With a crowd on the *Buford* that had no respect for epaulets and gold braid, with two hundred and forty-nine radicals on hand who believed in strikes and direct action, the warship was a veritable godsend.

Another reason was the *Buford* itself. The battered old tub had been unseaworthy at the start, and the long journey had not improved her condition. The United States Government had been fully aware that the boat was unsafe, yet it had entrusted five hundred or more lives to it. We were heading for German waters and the Baltic Sea, the latter still thickly dotted with mines. The British destroyer was sadly needed in such a hazardous situation. The captain realized the imminent peril. He ordered the life-boats held in readiness and authorized Sasha to take charge of twelve of them and organize the men for quick action in case of alarm.

Many of the deportees had left considerable sums in American banks and postal savings. They had been denied time to draw their money, nor had they been given an opportunity to transfer it to their families. Sasha proposed to Berkshire that a statement be prepared of their holdings, to be sent to America with authorization for their kin to collect. The inspector seized upon the idea, but he left the work to Sasha. For days and late into the nights he worked tirelessly, collecting data and taking down depositions. When he got through, thirty-three affidavits were completed, disclosing that $45,470.39 had remained in the States. Some of the men had deposited their money in private banks and they preferred not to trust the government that had driven them out like dogs. It was all they had from long years of drudgery and economy.

After nineteen days of dangerous cruising we at last reached the Kiel Canal. Badly battered, the *Buford* had to remain for twenty-four hours for repair. The men were locked below deck, and special guards stationed on watch. German barges came alongside of our ship. They were in front of our cabin, and I threw them a note through the port-hole, telling them who we were. They consented to forward a letter, and I covered two sheets in the smallest German script I could write, describing our deportation, the reaction we left behind, and the treatment of the revolutionists imprisoned without benefit of amnesty. I addressed the letter to the *Republik,* organ of the Independent Socialists, and I added an appeal to the German workers to make their revolution as fundamental as that of Russia.

The men locked in the steerage and almost suffocating in the vile air made vigorous protests, demanding the daily exercise they had won after the first days of the journey. Meanwhile they were bombarding the German workers on the dock with missiles in which messages had been secreted. Presently the repair men, their work done and my letter safe in their hands, pulled away, shouting cheers for the political deportees from America and *die soziale Revolution.* It was a stirring demonstration of comradely solidarity which even war could not destroy.

We learned that our destination was Libau, in western Latvia, but two days later a radiogram notified the captain that fighting was continuing on the Baltic front, and the course of the *Buford* was changed. Again we were at sea in more senses than one. Deportees and crew became impatient and irritable with the drawn-out, perilous voyage. Longing filled me for those I had left behind and sickening uncertainty of the things ahead. Roots embedded in the soil of one's entire life are not easily transplanted. I felt uneasy and restless, between hope and doubt. My spirit was still in the United States.

The ghastly trip was over at last. We had reached Hango, a Finnish port. Supplied with three days' rations, we were turned over to the local authorities. America's obligation was at an end and so were her fears.

On our trip through Finland we were kept locked in the train, with sentries with fixed bayonets inside the cars and on the platforms. Ethel and Dora, as well as a number of the men comrades, were ill, but though our train stopped at stations having buffets, no one was allowed to step out for purchases. On the border, at Teryoki, our compartments were unlocked and the sentries withdrawn. We were permitted to look after our supplies, but to our consternation we discovered that the greater part of our provisions had been appropriated by the Finnish soldiers. Presently there appeared a representative of the Finnish Foreign Office and a military officer of the General Staff. They were very anxious to be rid of the American political deportees and they demanded that we cross over at once to Russia. We refused to comply without first notifying Soviet Russia of our arrival. There followed negotiations with the Finnish authorities, and finally we were granted permission to send two radios, one to Moscow, addressed to Chicherin, People's Commissar for Foreign Affairs, the other to our old friend Bill Shatoff in Petrograd. Within a short time the Soviet committee arrived. Chicherin had sent Feinberg as his representative, while the Petrograd Soviet delegated Zorin, Secretary of the Communist Party of that city, to receive us. Mme Andreyeva, Gorki's wife, accompanied them. Arrangements were quickly made to transfer our luggage from the train across the border. Just at that moment the complete rout of Denikin by the valiant Red Army was announced, and the air was rent by the joyous hurrahs of our two hundred and forty-nine deportees.

All was ready. It was the twenty-eighth day of our journey, and at last we were on the threshold of Soviet Russia. My heart trembled with anticipation and fervent hope.

# CHAPTER LII

SOVIET RUSSIA! SACRED GROUND, MAGIC PEOPLE! YOU HAVE COME to symbolize humanity's hope, you alone are destined to redeem mankind. I have come to serve you, beloved *matushka*. Take me to your bosom, let me pour myself into you, mingle my blood with yours, find my place in your heroic struggle, and give to the uttermost to your needs!

At the border, on our way to Petrograd, and at the station there, we were received like dear comrades. We who had been driven out of America as felons were welcomed on Soviet soil as brothers by her sons and daughters who had helped to set her free. Workers, soldiers, and peasants surrounded us, took us by the hand, and made us feel akin to them. Pale-faced and hollow-cheeked they were, a light burning in their sunken eyes, and determination breathing from their ragged bodies. Danger and suffering had steeled their wills and made them stern. But underneath beat the old childlike, generous Russian heart, and it went out to us without stint.

Music and song greeted us everywhere and wondrous tales of valour and never-failing fortitude in the face of hunger, cold, and devastating disease. Tears of gratitude burned in my eyes and I felt great humility before those simple folk risen to greatness in the fire of the revolutionary struggle.

In Petrograd, after a third reception, *Tovarishtch* Zorin, in whose company we had made the trip, invited Sasha and me to come with him to a waiting automobile. Darkness covered the big city, fantastic shadows over the glistening snow on the ground. The streets were entirely deserted, the grave-like silence disturbed only by the rattling of our car. We sped on, several times halted by human forms suddenly emerging from the blackness of the night. Soldiers they were, heavily armed, their flashlights searchingly on us. "*Propusk, tovarishtch!*

(Pass-card, comrade!)," was their curt demand. "Military precautions," our escort explained; "Petrograd has only recently escaped the menace of Yudenich. Too many counter-revolutionists are still lurking about for us to take any chances." We continued on our way, and as the automobile turned a corner and passed a brightly lighted building, Zorin remarked: "The Cheka and our jail—generally empty, though." Presently we halted before a large house, lights streaming from its many windows. "The Astoria, a fashionable hotel in tsarist times," Zorin informed us, "now the First House of the Petro-Soviet." We were to room there, he added, while the rest of the deportees would be housed in the Smolny, formerly the most exclusive boarding-school for the daughters of the aristocracy. "And the girls?" I inquired. "Ethel Bernstein and Dora Lipkin — I could not bear to be separated from them." Zorin promised to secure a room for them in the Astoria, although only party members were quartered in that Soviet house, mostly high officials, as well as special guests. He led us to his apartment, while places for us were being prepared.

Liza, Zorin's wife, bade us a hearty welcome, her greeting as kindly as Zorin's attitude had been throughout the day. She felt sure we were hungry. She had not much to offer us, but we should partake of everything she had, which proved to be herring, *kasha,* and tea. The Zorins looked none too well fed themselves, and I promised myself to replenish their scanty larder when our trunks were unpacked. Our American friends had provided us with a huge trunkful of supplies and we had also rescued some of the rations given us on leaving the *Buford.* I chuckled inwardly at the thought of the United States Government unwittingly feeding the Russian Bolsheviks.

The Zorins had lived in America, though we had never met them there. But they knew us, and Liza said that she had attended some of my lectures in New York. Both spoke English with a strong foreign accent, but more fluently than we did Russian. Thirty-five years in the States with almost no practice in our native tongue had paralysed our ability to use it. Besides, the Zorins had much to relate to us and they could do it in English. They told us of the Revolution, its achievements and hopes, and many other things we wanted to learn about. Their story of the events leading up to October and the developments since, though more detailed, was somewhat repetitious of what we had already heard at our receptions. It concerned the blockade and its fearful toll; the iron ring that surrounded Russia and the devastating sabotage of the interventionists; the armed attacks by Denikin, Kolchak, and Yudenich; the havoc wrought by them and the revolutionary spirit that kept at its height against terrible odds, fighting on numerous fronts and routing its enemies. Fighting also on the industrial front, building the new Russia out of the ruins of the old. Already much constructive work had been achieved, they informed us; we should have the opportunity to see it with our own eyes. Schools, workers' colleges, social protection of mother and child, care of the aged and the sick, and much more were made possible by the dictatorship of the proletariat. Of course, Russia was very far yet from perfection, with every hand raised against her. The blockade, the intervention, the counter-revolutionary plotters — foremost amongst them the Russian intelligentsia — they were the greatest menace. It was they who were responsible for the fearful obstacles the Revolution encountered and for the ills the country was suffering.

The herculean tasks facing Russia now made our past struggles in America appear pitifully insignificant; our real test by fire was yet before us! I trembled at the thought of my possible failure, my inability to scale the heights already attained by the obscure and dumb millions. In their earnestness and obvious consecration the Zorins symbolized this greatness and I felt proud to have them as friends. It was past midnight before we could tear ourselves away from them.

In the hotel corridor we ran into a young woman who told us that she was on her way to the Zorins' to call us. A friend from America was waiting, eager to see us. We followed her to an apartment on the fourth floor, and when the door was opened, I found myself in the embrace of our old comrade Bill Shatoff. "Bill, you here!" I cried in surprise; "why, Zorin told me you had left for Siberia!"

"Why were you not at the border to meet us? Didn't you receive our radio?" Sasha chimed in.

"None of your American speed," Bill laughed: "let me hug you first, dear Sasha, and let's have a glass to your safe arrival in revolutionary Russia. Then we'll talk." He led us to a divan, placing himself between us. The others present greeted us warmly: Anna (Bill's wife), her sister Rose, and the latter's husband. I had met the girls in New York, but I had not recognized Rose in the dim light of the corridor.

Bill had put on considerable weight since the farewell send-off we had given him in New York. His military uniform accentuated his bulging lines and made his face look rather hard. But he was the same old Bill, impulsive, affectionate, and jovial. He pelted us with a volley of questions about America, the San Francisco labour cases, our imprisonment and deportation. "Never mind all that for the present," we parried; "better tell us first about yourself. How do you happen still to be in Petrograd? And why were you not on the reception committee for the American deportees?" Bill looked somewhat embarrassed and sought to dodge our questions, but we were insistent. I could not bear the uncertainty about Zorin and I was not willing to suspect him of deliberate deception. "I see you have not changed," Bill teased; "you are the same old persistent pest." He tried to explain that in the strenuous life of Russia people had no time for mere sociability. He and Zorin, having different duties, rarely met. That might explain Zorin's impression that he had departed. His Siberian journey had been settled upon weeks previously, but, owing to the difficulty of procuring the necessary equipment for his trip, had been delayed. Even now much was to be attended to before he would be ready to leave. It might keep him in the city for another fortnight, but he did not mind it now that we were with him — it would give us time to talk things over, about America and Russia. He had received our radio and he had asked to be on the committee, but he was refused. It had been considered unwise to allow him to give us our first impressions of Russia, in order not to prejudice us. "It! It!" both Sasha and I exclaimed. "Who is that dictatorial 'it' that orders your Siberian trip and that refuses you the right to meet your old comrades and friends? And why could you not have come on your own account?" "The dictatorship of the proletariat," Bill replied, patting me on the back indulgently; "but of that some other time. Now I just want to tell you," he continued earnestly, "that the Communist State in action is exactly what we anarchists have always claimed it would be — a tightly centralized power, still more strengthened by the dangers to the Revolution. Under such conditions one cannot do as one wills. One does not just hop on a train and go, or even ride the bumpers, as I used to in the United States. One needs permission. But don't get the idea that I miss my American 'blessings.' Me for Russia, the Revolution, and its glorious future!"

Bill was certain we would come to feel just as he did about things in Russia. No need to worry about trifles like *propusks* during our first hours together. "*Propusks!* I have a whole trunkful of them, and so will you soon," he concluded, a mischievous twinkle in his eye. I caught his mood and dismissed my questions. I was dazed by the impressions that had crowded the day. Was it really only one day, I wondered. I seemed to have lived years since our arrival.

Bill Shatoff did not leave for another fortnight, and we spent together most of our time, often into the wee hours of the morning. The revolutionary canvas he unrolled before us was of far larger scope than had been painted before by anyone else. It was no longer a few individual figures thrown on the picture, their rôle and importance accentuated by the vast background. Great and small, high and low, stood out in bold relief, imbued with a collective will to hasten the complete triumph of the Revolution. Lenin, Trotsky, Zinoviev, with their small band of inspired comrades, had a tremendous part to play, Bill declared with enthusiastic conviction; but the real power behind them was the awakened revolutionary consciousness of the masses. The peasants had expropriated the masters' land all through the summer of 1917 . . . workers had taken possession of the factories and shops . . . the soldiers had flocked back by the hundred thousands from the warring fronts . . . the Kronstadt sailors had translated their anarchist motto of direct action into the everyday life of the Revolution . . . the Left Socialist Revolutionists, as also the anarchists, had encouraged the peasantry in socializing the land. . . . All these forces had helped to energize the storm that broke over Russia, finding full expression and release in the terrific sweep of October.

Such was the epic of dazzling beauty and overwhelming power, infused with palpitating life by the ardour and eloquence of our friend. Presently Bill himself broke the spell. He had shown us the transformation in the soul of Russia, he continued; he would have to let us see her ills of the body as well. "Not to prejudice you," he emphasized, "as has been feared by people whose criterion of revolutionary integrity is a membership card." Before long we would ourselves meet the appalling afflictions that were sapping the country's strength, he said. His object was merely to prepare us — to help us diagnose the source of the disease, to point out the danger of its spreading and enable us to see that only the most drastic measures could effect a cure. The Russian experience had taught him that we anarchists had been the romanticists of revolution, forgetful of the cost it would entail, the frightful price the enemies of the Revolution would exact, the fiendish methods they would resort to in order to destroy its gains.

One cannot fight fire and sword with only the logic and justice of one's ideal. The counter-revolutionists had combined to isolate and starve Russia, and the blockade was taking frightful toll of human life. The intervention and the destruction in its wake, the numerous White attacks, costing oceans of blood, the hordes of Denikin, Kolchak, and Yudenich; their pogroms, bestial revenge, and the general havoc wrought had imposed on the Revolution a warfare that its most far-sighted exponents had never dreamed about. A warfare not always in keeping without romantic ideas of revolutionary ethics, indispensable none the less to drive off the hungry wolves ready to tear the Revolution limb from limb. He had not ceased to be an anarchist, Bill assured us; he had not become indifferent to the menace of a Marxian State machine. That danger was no longer a subject for theoretic discussion, but an actual reality because of the existing bureaucracy, inefficiency, and corruption. He loathed the dictatorship and its handmaiden, the Cheka, with their ruthless suppression of thought, speech, and initiative. But it was an unavoidable evil. The anarchists had been the first to respond to Lenin's essentially anarchistic call to revolution. They had the right to demand an accounting. "And we will! Never doubt that," Bill fairly shouted, "we will! But not now, not now! Not while every nerve must be strained to save Russia from the reactionary elements which are desperately fighting to come back to power." He had not joined the Communist Party, and never would, Bill assured us. But he was with the Bolsheviki and he would continue until every front had been liquidated and the last enemy driven to cover, like Yudenich, Denikin, and the rest of the tsarist gang. "And so will you, dear Emma and Sasha," Bill concluded; "I am certain of it."

Our comrade was the enthusiastic bard of old, his song the saga of the Revolution, the most stupendous event of our time. Its miracles were many, its horrors and woe the martyrdom of a people nailed to the cross.

Bill was entirely right, we thought. Nothing was of moment compared with the supreme need of giving one's all to safeguard the Revolution and its gains. The faith and fervour of our comrade swept me along to ecstatic heights. Yet I could not entirely free myself from an undercurrent of uneasiness one often feels when left alone in the dark. Resolutely I strove to drive it back, moving like a sleep-walker through enchanted space. Sometimes I would stumble back to earth only half-aroused by a harsh voice or an ugly sight. The gagging of free speech at the session of the Petro-Soviet that we had attended, the discovery that better and more plentiful food was served Party members at the Smolny dining-room and many similar injustices and evils had attracted my attention. Model schools where the children were stuffed with sweets and candies, and side by side with them schools dismal, poorly equipped, unheated, and filthy, where the little ones, hungry all the time, were herded together like cattle. A special hospital for Communists, with every modern comfort, while other institutions lacked the barest medical and surgical necessities. Thirty-four different grades of rations — under alleged *Communism!* — while some markets and privileged stores were doing a lively business in butter, eggs, cheese, and meat. The workers and their womenfolk standing long hours in endless queues for their ration of frozen potatoes, wormy cereals, and decayed fish. Groups of women, their faces bloated and blue, accompanied by Red soldiers and bargaining with them for their pitiful wares.

I talked to Zorin about these things, to the young anarchist Kibalchich, living in the Astoria, to Zinoviev and others, pointing out these contradictions. How were they to be justified or explained? All of them repeated the same refrain: " What will you, with the blockade around us, the sabotage of the intelligentsia, the attacks of Denikin, Kolchak, and Yudenich!" They alone were to blame, they reiterated. Old evils could not be eradicated until the fronts were liquidated. " Come and work with us," they said, " you and Berkman. You can have any position you choose and you can help us a great deal."

I was profoundly moved to see these people reaching eagerly out for willing hands. We would join them; we would work with them with our best energy and strength as soon as we found our bearings, knew where we belonged and where we could be of greatest use.

Zinoviev did not look the formidable leader his reputation would have led one to assume. He impressed me as flabby and weak. His voice was adolescent, high-pitched and lacking in appeal. But he had faithfully helped the Revolution to its birth and he was indefatigably working for its further development, we had been told. He certainly deserved confidence and respect. " The blockade," he reiterated, " Kolchak, Denikin, Yudenich, the counter-revolutionist Savinkov, as well as the Menshevik traitors and the Socialist Revolutionists of the Right, are a constant menace. They are eternally plotting vengeance and the death of the Revolution." Zinoviev's plaint added tragic momentum to the general chorus. I joined in with the rest.

Soon, however, other voices rose from the depths, harsh, accusing voices that greatly disturbed me. I had been asked to attend a conference of anarchists in Petrograd, and I was amazed to find that my comrades were compelled to gather in secret in an obscure hiding-place. Bill Shatoff had spoken with great pride of the courage shown by our comrades in the Revolution and on the military fronts, and he had extolled the heroic part they had played. Why should people with such a record, I wondered, be driven under cover.

Presently came the answer — from workers in the Putilov Iron-works, from factories and mills, from the Kronstadt sailors, from Red Army men, and from an old comrade who had escaped while under sentence of death. The very brawn of the revolutionary struggle was crying out in anguish and bitterness against the people they had helped place in power. They spoke of the Bolshevik betrayal of the Revolution, of the slavery forced upon the toilers, the emasculation of the soviets, the suppression of speech and thought, the filling of prisons with recalcitrant peasants, workers, soldiers, sailors, and rebels of every kind. They told of the raid with machine-guns upon the Moscow headquarters of the anarchists by the order of Trotsky; of the Cheka and the wholesale executions without hearing or trial. These charges and denunciations beat upon me like hammers and left me stunned. I listened tense in every nerve, hardly able clearly to understand what I heard, and failing to grasp its full meaning. It couldn't be true — this monster indictment! Had not Zorin pointed the jail out to us and assured us that it was almost empty? Capital punishment, he had said, had been abolished. And had not Bill Shatoff paid glowing tribute to Lenin and his co-workers, glorifying their vision and valour? Bill had not covered up the dark spots on the Soviet horizon; he had explained the reason for them and the methods they had forced upon the Bolsheviki, and indeed upon all rebels serving the Revolution.

The men in that dismal hall must be mad, I thought, to tell such impossible and preposterous stories, wicked to condemn the Communists for the crimes they must know were due to the counter-revolutionary gang, to the blockade and the White generals attacking the Revolution. I proclaimed my conviction to the gathering, but my

voice was drowned in the laughter of derision and jeers. I was roundly
denounced for my wilful blindness. " That's the gag they have given
you!" my comrades shouted at me. " You and Berkman have fallen
for it and swallowed it whole. And Zorin, the bigot who hates anarchists and would shoot them all in cold blood! Bill Shatoff, too, the
renegade!" they shouted; " you believe them and not us. Wait, wait
until you have seen things with your own eyes. You will sing another
song then."

When the indignant uproar had subsided, the fugitive from the
death-sentence demanded the floor. His pale face was deeply fur-
rowed, suffering spoke from his large, hunted eyes, and he talked in
a voice trembling with suppressed excitement. He dwelt at length on
the recent events and the difficulties in the way of the Revolution.
The anarchists did not close their eyes to the counter-revolutionary
menace, he said. They were fighting it tooth and nail, as proved by
the numerous comrades on the fronts and the great numbers that had
laid down their lives in the battles against the enemy. In fact, it was
Nestor Makhno, an anarchist, who with his peasant rebel army of
*povstantsy* had helped to rout Denikin and thus saved Moscow and
the Revolution at the most critical period. Anarchists in every part of
Russia were at the very moment on the firing line, driving back the
enemies of the Revolution. But they were also fighting the plague
that had brought in the counter-revolutionary pest: the Brest-Litovsk
peace, which had disintegrated the revolutionary spirit of the masses
and had been the first wedge to break the proletarian forces and their
unity. The anarchists and the Left Social Revolutionists had opposed
it from the very first as a perilous step and a breach of faith on the
part of the Bolsheviki. The policy of the *razverstka*, introduced by
the Bolsheviki, the forcible gathering of products by irresponsible
military detachments, had added fuel to the fires of popular bitterness. It had aroused hatred among the peasants and workers and had
made them fertile soil for counter-revolutionary plots. " Shatoff knows
all this," the man cried; " why did he hide these facts from you? But
Bill Shatoff has become a 'Sovietsky' anarchist and he is serving the
men in the Kremlin. That is why Lenin has saved him from the Cheka
and has exiled him to Siberia instead. Workers and peasants, soldiers
and sailors had been shot for lesser offences than the shady manipulations with his *bourgeois* cronies that Shatoff engaged in as virtual
governor of Petrograd. The Bolsheviki are grateful masters. Shatoff

had ruled Petrograd with an iron hand. He had himself rushed after the fleeing Kanegiesser, the slayer of the sadist Uritsky, chief of the Petrograd Cheka. Shatoff, the anarchist, had caught the unfortunate prey, brought him back in triumph, and turned him over to the Cheka to be shot!"

"Stop, stop!" I screamed; "I've had enough of your lies! Bill would never do such a thing. I have known Bill for years as the kindest and gentlest of beings. I could never believe him capable of such things." In rage I struck out at these people who called themselves anarchists and yet were so vindictive and mean-spirited. I fought for the integrity of Zorin and defended Zinoviev as an able and energetic leader. I championed Bill, my old comrade and friend, extolling the nobility of his character, his big spirit and clear vision. I refused to have my burning faith extinguished by the poisonous fumes I had been inhaling for three days.

Sasha had been laid up with a severe cold and was too ill to attend the conference of the anarchist group. But I had kept him informed, and now I burst into his room in great mental turmoil to tell him of this last dreadful day. He dismissed the charges as the irresponsible prattle of ineffective and disgruntled men. The Petrograd anarchists were like so many in our ranks in America who used to do least and criticize most, he said. Perhaps they had been naïve enough to expect anarchism to emerge overnight from the ruins of autocracy, from the war and blunders of the Provisional Government. It was absurd to denounce the Bolsheviki for the drastic measures they were using, Sasha urged. How else were they to free Russia from the stranglehold of counter-revolution and sabotage? So far as he was concerned, he did not think any methods too harsh to deal with this. Revolutionary necessity justified all measures, however we might dislike them. As long as the Revolution was in jeopardy, those seeking to undermine it must pay the penalty. Single-hearted and clear-eyed as ever was my old pal. I agreed with him; still, the ugly reports of my comrades kept disturbing me.

Sasha's illness had driven back the phantoms of my sleepless nights. Physicians were few, medicine scarce, and disease rampant in Petrograd. Zorin had immediately sent out for a doctor, but the patient's fever was too alarming for a long wait. My old professional experience never served a better purpose. With the help of my small, well-equipped medicine chest which the kindly doctor of the *Buford* had given me, I succeeded in breaking Sasha's fever. Two weeks of careful nursing brought him out of bed, looking thin and pale, but on the road to complete recovery. About this time two men were sent up to see us: George Lansbury, editor of the London *Daily Herald,* and Mr. Barry, an American correspondent. They had not been expected and no provision had been made for an English-speaking person to meet them. They did not understand a word of Russian and they wanted to get to Moscow. We communicated their plight to Mme Ravich, head of the Interior Department and chief of the Foreign Office in Petrograd. She requested Sasha to accompany the English visitors to Moscow, and he consented.

His departure left me free to go about again. The Zorins were always willing to take me to places of interest, but I was beginning to pick up my Russian and I preferred to go alone. The anarchist conference having been held under cover, I had not been in a position to talk to the Zorins about it, much less tell them what I had heard. It made me feel somewhat guilty in their presence. Added to it was my impression that Zorin was purposely keeping me away from certain things. I had asked him whether I could visit some factories. He had promised to secure a *propusk* for me, but he had failed to do so. He had also shown impatience with Liza when she had asked me to address the girls of a shop-collective. Not that I had consented; my Russian was still too halting. Moreover, I had come to Russia to learn and not to teach. Zorin seemed greatly relieved at my refusal. I had paid no attention to his peculiar attitude at the time, but when he also broke his promise to take me to the mills, I began to wonder whether there was not something wrong there. I did not believe that conditions were as bad as described at the conference; why, then, should Zorin refuse to let me see them? However, my relations with the Zorins continued very friendly. They were ardent rebels, utterly without thought of themselves and their needs. They were unwilling to accept anything from us, though always ready to share their own meagre supplies. Zorin was particularly adamant. Every time I would bring some of our American provisions, he would warn me that we should soon go hungry ourselves if we continued giving our things away. Liza also was difficult to persuade. She was expecting her baby, and I was urging her to let me help her prepare a few things for the new arrival. "Nonsense," she would reply; "in proletarian Russia no one fusses about baby clothes; we leave that to the pampered *bourgeois* women in capitalist countries. We have more important things to do."

I would argue that the babies of today were going to be the inheritors of that future she was working for. Shouldn't their first needs be considered even before their birth? But Liza would laugh it off and call me sentimental, not at all the fighter she had thought me. I liked and admired their sterling qualities, in spite of their narrow partisan traits. I did not see quite so much of them, however, as in the first weeks. There was no need for it, as I could now go about by myself; moreover, other people had come into my life.

One thing Bill Shatoff had told us about was certainly not overdrawn: the matter of *propusks*. They played a greater rôle in Soviet Russia than passports had under the tsars. One could not even get in or out of our hotel without a permit, not to speak of visiting any Soviet institution or important official. Almost everyone carried portfolios stocked with *propusks* and *oodostoverenyas* (identification papers). Zorin had told me that they constituted a necessary precaution against counter-revolutionary plotters, but the longer I stayed in Russia, the less I saw their value. Paper was at a high premium, yet reams upon reams of it were used for " permits," and much time was wasted in securing them. On the other hand, the very quantity of them defeated any real control. What sane counter-revolutionist, I argued, would expose himself to discovery by standing for hours in line waiting for a *propusk*? He could more easily secure it in other ways. But it was useless; every Communist I met seemed to suffer from counter-revolutionary fixation, no doubt due to the attacks already endured. How could I take issue with them? My stay in Russia had been too short for me to advise them on the most practical method of coping with the enemies of the Revolution. And what did the pesky pieces of paper matter in view of the great things already achieved? Everywhere I witnessed sublime courage, selfless devotion, and simple grandeur on the part of those holding the revolutionary fort against the entire inimical world. Thus I reasoned with myself, determinedly refusing to see the reverse side of Russia's face. But its scarred and twisted countenance would not be ignored. It kept calling me back, urging me to look, forcing me to view its suffering. I wanted to see only its beauty and radiance, longed passionately to believe in its strength and power, yet the very hideousness of the other side

compelled with an irresistible appeal. " Look, look ! " it grinned,
" within reach of Petrograd are vast stretches of forest, enough to
heat every home and make every factory wheel turn. Yet the city is
perishing from cold, and the machines are frozen. The *razverstka*
(forcible collection of food) drains the peasantry to feed Petrograd,
they are told; fertile Ukraine is forced to ship carloads of provisions
northward, yet the population of the cities is starving. A goodly half
of the provisions somehow vanishes along the route, the rest reaching,
in the main, the markets rather than the hungry masses; and the constant shootings on the Gorokhovaya (Cheka headquarters), have you
been deaf to those? And the planned prison for morally defective children — has your indignation not been aroused by this, you who have
for thirty-five years hurled anathema at the traducers of child-life?
What about all these ghastly blotches so skilfully hidden by Communist rouge? "

Like a rabbit in a trap I dashed about in my cage, beating against
the bars of these fearful contradictions. Blindly I reached out for
someone to ward off the mortal blow. Zinoviev and John Reed, who
had just returned from Moscow, could explain, I thought. And Maxim
Gorki, he would surely tell me which side of the Russian face was the
real one and which one false. He would help me, he the great realist,
whose clarion voice had thundered against every wrong and who had
castigated the crimes against childhood in words of fire.

I dispatched a note to Gorki, requesting him to see me. I felt lost
in the labyrinth of Soviet Russia, stumbling constantly over the many
obstacles, vainly groping for the revolutionary light. I needed his
friendly, guiding hand, I wrote him. Meanwhile I turned to Zinoviev.
" Forests within easy reach of Petrograd," I said; " why must the
city freeze? " " Any amount of fuel," Zinoviev replied; " but of what
avail? Our enemies have destroyed our means of transportation; the
blockade has killed off our horses as well as our men. How are we to
get at the woodland? " " What about the population of Petrograd? "
I persisted. " Could it not be appealed to for co-operation? Could it
not be induced to go *en masse* with pick and ax and ropes to haul wood
for its own use? Would not such a concerted effort alleviate much suffering and at the same time decrease the antagonism against your
party? " It might help to diminish the misery from cold, Zinoviev
replied, but it would interfere with the carrying out of the main political policies. What were they? " Concentration of all power in the

hands of the proletarian *avant-garde,*" Zinoviev explained, "the *avant-garde* of the Revolution, which is the Communist Party." "Rather a dear price to pay," I objected. "Unfortunately," he agreed; "but the dictatorship of the proletariat is the only workable program during a revolutionary period. Anarchist groups, free initiative of communes, as your great teachers have suggested, may be feasible in centuries to come, but not now in Russia, with the Denikins and Kolchaks ready to crush us. They have doomed the whole of Russia, yet your comrades fret about the fate of one city." One city, with a million and a half inhabitants reduced to four hundred thousand! A mere bagatelle in the eyes of the Communist political program! Disheartened, I left the man so cock-sure of his party's wisdom, so ensconced in the heavenly Marxian constellation and self-conscious of being one of its major stars.

John Reed had burst into my room like a sudden ray of light, the old buoyant, adventurous Jack that I used to know in the States. He was about to return to America, by way of Latvia. Rather a hazardous journey, he said, but he would take even greater risks to bring the inspiring message of Soviet Russia to his native land. "Wonderful, marvellous, isn't it, E.G.?" he exclaimed. "Your dream of years now realized in Russia, your dream scorned and persecuted in my country, but made real by the magic wand of Lenin and his band of despised Bolsheviks. Did you ever expect such a thing to happen in the country ruled by the tsars for centuries?"

"Not by Lenin and his comrades, dear Jack," I corrected, "though I do not deny their great part. But by the whole Russian people, preceded by a glorious revolutionary past. No other land of our days has been so literally nurtured by the blood of her martyrs, a long procession of pioneers who went to their death that new life may spring from their graves."

Jack insisted that the young generation cannot for ever be tied to the apron-strings of the old, particularly when those strings are tightly drawn around its throat. "Look at your old pioneers, the Breshkovskayas and Tchaikovskys, the Chernovs and Kerenskys and the rest of them," he cried heatedly; "see where they are now! With the Black Hundreds, the Jew-baiters, and the ducal clique, aiding them to crush the Revolution. I don't give a damn for their past. I am concerned only in what the treacherous gang has been doing during the past three years. To the wall with them! I say. I have learned one mighty expressive Russian word, ' *razstrellyat* '! " (execute by shooting).

" Stop, Jack! Stop! " I cried; "this word is terrible enough in the mouth of a Russian. In your hard American accent it freezes my blood. Since when do revolutionists see in wholesale execution the only solution of their difficulties? In time of active counter-revolution it is no doubt inevitable to give shot for shot. But cold-bloodedly and merely for opinion's sake, do you justify standing people against the wall under such circumstances? " I went on to point out to him that the Soviet Government must have realized the futility of such methods, not to speak of their barbarity, because it had abolished capital punishment. Zorin had told me that. Was the decree revoked, that Jack spoke so glibly of standing men against the wall? I mentioned the frequent shooting I heard in the city at night. Zorin had said that it was target practice of *kursanty* (Communist students at the military training-school for officers). "Do you know anything about it, Jack? " I questioned. " Tell me the truth."

He did know, he said, that five hundred prisoners, considered counter-revolutionists, had been shot on the eve the decree was to go into force. It had been a stupid blunder on the part of over-zealous Chekists and they had been severely reprimanded for it. He had not heard of any other shootings since, but he had always thought me a revolutionist of the purest dye, one who would not shirk any measure in defence of the Revolution. He was surprised to see me so worked up over the death of a few plotters. As if that mattered in the scales of the world revolution!

" I must be crazy, Jack," I said, " or else I never understood the meaning of revolution. I certainly never believed that it would signify callous indifference to human life and suffering, or that it would have no other method of solving its problems than by wholesale slaughter. Five hundred lives snuffed out on the eve of a decree abolishing the death-penalty! You call it a stupid blunder. I call it a dastardly crime, the worst counter-revolutionary outrage committed in the name of the Revolution."

" That's all right," said Jack, trying to calm me; " you are a little confused by the Revolution in action because you have dealt with it only in theory. You'll get over that, clear-sighted rebel that you are, and you'll come to see in its true light everything that seems so puzzling now. Cheer up, and make me a cup of the good old American coffee you have brought with you. Not much to give you in return for all my country has taken from you, but greatly appreciated in starving Russia by her native son."

I marvelled at his capacity to change so quickly to a light tone. It was the same old Jack, with his zest for the adventures of life. I longed to join in his gay mood, but my heart was heavy. Jack's appearance had brought back memories of my recent life, my people, Helena and those dear to me. Not a word from anyone had reached me in two months. Uncertainty about them added to my depression and restlessness. Sasha's letter, suggesting that I come to Moscow, put new energy into me. Moscow was much more alive than Petrograd, he wrote, and there were interesting people to meet. A few weeks in the capital might help to clarify the revolutionary situation to me. I wanted to go immediately. I had already learned, however, that in Soviet Russia one does not just buy a ticket and board a train. I had seen people standing in queues for days and nights to obtain a permit for their journey and then again wait in long lines to purchase their tickets. Even with the helpful co-operation of Zorin it required ten days before I could leave. He had arranged for me to be in the party of Soviet officials going to Moscow, he informed me. Demyan Bedny, the official poet, would be there and he would place me in the Hotel National. Zorin was as obliging as ever, though somewhat distant.

Arrived at the station, I found myself in distinguished company. Karl Radek, who had escaped the fate of Liebknecht, Rosa Luxemburg, and Landauer, was there. Chiperovich, head of the Petrograd labour unions, Maxim Gorki, and several lesser lights were also in the same car with me.

Gorki had previously replied to my letter and had asked me to call for a talk. I did, but there was no talk. I found him suffering from a heavy cold and constantly coughing, while four women were fluttering about him, ministering to his needs. When he saw me in the car, he said we could have our postponed talk *en route;* he would come to my compartment later. I waited eagerly the largest part of the day. Gorki did not appear, nor anyone else except the porter with sandwiches and tea for the Soviet party. Radek, in the next compartment, was evidently holding court. In true Russian fashion everybody talked at once. But the little, nervous Radek managed to outstrip the others. For hours he rattled on. My brain grew weary and I dozed off.

I was roused from my sleep by a gaunt and lanky figure towering above me. Maxim Gorki stood before me, his peasant face deeply lined with pain. I asked him to sit down beside me and he crumpled into the seat, a tired and languid man, much older than his fifty years.

I had looked forward with much anticipation to the chance of talking to Gorki, yet now I did not know how to begin. " Gorki knows nothing about me," I was saying to myself. . . . " He may think me merely a reformer, opposed to the Revolution as such. Or he may even get the impression that I am just fault-finding on account of personal grievances or because I could not have ' buttered toast and grape-fruit for breakfast ' or other material American blessings." Such an interpretation had actually been given to the complaint of Morris Becker about the unbearably putrid air in the shop where he was working, the unnecessary filth and dirt. "You are a pampered *bourgeois*," the Commissar had bellowed at him; " you pine for the comforts of capitalist America. The proletarian dictatorship has more important things to consider than ventilation or lockers to keep your bread and tea clean." I had laughed to tears over that story, but now I was upset by the apprehension lest Maxim Gorki consider me also a pampered *bourgeois,* dissatisfied because I had failed to find in Soviet Russia the flesh-pots of capitalist America. But it was ridiculous to think Gorki capable of the silly prattle of a subordinate Bolshevik official, I sought to reassure myself. Surely the seer who could detect beauty in the meanest life and discover nobility in the basest was too penetrating to misunderstand my groping. He more than any other man would grasp its cause and its pain.

At last I began by saying that I should first have to introduce myself before I could talk to him about the things that were distressing me. " Hardly necessary," Gorki interrupted; " I know a good deal about your activities in the United States. But even if I knew nothing about you, the fact that you were deported for your ideas would be proof enough of your revolutionary integrity. I need nothing more." " That is most kind of you," I replied, " yet I must insist on a little preliminary." Gorki nodded, and I proceeded to tell him of my faith in the Bolsheviki from the very beginning of the October Revolution, and my defence of them and of Soviet Russia at a time when even very few radicals dared speak up for Lenin and his comrades. I had even turned from Catherine Breshkovskaya, who had been our torch for a generation. It had been no easy task to cry in the wilderness of fury and hate in defence of people who in point of theory had always been my political opponents. But who could think of such differences when the life of the Revolution was at stake? Lenin and his co-workers personified that life to me and to my nearest comrades and friends. Therefore we had fought for them and we would have cheerfully given our lives for the men who were holding the revolutionary fort. " I hope you will not consider me boastful or think that I have exaggerated the difficulties and dangers of our struggle in America for Soviet Russia," I said. Gorki shook his head and I continued: " I also hope you will believe me when I say that, though an anarchist, I had not been naïve enough to think that anarchism could rise overnight, as it were, from the debris of old Russia."

He stopped me with a gesture of his hand. " If that is so, and I do not doubt you, how can you be so perplexed at the imperfections you find in Soviet Russia? As an old revolutionist you must know that revolution is a grim and relentless task. Our poor Russia, backward and crude, her masses, steeped in centuries of ignorance and darkness, brutal and lazy beyond any other people in the world! " I gasped at his sweeping indictment of the entire Russian people. His charge was terrible, if true, I told him. It was also rather novel. No Russian writer had ever spoken in such terms before. He, Maxim Gorki, was the first to advance such a peculiar view, and the first not to put all the blame upon the blockade, the Denikins and Kolchaks. Somewhat irritated, he replied that the " romantic conception of our great literary genuises " had entirely misrepresented the Russian and had wrought no end of evil. The Revolution had dispelled the bubble of the goodness and naïveté of the peasantry. It had proved them shrewd, avaricious, and lazy, even savage in their joy of causing pain. The rôle played by the counter-revolutionary Yudeniches, he added, was too obvious to need special emphasis. That is why he had not considered it necessary even to mention them, nor the intelligentsia, which had been talking revolution for over fifty years and then was the first to stab it in the back with sabotage and conspiracies. But all these were contributory factors, not the main cause. The roots were inherent in Russia's brutal and uncivilized masses, he said. They have no cultural traditions, no social values, no respect for human rights and life. They cannot be moved by anything except coercion and force. All through the ages the Russians had known nothing else.

I protested vehemently against these charges. I argued that in spite of his evident faith in the superior qualities of other nations, it was the ignorant and crude Russian people that had risen first in revolt. They had shaken Russia by three successive revolutions within twelve years, and it was they and their will that gave life to " October."

" Very eloquent," Gorki retorted, " but not quite accurate." He admitted the share of the peasantry in the October uprising, though even that, he thought, was not conscious social feeling, but mere wrath accumulated for decades. If not checked by Lenin's guiding hand, it would have surely destroyed rather than advanced the great revolutionary aims. Lenin, Gorki insisted, was the real parent of the October Revolution. It had been conceived by his genius, nurtured by his vision and faith, and brought to maturity by his far-sighted and patient care. Others had helped to deliver the lusty child, particularly the small band of Bolsheviki, aided by the Petrograd workers, together with the sailors and soldiers of Kronstadt. Since the birth of October it was again Lenin who was steering its development and growth.

" Miracle-worker, your Lenin," I cried; " but I seem to remember that you have not always thought him a god or his comrades infallible." I reminded Gorki of his scathing arraignment of the Bolsheviki in the journal *Zhizn,* edited by him in the days of Kerensky. What had caused his change? He had attacked the Bolsheviki, Gorki acknowledged, but the march of events had convinced him that a revolution in a primitive country with a barbarous people could not survive without resort to drastic methods of self-defence. The Bolsheviki had made many mistakes and they continued doing so. They admitted it themselves. But the suppression of the rights of the individual for the sake of the whole, the Cheka, prison, terror, and death were not of their choice. These methods had been forced upon Soviet Russia and they were unavoidable in the revolutionary struggle.

He looked exhausted, and I did not detain him when he rose to leave. He shook my hand and walked out with a weary gait. I, too, was tired and unutterably sad. Which of the two Gorkis, I wondered, had come closer to the Russian soul. Was it the creator of *Makar Tchudra* and *Tchelkash,* the author of *In the Depths,* of *Twenty-six and One,* the " dumb and cruel savages " of the Russian mass? How human Gorki had made them, how childlike and guileless, how moving in their frustration! He had lived with them, in the " nethermost where there is naught but murk and slush "; he had heard their " harsh cry for life," and he had " come up to bear witness to the suffering he had left behind." Was that the true soul of Russia, or was it as pictured by

Gorki the worshipper of Lenin? "A hundred million people, cruel savages needing barbarous methods to keep them in leash." Did he actually believe such monstrous things, or had he invented them to enhance the glory of his god?

Maxim Gorki had been my idol, and I would not see his feet of clay. I became convinced, however, of one thing: neither he nor anyone else could solve my problems. Only time and patient seeking could do it, aided by sympathetic understanding of cause and effect in the revolutionary struggle of Russia.

The occupants of the car had retired, and all was quiet. The train sped on. I tried to gain some sleep, but found myself thinking of Lenin. What was this man and what the power that drew everyone to him, even those who disagreed with his course? Trotsky, Zinoviev, Bukharin, and the other prominent men I had come across, all differed on many problems, yet were unanimous in their appraisal of Lenin. His was the clearest mind in Russia, everyone assured me, of iron will and dogged perseverance in pursuit of his aims, no matter what the cost. It was peculiar, though, that no one ever referred to any generous impulses of the man. I thought of Dora Kaplan, Lenin's assailant. Her story, told me by a friend of Bill Shatoff, who was entirely for the Bolsheviki and Lenin, had been among the first shocks of my Petrograd days. He roundly condemned the attack on Lenin as fraught with most disastrous effects on Russia had Lenin not survived his wounds. But he spoke with the highest regard of Dora and her revolutionary idealism and strength of character, which baffled even her Cheka tormentors. She had been motivated by her conviction that Lenin had betrayed the Revolution by his Brest-Litovsk negotiations. Her attitude was shared by her entire party, the Left Socialist Revolutionists, as well as by the anarchists. Even a goodly number in Communist ranks held the same view. Trotsky, Bukharin, Joffe, and other foremost Bolsheviki had strenuously fought their leader on the issue of making peace with the Kaiser. Lenin's influence, supported by his ingenious slogan of a *peredishka* (getting one's breath), had conquered all opposition. Many claimed that the *peredishka* would, in reality, prove a *zadishka* (death by strangulation). It would mean the end of the Revolution, they insisted, and Lenin would be responsible for it. Dora Kaplan, a mere slip of a girl, had translated the mental turmoil of the moment into action. She had attempted to slay Lenin before he could slay the Revolution!

"Only the Cheka works fast in Russia," my informant had

remarked with a cynical smile. " No time was wasted on a trial, and no chances were taken with a hearing." Torture having failed to induce Dora Kaplan to involve others in her act, she was put out of her agony by a steadier hand than hers. Lenin had gained the love and adulation of millions in every land, but he did nothing to save that unfortunate young woman. The ghastly story had haunted me for weeks. Relief came and renewed faith in Lenin's humanity when I learned that he had saved Bill Shatoff from the " quick action " of the Cheka. He could rise to generous heights, after all, I thought. Perhaps he had been too ill to intercede for Dora in time; possibly, also, the fact of her being tortured had been kept from him. Almost two months had passed since then. Now I was on my way perhaps to meet the man once hounded as a criminal and exile and who was now holding the fate and future of Russia in his hands.

Half asleep I heard the porter call out " Moscow!" When I reached the platform, I found that my fellow-passengers had already departed, including Demyan Bedny. I had had no means of notifying Sasha of my arrival, and no one else in the capital knew of my coming. I felt quite lost in the noise and bustle of the station and helpless with my bags and bundles. I had been warned that things had a way of vanishing in Russia under one's very eyes. I could not go in search of an *izvostchik* and I stood irresolutely wondering what to do. Presently a familiar voice struck my ears. It was Karl Radek talking to some friends. He had not come near me during the entire journey, nor did he show any sign that he knew my identity. I felt awkward about turning to him for help. Suddenly he wheeled round and approached me. Was I waiting for anyone, he inquired, or could he be of aid? I could have hugged the dear little man for his kindly interest, but I was afraid of scandalizing him by such a display of " *bourgeois* sentimentality." I had frequently heard the expression used with great derision. I assured Radek that he was more chivalrous than the chaperon Zorin had given me. He had faithfully promised to see me safely to Moscow and secure a room for me there, and he had basely run away. " Chivalry, nonsense! " laughed Radek; " we are comrades, aren't we, even if you are not a member of my party? " " But how do you know who I am? " " News travels quickly in Russia," he replied. " You're an anarchist, you are Emma Goldman, and you were driven out of plutocratic America. That's three good reasons to entitle you to my comradeship and assistance."

He invited me to accompany him and to give the " comrade chauffeur " directions where to let me off. I explained that I had only the name and number of the street where my comrade Alexander Berkman was stopping. He was not expecting me and he would probably not be in. Moreover, he had no room of his own. Radek demanded to know " what swine " had left me " in such a predicament." I remarked that he would not apply such a term to the man if he knew how important he was. " Why, he is substituting official jingles for the daily bread," I said. " Demyan! " Radek shrieked; "just like that fat pig to shirk a difficult task." It was certainly not going to be easy to secure a room for me in Moscow, he remarked; the city was over-crowded and few quarters were available. But I should not worry; he'd take me to his apartment in the Kremlin and then we should see.

After the desolation of Petrograd, Moscow appeared a veritable cauldron of activity. Crowds everywhere, almost everyone lugging bundles or pulling loaded sleighs, rushing about and jostling, pushing and swearing as only Russians can. Very conspicuous was the number of soldiers and hard-faced men in leather jackets, with guns in their belts. Jack Reed had not exaggerated when he told me that Moscow was like an armed camp. Petrograd also did not lack military display, but in the ten weeks I had spent there, I did not see so many men in uniform, much less Chekists, as on my first morning in Moscow.

Radek and his car were evidently well known to the sentries along our route. We were not halted, not even when the auto dashed through the portals of the Kremlin. The sight of its stone walls brought back to me memories of the tsarist régime. Through the centuries its rulers had dwelt in the magnificence of the huge palaces, their drunken orgies and black deeds echoing through the vast halls. More miraculous than legend, I mused, were the changing faces of time. But yesterday entrenched in inviolate power, their authority inalienable as the stars, today hurled from their thrones, bemoaned by a handful, by the many forgot. The builders of the new Russia in the seats of the mighty of old seemed incongruous in the extreme. How could they feel comfortable or at ease in the creeping shadows of the gruesome past, I wondered. A few hours in the Kremlin were enough to give me the uncanny feeling of the dead trying to come to life again. The generous hospitality of Mme Radek, and her chubby baby blissfully unconscious of the surroundings of the bygone days, helped to dispel my oppressive thoughts. Karl Radek was a veritable dynamo of energy, all the time rushing about, hastening to the telephone, dashing back to pick up the baby and dandle it on his knees, talking and giggling like a schoolgirl. He apparently could not sit still a minute, not even during the meal. He seemed everywhere and nowhere at the same time. Mme Radek, who mothered her husband more than her baby, did not seem to mind his nervous state. Every time he went up like a balloon, her restraining hand would gently detain him and threaten to feed him like the infant if he did not finish the morsel she had set before him. It was an amusing scene, though somewhat wearing through constant repetition.

After luncheon my host invited me to his study. We entered a tall and stately room flooded with sunshine. Beautifully carved old furniture was about, the walls lined with books from floor to ceiling. Here Radek became a changed man. His nervousness disappeared and a strange poise was upon him. He began speaking of the German Revolution and the failure of the Socialists to make it as thorough as the Russian October. No fundamental changes had taken place, he declared. The few radical achievements were insignificant, and the cowardly Socialist Government had not even disarmed the counter-revolutionary Junkers. No wonder the Spartacus uprising had been stifled in the blood of the workers. He spoke with deep feeling about the dreadful end of Karl Liebknecht, Rosa Luxemburg, and the anarchist Gustav Landauer. I had reason to be proud of my comrade, he said, for he was a great mind and a rare spirit. Though scholar and humanist, Landauer had joined the masses in the Revolution and died as he lived, heroic to the end. " If only we had such anarchists as Gustav Landauer to work with us! " Radek exclaimed enthusiastically. " But you do have many anarchists working with you," I replied, " some of them extremely able, I understand." " True," he admitted, " but they are not Landauers. Many of them have a *bourgeois* ideology, *kleinbürgerlich* in their interpretation of the revolutionary struggle. Others again are positively counter-revolutionary and a direct danger to Soviet Russia." His tone now was different from his manner at the station or at the luncheon a while ago. It was harsh and intolerant.

Our talk was interrupted by visitors, which I did not regret. I felt much indebted to Radek, but his Communist omnipotence was too much for me. I went back to play with the baby, still free from dogma and creed and refreshing in its innocence of the puerile efforts of all authorities to cast humanity into one mould.

The repeated telephoning of Radek to the commandant of the National about a room for me finally brought results. At ten in the evening he sent me off in his car to the hotel, bundles and all. He was most cordial, assuring me that I could call on him in any emergency.

Moscow at that hour was as deserted as Petrograd and equally dark. Numerous sentries were along the route, halting our automobile with the same stereotyped: " *Propusk, tovarishtch.*" My thoughts were still at the Radeks'. They had given out of the fullness of their hearts to a stranger. But would they have done so if they had found me wanting in their political faith? Poor, loving human heart, so kind and generous when free from class and party strife, so warped and hardened by both.

It was a novel sensation to be with Sasha in the same city and not be able to reach him. Radek had tried all through the day to get hold of him, but he was not in. Seeing my anxiety, Radek had assured me that Berkman would surely be at his lodgings before midnight. He could remain nowhere else, it being strictly prohibited as a protectionary measure against counter-revolution. No one would dare keep him overnight without registering him with the house commandant, and the latter would not permit a person unknown to him to stay after hours. But how could Radek offer to let me pass the night in his apartment, I asked. The Kremlin, he explained, was an exception. It was heavily guarded against unwelcome guests, and as only the most responsible party members lived there, they could be trusted not to harbour undesirable or suspicious strangers. Anyway, I could call Berkman again after midnight, Radek advised; he would surely be in then.

Radek proved right. At one o'clock I reached Sasha. Not having expected me, he had left for the day. He could not come to me then, because his *propusk* was good only till midnight, but he would call in the morning.

Sasha's voice over the telephone was already a great comfort. It helped to take the edge from the loneliness I felt in the great, strange city. My dear old pal arrived bright and early " to drink a cup of coffee with you," he said. He had had nothing like it since he had left Petrograd, he told me, nor much of anything else. A glance at his hollow cheeks convinced me that he had gone hungry. I thought it strange, as I knew he had taken enough provisions from our American supplies to last him several weeks. Lansbury had even teased him about it. As the guest of the Soviet Government he would not go short, Lansbury had said, and of course he would also share with his " comrade Berkman." Sasha had mentioned in his letter to me that he was not feeling well, but not a word about scarcity of food or whether Lansbury had kept his promise. I inquired if he had undergone a cure to reduce for beauty's sake. " No need for that in Russia," Sasha laughed; but his supplies did not go very far, he explained, because he had found so many starving, even if his loaves outdid Christ's in feeding large numbers on a few pieces. As to the comradeship of Mr. Lansbury, it had lasted only until the latter was taken in charge by an official representative of the Foreign Office. The English editor was housed in the palatial home of a former sugar-king, now the residence of Assistant Foreign Commissar Karakhan; but apparently no room could be found there for Sasha, nor had Lansbury shown any interest in whether his travelling companion and interpreter could find lodgings anywhere else. Sasha was informed that he had not been expected. Moreover, he had not a scrap of paper to identify himself. Finally it was decided to send him to a Soviet house on Kharitonenskaya Street. There also the commandant declared that he had no spare room. Sasha was saved from his predicament by a Socialist Revolutionist staying in the house. The man had recently come from Siberia to bring a report to headquarters from the local Communists with whom he was working. He invited Sasha to share his room, even at the risk of rousing the ire of the all-powerful house commandant. This difficulty temporarily solved, Sasha called on Chicherin, who immediately provided him with a credential. That piece of paper proved a veritable magic key, which had already unlocked many doors for him, as well as some hearts. The commandant of the Kharitonensky Soviet house suddenly discovered that there was a vacant room there, after all, and other officials became friendly the moment Sasha produced his talisman!

The food at the Kharitonensky was not bad, but entirely insufficient for adults. The other guests at the house somehow managed to supply themselves with extra morsels, which they would bring to the common dinner-table, but Sasha did not care to do this. His main difficulty, however, was the black bread, which was causing him serious stomach trouble. In fact, he had been compelled to stop eating it altogether. But now he would pick up lost weight quickly, he joked; now that I was in Moscow, he was sure I would manage to prepare good meals out of scraps, as I had always done. My dear Sasha! What amazing capacity for adaptation and what splendid sense for the comic sides of life!

The main attraction of the place where he lived, Sasha related, was the interesting types of humanity domiciled there. Chinese, Koreans, Japanese, and Hindu delegates, come to study the achievements of " October " and to enlist aid for the work of liberation in their native countries.

Our comrades in Moscow, Sasha informed me, seemed to enjoy considerable freedom. The Anarcho-Syndicalists of the group Golos Truda were publishing anarchist literature and selling it openly at their book-shop on the Tverskaya. The Universalist Anarchists had club-rooms with a co-operative restaurant and held open weekly gatherings at which revolutionary problems were freely discussed. A little anarchist sheet was also published by our old Georgian comrade Attabekian, a close friend of Peter Kropotkin, who had his own print-shop. " What an extraordinary situation," I remarked, " to grant anarchists in Moscow so much freedom, and none at all to the Petrograd circle! Most of the dreadful charges I heard there against the Bolsheviki must have been mere fabrication, but one thing was obvious : they were compelled to meet in secret." Sasha explained that he had come upon quite a number of strange contradictions. Thus, many of our comrades were in prison, for no cause apparently, while others were not molested in their activities. But I would have ample opportunity to learn everything at first hand, he added; the Universalist group had invited us to a special conference where the anarchist angle of the Revolution and current events would be presented by three able speakers.

I could hardly wait for the approaching meeting, which held out the hope of better understanding of Russian reality. In the meantime I tramped Moscow many hours a day, sometimes with, but more often without, Sasha. He lived too far away, a full hour's walk from the National, and there were no street-cars and but few *izvostchiky*. But I urged Sasha to have at least one meal a day with me. He needed building up, and I had brought with me part of our groceries from Petrograd. The markets in Moscow were wide open, doing a rushing business. I saw no betrayal of the Revolution in buying necessaries there. Zorin had indeed told me that trading of any kind was the worst counter-revolution and was strictly prohibited. When I had called

his attention to the open markets, he had assured me that only speculators were to be found there. I thought it was sheer nonsense to expect people to starve to death in sight of food. There was no heroism
in that, nor could the Revolution profit by it. Starving people could
not produce, and without production revolution is doomed to failure.
Zorin had insisted that the blockade, the Allied intervention, and the
White generals were responsible for the lack of food. But I had grown
weary of the same rosary about the causes of Russia's ills. I did not
dispute the facts as presented by Zorin and other Communists, but I
did think that if the Soviet Government failed to prevent food reaching the markets, it should at least close them. If food was allowed to
be sold in public places, it was adding insult to injury to forbid the
masses to take advantage of securing provisions, the more so as
money was permitted to circulate, the Government coining it wholesale. To such arguments Zorin replied that only my theoretic concep-
tions of revolution were obscuring the needs of the practical situation.

The main market in Moscow was the once famous Soukharevka,
which presented the most amazing picture of incongruity I had yet
seen in Russia. People of every kind and station were gathered there,
stripped of the trappings of caste and station. The aristocrat and the
peasant, the cultured and the uncouth, the *bourgeois,* the soldier, and
the worker rubbed elbows with the enemy of yesterday, pitifully crying out their wares or feverishly buying. Former barriers were broken
down, not by the equity of communism, but by the common need for
bread, bread, bread. Here one could find exquisitely carved ikons and
rusty nails, beautiful jewelry and gaudy trinkets, damask shawls and
faded cotton quilts. Amidst the remnants of former luxury and the
last cherished objects of wealth, the crowds jostled, motley gatherings
scrambling to possess themselves of coveted articles. Truly an overpowering spectacle of primitive instincts, asserting themselves without
restraint or fear.

The Soukharevka made more flagrant the discrimination against
smaller places of barter. The little market near the National was being constantly raided. Yet there were but the poorest of the poor
desperately trying to keep alive: old women, children in tatters,
derelict men, their wares as wretched as themselves. Ill-smelling
*tshchi* (vegetable soup), frozen potatoes, biscuits black and hard, or
a few boxes of matches — they held them out to the passers-by with
trembling hands, in trembling voices pleading: " Buy, *barinya* (lady),

buy, for the love of Christ, buy!" In the raids their measly wares
would be seized, their soup and kvass poured out on the square, and
the unfortunates dragged off to prison as speculators. Those lucky
enough to escape the raiders would soon crawl back, gather up the
matches and cigarettes strewn about, and begin their wretched trade
again.

The Bolsheviki, in common with other social rebels, had always
stressed the potency of hunger as the cause of most of the evils in
capitalist society. They never grew tired of condemning the system that
punished the effects while leaving their sources intact. How could they
now pursue the same stupid and incredible course, I wondered. True,
the appalling hunger was not of their making. The blockade and the
interventionists *were* chiefly responsible for that. More reason, then,
it seemed to me, why the victims should not be hounded and punished.
Witnessing such a raid, Sasha had been aroused by its cruelty and
inhumanity. He had vigorously protested against the brutal manner
in which the soldiers and the Chekists dispersed the crowd, and he had
been himself saved from arrest only by the credential Chicherin had
given him. Forthwith the Chekist had changed his tone and manner,
offering profuse apologies to the "foreign *tovarishtch.*" He was only
doing his duty, he said, carrying out the orders of his superiors, and
he could not be blamed.

It was evident that the new power in the Kremlin was feared no
less than the old, and that its official seal had the same awesome
effect. "Wherein is the change?" I asked Sasha. "You can't measure
a gigantic upheaval by a few specks of dust," he replied. But were they
mere specks, I wondered, for they seemed to me gusts that were
threatening to pull down the entire revolutionary edifice I had constructed in America around the Bolsheviki. Yet my faith in their
integrity was too strong to charge them with responsibility for the
evils and wrongs I was witnessing at every step. These kept growing
daily, ugly facts utterly at variance with what Soviet Russia had been
proclaiming to the world. I tried to avoid facing them, but they lurked
in every corner and would not be ignored.

The National, almost exclusively occupied by Communists, was
manned by a large kitchen force that was wasting time and precious
foodstuffs in preparing uneatable meals. Next to it was another
kitchen with private servants cooking all day for their masters, prominent Soviet officials. They and their friends were permitted special

privileges, often receiving three and even more rations, while the ordinary mortals were wearing out their depleted strength to attain their meagre due.

The housing arrangements disclosed similar favouritism and injustice. Large and well-furnished apartments were easily obtainable for a monetary consideration, but it required weeks of humiliation before petty officials to secure one room in a dismal flat without water, heat, or light. Lucky indeed the person if, after all his exhausting efforts, he did not find someone else occupying the same room. This seemed entirely too fantastic to believe, but the personal experience of various friends, among them a young girl I knew, as well as of Manya and Vassily Semenoff, old comrades from the States, left no doubt. They had been among the first to hasten back to Russia at the very outbreak of the Revolution. Since then they had faithfully worked in Soviet institutions at the hardest tasks, yet they had been compelled to wait months and canvass numerous departments before they were granted lodgings. Their happiness was, however, short-lived. On reaching the place assigned to her the young woman found a man already in possession of it. " But we can't both live in the same room," she had told him. " Why not? " he replied; " in Soviet Russia one mustn't be so particular. I worked too hard to secure this hole and I can't afford to give it up. But I can sleep on the floor and let you have the bed," he offered. " It was very decent of him," the girl said, " but I could not face such close proximity with an utter stranger. I left the room and resumed my search for another place."

The hideous sores on revolutionary Russia could not for long be ignored. The facts presented at the gathering of the Moscow anarchists, the analysis of the situation by leading Left Socialist Revolutionists, and my talks with simple people who claimed no political affiliations enabled me to look behind the scenes of the revolutionary drama and to behold the dictatorship without its stage make-up. Its rôle was somewhat different from the one proclaimed in public. It was forcible tax-collection at the point of guns, with its devastating effect on villages and towns. It was the elimination from responsible positions of everyone who dared think aloud, and the spiritual death of the most militant elements whose intelligence, faith, and courage had really enabled the Bolsheviki to achieve their power. The anarchists and Left Socialist Revolutionists had been used as pawns by Lenin in the October days and were now doomed to extinction by his creed and policies. It was the system of taking hostages for political refugees, not exempting even old parents and children of tender age. The nightly *oblavas* (street and house raids) by the Cheka, the population frightened out of sleep, their few belongings turned upside down and ripped open for secret documents, the dragnet of soldiers left behind to haul in the crop of unsuspecting callers at the besieged house. The penalties for flimsy charges often amounted to long prison terms, exile to desolate parts of the country, and even execution. Shattering in its cumulative effect, the essence of the story was the same as told me by my Petrograd comrades. I had been too dazzled then by the public glare and glitter of Bolshevism to credit the veracity of the accusations. I had refused to trust their judgment and their view-point. But now Bolshevism was shorn of its pretence, its naked soul exposed to my gaze. Still I would not believe. I would not see with my inner eye the truth so evident to my outer sight. I was stunned, baffled, the ground pulled from under me. Yet I hung on, hung on by a thread as a drowning man. In my anguish I cried: " Bolshevism is the *mene, tekel* over every throne, the menace of craven hearts, the hated enemy of organized wealth and power. Its path has been thorny, its obstacles many, its climb steep. How could it help falling behind at times, how could it help making mistakes? But to belie itself, to play Judas to the fervent hope of the disinherited and oppressed, to betray its own ultimate aims? No, never could it be guilty of such an eclipse of the world's most luminous star! "

Even the Moscow Anarchist Conference had not gone so far in its indictment. The Soviet State was different from capitalist and *bour-geois* governments, they had told us when we objected to their absurdly illogical resolution asking for the legalisation of their work and the release of our comrades from prison. " In no country have the anar-chists ever begged favours from the government," we argued, " nor do they believe in loyalty to the State. Why do it here, if the Bolsheviki have broken faith? " The Bolshevik government was revolutionary in spite of its offences; it was proletarian in its nature and purposes, the Russian comrades insisted. Whereupon we had signed the peti-tion and agreed to present it to the proper authorities.

Both Sasha and I held on to the firm belief that the Bolsheviki were our brothers in a common fight. Our very lives and all our revolu-tionary hopes were staked upon it. Lenin, Trotsky, and their co-workers were the soul of the Revolution, we were sure, and its keenest defenders. We would go to them, to Lunacharsky, Kollontay, Bala-banoff. Jack Reed had spoken of them with deepest admiration and affection. They were capable of other criteria than a membership card in estimating people and events, Jack had said. They would help me see things in their proper light. I would seek them out. And our old teacher, Peter Kropotkin — we had drifted apart over our stand on the World War, but our love and esteem for his great personality and acute mind had not changed. I was certain that his feeling for us had also remained the same. We had been eager to see our dear comrade immediately upon our arrival in Russia. He was living in the village of Dmitrov, we had been informed, about sixty versts from Moscow, in his own little house, and he was well supplied with all necessaries by the Soviet Government. Travel was impossible then, but our trip would be arranged in the spring, Zorin had assured us.

Seeing Peter was too imperative for me now to stop at the hardships of travel. I would reach him somehow, I decided. He, of all people, would best be able to help me out of the pit of doubt and despair. He had returned to Russia after the February Revolution and he had witnessed the " October." He had seen some part of his cherished dream realized. His was a penetrating mind. He would strike the right key. I must go to him.

Alexandra Kollontay and Angelica Balabanoff were within easy reach, as they were living in the National. I sought out the former first. Mme Kollontay looked remarkably young and radiant, considering her fifty years and the severe operation she had recently undergone. A tall and stately woman, every inch the *grande dame* rather than the fiery revolutionist. Her attire and suite of two rooms bespoke good taste, the roses on her desk rather startling in the Russian greyness. They were the first I had seen since our deportation. Her handshake was limp and aloof, though she did say that she was glad to meet me at last in " great, vital Russia." Had I already found my place, she inquired, and the work I wanted to do? I replied that I still felt too uncertain of my ground to decide where I could be of best use. Perhaps I should know better after I had talked with her about the things that disturbed me, the contradictions I had found. I should tell her everything, she said; she was sure she could help me over my first difficult period. Every new-comer passes through the same state, she assured me, but everyone soon learns to see the greatness of Soviet Russia. The little things do not matter. I tried to tell her that my problems did not concern themselves with little things; they were vital and all-important to me. In fact, my very being depended on their right interpretation. "All right, go ahead," she remarked nonchalantly. She leaned back in her arm-chair and I began speaking of the harrowing things that had come to my knowledge. She listened attentively without interrupting me, but there was not the slightest indication in her cold, handsome face of any perturbation on account of my recital. "We do have some dull grey spots in our vivid revolutionary picture," she said when I had concluded. "They are unavoidable in a country so backward, with a people so dark and a social experiment of such magnitude, opposed by the entire world as it is. They will disappear when we have liquidated our military fronts and when we shall have raised the mental level of our masses." I could help in that, she continued. I could work among the women; they were ignorant of the simplest principles of life, physical and otherwise, ignorant of their own functions as mothers and citizens. I had done such fine work of that kind in America, and she could assure me of a much more fertile field in Russia. "Why not join me and stop your brooding over a few dull grey spots?" she said in conclusion; "they are nothing more, dear comrade, really nothing more."

People raided, imprisoned, and shot for their *ideas*! The old and the young held as hostages, every protest gagged, iniquity and favouritism rampant, the best human values betrayed, the very spirit of revolution daily crucified — were all these nothing but "grey, dull spots," I wondered! I felt chilled to the marrow of my bones.

Two days later I went to see Anatol Lunacharsky. His quarters were in the Kremlin, the impenetrable citadel of authority in the popular mind of Russia. I bore several credentials, and my escort was a "Sovietsky" anarchist held in high esteem by the Communists. Nevertheless we made very slow progress in reaching the seat of the People's Commissar for Education. Repeatedly the sentries scrutinized our *propusks* and asked questions regarding the purpose of our coming. At last we found ourselves in a reception room, a large salon filled with many objects of art and a crowd of people. They were artists, writers, and teachers awaiting an audience, my companion explained. A sorry and undernourished lot they were, their gaze steadily riveted on the door leading to the Commissar's private office. Hope and fear burned in their eyes. I too was anxious, though my rations did not depend on the man who presided over the cultural positions. Lunacharsky's greeting was warmer and more cordial than Kollontay's. He also inquired whether I had already found suitable work. If not, he could suggest a number of occupations in his department. The American system of education was being introduced in Soviet Russia, he said, and I, coming from that country, would undoubtedly be able to make valuable suggestions in regard to its proletarian application. I gasped. I forgot all about the purpose of my visit. The educational system found wanting and rejected by the best pedagogues in the United States now accepted as a model in revolutionary Russia? Lunacharsky looked much astonished. Was the system really being opposed in America, he inquired, and by whom? What changes had they suggested? I should explain the whole matter to him and his teachers, and he would call a special conference for the purpose. I could do much good, he urged, and I could be of great help to him in his struggle with the reactionary elements among the teachers who were clamouring for the old methods in dealing with the child and who even favoured prison for the mental defectives.

His eagerness to learn lessened somewhat my resentment at the attempt to transplant to Russia the American public-school system. It was evident that Lunacharsky knew nothing of the insurgent movement that had for years been trying to modernize that hoary and futile institution. I must point out to the educators of Russia the absurdity of aping those antiquated methods in the land of new life and values. But America was millions of miles away from my mind. Russia was consuming me, Russia with all her wonders and woes.

Lunacharsky continued to talk of his difficulties with the conservative instructors and of the controversy raging in the Soviet press about defective children and their treatment. He and Maxim Gorki were standing out against prison as a reformative influence; he himself was even opposed to milder forms, in fact to any form, of coercion in dealing with the young. "You are more in tune with the modern approach to the child than Maxim Gorki," I said. In part, however, he agreed with Gorki, he replied, for most of Russia's young generation were tainted with bad heredity, which the years of war and civic strife had accentuated. But rejuvenation could not be brought about by punishment or terror, he emphasized. "That is splendid," I remarked; "but are not terror and punishment the methods of dictatorship? And do you not approve of the latter?" He did, but only as a transitory factor, while Russia was being bled by the blockade and attacked on numerous fronts. "Once these have been liquidated, we will begin in earnest to build the real Socialist Republic, and the dictatorship will then go, of course." He considered it stupid to hold Denikin, Yudenich, and their kind responsible for all the shortcomings of Soviet Russia while ignoring the evil of the growing new bureaucracy and the increasing power of the Cheka. It was also very bad policy to proclaim Russia's educational achievements from the house-tops, he thought. Much was being done for the child, but the real herculean task was still ahead. "Rather heretical!" I remarked. He replied laughingly that he was considered even worse than a mere heretic because he had insisted that the intelligentsia, besides being indispensable, was, after all, also human and should not be forced to die by starvation. He had great faith in the proletariat, but he refused to swear by its infallibility. "If you don't look out, you'll be excommunicated," I warned him. "Yes, or put in a corner under the watchful eye of a teacher," he countered, with a knowing smile.

Lunacharsky did not give the impression of a vital personality, but he had broad humanity and I liked him for that. I wanted to broach my own problems, but I had already taken up too much time and I was conscious of the people waiting behind the door and undoubtedly cursing me. Before I left, Lunacharsky once more reiterated that his department was the right place for me, and that I must not leave Moscow until I had addressed the conference he was going to call.

On my way back to the National I learned from my escort that the People's Commissar for Education was considered not only sentimental, but also a scatter-brain and a wastrel. He was doing very little for the *proletcult* (proletarian culture), spending huge sums instead to protect *bourgeois* art. Worst of all, he was devoting most of his time to saving the last remnants of the counter-revolutionary intelligentsia. With the co-operation of Maxim Gorki he had succeeded in reinstating the old professors and teachers in the Dom Utcheniy (Home of the Learned). There they could keep warm while at work and get their rations without standing in line. He had also committed a grave offence in establishing the so-called academic ration for the more noted writers, thinkers, and scientists of Russia, irrespective of party affiliation. The academic ration was far from luxury and by no means too plentiful; many of the responsible Communists received even better provisions, but they were bitter against Lunacharsky for " favouring " the intelligentsia, my informant declared.

The poor bigots, I thought, to whom the Revolution meant only vengeance and a rung on the social ladder! They were the dead weight threatening to sink the revolutionary ship. Lunacharsky was aware of it. And Kollontay? I was certain she too knew better. But she was a diplomat trying to smooth over crude and hard places. Would Balabanoff also turn out to be of the same type, I wondered. Presently I had an opportunity to convince myself that she was quite the reverse.

The two leading Communist women of Russia proved the greatest contrast. Angelica Balabanoff lacked what Kollontay possessed in abundance: the latter's fine figure, good looks, and youthful litheness, as well as her worldly polish and sophistication. But Angelica had something that far outweighed the external attributes of her handsome comrade. In her large sad eyes there shone profundity, compassion, and tenderness. The tribulations of her people, the birth-pangs of her native land, the suffering of the downtrodden she had served her whole life were deeply graven on her pallid face. I found her ill, crumpled up on the couch of her small room, but she immediately became all interest and concern for me. Why had I not let her know that I was her neighbour, she asked. She would have come to me at once. And why had I waited so long before seeking her out? Did I need anything? She would see to it that my wants should be looked after. Coming from the States, I must find it very hard to adjust myself to Russia's poverty. It was different with the native masses, who had never known anything except hunger and want. Ah, the Russian masses, their power of endurance, their capacity for suffering, their heroism in the face of such fearful odds! Children in their weakness, giants in their strength! She had come to know them better since " October " than in all her previous years in Russia. She had grown to believe in them with a more abiding faith and to feel with them an all-embracing love.

It was dusk; the city's noises did not penetrate the cell-like room. Yet it was vibrant with stirring sounds. The face before me, shrunken and ashy, was beauteous now in the glow of its inner light. Without a word from me Angelica Balabanoff had guessed my doubts and travail. I sensed that her tribute to the Russian masses was her unique way of making me feel that nothing mattered so much to the ultimate triumph of the Revolution as the spiritual resources of the people themselves. I inquired whether that was her meaning, and she nodded assent. She knew from her own struggle that mine must be very hard and she wanted me never to lose sight of the peaks of the " October " ascendancy.

I walked to her couch and stroked her thick braided black hair, already streaked with grey. I must call her Angelica, she said, drawing me to her heart. She asked me to ring for a comrade on the same floor to bring the samovar. She had some *varenya* (fruit jelly), and Swedish comrades had given her some biscuits and butter. She felt very guilty to enjoy such luxuries when the people did not have enough bread. But her stomach was bad; she could digest nothing, and so perhaps she was not so inconsistent as it might appear. Such selflessness amidst the callous indifference I had found everywhere moved me deeply. I broke down and wept as I had not since I had held my dear Helena in my arms at our final parting. Angelica became frightened. Had she said anything to cause me pain, or was I ill or in trouble? I opened my heart to her and poured out everything, my shocks, disillusionments, and nightmares, all the dreadful things and thoughts that had been oppressing me since my arrival. What was the answer, what the explanation, and where the responsibility?

Life itself is behind all frustration, Angelica replied, in an individual as well as in a social sense. Life was hard and cruel, and those who would live must also grow cruel and hard. Life is replete with eddies and whirlpools; its currents are violent and destructive. The sensitive, those shrinking from hurt, cannot hold their own against it. As with man, so with his ideas and ideals. The finer they are, the more humane, the sooner their death from the impact of Life. " But this is fatalism with a vengeance," I protested; " how can you harmonize such an attitude with your socialistic views and materialistic conception of history and human development? " Angelica explained that Russian reality had convinced her that life, and not theories, dictates the course of human events. " Life! Life! " I cried impatiently, " what is it but what the genius of man imparts to it? And what is the use of human striving if some mysterious power called Life can turn it to naught? " Angelica replied that there really was no particular sense in our efforts, except that living meant striving, reaching out for something better. But I should not mind her, she hastened to add. She was probably all wrong, and those others right who could pay the full measure life exacts. " You must go to see ' Ilich,' " she advised; only he, Lenin, could help me, for he knew how to meet the demands of Life. She would arrange an interview for me.

I left the dear little woman with mixed feelings. Soothed and comforted by her rich fount of love, I at the same time disapproved of her acquiescence in the evils and abuses about her. I had known of her as a fighter, always firm and unflinching in her stand. What had made her so passive now, I wondered. Communists enjoyed the right of criticism, as I had learned from the Bolshevik press. Why, then, did Angelica not use her pen and voice in and out of the party? It kept worrying me and I sought an opportunity to speak to her woman comrade who had served us tea. From her I learned that Angelica had been secretary of the Third International. In that capacity she had fought determinedly against the growing bureaucracy of the clique led by Zinoviev, Radek, and Bukharin. As a result she was most unceremoniously kicked out and denied all responsible work. It was not that Angelica cared about the personal injustice and insult. But she felt that the methods of intrigue and slander employed against her were also being used against other sincere comrades at variance with the leaders. This poison was eating into the very body of the party, and Angelica knew that it was fraught with disastrous results to the Revolution. " Is there no way of putting a stop to such nefarious methods? " I asked Angelica's friend. There was none, she assured me, none within Russia, and no one would think of a protest abroad as long as the Revolution was in danger. This awareness had undermined Angelica's health and had paralysed her will. Her mental state was due to the methods employed by her party, including the widespread suffering, the terror, and the cheapness of human life. Angelica could not face them.

Dear, sweet Angelica — I began to understand her better and what she meant by the currents of life. But I could not share her attitude. I could not submit. I must probe into the hidden sources of Russia's ills, I felt; I must unearth their causes and proclaim them aloud. No party clique should tie my tongue.

I had not seen Sasha for several days. The long trip from Kharitonenskaya to the National was too exhausting, he said. But the morning after my visit with Angelica I received a hurry call to come to his lodgings. I found Sasha ill in bed, with no help near. I dropped everything and took up my old profession of nursing. His fever was stubborn, but his dogged will to live presently won out. His illness left him weak and spent, however, and in no condition to remain alone. I could not stop at the Kharitonenskaya, nor could Sasha, for that matter, for the house commandant had informed him that his time had expired and that he would have to vacate his room. We were planning to leave for Petrograd within a week and it was therefore useless to argue with the official *tovarishtch*. We went to the National, my room fortunately being larger than the one I had occupied in the Astoria, and provided with an extra couch. When Angelica learned of Sasha's illness and his presence in the National, she immediately constituted herself his guardian angel. Her family of Swedish, Norwegian, and Dutch comrades seemed to increase all the time, and from them she would bring Sasha same delicate morsels. I had learned through various sources that Angelica was looked upon by her comrades as a " sentimental *bourzhooy*." She was wasting her time, they said, on philanthropy, always trying to procure milk for some sick baby, extra things for a pregnant woman, or old clothes for people of useless age.

When Angelica had suggested that I go to see Lenin, I decided to work out a memorandum of the most salient contradictions in Soviet life, but, not having heard anything more about the proposed interview, I had not done anything about the matter. Angelica's telephone message one morning, informing me that " Ilich " was waiting to see Sasha and me, and that his auto had come for us, was therefore most disconcerting. We knew Lenin was so crowded with work that he was almost inaccessible. The exception in our favour was a chance we could not miss. We felt that even without our memorandum we should find the right approach to our discussion; moreover, we should have the opportunity to present to him the resolutions our Moscow comrades had entrusted to us.

Lenin's auto rushed at furious speed along the congested streets and into the Kremlin, past every sentry without being halted for *propusks*. At the entrance of one of the ancient buildings that stood apart from the rest, we were asked to alight. An armed guard was at the elevator, evidently already apprised of our coming. Without a word, he unlocked the door and motioned us within, then locked it and put the key into his pocket. We heard our names shouted to the soldier on the first floor, the call repeated in the same loud voice at the next and the next. A chorus was announcing our coming as the elevator slowly ascended. At the top a guard repeated the process of unlocking and locking the elevator, then ushered us into a vast reception hall with the announcement: " *Tovarishtchy* Goldman and Berkman." We were asked to wait a moment, but almost an hour passed before the ceremony of leading us to the seat of the highest was resumed. A young man motioned us to follow him. We passed through a number of offices teeming with activity, the click of typewriters, and busy couriers. We were halted before a massive door ornamented with beautifully carved work. Excusing himself for just a minute, our attendant disappeared behind it. Presently the heavy door opened from within, and our guide invited us to step in, himself vanishing and closing the door behind us. We stood on the threshold awaiting the next cue in the strange proceedings. Two slanting eyes were fixed upon us with piercing penetration. Their owner sat behind a huge desk, everything on it arranged with the strictest precision, the rest of the room giving the impression of the same exactitude. A board with numerous telephone switches and a map of the world covered the entire wall behind the man; glass cases filled with heavy tomes lined the sides. A large oblong table hung with red; twelve straight-backed chairs, and several arm-chairs at the windows. Nothing else to relieve the orderly monotony, except the bit of flaming red.

The background seemed most fitting for one reputed for his rigid habits of life and matter-of-factness. Lenin, the man most idolized in the world and equally hated and feared, would have been out of place in surroundings of less severe simplicity.

" Ilich wastes no time on preliminaries. He goes straight to his objective," Zorin had once said to me with evident pride. Indeed, every step Lenin had made since 1917 testified to this. But if we had been in doubt, the manner of our reception and the mode of our interview would have quickly convinced us of the emotional economy of Ilich. His quick perception of its supply in others and his skill in making the utmost use of it for his purpose were extraordinary. No less amazing was his glee over anything he considered funny in himself or his visitors. Especially if he could put one at a disadvantage, the great Lenin would shake with laughter so as to compel one to laugh with him.

His sharp scrutiny having bared us to the bone, we were treated to a volley of questions, one following the other like arrows from his flint-like brain. America, her political and economic conditions — what were the chances of revolution there in the near future? The

American Federation of Labor — was it all honeycombed with *bourgeois* ideology or was it only Gompers and his clique, and was the rank and file a fertile soil for boring from within? The I.W.W. — what was its strength, and were the anarchists actually as effective as our recent trial would seem to indicate? He had just finished reading our speeches in court. " Great stuff! Clear-cut analysis of the capitalist system, splendid propaganda! " Too bad we could not have remained in the United States, no matter at what price. We were most welcome in Soviet Russia, of course, but such fighters were badly needed in America to help in the approaching revolution, " as many of your best comrades had been in ours." "And you, *Tovarishtch* Berkman, what an organizer you must be, like Shatoff. True metal, your comrade Shatoff; shrinks from nothing and can work like a dozen men. In Siberia now, commissar of railroads in the Far Eastern Republic. Many other anarchists hold important positions with us. Everything is open to them if they are willing to co-operate with us as true *ideiny* anarchists. You, *Tovarishtch* Berkman, will soon find your place. A pity, though, that you were torn away from America at this portentous time. And you, *Tovarishtch* Goldman? What a field you had! You could have remained. Why didn't you, even if *Tovarishtch* Berkman was shoved out? Well, you're here. Have you thought of the work you want to do? You are *ideiny* anarchists, I can see that by your stand on the war, your defence of ' October,' and your fight for us, your faith in the soviets. Just like your great comrade Malatesta, who is entirely with Soviet Russia. What is it you prefer to do? "

Sasha was the first to get his breath. He began in English, but Lenin at once stopped him with a mirthful laugh. " Do you think I understand English? Not a word. Nor any other foreign languages. I am no good at them, though I have lived abroad for many years. Funny, isn't it? " And off he went in peals of laughter. Sasha continued in Russian. He was proud to hear his comrades praised so highly, he said; but why were anarchists in Soviet prisons? " Anarchists? " Ilich interrupted; " nonsense! Who told you such yarns, and how could you believe them? We do have bandits in prison, and Makhnovtsy, but no *ideiny* anarchists."

" Imagine," I broke in, " capitalist America also divides the anarchists into two categories, philosophic and criminal. The first are accepted in the highest circles; one of them is even high in the councils of the Wilson Administration. The second category, to which we have the honour of belonging, is persecuted and often imprisoned. Yours also seems to be a distinction without a difference. Don't you think so?" Bad reasoning on my part, Lenin replied, sheer muddle-headedness to draw similar conclusions from different premises. Free speech is a *bourgeois* prejudice, a soothing plaster for social ills. In the Workers' Republic economic well-being talks louder than speech, and its freedom is far more secure. The proletarian dictatorship is steering that course. Just now it faces very grave obstacles, the greatest of them the opposition of the peasants. They need nails, salt, textiles, tractors, electrification. When we can give them these, they will be with us, and no counter-revolutionary power will be able to swerve them back. In the present state of Russia all prattle of freedom is merely food for the reaction trying to down Russia. Only bandits are guilty of that, and they must be kept under lock and key.

Sasha handed Lenin the resolutions of the anarchist conference and emphasized the assurance of the Moscow comrades that the imprisoned comrades were *ideiny* and not bandits. " The fact that our people ask to be legalized is proof that they are with the Revolution and the Soviets," we argued. Lenin took the document and promised to submit it to the next session of the Party Executive. We would be notified of its decision, he said, but in any event it was a mere trifle, nothing to disturb any true revolutionist. Was there anything else? We had fought in America for the political rights even of our opponents, we told him; the denial of them to our own comrades was therefore no trifle to us. I, for one, felt, I informed him, that I could not co-operate with a régime that persecuted anarchists or others for the sake of mere opinion. Moreover, there were even more appalling evils. How were we to reconcile them with the high goal he was aiming at? I mentioned some of them. His reply was that my attitude was *bourgeois* sentimentality. The proletarian dictatorship was engaged in a life-and-death struggle, and small considerations could not be permitted to weigh in the scale. Russia was making giant strides at home and abroad. It was igniting the world revolution, and here I was lamenting over a little blood-letting. It was absurd, and I must get over it. " Do something," he advised; " that will be the best way of regaining your revolutionary balance."

Lenin might be right, I thought. I would take his advice. I would start at once, I said. Not with any work within Russia, but with something of propaganda value for the United States. I should like to organize a society of Russian Friends of American Freedom, an active body to give support to America's struggle for liberty, as the American Friends of Russian Freedom had done in aid of Russia against the tsarist régime.

Lenin had not moved in his seat during the entire time, but now he almost leaped out of it. He swung round and stood facing us. " That's a brilliant idea ! " he exclaimed, chuckling and rubbing his hands. " A fine practical proposal. You must proceed to carry it out at once. And you, *Tovarishtch* Berkman, will you co-operate in it ? " Sasha replied that we had talked the matter over and had already worked out the details of the plan. We could start immediately if we had the necessary equipment. No difficulty in that, Lenin assured us ; we would be supplied with everything — an office, a printing outfit, couriers, and whatever funds would be needed. We must send him our prospectus of work and the itemized expenses involved in the project. The Third International would take care of the matter. It was the proper channel for our venture, and it would afford us every help.

In blank astonishment we looked at each other and at Lenin. Simultaneously we began to explain that our efforts could prove effective only if free from any affiliation with known Bolshevik organizations. It must be carried out in our own way ; we knew the American psychology and how best to conduct the work. But before we could proceed further, our guide suddenly appeared, as unobtrusively as he had left, and Lenin held out his hand to us in good-bye. " Don't forget to send me the prospectus," he called after us.

The methods of the " clique " in the *politbureau* of the party were also pervading the International and poisoning the entire labour movement, Angelica's friend had told me. Was Lenin aware of it? And was that also a mere trifle in his estimation? I was certain now that he knew everything that was going on in Russia. Nothing escaped his searching eye, nothing could take place without first having been weighed in his scale and approved by his authoritative seal. An indomitable will easily bending everyone to its own curve and just as easily breaking men if they failed to yield. Would he also bend or break us ? The danger was imminent if we made the first false step, if we accepted the tutelage of the Communist International. We were eager to help Russia and to continue our work for America's liberation, to which we had given the best years of our lives. But it would mean a betrayal of our entire past and the complete abrogation of our independence to submit to the control of the clique. We wrote Lenin to that effect and enclosed a detailed outline of our plan, carefully prepared by Sasha.

We agreed with Lenin in one thing, the need of getting to work. Not, however, in any political capacity or in a Soviet bureau. We must find something that would bring us in direct touch with the masses and enable us to serve them. Moscow was the seat of the Government with more State functionaries than workers, bureaucratic to the last degree. Sasha had visited a number of factories, all of them in a palpably neglected and deserted condition. In most of them the Soviet officials and members of the Communist *yacheika* (cell) far outnumbered the actual producers. He had talked with the workers and found them embittered by the arrogance and arbitrary methods of the industrial bureaucracy. Sasha's impressions only served to strengthen my conviction that Moscow was no place for us. If at least Lunacharsky had kept his promise! But he was swamped with work, he wrote, and unable just then to call the teachers' conference. It might take weeks before it could be done. He understood how difficult it was for people used to doing things in their own independent manner to fit themselves into a groove. But it was the only effective place in Russia and I would have to reconcile myself to that. Meanwhile I must keep in touch with him, his letter concluded.

It was a subtle hint that the dictatorship was all-pervading and that it would brook no independent effort. Not in Moscow, at any rate. After all, every seat of government inevitably breeds the martinet and the flunkey, the courtier and the spy, a herd of hangers-on fed by the official hand. Moscow was evidently no exception. We could not find our place there, nor come close to the toiling masses. One more thing we would attempt — get to see our comrade Kropotkin and then back to Petrograd, we decided.

We learned that George Lansbury and Mr. Barry were about to go to Dmitrov in a special train. We decided to ask permission to join them, though we were not elated over the prospect of seeing Peter in the presence of two newspaper men. We had not been able to arrange a trip to Dmitrov, and this was an unexpected and exceptional opportunity. Sasha hastened to see Lansbury. The latter consented to have us accompany him and even expressed his willingness that we bring with us anyone else we might want. He assured Sasha that he had long wanted to see me again and that he would be delighted at the chance. Considering that he had all along known of my presence in Moscow and that he had not taken the trouble to look me up, his delight seemed rather questionable. But the main thing was to meet Peter, and we also invited our comrade Alexander Schapiro to come with us.

The train crawled snail-like, stopping at every water-tank. It was late evening when we at last reached the house. We found Peter ill and worn-looking. He appeared a mere shadow of the sturdy man I had known in Paris and London in 1907. Since my coming to Russia I had been repeatedly assured by the most prominent Communists that Kropotkin lived in very comfortable circumstances and that he lacked neither food nor fuel; and here were Peter, his wife, Sophie, and their daughter, Alexandra, actually living in one room by no means sufficiently heated. The temperature in the other rooms was below zero, so that they could not be inhabited. Their rations, sufficient to exist on, had until recently been supplied by the Dmitrov co-operative society. That organization had since been liquidated, like so many other similar institutions, and most of its members arrested and taken to the Butirky prison in Moscow. How did they manage to exist, we inquired. Sophie explained that they had a cow and enough produce from her garden for the winter. The comrades from the Ukraine, particularly Makhno, had contrived to supply them with extra provisions. They would have managed to better advantage had not Peter been ailing of late and in need of more nourishing food.

Could nothing be done to rouse the responsible Communists to the fact that one of the greatest men of Russia was starving to death? Even if they had no interest in him as an anarchist, they must know his worth as a man of science and letters. Lenin, Lunacharsky, and the others in high position were probably not informed about Peter's situation. Could I not call their attention to his condition? Lansbury agreed with me. "It is impossible," he said, "that the big people in the Soviet Government would let so great a personality as Peter Kropotkin want for the necessaries of life. We in England would not stand for such an outrage." He would immediately take the matter up with the Soviet comrades, he declared. Sophie had been repeatedly pulling at his sleeve to make him stop. She did not want Peter to hear our talk. But that dear soul was deeply immersed in conversation with the two Alexanders, quite unaware that we were discussing his welfare.

Peter would accept nothing from the Bolsheviki, Sophie told us. Only a short time previously, when the rouble still stood well, he had refused the offer of 250,000 roubles from the Government Publication Department for the right to issue his literary work. Since the Bolsheviki had expropriated others, they might as well help themselves to his books, he had said. But it would not be done with his consent. He had never willingly dealt with any government and he had no intention of doing so with the one that in the name of socialism had abrogated every revolutionary and ethical value. Sophie had not even been able to induce Peter to accept the academic ration Lunacharsky had ordered for him. His increasing feebleness had compelled her to take it without his knowledge. His health, she apologized, was more important to her than his scruples. Besides, as a scientific botanist she was herself entitled to the academic ration.

Sasha was speaking to Peter of the maze of revolutionary contradictions we had found in Russia, the varied interpretations we had heard of the causes of the crying evils, and our interview with Lenin. We were eager to hear Peter's view-point and get his reactions to the situation. He replied that it was what it had always been to Marxism and its theories. He had foreseen its dangers and he had always warned against them. All anarchists had done so, and he himself had dealt with them in nearly every one of his writings. True, none of us had fully realized to what proportions the Marxian menace would grow. Perhaps it was not so much Marxism as the Jesuitical spirit of its dogmas. The Bolsheviki were poisoned by it, their dictatorship surpassing the autocracy of the Inquisition. Their power was strengthened by the blustering statesmen of Europe. The blockade, the Allied support of the counter-revolutionary elements, the intervention, and all the other attempts to crush the Revolution had resulted in silencing every protest against Bolshevik tyranny within Russia itself. " Is there no one to speak out against it? " I demanded, " no one whose voice would carry weight? Yours, for instance, dear comrade? " Peter smiled sadly. I would know better, he said, after I had been awhile longer in the country. The gag was the most complete in the world. He had protested, of course, and so had others, among them the venerable Vera Figner, as well as Maxim Gorki on several occasions. It had no effect whatever, nor was it possible to do any writing with the Cheka constantly at one's door. One could not keep " incriminating " things in one's house nor expose others to the peril of discovery.

It was not fear; it was the realization of the futility and impossibility of reaching the world from the inner prisons of the Cheka. The main drawback, however, was the enemies surrounding Russia. Anything said or written against the Bolsheviki was bound to be interpreted by the outside world as an attack upon the Revolution and as alignment with the reactionary forces. The anarchists in particular were between two fires. They could not make peace with the formidable power of the Kremlin, nor could they join hands with the enemies of Russia. Their only alternative at present, it seemed to Peter, was to find some work of direct benefit to the masses. He was glad that we had decided on that. " Ridiculous of Lenin to want to bind you to the apron-strings of the party," he declared. " It shows how far mere shrewdness is from wisdom. No one can deny Lenin's shrewdness, but neither in his attitude to the peasants nor in his appraisal of those within or outside the reach of corruption has he shown real judgment or sagacity."

It was growing late and Sophie had been trying to prevail upon Peter to retire. But he persistently declined. He had been so long cut off from his comrades — indeed, from any kind of intellectual contact, he said. Our visit at first seemed to exert a bracing effect upon him. But presently he began to show signs of exhaustion, and we felt it was high time to go. Gentle and gallant was our Peter even in his fatigue. Nothing would do but he must see us to the exit and once more clasp us lovingly to his heart.

Our train was not to start till two a.m., and it was only eleven. The woman porter was fast asleep. She had forgotten to look after the fire, and the car was bitterly cold. The boys set to work over the stove, but it would yield nothing except smoke. Meanwhile Lansbury, wrapped up to his ears in his great fur coat, held forth on what a pity it was that Peter Kropotkin's age disqualified him from taking an active part in Soviet affairs. Living away from the centre, Kropotkin was not in a position to do justice to the grandiose achievements of the Bolsheviki, he reiterated. I was almost frozen and too miserable over Peter's condition to argue. But the boys did it for the three of us. At the Moscow station Sasha had another tilt with the London editor. Starved and half-naked children besieged us for a piece of bread. I had sandwiches on hand and we gave them to the kids, who devoured them ravenously. "A terrible sight," Sasha remarked. "Look here,

Berkman, you are too sentimental," Lansbury retorted; " I could show you any number of poverty-stricken children in the East End of London." " I am sure you could," Sasha replied, " but you forget that the Revolution *has* taken place in Russia, not in England."

Our journey laid me up with a heavy cold and fever for a fortnight. Angelica was again beautifully solicitous, calling every day to look after me and never empty-handed. The comrades of the Universalist Club were also very helpful. Their care and that of gentle Angelica enabled me to leave my sick-bed much quicker than if I had been less fortunate in friends and attention. They urged me to stay at least another week. Travelling was dangerous at best and I was not yet completely recovered. But I could not bear Moscow any longer. It had grown into a veritable monster that I had to escape lest it destroy me. Petrograd held out the hope of relief in useful labour. And there was also my gnawing longing for news from my old home. Five months had passed without a word from anyone. The address we had left with our friends in America was Petrograd. My yearning was mingled with some unaccountable apprehension, both combining into the *idée fixe* that I must hasten back to the northern city.

Mail was actually awaiting us there, received four weeks previously. Why had it not been forwarded, we asked Liza Zorin. " What was the use ? " she replied; " I did not think anything from America so important and interesting as what you must have seen and heard in Moscow." The letters were from Fitzi and Stella. Not " so important " — only news of the death of my beloved Helena. What could personal sorrow mean to people who had become cogs in the wheel that was crushing so many at every turn? I myself seemed to have turned into one of the cogs. I could find no tears for the loss of my darling sister, no tears or regrets. Only paralysing numbness and a larger void.

My deportation, Stella wrote, had proved the last blow to Helena's shattered condition. She had grown steadily worse from the moment she had heard about it. Death was more kind to her than life : it came quickly through a stroke. Dear, sweet sister, merciful indeed was your end, your supreme wish fulfilled since David's loss. Your tortured spirit at last found release in eternal rest, my beloved. You are at peace. Not so those whose lives are strewn with the autumn leaves of hope, the withered branches of a dying faith.

Fitzi's letter contained another blow. Our friend Aline Barnsdall had made all arrangements to go to Russia and she had invited Fitzi to come with her. But at the last moment Washington had refused them passports. M. Eleanor Fitzgerald was too well known as " a notorious anarchist, the co-worker of Alexander Berkman and Emma Goldman," the authorities had declared, and she was therefore not allowed to leave the country. Aline Barnsdall's affiliations with radicals had also been traced through the cheque she had given me. Fitzi had no means, even if she could have found some *sub rosa* way of reaching Russia. She was all broken up over her failure to join us, but she knew we would understand.

On our return to Petrograd we found our fellow-passengers of the *Buford* considerably dimininished in numbers. Some of them had succeeded in getting sent to their native places. Others, who in America had been bitter opponents of our defence of the Bolsheviki, became reconciled to the Soviet régime. In Rome now, they argued, they would howl with the Romans. The eleven Communists among the deportees were entirely in clover. They found the flesh-pots prepared for them, and the tables laden. They had but to grab the best place and morsels.

The remaining group was in a deplorable condition. Their attempts to secure useful work, for which years of labour in the United States had qualified them, brought no results. They were being sent from one institution to another, from commissar to commissar, without anyone able to decide whether their efforts were needed and where.

Here was Russia, famished for what these men could and longed to give, yet their productive capacities were compelled to lie fallow, and everything was being done to turn their devotion to hatred. Was this to be the lot of other workers to be deported from the United States and of those who would flock to Soviet Russia to aid the Revolution, we wondered. We could not sit by without at least essaying some effort to prevent the repetition of such criminal stupidity. Sasha proposed a clearing-house for the American deportees, those already in Russia and the others that were being expected. He worked out a plan for their reception, which was to be less ostentatious than on the occasion of our arrival, but which would assure greater security of food and lodging, better economy and practical sense. His project included the classification of the refugees by trade and occupation and assignment to useful and needed work. "Think of the gain to the Revolution if American training and experience were sensibly directed into productive channels," Sasha commented. His plan also provided an immediate opening for our own usefulness and that of other deportees in the city.

I suggested that we get in touch with Mme Ravich about the matter. Herself a prodigious worker and very efficient, she would be quick to see the value of Sasha's idea. Chicherin's representative in the Petrograd Foreign Office was also chief of the city's militia as well as commissar of the factory women's collectives. She lived in the Astoria and we knew the long hours she remained at her desk. I phoned to her at two a.m. and asked for an appointment. She requested me to call at once, adding that she had just received a message from Chicherin for " *Tovarishtchy* Goldman and Berkman."

A large contingent of American deportees were on their way to Russia, Mme Ravich informed us, and Comrade Chicherin had instructed her to put us in charge of their reception. It was a most propitious occasion to broach Sasha's plan. Regardless of the late hour and her fatigue, Mme Ravich would not consent to our leaving until we had fully explained the project. We could count entirely on her co-operation, she assured us, and she would immediately issue directions to her secretary to facilitate our work in every way.

Mme Ravich kept her word, even supplying us with an automobile to save time in getting about. Her assistant, Kaplan, proved an earnest and willing aid, arming us with numerous *propusks* to secure us access to various departments. In his eagerness to help he even proposed to have a *tovarishtch* Chekist accompany us, to enable us to get quicker results. I assured him that I knew of a less drastic and more effective way, ironic and humbling though it was to admit it. Was there really such a method in the Soviet Republic, he inquired. Alas, not homegrown, but imported from the United States, I told him. It was American chocolate, cigarettes, and condensed milk. Their softening and soothing effect had proved irresistible to many Soviet hearts, inducing action and willingness where coaxing, commands, and threats had failed.

Now they achieved in a fortnight what Ravich and Kaplan admitted would have ordinarily taken months to accomplish. Three old germ-eaten buildings were renovated and equipped for the use of the expected deportees; the distribution of their rations organized so as to save their standing in queues, medical attention prepared in case of need, and employment secured for the " swimming " contingent.

Sasha and Ethel had in the meantime taken charge of the welcome to be given the deportees on the Latvian border. They were awaiting them there, with two trains held in readiness to bring the expected thousand refugees to Petrograd. They spent two weeks in vain waiting, only to find out that another blunder had been added to the chaos and confusion of the Soviet situation. The wireless announcing returning war prisoners had been misread by the Foreign Office to mean American deportees. Sasha had repeatedly telegraphed to Chicherin to explain the mistake and offering to use his trains for bringing the war prisoners to Petrograd. He was ordered, however, to remain on the border to await the American deportees; the war prisoners would be taken care of by the War Commissariat. But Sasha had positively ascertained from the war prisoners' convoy that no political refugees were on their way from America. Instead of keeping his trains and provisions for the mythical deportees, as directed by Moscow, and leaving the fifteen hundred war prisoners to their fates on the uninhabited plain, without food or medical aid, Sasha decided to put his trains at their disposal and send them on to Petrograd.

We proposed to use the buildings we had prepared for the benefit of the war prisoners, and Mme Ravich favoured the suggestion. But the men were under the jurisdiction of the War Department, and she felt she must first get permission. Nothing further was heard of the matter. The quarters renovated with so much effort and time were sealed up and three able-bodied militiamen stationed on guard. All our labour was wasted, and Sasha's plan of organizing the deportees or the war prisoners for useful work was allowed to go by the board.

The same disheartening results met our other attempts to do practical work outside of the State machine. We would not be daunted, however.

The palatial residences of the former rich in the part of Petrograd known as Kammenny Ostrov (Island) were to be turned into rest-homes for toilers. "Marvellous idea, isn't it?" Zorin remarked to us; "we must complete it within six weeks." Only American speed and efficiency could accomplish the job on time. Would we help? We took the work in hand and became absorbed in it, until again we struck the impassable wall of Soviet bureaucracy.

From the start we had insisted that at least one warm meal a day should be provided for the workers employed in the preparation of rest-homes for their brothers. I had undertaken to supervise the cooking and the equitable distribution of the rations. For a while all went well; the men were satisfied with the arrangements, and their labours were making unusual progress — unusual for Russians, at any rate. But presently the Bolshevik staffs and their favourites began to increase and the rations of the workers to diminish. The latter were not long in perceiving that they were being robbed of their share for the sake of unnecessary office-holders and hangers-on. Their interest in the work showed signs of waning and presently the effects became apparent. We protested to Zorin against the farce of ill-treating one set of workers to enable another set to enjoy leisure and a rest. Equally we objected to the peremptory eviction from their homes of people whose only offence was a university degree. Old teachers and professors had been occupying some houses on the island ever since October, and no one had troubled them in any way. Now they and their families were to be deprived of home without any possibility of securing another roof over their heads. Zorin had requested Sasha to have the eviction orders carried out. But Sasha emphatically refused to act as the bully of the Communist State.

Zorin felt indignant at our " rank sentimentality." A man with Berkman's revolutionary record, he said, should not shrink from any task; it made no difference whether the *bourgeois* parasites ended in the gutter or threw themselves into the Neva. We replied that translating Communism into the everyday life of Russia was more revolutionary than its denial and betrayal in behalf of an alleged future. But Zorin had become too blinded by his creed to see its disintegrating and devastating effect. He ceased calling for us on his daily ride to the island. We did not want him to think that our interest in the work depended on the comfort of his car and we continued to make the long journey on foot, which required about three hours' walk. Before long, however, we found others in our places, persons more pliable in the hands of the political machine. We understood.

The rest-homes were inaugurated with much éclat. To us the rows of rusty iron bedsteads in the vast salons, with their furniture of faded silk and plush, looked tawdry, cold, and uninviting. No worker with any self-respect could feel at ease or enjoy a rest in such surroundings. Many shared our views, and some even felt convinced that none but those within the party or hanging on to its coat-tails would ever see the inside of the Rest Homes for Workers on the Kammenny Ostrov.

We went our way in painful contemplation of the real tragedy of the Revolution become overgrown with poisonous weeds sapping its precious life. Still we would not despair or give up. Somewhere, somehow it must be possible to undertake the clearing of the path. The smallest beginning, we wanted nothing more. Surely we should find that much, if only we persevered in our search.

The Sovietsky soup-kitchens were an abomination, Zorin had repeatedly told us. Could we suggest some improvement, he asked. Sasha again became all interest, completely immersing himself in his new project of reorganizing the nauseating dining-rooms. In a few days he had outlined a complete project, every item provided for in his usual painstaking manner. A chain of cafeterias was to cover the entire city, planned to eliminate the great waste of food and the superfluous employees in the existing kitchens. Even with the given supplies, scarce though they were, simple but palatable dishes would be served in clean and cheerful surroundings. Sasha would undertake the work, and he was sure I would assist. A few cafeterias to begin with, later to be extended.

An amazing idea, Zinoviev said approvingly. Why had no one thought of it before? Very simple and easily carried out. There was great enthusiasm over it on all sides, and plenty of promises. Petrograd was filled with stores, locked and sealed since the Revolution. Sasha could select the necessary furnishings, get men to remodel the places and have the supplies and everything else needed. My pal was again on deck, his organizing ingenuity on fire in behalf of his plan.

This time there could be no hitch, we were assured. But again the bureaucracy blocked every move initiated without them. Difficulties began to appear in the most unexpected quarters. Officials were too busy to aid Sasha's work, and, after all, wholesome eating-places were not so important in the scale of the world revolution that was expected to break out momentarily. It was absurd to lay stress on immediate amelioration in the face of the general situation. At best it could have no vital effect on the course of the Revolution. And Berkman could do more important work. He should not busy himself as a reformer. It was most disappointing, for everyone had thought him to be a revolutionist of steel and iron. It was naïve of Berkman to claim that feeding the masses was the first concern of the Revolution, the care of the people, their contentment and joy, its main hope and safety, and indeed its only *raison d'être* and moral meaning. Such sentimentality was the purest *bourgeois* ideology. The Red Army and the Cheka were the strength of the Revolution, and its best defence. The capitalist world knew it and was trembling before the might of armed Russia.

One more hope perished, like the preceding ones. Yet to be reborn again in every pulse-beat of a stout heart. Sasha's determination and strength had never been greater. My Yiddish perseverance also refused to surrender. All Soviet streams do not lead to the same muddy pools, we thought. There must be others running into the deep, bracing sea. We must persevere and strike out for other fields.

I talked to the wife of Lashevich, Zinoviev's friend, high in the Bolshevik councils, about the condition of the hospitals. I was a trained nurse and I should be happy to give my services in improving them. She volunteered to call the matter to the attention of Comrade Pervoukhin, the Petrograd Board of Health Commissar. Weeks passed before I received word to call on him. I hastened to the Board of Health.

A trained nurse, months in Russia already and yet not assigned to him for service, Pervoukhin exclaimed. I should have known that he was desperately in need of just such aid. The hospitals were in a wretched condition; there was great scarcity of dispensaries and a lack of trained help, not to speak of the dearth of medical facilities and surgical instruments. He could use several hundred American nurses and here I had been doing nothing all this time. I must start in at once, he urged. As to co-operation, I could count on him to the limit, including an auto to make my rounds. He would take me for the first tour of inspection as soon as I was ready to start. Could I report to him in the morning?

I would come early, I replied, but he should not over-estimate my abilities and importance in the colossal task on hand. I would do my utmost, of course, I could promise him that. He would expect nothing else from a *tovarishtch,* he replied, from an old revolutionist and Communist, as he had been informed. I was indeed a Communist, I assented, but of the anarchist school. Oh yes, he understood that, but there was really no difference. Many anarchists had realized this and they were entirely with the party, working with the Bolsheviki and doing finely. "I also am with you," I said, "in the defence of the Revolution, even to my last breath." Not with the Communism of the dictatorship, however, I explained. I had not been able to reconcile myself to that, for I could not see the remotest relationship between the coerced and forced form of State communism and that of the free and voluntary co-operation of anarchist communism.

I had so often seen Communists on such occasions instantly alter their tone and manner that I was not surprised at the sudden change in Commissar Pervoukhin. The kindly physician so deeply concerned in the people's health, the humanitarian who had a moment previously so lamented his lack of nurses to minister to the ill and afflicted, immediately became the political fanatic fairly oozing antagonism and resentment. Did my differing view-point matter in the care of the sick, or did he think it would affect my usefulness as a nurse, I inquired. He forced a sickly smile, replying that in Soviet Russia everyone who wants to work is welcome. His ideas are not questioned, provided he is a true revolutionist willing to set all political considerations aside. Would I do so? I could make no pledges except one, I replied. I would help him to the best of my ability.

I called the next day and every day for a week. Pervoukhin did not take me on the planned tour of inspection. For hours he kept me in his office arguing the infallibility of the Communist State and the immaculate conception of the Bolshevik dictatorship. One must either accept them without question or be shut out of the fold. Ghastly hospitals, lack of medical supplies, no adequate care of the patients — those were piffling matters as compared with the required faith in the new trinity. I was evidently no longer " desperately needed." I was shut out.

With the help of my Astoria Hotel neighbour, young Kibalchich, I succeeded in visiting a few hospitals. Their condition was appalling. The true cause of it was not so much poor equipment or the lack of nurses. It was the omnipresent machine, the Communist " cell," the commissars, the eternal suspicion and surveillance. Physicians and surgeons with splendid records in their profession, touchingly devoted to their work, were hampered at every turn and paralysed in the atmosphere of dread, hatred, and fear. Even the Communists among them were helpless. Some of them had not yet been entirely divested of human feeling by the régime. Being of the intelligentsia, they were considered doubtful characters and were kept in leash. I understood why Pervoukhin could not have me on his staff.

These rude awakenings in the Soviet Arcadia of dictatorship were followed by repeated and more forcible jolts. They helped still further to uproot my cherished belief in the Bolsheviki as the clarion voice of " October."

The militarization of labour, rushed through the ninth Party Congress with typical Tammany Hall steam-roller methods, definitely turned every worker into a galley-slave. The substitution of one-man power in the shops and mills in place of co-operative management placed the masses again under the thumb of the very elements they had for three years been taught to hate as the worst menace. The " specialists " and professional men of the intelligentsia, formerly denounced as vampires and enemies guilty of sabotaging the Revolution, were now installed in high positions and clothed with almost supreme power over the men in the factories. It was a step that with one stroke destroyed the principal achievements of " October," the right of the workers to industrial control. Insult was added to injury by the introduction of the labour book, which virtually stamped everyone a felon, robbed him of the last vestiges of freedom, deprived him of the choice of place and occupation, and fastened him to a given district without the right of straying too far, on pain of severest penalties. True, these reactionary and anti-revolutionary measures were determinedly fought by a substantial minority within the party, as well as denounced by the people at large. We were among them, Sasha even more vigorously than I, although his faith in the Bolsheviki was still very strong. He was not yet ready to see with his inner vision the things already obvious to his outer eye, nor prepared to admit the tragic fate that the Bolshevik Frankenstein monster was pulling down the " October " edifice.

For hours he would argue against my " impatience " and deficient judgment of far-reaching issues, my kid-glove approach to the Revolution. I had always depreciated the economic factor as the main cause of capitalist evils, he declared. Could I fail to see now that economic necessity was the very reason which was forcing the hand of the men at the Soviet helm? The continued danger from the outside, the natural indolence of the Russian worker and his failure to increase production, the peasants' lack of the most necessary implements, and their resultant refusal to feed the cities had compelled the Bolsheviki to pass those desperate measures. Of course he regarded such methods as counter-revolutionary and bound to defeat their purpose. Still, it was preposterous to suspect men like Lenin or Trotsky of deliberate treachery to the Revolution. Why, they had dedicated their lives to that cause, they had suffered persecution, calumny, prison, and exile for their ideals! They *could* not go back on them to such an extent!

I assured Sasha that nothing was further from my thought than to charge the Bolsheviki with treachery. Indeed, I considered them quite consistent, truer to their aims than those of our own comrades who were working with them. Especially did I feel Lenin as a man hewn out of one piece. To be sure, his policies had undergone extraordinary changes; there was no denying his great agility as a political acrobat. But he had never deviated from his objective. His bitterest enemies would not accuse him of that. But his objective was the very crux of Russia's tragedy, I insisted. It was the Communist State, its absolute supremacy and exclusive power. What if it destroy the Revolution, condemn millions to death, and drench Russia in the blood of its best sons and daughters? That could not dismay the iron man in the Kremlin. They were " trifles, a little blood-letting." It could not affect his ultimate purpose. In point of clarity of vision, concentration of will, and unflagging determination Lenin had my respect. But as to the effect of his purposes and methods upon the Revolution, I considered him the greatest menace, more pernicious than the combined interventionists, because his objective was more elusive, his methods more deceptive.

Sasha did not gainsay this, nor was he less convinced than I of the hopelessness of our further attempts to fit into the garrotte of the political machine. But he thought that I was holding Lenin and his co-workers responsible for methods imposed upon them by dire revolutionary necessity. Shatoff had been the first to emphasize this. All the level-headed comrades, Sasha claimed, shared that attitude. And he himself had come to see that revolution in action is a quite different thing from revolution in the realm of theory mouthed by parlour radicals. It meant blood and iron, and it was unavoidable.

The dear companionship of my old pal and our intellectual harmony had mitigated much of the lacerating process of finding my way through the Soviet labyrinth. Sasha was all that had been left me from the tornado that had swept over my life. He represented everything dear to me, and I felt him a safe anchor in the roaring sea of Russia. Our disagreement, springing up so suddenly, overwhelmed me like a mighty wave, leaving me bruised and battered. I was certain my friend would in time realize the falsity of his position. I knew that his desperate attempt to defend Bolshevik methods was his last stand in a lost battle, the battle we had been the first to wage in the United States in behalf of the October Revolution.

Among our many callers during our Moscow stay had been an interesting young woman, Alexandra Timofeyevna Shakol. She had learned from Schapiro of our presence in the city, and, an anarchist herself, she was eager to meet her famous American comrades. Besides, she wanted to talk to us about a project initiated by the Petrograd Museum of the Revolution. An expedition was being planned, she explained, that was to cover the length and breadth of the country in search of documents bearing on the Revolution and the revolutionary movement of Russia since its inception. The collected material would ultimately serve as archives for the study of the great upheaval. Would we join such a venture?

For a moment we had been carried away by the plan and by the opportunity it offered to see Russia in her Revolutionary everyday life, to learn at first hand what the Revolution had done for the masses and how it affected their existence. We might never have such another chance. But on second thought we felt it bitter irony that would condemn us to collect dead material amidst the raging life of Russia. Thirty years long we had stood in the very thick of the social battle, always on the firing line. Could we now be content with anything less in our reborn native land? We longed for more vital work, something that would enable us to give out of the fullness of our hearts and the best of our abilities to the great task.

Since our return to Petrograd we had been so busy chasing Soviet windmills, so eagerly reaching out for a new hold, that we had hardly thought of our comrade Shakol and her proposal. But with every hope of useful work gone, her offer once more came to our minds. It might afford an escape from our meaningless existence. If the material we should collect would aid future historians in establishing the right relationship between the Revolution and the Bolsheviki, it would be worth the effort, Sasha and I agreed. Perhaps it would also help us to get the right perspective. The various parts of the country we should visit, the people we should come in contact with, their lives, customs, and habits, would prove a useful school, we comforted each other. We finally decided to try it, since nothing else was open to us. "If only the new project will also not turn out a bubble," I said to

Sasha on our way to the Winter Palace, where the Museum of the Revolution was located.

We found Shakol absent and we were distressed to learn that she had barely escaped death from typhus, which she had contracted in Moscow. She was convalescing now, but she would not be back to work for another fortnight. She had informed the museum, however, that we had promised to visit it, and we were received by the secretary, M. B. Kaplan, a man in the middle thirties, of pleasant and intelligent appearance. He offered to take us through the institution and show us what had already been accomplished. A number of rooms were filled with valuable material, among them the secret archives of the tsarist régime, including the records of the Third Political Section, disclosing the workings of its spy system. Much of the vast collection had already been arranged, classified, and prepared for exhibition in the near future. "Our task is only beginning," the secretary explained; " it will require years to achieve our object of establishing in Russia a museum more complete and unique than anything existing at present in any other country, not excepting the British Museum, the more so as no country contains such a wealth of revolutionary treasures scattered about the land and waiting to be rescued from loss and destruction." It was for that reason that the museum was anxious to send the collecting expedition as soon as possible, because much was being lost by delay. Kaplan was heart and soul for the project, and his collaborators were equally enthusiastic about the future of the museum and the work planned by it. All were anxious to secure our help.

Though it was the latter part of May, the vast chambers of the Winter Palace were breathing a penetrating chill. We were warmly clad, yet we quickly felt benumbed with the cold. We marvelled at the men and women working in the fearful dampness all through the severe months of the Petrograd winter. They had been employed there for almost three years now. Their faces were streaked with blue blotches, their hands frost-bitten. Some had contracted severe cases of rheumatism and tubercular affections. His own health had become undermined, the secretary admitted. But it was revolutionary Russia, and he and his co-workers were happy to be privileged to help in building its future. Most of them, like himself, were non-partisan.

He was all eagerness to be able to count on our aid. His enthusiasm was too infectious to resist, and we agreed. " Then you had better report for duty at once," he suggested. There was a great deal to be done yet to get the expedition under way. The necessary equipment for the journey was to be procured and two railroad cars prepared, one for the staff, which was to consist of six persons, the other to hold the material to be collected. Various formalities had also to be looked after, the consent of numerous departments, *propusks,* and supplies to be secured, and the right of way for the expedition. Haste was imperative and we must begin immediately.

We left the genial secretary and his collaborators in a more cheerful frame of mind. We did not yet feel about the work before us as did the other members of the museum. We knew we could not for long be content with merely collecting parchments when more important work was so urgently needed which we might do. But the devotion and fortitude of those people had lifted the weight of despair from our hearts. It was the most encouraging feature of Soviet life. Frequently we had come upon this new spirit of Russia, even in entirely unexpected places. In the darkest hours of our groping we would often discover the most heroic endurance and devotion hidden under the official Soviet surface. Not the kind daily acclaimed in public places and feasted with showy demonstrations and military display. No one outside the party believed in that official brand. Even within its ranks there were large numbers who hated the empty bombast and pretence, though they were powerless against the machine. They made up for the vulgar ostentation by their own singleness of purpose and probity. Silently they plodded at their tasks, giving their all to the Revolution and asking nothing in return for themselves either in rations, praise, or other recognition. These great souls redeemed for us much that was hateful in the Bolshevik régime.

Preparations for the expedition were progressing rather slowly, leaving us time to visit museums, art galleries, and similar places of interest, as well as to attend to other things. A report had reached us of the arrest of two anarchist girls, aged fifteen and seventeen, charged with the circulation of a protest against the degrading aspects of the labour book and also against the unbearable conditions of the politicals in the Shpalerny and Gorokhovaya jails in the city. Several Petrograd comrades called on us in the matter and we immediately addressed ourselves to the leading Bolsheviki. Zorin had long ago given us up as lost for his heaven. Zinoviev did not seem to like me particularly; the sentiment was, indeed, mutual. He was always extremely nice to Sasha, however, and the latter therefore called to see him about the arrested anarchists. On the same errand I visited Mme Ravich, whom I still greatly admired for her simple and unassuming personality and her readiness to admit and undo official abuses. Unfortunately, political prisoners were outside her jurisdiction. Such matters were under the control of the Cheka, whose Petrograd chief, the Communist Bakayev, was known as very vindictive towards anarchists. On the very first day of the arrival of the *Buford* deportees Bakayev had impressed upon them that " no anarchist foolishness is tolerated in Soviet Russia." Such luxuries were fit only for capitalist countries, he had told them. Under the proletarian dictatorship anarchists had either to submit or to be squelched. Upon our boys' resenting such a greeting, Bakayev had ordered the entire group of two hundred and forty-seven under house arrest. We had learned of it only the third day and we had been much wrought up over it. Zorin had minimized the occurrence as an unfortunate misunderstanding and had also prevailed upon his Chekist comrade to withdraw the armed guard from the dormitories of our people in the Smolny. Alas, since then we had seen too many of such " unfortunate misunderstandings."

On this occasion a wink from Zinoviev and Mme Ravich had immediate effect upon Bakayev. He also lived at the Astoria and he phoned me to call on him. He would release the arrested anarchist girls, he informed me, provided we were willing to vouch for it that that would stop their " bandit activities." I expressed amazement at his application of the term to two young girls guilty only of publishing a protest against the methods they considered counter-revolutionary. "Your party cannot be very sure of itself or it would not be constantly haunted by imaginary bandits and counter-revolutionists," I said. I declined to vouch for anyone, knowing that I myself would not keep silent if I saw the need of voicing my sentiments. Nor could I speak for Comrade Alexander Berkman, I informed Bakayev, though I knew that he would refuse to bind anyone by making promises for him. As to the ill treatment of political prisoners, I assured the Cheka chief that it would be grist to the American prison mills to learn that the jails in Soviet Russia were no better than those in the States. This seemed to reach Bakayev in the right spot. He would give the girls another chance, he declared, for, after all, they were proletarians even if they had not yet realized that they must not injure their own class by criticizing the dictatorship. He would also see what improvement the jails required, though conditions had been greatly exaggerated.

Getting people out of jail had been among our various activities in America. But we had never dreamed that we should find the same necessity in revolutionary Russia. Certainly not we who had fought fiercely the least suggestion of such a preposterous eventuality. Yet our only positive work so far had been just that — pleading for our imprisoned comrades with Lenin, with Krestinsky, and now with a lesser light. We were still able to see the pathos and the humour of the situation and we had not yet forgotten how to laugh at our own follies, though more often my laughter only thinly veiled my tears.

Nevertheless we had reason not to regret our efforts, particularly in the case of one of our finest comrades, Vsevolod Volin. He had been educationally active in the ranks of the Ukrainian peasant rebels headed by the anarchist Nestor Makhno, whom the Bolsheviki had formerly acclaimed as an effective leader of the masses, a man of great strategic acumen and exceptional courage. Not without reason, since it had been Makhno and his *povstantsy* army who had routed various counter-revolutionary adventurers and who had materially helped the Red forces to drive back the hordes of General Denikin. For refusing to submit his army to the absolute command of Trotsky, Makhno had been declared an enemy and bandit and his entire forces denounced as counter-revolutionary. Volin was an educator and in no way a participant in the military operations of Makhno. But the Ukrainian Cheka made no such fine distinction. At the first opportunity they had arrested Volin and held him incommunicado in the Kharkov prison, dangerously ill with fever though he was. Our comrades in Moscow realized the perilous position of Volin, for Trotsky had in the meantime sent telegraphic orders to have him executed. They tried to get the prisoner transferred to Moscow, where he was well known to the leading Communists as a man of revolutionary integrity and high intellectual attainments. They had circulated an appeal for his transfer, which was signed by every anarchist then present in the capital, and they had chosen Sasha and the local comrade Askaroff to present the petition to Krestinsky, Secretary of the Communist Party.

Krestinsky proved very fanatical and bitter against the anarchists, claiming at first that Volin was a counter-revolutionist deserving death, and again pretending that he had already been brought to Moscow. Sasha succeeded in convincing him that he was wrong on both points and that Volin be at least given a chance to state his case, which opportunity he would not have in Kharkov. Krestinsky finally yielded to Sasha's arguments. He promised to telegraph to the proper authorities in Kharkov to have Volin removed to the capital. Apparently he kept his word, because before long our comrade was brought to Moscow and placed in the Butirky prison. Shortly after that Vsevolod Volin was entirely released.

Having finally effected the release of the two Petrograd girls, we felt we might turn to other things before the expedition would be ready to start on its long journey. First of all we proceeded to visit the industries.

I had heard various rumours about factory conditions, but as I had not yet been able to gain access to the factories, I was loath to credit the stories. I had long ago realized that in a country deprived of press and speech, public opinion must needs be based on exaggerations and falsehoods. I would have to inspect the mills and shops myself, I always told my informants, before reaching conclusions.

My long-awaited opportunity to visit factories and possibly to talk to the workers at the bench came when Mme Ravich requested me to act as guide to a certain American journalist who had suddenly appeared in Petrograd. It was, I discovered, one of the newspaper men who had interviewed us on our landing in Terryoki, on our way through Finland. It seemed ages and ages ago. The man had repeatedly tried to get into Soviet Russia, as he had informed Sasha on the border, requesting him at the same time to speak a good word for him to Chicherin, in whose hands lay the decision about the admission of journalists. The young man had made a favourable impression by his frank expression and manner, but aside from that we knew about him nothing whatever, not even his name nor the paper he represented. Only at the last moment, as we walked across the border, did he hand us his card. Sasha had promised to transmit his message to the People's Commissar for Foreign Affairs, stating, however, that he could not plead in his behalf. Sasha had indeed kept his promise, having informed Chicherin that the young journalist, John Clayton by name, was anxious to come to Russia, and that he represented the Chicago *Tribune,* one of the reactionary newspapers in the United States.

We had heard no more about the matter, and in the hectic life of Russia we had forgotten all about Clayton's existence. I was therefore not a little surprised when on my return to Petrograd Mme Ravich telephoned me to inquire whether I knew a man by the name of John Clayton. He had been arrested on the border trying to cross over to Russia and he was being held by the Cheka. He had given our names as proof that he knew trustworthy people and that they would intercede for him. I repeated to Ravich what Sasha had previously told Chicherin, adding that, since the man was already on Soviet soil, it would be better policy to set him free. He could not see more than the Soviet government would permit, and he could not send out any news without the Bolshevik censorship passing upon it. Why, then, be afraid? Mme Ravich decided to report to the border Cheka what I had said and leave the matter to them for final action. Again there was nothing more heard about Clayton, and great was my astonishment to meet him one day at the door of my room in the Astoria. " Where do you come from? " I blurted out before even inviting him in. " Oh, don't ask me," he replied piteously; " I have risked my life to get into the country. I come with the best intentions and am treated worse than a dog." " What has happened? " I demanded. " For the love of Mike," Clayton cried, " aren't you mean not even to ask me to step into your room? I need a whole day to tell you all my adventures." The poor man did look forlorn, and I never liked to be rude, even to an American reporter, though few people had as good reason as I to be so. " Come in, old fellow, and make a clean breast of it," I said lightly. His face brightened. " Thanks, E.G.," he replied, " I knew they couldn't turn you into a hardened Bolshevik." " Nonsense," I corrected him, " all Bolsheviki are not hardened, and those that are have been made so largely by the grace of your Government in league with the others to starve the Russian masses."

Clayton related that he had ski'd and bribed his way from Finland, had been caught, thrown into a filthy Cheka prison, and finally

shipped to Moscow, where he had been " free " the past six weeks.
" Free? " I inquired in surprise. Yes, but he might as well not have
been for all he had got to see or to hear. Not a scrap of anything
even for a first measly story. As for himself, every kind of discrimination and chicanery had been employed against him ever since
he had reached Moscow. " Rotten I call it, and bad judgment to
treat a newspaper man so," he declared bitterly.

The way to a man's heart is proverbially through his stomach, and
something was needed to sooth Clayton's ruffled spirit. " Plenty of
time to discuss all that," I said, " after you have had a cup of coffee."
" Gee, that would be a real treat," he cried in glee. After having
partaken of two cups his chagrin somewhat subsided and he became
more amenable to reason. Before we started on our factory-inspection
tour, Clayton was willing to admit how untenable his position was
and how absurd it was to feel hurt. After all, he was an unknown
quantity, and his credentials from the Chicago *Tribune* anything but
reassuring. Spies and conspiracies had become a mania with the Communists. It was natural in view of the persecution Russia was enduring from the enemies of the Revolution. He would have to see
his unpleasant experiences in a larger light if his intentions were
really as good as he had assured me. Else he would be able to report
only the same stupidity as his colleagues about the alleged nationaliza-
tion of women, *bourgeois* ears and fingers fed to the people, and
similar juicy atrocities that had been published by the American press.
Clayton swore he would never be guilty of such misrepresentation.
" Wait and see," he assured me. I had waited for thirty years, searching all the time with a Diogenes lantern for fairness or accuracy
among American newspaper men. I had found some exceptions, of
course, very few and far between. None of them, however, on the
Chicago *Tribune*. I hoped he would prove to be one of the exceptions.

The function of an official cicerone was not exactly to my liking.
But I did not care to refuse Ravich who had always been responsive
to my intercession for unfortunates. Moreover, I felt that the Russian
situation was too great and vital and that I had not yet grasped it
fully, though I had reached a definite decision not to work within
Bolshevik political confines. Most important to me was it not to be
quoted by any American paper against Soviet Russia, not while the
latter was still forced to fight for life itself on so many fronts. I was
therefore in the predicament of not wanting Clayton to secure

information by my aid and I did not cherish the prospect of having to tell him deliberate lies. I reasoned that Mme Ravich knew what she was about when she had given Clayton permission to visit factories. They were probably not so bad as had been reported to me. Or she may have thought that with me as guide things would be made to appear less harsh. Fortunately Sasha was accompanying us. That would give one of us a chance to lag behind and talk to the workers while the other would interpret to Clayton the official version of conditions.

The Putilov works proved to be in a forlorn state, most of the machines deserted, others out of repair, the place filthy and neglected. While Sasha was explaining to Clayton what the superintendent of the shop was relating, I lingered behind. I found the men very unwilling to talk until I mentioned that I was a *tovarishtch* from America and not a Bolshevik. That made a big difference. They could tell me a great deal, they said, but even the walls had ears. Not a day passed but what some of their fellows failed to return to work. Sick? No, but they had protested a little too loud. I urged that, as the authorities had informed me, the workers in the Putilovsky, being engaged in one of the vital industries, received considerably better rations than other toilers — two pounds of bread a day and special shares of other products. The men stared at me in amazement. I might try their bread, one of them suggested, holding out a black chunk to me. " Bite hard," he said ironically. I tried, but knowing I could ill afford a dentist's bill, I had to return the leathery piece, much to the amusement of the group clustered about me. I suggested that the Communists could not be blamed for the bad bread and the scarcity of it. If the Putilov workers and their brothers in other industries would increase production, the peasants would be able to raise more grain. Yes, they replied, that was the yarn given them every day in explanation of the militarization of labour. It had been hard enough to work on empty stomachs when they were not being driven. Now it was altogether impossible. The new decree had only added to the general misery and bitterness. It was taking the workers too far away from their villages, which formerly had helped them out with provisions. Besides, the number of officials and overseers had been increased and they too had to be fed. " Of the seven thousand employed here, only two thousand are actual producers," an old worker near me remarked. Hadn't I seen the markets, another man demanded in a whisper. Had I noticed much scarcity there for those who had the price to pay? There was no time for a reply. At a warning from their neighbours the men hastened back to their benches and I joined my companions.

Our next objective looked like a military camp, with armed sentinels stationed all around the huge warehouse and about the mill inside. "Why so many guards?" Sasha asked the Commissar in charge. The flour had of late been disappearing by the carload, came the reply, and the soldiers were there to cope with the evil. They had not succeeded in stopping the thefts, but some offenders had been apprehended. They had proved to be workers misled by a gang of speculators. Somehow the official explanation did not sound plausible. I slackened my pace in the hope of getting close to some of the millmen. I knew the right password: "From America, bringing you the solidaric greetings of the militant proletariat and their gift of cigarettes." A young chap with a firm jaw and intelligent eyes attracted my attention as he passed me with a sack of flour on his shoulders. When he returned to pick up another, I tried my magic key. It worked. Would he tell me why armed soldiers were there? Didn't I know of the new decree *militarizing* labour, he demanded. The workers had resented it as an insult to their revolutionary manhood. As a result their brother soldiers, who had helped them during the October days, were now installed over them as watch-dogs. I asked about the theft of flour and whether the guards were not there to prevent it. The man smiled sadly. No one knew better than the commissars, he said, who was stealing the flour, for they themselves passed it through the gates. "And the Revolution? Has it given you workers nothing?" I questioned. "Oh, yes," he replied, "but it has been checked long ago. Now it is a stagnant pool. It will break out again, though, never fear."

In the evening, when Sasha and I compared notes, we agreed that we had seen all we wanted to know of Soviet factory conditions. We could leave the doubtful honour to the official guides, who were less squeamish about turning black into white, and grey into crimson hues. Sasha emphatically refused to act again as cicerone and I completed my unsolicited job by taking Clayton the next morning to the Laferm Tobacco Works. We found them in good condition, because the former owner and manager himself was still in charge.

Before long, Clayton departed, declaring that he would soon return for a longer stay and a more thorough study of conditions. His wife was Russian, he said, and she would serve as his guide, which would make it unnecessary for him to impose on our time and good will. He would guard against making misleading statements concerning Russia, he faithfully promised.

" Misleading," I mused. The poor chap could not know that every day of my Russian existence was misleading, misleading others as well as myself. Would the time ever come when I should once more stand firmly in my own boots, I wondered.

Preparations for the expedition were progressing very slowly, while my nervous tension almost reached breaking-point. Whatever poise I had of late gained had been destroyed by my recent impressions of the appalling conditions under which the masses were living and toiling. The arrival of Angelica Balabanoff somewhat helped to lighten my frame of mind.

She had been sent from Moscow to complete arrangements for the reception of the expected British Labour Mission. Poor Angelica, she too had been relegated to the rôle of guide, and I was certain she would agonize as much as I in having to play hide-and-seek with the shadow of her once glowing faith.

The Narishkin Palace on the Neva, one of the most beautiful in the capital, was assigned to the use of the distinguished English guests. It had been locked up since the October days, and Angelica asked me to help her put it in order. I cheerfully consented, though she really did not need me for the work. An array of servants had been commandeered to do the cleaning that three efficient persons could have accomplished in less time. I guessed that Angelica was lonely, and a glance at her showed me that she was again in bad health. She felt at home with me and I loved to be with her even if I could never get myself to talk frankly to her about the subject we both had most at heart. It would have been like digging into an open wound. Angelica was also very fond of Sasha and she had already secured his help as interpreter and translator of the testimonials of welcome that were being prepared in honour of the visitors.

The mission at last arrived, most of its members of the usual Anglo-Saxon better-than-thou attitude. They were against intervention, of course, and they boasted of having repudiated the attacks on Soviet Russia, but as to revolution or communism, no, thank you, none of that for them. Their reception was calculated to speak to the larger audience of the British labouring masses and to the workers of the entire world. No effort was to be spared to make the occasion propagandistically effective. The grand military display on the square of the Uritsky Palace was but the initial part of the program. Other functions were to prove even more persuasive. The dinners at the Narishkin Palace, its tables laden with the best starving Russia could command, the personally conducted tours through the model schools, selected factories, and rest-homes, theatrical performances, ballets, concerts, and opera, with the members of the mission in the former Tsar's loge, composed some of the festivities. British reserve could not resist such hospitality. Most members of the mission fell for the show and became the more pliable the longer they stayed.

Some of them exerted their best logic to persuade me that the dictatorship and the Cheka were inevitable in a country as backward as Russia, with her people for centuries used to despotic rule. " We Englishmen would not stand for it," one delegate declared, " but it is different with the ignorant Russian masses, strangers to civilized ways." The Soviet Government, he argued, had shown amazing intelligence and skill in having succeeded so well with its raw human material. But the average Englishman, of course, would not put up with such things. " The average Englishman," I retorted, " prefers to run three blocks after a cab so he can act the flunkey for a gentleman and earn the munificent sum of twopence." " If you saw such a sight in London, it was certainly only the dregs of the city," he replied. " Precisely," I said; " there is more than enough of such dregs in England and they would be the worst stumbling-block to any fundamental economic changes in your country. But I forget that you Englishmen will have none of revolution. That could only happen in ignorant and uncivilized Russia."

I walked away to the rear of the box to watch the rest of the ballet undisturbed by British complacent superiority. Presently the door opened and a man in military uniform entered. When the lights went on again, I recognized him as Leon Trotsky. What a change in his appearance and bearing within three years! He was no longer the pale, lean, and narrow-chested exile I had seen in New York in the spring of 1917. The man in the box seemed to have grown in breadth and height, though he showed no superfluous flesh. His pale face was bronze now, his reddish hair and beard considerably streaked with grey. He had tasted power and he looked conscious of his authority. He carried himself with proud mien, and there was disdain in his eyes, even contempt, as he glanced at the British guests. He spoke to no one and soon left. He did not recognize me, nor did I make myself known to him. The gulf between our worlds had widened too far to be reached across.

There were certain members of the British Mission, however, not entirely inclined to look in open-mouthed wonder at the things about them, with their mental eyes shut. These were not of the labouring element. One of them was Mr. Bertrand Russell. Very politely but decisively he had from the very first refused to be officially chaperoned. He preferred to go about himself. He also showed no elation over the honour of being quartered in a palace and fed on special morsels. Suspicious person, that Russell, the Bolsheviki whispered. But then, what can you expect of a *bourgeois*? Angelica almost broke her heart over such talk. She argued that it was stupid and criminal to try to pull the wool over everybody's eyes. People should be allowed to see conditions as they were, she insisted, to realize the harrowing want and misery of blockaded Russia. Perhaps that would help to arouse the conscience of the world against the powers that were starving the country. But the Cheka thought otherwise, though it did not too obviously interfere with the movements of the delegates.

Mr. Russell called on us one day with Henry G. Alsberg, an American correspondent accompanying the mission, who was representing the New York *Nation* and the London *Daily Herald*. John Clayton, whom Alsberg had met in Esthonia, had informed him that we were staying at the Astoria and had also given him some provisions for us. The unexpected replenishment of our larder deserved some kind of celebration, and we invited our callers to stay for lunch, which I proceeded to prepare in my improvised kitchenette. It was by no means an elaborate meal, but our guests assured me that they enjoyed it more than they would have the repast at the palace served in the festal Narishkin salon on damask and fine plate. With us, they said, one could speak freely and get a segment of Russian reality free from fear or favour. It was our first contact with the world outside of Russia, with persons earnestly concerned in the weal of the country. We cherished every moment with our visitors and I liked Henry Alsberg in particular. He brought with him a whiff of the best that was in America — sincerity and easy joviality, directness and *camaraderie*. Mr. Russell was of a more reserved nature, but of gracious and simple personality. Angelica had invited us to the last social function for the Mission before its departure for Moscow. We went in the capacity of interpreters. The same evening she left with the delegates. Nothing would do but she must have Sasha with her. He had much to attend to for the museum expedition, as no car had yet been secured for our journey. But who could refuse Angelica?

All was ready for our expedition except the principal thing — a railroad car. The Commissar of the Museum of the Revolution, Yatmanov, a prominent Communist, and Secretary Kaplan had for weeks been trying to get one for us, but without success. They were sure Sasha could manage the matter through Zinoviev, with whom he seemed to have a pull. But Sasha was still in Moscow with the British Labour Mission. It was exasperating to remain idle for one whose whole life had been filled with intense activity. I had learned, however, since I came to Russia, to possess my soul in patience. The dictatorship of the proletariat was building for eternity; what could a few weeks, months, or even years matter?

Sasha presently returned and with him a more intense drive for a car. He had not been happy in the capital. The Punch and Judy show for the British Labour Mission had distressed him. Poor Angelica had of course nothing to do with it. She had been thrust aside as soon as she had delivered the guests to Karakhan and his hosts of managers at the Moscow station. They had carried the Britishers off, leaving only Bertrand Russell behind. No one seemed to know him or his place in the world of science and advanced thought. Sasha had saved the situation by hailing Karakhan, who was about to drive off in his luxurious automobile, which he was occupying alone. Karakhan inquired who the man was, remarking that he had never heard of Bertrand Russell. However, he would take Sasha's word for it that the man with him was worth bothering about, upon which he invited Sasha and Russell to his car.

Sasha had absented himself from the public exhibitions and demonstrations in honour of the British Mission. He had had enough of those shows. Nor did he feel that he could serve as interpreter of the bombastic speeches at the public functions and the falsehoods palmed off on the unsuspecting Englishmen. He had translated for Angelica some resolutions and he had accompanied the delegates to shops and factories on tours of inspection. Karl Radek had asked him to translate something Lenin had written and had sent one of the official autos to bring Sasha to the headquarters of the Third International. There Radek had handed him Lenin's manuscript on the " Infantile Diseases of Leftism." " Imagine my surprise," Sasha related, " when a glance at the pages showed me that it was a vitriolic attack on all the revolutionists differing from the Bolshevik attitude. I told Radek I would translate it only on condition of being permitted to write a preface to the brochure." " Radek must have thought you mad to be guilty of such *lèse-majesté,*" I remarked. " Yes, he was so mad he took me for his brother lunatic," my humorous friend replied. Radek did not press the matter any further and Sasha had gone his way. But there were other things that soon engaged his entire attention in Moscow. A number of our people were in prison again, among them our comrade Abe Gordin, of the Universalist Club, who had taken a prominent part in the revolutionary events of 1917. They were being held without any charges made against them. Their repeated demands to know the reason for their arrest having failed to bring results, they had declared a hunger-strike in protest. Sasha had been kept busy trying to induce the authorities to specify our comrades' offence or release them. After much difficulty he had succeeded in getting an audience with Preobrazhensky, Secretary of the Communist Party. Sasha urged that the men in jail had grown dangerously weak from their long hunger-strike, and Preobrazhensky coldly declared that " the quicker they died, the better for us." Sasha had assured him that the Russian anarchists had no intention of obliging him or his party. Moreover, if his régime continued to persecute his comrades, it would have only itself to blame for anything that might happen. " Is this a threat? " the Secretary had demanded. " Only an unavoidable fact, which you as an old revolutionist should know," Sasha had replied.

Our Moscow comrades had enjoyed a modicum of freedom. What could be the purpose of the new policy of deliberate extermination, we wondered. Sasha thought it was due to the stand of the Moscow anarchist conference expressed in the resolutions we had handed to Lenin. The reply of the Communist Party Executive, a copy of which had been expressly sent to us, declared that " *ideiny* anarchists are working with the Soviet Government." The others, who did not, were considered enemies of the Revolution and as such not entitled to more consideration than counter-revolutionists like the Social Revolutionists or the Mensheviki. The Cheka had taken the hint and proceeded accordingly.

It was a terrible situation, but we were powerless. Any protest on our part within Russia would have no greater effect than that of Peter Kropotkin or Vera Figner. With the country endangered on the Polish front, we felt we could not issue any appeal to the workers abroad.

At the first news of war with Poland I had set aside my critical attitude and offered my services as nurse at the front. Mme Ravich was absent from Petrograd at the time and I went to Zorin about it. Since the birth of Liza's child I was again seeing a great deal of the Zorins. Mother and child had been very ill and I had taken care of them. This somewhat softened Zorin's disapproval of us since our disagreement over the rest-homes. My offer to aid Soviet Russia in her hour of need seemed to move him deeply. He had known that Sasha and I would finally come to collaborate with his party, he declared. We only needed time, he thought, to realize that the dictatorship and the Revolution were identical and that to serve one meant to work for the other. He promised to see the proper authorities about my offer and to inform me of results. But he never did. That of course could have no bearing on my determination to help the country, in whatever capacity possible. Nothing seemed so important just then.

Sasha had in the meantime succeeded in securing a car for the Museum Expedition. It was an old dilapidated Pullman containing six compartments, but soon he had it cleaned up, painted, and disinfected for our use. Having proved so successful where others had failed, the museum appointed Sasha general manager of the expedition. Shakol was nominated secretary, while I was entrusted with three jobs, besides the work of collecting historical material, in which we all shared. I was chosen treasurer, housekeeper, and cook. A Russian couple on our staff were supposed to be experts on revolutionary documents. The sixth in our group was a young Jewish Communist, whose special work was to visit local party institutions. As the only Communist in our circle he felt at first quite lost, being among three anarchists and two non-partisans.

Our car needed mattresses, blankets, dishes, and similar utensils, for which I received an order from Yatmanov on the supplies of the Winter Palace. Equipped with this " order," I went down to the basements of the palace, where the Tsar's household goods were stored. The transitoriness of station and power had never before struck me so forcibly as when looking at the wealth that had but recently been used by the reigning family on its State occasions. The toil of every country and clime was gathered there in priceless porcelain, rare silver, copper, glass, and damask. Room after room was stacked to the ceiling with utensils and plate, thickly covered with dust, mute witnesses to the glory that was no more. And there I was, rummaging in all that magnificence for dishes for our expedition! Could any legend be more fantastic, more significant of the ephemeral nature of human destiny?

It took a whole day to select what was suitable for our use, and even at that the things were more fit for a museum. I could not get excited over the fact that we should eat our herring and potatoes, and if lucky also *borscht,* from the plate that had fed the Lord of all the Russias and his family. It amused me to think, however, how the newspapers in America would play up such an incident. Berkman and Goldman, arch-anarchists, using the crested linen and china of the Romanovs! And the free-born Americans, such as the Daughters of the Revolution, dying for the sight of royalty, dead or alive, or even for some souvenir of an old boot that had squeezed a royal foot!

On June 30, 1920, just seven months after we had landed on Soviet soil, our renovated car was hitched to a night train, known as " Maxim Gorki," and headed for Moscow. It being the "centre," we had to stop off there for additional credentials from various departments, including those of education and public health, and from the Foreign Office, not forgetting also the Cheka. From the latter we had to secure a document giving us immunity for the possession of counter-revolutionary documents, the collection of which was part of our task. We expected that a few days in the capital would suffice to complete our arrangements, but it took two weeks instead.

The city was in a ferment over incidents of recent occurrence. The bakers had been on strike; their entire executive committee was now dissolved and its members in prison. The Printers' Union had met a similar fate for a more heinous offence. They had organized a meet-

ing with the members of the British Labour Mission as their guests.
The surprise of the occasion was the sudden appearance on the platform of Tchernov, leader of the Social Revolutionists and former
President of the Constituent Assembly. The Cheka had for a long
time been looking for Tchernov, who was in hiding. He appeared
disguised by a long black beard, and he was not at first recognized.
His impassioned speech against the Bolsheviki roused the assembly
to an ovation, but when the communist chairman of the meeting called
for the arrest of the man, he had disappeared in the crowd about
him.

There was great excitement in the city, due to the arrival of a
number of foreign delegates for the Second Congress of the Red
Trade-Union International. Among them we were delighted to find
some Anarcho-Syndicalists from Spain, France, Italy, Germany, and
Scandinavia. There were also labour men from England, more militant and less comfortable than their countrymen on the British Mission. Learning of our presence in Moscow, they sought us out and
we had many conferences together. The clearest minds among them
were two anarchists, Pistania from Spain and Augustin Souchy from
Germany, representing the Anarcho-Syndicalists labour bodies of
their respective countries. These two men were entirely with the
Revolution and sympathetic with the Bolsheviki. They were, however,
not the kind who could be fêted into seeing everything in roseate
colours. They came as earnest students of the situation, desirous of
getting the facts at first hand and of observing the Revolution in
action. They inquired, among other things, how our comrades were
faring under the Communist State. All sorts of rumours had filtered
to Europe about the persecution of anarchists and other revolutionists. The comrades abroad, they told us, had refused to credit
such reports as long as they had not heard from us about the
matter. They had asked that we send back word through Souchy
and Pistania about the actual state of affairs. Sasha explained that
the rumours were unfortunately not unfounded. Anarchists, Left
Socialist Revolutionists, militant workers and peasants were imprisoned in Soviet jails and detention camps, denounced as bandits and
counter-revolutionists. They were nothing of the kind, of course, but
sincere comrades, most of whom had taken an active part in the
October days. Our efforts had been effective for but few of them.
Possibly the Anarcho-Syndicalist delegates, as representatives of

large Left labour organizations abroad, would be more successful with the Soviet authorities. They should insist on their right to visit the prisons and talk to the prisoners. Sasha also suggested that the delegates demand redress for our people. But he was reluctant to talk to the men of the general situation. His own impressions had not yet sufficiently clarified, he said; he could not speak the final word and he did not want to prejudice the delegates. They would have to learn for themselves.

I felt differently on the matter. Our foreign comrades were accredited representatives of militant labour bodies. They were not likely to use anything I might tell them to the detriment of the Revolution, as newspaper reporters might do. I had no intention of biasing them, but neither did I think that I should keep the facts from them. I wanted at least our own comrades in Europe and America to behold the reverse side of the shiny Soviet medal. Souchy, Pistania, and a British I.W.W. man attentively listened to my narrative, but I could read on their faces that they were as incredulous as I had been of Breshkovskaya, Bob Minor, and the other friends who had told me of the actual conditions in Russia. Nor did I blame them. To the oppressed of the world the Bolsheviki had become the synonym of the Revolution itself. The revolutionists outside of Russia could not easily credit how far that was from the truth. One seldom learns from the experience of others. Nevertheless I did not regret having talked frankly to the delegates. Whatever their own impressions, they would know that I had not denied them my confidence and trust.

Europe and America seemed removed from me by decades. It was gratifying to have them brought closer by our foreign visitors and to learn from them about the anarchist and revolutionary labour activities outside of Russia. To the request of the delegates that I send a message to the workers abroad, I replied: " May they emulate the spirit of their Russian brothers in the coming revolution, but not their naïve faith in political leaders, no matter how fervent their protestations and how red their slogans! That alone can safeguard future revolutions from being harnessed to the State and enslaved again by its bureaucratic whip."

A great and most welcome surprise came to me in Moscow with the opportunity to see the famous Maria Spiridonovna and her friend Kamkov, leaders of the Left Socialist Revolutionists. Maria was living under cover, disguised as a peasant, and great precaution was necessary to keep her whereabouts from the Cheka. She therefore sent a trusted comrade to bring Sasha and me to her place.

Spiridonovna occupies one of the highest places in the galaxy of the heroic women of Russia. Her attack on General Lukhanovsky, Governor of Tambov Province, had been an extraordinary feat for a girl of eighteen. Maria had dogged the man's steps for weeks, patiently waiting for a chance to strike the notorious executioner of the peasants. When the train bearing Lukhanovsky steamed into the station, Maria jumped on to the running-board and shot the Governor dead before his guards realized what the girl was about. No less remarkable had been her behaviour during the tortures she had been subjected to after her arrest. Pulled about by her hair, her clothes torn off, and her naked flesh burned with cigarettes, her face beaten into a pulp, Maria Spiridonovna had remained silent and contemptuous of her tormentors. When this treatment had failed to force her to involve others in her act or to break her spirit, she was tried behind closed doors and condemned to die. She was saved by the tremendous protest in Europe and America, and her sentence was commuted to exile to Siberia for life. Twelve years later the historic tables were turned. Tsar Nikolas was hurled from his throne, and the victims of absolutism, numbering into the thousands, were brought back in triumph from their dungeons and exile. Among them was Maria Spiridonovna, whose Calvary was well known to the radicals everywhere. Her glowing personality had exalted and spurred me on in my work in the United States, and she was among the first I longed to meet when I came to Russia. But no one seemed to know her whereabouts. The Communists I had questioned, including Jack Reed, had told me that she had suffered a nervous break-down and was being nursed back to health in a Soviet sanatorium. It was only when I got to Moscow the first time that I learned from her comrades about the life and struggle of Maria Spiridonovna since her liberation from Siberia. Shattered in health from the agonies she had suffered, and broken down by tuberculosis contracted in prison, she had nevertheless refused to spare herself. Russia needed her, and the peasants to whom she had dedicated her young life were calling her. Now more than ever they needed her, having been betrayed by Kerensky and his party, which had also been hers and by whose order she had killed Lukhanovsky. The Socialist Revolutionist

Provisional Government was forcing the people to continue the world slaughter, and Maria would have nothing to do with it. Together with the more radical wing of the party, including Kamkov, Dr. Steinberg, Trutovsky, Izmailovich, Kakhovskaya, and others, Maria Spiridonovna organized the Left Socialist Revolutionist Party. Side by side with Lenin and his comrades they worked for the October upheaval and unwittingly helped the Bolsheviki to power. Not unmindful of the ardent support of Spiridonovna and her comrades, Lenin had approved the choice of Maria by the Peasant Congress as its president, his own party's appointment of Dr. Steinberg as People's Commissar for Justice, and Trutovsky as Commissar for Agriculture. But the break with the Bolsheviki came over Brest-Litovsk, the Left Socialist-Revolutionists considering peace with the Kaiser a fatal betrayal of the Revolution. Maria was the first to refuse further co-operation with the Bolsheviki. With her wonted determination she turned from the Communist Government as she had from Kerensky's régime, and her comrades followed her lead. Then her martyrdom began all over again. There followed arrest and incarceration in the Kremlin prison, escape, re-arrest, and more prison. Her influence among the peasantry continued, however, even growing with her persecution. The Communists resorted to the convenient explanation that Maria had gone mad and had to be restrained.

On the sixth floor of a large tenement in Moscow, in a room not much larger than my cell in the Missouri penitentiary, a little old woman embraced me tenderly, without uttering a word. It was Maria Spiridonovna. Though only thirty-three years of age, she was shrivelled in body; a hectic flush was on her emaciated face, her eyes were feverishly brilliant, but her spirit remained unchanged and unfettered, still scaling the heights of her indomitable faith. Anything I could have said at that moment would have sounded banal. Nor did I trust myself to speak. Her hands in mine had a steadying effect and the silence about us was soothing, like her tender touch. Maria spoke and I listened. For three days, with little interruption, I listened tense in every nerve. Her tone was calm, her mind clear, and her presentation keen. Her facts were incontestable and documented by peasant letters from every part of Russia. They cried to her to enlighten them on the great misfortune that had befallen their beloved *matushka Rossiya*. They had believed in the Revolution as in the second coming of Christ. They had prepared for its promised blessings, the freeing of the soil from the masters, the peace and brotherhood it would bring. She knew best, they wrote, how hard they had worked and how fervently they had believed in the holy power of the revolution. Now everything was crushed, their hopes turned to ashes. They had taken the land from their old masters, but their produce was now being taken from them by the new bosses, even to the last seeds for planting. Nothing had changed except the methods of robbing them. It was the Cossack and the *nagaika* before, the Chekists and shooting now. The same browbeating and arrests, the same heartless brutality and drive. Everything the same. They could not grasp it, could not understand it, and there was no one to explain, whose word they could believe. They still had her, their *angel Maryussa*. She had never played them false and she must now tell them whether the new Christ also was crucified and whether he would rise still once more to redeem their suffering land.

Maria was in possession of scores of these pitiful outpourings, written on slips of coarse paper or dirty cloth and smuggled to her under the greatest difficulties.

" The Bolsheviki maintain that forcible confiscation has been imposed on them by the peasants' refusing to feed the cities," I remarked. There was no truth in it, Maria assured me. The peasants had indeed refused to deal with the " centre " through its commissars. They had their soviets and they insisted that the latter be in direct touch with the soviets of the workers. They had taken the meaning and purpose of the soviets literally, as simple folk always do. The soviets were their medium of keeping in touch with the city toilers and exchanging with them needed products. When this was denied them and in addition their General Soviet dissolved and its members imprisoned, the peasants became aroused against the dictatorship. Moreover, the forcible collection of produce and the punitive expeditions against the villages had antagonized and embittered the rural population. These methods could not win with the peasants. The saying among them was that Ilich could exterminate the peasants, but he could not conquer the peasantry. " They are right," Maria commented, " for Russia is eighty per cent agricultural, and that is the very backbone of the country. It may take some time for Lenin to find out that the peasant will force his hands, not he the peasant's."

All through her recital Spiridonovna had said not a word about herself, her persecution, illness, or want. Her mainsprings poured into the vast human sea, I felt, each ripple rushing back to her all-embracing heart. I saw no sign of any personal current crossing her universal stream until just shortly before we bade her good-bye on the third day of our visit.

Sasha had been present at our sessions, together with Boris Kamkov. The latter, like his friend Maria, was also calm and collected in his arraignment of the evils wrought among the peasantry by the three years of the dictatorship. At no time during our stay did Maria betray by word or look that the man stirred in her other emotions than those of the solidarity of a common ideal. Now Kamkov was about to leave on a journey to the interior and he very emphatically insisted that he needed nothing for his trip except some bread. He would take nothing from Maria's share. Someone had brought her eggs and cherries, and while Kamkov was talking to Sasha, Maria stealthily stuck her little bundle of provisions, packed in a handkerchief, into the sack of literature her friend was taking with him. She stood near him, diminutive alongside of his great height and breadth. She did not speak, she only looked up into his eyes and lightly brushed her slender white hand over his sleeve, imperceptibly leaning against him. He was going on a dangerous mission and Maria felt that he might never return. No poet ever sang of greater love and longing than her simple gesture expressed. It was beautiful and moving beyond words, laying bare in a flash the rich fount of her soul.

Our red-painted car on a side track at the Moscow railroad station attracted many visitors, among them Henry G. Alsberg and Albert Boni, who had come to Russia. Both were envious of our trip and eager to come with us. Of the two men, Sasha and I liked Alsberg the best. We told him we would prevail on the members of our expedition to allow him to come with us if he would get the necessary credentials from the Soviet authorities.

On the day of our departure he arrived with written permission from Zinoviev, the Foreign Office and the Cheka. The representative of the Cheka in the Foreign Office insisted, however, Alsberg would have to secure an additional visa from the local Moscow Cheka. Karakhan's secretary (Foreign Office), under whose jurisdiction he was, definitely informed him that he did not need this extra visa and the Foreign Office "guaranteed" he would not be molested if he went on the expedition. Alsberg hesitated but we urged him to take a chance without the *proposk* of the Moscow Cheka. His American passport and the fact that he represented two pro-Soviet newspapers should save him from serious difficulties. Our secretary consented that he should join us, and there was an extra bunk in Sasha's compartment. Thereupon he decided to become the seventh member of our company.

Our Moscow stay had been rich in surprises. The final one came just an hour before our departure. A man dashed up, all out of breath, in search of us. " Why, E.G., don't you recognize me? " he cried; " I am Krasnoschokov, formerly Tobinson, of Chicago. Have you forgotten your chairman at the Workers' Institute meeting, your and Sasha's co-worker in the Windy City? " The change in him was as complete as Trotsky's. He seemed taller and broader, of proud carriage, but without the military severity and disdainful expression of the Commissar of the Red Army. He was, Tobinson-Krasnoschokov related, President of the Far Eastern Republic, and he had come to Moscow for an important conference with the Party Executive. He had been in the city for a week, eager to meet us again, but he had failed to locate us till the very last moment. He had many things to talk over and we must remain a few days to celebrate our reunion, he insisted. He had travelled from Siberia in his own railroad car, bringing plenty of provisions and his own cook, and he would give us our first real feast in Soviet Russia. Krasnoschokov had remained the same free and generous fellow he had been in the States, but we could not alter our plans and we had only a few hours to spend with him.

Sasha was still in the city, attending to last-hour commissions, but he would soon be back. Meanwhile Krasnoschokov was regaling me with his adventures since his arrival in Russia. He had become the chief executive of the Far Eastern Republic; Bill Shatoff was also there, as well as other anarchists from America, all working together with him. Free speech and press prevailed in his part of Russia, he assured me, and there was every opportunity for our propaganda. Sasha and I must come, he insisted. He needed our help and we could count on him. Shatoff was doing great work as Commissar of Railroads and he had warned him not to dare return without us. " Free speech and free press — how does Moscow stand for that? " I asked.

Conditions were different in that far country, Krasnoschokov explained, and he had been given a free hand there. Anarchists, Left Socialist Revolutionists, and even Mensheviki were co-operating with him and he was proving that free expression and joint effort were giving the best results.

An enchanting picture indeed, I commented, and I should certainly like to see it for myself. Perhaps when we had completed our present tour, we might induce the museum to send our expedition to Siberia. Presently Sasha arrived and there was renewed rejoicing. Alas, only for a short hour. Our visitor was loath to let us depart and we had to promise faithfully to let him know when we would be ready to come to his Far Eastern Republic. He would facilitate our journey and promise us all the liberty we wanted and carloads of material for the museum.

Our first important stop was at Kharkov. It looked prosperous after Petrograd and Moscow. The people, fine physical types of humanity, appeared well fed and carefree in spite of the numerous invasions, changes of government, and the ravages the city had experienced. There was evident a scarcity only of wearing-apparel, particularly of shoes, hats, and hosiery. Men, women, and children were bare-legged, some wearing queer-shaped sandals of wood and straw. The women were especially incongruously attired in dresses of the finest linen and batiste, wearing hand-made lace and multi-coloured kerchiefs. The brightly embroidered native costumes predominated, presenting a pleasant sight after the monotony of the Moscow streets. And the people! I had never seen such a collection of beauty in one place. The men dark-haired and bearded, bronze of skin, with dreamy eyes and shining teeth. The women with crowns of hair, lovely complexions, and flashing black eyes. They seemed a race entirely different from their northern brothers.

The markets were the main gathering-places and centres of attraction. The stalls spread for blocks, piled high with fruit, vegetables, butter, and other provisions. One had no longer believed such profusion existed in Russia. Some of the tables were laden with toys in carved and painted wood, mountains of them of curious shape and design. My heart ached for the children of Petrograd and Moscow, with their broken and mis-shaped dolls and the battered wooden monstrosities they called Cossack steeds. For two dollars in Kerensky

paper money I carried off an armful of wonderful toys. I knew that the joy they would give to my Petrograd youngsters would transcend any monetary value.

Bringing anything into another city without special permission was considered speculation and treated as a counter-revolutionary offence, often subject to the " supreme penalty," which meant death. Neither Sasha nor I could see the wisdom or justice, let alone the revolutionary necessity, of such a prohibition. We agreed that speculation in food-stuff was indeed criminal. But it was absurd to decry everyone as a speculator who tried to bring in half a sack of potatoes or a pound of bacon for his family use. Far from deserving punishment, we argued, one should be glad that the Russian masses still possessed such indomitable will to live. Therein alone was the hope of Russia, rather than in mute submission to a slow death by starvation.

Long before we had started on our expedition, we had agreed that if it was right to import dusty documents for future historians, it could not be wrong to bring back some provisions for the relief of present want, particularly for the sick and needy among our friends. The abundance of food on the Kharkov markets made us more determined to lay in a supply on our return trip. We only regretted that we could not take with us enough to feed every man, woman, and child in the stricken cities.

Moscow had been hot, but Kharkov was ablaze, with the railroad station miles from the town. It was physically impossible to spend the day in collecting material and then return to our car for meals. Comrades in the city helped me to secure a room where I could also prepare meals for our secretary, Alexandra Shakol, Henry Alsberg, Sasha and myself. As a pro-Soviet American correspondent Henry had no difficulty in getting a room, which he invited Sasha to share with him. Shakol preferred to sleep in the car. The Russian couple shifted for themselves, having friends in the city, and our Communist member was taken care of by his party comrades. These arrangements completed, we set out on our labours, each member being assigned to cover certain Soviet institutions. Sasha's task was to visit labour, revolutionary, and co-operative organizations; mine included the departments of education and social welfare.

Our reception at those institutions was anything but cordial. Not that the officials were openly disagreeable, but one could sense the frigidity of their manner. I wondered what could be the reason until

Sasha reminded me of the resentment the Ukrainian Communists felt against Moscow for depriving them of self-determination in their local affairs. They saw in our mission a new imposition of the centre. Not daring to ignore orders from Moscow, they could yet sabotage our work. We therefore decided to fall back on our old talisman, emphasizing that we were *tovarishtchy* from America on a tour of study of the revolutionary achievements of the Ukraine, about which we were to write. The change was instantaneous. No matter how busy the officials happened to be, they would drop their work, become wreathed in smiles, supply us with the information we needed, and send us away with stacks of material. In that manner we succeeded in seeing and learning more of the methods and effects of the dictatorship in the Ukraine than would have been possible in any other manner. We were able to collect more than the Russian members of the expedition, including even the Communist in our party.

The poor boy was really treated abominably by his southern comrades. They refused to give him data or documents. Moscow was on their backs heavily enough, they said, directing their every move. They were not going to let the centre rob them of their historical wealth to boot.

The amusing side of the family quarrel was that whenever we came upon some mismanaged institution or ugly state of affairs, the Ukrainians would explain them away by the interference of Moscow. On the other hand, if the Communist in charge was from the centre, he would argue that the Ukrainians were sabotaging the work of Moscow because they were anti-Semites and obsessed by the notion that almost the entire northern Communist Party consisted of Jews. Between the two we had little difficulty in learning the facts of the situation and the real cause of the widespread antagonism towards Moscow.

A Russian engineer who had just returned from the Don basin and whom we met in Kharkov threw considerable light on the Ukrainian situation. It was silly to put the entire blame for conditions on Moscow, he said. The Communists in the south in no way differed from the followers of Lenin in the north in their methods of dictatorship. If anything, their despotism was even more irresponsible in the Ukraine than anywhere else in Russia. His experience in the mines had convinced him of their ruthless persecution of those of the intelligentsia who were unwilling to co-operate with them. As to their inefficiency and inhumanity, a visit to the prisons and concentration camps would convince us as it did him. Only in one thing they differed from their comrades in the north : they took no stock in the imminence of the world revolution and they were not interested in it or in the international proletariat. All they wanted was to have their own independent Communist State and to command in the Ukrainian instead of in the Russian language. That was their main reason for dissatisfaction with Moscow, he thought.

I inquired about the feeling of anti-Semitism in the Ukraine. The engineer admitted that it was widespread, though it was not true that all Ukrainian Communists were against the Jews. He knew many Bolsheviki who were free from that racial prejudice. In any event, it was unjust of the northern Communists to charge their Ukrainian brothers with anti-Semitism, for they knew very well how prevalent the feeling was among themselves. There was a great deal of it in the Red Army. Moscow was trying to keep it down by iron force, though it did not entirely succeed in preventing anti-Jewish outbreaks on a small scale. In the Ukraine the Whites had so far been the only ones responsible for pogroms. Whether the Ukrainian Red forces would be willing and able to cope with the evil was yet to be seen.

We decided to visit the local prison and detention camp. The greatest difficulty, however, we met from the woman superintendent at the head of the Workers' and Peasants' Inspection, a sort of super-watch recently instituted over the other watchers of abuses in Soviet institutions. Concentration camps and prisons being under her jurisdiction, we presented our credentials to her. She frowned. The prison conditions in Kharkov were the concern of the local authorities and of no one else, she declared categorically. Disappointed, we left her office, meeting on the way a man who introduced himself as *tovarishtch* Dibenko, the husband of Alexandra Kollontay. He had heard from her about me, he explained, and he would be glad to be of help. He requested us to wait while he talked matters over with the superintendent. He was evidently in her good graces, because presently she returned with him quite softened. She had not known that we were such well-known American *tovarishtchy*, she said, and of course we could visit the prison and camp. She would immediately take us there in her auto.

Both penal institutions bore out the statement of our engineering

acquaintance as regards Ukrainian Communist management and despotism. The camp, called *kantslager*, occupied an old building without
any provisions for sanitation and not half large enough for its thousand inmates. The dormitories, overcrowded and smelly, were barren
except for wide boards that served as beds and had to be shared by
two and sometimes three persons. During the day they had to squat
on the floor and even eat their meals in that position. For an hour
they were taken out in sections to the yard, the rest of the time being
kept indoors without anything to occupy their time and minds. Their
offences ranged from sabotage to speculation, and they were all
counter-revolutionists, as our stern guide impressed upon us. " Could
not some useful occupation be provided for the prisoners? " I inquired.
" No time for such *bourgeois* dilly-dallying with the enemies of the
Revolution," she replied; " after the fronts are liquidated, we will
send them away where they can do no more harm."

The political prison of tsarist times was again in full operation.
Those who dared question the right of rulers, divine or self-appointed,
were held captive, now as then. The old régime prevailed, with most
of the former guards as keepers. During our inspection we halted before two locked doors. The others having been open, we inquired the
reason. Our woman escort was evasive at first. We remarked that
prison-investigators in America were usually shown only the most
obvious things and then wrote knowingly about penology. But we
could not be content with such superficiality. Finally the superintendent consented to make an exception in our case. We would understand, she hoped, that behind all measures in Soviet Russia, including
the prison régime, was revolutionary necessity. The occupants of
locked cells were dangerous criminals, she assured us, one, a woman,
was a member of the counter-revolutionary bandit army of Makhno,
and the man occupying the adjoining cell had been caught in a counter-
revolutionary plot. Both deserved severest treatment and the supreme
penalty. Nevertheless she had ordered their cell opened for several
hours a day and she had given permission to the other prisoners to
talk to them in the presence of a guard.

The Makhnovka, an old peasant woman, was crouching in the corner of her cell like a frightened hare. She blinked stupidly when the
door was opened. Suddenly she threw herself headlong before me and
shrieked: " *Barinya*, let me out, I know nothing, I know nothing! "
I tried to quiet her and get her to tell me about her case. Maybe I
could help her, I urged. But she was frantic, whining piteously that

she knew nothing about Makhno. In the corridor I told our guide that it seemed absurd to consider that stupefied old creature dangerous to the Revolution. She was half-crazed with the solitary and the fear of execution, and if kept locked up much longer, she would surely go stark mad. " It is mere sentimentality on your part," the guide upbraided me; " we live in a revolutionary period, with enemies on all sides."

The man in the next cell was sitting on a low stool, his head bent. With a sudden jerk he turned his eyes on the door, a terrorized and hunted look in their anticipation. Just as quickly he pulled himself together, his body stiffened, and his look fastened on our guide with concentrated contempt. Two words, no more audible than a sigh, yet petrifying in their effect, broke the silence. " Scoundrels! Murderers! " A horrible feeling overcame me that he believed us to be officials. I took a step towards him to explain, but he turned his back upon us and was standing erect and forbidding beyond my reach. With heavy heart I followed my companions out of the corridor.

Sasha had said nothing, but I felt that he was affected no less than I. With seeming nonchalance he sauntered along the corridors, his object being to find a young anarchist imprisoned in the place, as we had been confidentially informed. I was kept back by the superintendent, enlarging on my *bourgeois* sympathies.

I let her talk to give Sasha an opportunity for his quest. My thoughts were with the two prisoners I had just left. I knew what doom was awaiting them. The man especially had shown pride and independence. Where was mine, I pondered, that I still kept holding on to the shell whose kernel I knew to be worm-eaten through and through.

When alone with Sasha, I learned what our imprisoned comrade had communicated to him. The head of the Workers' and Peasants' Inspection was a former Chekist and she attempted to run the prison in the usual Cheka manner. She had introduced most severe restrictions, including solitary confinement for the politicals. The inmates sought to effect a change without resorting to drastic methods. But when the half-witted peasant woman and the man doomed to die were isolated from the rest and kept under lock, the entire prison protested. A hunger-strike followed. Though it failed of the desired results, it succeeded in opening the cells part of the day for their two fellow inmates. Another hunger-strike was being planned in the near future to compel a change in the despotic régime.

I understood the terrorized expression on the face of the man and the hate in his cry: " Scoundrels! Murderers!" He was being kept in isolation previous to execution, all the time in uncertainty as to when the fatal shot would silence his palpitating heart. Could any " revolutionary necessity " explain such refined cruelty? If only I had come to Russia in the October days, I thought, I might have found the answer or a fitting end to my past. Now I felt caught in a coil that was growing more strangling every day.

The people who least understood my travail were my own comrades in Kharkov. Most of them were from America and had been affiliated with my work there, among them Joseph and Leah Goodman, Aaron and Fanya Baron, Fleshin, and others. Fleshin had been working with us in the *Mother Earth* office and knew me more intimately. The Kharkov comrades, with the heroic personality of Olga Taratuta at their head, had all served the Revolution, fought on its fronts, endured punishment from the Whites, persecution and imprisonment by the Bolsheviki. Nothing had daunted their revolutionary ardour and anarchist faith. They had no painful hesitations, no torturing doubts, no unanswerable questions. They were shocked to find me so undecided. I had always been sure of myself, they said, unswerving in every issue. Yet in Russia, where I was so badly needed, I seemed to have lost my grip. And Sasha, always so clear and determined — why did he at least not join them in organizing and propaganda work instead of wasting his energies on collecting dead parchments?

Our coming to Russia had been a great impetus to them, they told us. They had been sure that we would continue on Soviet soil the work we had so energetically carried on in the United States. They knew, of course, that we would not give up our faith in the Bolsheviki until we became convinced that they had gone back on their revolutionary slogans. For that purpose Joseph and Aaron Baron had been sent to us by their organization, the Nabat, risking their very lives in the attempt to reach us in Petrograd. Had not their story of the Bolshevik emasculation of the Revolution sufficed to convince us? Their persecution of the anarchists, their perfidy and double-dealing in regard to Nestor Makhno? Had not their proofs demonstrated to us that the dictatorship had betrayed the very spirit of the Revolution? Surely we had heard and seen enough to make up our minds as to where we stood in regard to the Communist State.

Aaron Baron and Joseph had indeed visited us in Petrograd. They had come secretly, both having been outlawed by the Bolsheviki. For two weeks they had held our tense interest by their vivid description of conditions and the causes that had gradually turned the Communists into traitors to the Revolution. But those who knew us could not expect us to give up our belief in the revolutionary integrity of men like Lenin, Trotsky and their co-workers because of their mistaken policy towards Makhno or even towards our own comrades. Our Kharkov people were willing to concede that they had been too hasty in their expectations. But now, they argued, after eight months in Soviet Russia, with all the opportunities we had enjoyed of learning conditions at first hand, why did we still hesitate? Our movement needed us. The field was large and promising. We could easily organize the anarchists of the Ukraine into a strong, federated body that would reach the workers and the peasantry by its propaganda. The latter in particular, through the aid of Nestor Makhno. He knew the peasants and they trusted him. He had repeatedly urged the anarchists throughout the country to take advantage of the propaganda possibilities the south offered. He would put everything necessary at our disposal, including funds, a printing-press, paper, and couriers, our comrades urged, pleading for our speedy decision.

If I should make up my mind to become active in Russia, I explained to them, the support of Makhno would lure me no more than Lenin's offer of aid through the Third International. I was not denying Makhno's services to the Revolution in the struggle against the White forces, nor the fact that his *povstantsy* army was a spontaneous mass movement of the toilers. I did not think, however, that anarchism had anything to gain from military activity or that our propaganda should depend on military or political spoils. But that was beside the point. I was not in a position to join their work, nor was it a question of the Bolsheviki any more. I was ready to admit frankly that I had erred grievously when I had defended Lenin and his party as the true champions of the Revolution. But I would not engage in active opposition to them so long as Russia was still being attacked by outside enemies. I was no longer deceived by their mask, but my real problem lay much deeper. It was the Revolution itself. Its manifestations were so completely at variance with what I had conceived and propagated as revolution that I did not know any more which was right. My old values had been shipwrecked and I myself thrown overboard to sink or swim. All I could do was to try to keep my head above water and trust to time to bring me to safe shores.

Fleshin and Mark Mratchny, the most intelligent comrades I had met in Kharkov, grasped my difficulties and supported my stand in refusing to lead others where I myself had lost my way. The rest of the group Nabat was dissatisfied and indignant. They refused to recognize the Emma Goldman of their American conception in her present pale image. They turned to Sasha with greater expectations. They knew that *he* would never doubt the Revolution, no matter what demands it made on him. He had always been a better conspirator than I and he would see the great value of working with Makhno or at least of accepting his co-operation. Joseph and Leah, most genuine and lovable people, were particularly set on winning Sasha for their plans. They were presently joined by Fanya Baron, who had just arrived from Makhno's camp with an invitation to us. Would we come? She would safely guide us to him. " Will you come? " Sasha asked. If he insisted on going, I should be with him, I replied; under no circumstances would I let him face such danger alone. But what about the expedition? We had given our word to remain with it to the end and he had undertaken most of the responsibilities of the venture. Could we go back on that? In the first flush of the chance to get to Makhno and his *povstantsy* army Sasha had given little thought to the museum and our expedition. However, " a pledge is a pledge," he declared; " We must stick; perhaps we shall find another opportunity to meet the peasant leader."

Our stay in Kharkov came to a sudden end. Our secretary learned that our material was in danger of being held up by the Party Executive and not permitted to leave the Ukraine. We needed no further hint. The same night we managed to get our car hitched to a train going to Poltava, and off we lurched.

We speed-spoiled Americans could scoff and make fun of such slow travel, but to the congested humanity at every railroad station in Russia, waiting for days and even weeks to get on a train, the creeping pace was of great advantage. An appalling sight they were — these rag-covered, bundle-loaded, exhausted people, shouting, cursing, and falling over each other in the mad skirmish to swing on. Pushed off, often by the butt of a soldier's gun, not once but many times, doggedly they would try again and again until they succeeded in clinging to the railing or steps. It was an Inferno awaiting the master hand of a Russian Dante.

An entire car occupied by only eight persons, including our porter, with hundreds clamouring for a place on the platform or roof or even on the bumpers was not an unalloyed comfort. Yet we could do nothing to aid. Aside from the imminent danger of typhus infection, the people being vermin-eaten, we could allow no one into our car on account of the valuable material we carried. Thievery, in places high and low, was no new phenomenon in Russia. Years of disintegration and want had increased its scope and perfected its dexterity. We could not hope to safeguard our collection or anything else in the car against such artistry. We could take none of the woeful mob into our car, that was certain. However, we might permit some women or children to ride on the platforms, I suggested. The Jews of our company favoured the plan, the Gentiles were against it. The Russian couple had proved very disagreeable from the start. It seemed their special mission to inject a jarring note. Shakol was Slavic with a vengeance, now bursting with sympathy and compassion for her fellow-men, now talking like a lady of a feudal manor. She could not bear to feel the filthy creatures so near, she said, and she was mortally afraid of catching typhus or some equally dangerous disease. She could not risk another infection. Poor child, she had had a narrow escape and I could not blame her. I promised to scrub and disinfect the platforms every morning, but even that did not prove as persuasive as Sasha's suavity. It was the art of my old chum to lead people gently to where he wanted them and make them think they had been dying to get there all along. With Shakol on our side, we were able to carry our point.

Everything in life is relative, looming in value according to one's necessity. The platforms of our car were coveted more than palaces. They offered to a few creatures a night's security against wind and hot soot and preserved them from falling off the roof of the car, a thing that was a common occurrence on the road. Life was cheap and people too preoccupied with their own little share of it to get excited over such matters. No one knew whether he might not come next and no one cared. Once squeezed past the soldiers to the tiniest spot on the train, they looked neither behind nor ahead. The present moment alone was theirs and they snatched at it greedily. Quickly they forgot their tears, their cursing and shrieking. They felt sociable again and capable of fun and frolic. Once more they could give vent to their rich imagery and song. What a people! What kaleidoscopic changes of spirit!

Our credentials from the centre found greater favour in Poltava than in Kharkov. The secretary of the *Revkom* (revolutionary committee acting as the local government) received us pleasantly and gave us *carte blanche* to every Soviet department. With such aid our expedition had no difficulty in gathering a goodly crop of material. It included a large amount of counter-revolutionary documents left behind by the various bands and the armies that had invaded Poltava, finally to be routed by the Red forces. Records, decrees, manifestoes, military emblems, and an assortment of curious weapons were unearthed by our secretary and Sasha and carried in triumph to our car.

Together with Henry Alsberg I made a tour of inspection. Henry wanted to interview the main local Soviet officials, as well as persons outside of the Communist Party. He invited me to act as his interpreter and I gladly accepted.

Curiously enough, Poltava showed but few physical traces of the numerous invaders. Hardly any damage had been done to buildings and parks. Her stately trees were in their appointed places, looking contemptuously down from their great height upon the puny thing called man. Flowers were profuse, vegetable patches at their side, with no armed guards or even a fence to protect them from despoilers. After the distressing scenes of our journey from Kharkov the sight of nature's bounty and a walk along the shady alleys were heaven indeed.

The Soviet institutions presented little interest. They were running true to type, managed in conformity with the established one-track idea and according to the Moscow formula. The official interviews added no new note. It gave us time to look for the tabooed part of the population. Inadvertently we came upon two of that class and by their aid met a larger group held together by their common fate, though widely separated in ideas. Our discovery was two women, one of them the daughter of Vladimir Korolenko, the last of the old school of Russian writers. The other was the head of the " Save the Children " organization, founded in 1914 and continued through all the vicissitudes of the intervening years. They invited us to their home, where we came in contact with others of their circle. They were of the old radical intelligentsia that had always been dedicated to the enlightenment and succour of the Russian masses. They were not able to reconcile themselves to the dictatorship, they frankly admitted; nor were they actively engaged against it. In fact, they were co-operating economically with the Bolsheviki and working in the social welfare departments. Nevertheless they were being persecuted as *sabotazhniky* and the " Save the Children " society had been repeatedly raided by the local authorities as a counter-revolutionary body. This in spite of Lunacharsky's express permission to continue their work.

Henry remarked to our hosts that, no matter what might be said against the Bolsheviki, they could not be charged with neglecting the children. They were doing more in that direction than any other country. Why, then, the need of private welfare associations? Our hostesses smiled sadly. They had no intention whatever, they said, to deprecate the sincerity of the Bolsheviki in relation to the child. They had done much for it and would no doubt do still more. That referred, however, only to a privileged class of children. The destitute ones had alarmingly increased in numbers, and thousands were constantly added. Prostitution, venereal diseases, and every form of crime were rampant among the children of even tender age, and pregnancies frequent among girls of ten and eight. The more thoughtful Communists were aware that the scourge could not be cured by political decrees or the Cheka. It had to be dealt with from other angles and by different means. They welcomed the co-operation of the " Save the Children " society. Lunacharsky, for instance, was most generous in aiding it. The trouble was with the *local* authorities. They cared nothing about Lunacharsky and his enlightened view-point. They saw a traitor, actual or potential, in every intelligent non-partisan and treated him accordingly.

The magnificent spirit I had so often found in the hated and harassed elements was also manifested by Miss Korolenko and her colleagues. They asked nothing for themselves, but they begged me to intercede with Lunacharsky in behalf of their work and the children in their charge. The handicraft of the young folks of the society consisted of toys made from waste paper, rags, straw, and even from discarded shoes. It presented a unique collection of animals, dolls, and fanciful beings, specimens of which the women pressed upon us " for the children in America." I assured my hostesses that they would be much more appreciated by my toy-starved young friends in Petrograd.

Vladimir Korolenko was convalescing after a severe illness and not accessible to visitors. His daughter promised, however, to see her father about us and invited us to come to the home of her parents the next day.

In the evening I called on Mme X, chairman of the Political Red Cross. In the past the organization had been aiding the political victims of the Romanovs. I was interested to learn what they were being permitted to do by the new régime. Mme X was a beautiful woman with snowy white hair and large, tender blue eyes. She was the best type of the old Russian idealist, rarely met with nowadays. Warmth, kindliness, and utmost hospitality had been their characteristics, and my hostess had lost none of these qualities, although she had lived through every phase of misery since 1914. It was a hot evening and we sat out on the little balcony, with the puffing *samovar* between us. The bright moon and the glowing coal in the large tea-urn lent romance to the scene. But our conversation was of Russian reality, of the unfortunates who had filled the Tsar's dungeons and places of exile. The activities of her group were more limited now, the old lady informed me. They were becoming more circumscribed all the time and harassed by many difficulties for reasons that had not existed in the past. The dictatorship and the persecution of everyone even remotely suspected of disagreement with the régime robbed the politicals of their former ethical status and the high regard they had enjoyed in all but the most reactionary circles. Now they were denounced as bandits, counter-revolutionists, and enemies of the people. The public at large, deprived of any means of verifying the terrible accusations, believed the Bolshevik charges. The new régime had thus gone further than the old in branding the flower of Russia with the mark of Cain and alienating from them popular esteem. " I consider it the blackest crime of the Bolsheviki, the most reprehensible even from their own view-point of so-called revolutionary necessity," Mme X said bitterly. The Red Cross was now compelled to operate on two fronts, she continued; to aid the politicals materially and save them from death by starvation, and to dispel the cruel lies spread against them. It was a most difficult task, for it was well-nigh impossible to reach the public mind, because the least attempt to enlighten the people on the subject was considered counter-revolutionary and would result in the entire suppression of the organization and the arrest of everyone connected with it. Another obstacle lay in the general disorganization of the railroads and other means of communication, which made it very hard to visit the imprisoned politicals or to keep in touch with them. The most vital thing, even more important than food, was denied the idealists of Bolshevik Russia — encouragement and the inspiration of their comrades at large. That was the hardest for them to bear, my hostess concluded.

I related to her my great shock on first learning of the Jesuitical methods resorted to by the Bolsheviki to slay their opponents, and my long struggle against crediting such things. I told her of my interview with Lenin and his contention that only bandits and counter-revolutionists were in prison. It seemed unbelievable that a man of his mental stature should stoop to such despicable falsehoods to justify his methods. Mme X shook her head. It was apparent, she said, that I was not conversant with Lenin's habitual ways. In his early writings I would find that he had for years advocated and defended such methods of attack against his political opponents, methods to " cause them to be loathed and hated as the vilest of creatures." He had used such tactics when his victims could defend themselves; why should he now not add insult to injury when he had the whole of Russia as his forum? " Yes, and the rest of the radical world," I added, " for in Lenin it sees the revolutionary Messiah. I had believed him that myself, as did also my comrade Alexander Berkman. We had been among the earliest crusaders in America in his behalf. Even now we find it bitter hard to free ourselves from the Bolshevik myth and its principal spook."

It was growing late and I was anxious to hear from the old lady about Korolenko. I knew that like Tolstoy he had for decades been a great moral force in Russia. I wondered what influence he had been able to exert since 1917. I had been informed that Mme X was Korolenko's sister-in-law and very close to the great writer. I begged her to tell me about him.

The prophet of Yasnaya Polyana, she said, had fortunately been spared the spectacle of the old autocracy surviving the Revolution in a new dress. He was saved the agony of writing letters of protest to the new Tsar. Not so her brother-in-law. Though almost seventy and in poor health, Vladimir Korolenko had to spend most of his time in the Cheka pleading for some innocent life or penning entreating letters to Lenin, Lunacharsky, and Maxim Gorki to put a stop to the wholesale executions. Maxim Gorki, she continued, had proved a great disappointment. No, Maxim found the company of Lenin a safer haven, and the Kremlin a pleasanter abode, than exile in a desolate village. Maxim Gorki had not even the courage, she added, to live up to the honoured tradition among Russian authors of encouraging and helping members of the profession and standing by them in distress.

My own experience with Maxim Gorki came to my mind. I recalled his lame apology for Bolshevik autocracy. Still I was not willing to impute ulterior motives to the man I had once so admired. After all, Gorki had done some good, I pleaded in his behalf. He had helped to organize the Dom Utchonikh for the benefit of old scientists and authors, and he had also protested against the system of taking hostages and had raised his voice against the Government monopoly of everything published in Russia. Mme X readily admitted where credit was due to Gorki. But she thought it insignificant for a man of Gorki's former wide and sympathizing humanity. What little good he had done was merely to salve his conscience; it was not prompted by a sense of justice and decency. Still I stressed the point that Maxim Gorki might really believe in the righteousness of Lenin's policies. He was a poet, not a politician; it was probably the glamour about Lenin's name that made him worship. I preferred to think so rather than to believe Gorki capable of selling his birthright for a mess of pottage.

I expressed my surprise that Korolenko was still permitted to be at large, in view of his repeated offences of *lèse-majesté*. Mme X did not consider it strange. Lenin was a very clever man, she explained. He knew his trump cards: Peter Kropotkin, Vera Figner, Vladimir Korolenko were names to reckon with. Lenin realized that if he could point to them as remaining at liberty, he could effectively disprove the charge that only the gun and the gag were applied under his dictatorship. The world actually swallowed that bait. It remained silent while the Calvary of the real idealists was going on. " The tsarist prisons are reaping a rich harvest, and shooting is being kept up as a matter of course," Mme X concluded.

I felt too stifled to return to the narrow quarters of my compartment. It was past two in the morning, the break of day already near. I suggested to the friend who accompanied me that we take a walk. The air outside was balmy, the streets deserted. Poltava was soothing in her sleeping peace. Silently we walked on, each absorbed in the impressions of the evening. I was trying to see beyond the immediate and reaching upward to a point that might hold out the hope of a renaissance in the life of Russia. Approaching steps, their thud falling regularly on the granite walk, startled me. A detachment of soldiers marched by, rifles slung over their shoulders, a group of huddled people in their midst. " And shooting is being kept up as a matter of course," flitted through my mind.

In the morning, still in the throes of the preceding evening, I went, together with Henry Alsberg, to the Korolenko home. It was a little green gem, entirely hidden from view by trees and vines — an enchanting place, with its old native furniture, ornate copper, brass, and colourful Ukrainian peasant handiwork.

Vladimir Korolenko, white of hair and beard, in girdled peasant tunic, suggested amid the surroundings of his home a world removed by centuries. But the illusion was quickly dispelled the moment he began to speak. He was intensely alive and deeply interested in everything we could tell him of America, of which he seemed very fond. He knew a great many persons there, he said; they had always responded generously to every appeal of the Russian people and he admired the country for its broad democracy. We assured him that he would find very little of it left now except in some small circles that were too timid and politically confused to exert any influence. We were much more interested, however, to hear Korolenko on Russia and we gently led the conversation into that channel. The subject was apparently an open wound with the old writer and I soon regretted having dug into it. He relieved my sense of guilt somewhat by remarking that he would give me copies of two letters he had written to Lunacharsky, treating the very problems on which we had come to interview him. They were the first of a series of six that Lunacharsky had asked him to write and which would contain the frank expression of his attitude towards the dictatorship. " The letters may never see the light of day," he commented, " but your museum shall have all of them when they have been written." Alsberg inquired whether Korolenko could be quoted in America, and our host replied that he had no objections, because the time for silence had long passed. He was aware of the danger still facing Russia, he said, but " great as it may be, it is not anything nearly so grave as the inner menace threatening the Revolution." It was the Bolshevik claim that every form of terror, including wholesale execution and the taking of hostages, is justifiable as a revolutionary necessity. To Korolenko it was the worst travesty on the basic idea of revolution and on all ethical values.

" It has always been my conception," he added, " that revolution means the highest expression of humanity and justice. The dictatorship has denuded it of both. At home the Communist State daily divests the Revolution of its essence, substituting for it deeds that far exceed in arbitrariness and barbarity those of the Tsar. His *gendarmes,* for instance, had the authority to arrest me. The Communist Cheka has the power to shoot me, as well. At the same time the Bolsheviki have the temerity to proclaim the world revolution. In reality their experiment upon Russia must retard social changes abroad for a long period. What better excuse needs the European *bourgeoisie* for its reactionary methods than the ferocious dictatorship in Russia?"

Mme Korolenko had cautioned us that her husband was yet far from recovered and should avoid much strain. But once the old man had started on Russia, it was difficult for him to stop. He seemed considerably spent and we dared not prolong our stay. I could not leave, however, without telling him that he had given new impetus to my revolutionary faith. His own fine view of the meaning and purpose of the Revolution had strengthened mine, which eight months in Soviet Russia had almost destroyed. I could never be sufficiently grateful to him for it.

I should have loved to remain awhile longer in beautiful Poltava and to spend some more time with the wonderful spirits I met there. But our expedition had finished its labours and we had to proceed. Our next destination was to be Kiev, but the contrariness of Russian engines compelled us to stop at Fastov.

We did not regret the delay. We had heard and read of ghastly anti-Jewish pogroms, but we had never before come face to face with their ravages. On our way to the town we met neither human being nor beast until we reached the market square. A dozen stands displayed a miserable assortment of cabbages, potatoes, herring, and cereals. Their owners were mostly women. Instead of showing some animation at the sudden avalanche of so many customers, they hurriedly pulled their handkerchiefs over their foreheads and shrank back in fright. But their eyes remained riveted in terror on the men with us, consisting of Sasha, Henry, and our young Communist collaborator. We were completely nonplussed. Being the best-versed in Yiddish, I addressed an old Jewess near by. Except for our woman companion, I told her, we were the children of *Yehudim,* and we had come from America. Would she not tell me why the women acted so strangely? She pointed to the men. "Send them away," she begged.

The men withdrew. I remained with our secretary, Shakol, and the women approached nearer. Soon the whole group surrounded us, each competing with the rest in their eagerness to tell us the story of their *tsores* (troubles). The news of the arrival of Americans spread quickly, and presently the whole village was on its feet. Men came running from the synagogue, women and children hurried towards us to behold the strangers from afar. We must come to the house of prayer, a man declared, to hear the story of the Fastov *goles* (servitude). The march began, and on the way we were met by the rabbi, the *khasin* (singer) and the *magid* (preacher) as honoured guests. Everybody was fearfully excited, gesticulating and talking, most of the women laughing and crying, as if Messiah had indeed come at last.

Our three male companions joined us in the synagogue. The whole assembly tried to tell us the tragic story of their town, all at once. We suggested that they choose a committee of three, each in his turn to relate to us what had happened. In that way we were able to get a coherent account of one of the worst pogroms that had taken place in the Ukraine. Fastov had repeatedly been the scene of Jewish massacres, perpetrated by the hordes of every White general who had invaded the district. They had suffered from Denikin, from Petlura and the other enemy forces. But the pogrom organized in 1919 by Denikin had been the most fiendish one. It had lasted a whole week and had taken the lives of four thousand persons outright and of several thousand more that had perished while escaping to Kiev. But death had not been the worst infliction, the rabbi said in a broken voice. Far more harrowing had been the violation of the women, regardless of age, the young among them repeatedly and in the presence of their male kin, whom the soldiers held pinioned. Old Jews were trapped in the synagogue, tortured, and killed, while their sons were driven to the market square to meet similar fates.

The old rabbi being too shaken to continue, the narrative was taken up by another of the committee. Fastov had been, he said, one of the most prosperous cities in the south. When the Denikin hordes tired of their blood orgy, they pilfered every home, demolished the things they could not carry away, and set the houses on fire. The larger part of the town was destroyed. The survivors, a mere handful, most of them old women and small children, were now doomed to slow extinction unless help quickly came from somewhere. God had heard their prayers and had sent us at the moment when they had almost despaired of the Jewish world's learning of their great calamity. " *Borukh Adonai!* " he cried solemnly, " blessed be Thy name." And everyone repeated after him : " *Borukh Adonai!* "

Their religious fervour was all these people had rescued from their hideous experiences, and, in spite of all certainty that there was no Jehovah to hear them, I was strangely stirred by the tragic scene in the poverty-stricken synagogue in outraged and devastated Fastov. The Jews of America were more likely to answer their prayers, and, alas, neither Sasha nor I had access to them. All we could do was to write about the dreadful pogroms. Excepting the anarchist press, however, we had no assurance that any paper would publish our account. It would have been too cruel to tell these people that in America we were considered *Ahasverus*. We could make known their great tragedy only to the radical labour world and to our own comrades. But there was Henry. He could do a great deal for these unfortunates, and I was sure he would. Our fellow traveller had been with us six weeks and he had witnessed some heart-rending scenes. Yet I had never seen him so affected as in Fastov. Not that he did not feel deeply in a universal sense. Henry was a bundle of emotions, though his male pride would have stoutly denied such an imputation from a mere woman. Nevertheless it was true that his kind heart ached more when Jews were being persecuted, which in view of the fearful Denikin atrocities was not at all surprising. The people gathered in the synagogue no doubt sensed that in him Heaven had sent them the right messenger. They threw themselves upon him with avidity and would not let him go.

We were besieged by the inhabitants with letters and messages for their kin in America. Truly pathetic were the women who brought their little scribbles to us to be forwarded to a son, a daughter, a brother, or an uncle. They were somewhere " in Amerike." We asked the addresses or at least the names of the places where their relatives lived. They had none. Some thought just the name of their loved ones would be enough. They wept bitterly when informed that " Amerike " was somewhat larger than Fastov. We should take their letters anyhow, they implored ; maybe they would be delivered somehow. We had not the courage to refuse. We could send them through our people to the Yiddish press in the States, Sasha suggested. No more solemn blessings were ever bestowed on anyone than were showered upon us at our departure.

In the whole gruesome picture of Fastov two redeeming features stood out. The Gentiles of the town had had no share in the massacres. And no pogroms had taken place since the Bolshevik forces had entered the district. Our informants admitted that the Red soldiers were not free from anti-Semitism, but the establishment of Soviet authority in Fastov had lifted the dread of new massacres, and the villagers had been praying for Lenin ever since. "Why only for Lenin?" we asked; "why not also for Trotsky and Zinoviev?" "Well, you see, Trotsky and Zinoviev are *Yehudim*," an old Jew explained with Talmudic intonation; "do they deserve praise for helping their own? But Lenin is a *goi* (Gentile). So you can understand why we bless him." We too felt grateful that the *goi* had at least one saving grace in his régime.

One Gentile was pointed out to us as a physician who had done heroic rescue work during the Denikin pogrom. Repeatedly he had braved grave danger to save Jewish lives. The community fairly worshipped him and gave us numerous instances of his noble valour. We invited the doctor to our car to share with us our evening meal. He had kept a diary of the pogroms in Fastov and he held our attention tense while reading from it till the dawn of morning.

The nightmare of travel we had experienced between Kharkov and Fastov was again repeated during the six days that it required to reach Kiev. It left us bruised and battered and made us realize anew the incredible persistency of the Slav in overcoming the greatest hardships.

The masses of desperate human beings fighting at every station to get on the train were increased by the village poor, the destitute and ragged children presenting the most awful sight. Of various ages and covered with filthy tatters, they besieged us with hungry eyes and pleading voices for a piece of bread. These innocent victims of war, strife, and inhumanity were to me always the most heart-breaking sight in the fearful panorama of our journey.

The crowds at the stations, Sasha and Henry reported, were as nothing compared with the swarms at the village markets. There they were thick as ants and as determined in their attacks. They were the torment of hucksters and of the militiamen ordered to drive them off the streets. No sooner were the markets cleared of them than they would flock back, apparently in even larger numbers. "Drive them away — what solution is that?" I remarked to Henry. "With the blockade starving Russia, there seems no other way," he replied. I wished I could still believe that it was only the blockade and not general inefficiency and the bureaucratic Frankenstein monster which were mainly responsible for the situation. No governmental machinery can cope with great social issues, I said to Henry. Even the United States, with its vast resources and powerful organization, had to enlist the co-operation of the social forces in the war. Trained and efficient men and women outside the Government limits won the World War for Woodrow Wilson rather than his generals. The dictatorship would have none of the social elements to help, and their energy and abilities were compelled to lie fallow. Thousands of Russia's public-spirited men and women were eager to render service to their country, but were refused participation because they could not swallow the twenty-one points of the Third International. How, then, could one hope that the Communist State would ever succeed in solving difficult social problems?

Henry insisted that my impatience with the Bolshevik régime was due to my belief that a revolution *à la Bakunin* would have brought more constructive results, if not immediate anarchism. Yet as a matter of fact the Russian Revolution had been *à la Bakunin,* but it had since been transformed *à la Karl Marx.* That seemed to be the real trouble. I had not been naïve enough to expect anarchism to rise phœnix-like from the ashes of the old. But I did hope that the masses, who had made the Revolution, would also have the chance to direct its course. Henry did not believe that the Russian people would have been capable of accomplishing constructive work even if the dictatorship had not monopolized all power. He was certain, however, that the Bolsheviki would do better, once the blockade had been lifted and the military fronts liquidated. How I wished I could share his hope! But I could not see the slightest sign of the reins being loosened. On the contrary, there was an unmistakable tightening up until all the life was pressed out of the original Revolution.

We never got much further in our discussions. Still it was a great relief to talk these matters over with Henry. One could never discuss them with the Russians in our party, least of all with our secretary, Shakol. She was as aware of conditions as I, but she could not bear the least derogatory remark regarding Russia or the régime. I loved her, though her Slav tendency to mope was very trying at times.

Our need for a thorough scrub and a real night's rest was compelling. Not less so was our eager anticipation of the rich material, particularly counter-revolutionary data, to be found in Kiev. The city on the Dnieper had been the pivot of all the battles in the Ukraine between the Red and the White forces. Only recently the Poles had invaded Kiev.

While still in Petrograd, Sasha and I had shared the indignation of the Soviet press over the vandalism of the Polish occupation. They had demolished all the art treasures of the city, Lunacharsky and Chicherin declared. The ancient cathedrals, the Sophia and the Vladimir, famous for their architectural beauty, had been wrecked. We feared that on our arrival we should find the greater part of the old Russ capital in ruins. But we had failed to take into account the Soviet methods of propaganda, of turning a mole-hill into a mountain. The Poles may have indeed intended much damage to Kiev, but they had evidently not succeeded in accomplishing their purpose. Several small bridges and some railroad tracks were all that had been destroyed. No other ruins were awaiting our arrival. On the other hand, we were assured that the enemy had left behind a wealth of material, but to get possession of it proved a most difficult task. The native Communists fairly oozed antagonism to Moscow, disdainfully ignoring our credentials from " the centre." They evidently had no love for any of their northern comrades, with the exception of Lenin, who seemed everybody's patron saint. They bristled at the very mention of Zinoviev, and apparently they thought us his personal emissaries come to spy on them. " Who is Zinoviev, indeed? " they cried bitterly; " who is he to order us to hand over our valuable historical material? " Safe in the luxurious Kremlin and Smolny, they said, it was easy for Zinoviev to issue commands. But they, the people of the Ukraine, and particularly of Kiev, were living in constant danger. Their *Ispolkom* (Executive Committee) was in hourly dread of a new invasion. Could they bother about Zinoviev's orders? They had more important things to look after. The life of the city had to be organized and they could waste no time on our mission.

Dispirited, our secretary returned from her interview with *Tovarishtch* Vetoshkin, chairman of the all-powerful *Ispolkom*. She was almost in tears. The official was adamant and absolutely refused to aid our efforts. It were better to continue our journey without further loss of time. In spite of her pessimism we decided to try our American sesame. It had worked in seemingly hopeless situations before.

Why not in Kiev? We had a real, honest-to-goodness native American son with us, and a full-fledged correspondent at that. The authorities would not be able to withstand his importance, we said. Henry grinned assent. With a mischievous twinkle in his fine eyes he declared that as his interpreter I had already induced people to say more than he had intended to ask them and that I had succeeded in making them think they would be serving posterity by helping the Museum of the Revolution. Between the two of us he was sure we should succeed in inducing the Ukrainians to co-operate with our mission.

Henry's press card worked like a charm. Not only did Vetoshkin come out in person to greet us, but we were invited into his sanctum and treated to a lengthy and interesting account of Petlura, Denikin, and other adventurers who had been driven out of the Ukraine by Red forces. When we emerged from Vetoshkin's office, we were equipped with an order to the housing-department for two rooms and with instructions to his secretary to give us all the assistance possible. I also received from Vetoshkin an order on the Party Commissary for rations, which I accepted for the Russian members of our group, but declined for Sasha and myself. The markets were well stocked with provisions, and trading was not interfered with, and we preferred to pay our way, I informed the chairman.

The return of the Bolsheviki to the city was but recent and we soon realized that the Soviet departments had almost no material that could serve our purpose. There was too much confusion in the new Government to keep any records. No one knew what anybody else was doing, and orders were given and countermanded with no rhyme or reason.

The Whites had also left very little valuable material. Fourteen different times Kiev had changed hands, and only in one thing the various governments had agreed and co-operated — in pogroms against the Jews.

In the Jewish hospital, now known as the Soviet Clinic, we came upon the victims of the Denikin outrages in Fastov. Though considerable time had elapsed since the last pogrom in that city, many of the women and girls were still very ill, some of them crippled for life as a result of their injuries. The most fearful cases were those of children suffering from the shock of having been forced to witness the torture and violent death of their parents. From Dr. Mandelstamm, the surgeon of the institution, we learned of his gruesome experiences during the pogroms, whose battle-field had been the hospital. He also spoke of the Denikin fury as the worst of all the attacks. Not a patient would have been left alive, he related, nor the building intact, but for the heroic resistance of his staff, most of whom were Gentiles. Bravely they had remained at their posts, rescuing many of their charges. " Fortunately the Bolsheviki came back, bringing with them security from further atrocities," he said.

One of the startling finds I made in Kiev consisted of copies of *Mother Earth*. They were given to me by a man we had called to see in reference to data on pogroms. He had shown little interest in our mission, but the next day he came to our car with a bundle of the magazine I had published in the States. Why had I not explained who Berkman and I were, he chided me; he would not have given us such an indifferent reception. He had received the copies only the previous evening from a friend whom he had told about the visit of " the Americans." Only then he learned whom the Jewish colony of his city had in their midst. How did the magazine get to Kiev, I wondered; I was sure it had never been sent to Russia. Our caller explained that his friend Zaslavsky had received some copies from his brother in America. "Zaslavsky?" I inquired; " not our old comrade of Brooklyn, New York?" "The very same," the man replied. Now that he knew of our identity, he declared, we must come to his house for tea, and he would also invite the local Jewish intelligentsia to meet us. They would never forgive him when they learned that we had been in Kiev and they were not apprised of our presence. Before leaving, the man informed me that he was Latzke, former Minister for Jewish Affairs in the Rada (Ukrainian National Assembly).

In the Russian cataclysm my former life in America had receded into pale memory, becoming a dream bereft of living fibre and I myself a mere shadow without firm hold, all my values turned to vapour. The sudden appearance of the *Mother Earth* copies revived the poignancy of my aimless and useless existence. Yearning, sickening yearning, possessed me, chilling the very marrow of my being. I was pulled back to reality by the arrival of Sonya Avrutskaya, a very sympathetic local comrade. With her was a stranger, a young woman in peasant costume, who was introduced to me as Gallina, the wife of Nestor Makhno. I forgot my distress at the peril that threatened her, Sonya, and all of us. I knew that the Bolsheviki had set a price on Makhno's head, dead or alive. They had already killed his brother and several members of his wife's family in vengeance for their failure to capture Makhno. Anyone even distantly suspected of having any relationship with him was in imminent jeopardy of his life. Discovery would mean certain death for Gallina. How could she risk coming to our place, well known to the authorities as it was and open to every caller, including Bolsheviki? She had faced danger too often to care, Gallina replied. The purpose of her visit was too important to be entrusted to anyone else. She was bringing a message from Nestor to Sasha and me, asking us to consent to a *coup* he was planning. He was not far from Kiev, with a detachment of his forces. His plan was to hold up our train on its journey south, to take us prisoners, as it were. The rest of our expedition could proceed on its way. He wanted to explain to us his position and aims and he would give us safe conduct back to Soviet territory. Such a manœuvre would clear us of suspicion of deliberate dealing with him. It was a desperate scheme, he was aware, but so was also his situation. Bolshevik lies and denunciations had blackened him and the revolutionary integrity of his *povstantsy* army and misrepresented his motives as an anarchist and internationalist. We were his only opportunity to give his side of the situation to the proletarian world outside Russia, to explain that he was neither bandit nor *pogromshtchik,* that he had in fact punished with his own hands individual *povstantsy* guilty of offences against the Jews. He was with the Revolution to the last breath and he hoped and urged that we would render him this vital and solidaric service, to let him talk to us and present his aims. Would we consent to his plan?

It was an ingenious scheme, recklessly daring, its adventurous quality enhanced by the beauty and youth of Makhno's messenger. Presently Sasha and Henry arrived and we were all held spellbound by the passionate pleading of Gallina. Sasha's conspiratory imagination caught fire and he was almost ready to consent. I also felt strongly tempted to accept. But there were others to consider, our companions of the expedition. We could not lead them blindly into something that was undoubtedly fraught with grave consequences. There was also something else that acted as a restraining influence. I had not yet been able to cut the last threads that bound me to the Bolsheviki as a revolutionary body. I felt I could not be guilty of deliberate deception towards those whom I was still trying to exonerate emotionally, though intellectually I could not longer accept them.

In the entire city there was no hiding-place for Makhno's wife. My room offered scant security, but it was her only cover for the night. Tense and moving were the hours spent with Gallina. We sat in darkness, except for the pale moonlight that lit up now and then her lovely face. She seemed completely oblivious of the danger of her presence in my quarters. She was vital, and hungry for information about the life and work of her sisters abroad, particularly in America. What were the women doing there, she questioned, and what have they accomplished in independence and recognition? What was the relationship of the sexes, woman's right to the child and to birth-control? Amazing was the thirst for knowledge and information in a girl born and bred in primitive surroundings. Her passionate eagerness was infectious and revived my own mainsprings for a while. The break of morning compelled us to part. Gallina walked out into the dawning day with brave and sure gait. I stood behind the portières, watching her receding figure.

After Gallina's visit I no longer felt at ease in accepting aid even for our official mission. Not that I was conscious of any breach of confidence so far as the Bolsheviki were concerned. Makhno's wife was in my estimation no counter-revolutionist; and even if I had thought her one, I should not have turned her over to certain death at the hands of the Cheka. Just the same, I realized that I had no business with the *Revkom* and I decided not to visit it any more.

The arrival of Angelica in Kiev brought a new interest. She came as the guide of the Italian and French Mission. Her greeting when I sought her out was so full of tenderness and love that the local Bolsheviki began to consider me as one of their very own. In addition dear Angelica had felt moved to disclose to Vetoshkin our American past and he reproached us for coming to him merely as members of the museum expedition. We had been nearly two weeks in the city and we had not even hinted at our real identity, he complained. He begged us to give up our quarters and become the guests of the Soviet house.

Alexandra Shakol had once told me that she would forgo half her life to wake up a Communist, so as to give herself unreservedly to the party's demands and service. Now I understood what she had meant. I felt that I would also give anything to be able to take Vetoshkin's hand and say: " I am with you. I see your cause with your eyes and I will serve with the same blind faith as you and your sincere comrades." Alas, there was no such short and easy way out of the mental anguish for those who seek for life beyond dogma and creed.

We did not move to the Soviet house and we assured Vetoshkin that we had no need of anything. We accepted, however, Angelica's invitation to the banquet arranged in honour of the Italian and French Mission that she was chaperoning. We had been south for over two months, completely cut off from the Western world as well as from the rest of Russia. Angelica was the first friend from the north we had met since our departure. Unfortunately she could tell us but little, as she herself had been constantly on the road. But she brought us the disturbing news of the arrest of Albert Boni. Suspected as a counter-revolutionary, she told us. " Absurd ! " I laughed. Albert was just a publisher and very far from rebelling against any established institution, whether revolutionary or otherwise. I hastened to call Sasha and Henry. They were much amused to hear that Boni was considered dangerous to the Soviet Government. We knew, however, that landing in the Cheka was no joking matter and we begged Angelica to send a telegram to Lenin, signed by us, to which she readily assented.

On the way to the banquet Sasha fell into a Cheka *oblava* that had encircled the entire street. Every pedestrian was halted and searched for documents. Though Sasha's were in perfect order, the officer held on to him as for dear life, and no explanations would induce the Chekist to permit him to go his way. Fortunately a heated argument was started by a near-by group in the same predicament. No Russian could escape the temptation to join in. The Chekist forgot for a moment his captive, and without much ceremony Sasha left.

The former Commercial Club and its elaborate rooms and gardens were brightly illuminated for the festive occasion and decorated with fresh-cut flowers. The wine and fruit on the tables gave little indication of the storms that had swept the city. It might still have been the good old time when stout ladies tightly laced, their necks and arms bedecked with jewels, sauntered about the place, and no less stodgy gentlemen in swallow-tails feasted in these halls. The gold and plush of the club made an incongruous background for the pale-faced proletarians in shoddy clothes. Of the hundred and fifty or more persons that sat down to the gala affair Angelica was probably the only Communist to suffer from the vulgar display. Even the presence of her beloved Italian comrades could give her little comfort. Serrati to her right and the French Communist Sadoul on her left kept her engaged in conversation. But her pained and roaming eyes expressed better than words how utterly out of place she felt and how out of touch with the entire farce in honour of Lenin, Trotsky, Zinoviev, the Red Army, the Third International, and the world revolution. Intoxicating words to those that had no ear for jarring dissonances. They made her wince as they did me, though our leitmotifs were in vastly different keys. Two Anarcho-Syndicalists whom we discovered among the French delegates induced us to remain at the affair till the end. They were to leave with the mission the same night and they invited us to accompany them to the station so that we could have a talk. They had been impressed by much that had been shown them, they told us, but they had also made disturbing observations. They had collected information and data about the political machine that convinced them that the proletariat had very little share in the actual dictatorship. They meant to use the material in their report to the syndicates on their return to France. They looked at us in amazement when we warned them to be careful about taking out their data. They might not be permitted to do so, we informed them. " Preposterous! We are not Russians, nor bound by the discipline of the Communist Party," they exclaimed. They were Frenchmen, representatives of large syndicalist organizations. Who would dare molest them? " The Cheka, of course," we explained. We were unduly anxious, they thought.

The evening arranged for us at Latzke's had none of the affluence of the mission banquet, though our hosts had spread the best they could afford. Its interest to us was not the repast, however, but the unrestrained good will and spirit that prevailed. Everyone felt free to express himself, and there was no lack in the variegation of opinion and sentiment. Every profession of the Yiddish intelligentsia was represented. All came to meet the American visitors, to exchange with them their views, hopes, and fears. None was a Communist, yet almost every one of them was an ardent defender of the régime, for racial reasons. Like Dr. Mandelstamm, who was also present, they frankly admitted that their main concern was the safety of the Jew. The Bolsheviki were preventing pogroms and therefore the Jews should support the Soviet Government, they argued. I inquired whether they were content with or could believe in permanent protection of their people in an atmosphere of general terror and insecurity. They agreed that the dictatorship was fatal to individual initiative and effort. But since they had no choice, it was gratifying to know that at least the Jews as a race had been freed from the discrimination suffered for centuries. Their feeling was the result of fear, understandable enough in surroundings surcharged with anti-

Semitism, as the Ukraine was. But as a criterion for releasing social energies it was worse than useless. To me that was the prime consideration. I could not translate the October upheaval into terms of Jew or Gentile, but only into values accruing to all of humanity, or at least to all the people in Russia.

The younger element at our gathering had a different view-point. They did not deny the Bolsheviki full credit for stopping pogroms, but they held that the Soviet régime itself was fertile soil for the poisonous weed of Jew-hatred. Under the tsarist autocracy the pest had been limited to the most reactionary elements. Now all sections of the country were infected by it. The peasant, the worker, and the intelligentsia all saw in Jews Communists and commissars responsible for punitive expeditions, forcible food-collection, militarization, and intimidation. Bolshevism was an impetus to Jew-baiting, they insisted, rather than a safety-valve against it.

Sasha stressed the point that both sides were making the mistake of denouncing the abuses of power, while the evil was in the thing itself. It was the Communist State and dictatorship that had subordinated the aims of the Revolution to those of the ruling party. The purpose of October was to release the creative energies of Russia for the free upbuilding of a new life. The object of the dictatorship was to organize a formidable political machine as the absolute master. That was the source of the disintegrating forces at work in the country. Increased anti-Semitism, return to the churches, anti-revolutionary feeling on the part of the peasantry and the workers, the cynicism of the young generation, and similar manifestations were the direct result of the failure of the Bolsheviki to keep the solemn promises made by them during the October days.

Some of those present favoured our view-point, others fought it determinedly, but without rancour or ill feeling, and therein lay the charm of the gathering at the home of Latzke.

Sasha gathered a wealth of material from the Mensheviki he had met. They had been a potent educational and social force during the first two years of the Revolution in the south, but they had since been liquidated by the Bolsheviki and the Social Democratic unions hitched to the Communist wagon. The Mensheviki had succeeded in rescuing valuable data bearing on the history of Ukrainian labour and of their party and they turned them over to Sasha, together with a lot of personal notes and diaries. He had also somehow ferreted out a counter-revolutionary archive in a desk drawer of the Labour Soviet head-quarters. It consisted of a strange conglomeration of police records, minutes of the Rada sessions, commercial statistics, and similar matter. In that helter-skelter Sasha had also chanced upon the first *Universal* issued by Petlura as dictator of the Ukraine, containing his official declaration of principles of the Southern National Democracy. A most important find was also made by our secretary, consisting of reams of Denikin material stored in the public library of the city and apparently forgotten. The librarian, a rabid nationalist, remained deaf to the pleas of Shakol. But he became all attention when faced with the argument that he could not afford the ridicule and disgrace if it should become known in America that he had preferred to leave the valuable documents to become the prey of rats in his cellar rather than have them preserved for future generations by the Museum of the Revolution.

Our last day in Kiev was a Sunday and we took the opportunity to journey along the beautiful Dnieper. Excursion boats enlivened the view, and in the distance lay the magnificent cathedrals and churches. At a point farther on along the river we came upon an old village with an ancient monastery. The hospitable nuns fed us on bread and honey from their own hives. Between their prayers and labours they had remained untouched by the events in their country and totally ignorant of all that had happened. Steeped in centuries of superstition, they could not realize the meaning of the new life struggling all about them to be born. Their saving grace was the work they were doing, raising vegetables, cultivating bees, teaching the village children to sew and mend, and their kindliness to strangers. Not so their brother monks in the Sophia and the Vladimir cathedrals. They continued to thrive on the credulity of their dupes, still very numerous, as we were assured. The solemn humbugs kept busy showing people through the caves and enlarging on the miracles performed by the saints whose dried bones were exposed to view. A strange sight, indeed, in revolutionary Russia!

On the way to Odessa we lost our good friend Henry Alsberg. Inadvertently he had caused his own arrest. Henry had joined the expedition without having secured the consent of the Moscow Cheka and he could have continued till the end of our journey without the eagle eye of the Soviet being able to discover his whereabouts. But he had added his signature to the telegram we had sent to Lenin in behalf of the arrested Albert Boni. As a result the All-Russian Cheka in the capital had at once sent orders to apprehend the criminal who had dared absent himself without its permission. Things moving at a snail's pace in Russia, the command failed to reach Kiev while we were there. It was wired to every station along our route and over-took us in Zhmerinka.

All our protests failed to save Henry. The Cheka in charge declared that Alsberg's papers were in perfect order and his credentials from Chicherin and Zinoviev valid, but he lacked permission from the Moscow Cheka, and they had strict orders to arrest him. We could not permit Henry to go alone, and we proposed that Sasha or I accompany him to Moscow. But Henry would not hear of it. He knew enough Russian, he joked, to keep his escorts in good humour. Why, he could say *pozhaluysta* (please), *nitchevo* (nothing), and *spassibo* (thank you), and was not that enough for all practical purposes? If need be, he could also muster up a few less polite expressions. Besides, he possessed something policemen everywhere appreciated best — *me-zuma*. He had no fear and we need not be anxious about him, he assured us. Brave old Henry! One thing I insisted on, however: that he should not take his notes with him. They would be sure to get him into trouble and they would be safer with us and he without them.

We immediately dispatched telegrams to Lenin, Lunacharsky, and Zinoviev in behalf of Alsberg, but we did not feel very sanguine that they would reach their destination.

Henry had endeared himself to us by his fine spirit, joviality, and ready wit. It was with a heavy heart that we saw him leave, led away by the Chekists. The poor boy had already met with misfortune recently, having been robbed of his wallet. The loss of one's last sou is nowhere very pleasant, but in Russia it was a calamity. I did not have a chance to console my friend, because the boys missed the train and did not rejoin us until many hours later. They were bubbling over with their adventure. "But the thief!" I exclaimed; "was your money recovered?" "Fine chance to find the one among the many," Henry laughed.

Alsberg's arrest proved the beginning of a chain of adversities that pursued us for the rest of our journey. Barely out of Zhmerinka we received the news of the defeat of the Twelfth Army and the advance of the Poles on Kiev. The line was clogged with military trains on their retreat, and at the stations everything was in the wildest confusion. Our car was repeatedly attached to trains ordered south and as many times detached again to be sent in the opposite way. At last we were lucky enough to get into an echelon actually going in the direction of our next destination, the great city on the Black Sea. From there we planned to reach the Caucasus, but the movements of General Wrangel decided otherwise. His forces had just invested Alexandrovsk, a suburb of Rostov, thus shutting off the route we were to take to the Crimea. Our credentials were to expire at the end of October and we knew that months would be required to get them renewed by mail. It would be courting danger to remain south longer than our documents permitted, but, once in Odessa, we hoped to find a way out of the difficulty.

At last we reached the great city on the Black Sea, only to find that a devastating fire had laid the main telegraph office and the electric station in ashes the previous day, leaving the city in utter darkness. The holocaust was declared to be the work of White incendiaries, and the city was placed under martial law. The general nervousness was increased by the report that the Poles had taken Kiev and that Wrangel was advancing north. The public had no means of learning the truth of the situation, which only increased their trepidation.

An atmosphere of suspicion and fear dominated the Soviet institutions. All eyes were turned on us as Shakol, Sasha, and I entered the *Ispolkom*. Our credentials were carefully scrutinized and we were examined as to our identity and purpose before we were permitted to come into the august presence of the *predsedatel*. He proved a rather youngish man, obviously conscious of the importance of his position. He neither responded to our greeting nor asked us to sit down. He kept buried in the papers on his desk, then examined our documents, studying them long and carefully, till at last he seemed satisfied with them. All he could do, he told us finally, was to supply us with a pass to the other Soviet departments and with written permission to be out on the streets "after permitted hours." He could aid us no more and he was not interested in museums, anyhow. It was a sinecure for the intelligentsia, but the workers had more important things to do to defend the Revolution. Everything else was a waste of time, he declared. The man's attitude and curt manner did not augur well for our efforts. Nor did his words sound convincing as to his own integrity. Sasha thanked him, remarking that we appreciated his revolutionary zeal and that we would not impose on his good nature any longer. His sarcasm was lost, however, on the man standing rigid at his desk.

My co-workers shared my impression that it was mostly hatred of the intelligentsia that motivated the chairman of the *Ispolkom*. I had met many proletarian Communists permeated with bitterest resentment against intelligent people, but never anyone so brutally frank about it as the Odessa *predsedatel*. I could not help feeling that such zealots were more harmful to the best interests of the Revolution than armed enemies. We decided that no member of our expedition should call again at the *Ispolkom* and that we would try to accomplish in the city whatever possible by ourselves.

As we were walking down the stairs, several young people approached us. They stared at us a moment and then shouted: " Hello, Sasha! Emma! You here? " The unexpected encounter with our comrades from America was a pleasant surprise after the sight of the Bolshevik martinet. When they learned of our mission, they assured us that we could take the next train out of the city; no help was to be expected from the officials, they were certain. With the *Ispolkom* chairman in the lead, most of them were anti-centre and anti-everything that was not local Communist. They were reputed as the worst *sabotazhniky*. The chairman, a dogmatic zealot, hated anyone whose education transcended the A.B.C.'s; he would have all intellectuals shot, one of the boys declared, if he had his way. Our comrades suggested that we might be aided in our efforts for the museum by our American comrade Orodovsky, who held a responsible position in the city, and there were several others who might also assist us. The Mensheviki, too, could supply us with information and material. They had recently been cleared out of the unions; still, some of them were so influential with the rank and file that the Bolsheviki had not dared to arrest them.

Orodovsky was a first-class printer and a man of a practical turn of mind. He had managed to get into the Government publishing house and he organized it in a manner to astonish the authorities. From the confiscated and neglected materials he formed the best printing shop in the city, and great was his pride in showing us through the place. It was a model of cleanliness, order, and efficient production. His efforts were hampered at every turn; he was not considered one of their " own " and therefore he was under suspicion. He loved the work and he felt he was doing something for the Revolution, but it made him sad to foresee the inevitable approaching. " Ah, the Revolution," he sighed, " what has become of it ? "

Through Orodovsky we were enabled to meet several other anarchists active in the economic department. All of them felt themselves, like Orodovsky, only temporarily tolerated and in constant danger of getting into trouble as men who were " not entirely " with the established standards of opinion. The most interesting of them was Shakhvorostov, of proletarian origin, whose whole life had been spent among the workers. He had fought for them under the autocracy and he continued to fight their battles even under the Bolsheviki. He was one of the most militant anarchists and was greatly beloved by the toilers.

On nearer acquaintance Shakhvorostov proved all we had been told of him, besides being most genuine and human. There was about him none of the rigidity and hardness of the chairman of the *Ispolkom*. He was all interest and kindliness, and his manner utterly simple.

" Sheer luck," he said, when asked how he managed to keep at liberty, " and the support of the workers," he added. They knew his sole purpose was to help them in their struggle against the constant encroachments of the Communist State. He realized that it was a losing battle, but all the same it was his duty to keep it up as long as he remained free.

Shakhvorostov substantiated the charges of widespread sabotage made by our young comrades. He added that, while most Soviet officials were simply inefficient, others were downright *sabotazhniky,* purposely hampering every effort for the welfare of the people. He related the particularly gross instance of the recent general raid on the *bourgeoisie* to apply Lenin's slogan: " Rob the robbers." Every house, shop, and shanty had been invaded and the last remnants ransacked and confiscated by the emissaries of the Cheka. It was a big haul, because the raid had taken the owners by surprise. The workers had been assured a supply of clothing and shoes, which they sorely stood in need of. When they learned of the new expropriation, they demanded that the promise be made good. " And it was," Shakhvorostov commented with a wry face; " we in the Public Economy Department received a dozen boxes of goods, but when we opened them, we found nothing but rags, old and torn things that one would not offer a beggar. The raiders had had first pick, and then they stocked the markets and the *bourgeoisie* quickly bought back everything they had lost. The scandal was so great that it could not be hushed up. The decent men in the party demanded an investigation, and the result was that some subordinates were shot. But corruption is rampant, and it is not to be eradicated by shooting."

Shakhvorostov and a comrade from the Metal Workers' Union promised to call a conference of the chairmen of the various labour bodies to acquaint them with the project of the Museum of the Revolution and interest them in our efforts. Sasha was to address the delegates and explain our mission.

A week's canvass of the Soviet institutions convinced us that, far from exaggerating, our comrades had not painted half the picture of Odessa sabotage. The local officials proved the worst shirkers we had ever come across in Russia. From the highest commissar to the last *barishnya* (young woman) typist they made it a habit of coming to work two hours late and quitting an hour earlier than closing time. Often the clerk's window would be shut right in the face of an applicant who had spent hours waiting his turn, only to be told that it was "too late" and to come tomorrow. We received almost no assistance in our work from the Soviet authorities. "Too busy, without a minute to spare," they would assure us. Yet most of them stood about smoking cigarettes and talking by the hour, while the "young ladies" were engaged in polishing their nails and rouging their lips. It was the most open and shameless official parasitism.

The Workers' and Peasants' Inspection, created specially to fight this kind of sabotage, seemed to take little interest in the purpose of their existence. Most of them were notorious speculators, and if anyone wanted tsarist or Kerensky money changed, though the practice was strictly forbidden, he would be advised to go to some well-known official to have the transaction attended to. "Ordinary citizens are shot for such speculation," a well-known Bundist [1] commented to us, "but who can touch these officials? They all work hand in glove." The corruption and autocracy of the highest Soviet circles were an open secret in the city, the man related. The Cheka in particular was nothing more than a gang of cut-throats. Extortion, bribery, and indiscriminate shooting of victims who could not pay

---

[1] Member of the *Bund*, Jewish Social Democratic organization.

were its common practices. It was a frequent occurrence that big speculators, sentenced to die, were set free by the Cheka for the payment of exorbitant ransom. Another practice was to notify the relatives of some prominent prisoner that he had been executed. While the family would be plunged in grief, a Cheka emissary would arrive to inform them that it had been a mistake. The condemned man was still alive, but only a certain sum, invariably very large, could save his life. Family and friends would divest themselves of everything to secure the necessary amount, and the money was always accepted. There would come no more emissaries to explain that the alleged mistake had been no mistake at all. If anyone dared show signs of protest, he would be arrested and shot for " attempting to corrupt " the Cheka. Almost every morning at dawn a truckload of those that were to die would clatter down " Cheka Street " at a furious pace towards the outskirts of the city. The doomed ones were forced to lie in the wagon face down, their hands and feet tied, armed guards standing over them. Chekists on horseback accompanied the truck, shooting at anyone who showed himself at an open window along their route. A narrow strip of red in the path of the returning truck would be all that was left to tell the story of those taken on their last ride to be *razmenyat* (destroyed).

The Bundist called again a few days later in the company of a friend whom he introduced as Dr. Landesman, a Zionist and member of a circle that included the famous Jewish poet Byalek and other public-spirited men. No doubt we knew, the doctor said, that Rosh Hashona was at hand, and he would be happy to have us celebrate the great day together in the company of his family. We confessed that we had not been aware of the approach of the Jewish New Year, but we were Jews enough to want to spend the holiday with him.

The home of the Landesman family, adjoining his former private clinic, now turned into a Soviet sanatorium, was beautifully situated. Perched on a high elevation, it was buried amidst a profusion of trees and shrubbery on one side, while the other faced the Black Sea, its waters beating against the foot of the hill. We arrived about tea-time, as requested, because some of the other guests had no permits to be out after dark, Odessa being under martial law.

Dr. Landesman's clinic had enjoyed the reputation of being the best in Odessa. The Bolsheviki had confiscated it for a workers' rest-home, but not a single proletarian had yet been sent there, not even the ordinary party member. Only the highest officials came, with their families. Just now the Chief of the Cheka, Deitsch, was taking the cure for a bad " nervous break-down."

" How can you bear to treat him? " I asked the doctor. " You forget that I have no choice," he replied; " besides, I am a physician and bound by professional ethics to refuse medical aid to no one." " Such *bourgeois* sentimentality! " I laughed. " With the Cheka Chief getting the benefit of it," he retorted in the same spirit.

We were sitting on the terrace, the *samovar* before us, the sky streaked with blue and amethyst, the sun a ball of fire slowly sinking into the Black Sea. The city with all its terror and suffering seemed far off, and the green bowered nook an idyll. If it would last awhile longer, I mused . . . but one lived in seconds only.

New guests arrived, Byalek among them, square-set and broad-shouldered, looking more like a prosperous merchant than a poet. A slender man with vibrantly sensitive features was introduced as a famous authority on Jewish persecution and pogroms. Sasha immediately engaged him in conversation on the subject, but in the midst of it, during the meal, he suddenly grew deathly pale and begged to be excused. Together with Doctor Landesman, I reached Sasha just in time to save him from falling in a faint. He was writhing in pain and gasping for breath, and presently he became unconscious. After a half-hour that seemed an eternity the good doctor had him somewhat restored. Packed in hot water bottles, he felt relieved, but still very weak. I told Landesman that my friend had been very ill when he left the United States, and that he had never been quite well since. The black bread in particular seemed to affect his condition, and he had showed considerable improvement since we had been able to procure white bread in the south. Our hosts insisted that we remain overnight with them in view of the possibility of Sasha's suffering another attack. " What good will it do? " the patient suddenly piped up. " The expedition must proceed to Moscow." The doctor suggested that the expedition proceed, but that Sasha and his nurse remain in Odessa until he could find out the cause of the trouble. Presently Sasha fell quietly asleep and I sat watching his thin, pale face intently. It had lost nothing of its endearment to me since we had met so many, many years ago. What would it mean to lose him, and in Russia? I shuddered at the thought, my mind unable to follow up the cruel possibility. My pal lay peacefully resting, and I went back to the dining-room, my thoughts upon my life and the struggle I had gone through together with my friend and comrade. The dishes were about to be cleared away when Sasha suddenly entered as if nothing had happened. Did they think he would be so easily done out of his share of the meal, he demanded with a broad grin. His appetite was great, he announced, and he would not think of allowing a little indisposition to stand between him and Mme Landesman's culinary art. The company roared with laughter. The doctor, however, vetoed heavy dishes, but Sasha read him the riot act about attempting to keep an anarchist from eating what he likes. I stared at him in wonder. It was the same boy who had called for extra steak and coffee in Sachs's restaurant in New York just thirty-one years before. The patient of an hour ago not only ate heartily, but became the spirit of the company. He had found the man for whom he had been looking for a long time, he declared, and he held on to the expert investigator of pogroms for the rest of the evening.

The man proved a walking encyclopædia on the subject. He had visited seventy-two cities where pogroms had taken place, and he had collected a wealth of data. Jew-baiting during the various Ukrainian régimes, he stated, had been of more fiendish character than the worst massacres under the tsars. He admitted that no pogroms had taken place since the Bolsheviki had come to power, but he agreed with the younger element of the Kiev writers that Bolshevism had intensified anti-Semitic feeling among the masses. Some day it would break out, he was certain, in the wholesale slaughter of vengeance.

Sasha argued heatedly with him. Speculations about future possibilities aside, he emphasized, it remained a generally recognized fact that the Bolsheviki had put the lid down on pogroms. Did that not point to a sincere and determined purpose to eradicate every violent manifestation of the old disease, if not the disease itself? The investigator denied it, asserting that the Bolsheviki had deprived the Jews of their right of self-defence, forbidding them to organize for the purpose. They were even suspected of plotting against the Soviet Government because they had applied for permission to arm themselves against future attacks. Doctor Landesman added that the local authorities had refused to allow him to form a Yiddish boy-scout unit. He had intended such a group to serve not only as a defence

for the Jews, but also for the protection of the citizens generally
against the notorious ruffian bands from whom no one was safe in
Odessa.

On closer examination the doctor found Sasha suffering from an
ulcerated stomach and offered to place him in his sanatorium for
treatment. " Give a doctor a chance at your insides and he is sure to
find something radically wrong there," Sasha joked, waving aside the
good physician's offer. The expedition had to proceed, he insisted,
and he with it.

We heartily thanked the Landesmans for their generous hospitality. In social ideas we were far removed from each other, but
they were among the most human and friendly beings that it had
been our good fortune to meet in Russia. We had exhausted the historical possibilities of Odessa and we had to leave. The Crimea was
definitely out of the question, the entire route being in the line of the
Wrangel advance. We were promised connexion with a train that was
to depart for Kiev within forty-eight hours. We hardly dared to
expect such luck, but we clung to the hope. Meanwhile our secretary
and Sasha decided to explore Nikolayevsk, where valuable archives
were supposed to await rescue. Shakol had been confidentially told
that a military auto truck was about to leave for that city and that
the soldiers might be persuaded to permit her and Sasha to join
them. It was but a slight chance, but nothing could stop those two
venturesome spirits.

I remained with the other members of the expedition in Odessa
to prepare our car for the journey to Kiev. In the midst of my washing and scrubbing a young woman entered. She addressed me in
English and, without stopping to introduce herself, began telling
me she had known me in the States. In Detroit she and her husband
had attended my lectures. She had learned of our presence in the
city and she had come to invite Comrade Berkman and me to her
home for a cup of tea. She regretted that her husband would not be
present. He was ill, in a hospital, but eager to see us. In fact, it was
he who had sent her to request us to visit him, since he could not
come to us, his old comrades. Berkman was away, I explained, and
I had a great deal of work on hand. I could not come to her home,
much as I appreciated her invitation. But I would call on the patient.
" One forgets the existence of flowers in Russia," I remarked, " else
I should be glad to take some to your husband." Then I asked my

caller's name and the address of the hospital. " My husband is in the former Landesman sanatorium," she replied; " his name is Deitsch." I jumped from my chair as if stung by a viper. The woman also sprang to her feet. For some seconds we stood glaring at each other. At last I found my voice. Pointing to the exit, I commanded: " Go, go at once! We want none of you or your husband." " What do you mean talking to me like that?" she cried wrathfully, " you probably don't know that my husband is Chairman of the Cheka!" " I know, I know too much to want to breathe the same atmosphere with you. Go!"

Instead of leaving she brazenly sat down and began upbraiding me for hob-nobbing with Zionists and *bourgeois*. Had I also become a counter-revolutionist, she demanded, that I preferred such bandits to her husband, a comrade who had worked himself ill in the service of revolutionary Russia. Deitsch could compel me to come to him, she said, and he probably would when she told him what his teacher E.G. had become. I let her talk. My social edifice had been crumbling piece by piece. One more edge ruthlessly chopped off could hardly matter. I had not the energy to argue or the faith that I could make that woman grasp the monstrous thing that was being acclaimed as the Revolution, and the monstrosities that were serving it.

Sasha returned with our secretary twenty-four hours later than they had expected. Only when the train pulled out of Odessa did I relate to them my encounter with the wife of the all-powerful Chekist.

My companions told the story of their exciting journey to Nikolay-evsk. They had gone through harrowing experiences, visiting villages devastated by the *razviorstka* (forcible collection of produce) and by the Bolshevik punitive expeditions. The Chekists accompanying the military supply truck on which my two friends had made the trip carried on as irresponsible autocrats in a conquered country, commandeering for their own use everything they could carry, even to the last chicken from the poorest farm-house. All along the route to Nikolayevsk, Sasha said, they had met long lines of peasants, flanked by Chekist troops, carting their confiscated grain to Odessa.

On our journey back to Kiev we did as the Romans. The markets still displayed quantities of foodstuffs, but the prices had risen enormously since our previous visit. We were sure that in Petrograd they

were even more prohibitive, if anything could be procured at all
We therefore felt it imperative not to return with empty hands to
our friends. Of course, there was the risk of arrest as speculators.
What other motive could induce anyone to expose himself to such
danger and obloquy? Sympathy, the desire to share with others, the
need of alleviating misery and suffering? These terms no longer
existed in the dictionary of the dictatorship. We knew too well that
we should be pilloried not only in Russia, but also abroad. We should
have no means of making ourselves heard, in our own defence, either
on the charge of speculation or on our present attitude to the Bolsheviki. Notwithstanding all this, it was impossible to forgo the
opportunity of securing food for starving friends in the north. Most
decisive, however, was my concern about Sasha and his health. We
had not gone very far out of Odessa when he again collapsed. This
time his attack lasted longer and was more serious. The black bread
and the wormy cereals would have been poison to him in his condition. I knew no law of the Communist State for which I would
jeopardize his life, least of all the absurd order that made it a
counter-revolutionary offence to bring provisions to a hungry population. I would therefore lay in a supply of food and take the consequences, I decided. No one would accept Soviet roubles as payment.
"What can we do with these scraps?" the peasants and shop-
keepers would ask. "They are of no use even as wrapping-paper,
and for cigarettes we already have sacks of them." Tsarist money
or even that of Kerensky they would accept, although they preferred
woollens, shoes, or other apparel.

Our return to Znamenka brought Henry back to our minds with
vivid sadness. Not that we had forgotten him or had ceased to be
concerned in his fate. But our experiences since he had been torn
from us had been so sapping that they had centred all our energies.
I felt his involuntary departure most because he had been such a
splendid companion and a most dependable help in our cuisine. No
one else in our group, outside of myself, knew how to cook. Henry
was an expert in making flapjacks, in which he took great pride, and
he was always ready to give me a vacation from the cooking of two
meals a day for seven persons. To do so on a primus in a small compartment on a moving train during the heat of a Ukrainian July
and August would have been a torture were it not for my willing
assistant. Znamenka revived these memories and made me feel doubly
hard the loss of our good old Henry.

Kiev had not been taken by the Poles, as had been reported, but the enemy was almost at its gates, we were informed on our arrival. The population was embittered even more than before, because it was continuously exposed to danger and hardships from whoever possessed itself of the city. They had become somewhat reconciled to the Soviet régime, and now the latter was about to evacuate. At the *Revkom* no one seemed better informed about the actual situation than the man in the street. Vetoshkin was out and his secretary would rather talk of Odessa. " *Tovarishtch* Rakovsky," he said, " recently returned with a glowing account of how well things are going there." We assured him that only in one thing had Odessa reached a high state of proficiency, and that was sabotage. " You really mean it? " he exclaimed in glee; " Rakovsky had given us the dickens that we had not succeeded as well as Odessa."

The Soviets would remain at their post, in spite of all danger, the officials declared, but they urged us to depart for Moscow before the roads became blocked. Sasha brought the good news that a train would be leaving the next day northward, and that he had arranged to have our car attached to it. We felt depressed at not being able to proceed farther on our journey to the Crimea, but that was out of the question under the circumstances. Yet Sasha would not allow us to remain long in bad humour. He was especially jolly that evening, relating anecdotes and cracking jokes and making us laugh in spite of ourselves.

Early in the morning Shakol and I were torn out of sleep by someone knocking on our door. Still dazed, we heard Sasha's voice demanding to know why we had played such a fool hoax on him. On opening the door of our compartment I saw him standing there wrapped in his blanket. " Where are my clothes? " he asked; " you girls have hidden them from me! " The secretary roared at the sight of him and we assured him that we were quite innocent of the prank. Thereupon he returned to his compartment. Presently he announced that excepting his portfolio of documents and some Sovietsky money, everything was gone. The robbers had made a clean haul, not leaving him a thing to put on. Even the valuable Browning which the secretary of Mme Ravich had lent Sasha for the journey, and a little gold watch, a gift from Fitzi, were missing. They had hung over Sasha's bed directly above his head, and the thief must have been very skilful not to have awakened him or anyone else in the car. Borrowing the most necessary things from the other men, Sasha rigged himself out and prepared to report his loss. In the midst of it he began chuckling to himself. " The fellow that swiped my pants will be fooled, though," he laughed, " for my money is in a secret pocket there that he'll never find." For a moment I did not grasp what he meant; then it struck me that Sasha had also been robbed of our entire fortune of sixteen hundred dollars. Six hundred of it I had turned over to him only the previous evening while my petticoat, in which I had kept it, was drying. " Our independence! " I screamed; " it's gone! "

Through all the bitter disappointments in Russia and our struggle to find ourselves and our work I had been sustained by one thought — our material independence. We did not have to beg or cringe like so many others who were driven by hunger. We had been able to keep our self-respect and to refuse any truck with the dictatorship because we had been made secure by our American friends. Now all was gone! " What now, Sasha? " I cried. " What is going to become of us? " Impatiently he replied: " You seem more concerned about the damned money than about our lives. Don't you realize that if I had stirred, or anyone else in the car, the burglars would have shot us dead? " He had never known me to cling to material things, he added; it was funny I should have thought of the money first of all. " Not so funny when one is compelled to forswear all one holds high in order to exist," I replied. I simply could not face the possibility of eating out of the hand of the Bolshevik State. For myself I should have preferred to be finished by our night callers.

I had been unable to sleep that night because of the stifling heat in our compartment and I had gone out several times into the corridor for a breath of air. Sasha had left the door of his compartment ajar in order to get some air from the corridor window opposite it. I had had a feeling that the window should be closed. Not that I anticipated robbery. Our car was in full view of the station, patrolled by Soviet soldiers. No one could enter or climb into it unobserved. But one could easily help himself to the large chunk of bacon that hung in a bag at the side of the window. It would be too hot for Sasha, I had decided. But the very thing I had thought might be stolen was still in its place. In Petrograd a thief would have certainly taken the meat, but in Kiev clothing was apparently more coveted. In any case it looked as if the robber must have been a railroad worker, since he had been able to enter our car, and undoubtedly he had the co-operation of the soldiers on guard. Our porter, who had been acting queerly for some time, was also not above suspicion. Sasha insisted on recovering his things or at least the money. While he was gone, our car was moved away from the spot where it had stood during the night. Such a proceeding was nothing unusual and we paid no attention to it. We realized its significance, however, when Sasha returned with two militiamen and a police dog. The hound sniffed about, but the traces had been destroyed by the steam of the engine. Undaunted, Sasha in the company of several comrades started a search of the markets in the hope that his clothes might be offered for sale. But apparently the thieves were too careful. They could afford to bide their time. Far from giving up the search, Sasha arranged with some comrades to visit the markets every day for at least a month and to buy back his trousers at any price. "Don't worry," he kept consoling me; "they'll never find that secret pocket with the money." I wished I could share the optimism of my irrepressible pal.

In Bryansk we were greeted with the joyful news of the complete rout of Wrangel. Strange to say, Nester Makhno was being proclaimed a hero who had materially helped to bring about the great victory. But yesterday denounced as a counter-revolutionary, a bandit, the aid of Wrangel, with a large price on his head — what had brought the sudden change of front on the part of the Bolsheviki, we wondered. And how long would the love-feast last? For Trotsky had in turn eulogized the leader of the rebel peasant army and in turn condemned him to death.

Sad news clouded our joy. In a Soviet paper we read of the death of John Reed. Both Sasha and I had been very fond of Jack and we felt his demise as a personal loss. I had last seen him the previous year when he returned from Finland, a very sick man indeed. I had learned that he was put up at the Hotel International in Petrograd, alone and without anyone to take care of him. I had found him in a deplorable condition, his arms and legs swollen, his body covered with ulcers, and his gums badly affected as a result of scurvy acquired in prison. The poor boy suffered even more spiritually, because he had been betrayed to the Finnish authorities by a Russian Communist, a sailor whom Zinoviev had sent with him as a companion. The valuable documents and the large sum of money Jack was taking to his comrades in America all fell into the hands of his captors. It was Jack's second failure of the kind and he took it much to heart. Two weeks' nursing helped put him on his feet again, but he remained fearfully distressed over the methods of Zinoviev and others in jeopardizing the lives of their comrades. " Needlessly and recklessly," he kept saying. He himself had twice been sent on a wild goose chase without any trouble having been taken to find out whether there was any possibility of the venture's succeeding. But at least he could take care of himself and he went into it with open eyes. Moreover, as an American he did not run the same grave risks as the Russian comrades. Communists, mere youngsters, were being sacrificed by the score for the glory of the Third International, he had complained. " Perhaps revolutionary necessity," I had suggested; " at least your comrades always say so." He had believed it also, he had admitted, but his experience and that of others had made him doubt it. His faith in the dictatorship was still fervent, but he was beginning to doubt some of the methods used, particularly by men who themselves always remained in safety.

In Moscow we learned of the presence in the city of Louise Bryant, Reed's wife. Ordinarily I should not have looked her up. I had known Louise for years, even before she was with Jack. An attractive, vivid creature, one had to like her even when not taking her social protestations seriously. On two occasions I had realized her lack of depth. During our trial in New York, when Jack had bravely come to our assistance, Louise had studiously avoided us. They were planning to go to Russia and she was evidently afraid of having her name connected with ours during that dangerous war period, though she had always protested her great friendship in times of peace. I considered it of no great importance, however.

A much graver offence, and one that had angered me considerably, was her misrepresentation of anarchism in her book on Russia. My niece Stella had sent me the volume at the Missouri prison and I was indignant to find repeated in it the stupid story of Russia's nationalizing women that had made its rounds in the American press. Louise charged the anarchists with having been the first to issue the decree. She had taken no trouble to adduce any evidence for her wild assertions, nor had she done so in reply to my letter demanding it. I considered it on a par with the cheap journalistic libelling of the Bolsheviki and I decided to have nothing more to do with Louise.

That seemed ages ago now. Louise had suffered the loss of Jack and she was all broken up over it, I was told by common friends. I went to her without any mental reservations, too deeply moved by her tragedy to remember the past. I found her a wreck, completely shattered. She broke down in convulsive weeping that no words could allay. I took her in my arms, holding her quivering body in a silent embrace. She quieted down after a while and began relating to me the sad story of Jack's death. She had made her way to Russia disguised as a sailor and under great difficulties, only to find on landing in Petrograd that Jack had been ordered to Baku to attend the Congress of Eastern Races. He had begged Zinoviev not to insist on his going, because he had not yet fully recovered from his experience in Finland. But the chief of the Third International was relentless. Reed was to represent the American Communist Party at the Congress, he had declared. In Baku Jack was stricken with typhus and he was brought back to Moscow shortly after Louise had arrived.

I sought to console her by the assurance that all possible care must have been given Jack after his return to Moscow, but she protested that nothing had been done for the boy. A whole week had been lost before the physicians agreed in their diagnosis, and after that Jack had been turned over to an incompetent doctor. No one in the hospital knew anything about nursing, and only after a protracted argument had Louise succeeded in getting permission to take care of Jack. But he had been delirious in his last days and he had probably not even been aware of the presence of his beloved. " Didn't he speak at all? " I inquired. " I could not understand what he meant," Louise replied, " but he kept on repeating all the time: ' Caught in a trap, caught in a trap.' Just that." " Did Jack really use that term? " I cried in amazement. " Why do you ask? " Louise demanded, gripping my hand. " Because that is exactly how I have been feeling since I looked beneath the surface. Caught in a trap. Exactly that."

Had Jack also come to see that all was not well with his idol, I wondered, or had it only been the approach of death that had for a moment illumined his mind? Death strips to the naked truth — it knows no deception.

We were to leave for Petrograd the next day to report to the Museum of the Revolution, but Louise begged us to remain for the funeral. She felt lonely and deserted, and we were the only friends she had, she implored. Now that Jack was gone, she had ceased to interest the Bolsheviki. She had already been made to feel that, she said. Public funerals had always been an abomination to me;

nevertheless I promised to remain to be near her and to help her over the painful ordeal. I told Louise that Sasha might also attend if he could prevail upon the other members of the expedition to postpone their departure for a day.

Louise gave me a message left by our friend Henry Alsberg. It was to the effect that, owing to the friendliness of the guard who had brought him back to Moscow, Alsberg had been saved from the Cheka prison. The *tovaritsch* had permitted him to see his friends in the Foreign Office before delivering him to the Cheka. Nuorteva, whom he was especially anxious to see, detained him there and arranged his release after communicating with the Cheka officials. Had he ever reached the Cheka building, Henry's message continued, it would have taken months for his friends to find him and get him away from their tender care. Henry had since departed for Riga, but he was planning to return in the spring. He had left with Louise the money we had given him at his arrest, which was only two hundred dollars, but a veritable fortune to us now. For a few months at least we should be materially independent, as we had been before Sasha was robbed.

No mail had reached us during our entire journey, but at the Foreign Office our old friend Ethel Bernstein now handed us quite a bundle of it from America. At the same time she gave me a clipping from the Chicago *Tribune*. It was by John Clayton and it told how " E.G. was praying before an American flag on her wall to get back to the States." I had complained to him bitterly, it stated, about the Bolsheviki and their treatment of me. " Of course no one here believes this rotten story," Ethel remarked, " but just the same you ought to see Nuorteva about it." The man she mentioned was in charge of the Publicity Department of the Foreign Office. I saw no reason for offering any apologies. But I was disgusted at having believed that Clayton would prove more honest and decent than the other American reporters who had pestered me in Russia. Yet Clayton had impressed me as trustworthy. Could it be that his story had been doctored by the desk editor? The flag he referred to was a miniature emblem that Jack Reed had once jokingly stuck over Fitzi's picture on my wall and that I had forgotten to take off. The innocent frolic of a friend turned into a fantastic lie! It was sickening. And my complaining about the régime, when I had been particularly reticent with Clayton in regard to such subjects! Well, the Soviet people might believe what they pleased, I decided, but they should get no explanation from me.

Nuorteva received me most kindly and gave me a large package of letters. He did not mention the Clayton story, nor did I. With considerable pride he spoke of having left America on the first Soviet passport submitted to Washington. He was now at the head of the Anglo-Russian Department of the Foreign Office and he would be glad to be of help in the matter of mail. I felt gratified at his tact in not bringing up the wretched matter of Clayton's write-up.

I hastened to our car to read my mail. Letters from Stella, Fitzi, and other friends expressed intense satisfaction at our having at last found a sphere of work. They did not doubt, they wrote, that now we would have the greatest expression for our energies and ideals. Letters of a later date contained clippings of the Clayton story, including one that I read and reread in utter stupefaction. It was a letter for Stella that I had given to Jack Reed to mail and that had been taken from him when he was arrested in Finland. After several readings it dawned on me that the newspaper editor had turned my epistle to Stella into a love missive to John Reed! " Poor Louise, how little she knows of my alleged love-affair with Jack! " I laughed to Sasha.

From our comrades in Moscow we learned of the city-wide raids that had taken place in the early part of October. Among the many victims was also Maria Spiridonovna. She had been ill with typhoid at the time, but the Cheka had arrested her and sent her to a prison hospital. Great, idealistic soul! There was no end to dear Maryusa's martyrdom.

Fanya and Aaron Baron, who were in Moscow, informed us about the developments in regard to Nestor Makhno. The Red forces had proved unable to stand up against Wrangel, and the Bolsheviki had turned to the *povstantsy* leader for aid. He and his army had consented on condition that all the anarchists and Makhnovtsy be released from prison, and that the Soviet Government grant them the right of a general conference. Makhno had named Sasha and me as his representatives in drawing up the agreement. This had never been communicated to us, but the Bolsheviki had accepted Makhno's demands and had actually released a number of the *povstantsy* and some of our comrades. They had also given permission for the gathering, which our comrades from all over Russia had agreed to hold in

Kharkov. Volin and others had already departed for that city, and comrades were expected from every part of the country.

A grey sky overhanging Moscow, rain steadily drizzling its melancholy tune, and artificial wreaths that had served at other funerals were Jack Reed's farewell in the Red Square. No beauty for the man who had loved it so, no colour for his artist-soul. No spark of the red-white flame of the fighter to inspire those who in bombastic speeches claimed him as their comrade. Alexandra Kollontay alone came close to the spirit of John Reed and found the words that would have pleased him most. During her simple and beautiful tribute to Jack, Louise crumpled to the ground in a dead faint just as the coffin was being lowered into the grave. Sasha had almost to carry her to the automobile Nuorteva had put at our disposal. Our old American friend Dr. W. Wovschin, a recent arrival, accompanied us to aid the desolate Louise.

In the Museum of the Revolution, in Petrograd, we were hailed as heroes come back from the front. It was a considerable achievement to return alive after four months of such a journey as we had made, they said, and to have also rescued a whole carload of material of historical value. The future, they assured us, would reward us according to our deserts. All the museum could do now was to give us a month's rest. We were henceforth on the permanent staff of the museum, Yatmanov and Kaplan informed us, and we need not look for other activities. Within a month we should start on a new journey. Our expedition would be granted the privilege of choosing its destination and route. Either the Crimea, which had since been entirely cleared of the Wrangel forces, or Siberia, where Semenoff and Kolchak had been finally routed, would be our objective point. In either place there was much material awaiting us, and we were expected to enrich the museum with it.

" Not to Siberia during the winter," shuddered our Russian members. We also did not particularly welcome the idea, though we remembered Krasnoschokov's invitation to come to the Far Eastern Republic. But there was no need for an immediate decision, the museum chief declared. Alexander Ossipovich and Emma Abramovna (meaning Sasha and me), he insisted, looked as if they indeed needed a vacation.

Sasha and I had definitely decided to apply to the Housing Department for rooms where we might live like the rest of the non-Communist population. The prospect of another trip within a month caused us to defer our plan till some other time, for it would take more than a month to secure lodgings. We should have liked to remain in our car, but there was the problem of heating and of reaching the city. Mme Ravich suggested that we take up our abode at the Hotel International. It was used for foreign visitors, the guests paying for their rooms and meals, and the charges were very reasonable, being fifteen dollars a month for a room and two daily meals. Its main attraction was cleanliness and an opportunity to take a bath. It was the first place of its kind in Russia for other mortals than Communists and we were relieved at the chance to be quartered there.

The museum material, not considered contraband, was easily transferred from our car. Not so the food we had brought with us. Entitled to pass freely through the railroad gates, we aroused no suspicion, though it required a week and four persons to remove the stuff. In the apartment of a friend everything was made up in parcels and sent to sick friends and to those who had children needing fats and sweets. Quite selfishly I had intended to keep enough white flour for the winter to safeguard Sasha from black bread. Now that we were soon to start on another journey, the unpleasant task became unnecessary. It was no small satisfaction to be able to relieve the need of a few more persons, if only for a little while.

In spite of all planning we went neither to the Crimea nor to the Far Eastern Republic. Instead we journeyed to Archangel, " to round out the year," as Yatmanov said. That district having been the centre of the interventionist operations, in which my erstwhile country had played such a disgraceful part, I was glad we were given the opportunity to explore it.

We were only three on that trip. The Russian couple preferred to hug their stove in Petrograd, while our young Communist collaborator had to resume his studies at college.

On the way to Archangel we made two stops, at Yaroslavl and Vologda. Both cities had served as centres for plotters against the Revolution. The former had been the base of the once celebrated revolutionist Savinkov's uprising, drenched in the blood of thousands.

Vologda had been the headquarters of the American Ambassador Francis and other wirepullers in favour of intervention.

Yaroslavl still bore witness to the fratricidal strife; its prison was filled with officers of the Savinkov army that had escaped death. In neither city did we find anything of special value for the museum.

Archangel, at the mouth of the northern Dvina, was separated from the railroad terminus by the frozen river. On arriving we found a temperature of fifty below zero, but the brilliant sun and the dry, crisp air made the cold far less penetrating than in Petrograd. My thoughtful niece, Stella, had pressed her fur coat on me on her last visit to Ellis Island. But I had never worn it because of an idiosyncrasy that made me feel as if the beast were alive and creeping over my neck whenever I put on furs. Everybody had warned us against the Archangel frosts, and as a precaution I had taken the coat with me. Great was my relief when I realized that I could go about in my old velour coat and sweater and even feel too warm in the sun. It was invigorating to walk across the frozen expanse of the river and along the clean streets of Archangel, quite a novelty in a Russian town. In fact, the city presented numerous surprises. Our credentials, scorned in the south, here proved a veritable magic wand, opening wide the doors of every Soviet institution. The chairman of the *Ispolkom* and all other officials went out of their way to aid the efforts of our mission. They exerted themselves to make our stay a memorable experience, as indeed it proved to be. Their fraternal attitude to the population, their equitable efforts to supply them with food and clothing so far as was in their power, made us feel that here principles different from those of " the centre " were operating. The men and women at the helm of affairs in Archangel had grasped the great truth that discrimination, brutality, and hounding were not calculated to convince the people of the beauty or desirability of communism or to cause them to love the Soviet régime. They sought more effective methods. They abolished speculation in food by organizing a more just distribution of rations. They did away with the humiliating and exhausting standing in line by instituting co-operative stores where the inhabitants received due attention and courteous treatment. They introduced a friendly tone and atmosphere in every Soviet institution. While this had not converted the whole community into disciples of Marx or Lenin, it had helped to eliminate the dissatisfaction and antagonism widespread in other parts of the country.

People said that the Communists had acquired organization, efficiency, and order from the example of the Americans quartered in the city. If so, they certainly proved apt pupils. For the usual characteristics of Soviet life, including sabotage, waste, and confusion, were almost entirely missing in Archangel.

Those sturdy sons of the north apparently had something that was very unsovietsky — respect for human life and recognition of its sanctity. Former nuns, monks, White officers, and members of the *bourgeoisie* put to useful work instead of against the wall were an extraordinary revelation. The mere suggestion of such a thing elsewhere in Russia would have marked us as very suspicious characters if not out and out counter-revolutionists. Here the new method had rescued hundreds of lives and had gained for the régime additional workers. Not that the Cheka was absent or capital punishment abolished. A dictatorship could hardly exist without these. But in Archangel the Cheka had not attained the unlimited powers it enjoyed in other places. It did not constitute a State within the State whose sole function was terror and vengeance. If these measures were really dictated by revolutionary necessity, the barbarous methods of the Whites in northern Russia would have certainly justified their use. Not only Communists, but even those remotely sympathetic with them had been subjected to torture and death. Entire families had been ruthlessly exterminated by the Whites. Kulakov, chairman of the *Ispolkom,* for instance, had lost every member of his family. Even his youngest sister, a mere child of twelve, had not escaped the fiendishness of the enemy, and there was hardly a radical or liberal home that had not felt the cruel hand of those that had come to crush the Revolution.

" Naturally we could not meet such fury with gloved hands," the chairman of the educational department said to us. " We fought back desperately, but when the enemy had been driven to flight, we saw no need of retaliation or terror. We felt that vengeance would serve no other purpose than to antagonize the population against us. We set to work to bring order out of the chaos left by the Whites and to reclaim as many lives as we could among our captives."

" Did all your comrades agree with such ' sentimental ' methods? " I asked in astonishment. " Of course not," he replied; " there were many who insisted on drastic measures, and there are those who still insist that we shall yet have to pay dearly for what they call our reformist attitude to those who had conspired against the Revolution."

However, the chairman continued, the more level-headed comrades
had prevailed, and experience proved that even former White officers could be utilized in various walks of life. A number of them
were employed as teachers and they were doing faithful and useful
work. The same held good of several other departments. Moreover,
even such dark and bigoted elements as nuns and monks had responded to humane treatment. It was not at all sentimentality, but
good common sense that taught him, he added, that the will to life
was not dictated by creeds. Nuns and monks were as subject to that
law of nature as any average person. After they had been dis-
possessed from the cloisters and monasteries and faced death if they
continued plotting, or starvation if they refused to work, they proved
themselves only too eager to make themselves useful in some way.
We could convince ourselves of it, he said, by visiting the schools,
nurseries, and arts and crafts studios.

We did. We went unannounced and unexpected and we found conditions in those institutions exemplary. I talked to some of the nuns
employed there, a number of whom had dwelt apart from the world
for a quarter of a century. Mentally they still lived in the cloisters.
They understood nothing of the new and changing forces at work
about them, but they were doing beautiful work, including pottery,
agriculture, illustrations for children's stories, stage scenery for their
theatre, and similar things. I also talked to some artisans and wood-
carvers of unusual skill. Several of them had been caught red-handed
in counter-revolutionary conspiracies. One lamented that his work
was not bringing him in as much money as in former days. But his
life had been spared and he was allowed to continue the labour he
loved. He wanted nothing better, he said.

A few days later I had occasion to meet one of the White officers
considered among the best teachers. He could not approve of the dictatorship, he frankly admitted, but he had come to realize the folly
and crime of foreign intervention. The Allies had promised much
to his country, but all they had done was to divide the Russian house
against itself. The Americans had been decent, he thought. They had
kept to themselves, their soldiers were off the streets after dark,
and they had also been generous with provisions and clothing. At their
departure they had distributed their surplus supplies with open hand.
The British were different. Their soldiers molested the native women,
their officers were arbitrary and haughty, and General Rollins had

ordered huge supplies sunk in the open sea before the British ships departed. He was through with intervention. He loved teaching and he was very fond of children and now he had the opportunity of his life.

Similar sentiments we found reflected by persons in various political groupings. Nearly every one agreed that the Soviet régime was sincerely and successfully carrying out the policy of reclamation, and that the social scope was being gradually widened for those even that did not agree with the Communist view-point. In other words, no one was being discriminated against on account of his past.

Among the vast material we gathered in the north were a number of revolutionary and anarchist publications that had appeared underground during the régime of the Tsar and all through the period of occupation. Most appealing was the last message of a sailor condemned to death by the invaders, containing a minute description of his torture by British officers to exact information. There were also photographs of men and women mutilated by the counter-revolutionists. In addition Sasha had also collected interesting material from Bechin, the chairman of the labour soviet, in whom the Provisional Government had tried to crush the revolutionary labour movement of the north. Together with others, but as the responsible factor, Bechin had been tried for treason and condemned to a slow death in the fearsome prison of Yokanan in the arctic zone. He had kept a diary of his arrest, trial, and imprisonment, and after much persuasion he had given it to Sasha for the museum.

Archangel proved so absorbing that we overstayed our time by two weeks. We still had Murmansk to visit, while our credentials were good only till the end of the year. With regret we left the friends we had made and the splendid people we had met in the city.

Within three days' distance from our objective we had to turn back. Heavy snow-storms blocked our route, and our progress resembled that of a snail. It would have required weeks to reach our destination, the road having first to be cleared of mountain-high snow. Fifty miles from Petrograd we were again stalled, this time by a blinding blizzard. Luckily we had fuel and provisions for several days. We settled down for a patient wait, for there was nothing else we could do under the circumstances.

On Christmas Eve, still held up on the road, Shakol and Sasha gave me a surprise. A wee pine-tree, decorated for the occasion and studded with coloured candles, gaily lit up our compartment. America contributed the gifts, or rather my women friends who had sent presents before we sailed. A good hot grog, brewed from the rum supplied us in Archangel, helped to make the festivity complete.

I thought of our Christmas of a year ago — of 1919. Sasha and I, together with many other undesirable rebels on the *Buford*, torn away from our work, our comrades, and our loved ones, cruising to an unknown destination. In enemy hands, under rigid military discipline, our male companions herded below deck like cattle and fed on wretched food, all of us exposed to imminent danger from war mines. Yet we did not care. Soviet Russia was beckoning us, liberated and reborn, the fulfilment of the heroic struggle of a hundred years. Our hopes ran high, our faith flamed red-white, all our thoughts centred on our *Matushka Rossiya*.

Now it was Christmas 1920. We were in Russia, her soil serene after the raging storms, her attire of white and green under a jewelled sky. Our house on wheels was warm and cozy. My old pal was at my side and a new dear friend. They were in a holiday mood and I longed to join in their merriment. But in vain. My thoughts were in 1919. Only a year had passed, and nothing was left but the ashes of my fervent dreams, my burning faith, my joyous song.

We reached Petrograd at the height of the excitement over the fate of the labour unions. The problem had already been discussed at the party sessions the previous October and ever since in preparation for the Eighth All-Russian Congress of the Soviets. The trade unions must serve as a school of communism, Lenin had declared, and the opposing views of Trotsky, of the old Marxian scholar Ryazanov, of Kollontay, leading the labour circles, had to capitulate to the dictum of Ilich. Trotsky insisted that the only thing that could save the Revolution was the militarization of labour and the entire subserviency of the unions to the needs of the State. Lenin treated all his opponents with equal contempt. Trotsky did not know his Marx, Lenin declared, while the views of Kollontay were half-baked. As to Ryazanov, he was forbidden all public utterance for a period of six months on the ground that he did not know what he was talking about.

The great explosion was finally precipitated by Kollontay and the old Communist Shlyapnikov, representing the labour opposition.

The Revolution had been fought by the workers, they insisted, and the world had been assured that the real dictatorship of Russia was that of the proletariat. Instead the masses were stripped of all rights and denied any say in the economic life of the country. These two daring leaders of labour were indeed articulating the thoughts and feelings of the toiling masses, of the rank and file of the Communists even, who had no way of making themselves heard.

The storm that followed threatened the disruption of the party. Something had to be done, and Lenin was equal to the occasion. He heaped ridicule upon the heretics who dared voice sentiments of " petty *bourgeois* ideology." Quickly the opposition was strangled. Kollontay's pamphlet on labour demands was suppressed and its author severely disciplined, while old Shlyapnikov, of weaker metal, was silenced by being made a member of the Executive Committee of the party and ordered to take a much-needed rest.

Our expedition was being reorganized and arrangements made for our third tour, which was definitely decided upon as a journey to the Crimea. But at the eleventh hour our plans were blocked by an order of the *Ispart,* the newly created Communist body for the purpose of collecting data on the history of the Communist Party. The Museum of the Revolution was curtly notified that henceforth the new organization would take charge of all expeditions, the *Ispart* claiming precedence, by virtue of its Communist character, in all such undertakings. It would also commandeer our car, though the Museum of the Revolution would be granted the privilege of assigning some of its members to the work of the *Ispart.*

The arbitrariness of the new institution was felt by every member of the museum as a deliberate attempt to curtail its independence and limit the scope of its work. Even Commissar Yatmanov, a devoted Communist, expressed himself in no gentle terms about the party zealots who insisted on having everything in their hold. It was unthinkable to submit to such methods without a fight, he declared. He would immediately take the matter up at the Petrograd end, while we must proceed to Moscow. Sasha was to see Zinoviev about it and I should see Lunacharsky, they being the chairmen of the Petrograd Museum. The decision of the *Ispart* was an infringement upon Zinoviev's jurisdiction over Petrograd; he would surely protest against it; while Lunacharsky, as the head of all the cultural efforts of

Russia, would not tolerate such invasion of his domain, Yatmanov asserted.

We had but little hope of success, but we consented to go to Moscow. We declared, however, that should the *Ispart* win in the matter, we would discontinue our affiliation with the museum, distressing as such a step would be to us. We knew too well the meaning of having a political commissar control our work and movements. It signified dictatorship and espionage and it involved clique interests, strife, and disruption. We had declined the offer of many high positions because we would not submit to such tutelage.

Zinoviev was indeed much incensed over the attempt of the *Ispart* to monopolize the work of the Petrograd Museum and to interfere with his program for it. He wrote a letter of protest to his comrades of the new institution and he turned it over to Sasha for presentation and argument. The Museum of the Revolution was not trespassing on the field of the *Ispart;* it had mapped out its own work, in no way in conflict with that of the Moscow body, and he as the head of the Petrograd Museum's executive committee would not tolerate such autocratic interference, Zinoviev wrote. He further assured Sasha that he would take the matter up with Lenin himself if the *Ispart* persisted in its arbitrary decision.

Lunacharsky also was angry with " the fools who would put all cultural endeavour under their own thumb." He promised to protest against such tactics, but soon I had occasion to learn that he was in reality quite without authority. The real power in the All-Russian Commissariat of Education was Pokrovsky, a Communist of old standing, and it was he who had founded the *Ispart*. Lunacharsky was a mere figure-head, exploited by the party because of his presumed European influence, since he had lived many years abroad and was well known in cultural circles there.

Finding lodgings in Moscow was always a difficult problem, but fortunately we were spared the disagreeable task of begging for a roof over our heads. Our good friend Angelica Balabanoff was in charge of a Russo-Italian bureau quartered in a house that had formerly been occupied by a foreign organization. She and her staff were now living there, and, having two vacant rooms, Angelica invited us to stay with her.

Our efforts in behalf of the Petrograd Museum were being blocked on every hand by the concentrated authority of Communist machinery and were proving fruitless. Petrograd urged a personal report and we decided to return there. We had already bought our tickets when word came from Dmitrov that our old comrade Peter Kropotkin had been stricken with pneumonia. The shock was the greater because we had visited Peter in July and had found him in good health and buoyant spirits. He seemed then younger and better than when we had seen him the previous March. The sparkle in his eyes and his vivacity had impressed us with his splendid condition. The Kropotkin place had looked lovely in the summer sunshine, with the flowers and Sophie's vegetable garden in full bloom. With much pride Peter had spoken of his companion and her skill as a gardener. Taking Sasha and me by the hand, he had led us in boyish exuberance to the patch where Sophie had planted a special kind of lettuce. She had succeeded in raising heads as large as cabbages, their leaves crispy and luscious. He himself had also been digging in the soil, but it was Sophie, he had reiterated, who was the real expert. Her potato crop of the previous winter had been so large that there was enough left over to exchange for fodder for their cow and even to share with their Dmitrov neighbours, who had few vegetables. Our dear Peter had been frolicking in his garden and talking about these matters as if they were world events. Infectious had been the youthful spirit of our comrade, carrying us along by its freshness and charm.

In the afternoon, assembled in his study, he had again become the scientist and thinker, clear and penetrating in his judgment of persons and events. We had discussed the dictatorship, the methods forced upon the Revolution by necessity and those inherent in the nature of the party. I wanted Peter to help me to a better understanding of the situation which was threatening to bankrupt my faith in the Revolution and in the masses. Patiently and with the tenderness one uses towards a sick child he had sought to soothe me. There was no reason to despair, he had urged. He understood my inner conflict, he had assured me, but he was certain that in time I should learn to distinguish between the Revolution and the régime. The two were worlds apart, the abyss between them bound to grow wider as time went on. The Russian Revolution was far greater than the French and of more potent world-wide significance. It had struck deep into the lives of the masses everywhere, and no one could foresee the rich harvest humanity would reap from it. The Communists, irrevocably adhering to the idea of a centralized State, were doomed to misdirect the course of the Revolution. Their end being political supremacy, they had inevitably become the Jesuits of socialism, justifying all means to attain their purpose. Their methods, however, paralysed the energies of the masses and terrorized the people. Yet without the people, without the direct participation of the toilers in the reconstruction of the country, nothing creative and essential could be accomplished.

Our own comrades, Kropotkin had continued, had in the past failed to give sufficient consideration to the fundamental elements of the social revolution. The basic factor in such an upheaval is the organization of the economic life of the country. The Russian Revolution proved that we must prepare for that. He had come to the conclusion that syndicalism was likely to furnish what Russia lacked most: the channel through which the industrial and economic upbuilding of the country could flow. He was referring to anarcho-syndicalism, indicating that such a system, by aid of the co-operatives, would save future revolutions the fatal blunders and fearful suffering Russia was passing through.

All this came vividly back to my mind at the sad news of Kropotkin's break-down. I could not think of leaving for Petrograd without seeing Peter again. Skilled nurses were scarce in Russia and I could take care of him and do at least that much for my dear teacher and friend.

I learned that Peter's daughter, Alexandra, was in Moscow and about to go to Dmitrov. She informed me that a very competent nurse, a Russian woman trained in England, was in charge of the case. Their little cottage was too crowded already, she said, and it was not advisable to disturb Peter at the moment. She was leaving for Dmitrov and she would telephone to me about father's condition and the advisability of my seeing him.

The Petrograd Museum was waiting for Sasha's report on his conferences with the *Ispart,* necessitating his immediate departure for the north, while I remained in Moscow ready for a call from Dmitrov. Several days passed without my receiving word from Alexandra, which led me to conclude that Peter was improving and that my services were not needed. I thereupon left for Petrograd.

I had hardly been in the city an hour when Mme Ravich telephoned to inform me that my presence was urgently called for from Dmitrov. She had received a message from Moscow on the long-distance wire urging my immediate coming. Peter had grown worse and the family had begged for me to be notified to come at once.

My train ran into a raging storm and we arrived in Moscow ten hours behind schedule. There was no train for Dmitrov until the following evening, and the roads were blocked by snow-drifts too great for an automobile. All telephone wires were down and there was no way to reach Dmitrov.

The evening train moved with exasperating slowness, repeatedly stopping to refuel. It was four in the morning when we arrived. Together with Alexander Schapiro, an intimate friend of the Kropotkin family, and Pavlov, a comrade from the Bakers' Union, I hastened to the Kropotkin cottage. Alas, too late! Peter had ceased breathing an hour before. He died at four a. m., February 8, 1921.

The distracted widow told me that Peter had repeatedly inquired whether I was already on my way and how soon I would arrive. Sophie was near collapse, and in the need of looking after her I forgot the cruel combination of circumstances that had prevented my rendering even the least service to him who had been such a potent inspiration in my life and work.

We learned from Sophie that Lenin, when informed of Peter's illness, had sent the best Moscow physicians to Dmitrov, together with provisions and delicacies for the patient. He had also ordered that frequent bulletins of Peter's condition should be sent him as well as published in the press. It was a sad commentary that so much attention should have been given on his death-bed to the man who had twice been raided by the Cheka and who had thereby been compelled to go into undesired retirement. Peter Kropotkin had helped to prepare the ground for the Revolution, but had been denied a share in its life and development; his voice had penetrated Russia in spite of tsarist persecution, but it was strangled by the Communist dictatorship.

Peter had never sought or accepted favours from any government nor tolerated pomp and display. We therefore determined there should be no intrusion from the State at his funeral, and that it should not be vulgarized by the participation of officialdom. Peter's last days upon earth should rest in the hands of his comrades only.

Schapiro and Pavlov departed for Moscow to call out Sasha and other Petrograd comrades. Together with the Moscow group they were to take charge of the obsequies. I remained in Dmitrov to help

Sophie prepare her precious dead for the transfer to the capital for burial.

In the silent presence of my comrade I came upon treasures in his being that his utter lack of egotism would not have permitted me to discover. I had known Peter for over a quarter of a century, was familiar with his life, his works and colourful personality. But only his death disclosed his cherished secret that he had also been an artist of unusual quality. I found, hidden away in a box, a number of drawings Peter had made in his all too few leisure moments. Their exquisite line and form proved that he might have achieved as much with his brush as he had with his pen had he cared to devote himself to it. In music also Peter would have excelled. He loved the piano and he could find expression and release in his fine interpretation of the masters. In the drab Dmitrov existence his sole delight consisted in the playing and singing of two young women friends of the family. With them he would feast his love of music on regular weekly evenings.

Richly endowed with creative ability, Peter had been still richer in his vision of a noble social ideal and in his humanity, which embraced all mankind. For that more than for anything else he had laboured during the conscious part of his almost fourscore years. In fact, until the very day when he had to take to his bed, Peter had continued working, under most distressing conditions, on his volume on *Ethics,* which he had hoped to make the supreme effort of his life. His deepest regret in his last hours was that he had not been given a little longer to complete what he had begun years before.

In the past three years of his life Peter had been cut off from close contact with the masses. In his death he found full contact with them. Peasants, workers, soldiers, intellectuals, men and women from a radius of many miles, as well as the entire community of Dmitrov, streamed through the Kropotkin cottage to pay their last tribute to the man that had dwelt among them and had shared their struggle and afflictions.

Sasha arrived in Dmitrov together with a number of Moscow comrades to assist in the removal of Peter's body to Moscow. Never had the little town rendered so great homage to anyone as it did to Peter Kropotkin. The children had known and loved him best because of his childlike playfulness with them. The schools were closed for the day in mourning for their departed friend. In large numbers they marched to the station and waved their farewell to Peter as the train slowly steamed out.

On the way to Moscow I learned from Sasha that the Peter Kropotkin Funeral Commission, which he had helped to organize and of which he was the chairman, had already been subjected to chicanery by the Soviet authorities. Permission had been granted the commission to publish two of Peter's pamphlets and to issue a special *Peter Kropotkin Memorial Bulletin.* Later the Moscow Soviet, under the presidency of Kamenev, demanded that the manuscripts of the *Bulletin* be submitted for censorship. Sasha, Schapiro, and other comrades protested that the proceedings would delay the publication. To gain time they had pledged that nothing but appreciations of Kropotkin's life and work should appear in the memorial issue. Then the censor suddenly remembered that he had too much work on hand and that the matter would have to await its regular turn. It meant that the *Bulletin* could not appear in time for the funeral, and it was evident that the Bolsheviki were resorting to their usual tactics of holding up things until too late for their effectiveness. Our comrades decided to resort to direct action. Lenin had repeatedly appropriated that anarchist idea, and why should the anarchists not recapture it from him? Time was pressing and the object was important enough even to risk arrest. They broke the seal the Cheka had placed on the printing establishment of our old comrade Atabekian, and our friends worked like beavers to prepare the *Bulletin* in time for the funeral.

In Moscow the expressions of esteem and affection for Peter Kropotkin became a tremendous demonstration. From the moment the body arrived in the capital and was placed in the Trade Union House, and all during the two days that the dead lay in state in the Marble Hall, there began an outpouring of the people such as had not been manifested since the days of " October."

The Funeral Commission had sent a request to Lenin to release temporarily the anarchists imprisoned in Moscow to enable them to take part in the last honours paid their dead teacher and friend. Lenin had promised and the Executive Committee of the Communist Party had directed the Veh-Cheka (the All-Russian Cheka) to free " according to its judgment " the imprisoned anarchists for participation in the obsequies. But the Veh-Cheka apparently was not disposed to obey even Lenin or the supreme authority of its own party. Would the Funeral Commission guarantee the return of the prisoners to jail, it demanded. The commission pledged itself collectively. Whereupon the Veh-Cheka declared that there were " no anarchists in the Moscow prisons." The truth, however, was that the Butirky and the inner jail of the Cheka were filled with our comrades arrested in the raid of the Kharkov Conference, though the latter had been officially permitted according to the Soviet agreement with Nestor Makhno. Moreover, Sasha had gained admission to the Butirky and there talked with more than a score of our imprisoned comrades. Accompanied by the Russian anarchist Yarchook, he had also visited the inner prison of the Moscow Cheka and there conversed with Aaron Baron, who represented on the occasion a number of other imprisoned anarchists. Still the Cheka insisted that there were " no anarchists imprisoned in Moscow."

Once again the Funeral Commission was compelled to resort to direct action. On the morning of the funeral it instructed Alexandra Kropotkin to telephone to the Moscow Soviet that a public announcement of its breach of faith would be made and that the wreaths laid on the bier of Kropotkin by Soviet and Communist organizations would be removed forthwith if the promise given by Lenin was not kept.

The large Hall of Columns was filled to the doors, among those present being also several representatives of the European and American press. Our old friend Henry Alsberg was there, recently returned to Russia. Another correspondent was Arthur Ransome, of the Manchester *Guardian.* They would be sure to make the Soviet breach of faith widely known. After the world had been daily apprised for weeks of the care and attention bestowed by the Soviet Government upon Peter Kropotkin in his last illness, the publication of such a scandal had to be avoided at all costs. Kamenev therefore pleaded for more time and solemnly promised to have the imprisoned anarchists released within twenty minutes.

The funeral was held up for an hour. The great masses of bereaved outside kept shivering in the bitter Moscow frost, all waiting for the arrival of the imprisoned pupils of the great dead. At last they came, but only seven of them, from the Cheka jail. There were none of the Butirky comrades, but at the last moment the Cheka assured the commission that they had been released and were on their way to the hall.

The prisoners on leave acted as the honorary pall-bearers. In proud sadness they carried the last remains of their beloved teacher and comrade out of the hall. In the street they were received in impressive silence by the vast assembly. Soldiers without arms, sailors, students, and children, labour organizations of every trade, and groups of men and women representing the learned professions, peasants, and numerous anarchist bodies, all with their banners of red or black, a multitudinous mass united without coercion, orderly without force, stretched along the long march of two hours to the Devichy Cemetery, on the outskirts of the city.

At the Tolstoy Museum the strains of Chopin's *Funeral March* greeted the *cortège,* and a chorus by the followers of the seer of Yasnaya Polyana. In appreciation our comrades lowered their flags, as a fitting tribute of one great son of Russia to another.

Passing the Butirky prison, the procession came to a second halt, and our flags were lowered in token of Peter Kropotkin's last greeting to his courageous comrades who were waving their adieu to him from their barred windows.

Spontaneous expressions of deep-felt sorrow characterized the speeches made by representative men of various political tendencies at the grave of our departed comrade. The dominant note was that the death of Peter Kropotkin was a loss of a great moral force, the equal of which was well-nigh extinct in their native land.

For the first time since my coming to Petrograd my own voice rang out in public. It sounded to me strangely hard and inadequate to express all that Peter had meant to me. My grief over his passing away was bound up with my despair over the defeat of the Revolution, which none of us had been able to avert.

The sun, slowly disappearing below the horizon, and the sky, bathed in dark red, made a fitting canopy over the fresh soil that was now Peter Kropotkin's eternal resting-place.

The seven paroled boys spent the evening with us, and it was late at night when they reached their prison-house. Not expecting them, the guards had locked the gates and retired. The men had fairly to break into the place, so astounded were the keepers to see anarchists foolish enough to live up to the pledge given for them by their comrades.

The anarchists in the Butirky prison had not appeared at the funeral, after all. The Veh-Cheka had assured our commission that they had declined to do so, though offered the opportunity. We knew that it was a lie; nevertheless I decided upon a personal visit to our prisoners to secure their side of the story. This unfortunately involved the hateful necessity of applying to the Cheka for a permit. I was taken into the private office of the presiding Chekist, who proved a mere youth with a gun in his belt and another on his desk. He met me with outstretched hands, profusely addressing me as his " dear comrade." His name was Brenner, he informed me, and he used to live in America. He had been an anarchist and of course he knew " Sasha " and me well and all about our activities in the States. He was proud to call us his comrades. Naturally he was now with the Communists, he explained, for he considered the present régime a stepping stone to anarchism. The Revolution was the main thing, and since the Bolsheviki were working in its behalf, he was co-operating with them. But had I ceased to be a revolutionist that I refused to grasp the proffered comradely hand from one of its defenders?

I had never in my life shaken hands with detectives, I replied, and much less would I do so with one who had been an anarchist. I came for a pass to the prison and I wanted to know whether I could secure one.

The Chekist turned white, but he kept his composure. " All right about the pass," he said, " but there is a little matter that needs explanation." He drew out a clipping from a desk drawer and handed it to me. It was the silly Clayton article that I had already seen months before. It was imperative that I retract its contents in the Soviet press, Brenner declared. I replied that I had long ago cabled my version of it to friends in America, and that I had no intention of doing anything more in the matter. My refusal was sure to go against me, the Chekist remarked. As a *tovarishtch* he felt it his duty to warn me. " Is it a threat? " I asked. " Not yet," he muttered.

He rose and walked out of the room. I waited for half an hour, wondering whether I was a prisoner. Everyone's turn comes in Russia; why not also mine, I mused. Presently steps approached and the door was thrown open. An old man, evidently a Chekist, gave me a slip of paper permitting me to enter the Butirky.

Among a large group of imprisoned comrades I met several I had known in the States: Fanya and Aaron Baron, Volin, and others who had been active in America, as well as the Russians of the *Nabat* organization whom I had met in Kharkov. They had been visited by a representative of the Veh-Cheka, they related, who had offered to release several of them individually, but not as a collective group, as had been arranged with the Funeral Commission. Our comrades had repudiated the breach of faith and insisted that they would attend the Kropotkin funeral in a body or not at all. The man informed them that he would have to report their demand to his superior officers and that he would soon return with the final decision. But he never came back. The comrades said it did not matter at all, because they had held their own Kropotkin memorial meeting in the corridor of their prison wing, and the occasion had been honoured by appropriate speeches and revolutionary songs. In fact, with the help of the other politicals they had turned the prison into a popular university, Volin remarked. They were conducting classes in social science, political economy, sociology, and literature, and they were teaching the common prisoners to read and write. They were enjoying more freedom than we on the outside and we should envy them, they joked. But their haven, they feared, would probably not last much longer.

Sophie Kropotkin, whose whole life had been wrapped up in Peter and his work, was completely shattered by her loss. She could not bear to go on without him, she told me, unless she could devote the rest of her days to the perpetuation of his memory and efforts. A Peter Kropotkin museum was her idea as a fitting testimonial, and she pleaded with me to remain in Moscow to help her realize the project. I agreed that her plan would be a most appropriate monument to Peter, though I did not consider Russia at present the best place for it. The work would involve continual begging from the Government, and that would certainly not be in conformity with Peter's views and wishes. But Sophie insisted that Russia was, everything considered, the most logical place for such a museum. Peter had loved his native land and had had the greatest faith in its people, notwithstanding the Bolshevik dictatorship. Heart-breaking as conditions were, he had often told her, he was determined to spend the rest of his life there. She also had always been devoted to Russia, and, with Peter now resting in Russian soil, it had become doubly sacred to her.

She felt that, with Sasha and me on the museum committee, the main support would come from America and very little would therefore have to be asked from the soviets. The members of the Kropotkin Funeral Commission favoured Sophie's plan. Whatever the nature of the dictatorship, they held, the fact remained that the great Revolution had taken place in Russia, and that country was therefore the proper home for a Kropotkin museum.

The Peter Kropotkin Funeral Commission reorganized itself into a Memorial Committee, with Sophie Kropotkin as its chairman, Sasha as general secretary, and me as manager. In addition I was also to substitute for Sophie during her absence in Dmitrov. The organization, which consisted of representatives of the various anarchist groups, decided to apply to the Moscow Soviet for the old Kropotkin family house as a home for the museum, as well as to request that the Kropotkin cottage in Dmitrov be secured for the widow of Peter.

Together with Sasha I returned to Petrograd to sever our connexions with the Museum of the Revolution. We both regretted having to give up our active association with its staff, who had been so splendid in their relationship with us. But the *Ispart* had irrevocably decided to set up a political commissar over the museum expeditions, and neither Sasha nor I would continue work under such conditions. Moreover, we considered the work of a Peter Kropotkin museum more vital than our labours for the Petrograd Museum and we were already in active charge of the preliminary work. Our presence in Moscow was urgent and we should have to live there. Alexandra Kropotkin was leaving for Europe, and Sophie had promised that we could have the two small rooms they had occupied in an apartment on the Leontevsky Pereulok. At last we should be able to live like the rest of the non-official population.

In my early Russian period the question of strikes had puzzled me a great deal. People had told me that the least attempt of that kind was crushed and the participants sent to prison. I had not believed it, and, as in all similar things, I had turned to Zorin for information. " Strikes under the dictatorship of the proletariat! " he had exclaimed; " there's no such thing." He had even upbraided me for crediting such wild and impossible tales. Against whom, indeed, should the workers strike in Soviet Russia, he had argued. Against themselves? They were the masters of the country, politically as well as industrially. To be sure, there were some among the toilers who were not yet fully class-conscious and aware of their own true interests. These were sometimes disgruntled, but they were elements incited by the *shkurniky*, by self-seekers and enemies of the Revolution. Skinners, parasites, they were, who were purposely misleading the dark people. They were the worst kind of *sabotazhniky*, no better than out and out counter-revolutionists, and of course the Soviet authorities had to protect the country against their kind. Most of them were in prison. Since then I had learned by personal observation and experience that the real *sabotazhniky*, counter-revolutionists, and bandits in Soviet penal institutions were a negligible minority. The bulk of the prison population consisted of social heretics who were guilty of the cardinal sin against the Communist Church. For no offence was considered more heinous than to entertain political views in opposition to the party, and to voice any protest against the evils and crimes of Bolshevism. I found that by far the greatest number were political prisoners, as well as peasants and workers guilty of demanding better treatment and conditions. These facts, though rigidly kept from the public, were nevertheless common knowledge, as were indeed most things that were secretly going on beneath the Soviet surface. How forbidden information leaked out was a mystery, but it did leak out and would spread with the rapidity and intensity of a forest fire.

Within less than twenty-four hours of our return to Petrograd we learned that the city was seething with discontent and strike talk. The cause of it was the increased suffering due to the unusually severe winter as well as partly to the habitual Soviet near-sightedness. Heavy snow-storms had delayed the meagre supplies of food and fuel for the city. In addition the Petro-Soviet had committed the stupidity of closing down several factories and cutting the rations of their employees almost in half. At the same time it had become known that the party members in the shops had received a fresh supply of shoes and clothing, while the rest of the toilers were wretchedly clad and shod. To cap the climax the authorities vetoed the meeting called by the workers to discuss ways of ameliorating the situation.

It was the common feeling in Petrograd among non-Communist elements that the situation was very grave. The atmosphere was charged to the point of explosion. We decided of course to remain in the city. Not that we hoped to avert impending trouble, but we wanted to be on hand in case we could be of help to the people.

The storm broke out even before anyone expected it. It began with the strike of the millmen at the Troubetskoy works. Their demands were modest enough: an increase in their food rations, as had long ago been promised them, and also the distribution of the foot-gear on hand. The Petro-Soviet refused to parley with the strikers until they returned to work. Companies of armed *kursanty*, consisting of young

Communists in military training, were sent to disperse the workers gathered about the mills. The cadets sought to incite the crowd by firing into the air, but fortunately the workers had come unarmed and there was no bloodshed. The strikers resorted to a more powerful weapon, the solidarity of their fellow-toilers, with the result that the employees of five more factories laid down their tools and joined the strike movement. To a man, they streamed from the Galernaya docks, the Admiralty shops, the Patronny mills, the Baltiysky and Laferm factories. Their street demonstration was promptly broken up by soldiers. From all accounts, I gathered that the handling of the strikers was by no means very comradely. Even such an ardent Communist as Liza Zorin had been aroused to protest against the methods used. Liza and I had drifted apart a long time ago and I was therefore much surprised that she should feel the need of unburdening her heart to me. Never would she have believed that Red Army men would rough-ride over workingmen, she protested. Some women had fainted at the sight of it, and others had become hysterical. A woman standing near her had evidently recognized her as an active party member and had no doubt held her responsible for the brutal scene. She turned on Liza like a fury and hit her full in the face, causing her to bleed profusely. Though staggered by the blow, dear old Liza, who had always teased me about my sentimentality, told her assailant that it did not matter at all. " To reassure the distracted woman I begged her to let me take her to her home," Liza related. " Her home — it was a dreadful hole such as I thought no longer existed in our country. One dark room, cold and barren, occupied by the woman, her husband, and their six children. To think that I have lived in the Astoria all this time! " she moaned. She knew it was not the fault of her party that such appalling conditions still prevailed in Soviet Russia, she continued. Nor was it Communist wilfulness that was responsible for the strike. The blockade and the world imperialist conspiracy against the Workers' Republic were to blame for the poverty and suffering. Just the same, she could not remain in her comfortable quarters any longer. That desperate woman's room and her frost-bitten children would haunt her days. Poor Liza! Loyal and staunch she was and of sterling character. But oh, so blind politically!

The plea of the workers for more bread and some fuel soon flared into decided political demands, thanks to the arbitrariness and ruthlessness of the authorities. A manifesto, pasted on the walls no one knew by whom, called for " a complete change in the policies of the Government." It declared that, " first of all, the workers and peasants need freedom. They don't want to live by the decrees of the Bolsheviki; they want to control their own destinies." Every day the situation grew more tense and new demands were being voiced by means of proclamations on the walls and buildings. At last appeared a call for the *Uchredilka,* the Constituent Assembly so hated and denounced by the ruling party.

Martial law was declared and the workers were ordered to return to the shops on pain of being deprived of their rations. This entirely failed of any effect, whereupon a number of unions were liquidated, their officials and the more recalcitrant strikers placed in prison.

In helpless misery we saw groups of men, surrounded by armed Chekists and soldiers, led past our windows. In the hope of making the Soviet leaders realize the folly and danger of their tactics Sasha tried to get hold of Zinoviev, while I sought Mme Ravich, Zorin and Zipperovich, head of the Petrograd Trade Union Soviet. But they all denied themselves to us on the excuse that they were too busy defending the city from counter-revolutionary plots hatched by the Mensheviki and Socialist-Revolutionists. This formula had grown stale by three years' repetition, but it still helped to throw sand into the eyes of the Communist rank and file.

The strike kept spreading, all extreme measures notwithstanding. Arrests followed upon arrests, but the very stupidity with which the authorities dealt with the situation served to encourage the dark elements. Anti-revolutionary and Jew-baiting proclamations began to appear, and the wild rumours of military suppression and Cheka brutality against the strikers filled the city.

The workers were determined, but it was apparent that they would soon be starved into submission. There was no means by which the public could aid the strikers even if they had anything to give. All avenues of approach to the industrial districts of the city were cut off by massed troops. Moreover, the population itself was in dreadful want. The little we could gather in foodstuffs and clothing was a mere drop in the ocean. We all realized that the odds between the dictatorship and the workers were too uneven to permit the strikers to hold out much longer.

Into this tense and desperate situation there was presently introduced a new factor that held out the hope of some settlement. It was the sailors of Kronstadt. True to their revolutionary traditions and solidarity with the workers, so loyally demonstrated in the revolution of 1905, and later in the March and October upheavals of 1917, they now again took up the cudgels in behalf of the harassed proletarians in Petrograd. By no means blindly so. Quietly and without outsiders knowing about it, they had sent a committee to investigate the claims of the strikers. Its report roused the sailors of the warships *Petropavlovsk* and *Sevastopol* to adopt a resolution in favour of the demands of their brother workers on strike. They declared themselves devoted to the Revolution and the soviets, as well as loyal to the Communist Party. They protested, however, against the arbitrary attitude of certain commissars and stressed the need of greater self-determination for the organized bodies of workers. They further demanded freedom of assembly for labour unions and peasant organizations and the release of all labour and political prisoners from Soviet prisons and concentration camps.

The example of these brigades was taken up by the First and Second Squadrons of the Baltic Fleet stationed at Kronstadt. At an open-air meeting on March 1, attended by sixteen thousand sailors, Red Army men, and workers of Kronstadt, similar resolutions were adopted unanimously with the exception of only three votes. The dissenters included Vassiliev, president of the Kronstadt Soviet, who was chairman of the mass meeting; Kuzmin, the Commissar of the Baltic Fleet; and Kalinin, President of the Federated Socialist Soviet Republics.

Two anarchists who had attended the gathering returned to tell us of the order, enthusiasm, and fine spirit that had prevailed there. Not since the early days of October had they seen such spontaneous demonstration of solidarity and fervent comradeship. If only we had been there, they lamented. The presence of Sasha, for whom the Kronstadt sailors had made such a valiant stand when he was in danger of extradition to California, in 1917, and of me, whom the sailors knew by reputation, would have added weight to the resolution, they declared. We agreed that it would have been a wonderful experience to participate in the first great mass meeting on Soviet soil that was not machine-made. Gorki had assured me long ago that the men of the Baltic Fleet were born anarchists and that my place was with them. I had often longed to go to Kronstadt to meet the crews and talk to them, but I had felt that in my disturbed and confused state of mind I could give them nothing constructive. But now I would go to take

my place with them, though I knew that the Bolsheviki would raise
the cry that I was inciting the sailors against the régime. Sasha said
he did not care what the Communists would say. He would join the
sailors in their protest in behalf of the striking Petrograd workers.
Our comrades emphasized that the expressions of sympathy on the
part of Kronstadt with the strikers could in no way be construed as
anti-Soviet action. In fact, the entire spirit of the sailors and the
resolutions passed at their mass meeting were thoroughly Sovietist.
They were strongly opposed to the autocratic attitude of the Petrograd authorities towards the starving strikers, but at no time had
the gathering shown the least opposition to the Communists. In fact,
the great meeting had been held under the auspices of the Kronstadt
Soviet. To show their loyalty the sailors had met Kalinin on his arrival
in their city with music and song, and his talk was listened to with
respect and attention. Even after he and his comrades had attacked
the sailors and condemned their resolution, Kalinin had been escorted
back to the station in the greatest friendliness, our informants stated.
   We had heard the rumour that at a gathering of three hundred
delegates from the fleet, the garrison, and the trade-union soviet
Kuzmin and Vassilev had been arrested by the sailors. We asked our
two comrades what they knew of the matter. They admitted that the
two men had been detained. The reason for it was that at the meeting
Kuzmin had denounced the sailors as traitors, and the Petrograd
strikers as *shkurniky,* and had declared that henceforth the Communist Party " would fight them to a finish as counter-revolutionists."
The delegates had also learned that Kuzmin had given orders for the
removal of all food and munitions from Kronstadt, thereby virtually
dooming the city to starvation. Therefore it was decided by the sailors
and the garrison of Kronstadt to detain Kuzmin and Vassilev and to
take precautions that no supplies be removed from the town. But that
was no indication whatever of any rebellious intentions or that they
had ceased to believe in the revolutionary integrity of the Communists.
On the contrary, the Communist delegates at the gathering were permitted an equal voice with the rest. Further proof of their confidence
in the régime was given by the delegates in sending a committee of
thirty men to confer with the Petro-Soviet with a view to an amicable
settlement of the strike.
   We felt elated over the splendid solidarity of the Kronstadt sailors
and soldiers with their striking brothers in Petrograd and we hoped

that a speedy termination of the trouble would soon result, thanks to the mediation of the sailors.

Alas, our hopes proved vain within an hour after we had received news of the Kronstadt proceedings. An order signed by Lenin and Trotsky spread like wildfire through Petrograd. It declared that Kronstadt had mutinied against the Soviet Government, and denounced the sailors as " tools of former tsarist generals who together with Socialist-Revolutionist traitors staged a counter-revolutionary conspiracy against the proletarian Republic."

" Preposterous! It's nothing short of madness! " Sasha cried as he read the copy of the order. " Lenin and Trotsky must be misinformed by someone. They could not possibly believe the sailors guilty of counter-revolution. Why, the crews of the *Petropavlovsk* and *Sevastopol* in particular had been the staunchest supporters of the Bolsheviki in October and ever since. And did not Trotsky himself greet them as ' the pride and flower of the Revolution '! "

We must go to Moscow at once, Sasha declared. It was imperative to see Lenin and Trotsky and to explain to them that it was all a horrible misunderstanding, a blunder that might prove fatal to the Revolution itself. It was very hard for Sasha to give up his faith in the revolutionary integrity of the men that had appeared as the proletarian apostles to millions throughout the world. I agreed with him that Lenin and Trotsky might have been misled by Zinoviev, who was nightly telephoning to the Kremlin detailed reports about Kronstadt. Zinoviev had never been famed even among his own comrades for personal courage. He had become panicky at the first symptoms of discontent shown by the Petrograd workers. When he learned that the local garrison had expressed sympathy with the strikers, he completely lost his head and had ordered a machine-gun placed at the Astoria for his protection. The stand of Kronstadt had put terror into his heart and had caused him to bombard Moscow with wild stories. I knew all that, as did also Sasha, but I could not believe that Lenin and Trotsky actually thought the Kronstadt men guilty of counter-revolution or capable of co-operating with White generals, as charged in Lenin's order.

Extraordinary martial law was declared over the entire Petrograd Province, and none but specially authorized officials could leave the city. The Bolshevik press opened a campaign of calumny and vituperation against Kronstadt, proclaiming that the sailors and soldiers had made common cause with the " tsarist general Kozlovsky," and declaring the Kronstadt people outlawed. Sasha began to realize that the situation involved a good deal more than mere misinformation on the part of Lenin and Trotsky. The latter was to attend the special session of the Petro-Soviet where the fate of Kronstadt was to be decided. We resolved to be present.

It was my first opportunity in Russia to hear Trotsky. We might remind him of his parting words in New York, I thought: the hope he had expressed that we should come to Russia soon to assist in the great work made possible by the overthrow of tsarism. We would plead with him to let us help settle the Kronstadt difficulty in a comradely spirit, to dispose of our time and energies, even of our lives, in the supreme test to which the Revolution was putting the Communist Party.

Unfortunately Trotsky's train was delayed and he failed to appear at the session. The men who addressed the gathering were beyond reason or appeal. Fanaticism run mad was in their words, and blind fear in their hearts.

The platform was heavily guarded by *kursanty,* and Chekist soldiers with fixed bayonets stood between it and the audience. Zinoviev, who presided, seemed on the point of a nervous collapse. Several times he rose to speak and then sat down again. When he finally began talking, he kept his head jerking to the left and right as if fearing a sudden attack, and his voice, always adolescently thin, rose to a high-pitched shrillness, extremely jarring and in no way convincing.

He denounced " General Kozlovsky " as the evil spirit of the Kronstadt men, though most of the audience knew that that military officer had been placed in Kronstadt by Trotsky himself as an artillery specialist. Kozlovsky was old and decrepit and of no influence whatever with the sailors or the garrison. That did not prevent Zinoviev, as chairman of the specially created Committee of Defence, from proclaiming that Kronstadt had risen against the Revolution and was seeking to carry out the plans of Kozlovsky and his tsarist aids. Kalinin shed his usually grandmotherly manner and attacked the sailors in vicious terms, forgetful of the honours paid him in Kronstadt but a few days previously. " No measure can be too severe for the counter-revolutionists who dare to raise their hand against our glorious Revolution," he declared. The lesser lights among the speakers followed in the same strain, rousing their Communist zealots, ignorant of the real facts, to revengeful frenzy against the men yesterday acclaimed heroes and brothers.

Above the din of the howling and stamping mob a single voice strove to be heard — the tense, earnest voice of a man in the front rows. He was a delegate of the striking employees at the arsenal works. He was moved to protest, he declared, against the misrepresentations uttered from the platform against the brave and loyal men of Kronstadt. Facing Zinoviev and pointing his finger directly at him, the man thundered: " It's the cruel indifference of yourself and of your party that drove us to strike and that roused the sympathy of our brother sailors, who had fought side by side with us in the Revolution. They are guilty of no other crime, and you know it. Consciously you malign them and call for their destruction." Cries of " Counter-revolutionist! Traitor! *Shkurnik!* Menshevik bandit! " turned the assembly into a bedlam.

The old worker remained standing, his voice rising above the tumult. " Barely three years ago Lenin, Trotsky, Zinoviev, and all of you," he shouted, " were denounced as traitors and German spies. We, the workers and sailors, had come to your rescue and saved you from the Kerensky Government. It was we who placed you in power. Have you forgotten that? Now you threaten us with the sword. Remember you are playing with fire. You are repeating the blunders and crimes of the Kerensky Government. Beware that a similar fate does not overtake you! "

The challenge made Zinoviev wince. The others on the platform moved uneasily in their seats. The Communist audience seemed awed for an instant by the portentous warning, and in that moment there rang out another voice. A tall man in a sailor's uniform stood up in the back. Nothing had changed in the revolutionary spirit of his brothers of the sea, he declared. To the last man they were ready to defend the Revolution with their every drop of blood. Then he proceeded to read the Kronstadt resolution adopted at the mass meeting on March 1. The uproar his daring evoked made it impossible for any but those nearest to hear him. But he stood his ground and kept on reading to the end.

The only reply to these two sturdy sons of the Revolution was Zinoviev's resolution demanding the complete and immediate surrender of Kronstadt on pain of extermination. It was rushed through the session amidst a pandemonium of confusion, with every opposing voice gagged.

The atmosphere, surcharged with the hysteria of passion and hate, crept into my being and held me by the throat. All evening I wanted to cry out against the mockery of men stooping to the lowest political trickery in the name of a great ideal. My voice seemed to have left me, for I could not utter a sound. My thoughts reverted to another occasion where the spirit of vengeance and hate had run amuck — the eve of registration, June 4, 1917, at Hunts Point Palace, New York. I had been able to speak out then, entirely oblivious of danger from the war-drunk patriots. Why could I not now? Why did I not brand the impending fratricide by the Bolsheviki, as I had Woodrow Wilson's crime that had dedicated the young manhood of America to the Moloch of war? Had I lost the grit that had sustained me all through the years of fighting against every injustice and every wrong? Or was it helplessness which paralysed my will, the despair that had settled on my heart with the growing realization that I had mistaken a phantom for a life-giving force? Nothing could alter that crushing consciousness or make any protest worth while.

Yet silence in the face of the threatened slaughter was also intolerable. I had to make myself heard. But not by the obsessed, who would choke back my voice as they had done with the others. I would make known my stand in a statement to the supreme power of the Soviet Defence, that very night.

When we were alone and I spoke to Sasha about the matter, I was glad to learn that my old pal had conceived the same plan. He suggested that our letter should be a joint protest and deal exclusively with the murderous resolution passed by the Petro-Soviet. Two comrades who had been with us at the session shared his view and offered to sign their names to our joint appeal to the authorities.

I had no hope that our message would exert any sobering or restraining influence on the events decreed against the sailors. But I was determined to have my attitude registered in a manner to bear future witness that I had not remained a silent party to the blackest betrayal of the Revolution by the Communist Party.

At two o'clock in the morning Sasha got in touch by telephone with Zinoviev, to inform him that he had something important to communicate to him regarding Kronstadt. Perhaps Zinoviev assumed that it was something that might aid the conspiracy against Kronstadt. Otherwise he would have hardly troubled to rush Mme Ravich over at that hour of the night, ten minutes after Sasha had talked to him. She could be trusted absolutely, Zinoviev's note said, and she was to be given the message. We handed her our communication, which read:

*To the Petrograd Soviet of Labour and Defence,*
*Chairman Zinoviev:*

To remain silent now is impossible, even criminal. Recent events impel us anarchists to speak out and to declare our attitude in the present situation.

The spirit of ferment and dissatisfaction manifest among the workers and sailors is the result of causes that demand our serious attention. Cold and hunger have produced dissatisfaction, and the absence of any opportunity for discussion and criticism is forcing the workers and sailors to air their grievances in the open.

White-guardist bands wish and may try to exploit this dissatisfaction in their own class interests. Hiding behind the workers and the sailors, they throw out slogans of the Constituent Assembly, of free trade, and similar demands.

We anarchists have long since exposed the fiction of these slogans, and we declare to the whole world that we will fight with arms against any counter-revolutionary attempt, in co-operation with all friends of the Social Revolution and hand in hand with the Bolsheviki.

Concerning the conflict between the Soviet Government and the workers and sailors, we hold that it must be settled, not by force of arms, but by means of comradely, fraternal revolutionary agreement. Resort to bloodshed on the part of the Soviet Government will not—in the given situation—intimidate or quiet the workers. On the contrary, it will serve only to aggravate matters, and will strengthen the hands of the Entente and of internal counter-revolution.

More important still, the use of force by the Workers' and Peasants' Government against the workers and sailors will have a reactionary effect upon the international revolutionary movement and will everywhere result in incalculable harm to the Social Revolution.

Comrades Bolsheviki, bethink yourselves before it is too late. Do not play with fire; you are about to make a most serious and decisive step.

We hereby submit to you the following proposition: Let a commission be selected, to consist of five persons, inclusive of two anarchists. The commission is to go to Kronstadt to settle the dispute by peaceful means. In the given situation it is the most radical method. It will be of international revolutionary significance.

*Petrograd*                                   ALEXANDER BERKMAN
*March 5, 1921*                            EMMA GOLDMAN
                                                       PERKUS
                                                       PETROVSKY

Proof that our appeal had fallen on deaf ears came to us the very same day on the arrival of Trotsky and his ultimatum to Kronstadt. By order of the Workers' and Peasants' Government, he declared to the Kronstadt sailors and soldiers, he would " shoot like pheasants " all those who had dared to " raise their hand against the Socialist fatherland." The rebellious ships and crews were commanded to submit immediately to the orders of the Soviet Government or be subdued by force of arms. Only those surrendering unconditionally might count on the mercy of the Soviet Republic.

The final warning was signed by Trotsky, as Chairman of the Revolutionary Military Soviet, and by Kamenev, the Commander-in-Chief of the Red Army. Daring to question the divine right of rulers was again to be punished by death.

Trotsky kept his word. Having been helped to authority by the men of Kronstadt, he was now in a position to pay his debt in full to the " pride and glory of the Russian Revolution." The best military experts and strategists of the Romanov régime were at his service, among them the notorious Tukhachevsky, whom Trotsky appointed commander-in-chief of the Kronstadt attack. In addition there were hordes of Chekists, with three years' training in the art of murder; *kursanty* and Communists specially picked for their blind obedience to orders; and the most trusted troops from various fronts. With such a force massed against the doomed city the " mutiny " was expected to be easily quelled. Especially after the soldiers and sailors of the Petrograd garrison had been disarmed and those that had expressed solidarity with their besieged comrades removed from the danger zone.

From my room window in the Hotel International I saw them led by in small groups, surrounded by strong detachments of Cheka troops. Their step had lost its spring, their hands hung at their sides, and their heads were bowed in grief.

The Petrograd strikers were no longer feared by the authorities. They were weakened by slow starvation and their energy sapped. They were demoralized by the lies spread against them and their Kronstadt brothers, their spirit broken by the poison of doubt instilled by Bolshevik propaganda. They had no more fight nor faith left to come to the aid of their Kronstadt comrades who had so selflessly taken up their cause and who were about to give up their lives for them.

Kronstadt was forsaken by Petrograd and cut off from the rest of Russia. It stood alone. It could offer almost no resistance. " It will go down at the first shot," the Soviet press proclaimed. They were mistaken. Kronstadt had thought of nothing less than of mutiny or resistance to the Soviet Government. To the very last moment it was determined to shed no blood. It appealed all the time for understanding and amicable settlement. But, forced to defend itself against unprovoked military attack, it fought like a lion. During ten harrowing days and nights the sailors and workers of the besieged city held out against a continuous artillery fire from three sides and bombs hurled from aeroplanes upon the non-combatant community. Heroically they repulsed the repeated attempts of the Bolsheviki to storm the fortresses by special troops from Moscow. Trotsky and Tukhachevsky had every advantage over the men of Kronstadt. The entire machinery of the Communist State backed them, and the centralized press continued to spread venom against the alleged " mutineers and counter-revolutionists." They had unlimited supplies and men whom they had masked in white shrouds to blend with the snow of the frozen Finnish Gulf in order to camouflage the night attack against the unsuspecting men of Kronstadt. The latter had nothing but their unflinching courage and abiding faith in the justice of their cause and in the free soviets they championed as the saviour of Russia from the dictatorship. They lacked even an ice-breaker to halt the onrush of the Communist enemy. They were exhausted by hunger and cold and sleepless nights of vigil. Yet they held their own, desperately fighting against overwhelming odds.

During the fearful suspense, the days and nights filled with the rumbling of heavy artillery, there sounded not a single voice amid the roar of guns to cry out against or call a halt to the terrible blood bath. Gorki, Maxim Gorki, where was he? His voice would be heard. " Let us go to him," I pleaded with some of the intelligentsia. He had never made the slightest protest in grave individual cases, neither in those concerning members of his own profession nor even when he knew of the innocence of doomed men. He would not protest now. It was hopeless.

The intelligentsia, the men and women that had once been revolutionary torch-bearers, leaders of thought, writers and poets, were as helpless as we and paralysed by the futility of individual effort. Most of their comrades and friends were already in prison or exile; some had been executed. They felt too broken by the collapse of all human values.

I turned to the Communists of our acquaintance, imploring them to do something. Some of them realized the monstrous crime their party was committing against Kronstadt. They admitted that the charge of counter-revolution was a downright fabrication. The supposed leader, Kozlovsky, was a nonentity too frightened about his own fate to have anything to do with any protest of the sailors. The latter were of sterling quality, their sole aim the welfare of Russia. Far from making common cause with the tsarist generals, they had even declined the help offered them by Chernov, the leader of the Socialist-Revolutionists. They wanted no outside aid. They demanded the right to choose their own deputies in the forthcoming elections to the Kronstadt Soviet and justice for the strikers in Petrograd.

These Communist friends spent nights with us — talking, talking — but none of them dared raise his voice in open protest. We did not realize, they said, the consequences it would involve. They would be excluded from the party, they and their families deprived of work and rations and literally condemned to death by starvation. Or they would simply vanish and no one would ever know what had become of them. Yet it was not fear that numbed their will, they assured us. It was the utter uselessness of protest or appeal. Nothing, nothing could stop the chariot-wheel of the Communist State. It had rolled them flat and they had no vitality left, even to cry out against it.

I was beset by the terrible apprehension that we also — Sasha and I — might reach the same state and become as spinelessly acquiescent as these people. Anything else would be preferable to that. Prison, exile, even death. Or escape! Escape from the horrible revolutionary sham and pretence.

The idea that I might want to leave Russia had never before entered my mind. I was startled and shocked by the mere thought of it. I to leave Russia to her Calvary! Yet I felt that I would take even that step rather than become a cog in the machinery, an inanimate thing to be manipulated at will.

The cannonade of Kronstadt continued without let-up for ten days and nights and then came to a sudden stop on the morning of March 17. The stillness that fell over Petrograd was more fearful than the ceaseless firing of the night before. It held everyone in agonized suspense, and it was impossible to learn what had happened and why the bombardment had ceased. In the late afternoon the tension gave way to mute horror. Kronstadt had been subdued — tens of thousands slain — the city drenched in blood. The Neva a grave for masses of men, *kursanty* and young Communists whose heavy artillery had broken through the ice. The heroic sailors and soldiers had defended their position to the last breath. Those not fortunate enough to die fighting had fallen into the hands of the enemy to be executed or sent to slow torture in the frozen regions of northernmost Russia.

We were stunned. Sasha, the last thread of his faith in the Bolsheviki broken, desperately roamed the streets. Lead was in my limbs, unutterable weariness in every nerve. I sat limp, peering into the night. Petrograd was hung in a black pall, a ghastly corpse. The street-lamps flickered yellow, like candles at its head and feet.

The following morning, March 18, still heavy with sleep after the lack of it during seventeen anxious days, I was roused by the tramp of many feet. Communists were marching by, bands playing military tunes and singing the *International*. Its strains, once jubilant to my ear, now sounded like a funeral dirge for humanity's flaming hope.

March 18 — the anniversary of the Paris Commune of 1871, crushed two months later by Thiers and Gallifet, the butchers of thirty thousand Communards. Emulated in Kronstadt on March 18, 1921.

The full significance of the "liquidation" of Kronstadt was disclosed by Lenin himself three days after the frightfulness. At the Tenth Congress of the Communist Party, staged in Moscow while the siege of Kronstadt was in progress, Lenin unexpectedly changed his inspired Communist song to an equally inspired pæan to the New

Economic Policy. Free trade, concessions to the capitalists, private
employment of farm and factory labour, all damned for over three
years as rank counter-revolution and punished by prison and even
death, were now written by Lenin on the glorious banner of the
dictatorship. Brazenly as ever he admitted what sincere and thoughtful persons in and out of the party had known for seventeen days:
that " the Kronstadt men did not really want the counter-revolutionists. But neither did they want us." The naïve sailors had taken
seriously the slogan of the Revolution: " All power to the Soviets,"
by which Lenin and his party had solemnly promised to abide. That
had been their unforgivable offence. For that they had to die. They
had to be martyred to fertilize the soil for Lenin's new crop of
slogans, which completely reversed the old. Their *chef d'œuvre* the
New Economic Policy, the NEP.

Lenin's public confession in regard to Kronstadt did not stop the
hunt for the sailors, soldiers, and workers of the defeated city. They
were arrested by the hundreds, and the Cheka was again busy " target-
shooting."

Strangely enough, the anarchists had not been mentioned in connexion with the Kronstadt " mutiny." But at the Tenth Congress
Lenin had declared that the most merciless war must be waged
against the " petty *bourgeoisie*," including the anarchist elements.
The anarcho-syndicalist leanings of the labour opposition proved that
these tendencies had developed in the Communist Party itself, he had
said. Lenin's call to arms against the anarchists met with immediate
response. The Petrograd groups were raided and scores of their
members arrested. In addition the Cheka closed the printing and publishing offices of the *Golos Truda,* belonging to the anarcho-syndicalist branch of our ranks. We had purchased our ticket to Moscow
before this happened. When we learned about the wholesale arrests,
we decided to stay a little longer in case we too should be wanted.
We were not molested, however, perhaps because it was necessary to
have a few anarchist celebrities at large to show that only " bandits "
were in Soviet prisons.

In Moscow we found all except half a dozen anarchists arrested
and the *Golos Truda* book-store closed. In neither city had any
charges been made against our comrades, nor had they been given
a hearing or brought to trial. Nevertheless, a number of them had
already been sent away to the penitentiary of Samara. Those still

in the Butirky and the Taganka prisons were being subjected to the worst persecution and even physical violence. Thus one of our boys, young Kashirin, had been beaten by a Chekist in the presence of the prison warden. Maximov and other anarchists who had fought on the revolutionary fronts, and who were known and respected by many Communists, had been forced to declare a hunger-strike against the terrible conditions.

The first thing we were asked to do on our return to Moscow was to sign a manifesto to the Soviet authorities denouncing the concerted tactics to exterminate our people.

We did so of course, Sasha now as emphatic as I that protests from within Russia by the handful of politicals still out of prison were entirely futile. On the other hand, no effective action could be expected from the Russian masses, even if we could reach them. Years of war, civil strife, and suffering had sapped their vitality, and terror had silenced them into submission. Our recourse, Sasha declared, was Europe and the United States. The time had come when the workers abroad must learn about the shameful betrayal of " October." The awakened conscience of the proletariat and of other liberal and radical elements in every country must be crystallized into a mighty outcry against the ruthless persecution for opinion's sake. Only that might stay the hand of the dictatorship. Nothing else could.

This much the martyrdom of Kronstadt had already done for my pal. It had demolished the last vestiges of his belief in the Bolshevik myth. Not only Sasha, but also the other comrades who had formerly defended the Communist methods as inevitable in a revolutionary period, had at last been forced to see the abyss between " October " and the dictatorship.

If only the cost for the profound lesson taught them had not been so terrific, I should have taken comfort in the knowledge that Sasha and I were again united in our stand, and that my Russian comrades hitherto antagonistic to my attitude to the Bolsheviki had now come closer to me. It would be a relief not to have to grope further in distressing isolation and not to feel so alien in the midst of people whom I had known in the past as the ablest among the anarchists, not to have to choke back my thoughts and emotions before the one human being who had shared my life, my ideals, and my labours through our common lot of thirty-two years. But there was the black cross erected in Kronstadt and the blood of the modern Christs trickling from their hearts. How could one cherish personal comfort and relief?

On our way to the Leontevsky we ran into a parade more demonstrative and showy than the usual variety. What was the special occasion, we inquired. Had we just come to Moscow that we were ignorant of the grand event? Why, it was the return of General Slaschov-Krimsky that was being celebrated. "What!" cried Sasha and I in the same breath, "the White General, the Jew-baiter, the man who had with his own hand snuffed out the lives of Red soldiers and Jews, the sworn and relentless enemy of the Revolution?" The very one, we were assured. He had recanted and had begged to be readmitted to the fatherland he loved so well, swearing to serve the Bolsheviki faithfully henceforth. He was now being received with military honours and fêted at the order of the Soviet Government by workers, soldiers, and sailors singing revolutionary songs for the edification of one of the most implacable foes of the Revolution. We walked over to the Red Square to see the spectacle of Leon Trotsky, the Commissar of the Revolutionary Army of the Socialist Republic, reviewing his forces before the tsarist general Slaschov-Krimsky. The grand stand was not far from John Reed's grave. Within its shadow Leon Trotsky, the butcher of Kronstadt, was clasping the blood-stained hand of his comrade Krimsky. A spectacle indeed to make the gods weep with laughter!

Shortly after this, General Slaschov-Krimsky was ordered to Karelia, a desolate district in the north, to "liquidate the counter-revolutionary uprising there." The simple Karelians, assured of their right to self-determination, had found the Communist yoke too irksome and had naïvely protested against the abuses they had been made to suffer. Who more competent to bring the "mutineers" to reason than General Slaschov-Krimsky?

One solace was left us. We did not have to eat out of the slayer's hand. My dear old mother and our friend Henry Alsberg had saved us from that degradation. Through a friend my mother had sent me three hundred dollars, and Henry had left Sasha some clothing to exchange for food. In our new mode of living these would go a long way to keep us above water.

We had not yet adapted ourselves to the process of existence that the bulk of the non-privileged were forced to undergo. Waylaying peasants at dawn for a supply of wood, pulling it home on a sleigh, chopping it with frozen hands, carrying it up three flights of stairs; then fetching water several times a day from a long distance and up to our quarters; cooking, washing, and sleeping in a little hall bedroom, Sasha's smaller even than mine and never quite warm — this was bitter hard, at first, and terribly exhausting. My hands were chapped and swollen, and my spine, never very strong, was full of aches. My dear friend also suffered a great deal, especially from the return of his old trouble with his legs, the ligaments of which he had stretched by his fall in New York and which had crippled him for a year.

However, physical pain and weariness were as nothing to our inner liberation — the spiritual release we felt that we no longer had to ask or accept anything from the powers that had dealt the final blow to " October " by the slaughter of Kronstadt.

Considering the complete collapse of all the revolutionary pretence of the dictatorship, a Peter Kropotkin museum under its protection struck me as a direct desecration of his name. Sasha had also come to see the incongruity of a memorial to Peter within the citadel of Lenin, Trotsky, and Slaschov-Krimsky. Our Russian comrades agreed with us. Still they clung to the idea of the museum as the only centre of anarchist thought that the Bolsheviki would not dare lay hands on. Sophie, however, did not want the Kropotkin museum turned into anarchist headquarters. Her ambition as the lifelong companion and co-worker of Peter was a testimonial to *all* of Peter's versatile activities — in the fields of science, philosophy, letters, humanism, and anarchism. While I understood Sophie and felt with her, I nevertheless had to sustain my comrades in their desire to emphasize the anarchist in Kropotkin. He himself had willed it so. He had chosen anarchism as his goal, and its exposition as his supreme interest in life. It was therefore Kropotkin the anarchist who should be given first place in a museum dedicated to him. Yet I could not ignore the importance of Sophie's part in the project. She alone had the devotion, the loving patience, the time and freedom necessary to bring the memorial to life and to watch over its development and growth. I pointed out to our comrades that, though they were still at liberty, they were in danger of arrest by the Cheka at any moment. How could they undertake to build and keep up the museum? Even when free, they could not do it. Their daily toil, added to the consuming task of securing their rations, would leave them neither time nor strength to accomplish anything for Peter's memorial. My part in the project would be limited to an appeal to our people in the United States, and even that I would make only because I wanted to help Sophie. I thought it very inconsistent to have a Kropotkin museum in present-day Russia, nor did I believe in asking or accepting help for it from the Soviet autocrats.

Sasha agreed to join me in the appeal, but under no circumstances would he have any further dealings with the men responsible for the Kronstadt blood bath, for the wholesale persecution of our comrades and the night assault on the politicals in the Butirky prison. The Romanov dynasty, he emphasized, had rarely been guilty of such a wanton attack on politicals. In the Socialist Republic Chekists and soldiers had fallen upon men and women asleep in their cells, beat them, dragged the women by the hair down the stairs, and thrown them into waiting trucks to be sent off no one knew where. No person with any humanity or revolutionary integrity could have anything to do with such criminals, Sasha declared passionately.

It was not often that my comrade was aroused to such a pitch or showed his indignation, no matter how deeply he felt it. But the letter we had received from one of the victims of the frightful night raid had been the last straw to Sasha's wrath, which had been accumulating for the past two months.

The letter bore out the rumours that had come to us during the day following the assault. It read:

*Concentration Camp, Ryazan*

On the night of April 25 we were attacked by Red soldiers and armed Chekists and ordered to dress and get ready to leave the Butirky. Some of the politicals, fearing that they were to be taken to execution, refused to go and were terribly beaten. The women especially were maltreated, some of them being dragged down the stairs by their hair. Many have suffered serious injury. I myself was so badly beaten that my whole body feels like one big sore. We were taken out by force in our night-clothes and thrown into wagons. The comrades in our group know nothing of the whereabouts of the rest of the politicals, including Mensheviki, Socialist-Revolutionists, Anarchists, and Anarcho-Syndicalists.

Ten of us, among them Fanya Baron, have been brought here. Conditions in this prison are unbearable. No exercise, no fresh air food is scarce and filthy; everywhere awful dirt, bed-bugs, and lice. We mean to declare a hunger-strike for better treatment. We have just been told to get ready with our things. They are going to send us away again. We don't know where to.

The reason for the outrage was that the Cheka could not tolerate the comparative freedom our men had established in the Butirky, and their organization of classes, lectures, and discussions. Also the politicals had pleaded for reforms in the treatment of the ordinary prisoners. Constantly locked in their cells, given abominable food, their excrement-buckets often not emptied for two days, fifteen hundred inmates had gone on strike. It had been entirely due to the politicals that the demands of the unfortunates had been satisfied and the trouble terminated. The Cheka had not forgiven the set-back it had received through the intervention of the politicals. Hence the night assault of April 25.

Repeated inquiries by the Moscow Soviet about the fate of the three hundred Mensheviki, Socialist-Revolutionists, and Anarchists forcibly removed from the Butirky elicited the information that they had been distributed among the Orlov, Yaroslavl, and Vladimir prisons.

Shortly after the raid students of the Moscow University protested in an open meeting against the horrors of April 25. The initiators were promptly arrested, the university closed, and the students, who had come from different parts of Russia, given three days to return to their native places. The official explanation given for these drastic measures was lack of rations. The young people declared that they would do without them if permitted to continue their studies. But they were ordered to leave just the same. A short time later the university was opened again. " Henceforth no political activities of any kind will be tolerated," declared Preobrazhensky, Dean of the university. Dropping professors from the faculty and suspending students if they dared to protest had been a daily occurrence. Only the public did not know about it. After Kronstadt and the New Economic Policy the academic gag became more severe and quite unashamed; it ceased to be a star-chamber proceeding. Alexey Borovoy, a well-known anarchist and professor of philosophy, who had been free to teach in the Moscow University during the régime of the Tsar, was forced to resign under the Bolshevik dictatorship. His offence consisted in that the students attended his classes *en masse* and heard him gladly.

The arrested students were exiled, among them even girls of the age of seventeen and eighteen, charged with belonging to a circle that was studying the works of Kropotkin. In view of the situation it was almost childish to think that the Bolsheviki would hesitate to lay hands on the Peter Kropotkin Museum. But most of the committee members refused to be convinced. Sasha and I needed no further justification for our stand. Besides, we had definitely decided to leave Russia.

In the first weeks of Sasha's anguish that followed the massacre of Kronstadt I had not dared to mention the idea of definitely leaving Russia that had come to me during the siege. I feared it might add to his agony. Later, when he had bravely pulled himself together, I broached the subject to him, not at all sure that he would want to go, but certain that I could not leave him behind under the murderous régime. I was therefore immensely relieved to find that Sasha had spent many sleepless nights brooding over the same idea. After we had discussed every possibility for making our lives count for more than mere existences in Russia, we had come to the conclusion that no word nor act of ours would be of value to the Revolution or to our movement or of the least help to our persecuted comrades. We might proclaim from the market-place the anti-revolutionary nature of Bolshevism, or we might hurl our lives against Lenin, Trotsky, and Zinoviev and go down with them. Far from serving our cause or the interest of the masses by such an act, we should be merely aiding the dictatorship. Its skilful propaganda would drag our names through the mire and brand us before the world as traitors, counter-revolutionists, and bandits. Nor could we continue gagged and chained. Therefore we decided to go. Once Sasha was clear that there was nothing vital for us to do in Russia, with the Revolution crushed by the iron hand of dictatorship, he insisted on our leaving soon and illegally. We should not be given passports, he said. Why, then, keep up the torture? Leave Russia like thieves in the night, I protested, Russia that had promised the fulfilment of our hopes? I could not do that, not until we had tried other means. I pleaded that we should get in touch with our comrades abroad to find out what country would admit us. Syndicalist delegates were sure to attend the Congress of the Red Trade Union International to be held in July in Moscow. We might entrust a message to them, or still better to Henry Alsberg, who was about to leave Russia. He would not be like the others who had promised to deliver our message to our people in America and to tell them frankly of the situation. Most of them either had not done so or had misquoted us. No wonder Stella and Fitzi still kept writing enthusiastically about our wonderful opportunity for activity in Russia. Henry was absolutely dependable;

we must wait until he saw our comrades in Germany. Sasha agreed, though reluctantly. He would find no more peace with Kronstadt on his mind, he said.

I shared his grief, as indeed did all our people and nearly everyone else who still had revolutionary fibre left. Our place in Moscow became the oasis for our comrades, as well as for others outside of our ranks. They came at all hours of the day and even late at night, hungry, spiritless, in black despair. The meals intended for ourselves and perhaps for one or two invited guests had to perform the miracle of Christ's loaves for the many who would drift in by the time we sat down to eat. To assure them that there was enough to go round I had to invent all kinds of reasons for my poor appetite: headaches, stomach trouble, and the vice of cooks who always have their pick of the best before the meal is served. I minded the faintness that would sometimes overcome me much less than the lack of privacy. But these people had no other place to go, nowhere where they might feel at home or free to communicate their troubled spirit. It was the only service we could render and we did so out of the fullness of our hearts.

We had other guests not quite so wearing, though no less distressed by the travail of their native land. Alexandra Shakol, our secretary of the expedition, arrived for a short stay in Moscow. It was good to see her again, to exchange thoughts with her, and to help dispel her gloom by treating her to the most cherished delicacy, gogglemoggle, as she called it (egg-nog), which she considered the acme of bliss.

Through Shakol we were able to renew our acquaintance with Vera Nikolayevna Figner, one of the loftiest figures in the pioneer revolutionary movement known as the *Narodnaya Volya* (the People's Will). I had met her the previous year and had been shocked to find her in poor health and underfed. I had inquired whether she was receiving the academic ration which, though not plentiful, was enough to live on. Vera Nikolayevna was too proud to ask for it and she had been overlooked, Shakol informed me. Lunacharsky, whom I had gone to see about the matter, was as indignant as I. He had known nothing about it and he immediately ordered the ration for Vera Figner. Now she looked better and younger. Despite her almost fourscore years, she was still a figure to feast one's eye upon, much of her former beauty being left, the beauty that had inspired poets. Equally marvellous was her spirit after twenty-two years spent in the Schlüsselburg Fortress and the years of struggle since the Russian drama unfolded itself before her. Gracious of manner, witty, and with infinite humanity, Vera Nikolayevna held us rapt by her reminiscences of the heroic revolutionary epoch, the comrades of the *Narodnaya Volva* period and their extraordinary fortitude and daring. They were the real precursors of anarchism, Vera thought, wholly dedicated to its realization by the masses, and without least thought of self. She had known almost all of them and her tribute reflected her own pure vision and grandeur, especially when she spoke of Sophie Perovskaya, the high priestess of the most significant revolutionary epoch in the world. Vera's narrative always renewed my hope that what had been might come again to life in our *Matushka Rossiya*.

An unexpected arrival from America was our old friend Bob Robins, of the quaint auto-house and the anti-Semitic dog. He also had " got religion " — Russia was in his blood. He had cut loose from his affiliations, comrades, and friends in the United States, and, taking his savings of years, he had come to the home of the soviets to help in its labours and to glory in its gains. His wife, Lucy, had chosen the smoother and safer way of the American Federation of Labor. Bobby was a strong link with our past. Poignantly real for a while, it was soon again overshadowed by the black clouds in the Russian sky. Louise Bryant suddenly appeared, no longer grief-stricken and in despair. Seven months had passed since Jack's death, and Louise was young and greedy for life. No wonder she aroused the misgivings and censure of her husband's comrades. She powdered her nose and rouged her lips and she was careful of her figure. Such heresies in Soviet Russia! Perhaps Louise had never been a Communist, but only the wife of one. Why might she not go her own way, I pleaded in her defence. That was grist to the Communist ascetics. I was a *bourzhouy* like Louise and others of her kind, they charged, always championing individual rights when there was only one purpose — the dictatorship and its aims.

Louise asked me to go with her to Stanislavsky for an interview. I was glad of the chance to meet the man whose great art and that of his group had often lifted me out of the drab reality. Lunacharsky had given me a letter of introduction to him as well as to Nemirovich-Danchenko on my first visit to Moscow. They had both been ill at the time, and since then Russia's wave had swept over me.

We found Stanislavsky among mountains of trunks, boxes, and bags. His studio had again been requisitioned. It had happened so many times before that he no longer minded it any more than his periodic house arrests, he told us. He felt much more discouraged about the poverty of the Russian drama. Nothing of any merit during the past four years, he said. The growth of a dramatic artist depends on the living source of creative art; when that is dried up, the greatest must needs become sterile. He was not despairing, he hastily added; no one could despair who knew the treasures of the Russian soil and soul. From Gogol to Chekhov, Gorki, and Andreyev the line has apparently broken, but is not entirely lost. The future will prove that, Stanislavsky prophesied.

The visitor closest to us was Henry Alsberg. He came often, somehow divining the moments when we were alone. He was always laden with gifts to replenish our larder, and his ready wit and fine human qualities helped dispel our gloom. Henry no longer talked about the great political changes that would follow when the fronts should be liquidated. Since he had returned to Russia, every front had indeed been terminated, even the Kronstadt front. The only one left was Karelia and General Slaschov-Krimsky was attending to that. Civil strife was at an end. The time had come for the hopes of Alsberg to be fulfilled: free speech, free press, and amnesty for the thousands of politicals in Soviet prisons. " Where are they, Henry? " I once asked him; " where are the liberties you had expected from Lenin and his party? " He was intellectually too honest to deny that he was haunted by Kronstadt, as all of us were, and oppressed by the wholesale arrests of the politicals and their inhuman treatment. His lack of clarity about the nature, meaning, and purpose of the Social Revolution was his trouble. He remained the knight-errant, blaming the Revolution, the backwardness of the country and its people, the interventionists, and the blockade for every crime that was inherent in the dictatorship, in the mania for power to subjugate everybody and everything for the greater glory of that cold monster the Communist State. His attitude sometimes taxed my patience, but never my affection for our easy-going, good-natured friend. Nor did it affect the bonds of our fellowship. In Bolshevik Russia perhaps more than anywhere else one had to laugh sometimes to keep back one's tears.

On one of his last calls at our place Henry again brought a large

bundle of clothing. " Well," he drawled to Sasha, " if Lenin can become a shopkeeper, why not also Alexander Berkman?" "Sure,"
Sasha replied, " it is kosher now, only I beat Lenin to it. I traded
things while we were in the Ukraine before the pope in the Kremlin
gave it his benediction." " You forget," I interjected, " that you engaged in trade as a ' speculator and bandit.' Lenin does it in the holy
name of Karl Marx. That's the difference."

Yes, therein was the difference. The unfortunates in the market in
front of the National Hotel had given way to a large pastry shop.
It was stacked with fresh loaves of white bread, cake, and *pyroshky.*
The owner, perhaps not a Communist, was a business man according
to Lenin's own heart. He knew how to attract customers. The place
was crowded and business brisk. Outside stood the rabble, pale-faced
and faint with hunger, their eyes bulging with craving for the miracle
displayed in the show-window, luxuries they had not seen in years.
" Where do these things come from ? " a woman protested as I was
passing there. " A little while ago it was dangerous to have a bit of
white bread in one's possession. And look at this. Look at those loaves
of fine cake! Is it for this that we have made the Revolution ? " she
moaned. " I thought we were through with the *bourgeoisie,*" a man
cried; " look at them going in and out of the place! What are they
and who are they ? " The crowd took up the refrain, and some
clenched their fists. " Go on now, disperse! " came the order of a
militiaman on guard at the store. The sacred rights of property had
to be protected.

A store on the Tverskaya that had been closed for three years now
opened its doors with a large stock of choice fruit, caviar, fowl, and
other things one would not have believed existed in Russia. The
crowd that gathered outside seemed too overwhelmed to realize what
it was all about. It was a brazen challenge to their hunger. Their
amazement soon turned to indignation and loud resentment. Those
nearest rushed into the store, the rest following. But Lenin's good
business man was prepared. Guards had been stationed inside to meet
such an emergency. They did their duty. They were the only force in
Soviet Russia that worked efficiently.

The Nep spread. The hour of the new *bourgeoisie* had arrived. No
further need to worry about Sovietsky soup or rations with such an
assortment of delicacies on hand. No further anxiety to hide the loot
taken from the predecessors of the new privileged class. I could

hardly trust my eyes when at the Stanislavsky First Studio I met a number of women dressed in velvet and silks, wearing costly shawls, and bedecked with jewelry. Why not? The Sovietsky ladies knew how to appreciate fine clothes, even if they were somewhat crumpled from their hiding-places and not exactly in keeping with the latest Parisian fashions!

The grey and drab continued, however, among the masses, wearing out their already depleted strength in the long wait for an order for a hole to live in, a bit of calico or medicine for their sick family or even a coffin for their dead. This was no hallucination of my exhausted brain. It was one of the many ghastly realities. One such case was related to me by Angelica Balabanoff. She had been sent back to a little room in the National and completely divested of her Soviet functions. Ill, disillusioned, and broken, she suffered more than most of her comrades from the latest somersault of her idol Ilich. To see constantly the hungry crowds around the bakeries and pastry-shops was torture to one who, like Angelica, felt guilty to accept the gift of even a few biscuits from her Swedish friends. It was a purgatory which only we, who knew her well, could appreciate.

In a feverish state she told me of the suicide of a friend, a Communist woman, who had been in the revolutionary ranks for a quarter of a century. Having heard of quite a number of Communists who had ended their lives after the new economic policy had been introduced, I thought it was a case of similar nature. But it was not that, Angelica explained. Her comrade had shot herself in the hope that her violent death would call attention to the plight of her son, who was ill in a hospital. She had lost one son at the revolutionary front. The second, a mere lad, was tubercular and the commissar had notified the mother that her boy had overstayed his time in the hospital and that she would have to take him home. She had tried to get an order for a room in the National, where the boy would be assured some comfort. Failing in that, she had decided to die so that her shot might induce the Party Executive Committee to secure a room for her child. " The poor creature must have been insane," I protested. Angelica assured me that the woman had been quite in her mind, but she had been unable to see her son die like a dog. The horror of it had completely overtaken Angelica on the day of the burial. She had gone with a comrade to the cemetery by the last request of their dead friend. No one else was there, nor the body of the deceased. Angelica was near a collapse and her escort insisted on turning back. On the way they met two Communist women with a pushcart for a hearse. The delay had been due to the difficulty of getting an order for the coffin and a burial certificate.

The Nep flourished, and the inspired, flocking to the holy grail, were assured that the proletariat was in full control and that money was no more needed in Soviet Russia because the workers had free access to the best the land produced. A large contingent of the devout believers from America had confidingly turned over to the reception committee on the border all their possessions. In Moscow they were packed like sardines in common quarters, given a small ration of bread and soup, and left to their fate. Within a month two children of the group died of undernourishment and infection. The men became despondent, the women ill, one of them going insane from anxiety about her children and the shock of the conditions she had found in Russia. Our friend, little Bobby, his hopes already shattered, came to tell us of the case on the very day when another woman and her two children had walked two miles from the Moscow station to lay their tragedy at our door. Mrs. Konossevich, her husband, their fourteen-year-old daughter and little boy had been deported from America after they had experienced a dose of Mitchell Palmer's régime. They came to Russia with high enthusiasm in their hearts, though not quite so credulous as the others who had been deported with them. They had heard that Russia was naked and starved and they decided to distribute their possessions among the needy. Two weeks later Konossevich, together with his family, were taken off the train on their way to their native village in the Ukraine. He was accused of being a Makhnovets. He had just arrived from the States, where he had been maltreated and deported for his pro-Soviet stand, he explained to the Cheka, and he had never even heard of Makhno. His protests did not help. He was arrested, his baggage confiscated, and his wife and two children left at the station without enough money to exist a week.

It was at any rate work for us to try to save the wife of one comrade from going mad, to find work for Mrs. Konossevich, and to rescue her husband from probable execution. Over and above this crazy pattern of Soviet life, the famine suddenly loomed across the land; want and death spread through the Volga region and threatened the rest of the country. The Soviet Government had known for two

months that millions were likely to perish unless immediate steps for
relief were taken. Agricultural specialists and economists had warned
the authorities of the impending calamity. They had frankly declared
that the main cause of the situation was inefficiency, mismanagement,
and bureaucratic corruption. Instead of setting the Soviet machinery
to work to relieve the calamity, to acquaint the public with the situation and rouse it to the danger, the report of the specialists had been
suppressed.

The few non-Communists who knew of it were powerless to do
anything. We were among the latter. In the heyday of our faith in
the Bolsheviki we should have knocked at the door of every leader
and given our help in relief work. We had learned better since Kronstadt. Nevertheless we informed the Left elements accessible to us of
the threatened calamity and begged to be permitted to join in a campaign to succour the famine-stricken. They hastened to offer suggestions and aid to the Government, but it was declined. The Right wing
was given a more favourable reception. Apart from Vera Figner,
who had joined that group out of human interest, most of the others
were Constitutional Democrats who had bitterly fought the October
Revolution. They had repeatedly been arrested as counter-revolutionists, but now they were accepted with open arms as the " Citizens'
Committee." Every facility was given them in their work: a building,
telephones, typists, and the right to publish a paper. Two numbers
appeared, the first containing an appeal by Patriarch Tikhon, who
called upon his flock to contribute their donations to him since he
would be responsible for their distribution. The irony of this love-
feast between the *avant-garde* of the proletariat and its enemies was
demonstrated by the *Bulletin* the latter issued. It was nothing else
than the resurrected old *Vyedomosty,* the blackest reactionary sheet
of the tsarist régime, which it resembled in every detail save in name.
It was now called *Pomoshch (Aid).*

Once more the geniuses of the Soviet circus had scored over Barnum
and Bailey. Indeed, western Europe would no more dare say that
political liberties were extinct in the Communist State, or that the
Soviet Government did not welcome the co-operation of all parties in
the crucial hour of famine.

After the glad tidings had been heralded abroad and generous aid
found in the American Relief Administration, the love-feast came to
a sudden end. The alliance was declared off, the bride not merely

jilted, but even thrown into the Cheka jail. The members of the " Citizens' Committee " were again denounced as counter-revolutionary, and its leaders exiled to distant parts of the country. Vera Figner was spared, but she refused the honour. She went to the Cheka and demanded to share the fate of her co-workers, but the Government did not think it wise to touch her for fear of the storm of indignation that would have been raised abroad.

President Kalinin, of Kronstadt infamy, travelled in a train *de luxe,* with carloads of Lenin's wisdom, and royally entertained a host of foreign correspondents. The world was to learn how solicitous the Soviet State was of its afflicted people.

The actual workers of the relief, however, were the foreign bodies that had meantime organized their aid. The workers of Russia and the majority of the non-Communist population were performing superhuman labour to succour the famine-stricken districts. The intelligentsia accomplished miracles. In their capacity as physicians, nurses, and distributors of supplies scores of them sacrificed themselves. Many died of exposure and infection, and a number were even killed by the dark and crazed people whom they had come to help. With millions of lives devoured by the famine, the loss of a few hundred *bourgeois* was hardly worth noticing by the Government. It was more important for the world revolution that the Soviet régime suddenly discovered the wealth contained in the churches. It could have been confiscated before without much protest from the peasantry. But now the expropriation of the Church treasures added fuel to the fires of hate which the dictatorship had engendered in all classes of the people. Another demonstration of the continued revolutionary zeal of the Communist State was to order its own members to deliver forthwith all the valuables they had in their possession, even to the last trinket. It was a shock to learn that Communists should be suspected by their own party of hoarding jewelry or other valuables. But apparently there actually were such members. The editor of the *Izvestia,* the well-known Communist Steklov, whose specialty was to hound non-Communist revolutionists as bandits, was discovered to have a large collection of silver and gold, things a Communist was not supposed to own. They could not shoot a prominent party editor as they had shot a Fanya Baron. Neither could he be allowed to remain in the sanctum. The rank and file might muster up courage to demand why such discrimination was practised. Steklov was therefore suspended from the paper, and other Communists were sent to the Crimea.

The famine continued its devastating march. But Moscow was far from the stricken region, and great events were being prepared for within its gates. Three international congresses were to take place: those of the Communist International, of the Women's Organizations, and of the Red Trade Unions. A number of buildings adjoining the Hotel de Luxe were being renovated and the city cleaned up and decorated for the occasion. The blue and gold of the cupolas on the forty times forty churches intermingled with the scarlet hues of the bunting and flags. All was ready for the reception of the foreign delegates and visitors from every part of the world.

Among the early arrivals were two I.W.W. delegates from America, Williams and Cascaden. Others also soon came, among them Ella Reeves Bloor, William Z. Foster, and William D. Haywood. How could "Big Bill" come, we wondered, for we knew that he was out on twenty-thousand-dollar bail and under sentence of twenty years' imprisonment. Was it possible that he had jumped his bond? Sasha was inclined to believe it; he had lost faith in Bill since 1914, when the latter had shown himself weak-kneed during the free-speech fights that Sasha had conducted in New York. I defended Bill hotly, pointing out that our actions are not always to be judged so easily. "Not even your own, old man," I said. But Sasha refused to come with me to the hotel where Haywood was lodged. "He will come to us if he is really anxious to see us," he declared. I laughed at such ceremony with Bill.

Bill Haywood had often been under our roof, by day and by night, always our welcome guest, our comrade in many battles, though not sharing the same ideas. I hastened to the Hotel de Luxe, where the most favoured delegates were quartered, to find the old war-horse, of whom I had always been very fond. Bill received me in the same warm and genial manner that had captured all his friends. In fact, he immediately embraced me, before the whole crowd. A roar went up from the boys, who began teasing Bill for keeping it secret that E.G. was among his many lady-loves. He laughed good-naturedly and drew me down to a seat at his side. I had come only for a moment, I told him, just to welcome him and to tell him where and when he could find us. I still could give him a cup of coffee " as black as night, as sweet as love, as strong as revolutionary zeal." Bill smiled in remembrance. "I'll come tomorrow," he said.

In the crowd surrounding Haywood I noticed several interpreters, whom I knew as Chekists. They were Russian-American Communists who had risen in station and importance for their services to the party. They felt ill at ease in my presence and eyed me suspiciously. I was glad to see Bill again and also several others from the States, including Ella Reeves Bloor, who had visited me in the Missouri penitentiary and who had always showed affection for me and interest in my work. I paid no further attention to the " interpreters " and soon I left.

Sasha was out when Bill arrived in the late afternoon the following day. My visitor transferred me back to America, my old arena of so many years' effort. I plied him with questions about my friends, about Stella and Fitzi, Elizabeth Gurley Flynn, and many others whom I still had in my heart. I wanted to hear about the general situation, the labour movement, and the I.W.W., which had since been all but demolished by the war phobia, as well as about my own comrades. Bill stopped my volley of questions. Before we proceeded, he said, he would first have to make his own position clear to me. I noticed that he was under the nervous tension that used to come over him when he stood before a large audience, his big frame shaking with suppressed feeling. He had jumped his bail, he said suddenly; he had run away. Not because of the twenty years of prison that faced him, though that was no small matter at his age. " Ridiculous, Bill," I interrupted; " you would never have to serve the whole sentence. Gene Debs was pardoned and Kate Richard O'Hare also." " Listen first," he interrupted; " the prison was not the deciding factor. It was Russia, Russia, which fulfilled what we had dreamed about and propagated all our lives, I as well as you. Russia, the home of the liberated proletariat, was calling me." He had also been urged by Moscow to come, he added. He was told he was needed in Russia. From here he would be able to revolutionize the American masses and to prepare them for the dictatorship of the proletariat. It had not been easy to decide to leave his comrades to face their long terms in prison alone. But the Revolution was more important and its ends justified all means. Of course, the twenty-thousand-dollar bail would be paid by the Communist Party. He had been given a solemn pledge for that. He hoped, he said, that I would understand his motives and not think him a shirker.

I did not ask any more about America, nor did I satisfy his request to tell him my impressions of Russia. With a shock I realized that Bill was as blindfolded as we had been on our arrival in the country. Would he also undergo the excruciating operation that would remove the scales from his eyes? And what would become of Bill when his house of cards had tumbled over him, and all his hopes were buried like ours? He had burned his bridges in America, and never again could he fire the imagination of the proletarian youth of his country and justify to them his escape at a time when they needed him so desperately. Who would again entrust his life to a captain who had been the first to abandon his sinking ship? And later on, when he would come to see Soviet Russia with open eyes, what would he do? He would be cast on the refuse-pile, like so many before him, after he had served the propaganda purposes of Moscow. Bill, so rooted in his native soil and its traditions, so alien to Russia, ignorant of her language and her people —

I had almost forgotten the presence of my guest in the contemplation of the tragic future that was awaiting him. " Why so silent? " he asked. " Because silence is more golden than speech," I joked. Later, after he had got his bearings in the new country, we might talk again, I added. Could he come often, he asked, " just as in the days of 210 East Thirteenth Street? " " Yes, dear Bill," I replied, " any time, if you still want to after you have been taken in hand." He did not understand, nor did I explain.

Sasha ridiculed the motives Bill had given for running away. Russia and all the other reasons were not convincing to him. They were no doubt contributory factors, but the main reason was that Bill quaked before the twenty years in Leavenworth. In late years he had repeatedly shown the white feather. I need have no anxiety about Bill's future, Sasha assured me. He would fit in, even when he came to see the stupendous delusion foisted on the world by Moscow. There was no reason why he shouldn't. Bill had always stood for a strong State and centralization. What was his One Big Union but a dictatorship? " Bill will be in clover here," Sasha concluded; " just wait and see."

Two days later William Z. Foster telephoned to ask whether he could come up. It was my wash-day and I was too busy, but Sasha offered to receive Foster in his room until I should be through with my work. It occurred to me that Foster might like to meet Schapiro and other comrades still free. But when I asked him about it, he said he was not interested in Russian syndicalists. He only wanted to talk to Sasha and me. Foster had been among the first in America to advocate revolutionary labour tactics in the economic struggle, which the Russian Anarcho-Syndicalists had applied. It seemed strange that he should decline to meet these rebels and to hear from them what place, if any, syndicalism had in the Communist régime.

He arrived in the company of Jim Browder, a Kansas boy, whom we used to know as an active I.W.W. Sasha took them in charge. At noon, when my work was finished and lunch prepared, I invited our guests to share it with us. Vegetables and fruit were plentiful on the market and much cheaper than meat and fish. We lived almost entirely on this diet. The boys had evidently not lost their American appetite. They ate with relish and expressed appreciation of E.G.'s skill in preparing such dishes. Foster said nothing during the meal except to inform us that he was in Russia in the capacity of a reporter for the Federated Labor Press. Browder talked a great deal about the marvels of the Communist State and the wonderful things the party had achieved. I inquired how long he had been in the country. "About a week," he replied. "And you have already discovered that all is wonderful?" "Indeed," he said, "it can be seen at a glance." I congratulated him on his extraordinary vision and turned our conversation into less turbulent waters. Our callers soon left, which I did not regret.

Two other Americans came to see us, Agnes Smedley and her Hindu friend Chato. I had heard a good deal about Agnes in the States in connexion with her Hindu activities, but I had never met her personally. She was a striking girl, an earnest and true rebel, who seemed to have no other interest in life except the cause of the oppressed people in India. Chato was intellectual and witty, but he impressed me as a somewhat crafty individual. He called himself an anarchist, though it was evident that it was Hindu nationalism to which he had devoted himself entirely.

Cascaden, the Canadian I.W.W. delegate, visited us often, daily looking more distressed over the political intrigues going on in the preliminary sessions. The other American delegates had already been roped in by the Communists, he told us, and made to dance to the tune played by Losovsky, the prospective president of the Red Union International. Cascaden was holding out against their wiles, but he foresaw that he would have no chance at the Congress. We consoled him by telling him that no one with independence and character would have any chance. The Congress would be packed by marionettes of the Russian Bolsheviki, who would vote on every subject as directed by " the centre." Cass, as we familiarly called him, was brave; he would fight to the last for the instructions given him by his organization, he assured us.

The other delegates kept aloof from us, including my erstwhile devoted Ella Reeves Bloor. Bill Haywood also did not return. They had all been warded off by their " interpreters," as were also Robert Minor, Mary Heaton Vorse, and Tom Mann. They were in Moscow and they could not help knowing that we were living in the city. Bob Minor had " changed his mind a little ": he had become a Communist. We had read his confession in the *Liberator,* which had, in effect, been an open letter to the man he had idolized, his closest friend and teacher, Alexander Berkman. Mary Heaton Vorse, an intimate of my New York circle, was a kind soul and a charming companion. Her political views came to her by proxy. She had been an I.W.W. when vivid Joe O'Brien was her husband, and no doubt she must be a Communist now that she was with Minor. Reason enough why Mary should not have allowed her superficial political leanings to obscure the friendship that she had formerly so often proclaimed.

There was also Tom Mann, the old champion of syndicalism and bitter foe of every political machine, the man who had shown the greatest concern for my welfare in London during the exciting days of the Boer War. He had been our guest in New York during his American tour, which the efforts of the *Mother Earth* group had saved from disaster. All these delegates lived in the Hotel de Luxe, a stone's throw from us. " How can human beings go back so easily on their old affiliations? " I remarked to Sasha. I should not take it so much to heart, he replied. They had been told that we were in ill repute with the Bolsheviki and therefore they were afraid to come near us. For himself, he didn't give a damn, and he did not see why I should. I wished I possessed his simple and direct attitude.

The Latin delegates had also been given a gentle hint in regard to us, we learned. But they were of different mettle from the Anglo-Saxons. They informed their " guides " that they did not propose to deny their comrades or to be dictated to about whom they should associate with. The French, Italian, Spanish, German, and Scandinavian Anarcho-Syndicalists lost no time in seeking us out. In fact, they made our place their headquarters. They spent with us every free hour they had, eager to know our impressions and views. They had heard of the alleged persecution of the Left-wing elements by the Communists, but they had taken it as a capitalist fabrication. Their French Communist friends, who had made the journey with them, were also sincerely desirous to learn the facts. Among them Boris Souvarine was the most intelligent and alert inquirer.

The Cheka was of course well aware that these men were coming in and out of our place. Our attitude since Kronstadt had also not remained a secret from them. In fact, Sasha had gone to the head of the Soviet printing house in Petrograd and had demanded back the copy of his *Prison Memoirs,* which they were to publish in Russian. He had openly declared on that occasion, as well as to Zinoviev personally, that he was through with the Bolsheviki because of Kronstadt and all that it involved. We were prepared to take the consequences and we spoke freely to our visitors. Souvarine was quite shaken by our account. It could not be that Lenin and Trotsky knew about the real state of affairs, he thought. Had we tried to talk to them? We had, but we had not been received. Yet Sasha had written a letter to Lenin explaining the situation and our stand in regard to it. But all such efforts were as futile as our protests and proposal to the Petrograd Soviet of Defence during the Kronstadt siege. Nothing was being done in Russia, we informed our visitors, without the knowledge and approval of the supreme authority, the Central Committee of the Communist Party, and Lenin was the head of it.

The Communists in France were co-operating on many occasions with their anarchist comrades, Souvarine argued. Why could not the same conditions be brought about in Russia? The reason was not far to see, we explained. The French Communists had not yet attained political power in their country. They had not yet achieved a dictatorship there, but when that hour arrived, their comradeship with the French anarchists would be at an end, we assured Souvarine. He thought it impossible and he insisted that he should discuss the subject with the leading Bolsheviki. He wanted to bring about an amicable relationship between his Russian comrades and ours.

Just at that moment Olya Maximova called. Pale and trembling, she told us that Maximov and twelve other comrades in the Taganka prison had declared a hunger-strike to the death. They had repeatedly demanded the reason for their imprisonment since March. Information was refused them, nor had any charges been brought against them. Having failed to receive a reply to their protests, they had decided to call the attention of the foreign delegates to their intolerable situation by means of a desperate hunger-strike. The syndicalists present jumped to their feet in great excitement. They would have never believed such a state of affairs possible in Soviet Russia, they declared, and they would immediately demand an accounting. They would raise the question at the opening of the Red Trade Union Congress the following morning. Souvarine implored them to wait and first to see the trade-union leaders, among them Tomsky, the labour head, Losovsky, and others. An open discussion at the public sessions would be working into the enemy's hand, he argued; the capitalist press and the *bourgeoisie* in France and other countries would make the most of it. The matter must be settled quietly and in a friendly way, Souvarine pleaded. The delegates left, assuring us that they would not rest until justice was done to our suffering comrades. They returned late at night to inform us that the trade-union leaders had begged them not to make the scandal public and had promised to do their utmost to get redress for the imprisoned anarchists. They had suggested a committee of one delegate from each country, including Russia, to confer with Lenin and Trotsky. Our comrades from Europe were only too glad to avoid a breach and they had willingly accepted the proposal.

I went with Sasha to the opening session of the Congress to see whom we might get to act on the committee. We were sure that Tom Mann would be anxious to serve on it, for had he not fought against political persecution all his life? And Bill Haywood would certainly not refuse. When on trial for his life in Idaho, he had faced death, from which the anarchists had helped to save him; they had always given him and his I.W.W. organization solidaric assistance at every arrest and during every trouble, as well as during the war. "Tom Mann may help," Sasha said, "but Haywood won't. I may try to get Bob; he would hardly refuse me," he added.

The Marble Hall in the Trade Union House was the theatre where the grand review had been carefully prepared and rehearsed. We found the principal performers all grouped on the stage. The orchestra seats were packed by delegates from every part of the world, the Russians predominating. Not the least important among them were the delegates of such large industrial centres as Palestina, Bokhara, Azerbaijan and similar countries.

Outside of the railing, separating the official representatives from the general audience, were benches for the public. We took our seats in the first row, which the delegates had to pass on their way to the platform. Bill Haywood was in the place of honour. He saw us come in and he turned his head away. Having gone back on his comrades in distress, it was not surprising that he should also deny his former friends. Sasha had been right: there was no need to worry about Bill's future. He could see no more with his good eye than with his blind one and he would " fit in." I felt no anger; I was only unspeakably sad.

Tom Mann stopped short when he recognized us. Like Bill's, his greeting had been profuse only a short time ago. He drew back, however, as soon as I mentioned the proposed committee. He knew nothing about the matter, he said, and he would first have to investigate. Sasha violently upbraided Tom for his lack of stamina and for his fear to displease the Bolshevik bosses. Tom winced at the rebuke from one who had paid with an agony of years for his loyalty and devotion, while Tom had merely been spouting. " All right, all right," he said, shamefacedly, " I'll serve on the committee."

As we walked out of the hall during the noon intermission, we collided with Bob Minor and Mary Heaton Vorse. They were startled at the unexpected meeting and looked very much embarrassed. They pretended a friendly grin, Bob hastening to say that he had meant to look us up, but had been too busy; he would call on us soon, however. " Why these apologies? " Sasha retorted; " they are unnecessary, and please don't come out of duty." He did not mention the committee to Bob.

On our way my dear chum kept silent. I knew how sad he felt. He cared a great deal about Bob and he had trusted in his sense of fair play.

The committee was at last organized and ready to call on Lenin. None of them was a match for the shrewd Grand Mogul. He knew better how to divert their attention than they to compel his. Tom Mann, always anathema to the ruling class of his country, now accepted and made much of by the head of the new dynasty, proved clay in Bolshevik hands. He was too weak to resist Lenin and he was overcome like a débutante first receiving male homage. No less overawed were most of the other members of the committee, but the Labour Syndicalists refused to be side-tracked by the solicitous inquiries of Ilich about the conditions of labour abroad, the strength of the Syndicalists and their prospects. They insisted on knowing what he had to say about the revolutionary hunger-strikers in Russia. Lenin stopped short. He did not care if all the politicals perished in prison, he declared. He and his party would brook no opposition from any side, Left or Right. He would consent, however, to have the imprisoned anarchists deported from the country, on pain of being shot if they should return to Soviet soil. Lenin's ears had become attuned for nearly four years to shooting and he had grown infatuated with the sound of it.

His proposal, submitted to the Central Committee of the Communist Party as a matter of form, was of course approved by it. A joint committee was formed, representing the Government and the foreign delegates, to arrange for the immediate release and deportation of the Taganka hunger-strikers and the imprisoned anarchists.

On the eighth day of the strike there was still no definite action taken, because the high authority of the All-Russian Cheka, with Dzherzhinsky and Unschlicht at its head, insisted that " there were no anarchists in Soviet prisons." There were only bandits and Makhnovtsy, they declared. They demanded that the foreign delegates first submit a list of those they wanted liberated for deportation. The ruse was an obvious attempt to sabotage the entire plan and to gain time till the Congress adjourned and the foreign delegates departed. Some of the latter began to realize that nothing would be done and that our comrades might starve to death. They again threatened to take the matter up at the Congress and have it discussed in open session. But this was just what the Soviet authorities were anxious to prevent. They pleaded for a private conference with the delegates and faithfully promised to bring about a satisfactory arrangement without further loss of time.

Our people in the Taganka were beginning to break down under the torture of the protracted hunger-strike. One of them, a young student of the Moscow University, a consumptive, had already collapsed. His co-strikers urged him to terminate his fast, but he loyally refused to desert them, even in the face of death. We were powerless to aid in any way. With heavy hearts Sasha and I kept after the syndicalist members of the joint committee, urging and pleading for speedy action. One day, while on our way to the Congress, we were met by Robert Minor, who handed Sasha a large bundle. " Some provisions," he said sheepishly; "we at the Luxe get too much. Maybe you'll give it to the hunger-strikers. Some light things — caviar, white bread, and chocolate. I thought — " "Never mind what you thought," Sasha interrupted; "you are a rotter to add insult to the injury the Taganka men have already endured. Instead of protesting against the hounding of men for their political views, you try to bribe our comrades into breaking their strike by offering the leavings of your overfed fellow delegates." "By the way," I added, "you had better stop Mary Heaton Vorse from her irresponsible talk about our friend Bob Robins. Does she want to land him in the Cheka?"

Bob mumbled that Lucy Robins had allied herself with Gompers, who was fighting the Russian Revolution. Sasha replied that the fact that Lucy was working with the American Federation of Labor, while showing poor judgment, did not stamp her husband as a counter-revolutionist. He had better curb Mary's tongue. It meant a man's life.

Bob grew pale, his eyes shifted uneasily from Sasha to me and back, and then he started to say something. I stopped him. "Give your parcel to the women and children shivering outside your Hotel de Luxe and greedily picking up the crumbs that fall from the wagonloads of white bread brought to feed the delegates." "You people make me sick," Bob cried, trying to control his rage; "you make a big fuss over the thirteen anarchists in the Taganka and forget that it is a revolutionary period. What do those thirteen matter, or thirteen hundred even, in view of the greatest revolution the world has ever seen?" "Yes, we've heard that before," Sasha retorted; "but I should really not be angry with you, considering that I myself believed the same stuff for fifteen months. But I know better now. I know that this 'greatest revolution' is the greatest fraud, masking every crime to keep the Communists in power. Some day, Bob, you may also come to realize it. We'll talk then. Now we have nothing more to say to each other."

On the tenth day of the hunger-strike the joint committee finally met in the Kremlin. Sasha and Schapiro had been asked by the Taganka prisoners to represent their demands. Trotsky was to be the spokesman of the Central Committee of the Communist Party, but he failed to appear and Lunacharsky took his place. Unschlicht, acting head of the All-Russian Cheka, treated the delegates with open scorn and finally left the room without even a greeting to them. The "comradely" session might have ended in the arrest of the foreign delegates had not the coolness of Sasha and Schapiro smoothed matters. It required all his self-restraint, Sasha later told me, not to hit Unschlicht for his arrogant behaviour, but the fate of our sufferers was at stake. The air was surcharged with antagonism, and it was only after long bickering that an agreement was reached. A letter signed by the joint committee, but not concurred in by Alexander Berkman, was forwarded through Unschlicht to the Taganka men, containing the following statement:

> Comrades, in view of the fact that we have come to the conclusion that your hunger-strike cannot accomplish your liberation, we hereby advise you to terminate it.
>
> At the same time we inform you that definite proposals have been made to us by Comrade Lunacharsky in the name of the Central Committee of the Communist Party. To wit:
>
> 1. All anarchists held in the prisons of Russia who are now on a hunger-strike will be permitted to leave for any country they may choose. They will be supplied with passports and funds.
>
> 2. Concerning other imprisoned anarchists or those out of prison, final action will be taken by the party tomorrow. It is the opinion of Comrade Lunacharsky that the decision in their case will be similar to the present one.
>
> 3. We have received the promise, endorsed by Unschlicht, that the families of the comrades to go abroad will be permitted to follow them if they so wish. For conspirative reasons some time will have to elapse before this is done.
>
> 4. The comrades before going abroad will be permitted two or three days at liberty before their departure, to enable them to arrange their affairs.
>
> 5. They will not be allowed to return to Russia without the consent of the Soviet Government.
>
> 6. Most of these conditions are contained in the letter received by this delegation from the Central Committee of the Communist Party, signed by Trotsky.
>
> 7. The foreign comrades have been authorized to see to it that these conditions are properly carried out.
>
> [Signatures]     Orlandi ⎱ Spain
>                   Leval   ⎰
>
>                   Sirolle ⎱ France
>                   Michel  ⎰
>                   A. Schapiro—Russia
>                   [signed] Lunacharsky

The above is correct.

Alexander Berkman declines to sign because:

    *a.* he is opposed to deportation on principle;

    *b.* he considers the letter an arbitrary and unjustified curtailment of the original offer of the Central Committee according to which all the anarchists were to be permitted to leave Russia;

    *c.* he demands more time at liberty for those to be released, to enable them to recuperate before deportation.

Kremlin, Moscow

13/VII/1921

I was glad Sasha had refused to concur in the outrageous decision that established the precedent of deportation of revolutionists from Soviet Russia, of men who had valiantly defended the Revolution, had fought on its fronts, and had suffered untold danger and hardships. What a commentary on the Communist State outdoing Uncle Sam! He, poor boob, went only as far as deporting his foreign-born opponents. Lenin and Company, themselves political refugees from their native land only a short time ago, were now ordering the deportation of Russia's native sons, the best flower of her revolutionary past.

Despair is often more compelling than hunger. The Taganka comrades were motivated by that, rather than by their eleven torturous days, in terminating their hunger-strike. They accepted the conditions that were to set them adrift. They were completely exhausted by their long fast, some of them laid up with a high temperature. The coarse prison food would have been fatal to them, but Lenin had declared that he did not care if they perished in jail. It would be absurd to look for more humanity from the prison authorities or to expect them to supply suitable light diet. Fortunately the Swedish delegates had given us a suitcaseful of provisions, and these served to feed our prisoners during the critical days of recuperation.

The sequel of the " amicable settlement " Souvarine and his fellow French delegates had hoped for was supplied by Bukharin at the eleventh hour of the Red Trade Union Congress. In the name of the Central Committee of the Communist Party he made a ferocious attack on the men in the Taganka and the Russian anarchists in general. They were all counter-revolutionists, he declared, who were plotting against the Socialist Republic. The whole Russian anarchist

movement was nothing but banditry, he charged, the ally of Makhno
and of his highwaymen who had fought the Revolution and had murdered Communists and Red Army men. The flagrant breach of the
agreement to avoid publicity in the Taganka trouble, which the Bolsheviki themselves had insisted upon, came like unexpected thunder
in the final session of the Congress. The Latin delegates, outraged by
such underhand tactics, were immediately on their feet. They demanded to be heard in protest, in rebuttal of the denunciation of their
Russian comrades. Chairman Lozovsky had obligingly given the
floor to Bukharin, though the latter was not a delegate and had no
right to address the Congress. But now Lozovsky resorted to every
possible trick to deprive the foreign delegates of a chance to answer
the libellous charges of Bukharin. Even some of the Russian Communist delegates were dismayed by the proceedings and supported the
demand of the Latin delegates to be heard. Of the Anglo-Saxon
delegates only Cascaden rose in protest. Tom Mann, Bill Haywood,
Bob Minor, William Foster, and Ella Reeves Bloor were silent in
the face of the crying injustice and suppression. The lifelong champions of free speech could find no word of protest against its denial
in Soviet Russia. In the tumult and uproar that followed Bukharin's
attack on the anarchists few persons in the hall noticed Rykov, chairman of the All-Russian Soviet of Economy, signalling to the attending
Chekists. A detachment of soldiers clattered into the hall, adding
fuel to the blaze ignited by Bukharin's speech.

Sasha and I elbowed our way to the platform. This time I should
speak, I told him, even if I had to resort to force, unless Schapiro
or some Syndicalist delegate got the floor. He would rush the platform, if necessary, Sasha said. In passing he caught sight of Bob
Minor. He gripped his cane, about to strike him. " You're a yellow
cur, you son of a b——," Sasha roared at him. Minor recoiled in fright.
Sasha took up his stand on one side of the platform steps, while I
stood on the other. The majority of the delegates were on their
feet, clamouring to be heard and protesting against Lozovsky's
autocratic conduct. Beset on all sides, he was finally forced to give
the floor to Sirolle, the French Anarcho-Syndicalist. Roused by the
Jesuitical machinations of the Communist Party, Sirolle in thunderous
voice denounced the double-dealing tactics of the Soviet Government
and brilliantly refuted the cowardly charges against the Taganka men
and the Russian anarchists.

When the news of the approaching deportation became known, the Left Socialist-Revolutionists, comrades of Maria Spiridonovna, decided to benefit by the presence of the foreign delegates and labour men. In a statement distributed among them they set forth that Maria, taken from her sick-bed the previous year, was still being kept in prison. She had undergone several hunger-strikes in protest and had demanded her release and that of her life-long friend and companion Izmailovich. She had twice been at death's door and was now in a most precarious state. Her comrades would supply the means of sending Maria abroad for medical treatment, the statement read, if the Soviet authorities would permit her to go.

Dr. I. Steinberg requested me to interest the delegates of the International Women's Congress, then taking place in Moscow. I went to see Clara Zetkin, the famous old Social Democrat, who was now high in the councils of the Government. She was working to rally the support of the women of every country for the world revolution, she informed me. Well, Maria Spiridonovna had already served that cause, I told her, served it the greater part of her life. She was indeed the very symbol of that revolution. It would do irreparable harm to the prestige of the Communist Party if Maria was to be extinguished in a Cheka prison, I urged, and it was Clara Zetkin's duty to prevail upon the Government to permit Maria Spiridonovna to leave Russia.

Zetkin promised to intercede in behalf of Maria. But at the close of the Congress she sent me word that Lenin was too ill to be seen. She had spoken to Trotsky in the matter, and the War Commissar had told her that Maria Spiridonovna was still too dangerous to be at liberty or to be permitted abroad.

The Red Trade Union Congress was over. Its most pathetic harlequin proved to be Bill Haywood. The founder of the I.W.W. in America and its dominant figure for twenty years, he allowed himself to be persuaded to vote at the Congress for the Communist plan to " liquidate " the militant minority labour organizations, including the I.W.W., and force their members to join the American Federation of Labor, which Haywood had for years denounced as " capitalistic and reactionary."

The smaller fry among his comrades, the Ella Reeves Bloors, the Browders, and Andreychins, took the cue from their chief. Andreychin

had never been blessed with much backbone. During the Mesaba
Range strike he had been willing to make any compromise to save
himself from deportation. Sasha had interested Amos Pinchot and
other influential liberals in his behalf and through them had stayed
the hand of the Immigration Bureau. While Andreychin was in
Leavenworth, he again showed the white feather. I ascribed his
weakness to the fear of tuberculosis, which had begun to undermine
his health. I was at the time in the Missouri prison, but in compliance with Andreychin's repeated requests I urged Stella and Fitzi
to raise the ten thousand dollars needed to release him on bail. The
faithful girls had worked like galley-slaves to secure bonds for many
other victims of the war mania, but they would not refuse me. They
procured part of the bail, while a friend gave the balance. Andreychin,
spineless creature that he was, emulated his teacher Bill Haywood
and jumped his bond. On the very first day of his arrival in Moscow
he delivered a public speech in which he denounced his I.W.W. fellows
in the United States and pledged the Bolsheviki his help in destroying
the organization. Yet I felt that this treachery was not so much the
fault of Andreychin, Bill Haywood, and the many others who were
on their knees before the holy shrine of the Kremlin. It was rather
the appalling superstition, the Bolshevik myth, that duped and en-
snared them, as it had also formerly done to us.

Soviet Russia had become the modern socialist Lourdes, to which
the blind and the lame, the deaf and the dumb were flocking for
miraculous cures. I was filled with pity for these deluded ones, but
I felt only contempt for those others who had come, had seen with
open eyes and understood, and had yet been conquered. Of these
was William Z. Foster, once the champion of revolutionary syndicalism in America. He was keen-eyed and he had come as a press
correspondent. He went back to do Moscow's bidding.

No word had arrived from our comrades in Germany in reply to
the letter sent them about securing visas. Sasha was chafing under
the delay of getting out of Russia. He could stand the fearful tragicomedy no longer, he said. A German Syndicalist delegate, member
of the Seamen's and Transport Workers' Union, had also taken a
letter from us and had promised to see our people in Berlin. There
was no news yet. As in his early days after his coming out of the
Western Penitentiary, Sasha became very restless. He could not endure being indoors or seeing people. He would roam the streets of

Moscow most of the day and late into the night, and my anxiety about him grew.

In his absence one day Bob Minor called. Not finding Sasha, he edged out. I did not try to detain him, for our old ties had snapped. Shortly after, there arrived a letter from him, addressed to Sasha. He read it and handed it to me without comment. Bob's letter dilated on the " momentous and world-revolutionizing resolutions " passed by the Congress of the Third International. He had always known Sasha as the clearest mind in the anarchist movement in America and as an indomitable and fearless rebel. Could he not see now that his place was in the Communist Party? He belonged there, and it offered him a large field for his abilities and devotion. He could not give up the hope that Sasha would yet come to realize the supreme mission of the Communist dictatorship in Russia and its approaching conquest of capitalism throughout the world.

Bob was sincere, Sasha commented, but the veriest blockhead politically and blind as a bat socially. He should have stuck to his real field, that of art. I urged Sasha to reply to Bob's letter, but he refused. It was useless, he said, and he was weary of talk and arguments. How well I understood his weariness! I also felt completely fagged out. The physical drudgery of our existence and the excessive summer heat had sapped my strength. The stream of visitors, the long hours without sleep, and the great strain of the Trade Union Congress made me feel tired to death.

Sasha returned from one of his long tramps in the city looking unusually pale and distressed. When he made sure that I was alone, he said in a whisper: " Fanya Baron is in Moscow. She has just escaped from the Ryazan prison and she is in great danger; without money or papers and no place to go."

I was struck dumb with horror of the fate awaiting Fanya if discovered. Fanya in the very fortress of the Cheka! " Oh, Sasha, why did she come here, of all places? " I cried. " That isn't the question now," he returned; " better let us think quickly how we can help her."

Our own place would be a trap for her. She would be discovered within twenty-four hours. The other comrades were also being watched. To give her shelter would mean death for them as for her. Of course, we would supply her with money, clothing, and food. But how about a roof over her head? She was safe for the night, Sasha said, but on the morrow something would have to be devised. There was no more sleep for me that night — Fanya weighed heavily on my mind.

Early next morning Sasha left the house with money and things for Fanya, and I remained in sickening suspense until the late afternoon, beset by fears for both. My friend had a less anxious look when he returned. Fanya had found shelter with a brother of Aaron Baron. He was a Communist and his place therefore safe for Fanya. I stared in amazement. " It's all right," Sasha said, trying to soothe my fears, " the man has always been fond of Aaron and Fanya. He will not betray her." I was dubious of a Communist allowing family ties or personal feelings to interfere with his party's commands. But I could suggest no safer place and I knew that Fanya could not remain out on the streets. Sasha felt so relieved that Fanya was under cover that I did not want to arouse his fears again. I plied him with questions about the daring girl — why she had come to Moscow and when I could see her.

That was entirely out of the question, Sasha declared. It was enough for one of us to take the risk. I had already courted enough danger, he argued, by my visits to the Arshinov family. The Bolsheviki had set a price on Pyotr Arshinov's head, dead or alive, as the closest friend and associate of Nestor Makhno. He was in hiding and he could only venture out after dark to call on his wife and infant in the city. I had indeed been repeatedly to see them and to take things for their baby, and once Sasha had accompanied me. Now he insisted that I promise not to attempt to see Fanya. My dear, faithful pal was so concerned about my safety that I would have promised anything to reassure him. But at heart I determined to visit my haunted comrade.

Fanya's mission in Moscow, Sasha confided to me, was to prepare the escape of Aaron Baron. She had learned of the persecution he was undergoing in prison and she had determined to rescue her lover from his living death. Her own escape was made for that very purpose. Brave, wonderful Fanya, dedicated to Aaron as few wives are, yet not tied by law! My heart went out to our splendid comrade in trembling fear for her mission, her sweetheart, and herself.

Sasha's account of his meetings with Fanya served to allay my anxiety about her and him. It even made me laugh. The city was crowded and the parks filled with spooning couples. Ladies of pleasure were about everywhere, entertaining some of the foreign delegates in return for real valuta or delicacies from the Hotel de Luxe. Sasha and Fanya were no doubt considered by the passers-by as engaged in similar propaganda activities. Fanya looked much improved physically and was in fine spirits. She was less worried about Aaron now, because his brother, to whom she had confided her mission, had promised to aid her scheme. Again I felt my heart flutter at the risk Fanya was taking, but I kept my own counsel.

Then the blow came and left us stunned. Two of our comrades fell into the Cheka net — Lev Tchorny, gifted poet and writer, and Fanya Baron! She had been arrested in the home of her Communist brother-in-law. At the same time eight other men had been shot at on the street by Chekists and taken prisoners. They were *existy* (expropriators), the Cheka declared.

Sasha had seen Fanya the preceding evening. She had been in a hopeful mood: the preparations for Aaron's escape were progressing satisfactorily, she had told him, and she felt almost gay, all unconscious of the sword that was to fall upon her head the following morning. "And now she is in their clutches and we are powerless to help," Sasha groaned.

He could not go on any longer in the dreadful country, he declared. Why would I persist in my objection to illegal channels? We were not running away from the Revolution. It was dead long ago; yes, to be resurrected, but not for a good while to come. That we, two such well-known anarchists, who had given our entire lives to revolutionary effort, should leave Russia illegally would be the worst slap in the face of the Bolsheviki, he emphasized. Why, then, should I hesitate? He had learned of a way of going from Petrograd to Reval. He would go there to make the preliminary arrangements. He was suffocating in the atmosphere of the bloody dictatorship. He could not stand it any more.

In Petrograd the "party" that traded in false passports and aided people to leave the country secretly turned out to be a priest with several assistants. Sasha would have nothing to do with them, and the plan was off. I sighed with relief. My reason told me that Sasha was right in ridiculing my objection to being smuggled out of Russia. But my feelings rebelled against it and were not to be argued away. Moreover, somehow I felt certain that we should hear from our German comrades.

We planned to remain in Petrograd for awhile, since I hated Moscow, so overrun by Chekists and soldiers. The city on the Neva had not changed since our last visit; it was as dreary in appearance and as famished as before. But the warm welcome from our former co-workers in the Museum of the Revolution, the affectionate friendship of Alexandra Shakol and of our nearest comrades, would make our stay more pleasant than in the capital, I thought. Plans in Russia, however, almost always go awry. Word reached us from Moscow that the apartment on the Leontevsky where we had stayed had been raided and Sasha's room in particular had been ransacked from top to bottom. A number of our friends, among them Vassily Semenoff, our old American comrade, had been caught in the dragnet laid by the Cheka. A *zassada* of soldiers remained in the apartment. It was apparent that our callers, who did not know we were away, were being made to suffer for our sins. We decided to return to Moscow forthwith. To save the expenses of our trip I went to see Mme Ravich, to inform her that we were at the call of the Cheka whenever wanted. I had not seen the Petrograd Commissar of the Interior since the memorable night of March 5 when she had come for the information Zinoviev had expected from Sasha regarding Kronstadt. Her manner, while no longer so warm as before, was still cordial. She knew nothing about the raid of our rooms in Moscow, she said, but would inquire by long-distance telephone. The next morning she informed me that it all had been a misunderstanding, that we were not wanted by the authorities, and that the *zassada* had been removed.

We knew that such " misunderstandings " were a daily occurrence, not infrequently involving even execution, and we gave little credence to Mme Ravich's explanation. The particularly suspicious circumstance was the special attention given to Sasha's room. I had been in opposition to the Bolsheviki longer than he and more outspoken. Why was it that his room was searched and not mine? It was the second attempt to find something incriminating against us. We agreed to leave immediately for Moscow.

On reaching the capital we learned that Vassily, arrested when he had called on us during our absence, had already been liberated. So were also ten of the thirteen Taganka hunger-strikers. They had been kept in prison two months longer, despite the pledge of the Government to free them immediately upon the termination of their hunger-strike. Their release, however, was the sheerest farce, because they were placed under the strictest surveillance, forbidden to associate with their comrades, and denied the right to work, although informed that their deportation would be delayed. At the same time the Cheka announced that none of the other imprisoned anarchists would be liberated. Trotsky had written a letter to the French delegates to that effect, notwithstanding the original promise of the Central Committee to the contrary. Our Taganka comrades found themselves " free," weak and ill as a result of their long hunger-strike. They were in tatters, without money or means of existence. We did what we could to alleviate their need and to cheer them, although we ourselves felt anything but cheerful. Meanwhile Sasha had somehow succeeded in communicating with Fanya in the inner Cheka prison. She informed him that she had been transferred the previous evening to another wing. The note did not indicate whether she realized the significance of it. She asked that a few toilet things be sent her. But neither she nor Lev Tchorny needed them any more. They were beyond human kindness, beyond man's savagery. Fanya was shot in the cellar of the Cheka prison, together with eight other victims, on the following day, September 30, 1921. The life of the Communist brother of Aaron Baron was spared. Lev Tchorny had cheated the executioner. His old mother, calling daily at the prison, was receiving the assurance that her son would not be executed and that within a few days she would see him at liberty. Tchorny indeed was not executed. His mother kept bringing parcels of food for her beloved boy, but Tchorny had for days been under the ground, having died as the result of the tortures inflicted on him to force a confession of guilt.

There was no Lev Tchorny on the list of the executed published in the official *Izvestia* the next day. There was " Turchaninov " — Tchorny's family name, which he almost never used and which was quite unknown to most of his friends. The Bolsheviki were aware that Tchorny was a household word in thousands of labour and revolutionary homes. They knew he was held in the greatest esteem as a beautiful soul of deep human kindliness and sympathy, a man known for poetic and literary gifts and as the author of the original and very thoughtful work on *Associational Anarchism*. They knew he was respected by numerous Communists and they did not dare publish that they had murdered the man. It was only Turchaninov who had been " executed."

And our dear, splendid Fanya, radiant with life and love, unswerving in her consecration to her ideals, touchingly feminine, yet resolute as a lioness in defence of her young, of indomitable will, she had fought to the last breath. She would not go submissively to her doom. She resisted and had to be carried bodily to the place of execution by the knights of the Communist State. Rebel to the last, Fanya had pitted her enfeebled strength against the monster for a moment and then was dragged into eternity as the hideous silence in the Cheka cellar was rent once more by her shrieks above the sudden pistol-shots.

I had reached the end. I could bear it no longer. In the dark I groped my way to Sasha to beg him to leave Russia, by whatever means. " I am ready, my dear, to go with you, in any way," I whispered, " only far away from the woe, the blood, the tears, the stalking death."

Sasha was planning to go to the Polish frontier, to arrange for our leaving by that route. I was afraid to let him go alone in his present condition, his nerves shattered by the fearful shock of recent events. On the other hand, it would arouse suspicion if both of us should disappear from our quarters at the same time. Sasha realized the danger and consented to wait another week or two. The idea was for him to proceed to Minsk; I was to follow when he should have made the necessary arrangements. As we should have to travel like the rest of the damned portion of the population, Sasha insisted that I take no baggage. He would carry with him what we absolutely needed; the rest of our things were to be distributed among our friends. We had come to starved and naked Russia overflowing with the need of giving of ourselves as well as of the trunkfuls of gifts we had brought with us. Our hearts were empty now and so must be our hands.

Our preparations had to be made in the strictest privacy, at night, when the rest of the tenants in the apartment were asleep. Manya Semenoff, her lovable Vassily, and a few other trusted ones knew of our plan. It was tragic indeed, this scheming to steal out of the country that had held our highest longings and hopes.

In the midst of the packing the long-expected letter from Germany arrived. It contained an invitation for Sasha, Schapiro, and me to attend the Anarchist Congress that was to take place in Berlin at Christmas. It sent me spinning round the room, weeping and laughing at the same time. " We shan't have to hide and cheat and resort to false papers, Sasha," I cried in glee; " we shan't have to sneak out like thieves in the night! " But Sasha did not seem elated over it. " Ridiculous," he retorted, " you don't mean that our Berlin comrades can exert any influence over Chicherin, the Communist Party, or the Cheka! Moreover, I have no intention of applying to them for anything. I've already told you that." I knew from experience that it was useless to argue with my stubborn pal when he was angry. I would wait for a more propitious time. The new hope held out by the letter had reawakened my objections to leaving secretly the land that had known the glory and the defeat of the great " October."

I sought out Angelica. She had told me that she would help us secure the consent of the Soviet authorities to leave the country. She herself was planning to go abroad to regain her health in some quiet spot. She, too, had reached the spiritual breaking-point, though she would not admit it even to herself. Dear Angelica immediately offered to get the necessary application blanks, and she would go to Chicherin and even to Lenin, if need be, to vouch for Sasha and me. " No, dear Angelica," I protested, " you shall do nothing of the kind." I knew what it meant to leave such security. We would not have anyone endangered for us, nor did we care to have the benediction of Lenin. I informed Angelica that all I wanted of her was to help quicken action if passports were to be granted at all.

In the space in the application reserved for the promise of loyalty and the signature of two party members vouching for the applicant I wrote: " As an anarchist I have never pledged loyalty to any government, much less can I do it to the R.S.F.S.R., which claims to be Socialist and revolutionary. I consider it an insult to my past to ask anyone to stand the consequences of anything I may say or do. I therefore refuse to have anyone vouch for me."

Angelica was considerably perturbed by my declaration. She feared it might spoil our chances of securing permission to leave the country. " Either we go out without any strings attached to us, or we will find another way," I declared. We would leave no hostages behind. Angelica understood.

I went to the Foreign Office to find out whether a request from our German comrades that we be permitted to attend the Anarchist Congress had been received. I was called before Litvinov, who was acting in behalf of Commissar Chicherin. I had never met him before. He looked like a *commis voyageur,* short and fat and disgustingly content with himself. Reclining in an easy chair in his luxurious office he began to ply me with questions as to why we wanted to leave Russia, what our intentions were abroad, and where we meant to live. Had the Foreign Office not received any communication from the Berlin anarchists, I inquired. It had, he admitted, and he knew we had been invited to attend the Anarchist Congress in Berlin. That was explanation enough, I told him; I could add nothing further. " But if you are refused? " he demanded suddenly. If his Government wanted it known abroad that we were being kept prisoners in Russia, it could certainly do so, for it had the power, I replied. Litvinov peered at me steadily out of little eyes bulging from his puffy face. He made no comment, but asked whether our Berlin comrades had made sure that the German Government would admit us. Certainly the latter would not be anxious to increase the number of anarchists in its territory. It was a capitalist country and we could not expect the reception there that Soviet Russia had given us. " Yet, strange to say," I replied, " the anarchists continue their work in most European countries, which cannot be said to be the case in Russia." " Are you singing the praises of the *bourgeois* countries? " he demanded. " No, only reminding you of facts. I have been strengthened in my anarchist attitude that all governments are fundamentally alike, whatever their protestations. However, what about our passports? "

He would let us know, he replied. At any rate, the Soviet Government would not undertake to supply us with visas. That was our own look-out, and, saying so, Litvinov closed the interview.

Sasha had left for Minsk, and ten days passed before I received a sign from him. Then a short note arrived in a roundabout way, informing me that the trip had been hideous, but that he had finally reached his destination and was busy "collecting historical material for the Museum of the Revolution." He had given this as a reason for his journey when he had purchased his ticket.

I was somewhat distracted from my anxiety and worry by the glad news that Maria Spiridonovna had been released. She was almost at death's door from another hunger-strike. Fearing she was about to die in prison, the Cheka had permitted her friends to take her out for a rest and recuperation. Should she get well and show the least sign of renewed activity, the authorities had warned, she would be immediately arrested and imprisoned again. Her friends had indeed to take Maria away bodily, as she was too weak and ill to walk. Her companion Izmailovich was permitted to accompany her, and both women were installed by their friends in Malakhovka, near Moscow. The Government stationed Chekists about the place to guard against any attempt to spirit Maria away.

There was to be no end to Maria's martyrdom, but I felt that she would at least be with her own friends and comrades, and those who loved her would be privileged to look after her needs. It was a comforting thought.

On the twelfth day, when I had about given up hope of hearing from the Foreign Office again, Angelica telephoned to me that passports had been issued to us. I should call for them at the Foreign Office, she said, and take with me dollars or English pounds to pay for them. Cabs were a luxury when so many of our people were in dire want, but I did not have the patience to walk. I wanted to see the passports with my own eyes before I would believe that they had actually been granted. It proved true, however, really true. Sasha and I would not have to hide and cheat to leave the country. We should be able to go as we had come — in the open, even if desolate and denuded of dreams.

Our comrade A. Schapiro had applied independently and I was happy to learn that his passport was also ready and awaiting his call.

I telegraphed Sasha: "This time I win, old scout. Come back quickly." It was probably cattish, but revenge was sweet. In my joyous exuberance I had not stopped to consider the anomaly of the Foreign Office demanding *valuta* when the possession of such currency was strictly prohibited. Well, I mused, laws were made to be broken, and none so skilful as the lawmakers themselves.

Passports on hand, I was now beset by other misgivings. Visas — how were they to be obtained? Our Berlin comrades notified us that they were trying their utmost to secure our admission to Germany. If we could somehow reach Latvia or Esthonia, it would be easier to get visas, they wrote.

Sasha burst into the house unannounced. He looked a fright, unshaven and apparently unwashed for days, tired and exhausted, and without the suit-case he had taken with him. " What's this? " he demanded; " just a hoax to get me back here? " He had made all preparations, he said, to cross the border and had come to fetch me. The papers would be awaiting us in Minsk and he had given fifty dollars' deposit on them. " Is the money to be lost? " he demanded. " And the suit-case," I returned, " is that to be lost too? " He grinned. " That's already lost," he replied; " you know, they are clever, these

Russians. I was told the safest way on trains is to tie your bags to your legs. I did so, and the rope was strong. But the car was pitch-dark — no lights whatever — and so crowded I had to stand all the way. The train stopped at innumerable stations and I must have dozed off. When I looked at my suit-case — well, the rope was there, but no suit-case. Couldn't find it anywhere in the car. Clever of them, wasn't it?"

"Clever of you, too — the third time, isn't it?" "You're a hard loser, old girl," he teased, "you ought to be glad it wasn't sixteen hundred dollars again." What could one do with such an irrepressible one? I had to laugh with him.

Triumphantly I held out the passports. He scrutinized them from every side. "Well," he drawled, "I was sure they'd refuse. A fellow may be wrong, sometimes."

But I could see he felt relieved that it would not have to be the Minsk route. His trip must have been ghastly. It took him a week to recuperate from it.

The Lithuanian visa was granted for two weeks. A transit through Latvia was obtained without much trouble. We could leave any day. The certainty made us feel doubly the plight of the comrades and friends whom we were leaving behind — in want, distress, fettered and utterly helpless in the Soviet void. The Taganka men awaiting deportation were still kept in uncertainty. Exhausted by their daily chase after the authorities to secure some definite statement or action, they were spending most of their time in the corridor of our apartment trying to reach the Cheka by telephone. There was no lack of promises, but not a single one of them had been kept during the four months that had passed since the agreement to deport the men. Every gamut of human suffering had been experienced by them, every physical and spiritual torture for opinion's sake. Yet they were undaunted. Nothing could affect their ideal or weaken their faith in its final triumph. Mark Mrachny, recently robbed by death of his young wife, with a poor little sickly infant on his hands, remained brave and unbent. Volin, with his four small children doomed to starvation before his very eyes, and with his wife ailing in their cold and barren quarters, still continued to write poetry. Maximov, his health broken by several previous hunger-strikes, had lost nothing of his studious interests. Olya Maximova, delicate and sensitive, who had for seven months twice weekly carried heavy loads of provisions to the Taganka prison in continuous stress and anguish about the fate of her beloved Maximov, could still crave beauty and social fellowship. Yarchook, a dauntless fighter, with trials and tribulations to break the strongest, had also withstood all the Taganka horrors. The rest of the men awaiting deportation were of the same fibre and grit. Amazing were they, and those other wonderful friends and comrades we had met in the Ukraine and all through Russia, men of courage, ability, and heroic endurance for the sake of their ideals. I owed much to them, and in my heart I felt grateful for having known them. Their staunch comradeship, understanding, and faith had helped to sustain me spiritually and had kept me from being swept away by the avalanche that had passed over all of us. Their lives had become one with mine; the approaching parting would, I knew, be a wrench and bitter hard. My special favourites were Alexey Borovoy and Mark Mrachny, the first because of his brilliant mind and gracious personality, the other for his sparkling vitality, ready wit, and understanding of human frailty. It was hardest for me to leave them behind; and of course also our dear Manya and Vassily. To ease the pangs of parting, our dear friends kept assuring us that by leaving our tragic Russia we should be aiding them, for we could do much more for the country abroad than in Russia, work for a better understanding of the chasm between the Revolution and the régime and for the political victims in Soviet prisons and concentration camps. They were certain our voices would be heard in western Europe and America to good advantage, and they were glad we were leaving. They pretended a gay mood to cheer us at our farewell party.

Belo-Ostrov, January 19, 1920. O radiant dream, O burning faith! O *Matushka Rossiya,* reborn in the travail of the Revolution, purged by it from hate and strife, liberated for true humanity and embracing all. I will dedicate myself to you, O Russia!

In the train, December 1, 1921! My dreams crushed, my faith broken, my heart like a stone. *Matushka Rossiya* bleeding from a thousand wounds, her soil strewn with the dead.

I clutch the bar at the frozen window-pane and grit my teeth to suppress my sobs.

# CHAPTER LIII

RIGA! JOSTLING CROWDS AT THE STATION, STRANGE SPEECH, laughter, and glaring lights. It was bewildering and it aggravated my feverish condition from the bad cold I had contracted on the way. We planned to go to our comrade Tsvetkov, who was employed in the Soviet transport department. He and his lovely wife Maryussa had been our close friends in the early Petrograd days. Little Maryussa, delicate as a lily, together with Tsvetkov and others, had guarded Petrograd against General Yudenich. Rifle over shoulder, brave Maryussa had been prepared to lay down her life for the Revolution. Later they had endured untold privation and hardships, which undermined Maryussa's health, and finally she succumbed to typhus. Both she and Tsvetkov were of sterling quality. He remained unchanged in his ideas, notwithstanding that he was compelled to earn his living in the employ of the Bolshevik régime. I knew he would bid us a hearty welcome. Still, I shrank from renewed contact with what I had left behind. Nor was I in a condition to meet people and argue the questions I had definitely settled for myself. I needed a rest and I wanted to forget — to shut out the nightmare behind me and not to have to think of the void before me. We considered it inadvisable to go to a hotel: we would arouse too much attention and we were particularly anxious to avoid newspaper men. At Tsvetkov's we could live quietly.

Our first thought was to prepare a manifesto setting forth the appalling conditions of the politicals in the Communist State and urging the anarchist press in Europe and America to help save them from a slow death. It was our desperate cry after twenty-one months of forced silence, the initial step of fulfilling the pledge given our people to make known to the world the colossal fraud wrapped in the Red mantle of " October."

News from Germany was reassuring. Our comrades were working to secure our admission and they were confident of success. But they needed a little more time and therefore we must get our Latvian visa extended for a few days. The few days dragged into three weeks. Owing to our persistency, the visas were renewed, but only in driblets. We would have to get out of their country, the local authorities informed us, go anywhere or back to Russia, where we belonged " as Bolsheviks." The officials were almost without exception mere youths. Their new statehood had evidently gone to their heads like suddenly acquired riches. They were " climbers," coarse and arrogant, overbearing to the point of disgust.

A ray of hope broke at last through our dark sky. " All is settled," our Berlin comrades notified us. The German Consul in Riga had been given instructions to issue the necessary visa. We hastened to the Consulate. It was all right about our visa, we were told there, but our application must first be sent on to Berlin. Within three days we would receive them.

In high spirits our boys again went to the Consulate, confident of securing the visas this time. When they returned, I knew the result without a word being spoken. Our application was refused.

Again it was necessary to procure a prolongation of our stay in Latvia. The sullen youngsters in office demurred, but finally permitted us another forty-eight hours. At the expiration of that time we must leave, they insisted, whether we procured any visa by then or not. " You'll go back to your own country," they declared peremptorily. Our country? Where was it? The war had destroyed the ancient right of asylum, and Bolshevism had turned Russia into a prison. We could not return even there. Nor would we if we could. We'll go to Lithuania, we thought, and we should have really gone there if we had not missed the train on our arrival in Riga.

Our friend Tsvetkov would not hear of it. Lithuania was a trap, he declared. It would be impossible for us to get to Germany from there, nor could we return to Riga again. He would arrange a *sub rosa* route. He knew some freighters whose crews were syndicalists, and he would manage the matter. But could Emma stand being stowed away? I bristled at the implication that I could stand less than the boys. " But your cough — it will give you all away! " he retorted. I protested vigorously. To escape my feminine indignation our friend left to establish the necessary connexions. But his scheme proved a bubble — luckily for us all. For on the following day, the last we could remain in Latvia, came Swedish visas that our syndicalist comrades in Stockholm had obtained. Mr. Branting, the Socialist Prime Minister, had proved more decent than his German comrades.

Accompanied by Tsvetkov and Mrs. C., Secretary Shakol's sister, who had befriended us and supplied us with a large lunch-basket for the journey, we went to the railroad station to board the train which was to take us to Reval. As it pulled out, we heaved a deep sigh of relief. For a while, at least, our visa troubles were over! But the train was barely out of the sight of our friends when we discovered that we had an escort with us. It proved to be three Latvian secret-service men. They demanded our passports, which they immediately confiscated, declaring that we were all under arrest. In vain were our protests against the sudden interruption of our journey, when they could have arrested us during our stay in Riga. The train was stopped and we were taken off, bag and baggage, bundled into an already waiting automobile, and driven by a roundabout route to the city. The car came to a halt before a large brick building, and great was our astonishment when, some feet distant, we recognized the house where we had occupied rooms in the apartment of Tsvetkov. It was the Political Police Department and we could not help laughing at the manœuvres of the authorities to " catch " us when all the time we had been so close at hand.

One by one we were taken into an inner office and examined about our " Bolshevism." I informed the official that, though I was not a Bolshevik, I refused to discuss the subject with him. He evidently realized that it was useless to threaten or coax me, and he ordered me taken to another room, for later disposition.

The room was filled with officials, sitting about, talking, apparently with nothing to do. I had a book with me, and as in the olden days in my adopted country — how far away and long ago it seemed now! — I was soon lost in reading. I did not even notice that the men had left and I was alone. Another hour passed and there was still no sign of my two companions. I grew somewhat uneasy, though I was not alarmed. I knew that Sasha was seasoned in handling difficult situations, and Schapiro was also no novice in such matters. He had had previous experience with the police. During the war, as editor of the London Yiddish weekly, the *Arbeiter Freund,* he had taken over the editorial duties of Rudolf Rocker, who had been interned. Before

long he was arrested and had to serve six months for an article someone else had written. He was a man of discretion and cool-headed. I
felt confident that whatever might happen to my two friends or to
me, we should at least have a chance for a fight. It would reach the
outside world and would thus serve our ideas.

Someone broke in on my reflections. A large policewoman stood
before me. She came to search me, she announced. " Really? " I remarked; " the three hours I was waiting here were more than enough
time to destroy any evidence of the conspiracy the police suspect us
of." Her stolidity was not affected by my raillery. She proceeded to
search me to the skin. But when she attempted to go further, I slapped
her face. She dashed out of the room vowing she would bring men to
finish the job. I dressed in order to receive the gentlemen without
shocking their modesty. Only one came, who invited me to follow him
to my cell, which he locked upon me. He was an obliging chap. Silently
he pointed to the adjoining cells, indicating that my two friends were
there. That was a pleasant surprise and gave me great relief. I was
in solitary confinement, yet I had not felt so free and at peace for the
past twenty-one months. I had ceased to be an automaton. I had regained my will. I was back where I had been in the past — in the
fight. And my comrades were near me, separated only by a wall.
Great peace came over me, contentment and sleep.

On the second day I was taken downstairs for examination. A youth
in his twenties was my inquisitor. He demanded to know about our
secret Bolshevik mission in Europe, why we had stayed in Riga so
long, with whom we had associated, and what had become of the
important documents he knew we had smuggled into the country. I
assured him he still had much to learn to achieve fame and fortune as
an interrogator of such an experienced criminal as he had before him.
I would not take him into my confidence, I told him, even if I had
any information that he might want. I would divulge, however, that
I was an anarchist not a Bolshevik. As he did not seem to know the
difference, I promised him some anarchist literature, which I would
forward to him after leaving the country. He might exchange information and tell me why we had been arrested and on what charge.

He would within a few days, he promised. Strange to say, he kept
his word. The day before Christmas he came to my cell to inform me
that " it was an unfortunate mistake." I started at the familiar phrase.
" Yes, an unfortunate mistake," he repeated, " and the fault is with

your friends the Bolsheviki, not my Government's." I scorned his insinuation. " The Soviet Government gave us passports and permitted us to depart. What interest could it have 'to land us all in your jail? " I demanded. " I cannot reveal State secrets," he replied, " but it is true, just the same." We would find out later that this was no idle talk. By right we should be immediately released, he added, but there were some formalities to attend to, and all the superior officials had already left for their holidays. I assured him it did not matter. I had spent more than the birthday of Jesus in prison, and that was, after all, the place where the Nazarene would now find himself if he happened to visit our Christian world. The man was duly scandalized, as behooved a prospective State prosecutor.

The guard did my Christmas shopping for me, bringing me fruit, nuts, cake, coffee, and a can of evaporated milk. Luxuries they were, but I was anxious to prepare a Christmas feast for my friends in the adjoining cells. In return for a tip the old guard's heart softened and he permitted me the use of the kitchen situated on the same floor. I took my time and found excuses for going back and forth to my cell, humming all the time: " Christ has risen, rejoice, ye heathen! " and finding a chance to whisper a few words to my invisible companions. Two neatly wrapped packages and a large thermos bottle of steaming coffee were carried by the guard to the two desperadoes next door in return for a little Christmas gift to his family.

We were finally released with profuse apologies. My friends related their experiences to me. They had also been searched to the skin, the lining of their coats ripped open, and the bottoms of their suit-cases torn out for the secret documents we were supposed to have brought out with us. It had been a real burlesque to watch the eager faces of the guards gradually turn to baffled disappointment. Sasha, old jail-bird that he was, had managed to signal at night with lighted matches to a young fellow who sat reading in a house opposite. He threw out notes to the man, one of which the latter picked up, and Sasha hoped it might reach our friends in the city. Schapiro had repeatedly tried to get in touch with me by tapping. I had answered, but he could not make me out. " Nor I you, old man," I confessed. " Next time we'll agree on the key." Even if I could not understand his good old Russian prison signals, he added, I somehow always managed to start a cuisine. " She loves to cook, and even prison can't stop her," Sasha interposed.

At last, on January 2, 1922, we departed from Reval, Esthonia. To avoid a repetition of our Riga adventure we went directly to the steamer, though the boat was not to leave until the following morning. We made good use of the free day to see the quaint town, much older and more picturesque than Riga.

Our reception in Stockholm was fortunately unofficial. Neither soldiers nor workers were ordered out to meet us with music and speeches, as on our arrival in Belo-Ostrov. Just a few comrades genuinely glad to see us. Our good chaperons were Albert and Elise Jensen, who steered us safely past the shoals of American newspaper men. Not that I was averse to greeting my enemies who had been so eager to lie about my doings in Russia. But I preferred not to be misquoted on the Soviet experiment until I had a chance to express my thoughts over my own signature. With the Stockholm *Arbetaren,* our daily syndicalist publication, and the *Brand,* an anarchist weekly, open to us to have our say, there was no need to be interviewed by reporters, and we were all grateful to our friends for saving us from falling into their hands.

Letters from Berlin explained the sudden change of heart on the part of the German Consul in Riga after he had led us to believe that the visa would be issued to us. He had been warned by a Chekist that we were dangerous conspirators on a secret mission to the Anarchist Congress in Berlin. This also shed a light on the insistence of the Lettish officials that " our friends the Bolsheviks " had been behind our trouble in Riga. The Latvian Government had known of our presence in Riga, and the repeated extensions of our stay had been registered with the local police. They would have hardly waited with our arrest till we were leaving the country, except that they were at the last moment supplied by the Soviet emissary with the same information he had given the German Consul in Riga. Our examiners everywhere stressed our alleged possession of secret documents. Their exceptionally thorough search also tended to indicate that our good friends in the Kremlin had denounced us.

I realized with a shock what strong hold the Bolshevik superstition still had on me. Well knowing the nature of the beast, I had yet protested vehemently against the insinuations of the Lettish officials in regard to the Soviet people in Moscow. Notwithstanding my two years' daily experience of Bolshevik political depravity, I was yet unable to credit such Jesuitism on their part — to give us passports and at the same time make it impossible for us to enter any other country. I fully understood now the significance of Litvinov's assurance that " the capitalistic countries will not be anxious to have you." But why, then, did they let us go out of Russia, I wondered. My companions said that the reason was obvious. To refuse us permission to leave would have caused too much protest abroad, as in the case of Peter Kropotkin. He had in fact never attempted to leave Russia, but the mere rumour that he had not been permitted to do so had aroused the entire revolutionary and liberal world abroad and rained endless inquiries on the Kremlin. Moscow evidently did not want to invite a similar uproar again. Our arrest in Russia would have caused undesirable publicity. On the other hand, the Cheka, aware of our stand on the dictatorship and of our part in the protest of the foreign delegates in regard to the Taganka hunger-strike, could not leave us at large much longer. The best solution of the situation was therefore to permit us to depart. It was better policy to appear magnanimous and do the dirty work against us outside the territory of the R.S.F.S.R. This was also the view expressed by our Berlin correspondents. The German Consul in Riga had communicated to his uncle Paul Kampfmeier, the well-known Social Democrat, the rôle played by the Bolshevik Chekist in the matter.

Our Swedish anarchists and anarcho-syndicalists were certain we could remain in their country as long as we pleased. We might as well live there as anywhere else and carry out our plan of writing about our Russian experiences. The *Arbetaren* was anxious for articles from us, as was also the *Brand*. But Sasha as well as I felt that America, our old home, had first claim on us. It had been our field of activity for over thirty years. For good or evil we were known there and we could reach a wider audience than in Sweden or in any other country. We agreed, however, to be interviewed for the *Arbetaren* and the *Brand* and to write appeals in them for the politicals imprisoned and exiled in Russia.

No sooner had our first article appeared in the *Arbetaren* than Mr. Branting had his secretary notify the Syndicalist Committee that had obtained our visa to Sweden that " it was inadvisable for the Russians to appear in print." Branting was a Social Democrat and was opposed to the Bolsheviki. But he was also Prime Minister, and Sweden was at the time discussing the recognition of the Russian Government. An additional reason was the bid the Bolsheviki were making for a united front with the Social Democrats, whom but yesterday they had been denouncing as social traitors and counter-revolutionists. Moreover, the reactionary press started a campaign of denunciation against Branting for having given asylum to anarchists and Bolsheviks. The latter charge referred to Angelica Balabanoff, who was then in Sweden. We were informed that another extension of one month had been given us, but at the expiration of that time we would be expected to shake the dust of Sweden off our revolutionary feet. Poor Branting seemed anxious to quiet the storm against him by securing our departure as soon as possible. He would not drive us out, of course, his secretary assured our people, but we should try at once to find some other country for our abode.

Comrades in half a dozen lands were working hard to secure asylum for us. Our Berlin friends kept up their strenuous efforts. In Austria our old comrade Dr. Max Nettlau was exerting himself in our behalf. In Czechoslovakia others were working to obtain visas. Also in France. The smaller countries were hopeless, Denmark and Norway having already signified to our comrades that there was " nothing doing."

The situation was rather desperate, made more so by several other circumstances. The cost of living in a Stockholm hotel had bankrupted us within a month. The hospitable Jensens invited me to share their two-room apartment, which I accepted in the belief that it would be only for a short time. Sasha had found a room with a Swedish family whose place was too small even for themselves. He regretted that we had not followed his original plan of going by the Minsk route. It had been stupid to ask Moscow for passports. At any rate, he would not apply for a visa any more and he was determined to leave without giving notice and to enter without permission. I could do as I pleased, he declared.

There was something else that had come between us — the question whether I should or should not permit the New York *World* to publish my series of articles on Soviet Russia. Stella had cabled me that the *World* was eager for the story of my Russian experience. I had already been informed to the same effect in Riga by a *World* representative. In fact, he told me his paper had tried to reach me several times while I was still in Moscow. If I had been informed about it there and even if I could have safely sent out an article from R.S.F.S.R., I should have declined to write for a capitalist paper on

so vital an issue as Russia. I was just as loath to consider the offer
that came through Stella. I wrote her that I preferred to have my
say in the liberal and labour press in the United States, and that I
should be willing to have them publish my articles without any pay
rather than have them appear in the New York *World* or similar
publications.

Stella tried the *Freeman* with an article on the martyrdom of
Maria Spiridonovna. It was declined. The other American liberal
papers showed equal illiberality. I realized that in addition to being
stamped an Ishmaelite I should also be gagged on the question of the
Bolsheviki. I had kept silent long enough. I had witnessed the slaughter of the Revolution and had heard its death-rattle. I had weighed
the evidence that was daily being added to the mountain of Bolshevik
crimes. I had seen the collapse of the last vestige of revolutionary pretence of the dictatorship. And all I had done during the two years was
to beat my chest and cry: " I have sinned, sinned." In America I had
presumed to write *The Truth about the Bolsheviki* and to uphold and
defend them in the sincere and ignorant belief that they were the
protagonists of the Revolution. Now that I knew the truth, was I to
be forced to slay it and keep silent? No, I must protest. I must cry
out against the gigantic deception posing as truth and justice.

This I told Sasha and Schapiro. They also were determined to
speak out, and, indeed, Sasha had already written a series of articles
dealing with various phases of the Bolshevik régime, and they
were being published in the anarchist press. But both he and Schapiro
emphasized that the workers would not credit my story if published
in a capitalist paper like the New York *World*. I did not mind Schapiro's objection because he was of the old sectarian school that had
always frowned on the idea of anarchists' writing for *bourgeois* publications, though nearly all of our leading comrades had done so.
But Sasha knew that the bulk of workers, particularly in the United
States, read nothing but the capitalist papers. It was they whom he
wanted to enlighten on the difference between the Revolution and Bolshevism. His attitude hurt me very much and we argued for days.
I had repeatedly written for the New York *World* in the past, as well
as for other similar publications. Was it not more important how and
what one said than where? Sasha insisted that it did not apply in this
case. Anything I might write in the capitalist press would inevitably
be used by the reactionaries against Russia and I would justly be

censured for it by our own comrades. I was well aware of it. Had I
not myself condemned the old revolutionist Breshkovskaya for speaking under the auspices of *bourgeois* sponsors? Nothing my comrades
would say against me could be so lacerating as the compunction I
suffered for having sat in judgment over *Babushka*. Fifty years of her
life had gone into the preparation of the Revolution, only to see it
exploited by the Communist Party for its political aims. She had
witnessed the great *débâcle* while I had been thousands of miles away.
And I had added my stone to the pile hurled against her when
she had been in America. For that very reason I must speak out
now. But Sasha urged that we could do so by means of pamphlets
that our people would circulate. He had several of them in preparation; a number of his articles had already appeared in our press;
three of them had also been published in the New York *Call,* the
Socialist daily. Why could I not do the same? The comrades of the
International Aid Federation in the United States were also urging
similar means for my presentation of the Russian situation. They had
cabled and written, stressing that I refrain from writing for the
capitalist press. Their main point was that it would hurt the cause.
Their condemnation left me cold. But it was different with Sasha.
He was my lifelong comrade in arms, my friend and fellow fighter in
a hundred battles that had scorched our beings and tested our souls.
We had gone our separate ways while in Russia regarding the question of " revolutionary necessity." There had been no break between
us, however, because I also had been uncertain for a long time in my
stand. Kronstadt had cleared our minds and had brought us closer
again. It was harrowing now to have to take a position so divergent
from my friend's attitude. Days and weeks went into the conflict, the
hardest life had allotted me. All through the spiritual torture it beat
against my brain: I must, I would be heard, even if it should be for
the last time. Finally I cabled to Stella to turn over the articles, seven
in all, to the New York *World.*

In my decision I was spared the bitterness of complete isolation.
Our Grand Old Man Enrico Malatesta, Max Nettlau, Rudolf Rocker,
the London *Freedom* group, Albert and Elise Jensen, Harry Kelly,
and several other friends and comrades whose opinion I valued expressed their approval of my stand. I should have walked the way of
Golgotha in any event. But it was balm to have their support.

I was too far away to witness the fury my articles aroused in the

Communist ranks or to be affected by their poisonous venom. But from the descriptions sent me about Communist meetings against me and from their press I could see the similarity between their blood-lust and that of Southern whites at Negro lynchings. One such occasion must have been most edifying: the gathering presided over by Rose Pastor Stokes. Once she had sat at E.G.'s feet — now she was calling for volunteers to burn E.G., at least in effigy. What a picture! The chairlady intoning the *International*, and the audience holding hands in an orgiastic dance round the flames licking Emma Goldman's body to the tune of the liberating song.

The stereotyped accusation that I had forsworn my revolutionary past, by people who had no past to forswear, was also nothing to worry about. What did trouble me was that the New York *World* had not rated my literary value as highly as did my Communist admirers. It had paid me a paltry three hundred dollars for each article, or twenty-one hundred dollars for the series of seven. And it was being heralded by the Communist chorus that thirty thousand dollars had been paid to the traitor E.G. I was wishing it were true! I might have saved at least some portion of it for the Russian political victims who were suffering cold, hunger, and despair in the prisons and exile of the Bolshevik paradise.

Under pressure from the Swedish syndicalists Branting had extended permission for us to stay for another month. It was to be the last. Visas to other countries were not in sight, and Sasha and Schapiro decided to take matters into their own hands. The latter soon left and Sasha was to go next. A comrade in Prague had secured a visa for me to Czechoslovakia and I implored Sasha to allow our friend to do the same for him. But the mere suggestion of it aroused his wrath.

Sasha stowed away on a tramp steamer, but before the boat pulled out of Stockholm word reached me from the Austrian Consulate that a visa had been granted us. Sick with fear that the boat might leave before I should have the visa in my hands, I did not care if the chauffeur broke all speed limits. I found the visa ready for all three of us, but with it a demand of the Austrian Minister for Foreign Affairs that we give a written pledge not to engage in any political activities in his country. I had no intention of doing so, and I was confident that neither of the boys would consent to it. However, I could not disclose the clandestine departure of the one and the impending going of the other. I would consult my comrades, I told the Consul, and return with the answer the next day. It was not altogether a lie, as I still had time to reach Sasha. A blizzard had descended on the city, and the boat was held up for forty-eight hours. It afforded me the chance to send word to Sasha about the Austrian visa and the string attached to it. I did not expect him to accept it, but I felt he should be informed about it. A young Swedish friend, the one comforting association of my dismal sojourn in Stockholm, brought back word that Sasha had decided on his course and would not be swerved from it. I hovered about the neighbourhood of the wharf in the deep snow to be near our stowaway, whom fate had woven into the very texture of my life.

A week after Sasha's departure I also decided on a *sub rosa* route. Accompanied by my young companion, I travelled to the southern part of Sweden in the hope of finding there means to be smuggled over to Denmark. Some sailors my friend knew had agreed to aid me for three hundred kronen, equal to about a hundred dollars. At the last moment they demanded double the amount. I was not impressed with their reliability and we dropped the scheme. We found a man with a motor boat. We were instructed to get aboard before midnight, the "lady to lie flat and covered with a blanket until the inspector had made his rounds." I did. It was not the inspector, however. It was a policeman. We explained that we were lovers and destitute, and we had taken refuge on the boat. He was a kindly man, but he wanted to arrest us just the same, until a generous tip changed his mind. I could not help laughing at our impromptu story, for it really expressed the situation.

My friend was crestfallen at the way things were bungled. I consoled him by saying that I had always been a bum conspirator and that I was glad the scheme had failed. It had certain advantages, however — did it not give me a chance to see a warmer part of Sweden and more attractive women than the capital, and — not the least — forty new varieties of hors-d'œuvre that would inspire the most fastidious gourmet.

Upon my return to Stockholm the next day, I found a letter from the German Consul. A visa for ten days had been granted me.

# CHAPTER LIV

AT THE GERMAN BORDER I FELL RIGHT INTO THE LOVING ARMS of two stalwart Prussian officials whose Kaiser Wilhelm moustaches had lost nothing of pride by the ignominious retreat of their namesake. Quickly they led me into a private office. I was confronted with a dossier comprising all the events of my life, almost from my cradle days, whereupon they began grilling me for an hour. I congratulated them on their German thoroughness in having kept such a complete record that there was nothing I could add. What were my intentions in Germany? Honourable, of course: to find a millionaire old bachelor in search of a handsome young wife. At the expiration of my visa I would proceed to Czechoslovakia on the same quest. "*Ein verflixtes Frauenzimmer*" they roared, and after a further exchange of compliments I was escorted back to the train.

Five months after our comrades had begun the campaign to enable me to enter Germany, I landed in Berlin, with no more hope that I should be more successful than they in securing a longer stay. I accepted Czechoslovakia as a last resort — a place of exile. I had no connexions or friends there; the comrade who had helped to secure my visa was about to leave the country. I knew I should be cut off from everybody I cared about. Moreover, the cost of living was high. But in Germany I was on familiar ground: its language was my mother tongue. Whatever schooling I had received was in that country, and my early influences were German. Most important, there was a strong anarchist and anarcho-syndicalist movement in which I might take root. My friends Milly and Rudolf Rocker and many other dear comrades were also in Berlin. I would try my luck there, and, should I have to leave, it would not be without a fight!

Much to everybody's surprise, the Foreign Office made no difficulties about granting me a month's stay. At its expiration I was informed that two more months had been secured for me, and that I was to call at the Foreign Office. I found the Secretary engaged with a man who looked like a Russian. The latter was evidently leaving for his native land; the Secretary was seeing him to the door and impressing upon his visitor not to forget to bring back caviar and *ein Pelz*. Then the official turned on me with good old Prussian politeness. What did I mean by coming back, he shouted, after he had told me I should have to leave at the end of the month? My time would be up tomorrow, he said, and I'd have to go or I should be forcibly put across the border. His changed manner made me think that Moscow and its Berlin satraps were again at my heels. The man who had just left was probably a Chekist.

However, I could not afford to lose my temper. I explained in as ladylike a tone as I could under the circumstances that another two months had been granted me and that I came to have my passport stamped for that. He knew nothing about it and he would not give me the extension if he did know, he declared. I had better leave the country quietly or be kicked out. In that case, I replied, he would have to send several men to carry me out. I left him confounded by my *Frechheit* and went to the Reichstag in search of my sponsors. They kept me waiting three hours, too busy with affairs of State to see me. I was in a disturbed state of mind, but soon I forgot my troubles in watching the antics of what Johann Most used to call "the House of Marionettes."

Judging by the continuous stream of deputies to the refreshment rooms, the latter seemed to be the real seat of the august body. There, amid quantities of *Stullen, Seidels* of beer, and gusts of cigar-smoke, the weal and woe of the German masses was being decided. In the legislative hall someone was talking against time, no doubt to hold the fort till his political group should have recouped themselves sufficiently to knock the other on the head. It was an entertainment I should have been sorry to miss.

The day's hard work over, my sponsors turned to me. After listening to my account of the interview at the Foreign Office, they took up the telephone. A rather warm argument followed, in the course of which the party at the other end was told that he would be reported to his chief for " suppressing the extension issued to Frau E. G. Kerschner." The threat seemed to be effective as indicated by " Well, then — we knew you'd be sensible." The following morning my passport was stamped for another two months' stay.

With this respite, I decided on a little apartment. I had been driven about so much that I felt bruised in every bone and I was in need of a rest under my own roof. I wanted some peace to collect my thoughts before beginning my book on Russia. I longed for my flaxen-haired, blue-eyed Swedish boy, whose tender devotion had been my mainstay in the three and a half months of my existence in Stockholm. I'd send for him and have two months of personal life in a lifetime that had never been my own. Vain hope! I realized it the moment I met my friend at the station. His fine eyes had not lost their friendliness, but the glow that had rekindled my soul was no longer there. They had come to see what I had known from the start, yet did not wish to realize — that he was twenty-nine and I fifty-three.

Would that the adventure had ended at its height, a golden memory on my thorny road! But his eagerness to rejoin me, and my own heart-hunger had been hard to resist. " Berlin soon! " had been our parting word. Only four weeks had passed since, and his flame had burned out. I was too staggered by the unexpected blow to think clearly and I clung to the straw that I might reawaken the love that had been mine.

There were various reasons why I could not tell him to go. He had avoided conscription and he had aroused the suspicion of the Stockholm police because of his attempt to help Sasha with some papers. He had no means and he would not be permitted to work in Germany. I felt I could not send him away. What if his love had died? Our friendship would still be sweet — my affection for him strong enough to be content with that, I reasoned. The rest and joy I had hoped for were turned into eight months of purgatory.

My misery was increased by Sasha's lack of sympathy with my struggle, the more surprising because he had been kind and solicitous when I fought against the growing infatuation for my friend. He had ridiculed the silly conventions regarding difference in age, and advised me to follow my desire for the youth who had come into my life. Sasha was fond of the boy, and as for the latter, he worshipped my old chum. But my young Swede's arrival in Berlin and his presence in the same apartment somehow changed their former fine comradeship into silent antagonism. I knew they did not mean to hurt me, and yet in their male short-sightedness they did nothing else.

I was in no state of mind for writing a book on Russia. The thought of that unfortunate country and of its political martyrs was ever present with me and I felt I was betraying their trust. I was doing nothing to make their condition and the even more poignant drama of " October " known. I tried to salve my conscience by a contribution I made from the sums earned by my articles and from the brochure the London group had published at my expense. Sasha was doing splendid work, writing articles and issuing pamphlets on *The Russian Tragedy, The Communist Party, Kronstadt,* and related subjects. Our Taganka deportees were now also in Germany and they were making themselves heard in the anarchist press and on the platform regarding the Soviet reality. And even before our voices were raised, our able comrades Rudolf Rocker and Augustin Souchy had been enlightening the German workers on the true conditions in Russia.

Through Herbert Swope, of the New York *World,* and Albert Boni, Clinton P. Brainard, then president of Harper's, became interested in my planned work on Russia. He proved a jovial old man, a breezy Westerner, expansive in manner and conversation; but he did not seem to have the slightest idea of books and their relation to their authors. " Six months for a book on the Soviets! " he exclaimed. " Nonsense! You ought to be able to dictate it right off the bat in a month." " Your name and the subject will make the book, not its literary quality," he asserted. He would bet anything that a volume by Emma Goldman on the Bolsheviki, with an introduction by Herbert Hoover, would prove the greatest thriller of the day. " Why, it means a fortune for you! Did you ever expect that, E.G.? " " No, never in all my life," I admitted, wondering whether he was joking or so incredibly ignorant of my life, my ideas, the importance of Russia to me, or why I wanted to write about it. I felt that Mr. Brainard was so naïve, so like the average American mind, that I could not take offence at his suggestion of Mr. Hoover, another perfect average American, to introduce my poor book to the world.

I expressed surprise to Albert Boni that anyone so limited as the president of Harper's should be at the head of a publishing house of quality and reputation. He explained that Mr. Brainard's domain was business and not the literary department, which was some relief.

I had had no experience with publishers, our books in America having always been issued by ourselves through the *Mother Earth* Publishing Association. Albert Boni, representing Brainard and the McClure Newspaper Syndicate, did not find it necessary to enlighten me on their commercial methods. The result was that I sold to Mr. Brainard the world rights to my book on Russia for $1,750 advance against the usual royalties and fifty per cent for the serial rights. It seemed a very satisfactory arrangement to me, the most gratifying provision in the agreement being that nothing could be changed in my manuscript without my knowledge and consent.

My visa was renewed for another two months and the hope held out that I could have further extensions. My living-expenses were now also secured. I could proceed with my book. I had lived with it since Kronstadt and had worked it out in all its aspects. But when I came to write it, I was overwhelmed by the magnitude of my subject. The Russian Revolution, greater and more profound than the French, as Peter had rightly said — could I do it justice in one volume and in the limited time set? Years were needed for such a work, and a far abler pen than mine to make the story as vivid and moving as its reality. Had I gained the necessary perspective and detachment to write without personal grievance or rancour against the men at the helm of the dictatorship? These doubts assailed me at my desk, gaining momentum the more I tried to concentrate on my task.

My immediate surroundings were anything but helpful. My young friend had got into the same slough as I. He had not the strength to leave, nor I to send him away. Loneliness, the yearning to be cared for in an intimate sense, made me cling to the boy. He admired me as a rebel and as a fighter; as a friend and companion I had awakened his spirit and had opened to him a new world of ideas, books, music, art. He did not want to live away from me and he needed the fellowship and understanding that he found in our relationship, he said. But the difference, the ever present difference of twenty-four years, he could not forget.

My friends Rudolf and Milly Rocker sensed the physical and mental stress I was going through. I had not seen them since 1907, when we had known each other only as comrades. During my stay in Berlin I came to appreciate and love their beautiful spirit. Rudolf was very much like my old companion Max, as understanding, tender, and generous, and not given so much to paralysing introspection. Intellectually brilliant and with a prodigious capacity for work, he was a force in the German anarchist movement and an inspiration to everyone who came in contact with him. Milly was also sensitively attuned to human suffering and unstinted in her sympathy and affection. They were a soothing help in the battle I was fighting to get control of myself. I desperately needed to begin my book.

The arrival of my beloved Stella and Ian, my baby almost as much as hers, somewhat dulled my gnawing pain. I had not seen them for three years and I had longed for their coming. One week went by in sweet harmony with my own, in reminiscences of the past, with all its joy and travail, of what is admirable and what is hateful in my adopted land.

A dissonant note soon disturbed our idyll. Stella had always kept me on a pedestal. She could not bear to see my feet of clay. She had suffered through my relation to Ben, and now again my dear one resented that her adored *Tante* should " throw herself away." My young Swede was quick to sense the disdain of my niece. He became more contrary and went out of his way to be particularly disagreeable to her.

Ian, a beautiful youngster of six, wild and unbridled as a young colt, found our apartment too small for his energies. He knew no German and he could not understand why everybody should walk as on glass because " granny's " nerves were on edge. There was wisdom from the mouth of a child. Even our baby had learned to go by years, and, fool that I was, I still felt young, reaching out hungrily for the fire of youth. Fortunately my sense of the ridiculous had not entirely forsaken me. I could still laugh at my own folly. But I could not write, or do as my Swede — run away!

He would go to the seashore for a few days, so that Stella and I could be with each other undisturbed, he said. I did not protest; I felt rather relieved. The two days lengthened into a week without a word to reassure me that all was well with him. My anxiety grew into an obsession that he had taken or lost his life. To escape the torturing thought I tried once more to start my book. As if by magic the load I had carried for months was lifted; the harrowing shadows disappeared together with the boy and my frustrations. I myself became dissolved into the picture that was taking form on the paper before me.

A storm began in the late afternoon and continued throughout the night. Thunder and lightning, followed by wind and rain, beat against the windows of my room. I wrote on, oblivious of everything except the storm in my own soul. I found release at last.

The storm outside had stopped. The air was still, the sun slowly

946 The Swede falls in love with my secretary

rising and spreading its red and gold over the sky in greeting of the new day. I wept, conscious of the eternal rebirth in nature, in the dreams of man, in his quest for freedom and beauty, in the struggle of humanity to greater heights. I felt the rebirth of my own life, to blend once more with the universal, of which I was but an infinitesimal part.

The Swede returned hale and sound. He had not written because he was trying to muster up courage to go his own way. He failed. He was drawn back by his need of me. Would I accept him again? I did, certain that he could not consume me as before. I was back in Russia now, in her triumph and defeat, my every fibre intent on re-creating the tremendous panorama I had witnessed for twenty-one months.

My dear old pal Sasha, though rarely sympathetic with my affairs of the heart, never failed me in our common activities or in his co-operation with my literary efforts. Just as soon as he saw me working in earnest, he came back with his old eagerness to help. I should have made considerable progress now but for a new disturbance.

Young people are rarely generous to each other, nor have they patience with each other's shortcomings. My secretary, an intelligent and efficient Jewish-American girl, and my young Swede could apparently not get on. They argued violently and quarrelled over every trivial matter. The strain was aggravated when the girl moved into our apartment. It was large enough, and each of us had his own room. But the two young things glared and fumed at each other every moment they were together.

Soon I discovered the truth of the German saying: *Was liebt sich, das neckt sich.* The two young people had fallen in love with each other and were fighting to distract my attention from their real feelings. They were too unsophisticated to be guilty of deliberate deception. They simply lacked the courage to speak and were perhaps afraid to hurt me. As if their frankness could have been more lacerating than my realization that their show of indifference was only a shield! At heart I had not ceased to believe that my love would rekindle his affection, so rich and abundant during our months in Stockholm.

I could not endure the silly hide-and-seek going on before my eyes. I assured them that nothing would change my affection for them, and that I wanted the girl to continue with me until the manuscript was typed, but I would ask them to find quarters of their own. It would be less wearing for the three of us.

They moved out. The girl continued to do my secretarial work, but her attitude towards me had changed. The young Swede kept coming to see me, generally in the evening, when his sweetheart was not present. She could not bear to see him with me, he said, or to be made to feel that I was his inspiration. I would always remain that, he reiterated. It was something of a consolation; still, it would be best if he stayed away altogether, I told him. I was past minding. Their love was young, and it was unkind to cause it pain. He took my advice and he did not come again until shortly before he left with the girl for America, and then only to say good-bye.

I still had the hardest part of my book to do — an Afterword that was to set forth the lessons of the Russian Revolution which our comrades and the militant masses will have to learn if future revolutions are not to be failures. I had come to realize that with all the Bolshevik mania for power they could never have so completely terrorized the Russian people if it were not inherent in mass psychology to be easily swayed. I was also convinced that the conception of revolution in our own ranks was too romantic, and that miracles cannot be expected even after capitalism shall have been abolished and the *bourgeoisie* eliminated. I knew better now and I wanted to help my comrades to a clearer understanding.

I felt that for an adequate treatment of the constructive side of revolution I myself had to get away from the phantom of the Communist State far enough for objective writing. I did not want my book to go out into the world without some definite conclusions. Yet in my state of mind I found it impossible to go into the complex problems of the subject. After weeks of conflict I decided to jot down a few thoughts, some fragments that might serve as a sketch for a larger work on the vital subject. Sasha agreed that in the light of the Russian events a thorough revision of the old conception of revolution had become imperative. He or I or both of us might undertake it later. There was no need to fret about the matter now. A book of impressions, such as mine, was no place for an analysis of theories and ideas. Rudolf also held this view. As a result of the advice of my two friends, whose judgment in such questions rarely erred, and because of my own feeling about it, I wrote a closing chapter suggesting in general outline the practical, constructive efforts during revolution.

I had reasons for a double celebration. I had regained my emotional sanity and I had completed the manuscript of " My Two Years in Russia." Sasha also had cause to be exceedingly glad. The precious diary he had kept in Russia, which had escaped the Chekists who ransacked his room because I had it hidden in mine, had been lost after it was smuggled out of Russia. While Sasha was in Minsk, a friend had taken his note-books to Germany, promising to deliver them to the Rockers. Great was our shock on learning that our Berlin friends had failed to receive the precious package. Nothing could replace the day-by-day record Sasha had kept of every incident and event during our stay in Russia. Luckily the priceless diary was discovered after many an anxious week.

Months passed after my manuscript had been mailed to the McClure Newspaper Syndicate, but no word came about its receipt. I wrote with every sailing and spent a little fortune on cables, but there was no reply. Stella and Fitzi, whom I had asked to see Brainard about it, reported that they had been told that the man had not appeared in his office since his return from Germany, and no one at the Syndicate knew anything about my manuscript. I then cabled Mr. Swope, of the New York *World,* begging him to go after the president of Harper's. I saw Garet Garrett, of the *Tribune,* while he was in Berlin and asked him to help me locate the manuscript. I gave Albert Boni no peace. All these frantic efforts brought no results. Unable to endure the worry about my book any longer, I turned the matter over to my old friend and counsellor Harry Weinberger. I was confident he would succeed in making the McClure people or Brainard give me an account.

In addition to this anxiety came the news of the frightful calamity that had happened to my Stella. She had lost the sight of her right eye. Specialists who had treated her nearly brought her to the grave by their experiments. One of them dismissed her case as a detached retina that could not be cured, and hinted at complete blindness. Germany is famous for its eye specialists and I was entirely free now to devote myself to my niece. I urged her to come to me at once. She came, a shadow of the radiant girl that had visited me the previous year. A specialist diagnosed her case as tuberculosis of the eyes and held out no hope for recovery.

Dr. Magnus Hirschfeld, whom I knew for his pioneer work in sex psychology, came to our rescue. He suggested Dr. Count Wiser, of

Bad Liebenstein, in Thüringen. He was a remarkable man, Dr. Hirschfeld said, a great diagnostician and an innovator in the treatment of eye affections. The doctor added that I should be particularly interested in Wiser because he had been proscribed and persecuted by the profession, as I had been in the political field and he himself in his humanitarian and social prophylactic work. I smiled at the idea that an aristocrat should meet with the same opposition as a social rebel or even as Dr. Hirschfeld, a Jew working to clear away the sexual prejudices of the German *Michel*. However, we were willing to try Count Wiser.

Though we had been informed about the attitude of the medical profession towards Dr. Wiser, we were rather dismayed by the circular handed us in his office when we arrived for a consultation. It was an appeal to the Medical Department of the War Ministry to have Dr. Graf Wiser suppressed on grounds of professional incompetence, quackery, and dishonesty, and it was signed by twenty-two of the foremost eye specialists of Germany. For a moment the thought came to me that there must be something wrong with Dr. Wiser to have called forth the enmity of his illustrious colleagues. Our unpleasant impression was somewhat mitigated by the fact that Wiser did not hesitate to let his patients know the professional attitude against him. He could not undertake to treat any person, he stated in a foot-note, unless assured of confidence in his method. This raised him considerably in my estimation and respect.

My first personal meeting with the proscribed doctor freed me entirely from the last doubt raised by the circular. His entire demeanour belied the accusation against him. His simplicity and sincerity were evident in every word. Though he had a line of people waiting, he took an hour and a half to examine Stella and then declined to form a definite opinion about her condition. He was certain, however, that she had neither a detached retina nor tuberculosis. He expressed the view that probable overstrain had resulted in excessive blood-pressure, causing a hæmorrhage that formed a blood clot over the optic nerve. He hoped he could treat it in such a manner that it would be absorbed in her system. Time and care would tell. Much would depend on the patient herself. His treatment was rather rigorous, and " The patience of an angel is required to keep it up," the doctor remarked, with a smile that lit up his fine features. Six hours or more of daily exercises with various lenses was a strenuous process that called for complete rest and relaxation after the ordeal. His charm and human interest convinced me that there was a beautiful personality beneath the physician who loved his profession. Every day strengthened my first impression of Dr. Wiser.

Our presence in Liebenstein brought to us many of our friends from America. Fitzi and Paula, whom we had not seen since our deportation, came for a stay. Ellen Kennan, our old Denver friend, Michael Cohn and his new wife, Henry Alsberg, Rudolf and Milly Rocker, Agnes Smedley, Chatto and comrades from England. My life had not been so replete with friendship and affection in many years. Joy over Stella's improvement filled my cup of happiness to the brim. " Queen E.G. and her court," teased Henry at the lovely surprise party my family arranged for my fifty-fourth birthday. This much life had given me: friends whose love neither faltered nor changed with the years, a treasure few possess.

Among the many birthday gifts and messages I received was also one from my faithful friend and counsellor, Harry Weinberger. It brought the good news that my manuscript had been sold by Brainard to Doubleday, Page and Company and that the book would be out in October of that year (1923). I cabled that page proofs be sent to me. The publishers replied that it would delay the issue of my book and assured me that they would keep strictly to the manuscript.

After three months' treatment by Dr. Wiser, Stella regained partial sight of her blind eye. Nor was that the only achievement of " our Graf," as we began to call him. Every day in his private clinic I had occasion to study various cases, afflictions similar to Stella's, that had been given up as hopeless and that Dr. Wiser succeeded in curing, partially or completely. I thought it incredible that anyone so skilled and eager to give relief should have been put in the pillory.

From my talks with Dr. Wiser's patients, some of whom had known him for years, I learned of the most amazing conspiracy I had ever heard of in the professional world. The statement sent to the War Ministry by the group of eye specialists was only a minor part of the dossier manufactured against the Graf. They had even gone to the extent of sending one of their worthies to spy on him. Among the accusations against him was that he was mercenary. I never knew anyone less concerned with money than Wiser. When the value of the mark was going down five times a day, he never asked a pfennig from his patients until they had finished their treatment. This in-

volved losses that caused him to close his public clinic, where the
poorest were given the same treatment and attention as those who
could afford to pay. Sixty-three years of age, in delicate health,
Dr. Wiser worked twelve hours a day, seven days a week, and tnough
he had scores of patients, he and his wife lived in the utmost fru-
gality. At the same time he freely helped everybody who came to
him, not only professionally, but from his limited means as well.

Dr. Wiser's greatest offence in the eyes of his detractors, apart
from the fact that he achieved results where they had failed, was
his reluctance to return soldiers to the front who had had their sight
impaired. In one of the many interviews I had with him, he remarked: " I know nothing about politics and I care little about it. I
only know suffering humanity, the flower of the land shot to pieces
by senseless hate. My aim, my sole interest, is to help them and instil
in them new faith in life."

Stella, having begun to show signs of strain from the three months
of daily application, Dr. Wiser ordered her to take a complete rest.
It was part of his general system to have his patients recuperate from
time to time before continuing the treatment. She was planning to
visit Munich for the approaching Wagner-Strauss festival, with the
latter conducting his own operas. Sasha, Fitzi, Paula, and Ellen were
also going and they all urged me to join them.

Bavaria being the stronghold of German jingoism, I was dubious
about the suggestion, but the girls insisted and I accompanied them.
Forty-eight hours after reaching Munich came again the familiar
knock on my door. Three men invited me to accompany them to the
*Polizei Presidium.* They were not nearly so polite as my early callers
in Berlin, but they consented to wait long enough to enable me to
apprise my friends of my arrest.

The dossier in the Munich rogues' gallery was as complete as the
one on the German border. It contained material dating back to 1892
— nearly everything I had ever written or said — all about Sasha's
activities and mine, and a complete collection of photographs. The
most surprising exhibit was a picture taken in New York by my uncle,
a photographer, in 1889. My vanity flattered at seeing myself so
young and attractive, I offered to buy a copy. The police grew quite
angry at such " flightiness " in the face of my arrest and certain deportation. After several hours inquisition I was permitted to return
to my hotel for lunch on condition that I come back again. I was

grateful for the hour with my family. My one regret was that I had heard only *Tristan and Isolde* and *Electra,* and that my subscription to the rest of the cycle would be lost.

Among the charges against me was that I had been in Bavaria in the Fall of 1893 on a secret mission. I denied the allegation because I had then been " otherwise engaged." " What was it? " they demanded. " I was taking a rest-cure at Blackwell's Island Penitentiary in New York." And I had the effrontery to admit it? Why not? I had not been there for stealing silver spoons or silk handkerchiefs. I was there for my social ideas, for the very ones for which they were about to expel me. " We know those ideas," they roared, " plotting conspiracies, bombs, killing of rulers." Were they still afraid of such trifles after the world slaughter they and their Government had helped to launch? Oh, that was for the protection of the Fatherland, but I could not be expected to understand such holy motives. I cheerfully admitted my limitations.

In the late afternoon I was sent back to the hotel with a body-guard and ordered to leave on the evening train. How to get Sasha away was my main problem. My young police escort unwittingly suggested a way. He complained that he had been on duty since early morning and now he would be unable to get back to his wife and child until he saw me leave Munich. I remarked that he could just as well turn me over to the hotel porter, who would take me to the station. He hesitated only long enough to see me pull out a five-dollar bill. The matter could be arranged, he said, if I would promise not to jump out of the train after it left the station. Reassured that I had no intention of committing suicide, he went his way.

In the hotel I held a hurried conference with the members of our party. We agreed that Sasha must get out of Munich at once, for it was certain that the police would find him if he remained another day. Fitzi, looking very ladylike in spite of her many " plots " while she had been with us in America, saw Sasha to the station. We met on the train when it was well out of Bavaria.

The police returned to the hotel the next morning in search of Alexander Berkman, and the same day Stella was expelled from the country because she was the niece of Emma Goldman. They did not bother the other girls, but the latter decided that they had had enough of Bavarian hospitality.

Stella went back to Wiser and I remained in Berlin till Fitzi's sailing. I planned to join my niece as soon as dear Fitzi should have departed. It became unnecessary, because Stella could not longer stand the separation from her son and his father. Moreover, Dr. Wiser felt anxious about her because of the threatening political situation in Germany. He knew the temper of the reactionaries in his country and he would not expose his foreign patients to it. He advised Stella to return to America, impressing upon her the necessity of the utmost precaution against exposing her sick eye. He also mapped out a system of treatment that she could continue herself until the spring, when he expected her to come back. I fought against her leaving. I dreaded some mishap — a cold, something unforeseen, that might throw her back. But there was no holding Stella any longer, and the reassurance of our *Graf* quieted my fears.

Stella had hardly left when I received a blow that staggered me. A copy of my book arrived with the last twelve chapters missing and with an entirely wrong title. As printed, the volume was an unfinished work, because the last chapters and particularly my Afterword, which represented the culminating essence of the whole, were left out. The unauthorized name was fearfully misleading: *My Disillusionment in Russia* was sure to convey to the reader that it was the Revolution that had disillusioned me rather than the pseudo-revolutionary methods of the Communist State. The title I had given my work was simply " My Two Years in Russia." The spurious title was a veritable misfit. I wrote a statement for the press, which I sent to Stella, explaining that my manuscript had been amputated, and I cabled Harry Weinberger to demand of the publishers an explanation. I wanted the sales stopped till the matter should be straightened out.

In reply, Doubleday, Page and Company cabled that they had bought from the McClure Syndicate the world rights to the twenty-four chapters in the belief that they comprised my complete story. They had also been authorized to use their own title. They had known nothing about the existence of the other chapters.

Energetic Harry Weinberger would not give up. He succeeded in inducing Doubleday, Page and Company to publish the missing chapters in a separate volume, the cost of printing to be guaranteed by us. I appealed to our comrade Michael A. Cohn to extend the loan, which he did without delay.

Meanwhile Stella had suffered a relapse. In crossing the Atlantic she had done the very thing the *Graf* had warned her against. She remained on deck during a storm without the prescribed bandage to protect her eye. On landing she was caught in the vortex of family worries, which helped to aggravate her condition. She regretted bitterly not having remained in Wiser's care, and I reproached myself for permitting her to leave when she was making such progress.

I had written a story on Wiser's work and planned to send it to the New York *World*. But it was out of the question now. My readers could not be expected to take my word that Dr. Wiser was not responsible for Stella's relapse. I decided to withhold my article until she could again come under his care. However, the story appeared after all, in the *New Review,* a magazine published in Calcutta in the English language. Agnes Smedley and Chatto, the latter having also been treated by the *Graf,* believed in the success of his new method and they wanted to make him known in India. Its publication resulted in a number of Hindus' coming to Dr. Wiser as patients. It was the only comfort in my grief over Stella's condition.

The reviews of *My Disillusionment in Russia* showed as much discernment as the representative of Doubleday, Page and Company who had bought three-quarters of a manuscript as a complete work. Among the scores of reviewers only one guessed that the book was an abortion. It was a Buffalo librarian, who pointed out in the *Journal* that Emma Goldman's narrative ended with Kiev, 1920, while in her Preface she stated that she had left Russia in December 1921. Had nothing happened in all the intervening time to impress the author? The man's perspicacity strikingly reflected on the dullness of the " critics " who presume to pass literary judgment in the United States.

The Communist response to my volume on Russia could have been foreseen, of course. William Z. Foster's " review " was to the effect that everybody in Moscow was aware that Emma Goldman was receiving support from the American Secret Service Department. Mr. Foster knew that I should not have lasted a day in Russia if the Cheka had believed such a thing. Other Communists, who wrote as kindly as Mr. Foster, also knew that I had not been bought. There was only one who had the courage to say so: René Marchand, of the French group in Moscow, who stated in his review that, though he regretted my misguided judgment, he could not believe that my stand against Soviet Russia was motivated by material reasons. I appreciated his giving me credit for my revolutionary integrity, and I wished he were brave enough to admit that he was unable to reconcile himself to some of the methods the Bolsheviki practised in the name of the Revolution. Commandeered to work in the Cheka, René Marchand had seen enough to plead for his removal, as otherwise he would be compelled to leave the Communist Party. Like many other sincere Communists he did not understand the Revolution in terms of the Cheka.

Not so Bill Haywood. As Sasha had foreseen, he easily took the Bolshevik bait. Three weeks after his arrival in Russia he wrote to America that the workers were in full control and that prostitution and drunkenness had been abolished. Lending himself to such obvious falsehoods, why should Bill not also credit me with motives he knew were absurd? "Emma Goldman did not get the soft jobs she was looking for; that was why she wrote against the Dictatorship of the Proletariat." Poor Bill! He began rolling down the precipice when he ran away to save himself from the burning house of the I.W.W. He could not stop himself in his fall.

My Communist accusers were not the only ones to cry " Crucify! " There were also some anarchist voices in the chorus. They were the very people who had fought me on Ellis Island, on the *Buford,* and the first year in Russia because I had refused to condemn the Bolsheviki before I had a chance to test their scheme.

Daily the news from Russia about the continued political persecution strengthened every fact I had described in my articles and in my book. It was understandable that Communists should close their eyes to the reality, but it was reprehensible on the part of people who called themselves anarchists to do so, especially after the treatment Mollie Steimer had received in Russia after having valiantly fought in America for the Soviet régime.

For her activities in behalf of Soviet Russia and against intervention Mollie Steimer had been railroaded by an American court to fifteen years in prison. Before she had begun her sentence in the Missouri State Prison, she had endured incredible cruelty for six months in the New York workhouse. After eighteen months in the Jefferson City Penitentiary Mollie, together with three other members of her group, had been released to be deported to Russia. Surely these young people deserved well of the Communist State. The boys, more adaptable to the new wrongs, managed to move safely among the cliffs of the dictatorship. Not so Mollie, who was of different fibre. She found the Soviet jails filled with her comrades, and, while she could not make her protest heard as she had against the crimes in the United States, she undertook to raise funds to supply food to the incarcerated anarchists in the Petrograd jails. Such counter-revolutionary work could not be tolerated on Soviet soil.

Eleven months after Mollie had come to Russia, she was arrested, charged with the heinous offence of feeding her imprisoned comrades and corresponding with Alexander Berkman and Emma Goldman. A protracted hunger-strike and the vigorous protest of the Anarcho-Syndicalist delegates to the Congress of the Red Trade Union International brought about Mollie's release, but not freedom of movement. She was forbidden to leave Petrograd, placed under Cheka surveillance, and ordered to report every forty-eight hours. Six months later Mollie's room was raided and she was again arrested. In the Cheka Mollie was grilled, kept in a filthy cell, and once more compelled to hunger-strike.

Finally Mollie was deported by the Russian Socialist Federated Soviet Republic which she had so staunchly championed in America and for which she had willingly taken fifteen years' imprisonment. Could anything express more forcibly the degeneration of the Kremlin rulers, once revolutionists themselves? Yet some anarchists censured me because I had refused to handle the Bolshevik fetish with kid gloves. The case of Mollie and of her friend Fleshin, both of whom had gone through the same persecution and suffering, would have been enough for me to brand the Moscow outfit. They came straight to us in Berlin — starved, ill, penniless, without a possibility of finding work in Germany or of being admitted to any other country. Yet their spirit was undaunted none the less. They had escaped the Bolshevik inferno. Not so thousands of other true rebels who remained in the Communist paradise. What mattered to me the condemnation and attacks of the zealots in comparison with my inability to help the Mollies and the thousands of others in prison and exile? I had done nothing for them since my arrival in Germany.

The German Revolution was only skin-deep, but it succeeded in establishing certain political liberties. Our comrades could publish their papers, issue books, and hold meetings. The Communists carried on their propaganda with little molestation, condemning in Germany the abuses they defended in Russia. The reactionary nationalist elements were also not interfered with. Their arrogance knew no bounds, equalling that of the militarists of the old Prussian régime. With two such I had an encounter in a subway train. They were railing against the *verdammte Juden* as idle vampires and the cause of the ruin of the Fatherland. I listened for a while and then remarked that they were talking nonsense. I had lived in a land where there were millions of Jewish workingmen, I told them, and many of them brave fighters for the betterment of humanity. " Where is that? " they demanded. " In America," I replied. It drew a volley of abuse from them. America had tricked Germany out of victory, they cried. As the train reached my station and I alighted, they shouted after me: " Wait till things change and we'll fix such as you just as we did Rosa Luxemburg."

Though in a desperate economic situation, Germany enjoyed considerable political freedom. That is to say, the natives. But I was not a German and consequently I had no right to express opinions. It was not a matter of mere arrest: it meant expulsion. There was apparently no other country willing to let me in, but I thought I might try Austria again. Like his tribe in other lands, the Austrian Minister for Foreign Affairs signified his readiness to admit me, but on condition that I abstain from all political activity. Naturally I refused.

My friends Rudolf and Milly Rocker favoured one of the two ways out of my dilemma: the legalization in Germany by marriage, or England. The first method had been a frequent practice among the Russian intelligentsia and revolutionists in the days when women had no political status apart from their husbands or fathers. In Germany Rosa Luxemburg had contracted such a nominal marriage to enable her to remain in the country and follow her work. Why couldn't I do the same? I, they said, should go through with the ridiculous ceremony and end my troubles. Such a step had long before been suggested in America. Several comrades had been willing to sacrifice themselves for the cause, among them my old friend Harry Kelly. It would have prevented the United States from deporting me, Milly reiterated. But I had been unable to do the ludicrous and inconsistent thing, having opposed the institution of marriage all my life. Moreover, there had been the lure of Russia, the glowing dream. That too was dead now, together with the notion that one could remain on earth without making compromises.

My difficulties in Sweden and other countries made me amenable to the suggestion of marriage in order to gain a foothold now in some corner of the world. Harry Kelly was still ready to keep his promise.

On his visit to Sweden he had again offered to take me back to America as his bride. Good old scout! He had been unaware of the new law by which an American husband was no longer a protection for his foreign-born wife.

No such law existed in Germany, Rudolf informed me, and I might as well give some man a chance to make a " respectable woman " of me! If not that, then I should go to Great Britain. It was still politically the freest country. He himself would go back there if he could. He had deeper roots in England than in his native land, having lived and worked in that country nearly as long as Sasha and I had in America. He could understand why I felt alien everywhere and why I did not want to be bound to Germany. I would probably never be content anywhere, cut off from my old moorings. The next best was England.

I was dubious. It did not seem possible that Great Britain had escaped the reaction following upon the war any more than had other countries; still, it might be worth trying. My present position was insupportable. The only public meeting I had addressed in behalf of the Russian politicals brought me an official warning against expressing any further criticism of the Soviet Republic.

Another difficulty was how to earn my living by my pen. The German press was out of the question; too many native writers were starving. At the same time America's hatred of Germany was still strong. Two articles I had sent the New York *World* were refused. One treated of Gerhart Hauptmann in connexion with his sixtieth anniversary, celebrated on a national scale. The *World* had cabled its consent to my going to Breslau, where the main festivities were taking place, but declined my article on the ground that it was " too high-brow." My second essay was on the Ruhr occupation, with its resulting bitterness and suffering. A third article, on the experimental new schools in Germany, and a fourth on the foremost women in German art, letters, and labour, were returned by a dozen magazines. I had not the least chance of earning my salt by writing on German topics. From Brainard, who had broken our agreement and botched my book, there was no hope of any income.

England did not appear very enticing. Still, it might afford me asylum with comparative political freedom, and perhaps also an opportunity to earn my livelihood through lectures and articles. Frank Harris was in Berlin, keeping open house. His interest and kindness, as when I was in the Missouri prison, had not changed. It would be quite easy to get me to England, he said. He knew almost everyone in the Labour Government and he would try for a visa for me. Soon after, Frank left for France, and several months passed before I heard from him again. He informed me that the Home Office had asked no questions about my political views or intentions. It had merely inquired whether I had means of support. Frank had replied that I was an able writer who earned my living by my pen. Moreover, he could name a dozen persons who would consider it a privilege to support his friend and he was one of them. Shortly afterwards I was notified by the British Consulate in Berlin that a visa had been granted me.

Except for the parting from Sasha and from the other friends who had endeared themselves to me, I had no regrets on leaving Germany. Vicissitudes of many kinds, not the least the death of my mother in America, had not brought me cheer and joy. Enforced inactivity embittered even the occasional hours of tranquillity during my stay of twenty-seven months. Sasha had finished his *The Bolshevik Myth;* he was in good health, had acquired a circle of friends, and was devoting himself to the work of aid for the revolutionary politicals in prison and exile in Russia. For the rest, I was glad to get away. England might let me take root, offer an outlet for my energies, respond to an appeal for the doomed and damned in the Soviet land. That was worth going to England for; it was a new hope to cling to.

With this thought to give me courage, I left Germany on July 24, 1924, via Holland and France, for England.

My Dutch visa permitted a stay of only three days, yet long enough to address the twentieth anniversary celebration of the Anti-Militarist Society, organized by our grand champion of peace, our old comrade, Domela Nieuwenhuis. Dutch secret-service men watched the house of my host, de Ligt. They followed us to the station and waited until my train pulled out. At the same time the Dutch Government was entertaining another visitor, a Soviet representative. No limit was put on his stay, nor were his movements shadowed. When I expressed surprise that a reactionary government like that of Holland should offer hospitality to an emissary of the Communist State, my friends smiled. " Russia is a wheat-producing country and Rotterdam a good centre for the distribution of her exports," they explained.

My French transit visa was for two weeks. The inspector at the border insisted that it did not permit me to stop and ordered me to connect immediately with the boat train for England. I refused to budge. After a long parley, greased by American cash, I was allowed to proceed.

The two weeks in Paris, the city I love best in Europe, were enjoyable in the company of friends from America. There were Paula, who had come from Berlin, Harry Weinberger, little Dorothy Miller, Frank and Nellie Harris, and many others, some of whom I had not seen in five years.

" Two weeks! " objected Weinberger; " I'll get you an extension for a month at least."

" How can you — an unknown person here? " I retorted.

" Unknown — me? And coming straight from the Lawyers' Congress, received by the King of England, and presented to the President of the French Republic? " Harry protested indignantly. " You wait and see."

Dressed in morning clothes, wearing a top hat, with ribbons on his coat, Harry presented himself with me at Quai d'Orsay. His client, Madame Kerschner, had come from Germany, he announced, to confer with him on important business matters that would take at least a month. One look at Harry's regalia, and the extension was granted.

" Unknown? " said Harry triumphantly. " Say it again if you dare." I was as meek as a lamb.

In appreciation I offered to chaperon him through Paris. In the same group with my friend were several of his colleagues. The one I liked best was Arthur Leonard Ross. He was of the rare type that one gets to consider in a short time as a good friend.

My dear old friends were thinning out. I had been more fortunate in my friendships than most people, and I gained new ones, among them Nellie Harris, Frank's wife. I had never met her before; it was love at first sight on my part, and Nellie seemed to like me also. Frank continued to be eternally young; at sixty-eight he could still run twelve blocks for exercise after an elaborate meal and enough drink to make most men unsteady. Wine only made him more witty and sparkling. What if he loomed largest in his own estimation? So do most people whose gifts are not nearly so brilliant as his. He was extremely entertaining with the stories of the people he had known in every clime and station in life, from bricklayers, cowboys, and statesmen to the geniuses of art and letters. Frank was an extremist in his loves and hates. If he cared for you, no praise was too generous; if he disliked you, he saw you all black. His enemies, real or imaginary, had no redeeming qualities. Often he was unfair and unjust and we gave and took many verbal blows from each other.

My stay in Paris served to increase my aversion to going to London. I dreaded its fogs, bleakness and chill. Frank urged me to delay no longer. He expected the Labour Government to be defeated in the coming elections; the Tories would probably ignore my visa. To encourage me he enlarged on the many interesting people I should meet there who would welcome me and help in my contemplated campaign in behalf of the Russian politicals, as well as in my lectures on the drama and literature.

Helpful as ever was Frank, but he could not make London's autumn and winter attractive to me. Perhaps if I could secure a return visa to France, I might find England less irksome. Harry Weinberger had sailed and most of the people I knew in Paris lacked the necessary connexions to help me to a return visa.

My meeting with Ernest Hemingway held out some hope. It was at a party given by Ford Madox Ford. The affair might have been duller had not Hemingway been there. He reminded me of both Jack London and John Reed because of his simplicity and exuberance of spirit. He invited me to dinner together with a newspaper friend of his who, Hemingway believed, could secure a French visa for me. Ernest, in his rôle as proud father of a buxom baby, looked younger and was gayer in his home setting. His journalist friend did not impress me, nor could he do anything about a visa, though he had promised much. Instead he wrote a silly story about me, purporting to be an interview on Russia, not one word of which was true.

# CHAPTER LV

ONE IS CERTAIN TO BE DISAPPOINTED IN AMERICAN REPORTERS, YET never in the London weather during autumn or winter. It was foggy and drizzling when I arrived in September, and it did not let up until May. Unlike my visit in 1900, when I lived in a basement, my quarters this time were on the heights: a bedroom on the third floor in the house of my old friend Doris Zhook. I even had the luxury of a gas-stove, which I kept going all day. The monster fog mocked my futile attempts to keep the chill out of my old bones, even when I tried to snatch a little cheer from an occasional ray of sunlight. Doris and the other comrades insisted that it was " not really cold." American steam-heated apartments had spoiled me for the " mild British climate," they said. They would not have their homes centrally heated if they could. Fire-places were " more sensible, more healthful, and pleasanter." I told my friends that I had been away from America five years and had forgotten its material blessings. I had been in Archangel when the temperature was fifty below zero and I had not felt so chilly. Poetic fancy, they teased. If the damp makes one miserable, it produces good complexions, rich foliage, and the strength of the British Empire. Delicate skins, the luscious green lawns and meadows, are due to the weather, and the need to escape from his own climate has made the Englishman foremost among globe-trotters and colonizers.

I soon realized that physical handicaps would be the least of my difficulties. The anarchists of London were my friends of many years, solicitous and willing to assist in anything I wanted to do. They were the remnant of the old guard of the pre-war groups, including John Turner, Doris Zhook, her brother William Wess, Tom Keell, and William C. Owen, a former co-worker of mine in America. But they were divided among themselves. Tom Keell, the publisher of *Free-*

*dom,* and Owen, its editor, had kept the paper alive in spite of all vicissitudes. But there was no real movement in London or in the provinces, I soon learned. Coming as I did from the seething anarchist activities in Berlin, the situation in England was depressing. The general political conditions were worse than I had anticipated. The war had created greater havoc with traditional British liberalism and the right of asylum than it had in other lands. Getting into the country was extremely difficult for anyone of advanced social ideas. More difficult to remain if one engaged in socio-political propaganda. The Labour Government was expelling people on as slight pretexts as had the Tories before. My comrades thought it extraordinary that I should have been granted a visa, and expressed doubt that I would be allowed to remain long if I became politically active. The anti-alien laws had almost destroyed the Yiddish anarchist movement, as everyone active in the East End feared expulsion at any time. The disruption in radical ranks brought about by the nefarious methods of Moscow served to strengthen the hands of reaction. In former days the liberal and radical groups used to take a common stand against every encroachment on political freedom and in opposition to economic injustice. Now they were all at each other's throats over the question of Russia.

The older rebels were disillusioned by the collapse of the Revolution. The younger generation, as far as it was at all interested in ideas (which was little enough), was carried away by the Bolshevik glamour. Communist intrigue and denunciation were doing the rest to widen the chasm.

It was a disheartening picture. But I was in England and I did not propose to run away, notwithstanding the odds against me. My comrades agreed that my name and knowledge of Russian conditions might rally the radical and Labour factions to the support of the political victims of the dictatorship. They were certain that my presence in England would be a stimulus to our own comrades. I did not feel sanguine about the situation. I did not know how to reach the British people, and the only suggestion I could make was a dinner at some restaurant as my début before the London liberal public. My comrades were elated over the idea, and set to work.

My note to Rebecca West brought a kind of reply and an invitation to lunch. I was pleasantly surprised to find her anything but English in her manner. But for her speech I should have thought her

an Oriental, she was so vivacious, eager, charming, direct. Her friendliness, the cosiness of her room, the hot tea, were grateful after a
long, cold ride in the drab autumn afternoon. She had not read my
writings, she frankly admitted, but she knew enough about me to
add her welcome to that of the others and she would be happy to
speak at the dinner. She would also arrange an evening to have her
friends meet me. I was not to hesitate to call on her for anything
I might need. I left my hostess with the comforting feeling that I had
found a friend, an oasis in the desert London seemed to me.

The day of the dinner began in darkness and ended in a downpour.
I went to the restaurant with a sinking heart. Doris tried to reassure
me that no one in England minded the weather; I was known and
would draw a crowd. " Scotland Yard, the newspapers, and perhaps
a few persons acquainted with American liberal thought," I retorted.
There was no use to deceive ourselves; I should not set England
afire. " An incurable pessimist," my friend laughed; she could not
understand how I had kept up the struggle for so many years. Poor
Doris nearly collapsed when we reached the hotel. There wasn't
a baker's dozen present at seven o'clock. But at eight she walked on
air; two hundred and fifty people had crowded into the dining-room,
and additional tables had to be laid for guests who continued to
come, even after the speeches had begun. I was profoundly moved
that so many should venture out on such a night to welcome me.

The spirit of the evening, the messages of greeting from Havelock
Ellis, Edward Carpenter, H. G. Wells, Lady Warwick, Israel Zang-
will, and Henry Salt, and the beautiful tributes paid to my past
efforts by Colonel Josiah C. Wedgwood, our chairman, by Rebecca
West, and by Bertrand Russell completely swept me off my feet.
Surely the hospitality and generosity shown political refugees in
England, often described to me by Peter Kropotkin, were not dead.
I should at last find my sphere of action. With a feeling of gratitude
I began my address on the purpose of my coming to England and
the things I wanted to do. I have rarely had a more attentive audience until I mentioned Russia. Shifting of chairs, turning of necks,
and disapproval on the faces before me were the first indications
that all was not going to be so harmonious as it seemed at first.
I went on with my speech. It was important that the main reason
for my presence in England should be clear to everyone. I reminded
my hearers of the Russian Revolution of 1905 and the horrors that

followed it. It was my illustrious comrade Peter Kropotkin, then living in England, who had aroused the conscience of the radical and liberal world to protest against the frightful persecution of politicals. His "*J'accuse!*" was taken up in the House of Commons, and it succeeded in checking the autocracy. "You will be shocked to learn that a similar situation exists in Russia today," I said. "The new rulers are continuing the old terror. Alas! There is no Kropotkin to indict them at the bar of humanity." I did not feel, I continued, the equal of my great teacher in brain or personality, but I was determined to do all I could to make known the fearful state of affairs in Russia. With whatever ability and voice I possessed I would cry out my "*J'accuse!*" against the Soviet autocracy responsible for political persecution, executions, and savage brutality.

The applause was interrupted by loud protests. Some diners jumped to their feet and demanded the floor. They never would have believed, they said, that the arch-rebel Emma Goldman would ally herself with the Tories against the Workers' Republic. They would not have broken bread with me had they known that I had gone back on my revolutionary past. It was growing late. The evening meant too much to me to have it end in a row. We were planning a meeting in Queen's Hall, I informed the audience, and there we all should have opportunity to discuss the matter in detail.

The reports of the dinner in the London daily press were copious and fair. Only the *Herald* was evasive about my talk, though it printed a short paragraph about the other speeches. I was informed that its editors, George Lansbury and Hamilton Fife, were indignant at my "breach of faith." They had added their names to that of George Slocombe, who had assured the Home Office that my sole purpose in coming to England was to do research work in the British Museum. I explained to my friends that Mr. Slocombe was the man through whom Frank Harris had got permission for me to enter England. Neither Harris nor I had authorized him to make any pledges on my behalf. As to the gentlemen of the *Herald,* their share in helping secure a visa for me was news to me. I did not know Mr. Fife. Mr. Lansbury I had met in Russia, and from what I knew of his attitude to the Communist State it would have never occurred to me to ask favours of him. But I could understand Mr. Lansbury's chagrin over my intended campaign to shed light on the Russian situation. The author of the statement that the teachings of Jesus had been realized in Russia could not afford to be made ridiculous.

My conviction that governmental scene-shifting does not alter the economic situation of the masses had not changed. The Socialists in power, including those of Great Britain, had strengthened my attitude on the question of the State. Nowhere had they helped to improve the life of the worker. I was certain that Mr. MacDonald would do no more during his second term than he had in his first. But there was one matter of utmost importance that the Labour Government could accomplish: recognition of the Soviet Government. I was vitally interested in that, because I knew it would remove the halo of martyrdom from the brow of the Communist State. The international proletariat would then realize that the Soviet Government was of the same clay as the others. I therefore decided not to talk about Russia during the campaign.

Now it was over and my speeches could not affect the fate of the Independent Labour Party. It was its own incompetence in dealing with the poverty and distress of the country while still in office that defeated it. I felt free to write for *The Times* and the London *Daily News* the articles they had requested. It was not only that I had financially reached bottom, but mainly because we needed funds for our mass meeting in Queen's Hall. The British anarchists were too poor to contribute more than a few shillings, and so far no one of means had volunteered to aid. I was glad to earn forty pounds and at the same time speak to a wider public.

Owing to the elections and the approaching holidays, our meeting had to be postponed till January. My friends insisted that the backing of a numerous committee was indispensable to the moral success of our undertaking. I chafed at the delay and resented the idea of a committee. I told my friends of the large birth-control meetings my co-worker Ben Reitman had managed with just a few comrades to assist him; the big demonstrations Sasha had organized and our antiwar protests. We had had no prominent support. Why was it necessary in London? In America Sasha and I were well known, but it was different in England, my friends replied. Here people moved in a herd, at the direction of their shepherd, and this applied alike to party organizations, societies, and clubs. We must have backing to reach the public ear. They agreed with what Rebecca West had told me about free-lance lecture work. " It is not done in England," she had said. London audiences paid admission to lectures only for charitable purposes.

In my public career I had been affiliated with groups only temporarily. I worked for them, not with them. Whatever value my activities had in America was due to my free-lancing and independent position. My London friends urged that my first large public appearance must have the proper support. The dinner had already called attention to my presence in London and to my purpose. The meeting would pave my way for further efforts. After all, they knew best how to reach the British public, and I was willing to follow their advice.

For two weeks I bombarded with letters every name on the list of the prospective committee, but the response was negligible. Most of them did not even reply. Others gave evasive reasons why they could not serve. Mr. Zangwill wrote that, owing to poor health, he had given up all public participation; besides, he did not believe that a committee of known Labour people would do me the slightest good. I might approach the Society for Democratic Control, of which both he and Bertrand Russell were members. He could suggest nothing more. He was sorry I had had to go to Russia to find out what he had known all along: that the Moscow dictatorship was tyranny.

Havelock Ellis sent a kindly note. While he was certain of the sincerity of my motives, he feared my criticism of Russia would give comfort to the reactionaries. They had never protested against the tsarist autocracy and he had no patience with their opposition to Bolshevism, which was only " inverted tsarism." At any rate he did not like committee functions.

The venerable Mrs. Cobden-Sanderson, an old friend of the Kropotkins, who had co-operated with them against the political persecutions of the tsarist régime, Lady Warwick, Bertrand Russell, and Professor Harold Laski invited me to come to them for a talk.

Two persons consented to be on our committee without any reservations: Rebecca West and Colonel Josiah Wedgwood. Edward Carpenter wrote that because of age he could not venture out in the evening, but he was ready to back my efforts, which, he was confident, stood for freedom and justice.

Rebecca West had already given me considerable help. At her home I had met her colleagues on the feminist publication *Time and Tide* — Lady Rhonnda, Mrs. Archdale, and Rebecca's sister, Dr. Letitia Fairfield, as well as a number of others interested in the women politicals in Russia. My circle of acquaintance kept enlarging, and invitations to luncheons, teas, and dinners began to pour in. Everyone was most hospitable, attentive, and cordial — all very pleasant if I had come to England for social entertainment only. But I had come for a purpose. I wanted to arouse the sensibilities of fair-minded Englishmen to the purgatory of Russia, to stir them to a concerted protest against the horrors parading as Socialism and Revolution. It was not that my hosts and their friends were not interested or that they questioned the facts I presented. It was their remoteness from the Russian reality, their lukewarmness to conditions they could not visualize and hence did not feel.

The Labour leaders were callous. In the words of a British Socialist, " It would spell political disaster to my party to declare to its constituents that the Bolsheviks had slain the Revolution." Mr. Clifford Allen, secretary of the Independent Labour Party, declared that " Emma Goldman is an old-time Christian, still believing in the Truth and speaking it out." The most important issue was trade with Russia, he asserted. I had met Mr. Allen in Petrograd, in 1920, when he had come with the British Labour Mission, for which Sasha had acted as interpreter in Moscow. Both of us had been impressed by Allen's independent and idealistic personality. It was somewhat of a shock to discover that in his official capacity he would allow considerations of business to loom higher than human values. I admitted that I was not a shopkeeper, but I believed enough in liberty to let his party be one. Yet I failed to see the connexion between " trade with Russia " and acquiescence in the criminal doings of the Cheka. England had traded with the Romanovs, but liberty-loving Englishmen had often protested against the horrors of the tsars, not merely by words, but by deeds. Why should it be different now? Had the British sense of justice and humanity been shell-shocked that they could remain deaf to the desperate cry of thousands in Soviet dungeons? Did I mean to compare the rule of the Tsar with that of the Bolsheviki? Politically their régime was worse, I told my hearers, its tyranny more irresponsible and Draconic. The Soviet Government was proletarian, after all, and its ultimate aim socialism, Mr. Allen expostulated. He did not approve of all the methods of the dictatorship, but neither he nor his party could afford to join a campaign against it. Most of the others shared his view.

Among the scores of people I met, very few showed such kindly concern as Lady Warwick. I had experienced so many setbacks and disappointments that I clung to the hope that her interest in Russia was vital and that she could be depended on to induce her comrades to join our committee, or at least do so herself. But presently Lady Warwick informed me that it would be necessary to postpone the conference arranged to meet at her house because she had been requested by the Labour men to await the return from Russia of the British Trade Union Delegation. She seemed to be very much afraid that any move on her part might bring back the Tsar. Apparently she continued in that fear, for I never heard from her again.

When I first called on Professor Harold Laski, he expressed the opinion that I ought to take some comfort in the vindication anarchism had received by the Bolsheviki. I agreed, adding that not only their régime, but their stepbrothers as well, the Socialists in power in other countries, had demonstrated the failure of the Marxian State better than any anarchist argument. Living proof was always more convincing than theory. Naturally I did not regret the Socialist failure, but I could not rejoice in it in the face of the Russian tragedy. If I could at least arouse the labour and radical elements! So far I had made no progress. Outside of Rebecca West and Colonel Wedgwood I had found no one who really cared about the woe of Russia. In America I had never met such lack of response to any appeal. Laski thought I would find even the most radical elements reluctant to oppose the Bolsheviki. They were too enthusiastic about the Revolution to draw lines of demarcation. In time I might interest the labour ranks. He would do his best to aid me; he would invite his friends for the next Sunday afternoon to hear my story. Once more hope sprang from what seemed a hopeless and futile quest.

It was impossible for me to speak dispassionately about Russia, but on this occasion I sought to suppress all personal feeling. I spoke in a conversational tone and as objectively as I could. At the conclusion of my talk most of my questioners demanded whether I could point out " any political group more liberal than the Bolsheviki, more efficient for establishing a democratic government should the Soviet régime be overthrown." I replied that I did not want the Communist State overthrown, nor would I aid any group that attempted such a *coup.* Fundamental changes were not made by parties, but by the awakened consciousness of the masses. That had happened in March and October 1917 and would happen again, though probably not in the near future. The dictatorship had discredited all social ideals, and the people were exhausted by years of civil strife. It would require a long time to rekindle their revolutionary fire. I was not interested in a change of rulers in Russia, but I was vitally concerned in the plight of the political victims of the Kremlin autocrats. I believed that strong radical opinion in the United States and Europe would affect the Soviet government as it had that of the Romanovs. It might help to curb their despotism, stop persecution for mere opinion, convictions without trial, and wholesale executions in the cellars of the Cheka. Were not these simple human demands worth trying for? " Yes, but it might lead to the return of autocracy."

The same evasions and objections, the same faint-heartedness, I came across in every group I addressed. It was appalling. At last realizing the futility of my efforts, I resolved not to waste more time on the élite, the Labour politicians, or the ladies dabbling in socialism. Anarchists had always carried on their work without so-called respectable backing and they would have to do so now. Better small meetings under our own auspices and without obligation to anyone than the support of the *bourgeois* world. The dozen members of our little group agreed to go ahead in any way I should suggest, and they procured South Place Institute for our meeting. They reminded me that many a brave voice had pleaded from that platform for freedom and justice. I recollected that I had spoken there in 1900, during the Boer War, under the chairmanship of Tom Mann. Many scenes had been shifted since. Mann was in the bosom of the new church and I was still proscribed by both sides, the capitalist and the Communist.

Professor Laski notified me that his friends were of the opinion that the I.L.P. should abstain from attacking Soviet Russia. He added that Bertrand Russell, though he disliked the Soviet methods, doubted the advisability of my propaganda. Others were convinced that I was more anxious to attack the Bolsheviki than to obtain redress for the politicals; they would not support such an outspoken opponent of Russia. Some held that action must come from the Trade Union Delegation and not from non-English sources. Professor Laski concluded by stating that the Labour leaders would do nothing that might involve them in a controversy with the Soviets. On the whole he agreed with Bertrand Russell that a campaign in behalf of the politicals must not be under anti-Bolshevik auspices " such as yours."

Bertrand Russell's stand was a disappointment to me. I had seen him and talked with him at length. While he had not promised to act on the proposed committee, saying he would have to think the matter over, he had shown no indication that he did not care to affiliate himself with an avowed anarchist. It was rather discouraging to find the brilliant critic of the State, the man whose spiritual attitude was anarchistic, fight shy of co-operation with an anarchist. And Laski, too, the bold exponent of individualism!

The Trade Union Delegation returned from Russia on fire with the wonders they had seen — rather, had been shown! They waxed enthusiastic in the *Daily Herald* and at meetings about the splendid Soviet achievements. They had spent all of six weeks in Russia; could one speak with greater knowledge and authority?

If I failed to arouse the Britishers, I succeeded in impressing a few Americans in England, most of them Rhodes scholars, who invited me to address them. My visit to Oxford was quite an event, not only on account of the splendid meeting the boys had arranged in spite of opposition from the "Coolidge gang," but also because of the hospitality and generous aid given me by Professor S. E. Morison, of the American History Department, and by the dozen young chaps, the most thoughtful and wide-awake of the group, who became my ardent friends. This at least I had gained after four months of effort. The genuine interest and the sincere desire to help of such new friends as David Soskice, the well-known Russian revolutionist and one-time editor of *Free Russia,* of Mrs. Soskice, the writer and sister of Ford Madox Ford, as well as their two vivid boys, was a most satisfying recompense.

Thanks to the faithful and energetic work of my comrades, among them Doris Zhook, William Wess, A. Sugg, Tom Keell, and William C. Owen, our South Place Institute meeting was crowded, notwithstanding the downpour and the admission charged. The tact of our chairman, Colonel Josiah Wedgwood, my American student friends, some "real" proletarians to keep order, and my usual sang-froid on the platform saved the situation.

We had reason to rejoice over our success. Without backing, either moral or financial, we covered the expenses of our meeting and had some surplus left to send to the Berlin Fund for political prisoners. With Tom Sweetlove as treasurer, and A. Sugg, as secretary, the committee was launched as a permanent body for systematic activity. Though numerically small, it had ambitious aims: a series of lectures on Russia, the circulation of the *Bulletin* of the Joint Committee for the Defense of the Imprisoned Revolutionists in Russia, published in the English language in Berlin under Sasha's editorship, and the raising of funds. The *Bulletin* contained accurate information and data on political persecution, as well as letters from the incarcerated and exiled which Sasha and other members of the Joint Committee were receiving *sub rosa* from Russia.

Our main trouble was that I found myself between two fires. I had no hope of a hearing by the Independent Labour Party or in the trade unions; neither would I speak under the auspices of the Tories. From the latter I received a number of invitations to lecture on Russia, but I had to decline because I learned that they were exclusive Conservative clubs. Another came from the Woman's Guild of the Empire in Paisley. I inquired about its political character and was informed that it stood for " God, King, and Country." I wrote to the Guild that as an anarchist I repudiated social arrangements which raised some to the throne and condemned others to pauperism. I did not discriminate against any audience, whatever its social, political, or religious beliefs; in the United States I had lectured before the most diversified crowds — longshoremen and millionaires, poor working and professional women; in halls behind saloons and in drawing-rooms, in mines hundreds of feet below the ground, from pulpits and soap-boxes. From our own platform I should be willing to treat the subject of Russia, no matter who came to hear me. On any other topic I should be willing to talk in the House of Lords, in Windsor Castle, or before the Conservative Party. But not on Russia.

I doubted that our committee could succeed with independent meetings in reaching the general public. The members were not dismayed. They would experiment with English lectures, and the *Arbeiter Freund* group volunteered to organize Yiddish meetings in the East End. Thus encouraged, I started my weekly rounds from one end of London to the other, in rain, sleet, fog, and chill, for three months. Not even in my pioneer days in the United States had I found it quite so bitter to break new ground as I did in this venture. The result was hardly worth the effort, though the committee insisted that it was. Expenses were covered, some money was added to the Political Prisoners' Fund, and conditions under the Communist State were made known to hundreds of people.

My tour through the north of England and south Wales was

little to boast of. The Welsh people were impressionable and easily aroused, but not always dependable, John Turner had once told me. After the English icicles I had tried to melt, I welcomed the Welsh crowds and their enthusiasm. The difficulty was not the indifference of the workers, but their dreadful poverty. Many had been unemployed for a long time, and those who were fortunate enough to have jobs earned the barest pittance. The amazing thing was that people living in such bleakness should come to meetings at all; it seemed extraordinary that they could muster up enough sympathy in their suffering brothers in far-away Russia. The pale, pinched faces of these toilers made me painfully aware of my own position. Like all missionaries I was appealing for " charity for China " when help was so desperately needed at home. If I could at least enter their lives, share in their struggles, show them that anarchism alone has the key that can transform society and secure their well-being, my begging would have some justification.

Already in London after my first lectures I had begun to chafe under my compulsory silence on the frightful economic conditions in England. The social wrongs in Great Britain could of course in no way justify similar evils in Russia. Nor did I feel it just to talk about the dictatorship and ignore the situation close at hand. This feeling was constantly increasing and adding to my inner struggle. I could not go on much longer with my anti-Soviet activities without voicing my stand on the general social question. That opportunity denied me in England, as indeed everywhere else, I should have to stop discussing the Bolshevik State. I could not close my eyes to the fact that I owed my asylum to my attitude on Russia — a doubtful and uncomfortable hospitality, which I could not accept indefinitely. My comrades urged me to remain for my work. I had no reason to feel that I must not appeal for the imprisoned revolutionists in Russia because I could not take part in the social struggle in England, they argued. I was the first anarchist returned from the Soviet country to explain in Great Britain the relation of the Bolsheviki to the Revolution; such knowledge was vital everywhere, but nowhere more so than in England, where many of the labour leaders were emissaries of Moscow. This applied particularly to south Wales, where certain officials of the Miners' Federation were espousing the miracle of the Communist State. The simple trust and faith of my comrades was deeply touching. Proletarian from infancy, their lives barren of beauty and joy, they clung to their ideal as the sole hope of a new and free world. Typical of them was James Colton, who at the age of sixty-five was still compelled to slave in the mines for his daily bread. He had given the greater part of his life to active service in our ranks, and with much pride he told me that, like myself, he had become an anarchist as a result of the judicial murder of our Chicago martyrs. With no chance for an education, he had picked up much knowledge and a clear understanding of social problems. He devoted his native ability as a speaker to the cause and he contributed to the propagation of anarchism from his meagre earnings. The comrades in his group, younger men with families to support, were carried along by " Jimmy's " energy and inspired by his love and consecration to the ideal.

The Trade Union Report on Russia, signed by all the delegates, including John Turner, proved a complete whitewash of the Soviet régime. The ground it covered would have required several years' study, extensive travel, and a long stay in the country. The Labour delegates had been in Russia six weeks, more than a week of which was spent in trains, as John told me. Obviously their report could not represent the personal knowledge and observation of its authors. As a matter of fact, it was a compilation of the documents specially prepared for them by the authorities. Inasmuch as most of the delegates had been pro-Soviet before coming to Russia, it was quite natural that they should swallow the whole Bolshevik bait. Their interpreters, one of them a naval attaché of the British Embassy in the tsarist days, another in the diplomatic service for a long time, were past masters in mustering official data to good effect. They had winked at the old autocracy in the interests of their Government, and now, as adherents of the I.L.P., they had also to do considerable winking. That was their profession and I had no quarrel with them. But I was shocked to see John Turner sign the report. The more so because his article in *Foreign Affairs,* the interview he gave to a representative of the New York *Forward,* as well as his talk at our meeting, flatly contradicted the pæans of the report. I wrote him frankly how he had disappointed me and the other comrades. He replied in almost the identical phrase Lansbury had used to Sasha in 1920 : he could show me " any number of poor, destitute and starved in London." I failed to see the connexion between the misery in England and the statement in the report that the Russian toilers, though politically bound, were economically free and contented. Turner and his co-delegates knew that this was no more true regarding the masses in Russia than in reference to the British workers. It was imperative to unmask the deception. I suggested to our committee a reply and I was instructed to prepare it, with the help of Doris Zhook. The brochure we issued compared the statements in the report with quotations from the Soviet press during the visit of the British delegates. It contained no comments whatever, as we were willing to let the Bolsheviki themselves disprove the extravagant claims of the report. The Communists immediately charged us with using material from the forged *Izvestia* and *Pravda*, allegedly published by counter-revolutionists abroad. It was absurdly silly, but it was sad to see even so good an insurgent as Colonel Josiah Wedgwood change front. He wrote me that he would take no responsibility for the pamphlet and requested that his name be taken off the committee. Wedgwood, like most of the others, including even my comrade John Turner, moved in a groove and lacked the independence to stand out against the Communist rooters.

The one exception in these ranks was Rebecca West, who did not permit her affiliations to influence her attitude or curtail her freedom of action. Though extremely occupied with her own work, she nevertheless found time to interest her friends in my efforts, to put me in touch with a literary agent who might place *My Disillusionment in Russia* with a British publisher, to write a preface for it, and to preside at one of my lectures. But, then, Rebecca West is an artist, not a politician.

Mr. C. W. Daniel was another unfettered spirit; a publisher, he did not consider trade the all-embracing issue of life. He cared more for the ideas and literary quality of works he was issuing than for the money they might bring him. Was he, too, an old-fashioned Christian to prefer truth to business, I inquired, adding that I was charged with that offence. I admitted that it was naïve of me to expect more from the I.L.P. than from any other political party. I had always known that, like the beasts, they never change their natures, however much they may shed their skins. Alas, one grows older but not wiser or I should not have been so shocked to find radicals argue the life and death of thousands in terms of commerce. On closer acquaintance Mr. Daniel did not prove wiser than I, even if younger. He undertook to publish a British edition of *My Disillusionment in Russia*, fully aware that though it might secure glory from posterity it could not bring him much trade. My book had already appeared in complete form in a Swedish edition, but it did not mean so much to me as to see my work, so atrociously bungled in America, in one volume in England, with a preface by Rebecca West.

*My Disillusionment*, the articles in the New York *World*, reprinted and circulated by the London *Freedom*, my contributions to the *Westminster Gazette* and the *Weekly News*, besides those that had appeared in the London *Times* and been syndicated in the provinces, the article in the *Daily News*, and, finally, our brochure refuting the fiction of the trade-union delegates contained a wealth of information accessible to all but the wilfully blind.

Sasha had also not been idle; his *The Bolshevik Myth* now appeared, published in New York by Boni and Liveright. But the latter had eliminated the concluding and most vital chapter as being an " anti-climax." Thereupon Sasha issued it as a brochure under that very title and circulated it at his own expense. Sheets of the book had been imported to England and the volume sold at a prohibitive price without the author's knowledge or consent, and without his receiving a cent of royalties. The reviews were splendid, the critics agreeing that *The Bolshevik Myth* was a convincing and moving work of first-rate literary merit. In addition Sasha had gathered a wealth of data and documents about political persecution under the Soviet dictatorship. He secured the stories and affidavits of numerous politicals who had escaped or been deported from Russia. Added to similar matter collected by Henry G. Alsberg and Isaac Don Levine, the whole constituted a collective indictment of Bolshevik terror overpowering in its effect. On the strength of it Alsberg and Levine procured letters of protest against the Moscow despotism by men and women of international fame, and the entire material was published in New York by the International Committee for Political Prisoners in a volume entitled *Letters from Russian Prisons*.

We kept our pledge to our suffering comrades in Russia. We made known their cause as well as that of all other persecuted revolutionists. We demonstrated the abyss between the Bolsheviki and "October." We would continue to do so, Sasha through the *Bulletin* of the Joint Committee for the Defense of Political Prisoners, and I whenever and wherever the opportunity presented itself. Now was the time for me to turn to other matters. After eight months' absorption in the Russian situation I felt justified in seeking different subjects for expression. This was especially imperative because I could not go on indefinitely accepting support from my family and American friends. I should not have been able to keep going but for such dear and devoted friends as Stewart Kerr, for instance, who never allowed a month to pass without a gift. Now that I might become self-supporting by means of lectures on the drama, I decided to discontinue my Russian work, at least for a while.

Shortly after my arrival in England Fitzi had appointed me her representative for the Provincetown Playhouse, to which she had already given years of labour and love. My credentials afforded me free access to some of the theatres, yet what I saw did not whet my appetite for further exploration of the London stage. English friends spoke highly of the Birmingham Repertory Theatre, the only outstanding group of artistic merit. It had grown out of amateur beginnings, they informed me, and it owed its first start and splendid development to the skill and generosity of its founder, Barry V. Jackson. My experience with British intellectual hospitality had made me somewhat sceptical. Opportunity to judge for myself came when the Birmingham Repertory Company opened in London with Shaw's *Cæsar and Cleopatra,* and I made haste to present my credentials as Fitzi's European ambassador. At no theatre in the British metropolis had I been received with greater courtesy. The performance proved to be a revelation. Such settings, atmosphere, and ensemble acting I had not seen since the Stanislavsky Studio days, and even there the scenery did not compare with this feast for the eyes. Cedric Hardwicke's Cæsar surpassed that of Forbes-Robertson, whom I had seen in New York. He succeeded in making the old Roman intensely human, with enough wit to laugh at himself. Miss Gwen Ffrangçon-Davies as Cleopatra was an exquisite creature. For the first time in England I was able to banish the gloom the travail of eight months had settled on my spirit.

Nearer acquaintance with Barry Jackson, Walter Peacock, Bache Matthews (Mr. Jackson's director), and several other members of the company saved me from judging the nature of a whole people by the bitter experiences I had with some groups. They knew I was a stranger struggling to gain a foothold in their country, and that was reason enough for them to offer their help. The possibility of losing votes or support and disagreement with my views on social subjects did not affect them. They were interested in the human, in a fellow-creature adrift in an alien land. They made me welcome at their theatres and put me in touch with circles that could enable me to establish myself by means of lectures on the drama.

Mr. Peacock introduced me to a number of people, among them Geoffrey Whitworth, the Honourable Secretary of the British Drama League. Mr. Matthews interested the secretary of the Birmingham Playgoers in my work, which soon brought me an engagement from that society; and Barry Jackson, one of the busiest men in London, always found time for me when I needed his kindly aid. Mr. Whitworth generously turned his entire office over to my work; the assistant secretary of the league, the library, and the list of affiliated societies were put at my disposal. Mr. Whitworth also invited me to speak at the conference of the Drama League, which was to take place in Birmingham.

In the lovely Repertory Theatre I lectured on the Russian theatre, discussing the studios, the Kamerny, and Meyerhold. The atmosphere was free from strife or rancour, the audiences were receptive, the questions keen and intelligent. Intermission brought everyone together in easy sociability that was most encouraging to me.

Too late I learned that in England it is customary for clubs and societies to arrange their lecture courses six months in advance. Still, I succeeded in securing seven engagements for the early autumn from the Playgoers in Manchester, Liverpool, Birkenhead, Bath, and Bristol. In the last city a series was also being planned by our own people. The Drama Study Circle I had organized in London was planning several lectures on the origin and development of the Russian drama, and the anarchists in the East End of London asked for the same course in Yiddish. I could look forward to a busy time doing work I had always loved.

During my early days in England, when everything seemed bleakest, Stella had written me that London was a cold beauty that required much wooing before revealing her charms. "Who cares to woo a cold beauty?" I replied. Now I had been paying court to her for nine months. Could it be that I was beginning to touch her heart?

London was really beautiful now in its profusion of green and abundance of flowers and sun, as if it would never wear mourning or weep torrents again. One begrudged every moment indoors, knowing how short-lived the glory was. But six hours every day was the very least I needed to cope with the historic treasures I discovered in the British Museum on the Russian theatre and drama. This institution had been one of my objectives in coming to England, but it was only now that I had the time, the interest, and the need for availing myself of all it offered. The longer I worked in the museum, the more information I unearthed on stage arrangement, old plays, scenery, and costumes. This led to wider fields, embracing the political and social backgrounds of the dramatists of different periods, and their correspondence that reflected their feelings and reaction to Russian life. It was a fascinating study and so absorbing as to make me forget the closing-hour. One thing became plain from the start. I could not hope to cover even a fraction of the material in six lectures, or in a dozen. An entire volume would be required. Professor Wiener, Peter Kropotkin, and others had written such works on Russian literature. It occurred to me that my drama series might serve as an introduction to a larger book to be written at some later date.

My meetings with Havelock Ellis and Edward Carpenter stood out as the fulfillment of a wish cherished for a quarter of a century. Not that I learned to know them better through our fleeting personal contact than I had through their works. I saw Ellis for a bare half-hour in his London apartment and we were both rather tongue-tied. But if I had lived near him for years, I should not have realized better the oneness of the man with his life's labours, so expressive of his unique personality and lofty vision was every line that had spoken to me out of the pages of his liberating work.

My visit with Edward Carpenter lasted the greater part of an afternoon in his modest cottage at Guildford. He was nearly eighty, frail and feeble. Alongside of his dapper companion, whom everybody addressed as George, his clothes looked shabby. But there was distinction in his carriage, and grace in every gesture. Dear Edward had little chance to be heard, for it was George who did most of the talking about the work " Edward and I " had written while they were in Spain, and the book " we're planning this summer." Patient and forbearing was Edward towards the conceit of small people, viewing it with the wisdom of the sage.

I attempted to tell him how much his books had meant to me —
*Towards Democracy, Angel Wings, Walt Whitman.* He stopped me, gently putting his hand over mine. Instead I should rather tell him about Alexander Berkman, he said. He had read his *Prison Memoirs,*

" a profound study of man's inhumanity and prison psychology, and of his own martyrdom, portrayed with extraordinary simplicity." He had always wanted to know " Sasha " and " the Girl " in the book. Havelock Ellis and Edward Carpenter! My summer was indeed enriched by these two grand seigneurs of intellect and heart.

It brought also other interesting events outside of my research work. Fitzi arrived for a brief visit, and through her I came to know Paul and Essie Robeson, as well as several of Fitzi's associates in the Provincetown Playhouse. They had come to London to put on *The Emperor Jones* with Paul Robeson. Essie was a delightful person, and Paul fascinated everyone. I first heard Robeson sing a group of spirituals at a party given by my American friend Estelle Healy. Nothing I had been told about his singing adequately expressed the moving quality of his voice. Paul was also a lovable personality, entirely free from the self-importance of the star and as natural as a child. He never refused to sing, no matter how small the circle, if the company was congenial. The Robesons liked my cooking, especially my coffee, and so we exchanged compliments. I would prepare dinner for a chosen few or arrange a party of my English friends to meet the Robesons, and Paul would hold everyone spellbound by his glorious voice.

The summer was rich, the richest in years. Now that the sunny days were drawing to an end, my friends were departing. Work I loved lay before me and I still had a stout heart. But by December there was little left of it or anything else to help face the London winter. My venture into the Playgoers' societies was quite satisfactory. Gratifying also were the Liverpool and Birkenhead organizations, because of their mixed membership. The others were purely middle-class, with no vital interest in the drama and no feeling for its social and educational value. Nevertheless the experience proved that I could establish myself with the Playgoers if I could hold out long enough to become better known in England, for a year or two. I had no means for it, nor the inclination to become an adjunct.

The independent lectures in London and Bristol again demonstrated the truth of the British saying that " it isn't done in England." The London failure was particularly disappointing because the work had started with every promise of success. Keats' House, quaintly beautiful and permeated by the genius and spirit of England's great poet, was our meeting-place; Claire Fowler Shone, our secretary, a skilful organizer and prodigious worker, widely known in labour and trade-union ranks, with a dozen friends to assist her. A review of my drama work by Rebecca West and Frank Harris circulated in thousands of copies; Barry Jackson, Geoffrey Whitworth, A. E. Filmer, and others, no strangers in the world of the drama, were announced as chairmen. Yet the attendance was small and the receipts barely covered the expenses. True, the audiences were of a high intellectual order. That and the joy of collecting my material were the only satisfaction I gained from nearly six months' effort.

I spent three weeks in Bristol with similar results. My second attempt to take root in the United Kingdom had thus also gone by the board. The fogs and wet remained faithful and wandered through my system at their own sweet will. I was laid up with chills and fever when an invitation came from my dear friends Frank and Nellie Harris to visit them in Nice.

In June I had married the old rebel James Colton. British now, I did as most natives do who can scrape up enough to escape their country's climate. The *American Mercury* had sent me a cheque for my sketch on Johann Most, so I was able to pay my fare to the south of France. The Harrises were marvellous hosts, sparing no pains to surround me with care and help restore my health and cheer. I had spent many interesting hours with Frank before, but never enough to see more than the artist, the man of the world, the interesting *causeur*. In the intimacy of his home I was able to penetrate beneath what everyone considered Frank's egotism and conceit. I found that my host knew himself much better than anyone else did. He knew the human, all too human in his make-up. He had his gnawing doubts whether he was indeed the supreme artist he proclaimed himself, whether his works would live and he be given an immortal niche. Frank was not deceived about his own foibles, however blind he might be to those of his friends or mistaken in those he looked upon as enemies. Frank Harris, when he turned himself inside out, far from lessening my affection, brought himself nearer to me. We had few ideas in common, especially on social problems. We fought often, but always in the best of feeling, for we knew that no matter how far apart we might drift, our friendship would not weaken.

My meeting with Nellie Harris in Paris the year before had shown me little of her personality, except for her obvious loveliness and charm. During my visit all her rare and exquisite qualities unfolded like a flower before me. I had met wives of creative men on previous occasions. I had seen their bitterness to their husbands' friends, their jealousy of female admirers, and well I knew how overbearing and cattish my sex can be to the wives of their idols. My sympathies were often with the wives, for it seemed martyrdom enough to be the spouse of an artist. I should have thought no less of Nellie had I found her ungenerous to the admirers of Frank. But Nellie was an angel, a large and loving spirit, incapable of harshness, and no mere reflection of her famous husband, but an individual in her own right, a keen observer of people and affairs, a better judge of human nature than dear old Frank, and more patient and understanding.

I was loath to leave my good friends, but necessary research in the Bibliothèque Nationale called me back to Paris before returning to England. I still had some engagements to fill with the Playgoers' societies in Liverpool on the little-theatre movement in America. I had addressed them before on the works of Eugene O'Neill, and a woman reporter had reviewed my " sensitive hands and gold coloured lining of the opera cloak, rather startling in an anarchist," but the Play-goers must have liked my talks, because they invited me again. I had also consented to deliver another course of lectures on Continental and American plays in a popular hall, with one-shilling admission. My comrades were sure it would bring a crowd, but on the appointed day there were no crowds. Strindberg, the German expressionists, Eugene O'Neill, and Susan Glaspell did not interest the British public when presented without the seal of an organization or party. " It isn't done in England." I was compelled to realize that a much longer period than I had thought would be necessary to break through the wall of what " isn't done." Five years, perhaps, if not more. But I did not have many more years to throw about. Meanwhile I was faced with the problem of making ends meet. Not till my deportation had I ever given a thought to this question; I had felt that as long as I could use my voice and pen, I could easily earn my living. Since then I had been haunted by the spectre of dependence, and it grew after my tour of south Wales and the provinces. I would rather take a job as a cook or housekeeper than get my living from my activities among the underpaid miners and cotton-mill workers. I could not allow them to defray my railroad fares, let alone the expenses of my lectures. The drama meetings not paying for themselves, I saw no way of continuing my work in England.

A friend had once said jokingly that I was like a cat; " drop her

out of a sixth-story window and she'll land on her paws." After the
last failure I felt as if I had indeed been thrown from the top of the
Woolworth Building. Two things brought me on my paws again. One
was my plan of a volume on " The Origin and Development of the
Russian Drama "; the other, a tour through Canada. The anarchists
there had invited me to come, and a New York comrade promised to
raise my expenses. I would go to some little place in France and devote the summer to writing and would leave for Canada in the fall.
The two ventures, I hoped, might secure me for a year or two to live
and be active in England. I made sure of my going to Canada by
immediately reserving my passage.

The incentive to devote the next four months to writing had come
from C. W. Daniel, my patron publisher. He had taken the keenest
interest in my lectures on the Russian dramatists, had sent a stenographer to take them verbatim, and held out the hope of issuing my book
in the not too distant future. Besides *My Disillusionment* he had also
published an English edition of Alexander Berkman's *Prison Memoirs
of an Anarchist,* for which Edward Carpenter had written a preface,
and he had imported sheets of *Letters from Russian Prisons,* neither
of which undertakings added much to his coffers. But it in no way discouraged him from wanting to try his luck again.

I was about to leave London when the general strike was declared.
I could not think of running away from an event of such overwhelming importance. Workers and helpers would be needed and I must
remain and offer my services. John Turner was the most likely man
to get me in touch with the people in charge of the strike. I explained
to him that I was willing to do any kind of work to aid the great
struggle: look after the relief of the strikers' families, organize the
care of their children, or take charge of feeding-stations. I wanted
to help the rank and file. John was delighted. It would dispel the
prejudice my anti-Soviet stand had created in trade-union circles and
would demonstrate that anarchists not merely theorized, but were
capable of practical work and were ready for any emergency. He
would take my message to the strike committee and put them in direct
touch with me. I waited for two days, but no word came either from
trade-union headquarters or from John. On the third day I again
made the long trip on foot to see John and to inquire about the matter.
He had been told that all help in the strike situation was drawn from
trade-union ranks, and that no outside aid was needed. The excuse

was flimsy; clearly the leaders feared it would leak out that the anarchist Emma Goldman had some connexion with the general strike. John was loath to admit my interpretation, nor could he deny that I might be right. It was the old story: the centralized machinery in every walk of British life left no room for individual initiative. It was torture to remain neutral where the line between masters and men was so sharply drawn, or to stand by idly while the leaders were making one blunder after another; nor would I leave by rail or ship manned by strike-breakers. I found some relief in being out on the streets mingling with the men and getting their reactions. Their spirit of solidarity was wonderful, their fortitude great, their disregard of the hardships the strike had already imposed admirable. No less extraordinary was their good humour and self-control in the face of provocation from the enemy: armoured cars rattling along the streets, taunts and ridicule from the young bullies in charge, and the affronts of the wealthy in their luxurious automobiles. A few encounters had taken place, but on the whole the strikers carried themselves with pride and dignity, confident of the justice of their cause. It was inspiring, but it also increased my misery at my own helplessness. On the tenth day of the strike, there still being no sign of a settlement, I decided to leave England by airplane.

## CHAPTER LVI

FRIENDS HAD UNEARTHED A LOVELY SPOT IN SAINT-TROPEZ, AN ancient, picturesque fishing-village in the south of France. An enchanted place it was: a little villa of three rooms from which one caught a view of the snow-covered Maritime Alps, with a garden of magnificent roses, pink and red geraniums, fruit-trees, and a large vineyard, all for fifteen dollars a month. Here I regained something of my old zest for life, and faith in my ability to overcome the hardships the future might hold. I divided my time between my writing-desk and my *ménage*. I even found time to learn to swim. I prepared the meals on a quaint, red-bricked Provençal stove in which only charcoal could be used. Many friends from America and other parts of the world found their way to my new home in Saint-Tropez.

Georgette Leblanc, Margaret Anderson, Peggy Guggenheim, Lawrence Vail, and many others came for an hour or a day to discuss serious matters or in jolly company. Peggy and Lawrence lived not far from us in a village called Pramousquier and there I first met Kathleen Millay and Howard Young. The latter reproached me for not writing my autobiography. " A woman of your past! " he exclaimed; " just think what you could make of it! " I would, I told him, if I could secure an income for two years, a secretary, and some-one to scour my pots and kettles. He would undertake to raise five thousand dollars on his return to America, Young promised. In honour of my prospective benefactor, Peggy added a few more bottles of wine to those already emptied at dinner.

The four months in Saint-Tropez passed all too quickly in labour and play. A golden dream, not without its rude awakening, however. Mr. Daniels informed me that conditions in England since the general strike had grown from bad to worse; there being no sign of coming improvement I should not feel bound to his firm with my manuscript on the Russian drama. That was the first ripple in my azure sky, yet not so disconcerting as the cable from the New York comrade who had promised to raise the initial fund for my Canadian tour. " It is off," he announced.

The Canadian Government had probably declared I would not be admitted, or our own people had reconsidered their invitation, I thought. But my conjectures proved false. Canada remained blissfully ignorant of the danger threatening it, and our comrades assured me they were expecting me without fail.

My sponsor was apparently afraid of the bodily harm I might meet at the hands of the Communists. His fears were not entirely groundless; Communists in New York had broken up radical meetings and had even physically attacked their opponents. The hard times would also affect the success of my lecture tour, the comrade wrote. I appreciated his good intentions to protect me and my interests, but I could not be very gracious about the right he had assumed to cancel my tour. Had this new blow come while I was yet in England, I should have thought my world at an end. But life in Saint-Tropez had restored my strength and with it my fighting spirit. I cabled three friends in the States for loans. They responded simultaneously, though they lived in different parts.

While in Paris, I lunched with Theodore Dreiser. " You must write the story of your life, E.G.," he urged; " it is the richest of any woman's of our century. Why in the name of Mike don't you do it? " I told him that Howard Young had put the question first. I had not taken it very seriously and I was not surprised that I had received no word from him, though he had been back in America several months. Dreiser protested that he was greatly interested in seeing my story given to the world. He would secure a five-thousand-dollar advance from some publisher and I would hear from him very soon. " All right, old dear, see what you can do! If you also forget or if you fail, I will not sue you for breach of promise," I laughed.

I entered Canada as unheralded as I had England two years previously. In Montreal I learned that no English anarchist had been heard in Canada for a great many years. The only active people were the Yiddish-language group, but they had no experience in organizing English lectures. My friend Isaac Don Levine had promised to help with the publicity work, but even before he reached Montreal, the newspapers announced that the dangerous anarchist Emma Goldman, masquerading under the name of Colton, had managed to get by the immigration authorities and had come to Montreal. To save the Montrealers further trepidation and to satisfy the curiosity of the press Don issued a statement setting forth how and why I had come to Canada and inviting press interviews. The telephone and door-bell of my hosts, the Zahlers, worked overtime, and the papers were lurid with the news that romance still lived in this crassly materialistic age: Emma Goldman and James Colton, a southern Welsh miner, had rediscovered their mutual affection after twenty-five years and had joined their lives in matrimony. The immigration authorities were reported to have stated that there was no intention of interfering with my presence in Canada as long as I " did not advocate bombs."

The Moscow fanatics sought to boycott my lectures by a house-to-house canvass of the radical Yiddish population. A few of the more decent and sensible Communists deprecated these tactics. They suggested a debate between Scott Nearing and myself. I should have preferred some Communist who had lived in Russia longer and knew the situation better than Mr. Nearing. Still, I was quite willing to discuss with him the question of Life under the Dictatorship. Not so Mr. Nearing. His reply was that if E.G. were dying and he could save her life, he would not go round the corner to do so.

Besides my lecture in the theatre and an address at the Eugene Debs Memorial gathering I delivered six Yiddish lectures and spoke at a banquet where several hundred dollars were subscribed for the Russian politicals. The most satisfying result of my visit in Montreal was the group of women I gathered into a permanent body to raise funds for the imprisoned revolutionists in the Communist State.

The Toronto anarchists were more numerous and better organized. They were carrying on intensive propaganda in Yiddish and exerting an influence in their community, but they sadly neglected the natives. They were eager, however, to assist me to any extent with my program of English lectures. They had done a great deal of preparatory work that promised success for my first appearance. Support came also from an unexpected quarter. I had notified the Toronto newspapers of my visit to their city, but only the *Star* showed sufficient interest to send a representative, Mr. C. R. Reade. I was amazed to find him thoroughly informed about the anarchist philosophy and familiar with its exponents and their works. He might as well be one of us, I joked. Life was difficult enough without being an adherent of such an unpopular cause or sharing its ideas with a dull world, he laughed. His understanding and friendly attitude exerted a proselyting effect on his editors. In the words of the Communists, the *Star* became an " Emma Goldman propaganda sheet." The explanation given for my " pull " with the paper was that its owner had in the past been a " philosophic " anarchist and remained hospitable to advanced ideas. But I felt that it was due mostly to Reade's good offices. Both he and Mrs. Reade became my enthusiastic sponsors. Mrs. Reade even volunteered to organize a course of my drama lectures. They were among the few kindred intellectual spirits I enjoyed during my stay in Toronto.

Dear members of my family came to visit me from the States, and it was a great joy to be within their reach, even if they had to come to me instead of my going to them. Not that the opportunity was not offered me. Various friends were eager to smuggle me across the border. With my picture in every rogues' gallery in the United States, I could not have remained there long without being recognized, and there was no object in hiding. Those of my friends and comrades who could afford it would come to see me. For the rest, I never liked sensation for its own sake. There still was a large place in my heart for my erstwhile country, regardless of her shabby treatment. My love for all that is ideal, creative, and humane in her would not die. But I should rather never see America again if I could do so only by compromising my ideas.

The expense of travel in Canada and the great distances between the larger cities decided me to go no farther than Edmonton, Alberta. Winnipeg nearly became my Waterloo. The city was extremely cold and in the throes of a grippe epidemic, to which I succumbed in the first twenty-four hours. Lack of cohesion in our ranks, badly organized meetings, and Communist obstruction at every gathering made the situation anything but a cheerful prospect. Hugging my bed by day, in a half stupor from drugs to break my cold, I managed to pull through the Sunday evening mass meeting in spite of the rough-house created by the Moscow bigots. Later I added a course of drama lectures to my schedule. The six weeks in Winnipeg, though strenuous to exhaustion, were not entirely without compensation. The alert and active young people in the *Arbeiter Ring* organization, and the girl students of the University who invited me to speak, were the saving grace of my ordeal. I also succeeded in welding together the radical women into a relief society for the imprisoned revolutionists in Russia and added some money to the fund.

Edmonton, Alberta, proved a record-breaker. I came there for two lectures. I stayed to deliver fifteen in one week, some days speaking three times. All the Jewish organizations in town and most of the Canadian labour, social, and educational groups invited me to speak. The two extremes of the variegated audiences I addressed that week were factory girls during their lunch hour in the shop and the faculties of Edmonton College and the University of Alberta at a tea arranged in one of the hotels by Mrs. H. A. Freedman, the president of the Council of Jewish Women. The extraordinary interest my presence in Edmonton aroused was entirely due to the kindly efforts of three people, none of whom was an anarchist. Mrs. Freedman was a staunch and sincere adherent of the present political order, E. Hanson was a Socialist-Nationalist, and Carl Berg was an I.W.W.

A note from Peggy Guggenheim on my return to Toronto expressed surprise that I had not answered Howard Young's letter regarding my autobiography. Had I changed my mind about permitting him to raise a fund to enable me to write the book? He was planning to proceed with it and she would open the subscription with five hundred dollars. I replied that I had never received Howard's letter, but it was all right for him to go ahead. Yet I should prefer to have my old friend W. S. Van Valkenburgh in charge of the hard work the appeal would entail. I knew that if energy and indefatigability could avail, Van was sure of success. With Peggy Guggenheim and Howard Young as my first sponsors, Kathleen Millay as the official secretary, and Van to do the heavy correspondence, the project was finally launched to secure funds for my writing the " masterpiece that would set the world afire."

Meanwhile my Toronto comrades kept on insisting that I was wanted in their midst. They had never believed that their city could respond so warmly to anarchist propaganda. They urged that I make Toronto my permanent home or that I remain there several years at least. They offered to foot all bills and I should consider myself engaged, they declared. Most of these Yiddish anarchists were working-men, barely earning their living: expansive Maurice Langbord and his wife, Becky, toiling to support their six adorable children, with large appetites; A. Judkin, weighing no more than ninety pounds, with a sick wife, running a newspaper delivery truck; genial and kindly Joe Desser, ill for months; Gurian, Simkin, Goldstein, and other comrades — every one of them with heavy burdens to carry. I would not consent to accept support even from Julius Seltzer, the only " millionaire " in our ranks, let alone from them. Nor could I think of spending the rest of my life in Canada. But I would risk it for a year.

The special drama course, arranged by my two artist friends Florence Loring and Frances Wylie, had left a surplus. My family sent cash as their birthday gifts. The two Bens, Big and Little, and other friends had also remembered me on the occasion. I would have enough to keep going for part of the summer. I thought I would rest up for a while and then buckle down to prepare a new lecture course. But I lost all desire for a rest with the impending murder of Sacco and Vanzetti.

The first knowledge of their arrest had reached me in Russia; then nothing more till I was in Germany. So overpowering were the proofs of their innocence, it seemed impossible that the State of Massachusetts would repeat in 1923 the crime Illinois had committed in 1887. Surely some progress had been made in America in the past quarter of a century, some change in the minds and hearts of the masses to prevent the new human sacrifice, I reasoned. Strange that I, of all people, should have thought so. I who had lived and struggled in the United States for more than half my life and had witnessed the inertia of the workers and the unscrupulousness and the inhumanity of the American courts! With our Chicago men innocently slain, with Sasha doomed to twenty-two years for an offence that legally called only for seven, with Mooney and Billings buried alive on perjured testimony, the victims of Wheatland and Centralia still in prison, and all the others I had seen railroaded! How could I have believed that Sacco and Vanzetti, however innocent, would escape American " justice "? The power of suggestion had taken me off my guard. The whole world had repudiated the monstrous possibility that Sacco and Vanzetti would be denied a new trial or that the sentence of death would be carried out. I had been influenced by it and had done little to help stay the hangman's hand reaching out for these two beautiful lives. Only after I had come to Canada did I fully realize my mistake. Talking seemed inconsequential and futile. Yet it was all I could do to call attention to the black deed about to be committed across the border, after the seven years' purgatory suffered by the two persecuted men. Alas, my feeble voice, like that of millions, cried in vain. America remained deaf.

My comrades organized a memorial meeting. I consented to speak, though I knew that no pæan of their valour and nobility could raise them to greater glory in the eyes of posterity than Vanzetti's own beautiful song or Sacco's last simple and heroic words.

Absorption in some vital interest had often helped me over the savagery man inflicts on his brother. Concentrated study of the material for my winter's work might dull the pain over our great and poignant loss.

The Public and University libraries in Toronto were lacking in modern works on the social, educational, and psychologic problems occupying the best minds. " We do not buy books we consider immoral," a local librarian was reported as saying. I acquired a librarian of my own in Arthur Leonard Ross, best of friends, who sent me two boxes of the latest reference books on the subjects I was preparing. I also came upon a rich Walt Whitman collection, owned by Mr. H. F. Saunders, secretary of the Toronto Walt Whitman Fellowship, who invited me to speak at the annual gathering in memory of the Good Grey Poet.

My luck in Toronto far exceeded my deserts. Kind hearts supplied my every wish. " A secretary? " " Why, there's Molly Kirzner — she'll do your work." Within the year Molly changed her name to Ackerman, but not her loyalty to me. " A centrally located place for our publicity? " " Why, there's C. M. Herlick, the lawyer. Don't you fear, he is also a Socialist and eager to put his office at your service." A physician, a dentist, and tailors at my call, and a kidnapper whose cozy home soon became mine. The dear woman, Esther Laddon, was about my own age, but she mothered me as if I were her child. She fretted about my health, worried about my meals, and buttonholed everybody to warn them not to dare miss hearing the great orator E.G. Indeed, my luck exceeded my deserts.

In January 1928 I delivered my final talk in a series of twenty, embracing various problems of our time. The last evening, on which I discussed Ben Lindsey's *Companionate Marriage,* brought out an audience equalling the total attendance of four other meetings. I was assured that I had performed a feat no public speaker had ever attempted in Toronto before. I had come as a stranger without funds or a manager. Within a year I had created enough interest to secure audiences twice a week for eight months. Most important, my friends thought, was the effect of my lecture on corporal punishment in the schools. The campaign organized to abolish the savage practice was the direct result of it, they said. I could not have achieved what I did had it not been for the effective support of such friends as the Reades, Robert Low, Mary Ramsey, Jane Cohen, the Hugheses, Florence Loring and Frances Wylie, and my comrades in Toronto. Their share was no less than mine, nor should their credit be.

The week in Montreal before sailing was free from the gloom and disappointments of my previous visit. I came as the guest of the Women's Aid Society, the group I had organized for the relief of the persecuted revolutionists in Russia. My year's absence had not dampened their ardour nor lessened their efforts. Mrs. Zahler, Lena Slackman, Minna Baron, Rose Bernstein, and the other hard workers had surpassed my expectations in the amount of financial aid they had succeeded in sending to Berlin for the Russian Political Prisoners' Fund. They proved equally efficient with the two meetings they arranged for me, the largest and most interesting I had had in Montreal. I greatly enjoyed the fine fellowship at the farewell dinner they gave me. Other friends added to the interest and pleasure of my stay, among them Mr. and Mrs. H. M. Caiserman, enthusiastic Judaists, who gathered the Yiddish intelligentsia to attend my lecture on Walt Whitman at their home. They were proud that I was one of their race, they reiterated. It was worth coming back to Montreal to reach their Yiddish hearts by the grace of the *goi* Walt Whitman.

Evelyn Scott was in the city and I spent some lovely hours with her. I had read and admired her *Escapade* years before we met. Our friendship began in London and was cemented by Evelyn's letters, no less masterly than her literary work. We laughed to tears over the recollection of our recent meeting in Cassis, France. She had invited Sasha and me to dinner and we had arrived in the company of Peggy and Lawrence at four in the morning, hungry as wolves. Dazed with sleep, Evelyn had announced that she could offer us only coffee; not a scrap had been left from the sumptuous dinner.

The call to arms for " E.G.'s Life " had not brought battalions to the fore, Van ruefully reported; no more than a thousand dollars had come in, though he had bombarded everyone within reach. His face lit up when he learned that the comrades of the *Freie Arbeiter Stimme* had, through the efforts of its editor, Joseph Cohen, B. Axler, and Sarah Gruber, raised nearly as much, and that Toronto and Montreal had not lagged behind. But we were still only half-way towards the needed five thousand dollars. Van was not discouraged: he would continue to pester those who had once proclaimed their friendship for E.G. What were my plans? Would I wait before beginning my work? Did he dare suggest that a good anarchist would stop half-way, I teased my impresario. In fifteen months I had raised over thirteen hundred dollars for the political fund, some money for the fight to rescue Sacco and Vanzetti and for similar causes. I had paid my debts, amounting to twelve hundred dollars, and I had enough left to cover my return passage, aside from the new fund for my autobiography.

I was returning to France, to lovely Saint-Tropez and my enchanting little cottage to write my life. My life — I had lived in its heights and its depths, in bitter sorrow and ecstatic joy, in black despair and fervent hope. I had drunk the cup to the last drop. I had lived my life. Would I had the gift to paint the life I had lived!

EMMA GOLDMAN (MOSCOW, 1921)

# INDEX

A CATALOGUE OF SELECTED DOVER BOOKS
IN ALL FIELDS OF INTEREST

# A CATALOGUE OF SELECTED DOVER BOOKS
## IN ALL FIELDS OF INTEREST

THE DEVIL'S DICTIONARY, Ambrose Bierce. Barbed, bitter, brilliant witticisms in the form of a dictionary. Best, most ferocious satire America has produced. 145pp.                                                           20487-1 Pa. $1.75

ABSOLUTELY MAD INVENTIONS, A.E. Brown, H.A. Jeffcott. Hilarious, useless, or merely absurd inventions all granted patents by the U.S. Patent Office. Edible tie pin, mechanical hat tipper, etc. 57 illustrations. 125pp.        22596-8 Pa. $1.50

AMERICAN WILD FLOWERS COLORING BOOK, Paul Kennedy. Planned coverage of 48 most important wildflowers, from Rickett's collection; instructive as well as entertaining. Color versions on covers. 48pp. 8¼ x 11.        20095-7 Pa. $1.50

BIRDS OF AMERICA COLORING BOOK, John James Audubon. Rendered for coloring by Paul Kennedy. 46 of Audubon's noted illustrations: red-winged blackbird, cardinal, purple finch, towhee, etc. Original plates reproduced in full color on the covers. 48pp. 8¼ x 11.                                        23049-X Pa. $1.50

NORTH AMERICAN INDIAN DESIGN COLORING BOOK, Paul Kennedy. The finest examples from Indian masks, beadwork, pottery, etc. — selected and redrawn for coloring (with identifications) by well-known illustrator Paul Kennedy. 48pp. 8¼ x 11.                                                           21125-8 Pa. $1.50

UNIFORMS OF THE AMERICAN REVOLUTION COLORING BOOK, Peter Copeland. 31 lively drawings reproduce whole panorama of military attire; each uniform has complete instructions for accurate coloring. (Not in the Pictorial Archives Series). 64pp. 8¼ x 11.                                              21850-3 Pa. $1.50

THE WONDERFUL WIZARD OF OZ COLORING BOOK, L. Frank Baum. Color the Yellow Brick Road and much more in 61 drawings adapted from W.W. Denslow's originals, accompanied by abridged version of text. Dorothy, Toto, Oz and the Emerald City. 61 illustrations. 64pp. 8¼ x 11.            20452-9 Pa. $1.50

CUT AND COLOR PAPER MASKS, Michael Grater. Clowns, animals, funny faces . . . simply color them in, cut them out, and put them together, and you have 9 paper masks to play with and enjoy. Complete instructions. Assembled masks shown in full color on the covers. 32pp. 8¼ x 11.          23171-2 Pa. $1.50

STAINED GLASS CHRISTMAS ORNAMENT COLORING BOOK, Carol Belanger Grafton. Brighten your Christmas season with over 100 Christmas ornaments done in a stained glass effect on translucent paper. Color them in and then hang at windows, from lights, anywhere. 32pp. 8¼ x 11.           20707-2 Pa. $1.75

CREATIVE LITHOGRAPHY AND HOW TO DO IT, Grant Arnold. Lithography as art form: working directly on stone, transfer of drawings, lithotint, mezzotint, color printing; also metal plates. Detailed, thorough. 27 illustrations. 214pp.
21208-4 Pa. $3.00

DESIGN MOTIFS OF ANCIENT MEXICO, Jorge Enciso. Vigorous, powerful ceramic stamp impressions — Maya, Aztec, Toltec, Olmec. Serpents, gods, priests, dancers, etc. 153pp. 6⅛ x 9¼.
20084-1 Pa. $2.50

AMERICAN INDIAN DESIGN AND DECORATION, Leroy Appleton. Full text, plus more than 700 precise drawings of Inca, Maya, Aztec, Pueblo, Plains, NW Coast basketry, sculpture, painting, pottery, sand paintings, metal, etc. 4 plates in color. 279pp. 8⅜ x 11¼.
22704-9 Pa. $4.50

CHINESE LATTICE DESIGNS, Daniel S. Dye. Incredibly beautiful geometric designs: circles, voluted, simple dissections, etc. Inexhaustible source of ideas, motifs. 1239 illustrations. 469pp. 6⅛ x 9¼.
23096-1 Pa. $5.00

JAPANESE DESIGN MOTIFS, Matsuya Co. Mon, or heraldic designs. Over 4000 typical, beautiful designs: birds, animals, flowers, swords, fans, geometric; all beautifully stylized. 213pp. 11⅜ x 8¼.
22874-6 Pa. $5.00

PERSPECTIVE, Jan Vredeman de Vries. 73 perspective plates from 1604 edition; buildings, townscapes, stairways, fantastic scenes. Remarkable for beauty, surrealistic atmosphere; real eye-catchers. Introduction by Adolf Placzek. 74pp. 11⅜ x 8¼.
20186-4 Pa. $2.75

EARLY AMERICAN DESIGN MOTIFS, Suzanne E. Chapman. 497 motifs, designs, from painting on wood, ceramics, appliqué, glassware, samplers, metal work, etc. Florals, landscapes, birds and animals, geometrics, letters, etc. Inexhaustible. Enlarged edition. 138pp. 8⅜ x 11¼.
22985-8 Pa. $3.50
23084-8 Clothbd. $7.95

VICTORIAN STENCILS FOR DESIGN AND DECORATION, edited by E.V. Gillon, Jr. 113 wonderful ornate Victorian pieces from German sources; florals, geometrics; borders, corner pieces; bird motifs, etc. 64pp. 9⅜ x 12¼.
21995-X Pa. $2.75

ART NOUVEAU: AN ANTHOLOGY OF DESIGN AND ILLUSTRATION FROM THE STUDIO, edited by E.V. Gillon, Jr. Graphic arts: book jackets, posters, engravings, illustrations, decorations; Crane, Beardsley, Bradley and many others. Inexhaustible. 92pp. 8⅛ x 11.
22388-4 Pa. $2.50

ORIGINAL ART DECO DESIGNS, William Rowe. First-rate, highly imaginative modern Art Deco frames, borders, compositions, alphabets, florals, insectals, Wurlitzer-types, etc. Much finest modern Art Deco. 80 plates, 8 in color. 8⅜ x 11¼.
22567-4 Pa. $3.50

HANDBOOK OF DESIGNS AND DEVICES, Clarence P. Hornung. Over 1800 basic geometric designs based on circle, triangle, square, scroll, cross, etc. Largest such collection in existence. 261pp.
20125-2 Pa. $2.75

VICTORIAN HOUSES: A TREASURY OF LESSER-KNOWN EXAMPLES, Edmund Gillon and Clay Lancaster. 116 photographs, excellent commentary illustrate distinct characteristics, many borrowings of local Victorian architecture. Octagonal houses, Americanized chalets, grand country estates, small cottages, etc. Rich heritage often overlooked. 116 plates. 11⅜ x 10.                22966-1 Pa. $4.00

STICKS AND STONES, Lewis Mumford. Great classic of American cultural history; architecture from medieval-inspired earliest forms to 20th century; evolution of structure and style, influence of environment. 21 illustrations. 113pp.
20202-X Pa. $2.50

ON THE LAWS OF JAPANESE PAINTING, Henry P. Bowie. Best substitute for training with genius Oriental master, based on years of study in Kano school. Philosophy, brushes, inks, style, etc. 66 illustrations. 117pp. 6⅛ x 9¼.        20030-2 Pa. $4.50

A HANDBOOK OF ANATOMY FOR ART STUDENTS, Arthur Thomson. Virtually exhaustive. Skeletal structure, muscles, heads, special features. Full text, anatomical figures, undraped photos. Male and female. 337 illustrations. 459pp.
21163-0 Pa. $5.00

AN ATLAS OF ANATOMY FOR ARTISTS, Fritz Schider. Finest text, working book. Full text, plus anatomical illustrations; plates by great artists showing anatomy. 593 illustrations. 192pp. 7⅞ x 10¾.                20241-0 Clothbd. $6.95

THE HUMAN FIGURE IN MOTION, Eadweard Muybridge. More than 4500 stopped-action photos, in action series, showing undraped men, women, children jumping, lying down, throwing, sitting, wrestling, carrying, etc. "Unparalleled dictionary for artists," American Artist. Taken by great 19th century photographer. 390pp. 7⅞ x 10⅝.                20204-6 Clothbd. $12.50

AN ATLAS OF ANIMAL ANATOMY FOR ARTISTS, W. Ellenberger et al. Horses, dogs, cats, lions, cattle, deer, etc. Muscles, skeleton, surface features. The basic work. Enlarged edition. 288 illustrations. 151pp. 9⅜ x 12¼.        20082-5 Pa. $4.50

LETTER FORMS: 110 COMPLETE ALPHABETS, Frederick Lambert. 110 sets of capital letters; 16 lower case alphabets; 70 sets of numbers and other symbols. Edited and expanded by Theodore Menten. 110pp. 8⅛ x 11.        22872-X Pa. $3.00

THE METHODS OF CONSTRUCTION OF CELTIC ART, George Bain. Simple geometric techniques for making wonderful Celtic interlacements, spirals, Kells-type initials, animals, humans, etc. Unique for artists, craftsmen. Over 500 illustrations. 160pp. 9 x 12.                USO 22923-8 Pa. $4.00

SCULPTURE, PRINCIPLES AND PRACTICE, Louis Slobodkin. Step by step approach to clay, plaster, metals, stone; classical and modern. 253 drawings, photos. 255pp. 8⅛ x 11.                22960-2 Pa. $5.00

THE ART OF ETCHING, E.S. Lumsden. Clear, detailed instructions for etching, drypoint, softground, aquatint; from 1st sketch to print. Very detailed, thorough. 200 illustrations. 376pp.                20049-3 Pa. $3.75

CONSTRUCTION OF AMERICAN FURNITURE TREASURES, Lester Margon. 344 detail drawings, complete text on constructing exact reproductions of 38 early American masterpieces: Hepplewhite sideboard, Duncan Phyfe drop-leaf table, mantel clock, gate-leg dining table, Pa. German cupboard, more. 38 plates. 54 photographs. 168pp. 8⅜ x 11¼.          23056-2 Pa. $4.00

JEWELRY MAKING AND DESIGN, Augustus F. Rose, Antonio Cirino. Professional secrets revealed in thorough, practical guide: tools, materials, processes; rings, brooches, chains, cast pieces, enamelling, setting stones, etc. Do not confuse with skimpy introductions: beginner can use, professional can learn from it. Over 200 illustrations. 306pp.          21750-7 Pa. $3.00

METALWORK AND ENAMELLING, Herbert Maryon. Generally coneeded best all-around book. Countless trade secrets: materials, tools, soldering, filigree, setting, inlay, niello, repoussé, casting, polishing, etc. For beginner or expert. Author was foremost British expert. 330 illustrations. 335pp.          22702-2 Pa. $3.50

WEAVING WITH FOOT-POWER LOOMS, Edward F. Worst. Setting up a loom, beginning to weave, constructing equipment, using dyes, more, plus over 285 drafts of traditional patterns including Colonial and Swedish weaves. More than 200 other figures. For beginning and advanced. 275pp. 8¾ x 6⅜.          23064-3 Pa. $4.50

WEAVING A NAVAJO BLANKET, Gladys A. Reichard. Foremost anthropologist studied under Navajo women, reveals every step in process from wool, dyeing, spinning, setting up loom, designing, weaving. Much history, symbolism. With this book you could make one yourself. 97 illustrations. 222pp.   22992-0 Pa. $3.00

NATURAL DYES AND HOME DYEING, Rita J. Adrosko. Use natural ingredients: bark, flowers, leaves, lichens, insects etc. Over 135 specific recipes from historical sources for cotton, wool, other fabrics. Genuine premodern handicrafts. 12 illustrations. 160pp.          22688-3 Pa. $2.00

THE HAND DECORATION OF FABRICS, Francis J. Kafka. Outstanding, profusely illustrated guide to stenciling, batik, block printing, tie dyeing, freehand painting, silk screen printing, and novelty decoration. 356 illustrations. 198pp. 6 x 9.
          21401-X Pa. $3.00

THOMAS NAST: CARTOONS AND ILLUSTRATIONS, with text by Thomas Nast St. Hill. Father of American political cartooning. Cartoons that destroyed Tweed Ring; inflation, free love, church and state; original Republican elephant and Democratic donkey; Santa Claus; more. 117 illustrations. 146pp. 9 x 12.
          22983-1 Pa. $4.00
          23067-8 Clothbd. $8.50

FREDERIC REMINGTON: 173 DRAWINGS AND ILLUSTRATIONS. Most famous of the Western artists, most responsible for our myths about the American West in its untamed days. Complete reprinting of *Drawings of Frederic Remington* (1897), plus other selections. 4 additional drawings in color on covers. 140pp. 9 x 12.
          20714-5 Pa. $3.95

CATALOGUE OF DOVER BOOKS

EARLY NEW ENGLAND GRAVESTONE RUBBINGS, Edmund V. Gillon, Jr. 43 photographs, 226 rubbings show heavily symbolic, macabre, sometimes humorous primitive American art. Up to early 19th century. 207pp. 8⅜ x 11¼.
21380-3 Pa. $4.00

L.J.M. DAGUERRE: THE HISTORY OF THE DIORAMA AND THE DAGUERREOTYPE, Helmut and Alison Gernsheim. Definitive account. Early history, life and work of Daguerre; discovery of daguerreotype process; diffusion abroad; other early photography. 124 illustrations. 226pp. 6⅙ x 9¼.
22290-X Pa. $4.00

PHOTOGRAPHY AND THE AMERICAN SCENE, Robert Taft. The basic book on American photography as art, recording form, 1839-1889. Development, influence on society, great photographers, types (portraits, war, frontier, etc.), whatever else needed. Inexhaustible. Illustrated with 322 early photos, daguerreotypes, tintypes, stereo slides, etc. 546pp. 6⅛ x 9¼.
21201-7 Pa. $5.95

PHOTOGRAPHIC SKETCHBOOK OF THE CIVIL WAR, Alexander Gardner. Reproduction of 1866 volume with 100 on-the-field photographs: Manassas, Lincoln on battlefield, slave pens, etc. Introduction by E.F. Bleiler. 224pp. 10¾ x 9.
22731-6 Pa. $5.00

THE MOVIES: A PICTURE QUIZ BOOK, Stanley Appelbaum & Hayward Cirker. Match stars with their movies, name actors and actresses, test your movie skill with 241 stills from 236 great movies, 1902-1959. Indexes of performers and films. 128pp. 8⅜ x 9¼.
20222-4 Pa. $2.50

THE TALKIES, Richard Griffith. Anthology of features, articles from Photoplay, 1928-1940, reproduced complete. Stars, famous movies, technical features, fabulous ads, etc.; Garbo, Chaplin, King Kong, Lubitsch, etc. 4 color plates, scores of illustrations. 327pp. 8⅜ x 11¼.
22762-6 Pa. $6.95

THE MOVIE MUSICAL FROM VITAPHONE TO "42ND STREET," edited by Miles Kreuger. Relive the rise of the movie musical as reported in the pages of Photoplay magazine (1926-1933): every movie review, cast list, ad, and record review; every significant feature article, production still, biography, forecast, and gossip story. Profusely illustrated. 367pp. 8⅜ x 11¼.
23154-2 Pa. $7.95

JOHANN SEBASTIAN BACH, Philipp Spitta. Great classic of biography, musical commentary, with hundreds of pieces analyzed. Also good for Bach's contemporaries. 450 musical examples. Total of 1799pp.
EUK 22278-0, 22279-9 Clothbd., Two vol. set $25.00

BEETHOVEN AND HIS NINE SYMPHONIES, Sir George Grove. Thorough history, analysis, commentary on symphonies and some related pieces. For either beginner or advanced student. 436 musical passages. 407pp.
20334-4 Pa. $4.00

MOZART AND HIS PIANO CONCERTOS, Cuthbert Girdlestone. The only full-length study. Detailed analyses of all 21 concertos, sources; 417 musical examples. 509pp.
21271-8 Pa. $6.00

## CATALOGUE OF DOVER BOOKS

THE FITZWILLIAM VIRGINAL BOOK, edited by J. Fuller Maitland, W.B. Squire. Famous early 17th century collection of keyboard music, 300 works by Morley, Byrd, Bull, Gibbons, etc. Modern notation. Total of 938pp. 8⅜ x 11.
ECE 21068-5, 21069-3 Pa., Two vol. set $15.00

COMPLETE STRING QUARTETS, Wolfgang A. Mozart. Breitkopf and Härtel edition. All 23 string quartets plus alternate slow movement to K156. Study score. 277pp. 9⅜ x 12¼. 22372-8 Pa. $6.00

COMPLETE SONG CYCLES, Franz Schubert. Complete piano, vocal music of Die Schöne Müllerin, Die Winterreise, Schwanengesang. Also Drinker English singing translations. Breitkopf and Härtel edition. 217pp. 9⅜ x 12¼.
22649-2 Pa. $4.50

THE COMPLETE PRELUDES AND ETUDES FOR PIANOFORTE SOLO, Alexander Scriabin. All the preludes and etudes including many perfectly spun miniatures. Edited by K.N. Igumnov and Y.I. Mil'shteyn. 250pp. 9 x 12. 22919-X Pa. $5.00

TRISTAN UND ISOLDE, Richard Wagner. Full orchestral score with complete instrumentation. Do not confuse with piano reduction. Commentary by Felix Mottl, great Wagnerian conductor and scholar. Study score. 655pp. 8⅛ x 11.
22915-7 Pa. $11.95

FAVORITE SONGS OF THE NINETIES, ed. Robert Fremont. Full reproduction, including covers, of 88 favorites: Ta-Ra-Ra-Boom-De-Aye, The Band Played On, Bird in a Gilded Cage, Under the Bamboo Tree, After the Ball, etc. 401pp. 9 x 12.
EBE 21536-9 Pa. $6.95

SOUSA'S GREAT MARCHES IN PIANO TRANSCRIPTION: ORIGINAL SHEET MUSIC OF 23 WORKS, John Philip Sousa. Selected by Lester S. Levy. Playing edition includes: The Stars and Stripes Forever, The Thunderer, The Gladiator, King Cotton, Washington Post, much more. 24 illustrations. 111pp. 9 x 12.
USO 23132-1 Pa. $3.50

CLASSIC PIANO RAGS, selected with an introduction by Rudi Blesh. Best ragtime music (1897-1922) by Scott Joplin, James Scott, Joseph F. Lamb, Tom Turpin, 9 others. Printed from best original sheet music, plus covers. 364pp. 9 x 12.
EBE 20469-3 Pa. $6.95

ANALYSIS OF CHINESE CHARACTERS, C.D. Wilder, J.H. Ingram. 1000 most important characters analyzed according to primitives, phonetics, historical development. Traditional method offers mnemonic aid to beginner, intermediate student of Chinese, Japanese. 365pp. 23045-7 Pa. $4.00

MODERN CHINESE: A BASIC COURSE, Faculty of Peking University. Self study, classroom course in modern Mandarin. Records contain phonetics, vocabulary, sentences, lessons. 249 page book contains all recorded text, translations, grammar, vocabulary, exercises. Best course on market. 3 12" 33⅓ monaural records, book, album. 98832-5 Set $12.50

# CATALOGUE OF DOVER BOOKS

THE BEST DR. THORNDYKE DETECTIVE STORIES, R. Austin Freeman. The Case of Oscar Brodski, The Moabite Cipher, and 5 other favorites featuring the great scientific detective, plus his long-believed-lost first adventure — 31 New Inn — reprinted here for the first time. Edited by E.F. Bleiler. USO 20388-3 Pa. $3.00

BEST "THINKING MACHINE" DETECTIVE STORIES, Jacques Futrelle. The Problem of Cell 13 and 11 other stories about Prof. Augustus S.F.X. Van Dusen, including two "lost" stories. First reprinting of several. Edited by E.F. Bleiler. 241pp.
20537-1 Pa. $3.00

UNCLE SILAS, J. Sheridan LeFanu. Victorian Gothic mystery novel, considered by many best of period, even better than Collins or Dickens. Wonderful psychological terror. Introduction by Frederick Shroyer. 436pp. 21715-9 Pa. $4.00

BEST DR. POGGIOLI DETECTIVE STORIES, T.S. Stribling. 15 best stories from EQMM and The Saint offer new adventures in Mexico, Florida, Tennessee hills as Poggioli unravels mysteries and combats Count Jalacki. 217pp. 23227-1 Pa. $3.00

EIGHT DIME NOVELS, selected with an introduction by E.F. Bleiler. Adventures of Old King Brady, Frank James, Nick Carter, Deadwood Dick, Buffalo Bill, The Steam Man, Frank Merriwell, and Horatio Alger — 1877 to 1905. Important, entertaining popular literature in facsimile reprint, with original covers. 190pp. 9 x 12. 22975-0 Pa. $3.50

ALICE'S ADVENTURES UNDER GROUND, Lewis Carroll. Facsimile of ms. Carroll gave Alice Liddell in 1864. Different in many ways from final Alice. Handlettered, illustrated by Carroll. Introduction by Martin Gardner. 128pp. 21482-6 Pa. $1.50

ALICE IN WONDERLAND COLORING BOOK, Lewis Carroll. Pictures by John Tenniel. Large-size versions of the famous illustrations of Alice, Cheshire Cat, Mad Hatter and all the others, waiting for your crayons. Abridged text. 36 illustrations. 64pp. 8¼ x 11. 22853-3 Pa. $1.50

AVENTURES D'ALICE AU PAYS DES MERVEILLES, Lewis Carroll. Bué's translation of "Alice" into French, supervised by Carroll himself. Novel way to learn language. (No English text.) 42 Tenniel illustrations. 196pp. 22836-3 Pa. $2.50

MYTHS AND FOLK TALES OF IRELAND, Jeremiah Curtin. 11 stories that are Irish versions of European fairy tales and 9 stories from the Fenian cycle — 20 tales of legend and magic that comprise an essential work in the history of folklore. 256pp. 22430-9 Pa. $3.00

EAST O' THE SUN AND WEST O' THE MOON, George W. Dasent. Only full edition of favorite, wonderful Norwegian fairytales — Why the Sea is Salt, Boots and the Troll, etc. — with 77 illustrations by Kittelsen & Werenskiöld. 418pp.
22521-6 Pa. $4.00

PERRAULT'S FAIRY TALES, Charles Perrault and Gustave Doré. Original versions of Cinderella, Sleeping Beauty, Little Red Riding Hood, etc. in best translation, with 34 wonderful illustrations by Gustave Doré. 117pp. 8⅛ x 11. 22311-6 Pa. $2.50

MOTHER GOOSE'S MELODIES. Facsimile of fabulously rare Munroe and Francis "copyright 1833" Boston edition. Familiar and unusual rhymes, wonderful old woodcut illustrations. Edited by E.F. Bleiler. 128pp. 4½ x 6⅜. 22577-1 Pa. $1.50

MOTHER GOOSE IN HIEROGLYPHICS. Favorite nursery rhymes presented in rebus form for children. Fascinating 1849 edition reproduced in toto, with key. Introduction by E.F. Bleiler. About 400 woodcuts. 64pp. 6⅞ x 5¼. 20745-5 Pa. $1.00

PETER PIPER'S PRACTICAL PRINCIPLES OF PLAIN & PERFECT PRONUNCIATION. Alliterative jingles and tongue-twisters. Reproduction in full of 1830 first American edition. 25 spirited woodcuts. 32pp. 4½ x 6⅜. 22560-7 Pa. $1.00

MARMADUKE MULTIPLY'S MERRY METHOD OF MAKING MINOR MATHEMATICIANS. Fellow to Peter Piper, it teaches multiplication table by catchy rhymes and woodcuts. 1841 Munroe & Francis edition. Edited by E.F. Bleiler. 103pp. 4⅝ x 6.
22773-1 Pa. $1.25
20171-6 Clothbd. $3.00

THE NIGHT BEFORE CHRISTMAS, Clement Moore. Full text, and woodcuts from original 1848 book. Also critical, historical material. 19 illustrations. 40pp. 4⅝ x 6. 22797-9 Pa. $1.25

THE KING OF THE GOLDEN RIVER, John Ruskin. Victorian children's classic of three brothers, their attempts to reach the Golden River, what becomes of them. Facsimile of original 1889 edition. 22 illustrations. 56pp. 4⅝ x 6⅜.
20066-3 Pa. $1.50

DREAMS OF THE RAREBIT FIEND, Winsor McCay. Pioneer cartoon strip, unexcelled for beauty, imagination, in 60 full sequences. Incredible technical virtuosity, wonderful visual wit. Historical introduction. 62pp. 8⅜ x 11¼. 21347-1 Pa. $2.50

THE KATZENJAMMER KIDS, Rudolf Dirks. In full color, 14 strips from 1906-7; full of imagination, characteristic humor. Classic of great historical importance. Introduction by August Derleth. 32pp. 9¼ x 12¼. 23005-8 Pa. $2.00

LITTLE ORPHAN ANNIE AND LITTLE ORPHAN ANNIE IN COSMIC CITY, Harold Gray. Two great sequences from the early strips: our curly-haired heroine defends the Warbucks' financial empire and, then, takes on meanie Phineas P. Pinchpenny. Leapin' lizards! 178pp. 6⅛ x 8⅜. 23107-0 Pa. $2.00

THE BEST OF GLUYAS WILLIAMS. 100 drawings by one of America's finest cartoonists: The Day a Cake of Ivory Soap Sank at Proctor & Gamble's, At the Life Insurance Agents' Banquet, and many other gems from the 20's and 30's. 118pp. 8⅜ x 11¼. 22737-5 Pa. $2.50

THE MAGIC MOVING PICTURE BOOK, Bliss, Sands & Co. The pictures in this book move! Volcanoes erupt, a house burns, a serpentine dancer wiggles her way through a number. By using a specially ruled acetate screen provided, you can obtain these and 15 other startling effects. Originally "The Motograph Moving Picture Book." 32pp. 8¼ x 11. 23224-7 Pa. $1.75

STRING FIGURES AND HOW TO MAKE THEM, Caroline F. Jayne. Fullest, clearest instructions on string figures from around world: Eskimo, Navajo, Lapp, Europe, more. Cats cradle, moving spear, lightning, stars. Introduction by A.C. Haddon. 950 illustrations. 407pp. 20152-X Pa. $3.50

PAPER FOLDING FOR BEGINNERS, William D. Murray and Francis J. Rigney. Clearest book on market for making origami sail boats, roosters, frogs that move legs, cups, bonbon boxes. 40 projects. More than 275 illustrations. Photographs. 94pp. 20713-7 Pa. $1.25

INDIAN SIGN LANGUAGE, William Tomkins. Over 525 signs developed by Sioux, Blackfoot, Cheyenne, Arapahoe and other tribes. Written instructions and diagrams: how to make words, construct sentences. Also 290 pictographs of Sioux and Ojibway tribes. 111pp. 6⅛ x 9¼. 22029-X Pa. $1.50

BOOMERANGS: HOW TO MAKE AND THROW THEM, Bernard S. Mason. Easy to make and throw, dozens of designs: cross-stick, pinwheel, boomabird, tumblestick, Australian curved stick boomerang. Complete throwing instructions. All safe. 99pp. 23028-7 Pa. $1.75

25 KITES THAT FLY, Leslie Hunt. Full, easy to follow instructions for kites made from inexpensive materials. Many novelties. Reeling, raising, designing your own. 70 illustrations. 110pp. 22550-X Pa. $1.25

TRICKS AND GAMES ON THE POOL TABLE, Fred Herrmann. 79 tricks and games, some solitaires, some for 2 or more players, some competitive; mystifying shots and throws, unusual carom, tricks involving cork, coins, a hat, more. 77 figures. 95pp. 21814-7 Pa. $1.25

WOODCRAFT AND CAMPING, Bernard S. Mason. How to make a quick emergency shelter, select woods that will burn immediately, make do with limited supplies, etc. Also making many things out of wood, rawhide, bark, at camp. Formerly titled Woodcraft. 295 illustrations. 580pp. 21951-8 Pa. $4.00

AN INTRODUCTION TO CHESS MOVES AND TACTICS SIMPLY EXPLAINED, Leonard Barden. Informal intermediate introduction: reasons for moves, tactics, openings, traps, positional play, endgame. Isolates patterns. 102pp. USO 21210-6 Pa. $1.35

LASKER'S MANUAL OF CHESS, Dr. Emanuel Lasker. Great world champion offers very thorough coverage of all aspects of chess. Combinations, position play, openings, endgame, aesthetics of chess, philosophy of struggle, much more. Filled with analyzed games. 390pp. 20640-8 Pa. $4.00

CATALOGUE OF DOVER BOOKS

DRIED FLOWERS, Sarah Whitlock and Martha Rankin. Concise, clear, practical guide to dehydration, glycerinizing, pressing plant material, and more. Covers use of silica gel. 12 drawings. Originally titled "New Techniques with Dried Flowers." 32pp. 21802-3 Pa. $1.00

ABC OF POULTRY RAISING, J.H. Florea. Poultry expert, editor tells how to raise chickens on home or small business basis. Breeds, feeding, housing, laying, etc. Very concrete, practical. 50 illustrations. 256pp. 23201-8 Pa. $3.00

HOW INDIANS USE WILD PLANTS FOR FOOD, MEDICINE & CRAFTS, Frances Densmore. Smithsonian, Bureau of American Ethnology report presents wealth of material on nearly 200 plants used by Chippewas of Minnesota and Wisconsin. 33 plates plus 122pp. of text. 6$^{1}$/$_{8}$ x 9¼. 23019-8 Pa. $2.50

THE HERBAL OR GENERAL HISTORY OF PLANTS, John Gerard. The 1633 edition revised and enlarged by Thomas Johnson. Containing almost 2850 plant descriptions and 2705 superb illustrations, Gerard's Herbal is a monumental work, the book all modern English herbals are derived from, and the one herbal every serious enthusiast should have in its entirety. Original editions are worth perhaps $750. 1678pp. 8½ x 12¼. 23147-X Clothbd. $50.00

A MODERN HERBAL, Margaret Grieve. Much the fullest, most exact, most useful compilation of herbal material. Gigantic alphabetical encyclopedia, from aconite to zedoary, gives botanical information, medical properties, folklore, economic uses, and much else. Indispensable to serious reader. 161 illustrations. 888pp. 6½ x 9¼. USO 22798-7, 22799-5 Pa., Two vol. set $10.00

HOW TO KNOW THE FERNS, Frances T. Parsons. Delightful classic. Identification, fern lore, for Eastern and Central U.S.A. Has introduced thousands to interesting life form. 99 illustrations. 215pp. 20740-4 Pa. $2.75

THE MUSHROOM HANDBOOK, Louis C.C. Krieger. Still the best popular handbook. Full descriptions of 259 species, extremely thorough text, habitats, luminescence, poisons, folklore, etc. 32 color plates; 126 other illustrations. 560pp. 21861-9 Pa. $4.50

HOW TO KNOW THE WILD FRUITS, Maude G. Peterson. Classic guide covers nearly 200 trees, shrubs, smaller plants of the U.S. arranged by color of fruit and then by family. Full text provides names, descriptions, edibility, uses. 80 illustrations. 400pp. 22943-2 Pa. $4.00

COMMON WEEDS OF THE UNITED STATES, U.S. Department of Agriculture. Covers 220 important weeds with illustration, maps, botanical information, plant lore for each. Over 225 illustrations. 463pp. 6$^{1}$/$_{8}$ x 9¼. 20504-5 Pa. $4.50

HOW TO KNOW THE WILD FLOWERS, Mrs. William S. Dana. Still best popular book for East and Central USA. Over 500 plants easily identified, with plant lore; arranged according to color and flowering time. 174 plates. 459pp. 20332-8 Pa. $3.50

DRIED FLOWERS, Sarah Whitlock and Martha Rankin. Concise, clear, practical guide to dehydration, glycerinizing, pressing plant material, and more. Covers use of silica gel. 12 drawings. Originally titled "New Techniques with Dried Flowers." 32pp. 21802-3 Pa. $1.00

ABC OF POULTRY RAISING, J.H. Florea. Poultry expert, editor tells how to raise chickens on home or small business basis. Breeds, feeding, housing, laying, etc. Very concrete, practical. 50 illustrations. 256pp. 23201-8 Pa. $3.00

HOW INDIANS USE WILD PLANTS FOR FOOD, MEDICINE & CRAFTS, Frances Densmore. Smithsonian, Bureau of American Ethnology report presents wealth of material on nearly 200 plants used by Chippewas of Minnesota and Wisconsin. 33 plates plus 122pp. of text. 6⅛ x 9¼. 23019-8 Pa. $2.50

THE HERBAL OR GENERAL HISTORY OF PLANTS, John Gerard. The 1633 edition revised and enlarged by Thomas Johnson. Containing almost 2850 plant descriptions and 2705 superb illustrations, Gerard's Herbal is a monumental work, the book all modern English herbals are derived from, and the one herbal every serious enthusiast should have in its entirety. Original editions are worth perhaps $750. 1678pp. 8½ x 12¼. 23147-X Clothbd. $50.00

A MODERN HERBAL, Margaret Grieve. Much the fullest, most exact, most useful compilation of herbal material. Gigantic alphabetical encyclopedia, from aconite to zedoary, gives botanical information, medical properties, folklore, economic uses, and much else. Indispensable to serious reader. 161 illustrations. 888pp. 6½ x 9¼. USO 22798-7, 22799-5 Pa., Two vol. set $10.00

HOW TO KNOW THE FERNS, Frances T. Parsons. Delightful classic. Identification, fern lore, for Eastern and Central U.S.A. Has introduced thousands to interesting life form. 99 illustrations. 215pp. 20740-4 Pa. $2.75

THE MUSHROOM HANDBOOK, Louis C.C. Krieger. Still the best popular handbook. Full descriptions of 259 species, extremely thorough text, habitats, luminescence, poisons, folklore, etc. 32 color plates; 126 other illustrations. 560pp. 21861-9 Pa. $4.50

HOW TO KNOW THE WILD FRUITS, Maude G. Peterson. Classic guide covers nearly 200 trees, shrubs, smaller plants of the U.S. arranged by color of fruit and then by family. Full text provides names, descriptions, edibility, uses. 80 illustrations. 400pp. 22943-2 Pa. $4.00

COMMON WEEDS OF THE UNITED STATES, U.S. Department of Agriculture. Covers 220 important weeds with illustration, maps, botanical information, plant lore for each. Over 225 illustrations. 463pp. 6⅛ x 9¼. 20504-5 Pa. $4.50

HOW TO KNOW THE WILD FLOWERS, Mrs. William S. Dana. Still best popular book for East and Central USA. Over 500 plants easily identified, with plant lore; arranged according to color and flowering time. 174 plates. 459pp. 20332-8 Pa. $3.50

THE STYLE OF PALESTRINA AND THE DISSONANCE, Knud Jeppesen. Standard analysis of rhythm, line, harmony, accented and unaccented dissonances. Also pre-Palestrina dissonances. 306pp. 22386-8 Pa. $4.50

DOVER OPERA GUIDE AND LIBRETTO SERIES prepared by Ellen H. Bleiler. Each volume contains everything needed for background, complete enjoyment: complete libretto, new English translation with all repeats, biography of composer and librettist, early performance history, musical lore, much else. All volumes lavishly illustrated with performance photos, portraits, similar material. Do not confuse with skimpy performance booklets.

CARMEN, Georges Bizet. 66 illustrations. 222pp. 22111-3 Pa. $3.00
DON GIOVANNI, Wolfgang A. Mozart. 92 illustrations. 209pp. 21134-7 Pa. $2.50
LA BOHÈME, Giacomo Puccini. 73 illustrations. 124pp. USO 20404-9 Pa. $1.75
ÄIDA, Giuseppe Verdi. 76 illustrations. 181pp. 20405-7 Pa. $2.25
LUCIA DI LAMMERMOOR, Gaetano Donizetti. 44 illustrations. 186pp.
22110-5 Pa. $2.00

ANTONIO STRADIVARI: HIS LIFE AND WORK, W. H. Hill, et al. Great work of musicology. Construction methods, woods, varnishes, known instruments, types of instruments, life, special features. Introduction by Sydney Beck. 98 illustrations, plus 4 color plates. 315pp. 20425-1 Pa. $4.00

MUSIC FOR THE PIANO, James Friskin, Irwin Freundlich. Both famous, little-known compositions; 1500 to 1950's. Listing, description, classification, technical aspects for student, teacher, performer. Indispensable for enlarging repertory. 448pp. 22918-1 Pa. $4.00

PIANOS AND THEIR MAKERS, Alfred Dolge. Leading inventor offers full history of piano technology, earliest models to 1910. Types, makers, components, mechanisms, musical aspects. Very strong on offtrail models, inventions; also player pianos. 300 illustrations. 581pp. 22856-8 Pa. $5.00

KEYBOARD MUSIC, J.S. Bach. Bach-Gesellschaft edition. For harpsichord, piano, other keyboard instruments. English Suites, French Suites, Six Partitas, Goldberg Variations, Two-Part Inventions, Three-Part Sinfonias. 312pp. 8⅛ x 11.
22360-4 Pa. $5.00

COMPLETE STRING QUARTETS, Ludwig van Beethoven. Breitkopf and Härtel edition. 6 quartets of Opus 18; 3 quartets of Opus 59; Opera 74, 95, 127, 130, 131, 132, 135 and Grosse Fuge. Study score. 434pp. 9⅜ x 12¼. 22361-2 Pa. $7.95

COMPLETE PIANO SONATAS AND VARIATIONS FOR SOLO PIANO, Johannes Brahms. All sonatas, five variations on themes from Schumann, Paganini, Handel, etc. Vienna Gesellschaft der Musikfreunde edition. 178pp. 9 x 12. 22650-6 Pa. $4.50

PIANO MUSIC 1888-1905, Claude Debussy. Deux Arabesques, Suite Bergamesque, Masques, 1st series of Images, etc. 9 others, in corrected editions. 175pp. 9⅜ x 12¼. 22771-5 Pa. $4.00

INCIDENTS OF TRAVEL IN YUCATAN, John L. Stephens. Classic (1843) exploration of jungles of Yucatan, looking for evidences of Maya civilization. Travel adventures, Mexican and Indian culture, etc. Total of 669pp.
20926-1, 20927-X Pa., Two vol. set $6.00

LIVING MY LIFE, Emma Goldman. Candid, no holds barred account by foremost American anarchist: her own life, anarchist movement, famous contemporaries, ideas and their impact. Struggles and confrontations in America, plus deportation to U.S.S.R. Shocking inside account of persecution of anarchists under Lenin. 13 plates. Total of 944pp.
22543-7, 22544-5 Pa., Two vol. set $9.00

AMERICAN INDIANS, George Catlin. Classic account of life among Plains Indians: ceremonies, hunt, warfare, etc. Dover edition reproduces for first time all original paintings. 312 plates. 572pp. of text. 6⅛ x 9¼.
22118-0, 22119-9 Pa., Two vol. set $8.00
22140-7, 22144-X Clothbd., Two vol. set $16.00

THE INDIANS BOOK, Natalie Curtis. Lore, music, narratives, drawings by Indians, collected from cultures of U.S.A. 149 songs in full notation. 45 illustrations. 583pp. 6⅝ x 9⅜.
21939-9 Pa. $6.95

INDIAN BLANKETS AND THEIR MAKERS, George Wharton James. History, old style wool blankets, changes brought about by traders, symbolism of design and color, a Navajo weaver at work, outline blanket, Kachina blankets, more. Emphasis on Navajo. 130 illustrations, 32 in color. 230pp. 6⅛ x 9¼.
22996-3 Pa. $5.00
23068-6 Clothbd. $10.00

AN INTRODUCTION TO THE STUDY OF THE MAYA HIEROGLYPHS, Sylvanus Griswold Morley. Classic study by one of the truly great figures in hieroglyph research. Still the best introduction for the student for reading Maya hieroglyphs. New introduction by J. Eric S. Thompson. 117 illustrations. 284pp.
23108-9 Pa. $4.00

THE ANALECTS OF CONFUCIUS, THE GREAT LEARNING, DOCTRINE OF THE MEAN, Confucius. Edited by James Legge. Full Chinese text, standard English translation on same page, Chinese commentators, editor's annotations; dictionary of characters at rear, plus grammatical comment. Finest edition anywhere of one of world's greatest thinkers. 503pp.
22746-4 Pa. $5.00

THE I CHING (THE BOOK OF CHANGES), translated by James Legge. Complete translation of basic text plus appendices by Confucius, and Chinese commentary of most penetrating divination manual ever prepared. Indispensable to study of early Oriental civilizations, to modern inquiring reader. 448pp.
21062-6 Pa. $3.50

THE EGYPTIAN BOOK OF THE DEAD, E.A. Wallis Budge. Complete reproduction of Ani's papyrus, finest ever found. Full hieroglyphic text, interlinear transliteration, word for word translation, smooth translation. Basic work, for Egyptology, for modern study of psychic matters. Total of 533pp. 6½ x 9¼.
EBE 21866-X Pa. $4.95

BUILD YOUR OWN LOW-COST HOME, L.O. Anderson, H.F. Zornig. U.S. Dept. of Agriculture sets of plans, full, detailed, for 11 houses: A-Frame, circular, conventional. Also construction manual. Save hundreds of dollars. 204pp. 11 x 16.
21525-3 Pa. $6.00

HOW TO BUILD A WOOD-FRAME HOUSE, L.O. Anderson. Comprehensive, easy to follow U.S. Government manual: placement, foundations, framing, sheathing, roof, insulation, plaster, finishing — almost everything else. 179 illustrations. 223pp. 7⅞ x 10¾.
22954-8 Pa. $3.50

CONCRETE, MASONRY AND BRICKWORK, U.S. Department of the Army. Practical handbook for the home owner and small builder, manual contains basic principles, techniques, and important background information on construction with concrete, concrete blocks, and brick. 177 figures, 37 tables. 200pp. 6½ x 9¼.
23203-4 Pa. $4.00

THE STANDARD BOOK OF QUILT MAKING AND COLLECTING, Marguerite Ickis. Full information, full-sized patterns for making 46 traditional quilts, also 150 other patterns. Quilted cloths, lamé, satin quilts, etc. 483 illustrations. 273pp. 6⅞ x 9⅝.
20582-7 Pa. $3.50

101 PATCHWORK PATTERNS, Ruby S. McKim. 101 beautiful, immediately useable patterns, full-size, modern and traditional. Also general information, estimating, quilt lore. 124pp. 7⅞ x 10¾.
20773-0 Pa. $2.50

KNIT YOUR OWN NORWEGIAN SWEATERS, Dale Yarn Company. Complete instructions for 50 authentic sweaters, hats, mittens, gloves, caps, etc. Thoroughly modern designs that command high prices in stores. 24 patterns, 24 color photographs. Nearly 100 charts and other illustrations. 58pp. 8⅜ x 11¼.
23031-7 Pa. $2.50

IRON-ON TRANSFER PATTERNS FOR CREWEL AND EMBROIDERY FROM EARLY AMERICAN SOURCES, edited by Rita Weiss. 75 designs, borders, alphabets, from traditional American sources printed on translucent paper in transfer ink. Reusable. Instructions. Test patterns. 24pp. 8¼ x 11.
23162-3 Pa. $1.50

AMERICAN INDIAN NEEDLEPOINT DESIGNS FOR PILLOWS, BELTS, HANDBAGS AND OTHER PROJECTS, Roslyn Epstein. 37 authentic American Indian designs adapted for modern needlepoint projects. Grid backing makes designs easily transferable to canvas. 48pp. 8¼ x 11.
22973-4 Pa. $1.50

CHARTED FOLK DESIGNS FOR CROSS-STITCH EMBROIDERY, Maria Foris & Andreas Foris. 278 charted folk designs, most in 2 colors, from Danube region: florals, fantastic beasts, geometrics, traditional symbols, more. Border and central patterns. 77pp. 8¼ x 11.
USO 23191-7 Pa. $2.00